OFFICE PROFESSIONAL'S DESK REFERENCE

WEBSTER'S
NEW W❂RLD™

OFFICE PROFESSIONAL'S
DESK REFERENCE

Edited by Anthony S. Vlamis

MACMILLAN • USA

PROPERTY OF
DAKOTA COUNTY
TECHNICAL COLLEGE

Copyright © 1999 by Macmillan USA

All rights reserved. No part of this book shall be reproduced, stored in
a retrieval system, or transmitted by any means, electronic, mechanical,
photocopying, recording, or otherwise, without written permission from the
publisher. No patent liability is assumed with respect to the use of the information contained herein. Although every precaution has been taken in the
preparation of this book, the publisher and author assume no responsibility
for errors or omissions. Neither is any liability assumed for damages resulting from the use of the information contained herein.

Macmillan General Reference
A Pearson Education Macmillan Company
1633 Broadway
New York, NY 10019-6785

A Webster's New World™ Book

Macmillan is a registered trademark of Macmillan USA.

Webster's New World is a registered trademark of Macmillan USA.

ISBN 0-02-862883-7

Library of Congress Catalog Card Number 99-70262

Manufactured in the United States of America

03   02   01   00   99   4   3   2   1

This book is printed on 50# Husky Offset.

Trademarks

All terms mentioned in this book that are known to be trademarks or service marks have
been appropriately capitalized. Webster's New World cannot attest to the accuracy of this
information. Use of a term in this book should not be regarded as affecting the validity
of any trademark or service mark.

ABOUT THE AUTHOR/CONTRIBUTORS

Anthony S. Vlamis (residing in River Vale, New Jersey) has been in the field of business, professional, technical, and reference publishing for 25 years. A former executive editor at Simon & Schuster, Prentice-Hall, Amacom Books, and Van Nostrand Reinhold, he edited and published hundreds of titles in the business, industrial engineering, finance, and technology areas. He was a founder of Alexander Publishing and Marketing, a newsletter publisher and direct-marketing services agency. He is the author of *Smart Leadership* published by the American Management Association.

Susan Heyboer O'Keefe is co-founder and editor of the monthly newsletter *Secrets and Strategies for the Office Professional* (Economics Press) and editor of Stroman and Wilson's *Administrative Assistant's and Secretary's Handbook* (AMACOM Books).

Florence Stone has over 25 years of experience in management publishing at the American Management Association, most recently as senior editor responsible for all the organization's newsletters and journals. She is author of the new AMACOM book *Coaching, Counseling & Mentoring*. During her association with AMA, she has become an authority on supervisory and middle management problems and concerns.

Geoffrey Steck heads Alexander Publishing Inc., headquartered in Englewood, New Jersey. The firm provides direct-marketing support, motivational and business skills training, and editorial and publishing services such as the monthly newsletter *Secrets & Strategies for Office Professionals* (formerly *Secretary's Letter*), the magazine *Leadership—with a Human Touch*, and the biweekly *First-Rate Customer Service Manager's Memo*.

E. Alexander Saenz is a New York–based communications specialist for one of the world's largest banks and regularly writes for the mutual fund industry. As a freelance writer in the business and finance area, his writings have also appeared in a variety of professional books and journals including *Management Review* and the *Take-Charge Assistant*.

M. Faunette Johnston is an experienced reference editor working on such titles as *Pocket Style Guide, Dictionary of Quotations, Dictionary of Science, Pocket Book of Facts, Dictionary of Computer Terms,* and *Pocket Internet Directory and Dictionary*. She has a Master's degree in Communications Development from Colorado State University.

Other contributors include: Susan C. Bauer, Jeanette L. Bely, Murray Bromberg, Linda A. Bruce, Lois M. Burns, William W. Cook, Rose A. Doherty, Julie Eichenberger, Joyce Gold, Charlotte B. Holmquest, Audrey Katz, Milton Katz, Ruth Kimball Kent, Doreen La Blanc, Sheryl Lindsell-Roberts, James C. Matthews, John I. McCollum, Ardis R. Morton, Emojean G. Novotny, Barry Persky, Naomi Dornfeld Platt, Warren T. Schimmel, Abba Spero.

CONTENTS

CHAPTER 2 Other Office Documents   73

CHAPTER 5 Computers   165

CHAPTER 7 Office Operations   255

CHAPTER 8 Organizing People and Time   303

SIDEBARS AND TABLES

1

COMMUNICATIONS

◆

- **Face-to-Face Customer/Client Relations**

  Basic Communication Techniques

  The Protocol of Introductions

- **Basic Principles of Organization and Effectiveness**

  Telephone Techniques

  Answering Services, Answering Machines, and Voice Mail

  Long-Distance Services

  Memos

  Minutes of a Meeting

- **Correspondence**

  Letters

  Faxes

  E-mail

- **For More Information**

An office professional always has needed strong communication skills—but never before has the ability to communicate been so critical to an office professional's job. The responsibilities of this position have grown tremendously—and likely will continue to grow. Those office professionals who will benefit most from these ever-increasing opportunities for recognition—including promotions and raises—are those with communication strengths. They are the office professionals who can communicate effectively with customers and vendors. They are the professionals who have the interpersonal communication skills to work well with all members of their organization, from peers to technicians, to other managers, to senior executives, to the CEO. And they have the ability to network outside the organization to bring ideas for operating improvement to their workplace.

This book examines the traditional tasks of office professionals and also explores new and growing responsibilities. The subject of communication is an ideal place to begin. Today's office professionals serve in their managers' place in certain meetings and act as representatives of their operating group in project team meetings. They are the contacts with clients—international as well as domestic. Assistants' roles have given them the opportunities to utilize their communication skills to make good impressions, not only with their bosses but also with others who make promotion decisions.

FACE-TO-FACE CUSTOMER/ CLIENT RELATIONS

Good customer relations is a competitive advantage—and one to which you can contribute.

You, as the office professional, create the first impression when a client or customer visits the office. You are usually the first person visitors meet; by your welcome, you can help a visitor believe that he or she has chosen well the organization with which to do business. You can ignore the presence of a visitor or glare at him as he enters the office area, or you can continue to socialize while the visitor waits to get your attention. *Or* you can greet the visitor and ask if you can assist her.

If the visitor has an appointment, all you need to do is make the person comfortable until your boss is free. But if the visit is unexpected, and if your boss is tied up elsewhere or away from the office, you might have to make the customer feel welcome. Introduce yourself and offer to help. If you don't know the answer to the person's question, contact someone within the organization who can help. Keep a list of persons within your organization by your phone so that you can refer the visitor's problem to someone who can answer his or her questions.

Adapt your response to the customer's own style. On some occasions, a friendly, informal style works best. At other times, it is better to be completely professional.

BASIC COMMUNICATION TECHNIQUES

An important function of every office professional involves receiving guests—important or otherwise. How smoothly you handle this duty can dramatically affect everything that happens after your greeting.

If an individual seems rushed, respond by being as efficient as you can be. If someone seems relaxed and is smiling and happy, smile back and soften your tone. Professionals who have studied such responses call this pacing, establishing rapport, or mirroring. Although this technique is used most often by salespeople, it can work as effectively for office professionals in the course of their work.

Use the "Magic Mirror" Approach

Psychologists conclude that, in the short run, 90 percent of what's communicated between people comes from body language and tone of voice. So show visitors what they like best to see: themselves.

How do you use mirroring? When someone first approaches your desk, pay attention to his or her mood and deportment, and then adapt your responses accordingly. Affect a non-intimidating manner if the person seems at ease. If the person seems intent and formal, respond formally. If the person appears jolly, extend a cheery greeting. If the person seems frazzled, be empathetic.

A reminder: You're not ridiculing visitors when you mirror them. You're trying to make them feel comfortable, showing them that although they're in unfamiliar surroundings, they've come across someone who is like themselves and who can identify with their feelings.

Add the Personal Touch

The next crucial decision when you greet someone is whether to shake hands.

Some individuals feel awkward shaking hands with members of the opposite sex or with people perceived as subordinates. If the situation feels awkward, or if you sense an awkwardness in the other person, don't press the issue.

Otherwise, extend your hand. Grip the person's hand firmly but not tightly. Let him or her dictate how long you shake.

People usually welcome a touch that reassures and relaxes, as long as it's respectful. But be sensitive to persons of other cultures who do not like being touched by strangers. If you expect cultural differences, either discover the proper behavior and follow it, or keep your gestures as neutral as possible.

THE PROTOCOL OF INTRODUCTIONS

Introducing people correctly is important because it makes people feel at ease, fosters interesting conversations, feeds the ego of the introduced, and enhances your professional image.

Introductions have to do with communicating naturally and gracefully, and making people feel that they are valuable and important—skills every businessperson must have.

On various occasions in business you must introduce one person to another, whether in team or group meetings, in visits to suppliers or customer organizations, in professional association meetings, or in social occasions in which family members might be invited. The key to making introductions is to remember that the person lesser in age, rank, achievement, and so on should be introduced to the higher; a member of your organization to a client or customer; someone from your country to a visitor from a foreign country; and someone without an official title (for example, judge or senator) to the person with the title. If you find yourself introducing family members to office colleagues, you would introduce family members to your business associates.

Besides greeting visitors to your office, you might be responsible for taking visitors to meet with others or leading tours of the office if your boss is busy or unavailable. During the course of your travel through the office, you might have to introduce a visitor to those within your organization. Keep these tips in mind:

- Always introduce people with whom you are standing or walking when another person joins you.

- If you can remember the first name and not the last, use the first name: "Jerry, this is an old friend from my Chicago days. George, this is Jerry Perkins, one of the partners." (No one will notice that you didn't mention George's last name.)

- If you can remember the last name but not the first, bluff around it: "Jerry, this is an old friend, the very respectable Mr. Anderson, the best squash player in Chicago."

- If you can't remember any part of the name, laugh and admit it: "I'm sorry, but I can't even remember my mother's name. I'm hopeless!" The people with you should laugh, put out their hands to shake, and give their own names.

- If you get the feeling that someone is having difficulty remembering your name, extend your hand to the person standing next to him or her and introduce yourself. In other words, alleviate the embarrassment and give your name right away.

- Write down a difficult-to-pronounce name phonetically as soon as you're able, and practice saying it aloud several times. You might be asked to introduce an international colleague at a corporate function—practice. Or, write the name on a card, and as you take the person around, glance at the card to make sure you're pronouncing his or her name correctly.

■ If you're being introduced and the person doing it makes a mistake with your name, whisper in his or her ear to correct the error. Don't allow him or her to continue inaccurately. If you correct someone with a big smile on your face, he or she won't feel intimidated—just grateful.

BASIC PRINCIPLES OF ORGANIZATION AND EFFECTIVENESS

We communicate our professionalism not only in the work we do, but also in our greetings to visitors, as mentioned. But with other communications we must be alert to the impression we leave others. Over the telephone, always exhibit a professional demeanor when talking to others, whether they are internal callers or external callers. Likewise, memos and written communications should display carefulness and conscientiousness. This is what professionalism is all about.

TELEPHONE TECHNIQUES

The telephone is the most frequently used audio communication medium in the business world, and dependency on this instrument continues to grow.

Receptionists use the phone all day; assistants answer calls directed to them as well as their bosses.

The reputation and goodwill of the employer and the firm might depend upon your approach and skill in using the telephone. Although most people begin to use the telephone in early childhood, perhaps the majority still need to be trained in proper telephone techniques. An impressive way to point out defects in techniques—and one that results in a rapid and desirable change— is to make a recording or tape of a telephone conversation. Such a recording emphasizes the faults in telephone techniques and vividly points out areas needing improvement. Many organizations—even those that aren't efficiently organized—lose customers, money, and goodwill simply because of employees' poor telephone habits.

Speaking Clearly and Pleasantly

People talking on a phone have no visual image on which to base impressions. The frame of reference is based entirely upon the voice coming over the wires. If these sounds are jarring or unpleasant, a busy executive might quickly lose patience and discontinue association with the firm in question. On the other hand, a pleasant and understanding voice coming over an inanimate instrument can accomplish wonders. The power of the spoken word can and does exert a great impact upon the listener. Knowing how to pick the right tone of professionalism, friendliness, matter-of-factness, or even irritation is the key to good telephone relationships.

To enhance your telephone personality, inject variety and flexibility into the voice, and convey mood and attitude conversations. These qualities can be obtained through pitch, inflection, and emphasis. A high-pitched voice might convey an impression of childishness and immaturity, or of impatience and irritability. On the other hand, a voice that is well-modulated carries the impression of culture and polish. Pitch in speaking (as in pitch in music), refers to the key in which one speaks. Everyone has a range of tone within which a pleasant speaking voice is possible, and this can be consciously controlled. Each person must be conscious of his or her own range and practice utilizing it. An individual is said to speak in a *modulated* voice when the pitch falls in the lower half of the possible range. This tonal range carries best and is easiest to hear over the telephone.

In cultivating an interesting telephone personality, the speaker must enunciate clearly and distinctly. A garbled and indistinct speech pattern will annoy the listener who cannot understand what is being said. Do not be afraid to move your lips: You can't form rounded vowel sounds or distinct consonants unless the lips accomplish their function—however, it is not necessary to exaggerate or to become stilted. Your telephone voice should reflect your personality and transmit alertness and pleasantness. Your voice should be natural, distinct, and expressive—and neither too loud nor too soft. Avoid repetitious, mechanical words and phrases.

Answering Promptly

Answering a business telephone call is similar to welcoming a visitor. Therefore, it is essential that each call be greeted by a prompt, effective, and pleasing answer. Some disagreement exists about the impact of voice mail on customer relations. Still, most organizations have some version of voice mail in their offices. You'll want to set your system to reflect the attitude of your organization and your manager toward answering calls: Do they prefer to pick up calls after the first ring, or is it acceptable to answer after the third or even fourth ring?

The telephone should sit on the desk so that it is readily accessible. If you are left-handed, place the telephone on your left side; if you are right-handed, the phone belongs on the right side of your desk. You want it within reach, which means that you don't have to reach across your computer to pick it up. Keep a pad and pencil or pen handy to jot down necessary information.

Assistants might be juggling many things when the phone rings, and consequently put the call on hold as soon as they pick it up. Don't do this unless

it is absolutely imperative. Many callers find this practice infuriating. Instead, allow voice mail to pick up a call, or arrange for a colleague to pick up your phone after three rings. A co-worker can take a message after explaining that you are presently busy and will return the call as soon as you are free.
Use the same procedure if you step away from your desk for some time.

Never leave a telephone unattended. An unanswered telephone becomes an instrument of failure—failure to the company because of the loss of customers and failure of the individuals responsible.

A receptionist might or might not handle incoming calls in addition to greeting visitors (and notifying staff that the visitors have arrived). If this is part of the receptionist's responsibility, he or she should complete a discussion on the phone before turning to help a visitor. A receptionist never should ask a caller to wait while they attend to a visitor or staff member.

The matter isn't so clear-cut for other office staff when handling incoming calls represents 50 percent or more of the job. You can put a caller on hold for a brief period, either to address another issue or to search for materials pertinent to the telephone conversation.

On the Phone

When you pick up the phone, identify your office and yourself immediately. Let the caller know that he or she has reached the person he intended to reach. Don't just say, "Hello." This advice applies to assistants as well as receptionists, who should simply identify the company, ask whom the caller wishes to contact, and speedily connect the call to the individual the caller wants.

If you pick up your boss's line, you might want to let the caller know that it is your boss's line by saying, "Mr. Crawford's line," or "Ms. Erick's line." If you want, you then can identify yourself—"This is Ms. O'Brien, his assistant"—or say, "Mr. O'Connor is away from his phone. May I help you? I'm Ms. O'Brien, his assistant."

Many phones in today's offices have caller ID. This is very helpful in giving you direction about whether to put another call on hold or to just let it ring through to voice mail. Let's say that you are planning for a corporate retreat, and you have several calls out to local people as well as the hotel folks in Florida. If you're on the phone with a local caterer, you can let the line ring through if you see it's another local call. If it's your boss, you might put the other call on hold and pick up, or if it's long distance, you might finish and answer the other line.

Handling Incoming Calls

The wise telephone user develops a keen ear and learns to recognize the voices of important or frequent callers. However, a word of caution: Do not become too sure of an infallible ear, for voices might sound different over the telephone. If you know the voice beyond a doubt, use the caller's name when speaking. If you identify the voice correctly, the caller will be pleased that you have recognized and addressed him or her by name. Then speak *to* the person at the other end of the wire, not *at* the telephone. If you are incorrect in identifying the voice before divulging any information, little harm will occur because the caller will make the correction. Apologize tactfully and take up the business at hand. However, when the name of the caller is not revealed and/or the nature of the business is not identified, you always can ask politely, "Who is calling, please?" or "May I ask what this refers to?"

Some executives prefer their support staff to screen incoming calls. Do so with tact and discretion. In some cases, the executive will speak with anyone who calls, but wants to know beforehand who is calling and the nature of the business. The screener must obtain this information before transferring the call to the executive. Avoid curtness and rudeness in doing so. It is correct to say, for example, "May I tell Mr. Brown who is calling?" or "Ms. Winslow is talking on another line. Would you care to wait, or may I have her call you? I believe her other call may take some time." Also consider saying, "Mr. Zobkiw is in conference. May I help you?" Be sincere and courteous in your explanation, but do not divulge information unnecessarily. Your goal is simply to find out tactfully who is calling.

Although some executives answer the telephone themselves (especially those with direct lines), many depend on a receptionist or their own assistant to answer all incoming calls. Whoever takes these calls, therefore, must be familiar with the executive's preferences. Learn which calls the assistant is expected to handle, which are to be referred to the executive, and which should be transferred to someone else. Telephone callers must be classified accurately and quickly. Every call is important, and you must ascertain enough information to classify the call. Never allow a caller to get to the end of a long inquiry before being referred to the proper person. To forestall this, make a discreet vocal sound that causes the caller to pause slightly so that you can say, "Mr. Chan in the shipping department should be able to help you with this. Please let me transfer your call to him."

Routing the Call

The following sections describe calls that the office professional usually can handle.

Requests for information. Such calls might come to the office receptionist or an assistant within the office. Either can handle the information if it's not confidential and if no doubt exists about the request. For instance, some organizations include a main number to handle requests for product information if they do not have a designated customer service operation. If they have placed an advertisement for a job vacancy, the company might want to set aside a phone to receive such calls without identifying the organization. If the latter is the case, then those who might pick up the phone will be told in advance not to identify their organization.

Sometimes, you might have to check with the employer before imparting information. If any complications arise, it is always wiser to turn the call over to the executive. In certain situations, the assistant can ask for a letter of request and respond upon its receipt and approval.

Requests for appointments. Such calls likely will go directly to the person with whom the caller wants an appointment, or to his or her assistant. If the assistant answers the call, he or she can place the appointment tentatively on the manager's calendar, and confirm once the manager returns.

After you have received and routed the call, take down the message or information. Remember always to write clearly, and always get the phone number and verify the caller's name. This information will help in returning calls.

You also might decide to transfer the call directly to the recipient or other appropriate person. Let the caller know you are transferring; if the caller would rather not be switched over, provide another phone number to call directly (or take a message). If the caller agrees to a transfer, make sure that the right office is reached, and give the person in that office sufficient information before hanging up so that the caller will not need to repeat it.

When taking calls from persons who wish to speak to the executive directly, the screener must know how to handle the following situations tactfully, discreetly, and diplomatically:

- *The employer is in and free.* Inform the executive of the caller. On occasion, if the caller is well-known to the employer and is someone to whom the executive talks frequently, the assistant may signal the executive to pick up the telephone.

- *The employer is in but does not want to be disturbed.* Tell the caller that the executive is engaged at the moment, and ask whether you can take a message to him or her as soon as the employer is free.

- *The employer is in another office in the building.* The assistant should ascertain whether the executive will be available for telephone calls when away from the office. Generally, only the most urgent calls should be transferred under such circumstances.

Taking Messages

It is good practice to keep a written record of all incoming calls, particularly when the executive is away from the office. Indicate the time the call was received; the name, business affiliation, and telephone number of the caller; and the message. Then sign the note with your initials. If the message comes from an out-of-town caller, also record the area code or the telephone operator's number. When taking a message, read it back to the caller to avoid errors or misunderstandings. Always take messages verbatim. Be patient and pleasant, but persistent. Ask the caller to spell out both first and last names, if necessary. If numbers are involved, repeat the sequence for verification.

A good way to keep track of these messages is to use a special phone message book that is available from most office supply stores and catalogs. This a spiral-bound book provides perforated rows of message slips that you can tear out and give to the recipient, as well as carbon copies of the message for later reference.

When taking a call, place the phone message slip on the executive's desk immediately. The heads-up assistant also should anticipate the executive's needs by attaching to the slips any material (possibly annotated) necessary for reference to conclude the transaction successfully—this can include back correspondence, a bill, price lists, or whatever might assist the executive in handling the call intelligently.

To handle the incoming calls more efficiently, the office staff should know where the executive will be when away from the office, whether urgent messages can be relayed, and the expected time of return to the office.

In taking calls for other persons in the office, it is helpful if you can state when that person will return or whether the call can be transferred somewhere else. Offer whatever information is possible; otherwise, the caller might get the impression of being put off with an excuse. Be courteous and use discretion in explaining an absence from the office. It is less offensive to say, "Ms. Jones is away from her desk just now. May I have her call you, or would you prefer to leave a message?" than to say bluntly, "She's out," or "This is her coffee break," or "I don't know where she is." The office professional must always use tact in dealing with callers, whether it be for one's own executive or for another co-worker.

Taking Action

If you promise the caller some definite action, you must see to it that the promise is kept. If the caller is told that the executive will call back, then this information must be conveyed to the employer so that the call can be made. A broken promise can result in a canceled order or a lost customer—and it might take many months to regain lost goodwill.

If, for some reason, you can't deliver on the action, it's always safe to call back and let the caller know the information might be delayed or is not available. He or she might be disappointed but will appreciate the effort made by the follow-up call.

On some calls that the office staff can handle, more information might be needed than is within immediate reach. In such a case, leave the telephone to look up the necessary information, and inform the caller of this fact and of the length of time that it could take to obtain the material. Offer the caller a choice of waiting or of being called back. The caller never should be left waiting for an unreasonable amount of time. If you make a promise to call back with the needed information, you must honor the promise.

If the caller is waiting to speak to the executive, the assistant should reassure the caller periodically that the call will be connected as soon as the employer is free. When you're ready to transfer the call, thank the caller for waiting.

Completing the Incoming Call

At the completion of the call, indicate its end by summing up the details. Use the caller's name when saying a pleasant "Good-bye." It is courteous to wait for the caller to end the call. Permitting the caller to say "Good-bye" first also allows time for last-minute orders or special instructions. Replace the receiver gently in its cradle—the most pleasant "Good-bye" can be spoiled by the jarring sound of a receiver dropped into position. Do not hang up until your caller has done so first.

ANSWERING SERVICES, ANSWERING MACHINES, AND VOICE MAIL

As mentioned earlier, office staff today frequently rely on answering services, answering machines, or voice mail to handle incoming calls when they are too busy to pick up or are away from the phones.

Answering Services

Before the advent of modern electronics, the outside answering service offered the only viable way to get calls answered when no business "insiders" were available. Services still exist as an option for all sorts of businesses, but these are used primarily when a human touch or human judgment concerning off-hours callers is important to the enterprise.

Many professionals (such as doctors, dentists, accountants, and financial advisors) still use answering services. These individuals prefer an answering service for two reasons: The call might be an emergency, and they might need to be notified immediately. The caller also might need the reassurance that the person being called will understand the urgency of his or her request. A pager might alert the owner that someone wants to speak with him or her, but it doesn't communicate the compelling need for the call to be returned, which an answering service hopefully will do. A person might leave an urgent message on voice mail, but he or she can't be sure that the person being called regularly checks messages.

A good answering service should act as if it were the company—in effect, as if it were a message center at another location. When choosing one to serve your company, look (and listen) for courteous, professional-sounding operators who are able to identify themselves as you would like to be identified when they're covering your company's calls.

Procedure setup is critical when using an answering service to ensure that you are notified of emergencies. Make sure that you've set up an acceptable routine for doing so.

Answering Machines

Chip-sized electronics make some fairly inexpensive machines quite sophisticated, adding features such as mailboxes for several people or departments. Despite their popularity, keep in mind some answering machine cautions:

- Don't overdo the outgoing message you record. Write it down and practice saying it before you record. You might announce your regular business hours and perhaps an alternative means to contact the company (such as a fax number). But then get quickly to the business of taking a message if that's what you want to do.

- Be prepared to retrieve messages when you push the playback button. Quickly convey each to the appropriate individual, or at least acknowledge receipt to the original caller.

Answering machines don't have all the functions of most voice-mail systems, however. Although they work well for smaller organizations, voice mail is more appropriate for larger organizations.

Voice Mail

By far the most common systems in use today, voice-mail systems work like answering machines on a grand scale. The system might be internal, using computers or equipment in your company, or it might be a service provided by the local phone company. Most offer a slew of options that make them either another valuable workplace tool or a maze that can turn off callers with their impersonality.

The guidelines for good answering machine messages apply systemwide to voice-mail setups—in fact, they're doubly important because a caller might face two tiers of messaging before he or she gets to leave one. You know what annoys you when you're caught in voice mail limbo. Remedy it in your system.

Telephone Directories

Once a mainstay of business information, the mushrooming of telephone numbers and telephone-related ways of contacting companies and individuals—fax lines, e-mail, Web sites, cell phones, pagers, and so on—has diminished the usefulness of the local directory. Still, these are good places to begin the search for contact information about a firm or individual.

Local directories are usually available free to local service subscribers, at least one per phone listing. Libraries often have out-of-town directories, or you

CREATING GREAT VOICE-MAIL MESSAGES

You want callers who get your voice mail to want to leave a message. You also want those whom you call to return your call when you leave a message on voice mail.

Here's how to marshal the many phone skills you already have to handle voice mail easily and effectively:

- *Put a smile in your voice.* What works as a good phone tip for "live" conversations works even better for voice mail. A smile on your face adds pleasantness to your voice. Imagine that the person you're talking to can see you that very moment. This will help add expression and variation to your words.

- *Address the individual by name.* This gives the call a personal touch. The individual also will pay greater attention to your message, having heard his or her name first.

- *Who, what, when, where, and why?* You know the purpose of your call; the other person doesn't. Make your message specific: Do you want the other person to return your call, or will you call back? Do you want that person to have information ready for the call back? Say so now.

- *Time is of the essence.* Just as you consider time zones when you make a call, keep them in mind when leaving messages. Whenever you mention a time, frame it with a "my time" or "your time" reference so there's no mistake.

- *Postmark your voice mail.* Although some voice mail services automatically date and time stamp messages, others do not. The best bet is always to add that information to your voice message. It might not seem necessary at the moment, but if a person is collecting more than a day's worth of mail at once, undated messages can be very confusing. Postmarking your mail is essential when you leave instructions such as "I need this information tomorrow."

- *Sign your letter.* Unless it's your mother, the other person might not recognize your voice. Leave your full name, even if you speak to the person frequently. What might seem like overkill to you can save frustration for the person who can't place you by your first name alone.

- *Sign off by leaving your phone number.* Even if you're sure that the other person already has your number, state it anyway. This saves the time of looking it up.

might acquire one for a modest fee for areas where your company might have greater than passing interest.

Most local directories now are arranged in general sections to facilitate your information search. As a rule, the introductory section contains useful information about phone company services and might present some local highlights. The White Pages embody the comprehensive phone number listing, although the number listed might represent one of many ways to reach the company or individual you seek. Remember that the printed book is dated as soon as it rolls off the press—new numbers are issued daily.

This is why phone companies put their directories, both White and Yellow Pages, online—so they can always be up-to-date. One site for all Yellow Pages in the United States is www.bigbook.com. Another site that offers online White Pages is www.whowhere.com. Still, we need paper editions because we don't always have access to the Internet.

Government-related phone information often is listed in a section of its own. Paid listings in the Yellow Pages might provide more detailed information about phoning businesses you wish to contact.

Personal Phone Directories

For numbers you use all the time, such as those for clients or vendors, you'll want to have a system for keeping personal numbers organized and handy. You could have a low-tech recipe box full of 3×5 cards or a Rolodex with hand-written contact information. You also can go high-tech by keeping an address book on your desktop in Outlook or another scheduler or database. Card files, such as Rolodex cards, are very popular because they offer an organized way to store and access cards, plus easy replacement or addition of addresses and numbers. If you travel or move between offices, you might even want to investigate a portable desktop address book. Most are the size of large calculators, run on battery power, and can store hundreds of names, addresses, and numbers.

Many office professionals also keep business cards. Some are organized separately (in a binder designed specifically to hold business cards in plastic sleeves) or as part of a card file system. At office supply stores, you even can buy a hole punch for business cards that will punch the slots required to fit it into a Rolodex system.

The key to any personal system is using it to keep information as up-to-date as possible. The record should identify individuals by noting title and company affiliations as well as address and phone number options, including extension listings, fax numbers, toll-free numbers, cell phones, pager numbers, e-mail addresses, and the like. Personal data (spouse: Connie; one son: Alex; likes fishing) also might go into the record.

> **TIP:** Be aware of what information is available on what scale. You don't want to publish personal home numbers or information in the company phone list, nor do you want to restrict access of general information. You must counterbalance the capability of recording many things in a semi-public company database with the need for privacy. Certain information to which you are privy might not warrant general circulation—particularly information about other employees. The in-house telephone list, if you have one, should be bare bones for general perusal.

Assembling Data for Outgoing Calls

To place outgoing calls quickly for the employer, the office support staff should master all the telephone techniques needed to do this skillfully. Be absolutely certain of the telephone number before calling. Then assemble all the information that might be necessary to conduct the business transaction when the call is put through. You might have to obtain materials from the files to refresh the executive's memory on previous business, or you might need to get other information that will help in making a successful call. All pertinent material should be placed on the executive's desk before the call is made. Don't call someone unless you have the materials you need in front of you. It is unfair to make the person you are calling have to wait while you hunt for the pertinent information.

If you are placing a call for someone else, it is also a good practice to be sure they will be free and available to take the call as soon as it goes through. Delays not only lower the prestige of the company and the executive and cause annoyance, but they also can prove costly to the firm making the call.

Even today, the question frequently arises about which executive should answer first. Courtesy prescribes that the caller should be on the line, ready to talk, when the person called is put on the line by his or her own staff member—particularly if the person called outranks the caller. Put the executive on the line immediately, if possible. This can he done readily if the assistant identifies the employer when the call is answered. The assistant at the other end then can transfer the call to the person called without delay, or immediately can inform the caller about how to reach that individual.

LONG-DISTANCE SERVICES

In addition to business calls within the local community or surrounding areas, you might have to place calls to more distant points.

When you call long distance, keep in mind that different types of long-distance calls exist, called *classes*. These classes determine how calls are billed; rates can vary, depending on time of day, area called, use of a live operator, direct dial, and so on. Keep in mind that long-distance calls do add up—and make for a large proportion of business expense. Try to be organized and aware of the cost, and avoid use of high-priced calls (such as operator assistance) when possible. Also, make sure you try to look up a number first instead of just calling directory assistance.

AREA CODES

U.S. Domestic

Until 1990, all area codes had either a "1" or a "0" as the middle number. However, with rapid population and technology growth in many regions, area codes now contain all numbers. This list might change because area codes are added and change often.

Alabama		Colorado		
north	205	Denver	303	
south	334	southeast	719	
Alaska	907	west and northwest	970	
Arizona	520	Connecticut		
Phoenix	602	east	860	
		west	203	
Arkansas	870	Delaware	302	
Little Rock	501			
California		District of Columbia	202	
central	209	Florida		
Los Angeles	213	east and central	407	
Los Angeles west	562	Gainesville	352	
north and central	530	Miami	305	
	916	north	904	
northwest	707	south	941	
northwest and central	510	southeast	561	
	925		954	
Pasadena	818	west and central	813	
south	310	Georgia		
San Diego	619	Atlanta	404	
San Francisco	415	Atlanta northwest	770	
southeast	760	north	706	
southwest	714	south	912	
	805			
	949	Guam	671	
west and central	408	Hawaii	808	
	650			
	909	Idaho	208	

Illinois			Massachusetts (cont'd)	
central	217		northeast	508
Chicago	312		southeast	978
	630		west	413
	708		Michigan	
	773		central	517
	847		Detroit	313
north	815		northeast	810
northwest	309		northwest	906
south	618		Oakland county	248
Indiana			southeast	734
central	765		west	616
Indianapolis	317		Minnesota	
north	219		Minneapolis	320
south	812		St. Paul	612
Iowa			north	218
central	515		south	507
east	319		Mississippi	228
west	712		Jackson	601
Kansas			Missouri	
Kansas City	913		east	573
north	785		northwest	816
south	316		St. Louis	314
Kentucky			southwest	417
east	606		Montana	406
west	502		Nebraska	
Louisiana			east	402
northwest	318		west	308
southeast	504		Nevada	702
Maine	207		New Hampshire	603
Maryland			New Jersey	
east	410		central	732
	443		northwest	201
west	240			973
	301		northwest and central	908
Massachusetts			south	609
Boston	617		New Mexico	505
	781			

continues

AREA CODES *continued*

New York	
northeast	518
northwest	315
south and central	607
southeast	914
west	716
New York City	718
cellular	917
Long Island	516
Manhattan	212
North Carolina	
central	910
east	919
west	704
North Dakota	701
Ohio	
Cleveland	216
Dayton	937
north and central	440
northeast	330
northwest	419
southeast and central	614
southwest	513
Oklahoma	
northeast	918
west and central	405
Oregon	541
northwest	503
Pennsylvania	
east	717
Philadelphia	215
southeast	610
southwest	412
	724
west	814
Puerto Rico	787
Rhode Island	401

South Carolina	
coastal	843
north and central	803
northwest	864
South Dakota	605
Tennessee	
east	423
north and central	615
south and central	931
west	901
Texas	
Arlington	817
Dallas	214
	972
east central	254
Houston	281
	713
north and central	940
northeast	903
northwest	806
San Antonio	210
south and central	512
southeast	409
southwest	830
	956
west	915
Utah	801
Vermont	802
Virginia	
central	804
east	757
north	703
west	540
Washington	
east	509
northwest	253
	425
Seattle	206
southwest	360

West Virginia	304	Wisconsin (cont'd)	
Wisconsin		southeast	920
Milwaukee	414	southwest	608
north	715	Wyoming	307

Canadian Domestic

Alberta	403	Ontario (cont'd)	
British Columbia	250	northwest	807
Vancouver	604	southeast	905
		southwest	519
Manitoba	204	Toronto	416
New Brunswick	506	Quebec	450
Newfoundland	709	Montreal	514
		Quebec City	418
Nova Scotia/Prince		Sherbrooke	819
Edward Island	902	Saskatchewan	306
Ontario		Yukon/Northwest	
central	705	Territories	867
east	613		

Caribbean Domestic

Anguilla	264	Jamaica	876
Antigua and Barbuda	268	Montserrat	664
The Bahamas	242	Northern Mariana Islands	670
Barbados	246	St. Kitts/Nevis	869
Bermuda	441	St. Lucia	758
British Virgin Islands	284	St. Vincent/Grenadines	784
Caribbean Islands	809	Trinidad and Tobago	868
Cayman Islands	345	Turks and Caicos Islands	649
Dominica	767	U.S. Virgin Islands	340
Grenada	473		

Time Differences

Check the differences in time when planning to place a long-distance call. Be aware not only that this country is divided into time zones, but also understand that differences in time exist in all countries. For example, the United States (excluding Alaska and Hawaii) is divided into four standard time zones:

800 NUMBERS FOR
LONG-DISTANCE SERVICE PROVIDERS

Chances are, you won't ever have to price or select long-distance service for your office or company, but sometimes billing questions, travel concerns, or other questions require a call to a long-distance provider.

Amnex	800-287-2646
AT&T	800-222-0400
Cable & Wireless	800-486-8686
Frontier	800-836-7000
INS	800-469-4000
LCI	800-860-1020
LDDS WorldCom	800-264-1000
MCI	800-950-5555
Network Phoenix	800-800-3002
One Star	800-950-4357
Sprint	800-877-4646
UniDial Communications/Solutions	800-832-7999
U.S. Long Distance	800-460-1111

Eastern, Central, Mountain, and Pacific. Each zone is one hour earlier than the zone immediately to the east of it: When it is noon Eastern Standard Time, it is 11 A.M. in the Central zone. Likewise, 10 A.M. in Mountain zone is 9 A.M. Pacific time. Greenwich Mean Time (which is the mean solar time of the meridian at Greenwich, England) is used as the basis for standard time throughout most of the world.

Teleconferencing

When you set up a teleconference, bring the telephone numbers of those who will be in conference with you. Depending on the number of individuals on the teleconference and the existing equipment, you might be able to set up the phone conference from a typical office phone, or you might need to work through either a telephone service company or your company's switchboard.

INTERNATIONAL COUNTRY AND CITY CALLING CODES

Albania	355	Santa Fe	42
Durres	52	Tandil	293
Elbassan	545	Armenia	374
Korce	824		
Shkoder	224	Aruba	297
Tirana	42	All cities	8
Algeria	213	Ascension Island	247
Adrar	7	Australia	61
Ain Defla	3	Adelaide	8
Bejaia	5	Ballarat	53
Guerrar	9	Brisbane	7
American Samoa	684	Canberra	6
		Darwin	89
Andorra	376	Geelong	52
Angola	244	Gold Coast	75
Luanda	2	Hobart	02
		Launceston	03
Anguilla	264	Melbourne	3
Antarctica		Newcastle	49
Casey Base	67212	Perth	9
Scott Base	672	Sydney	2
		Toowoomba	76
Antigua and Barbuda	268	Townsville	77
Argentina	54	Wollongong	42
Babia Blanca	91	Austria	43
Buenos Aires	1	Bludenz	5552
Cordoba	51	Graz	316
Corrientes	783	Innsbruck	512
La Plata	21	Kitzbuhel	5356
Mar Del Plata	23	Klagenfurt	463
Mendoza	61	Krems An Der Donau	2732
Merlo	220	Linz Donau	70
Posadas	752	Neunkirchen	
Resistencia	722	Niederosterreich	2635
Rio Cuatro	586	St. Polten	2742
Rosario	41	Salzburg	662
San Juan	64	Vienna	1
San Rafael	627	Villach	4242

continues

INTERNATIONAL COUNTRY AND CITY CALLING CODES *continued*

Wels	7242	Mons	65
Wiener Neustadt	2622	Namur	81
		Ostend	59
Azerbaijan	994	Verviers	87
Baku	12		
Daskasan	216	Belize	501
Sumgayit	164	Belize City	2
		Belmopan	8
The Bahamas	242	Benque Viejo Del	
		Carmen	93
Bahrain	973	Corozal Town	4
		Dangriga	5
Bangladesh	880	Independence	6
Barisal	431	Orange Walk	3
Bogra	51	Punta Gorda	7
Chittagong	31	San Ignacio	92
Comilla	81	Stan Creek	5
Dhaka	2		
Khulna	41	Benin	229
Maulabi Bazar	861		
Mymensingh	91	Bermuda	441
Narayangon	671		
Rajshaki	721	Bhutan	975
Sylhet	821		
		Bolivia	591
Barbados	246	Cochabamba	42
		Cotoga	388
Belarus	375	Guayaramerin	855
Loev	2347	La Belgica	923
Minsk	172	La Paz	2
Mogilev	222	Mineros	984
		Montero	92
Belgium	32	Oruro	52
Antwerp	3	Portachuelo	924
Bruges	50	Saavedra	924
Brussels	2	Santa Cruz	3
Charleroi	71	Sucre	64
Courtrai	56	Trinidad	46
Ghent	9	Warnes	923
Hasselt	11		
La Louviere	64	Bosnia Herzegovina	387
Leuven	16	Mostar	88
Libramont	61	Sarajevo	71
Liege	41	Zenica	72
Malines	15		

Botswana	267	Burkina Faso	226
Jwaneng	380	Burundi	257
Kanye	340	Bujumbura	2
Lobatse	330	Buruchi	50
Mahalapye	410	Gitega	40
Mochudi	377	Muyinga	30
Molepolole	320	Rutana	50
Orapa	270		
Palapye	420	Cambodia	855
Serowe	430	Phnom Penh	23
		Cameroon	327
Brazil	55		
Belem	91	Cape Verde Islands	238
Belo Horizonte	31		
Brasilia	61	Cayman Islands	345
Curitiba	41	Central African Rep.	236
Fortaleza	85		
Goiania	62	Chad	235
Niteroi	21	Moundou	69
Pelotas	532	N'djamena	51
Porto Alegre	51		
Recife	81	Chile	56
Rio de Janeiro	21	Chiguayante	41
Salvador	71	Concepcion	41
Santo Andre	11	La Serena	51
Santos	132	Penco	41
Sao Paulo	11	Recreo	32
Vitoria	27	San Bernardo	2
		Santiago	2
British Virgin Islands	284	Talcahuano	41
		Valparaiso	32
Brunei	673	Vina del Mar	32
Bandar Seri Bagawan	2	China	86
Kuala Belait	3	Beijing	10
Mumong	3	Fuzhou	591
Tutong	4	Guangzhou	20
		Shanghai	21
Bulgaria	359		
Kardjali	361	Christmas Island	672
Pazardjik	34	Christmas	4
Plovdiv	32		
Sofia	2	Cocos Islands	672
Varna	52	Cocos	3

continues

INTERNATIONAL COUNTRY AND CITY CALLING CODES *continued*

Colombia	57	Platres	5
Armenia	67	Polis	6
Barranquilla	58	Czech Republic	42
Bogota	1	Brno	5
Bucaramanga	76	Havirov	6994
Cali	2	Ostrava	69
Cartagena	5	Prague	2
Cartago	656	Denmark	45
Cucuta	75		
Giradot	834	Djibouti	253
Ibague	82	Dominica	767
Manizales	68		
Medellin	4	Dominican Republic	809
Neiva	88	Ecuador	593
Palmira	22	Ambato	3
Pereira	63	Cayambe	2
Santa Marta	54	Cuenca	7
Comoros	269	Esmeraldas	6
Congo	242	Guayaquil	4
		Ibarra	6
Cook Islands	682	Loja	7
Costa Rica	506	Machachi	2
Croatia	385	Machala	7
Dubrovnik	20	Manta	4
Rijeka	51	Portoviejo	5
Split	21	Quevedo	5
Zagreb	41	Quito	2
		Salinas	4
Cuba	53	Santo Domingo	2
Havana City	7	Tulcan	6
Santiago de			
Cuba Santia	226	Egypt	20
		Alexandria	3
Cyprus	53	Aswan	97
Famagusta	392	Asyut	88
Kyrenia	581	Benha	13
Larnaca	4	Cairo	2
Lefkonico	3	Damanhour	5
Limassol	5	El Mahallah	43
Nicosia	2	El Mansoura	50
Paphos	6	Luxor	95

Port Said	66	French Antilles	596
Shebin El Kom	48	French Guiana	594
Sohag	93		
Tanta	40	French Polynesia	689
El Salvador	503	Gabon	241
Equatorial Guinea	240	Gambia	220
Bata	8	Georgia	995
Malabo	9	Suhumi	881
Qaliub	2	Tblisi	883
Eritrea	291		
Estonia	372	Germany	49
Rakvere	32	Bad Homburg	6172
Tallinn	2	Berlin	30
Tartu	7	Bonn	228
		Bremen	421
Ethiopia	251	Cologne	221
Addis Ababa	1	Cottbus	355
Awassa	6	Dresden	351
Dire Dawa	5	Dusseldorf	211
Jimma	77	Erfurt	361
Nazareth	2	Essen	201
		Frankfurt am Main	69
Faroe Islands	298	Frankfurt an der Oder	335
Falkland Islands	500	Gera	365
		Halle	345
Fiji Islands	679	Hamburg	50
Finland	358	Heidelberg	6221
Helsinki	09	Karl-Stadt	9353
Joensuu	013	Koblenz	261
Jyvaskyla	014	Leipzig	341
Kuopio	017	Magdeburg	391
Lahti	03	Mannheim	621
Lappeenranta	05	Munich	89
Oulu	08	Neubrandenburg	395
Pori	02	Nurnberg	911
Vaasa	06	Potsdam	331
France	33	Rostock	381
Aix-en-Provence	4	Saal	38223
Bordeaux	5	Schwerin	385
Cherbourg	2	Stuttgart	711
Paris	1	Wiesbaden	611

continues

INTERNATIONAL COUNTRY AND CITY CALLING CODES *continued*

Ghana	233		Labe	51
Accra	21		Mamou	68
Koforidua	81			
Kumasi	51		Guinea-Bissau	245
Takoradi	31		Guyana	592
			Anna Regina	71
Gibraltar	350		Bartica	5
Greece	30		Beteryerwaging	20
Argos	751		Georgetown	2
Athens	1		Ituni	41
Corfu	661		Linden	4
Corinth	741		Mabaruma	77
Iraklion	81		Mahaica	28
Kavala	51		Mahaicony	21
Larissa	41		New Amsterdam	3
Patrai	61		New Hope	66
Rodos	241		Rosignol	30
Salonica	31		Timehri	61
Sparti	731		Vreed-En-Hoop	64
Tripolis	71		Whim	37
Volos	421			
Zagora	426		Haiti	509
Greenland	299		Honduras	504
Grenada	473		Hong Kong	852
Guadeloupe	590		Hungary	36
Basse-Terre	81		Abasar	37
Capesterre	86		Balatonaliga	84
Gosier	84		Budapest	1
Grand Bourg	97		Dorgicse	80
Jarry	26		Fertoboz	99
Pointe-a-Pitre	8		Gyor	96
			Kaposvar	82
Guam	671		Kazincbarcika	48
			Komlo	72
Guatamala	502		Miskolc	46
Guatamala City	2		Nagykanizsa	93
			Szekesfehervar	22
Guinea	224		Szolnok	56
Conakry	4		Varpalota	80
Faranah	81		Zalaegerszeg	92
Kindia	61			

Iceland	354	Surabaya	31
Akureyri	6	Tanjungkarang	721
Hafnarfjorður	1	Yogyakarta	274
Husavik	6	Iran	98
Keflavik Naval Base	2	Abadan	631
Sandgerði	2	Ahwaz	61
Selfoss	8	Arak	861
Siglufjorður	6	Esfahan	31
Stokkseyri	8	Ghazvin	281
Suðavik	4	Ghome	251
Vik	8	Hamadan	81
India	91	Karadj	261
Ahmedabad	79	Kerman	341
Amritsar	183	Mashad	51
Bangalore	80	Rasht	231
Baroda	265	Rezaiyeh	441
Bhopal	755	Shiraz	71
Bombay	22	Tabriz	41
Calcutta	33	Tehran	21
Chandigarh	172	Iraq	964
Hyderabad	40	Baghdad	1
Jaipur	141	Basra	40
Jullunder	181	Kerbela	32
Kanpur	512	Kirkuk	50
Madras	44	Mousil	60
New Delhi	11	Najaf	33
Poona	212	Ireland, Republic of	353
Surat	261	Arklow	402
Indonesia	62	Cork	21
Bandung	22	Dingle	66
Cirebon	231	Donegal	72-75
Denpasar	361	Drogheda	41
Jakarta	21	Dublin	1
Madiun	351	Dundalk	42
Malang	341	Ennis	65
Medan	61	Galway	91
Padang	751	Kildare	45
Palembang	711	Killarney	64
Sekurang	778	Limerick	61
Semarang	24	Sligo	71
Solo	271		

continues

Tipperary	62	Verona	45
Tralee	66	Vatican City	6
Tullamore	502	Ivory Coast	225
Waterford	51		
Wexford	53	Jamaica	876
Israel	972	Japan	81
Afula	6	Chiba	43
Ako	4	Fuchu	423
Ashkelon	7	Hiroshima	82
Bat Yam	3	Kawasaki	44
Beer Sheva	7	Kobe	78
Dimona	7	Kyoto	75
Hadera	6	Nagasaki	958
Haifa	4	Nagoya	52
Holon	3	Naha	98
Jerusalem	2	Osaka	6
Nazareth	6	Sapporo	11
Netania	9	Sasebo	956
Ramat Gan	3	Tachikawa	425
Rehovot	8	Tokyo	3
Tel Aviv	3	Yokohama	45
Tiberias	6	Yokosuka	468
Tsefat	6	Jordan	962
Italy	39	Amman	6
Bari	80	Aqaba	3
Bologna	51	Irbid	2
Brindisi	831	Jerash	4
Capri	81	Karak	3
Como	31	Maa'n	3
Florence	55	Mafruq	4
Genoa	10	Ramtha	2
Milan	2	Sueeleh	6
Naples	81	Sult	5
Padova	49	Zerqa	9
Palermo	91	Kazakhstan	7
Pisa	50	Alma-Ata	3272
Rome	6	Chimkent	325
Torino	11	Guryev	312
Trieste	40	Petropavlovsk	315
Venice	41		

Kenya	254	Laos	856
Anmer	2845	Vientiane	21
Bamburi	11	Latvia	371
Embakasi	2	Daugavpils	54
Gigiri	2	Jelgava	30
Kabete	2	Liepaja	34
Karen	2882	Riga	2
Kiambu	154	Ventspils	36
Kikuyu	154		
Kisumu	35	Lebanon	961
Langata	2	Beirut	1
Mombasa	11	Tripoli	6
Nairobi	2	Zahle	8
Nakuru	37	Lesotho	266
Shanzu	11		
Thika	151	Liberia	231
Uthiru	2	Libya	218
Kiribati	686	Angelat	282
		Benghazi	61
Korea, North	850	Benina	63
Pyong Yang	2	Derna	81
		Misuratha	51
Korea, South	82	Sabratha	24
Chuncheon	361	Sebha	71
Chung Ju	431	Taigura	26
Icheon	336	Tripoli	2133
Inchon	32	Zawai	23
Kwangju	62	Zuara	25
Masan	551		
Osan	339	Liechtenstein	41
Pohang	562	Kaunas	7
Pusan	51	Klaipeda	6
Seoul	2	Panevezys	54
Suwon	331	Siauliai	1
Taegu	53	Vilnius	2
Uijongbu	351		
Ulsan	522	Lithuania	370
Wonju	371	Luxembourg	352
Kuwait	965	Macau	853
Kyrgyzstan	7	Montserrat	664
Osh	33222		

continues

INTERNATIONAL COUNTRY AND CITY CALLING CODES *continued*

Morocco	212	Okahandja	6228
Agadir	88	Olympia	61
Beni-Mellal	348	Otjiwarongo	651
Berrechid	2	Pioneerspark	61
Casablanca	2	Swakopmund	641
El Jadida	334	Tsumeb	671
Fez	5	Windhoek	61
Kenitra	73	Nauru	674
Marrakech	4		
Meknes	55	Nepal	977
Mohammedia	332	Bhaktapur	1
Nador	660	Dhangadi	91
Oujda	668	Gorkha	64
Rabat	7	Kathmandu	1
Tangiers	99	Nepalgunj	81
Tetouan	996	Netherlands	31
Mozambique	258	Amsterdam	20
Beira	3	Arnhem	85
Chimolo	51	Eindhoven	40
Chokwe	21	Groningen	50
Maputo	1	Haarlem	23
Matola	4	The Hague	70
Nampula	6	Heemstede	23
Quelimane	4	Hillegersberg	10
Tete	52	Hoensbroek	45
Xai-Xai	22	Hoogkerk	50
		Hoogvliet	10
Myanmar	95	Loosduinen	70
Bassein	42	Nijmegen	80
Mandalay	2	Oud Zuilen	30
Monywa	71	Rotterdam	10
Prome	53	Utrecht	30
Rangoon	1	Netherlands Antilles	599
Namibia	264	Bonaire	7
Gobabis	681	Curacao	9
Grootfontein	6731	Saba	46
Industria	61	St. Eustatius	38
Keetmanshoop	631	St. Maarten	5
Luderitz	6331		
Mariental	661	New Caledonia	687

New Zealand	64	Norfolk Island	672
Auckland	9	Norway	47
Christchurch	3		
Dunedin	3	Oman	968
Hamilton	7	Pakistan	92
Hastings	6	Abbotabad	5921
Invercargill	3	Bahawaipur	621
Napier	6	Faisalabad	411
Nelson	3	Gujranwala	431
New Plymouth	6	Hyderabad	221
Palmerston, N	6	Islamabad	51
Rotorua	7	Karachi	21
Tauranga	7	Lahore	42
Timaru	3	Multan	61
Wanganui	6	Okara	442
Wellington	4	Peshawar	521
Whangarei	9	Quetta	81
Nicaragua	505	Sahiwal	441
Boaco	54	Sargodha	451
Chinandega	341	Sialkot	432
Diriamba	4222	Sukkur	71
Esteli	71	Palau	680
Granada	55	Panama	507
Jinotepe	41		
Leon	311	Papua New Guinea	675
Managua	2	Paraguay	595
Masatepe	44	Asuncion	21
Masaya	52	Ayolas	72
Nandaime	4522	Capiata	28
Rivas	46	Concepcion	31
San Juan Del Sur	4682	Coronel Bogado	74
San Marcos, Titipapa	53	Coronel Oviedo	521
Niger	227	Encarnacion	71
		Hernandarias	63
Nigeria	234	Ita	24
Badagry	1	Pedro J. Caballero	36
Kaduna	62	Pilar	86
Lagos	1	San Antonio	27
Port Hartcourt	84	San Ignacio	82
Niue Island	683		

continues

INTERNATIONAL COUNTRY AND CITY CALLING CODES *continued*

Peru	51		Portugal	351
Arequipa	54		Almada	1
Ayacucho	6491		Angra Do Heroismo	95
Callao	14		Barreiro	1
Chiclayo	74		Braga	53
Chimbote	44		Caldas Da Rainha	62
Cuzco	84		Coimbra	39
Huancavelica	6495		Estoril	1
Huancayo	64		Evora	66
Ica	34		Faro	89
Iquitos	94		Lajes Air Force Base	95
Lima	14		Lisbon	1
Piura	74		Madalena	92
Tacna	54		Madeira Islands	91
Trujillo	44		Motijo	1
			Ponta Delgada	96
Philippines	63		Porto	2
Angeles	455		Santa Cruz	92
Bacolad	34		Setubal	65
Baguio City	74		Velas	95
Cebu City	32		Vila Do Porto	96
Dagupan	75			
Davao	82		Puerto Rico	787
Iloilo City	33			
Lucena	42		Qatar	974
Manila	2			
			Reunion Island	262
Poland	48		Romania	40
Bialystok	85		Arad	57
Bydgoszcz	52		Bacau	34
Crakow	12		Brasov	68
Gdansk	58		Bucharest	0
Katowice	3		Cluj-Napoca	64
Lodz	42		Constanta	41
Lublin	81		Craiova	51
Olsztyn	89		Galati	36
Poznan	61		Iasi	32
Radom	48		Oradea	59
Sopot	58		Pitesti	48
Torun	56		Ploiesti	44
Warsaw	22		Satu-Mare	61
			Sibiu	69

Timisoara	56	Sierra Leone	232
Tirgu Mures	65	Freetown	22
Russia	7	Singapore	65
Magadan	413	Slovak Republic	42
Moscow	095	Bratislava	7
St. Petersburg	812	Presov	91
Rwanda	250	Slovenia	386
St. Helena	290	Ljubljana	61
St. Kitts/Nevis	869	Maribor	62
St. Lucia	758	Solomon Islands	677
St. Pierre and Miquelon	508	South Africa	27
St. Vincent and		Bloemfontein	51
Grenadines	784	Cape Town	21
San Marino	378	De Aar	571
Sao Tome	239	Durban	31
Saudi Arabia	966	East London	431
Abha	7	Gordons Bay	24
Abqaiq	3	Johannesburg	11
Al Khobar	3	La Lucia	31
Al Markazi	2	Pretoria	12
Al Ulaya	1	Sasolburg	16
Damman	3	Somerset West	24
Dhahran	3	Uitenhage	41
Hofuf	3	Welkom	57
Jeddah	2	Spain	34
Khamis Mushait	7	Barcelona	3
Mecca	2	Bilbao	4
Medina	4	Cadiz	56
Najran	7	Ceuta	56
Qatif	3	Granada	58
Riyadh	1	Igualada	3
Taif	2	Las Palmas de	
Yenbu	4	Gran Canaria	28
Senegal	221	Leon	87
Seychelles	248	Madrid	1
		Malaga	5
		Melilla	52
		Palma de Mallorca	71
		Pamplona	48

continues

Santa Cruz de Tenerife	22	Switzerland	41
Sandander	42	Baden	56
Seville	5	Basel	61
Torremolinos	52	Berne	31
Valencia	6	Davos	81
		Fribourg	37
Sri Lanka	94	Geneva	22
Ambalangoda	97	Interlaken	36
Colombo Central	1	Lausanne	21
Galle	9	Lucerne	41
Havelock Town	1	Lugano	91
Kandy	8	Montreux	21
Katugastota	8	Neuchatel	38
Kotte	1	St. Gallen	71
Maradana	1	St. Mortiz	82
Matara	41	Winterthur	52
Negombo	31	Zurich	1
Panadura	34		
Trincomalee	26	Syria	963
		Aleppo	21
Suriname	597	Banias	43
		Damascus	11
Swaziland	268	Deir Ezzor	51
Villaverde de		Gableh	491
Gualalimar	67	Halab	21
		Hama	33
Sweden	46	Hasake	52
Alingsas	322	Homs	31
Boras	33	Idleb	23
Boteborg	31	Jebleh	41
Eskilstuna	16	Jisr Shogoor	441
Gamleby	493	Kamishly	53
Helsingborg	42	Kerdaha	492
Karlstad	54	Kuneitra	141
Linkoping	13	Lattakia	412
Lund	46	Nebek	12
Malmo	40	Rakka	22
Norrkoping	11	Safita	32
Stockholm	8	Sweida	16
Sundsvall	60	Tartous	43
Trelleborg	410	Yabroud	192
Uppsala	18	Zabadani	131
Vasteras	21		

Taiwan	886	Togo	228
Changhua	4	Tonga Islands	676
Chunan	37		
Chunghsing-Hsintsun	49	Trinidad and Tobago	868
Chungli	3	Tunisia	216
Fengyuan	4	Agareb	4
Hsiaying	6	Beja	8
Hualien	38	Bizerte	2
Kaohsiung	7	Carthage	1
Keelung	2	Chebba	4
Lotung	39	Gabes	5
Pingtung	8	Gafsa	6
Taichung	4	Haffouz	7
Tainan	6	Hamman-Sousse	3
Taipei	2	Kairouan	7
Taitung	89	Kef	8
Taoyuan	3	Khenis	3
		Medenine	5
Tajikistan	7	Tabarka	8
Dushanbe	3772	Tozeur	6
		Tunis	1
Tanzania	255		
Dar Es Salaam	51	Turkey	90
Dodoma	61	Adana	322
Mwanza	68	Ankara	312
Tanga	53	Antalya	242
		Bursa	224
Thailand	66	Eskisehir	222
Bangkok	2	Gaziantep	851
Burirum	44	Istanbul Asya	216
Chanthaburi	39	Istanbul Avrupa	212
Chiang Mai	53	Izmir	232
Chiang Rai	54	Izmit	262
Kamphaengphet	55	Kayseri	352
Lampang	54	Konya	332
Nakhon Sawan	56	Malatya	422
Nong Khai	42	Samsun	362
Pattani	73		
Pattaya	38	Turkmenistan	7
Ratchaburi	32	Ashkhabad	3632
Saraburi	36	Chardzhou	378
Tak	55		
Ubon Ratchathani	45		

continues

INTERNATIONAL COUNTRY AND CITY CALLING CODES *continued*

Turks and Caicos		London	181
Islands	649	Manchester	161
		Nottingham	115
Tuvalu	688	Prestwick	1292
		Sheffield	114
Uganda	256	Southampton	1703
Entebbe	42		
Jinja	43	Uruguay	598
Kampala	41	Canelones	32
Kyambogo	41	Florida	352
		Las Piedras	324
Ukraine	380	Maldonado	42
Kharkov	572	Mercedes	532
Kiev	44	Minas	442
L'viv	322	Montevideo	2
		Paysandu	722
United Arab Emirates	971	Punta Del Este	42
Abu Dhabi	2	San Jose	342
Ajman	6	San Jose De Carrasco	38
Al Ain	3		
Aweer	58	U.S. Virgin Islands	340
Dhayd	6		
Dibba	9	Uzbekistan	7
Dubai	4	Karshi	375
Falaj-al-Moalla	6	Samarkand	3662
Fujairah	9	Tashkent	3712
Khawanij	487		
Ras-al-Khaimah	7	Vanuatu	678
Sharjah	6		
Tarif	88	Vatican City	6 & 39
Umm-al-Qaiwain	6		
		Venezuela	58
United Kingdom	44	Barcelona	81
Belfast	1232	Barquisimeto	51
Birmingham	121	Cabimas	64
Bournemouth	1202	Caracas	2
Cardiff	1222	Ciudad Bolivar	85
Durham	191	Coro	68
Edinburgh	131	Cumana	93
Glasgow	141	Los Teques	32
Gloucester	1452	Maiquetia	31
Ipswich	1473	Maracaibo	61
Liverpool	151	Maracay	43
London	171	Maturin	91
		Merida	74

Puerto Cabello	42	Taiz	4
San Cristobal	76	Yarim	4
Valencia	41	Zabid	3
Vietnam	84	Zaire	243
Hanoi	4	Kinshasa	12
Ho Chi Minh City	8	Lubumbashi	2
Virgin Islands	284	Zambia	260
Wallis and Futuna		Chingola	2
Islands	681	Kitwe	2
		Luanshya	2
Western Samoa	685	Lusaka	1
		Ndola	2
Yemen	967		
Aden	2	Zimbabwe	263
Almahrah	5	Bulawayo	9
Amran	7	Harare	4
Sana'a	1	Mutare	20

Setting up anything but a basic conference call requires more than a little preplanning. A teleconference deserves at least the same degree of thoughtful preparation as the face-to-face meeting it is intended to replace.

Cellular Guidelines

The etiquette of cellular phone use fundamentally relies on common sense. For instance, you should not pull out your cellular phone in a quiet restaurant and begin yakking in a loud voice. You also shouldn't answer your cellular phone in the middle of a conversation. Check the caller number. If it is a call you must take, excuse yourself and step aside so you don't interrupt the conversation around you. Find a private place where you won't disturb others and then take the call. At the least, if you are with others, excuse yourself for a moment to take the call. Tell the caller that you are busy and that you will call him or her back as soon as you are free.

What if your boss calls you on his or her cellular phone? That call is important. If you get interrupted, don't leave the vicinity of your phone or pick up the phone and make a call yourself. It's likely that your boss will call back.

Because cellular rates are still higher than regular telephone rates, your boss might prefer to have you call him or her on the office phone instead of calling you. Discuss this with your boss and decide how you will handle cellular calls, either incoming or outgoing.

The cell phone system still suffers from frequent service interruptions, so it's wise to avoid putting incoming cell phone callers on hold. Likewise, when transferring a call, try to be quick and prepare the party receiving the transfer by telling them that their caller is on a cell phone.

Always keep in mind that the confidentiality of a cell phone conversation is easily compromised—by malicious intent or just by pranksters. Watch what you say. Discourage any indiscreet caller from speaking too freely. Wait until a secure line can be used to spell out important confidential details or reveal account numbers, credit card information, and the like.

MEMOS

A memo, short for memorandum, is basically written correspondence between company employees that is less formal than a traditional letter. A memo might be short or long, single- or multipage. An office assistant might be asked to compose memos as well as type them for executives.

Ideally, memos should be no more than a single page or two. Anything longer really needs more formatting than a typical memo—more like a report. Some managers believe that a memo is needed to record every decision they make, or that everyone within their organization—from janitor to CEO—needs to receive a memo on an issue, regardless of whether it is relevant to their work. Sending unnecessary memos only adds to the junk mail in your office. Limit copies of memos to those with a need to know. Send memos only when the recipient must know the information in the memo to do his or her job, when he or she needs to respond to the work you have done, or when he or she needs to appreciate the work you are doing.

Depending on distribution lists and the amount of contents, many memos today can be sent as e-mail.

Office memos are used for various purposes:

■ To supplement face-to-face discussions on complex issues

■ To avoid making unnecessary telephone calls for business that might not be urgent

■ To create a written record

Memos not only avoid situations that might be misunderstood, but they also protect people by having a written record. Usually, office memos are brief and direct. However, some exceptions exist, depending upon the nature, purpose, and scope of the subject discussed and the writer's purpose and intent. For instance, memos should not be used to inform employees of anything related to their position, whether it is a promotion or a layoff. These subjects should be discussed in person, although you might want to record the particulars in a memo after the fact.

> **TIP:** The plural form of memorandum may be either *memorandums* (add an "s") or *memoranda* (add an "a" for the Latin form). When composing or writing, be consistent and use only one form for the plural.

Types of Memos

Memos come to our desks two ways: through the mail room and through our computer network as e-mail:

- *E-mail.* As companies become more global, distribution of paper memos is decreasing. E-mail offers a much faster way to send a message to individuals who are not located at one site, but rather at various corporate locations around the world.

- *Paper memos.* Although e-mail memos can be printed and stored in a file drawer, some managers still feel more comfortable issuing memos on paper. The speed with which these memos on paper are read depends on corporate culture. As organizations become more electronic, it is less likely that memos on paper will get as speedy attention as e-mail.

Different organizations have different formats for their memos. See examples of each type on pages 40 and 42. However, all the principles of writing and business correspondence apply to memos, just as they do to letters.

One principle includes the issue of confidentiality. As assistant, you might be privy to confidential correspondence—including memos. It is your professional responsibility to keep to yourself what you see in these memos.

Parts of a Memo

All memos, whether in print or e-mail, should be composed of a few essential parts. Formats might differ, but the parts still include the name of the sender, the name of the recipient(s), the date, the subject, the body, and sometimes end references (for example, reference initials, distribution of copies, and so on).

To/From

The To/From section can be reversed. Some feel that using "To" first is more courteous to the reader. However, follow the company preferences. Omit personal titles (Mr., Ms.), but use professional titles (Prof., Dr., and so on).

In e-mail memos, the "To" sometimes is omitted if it's clear who the memo is reaching by the other addresses. If not, it's appropriate to note the person to whom the memo is being distributed, as in, "All employees," or "All employees at the main location," or "All members of Joe Stack's product development team."

INTEROFFICE COMMUNICATION

TO: Horace Denize, Executive Director

FROM: Julia Brown, Chairperson, Board of Directors

DATE: October 15, 200_

SUBJECT: Organizational Meeting

A Board of Directors meeting has been scheduled for Wednesday, October 30, 1999, in Conference Room A, East Building.

The agenda will include:

- Approval of Minutes
- Report for the Chairperson
- Discussion of Goals
- New Business

Since this is the first meeting, your attendance is necessary. Please bring business report No. 23-A, located in the central database file.

JB/TS 8.8a

Distribution:

Jerome L. Abrams
Bennette Von Brun
Josephine D'Allo
Maye Santiago
Norman Zapper

Sample Typed Memo

In formal use, a name and a title exist in both the "To" and "From" sections, as in the following:

TO: Horace Denize, Executive Director

FROM: Julia Brown, Chairperson, Board of Directors

No salutation, complimentary close, or signature exists. However, the person sending the memorandum might initial it between the name and title, or at the end of the "From" line.

Date

The date always should be included in e-mail memos because the date the memo was prepared or sent could differ from the date you read it or the date your e-mail system tags it.

Follow a standard format; do not use shortcuts. Type the date in one of the two following ways:

September 19, 1999

9/29/99

Subject

The "Subject" line provides a short description of what the memorandum is about. It focuses attention and serves as a subject category for filing and retrieval. This line should be brief and to the point: Delete unnecessary words.

Body

This section contains the main idea and purpose of the memo. If enumerations are present, use an acceptable format, such as (1), (2); or (a), (b).

You might use some special keyboarding symbols before the enumeration to capture the reader's attention. These include dashes (—) and bullets (■).

- Call Mr. Gomez and make an appointment.

- Cancel the Simmons' contract (No. 23-A).

- Print file #23.A-9 (4.1).

This technique calls immediate attention to enumerations and enhances the appearance. Numbering and/or lettering the items or points also makes it easier for the reader to follow the sequential development of ideas and comments.

Reference Information

Several types of reference information might be located at the end of a memo. These include reference initials, copy notations, enclosures, filing code, and word processing code. Reference initials may be typed in lowercase or uppercase.

At times, the composer or originator of a document might be someone other than the executive or principal. If this is the case, use the following:

MC:CH:MI (Executive, composer or originator, transcriber)

Word/Information Processing Codes

Many documents are electronically stored and processed. For ease of retrieval in these cases, codes are necessary:

MJ/e 8.8

MJ/CH 8.8a

A colon (:) may be substituted for the slash (/). The code 8.8 represents month, day, disk number, or another meaning, such as file No. 8.8. Because such codes are not necessarily standardized, the office should create a system.

```
Author:   Samuel Walt
Date:     1/27/00  1:27 AM
Priority: Normal
TO: Rose Wilt/CPG; Len Texman/CPG
CC: Michael James/DC; John Wilson/DC
BCC: Harrison DeWitt/VP Finance
Subject: Meeting/Project X
------------------- Message Contents --------------------

The next meeting of the Project X team will be held in Room
79A at 9:00 a.m. Tuesday, January 19. Let me know if you
can make presentations on your assignments at that time.
```

Sample E-mail Memo

Copies and Distribution

This final section of the memo alphabetically lists the names of those who were sent copies. The list may be ordered by seniority or by rank: Follow the company policy and check with your superior. The omission of a name might be an oversight, or it might be deliberate.

With e-mail, copies may be sent through a network to various terminals. If this procedure is used, the usual distribution lists should be keyed into a database. The receipt of a transmission easily can be acknowledged by return transmission; a reply also can be keyed. If electronic messages are stored, keep an index. These data then can serve as boilerplates and standard paragraphs that can be inserted into other future memorandums without rekeying.

Formatting a Memo

Paper memos often are typed on plain paper or on printed forms that contain standard parts. If plain paper is used for one or more pages, use quality paper. If the memorandum is short, use a half-sheet. If a preprinted form is used, align the typing evenly with the printed headings.

TIPS FOR WRITING EFFECTIVE MEMOS

- If your company has guidelines for memos, follow that standard format.

- Set a consistent, professional, and objective tone in your memos.

- Be clear about the information you're conveying.

- Be direct in your requests.

- Make sure that your expectations of the recipients are reasonable and attainable.

- Focus on one single idea or objective; do not digress.

- Keep your memos brief and free of unnecessary details.

- Although more informal than business letters, memos still should follow the principles of good writing.

- Proofread carefully, checking all facts and figures before sending.

- Remember, memos are often the only written record of an event or conversation.

The background for e-mail memos can vary, depending on templates available through a company's communication network. Beyond this, the formatting of memos, whether on paper or e-mail, is similar.

Margins on paper are usually 1 inch from all sides—left, right, top, and bottom. If the memo is electronic, the template will have set margins.

For printed forms, the left margin should begin evenly with the "To/From" element printed on the form.

Whether using typed or preprinted forms, begin two or three spaces from the colon. Triple-space between the subject line and the beginning of the text. Single-space the content of each paragraph, but double-space between paragraphs.

MINUTES OF A MEETING

If you work as an assistant to an executive or for an organization with either a board of directors or another group that meets formally, you might be called upon to produce minutes of a meeting. *Minutes* is a term used to describe an official record of the proceedings of a meeting. Keeping minutes of meetings is always advisable. Although the minutes might not be disseminated, they should be filed in case they are needed at a later date.

Producing minutes usually involves "taking" them and then typing them. To take minutes, you should be present at the meeting. If you will type them up later, take detailed notes or use shorthand. If the meeting is conducted by phone or involves legalities, you often will take a formal transcription. However, it is helpful to take notes to maintain the structure of the meeting and isolate key points and issues. The minutes you type up are not meant to serve as a word-for-word account of the meeting; rather they act as a written record of the items discussed, issues raised, and business conducted.

Types of Meetings

Basically two types of meetings exist: formal and informal. A formal meeting is a preplanned, structured event, such as an annual conference or convention. Usually a prepared agenda is drawn up. An informal meeting may be short and may be announced only a short time before it is held; it usually takes place on company premises. To inform staff members of a quickly scheduled meeting, the assistant might use electronic calendaring, e-mail, or, if on very short notice, the telephone. In such a case, always confirm by sending a follow-up e-mail.

A formal meeting requires a slight knowledge of formal meeting flow, such as the formal reading or acceptance of the minutes from the previous meeting; a formal recorder or recording secretary, the opening of old business and new business; and votes, including motions and seconds. It's not required that you know *Robert's Rules of Order* inside and out, but it might be helpful to get an idea—and might make it easier to keep up!

Preparing the Minutes

The most important phase of preparing minutes involves the accurate recording and reporting of the actions taken and what was said. At times, it is difficult to report what is done. For informal meetings, the minutes are compact and simple; for formal meetings, the minutes are complex. If you find that grouping the minutes around a central theme is clearer, do so. On the other hand, the executive might prefer chronological order.

Corporate minutes (official minutes of a formal nature) must be prepared in the order of occurrence, showing details and the exact wording of motions, resolutions, and so forth. By law, corporations are required to keep minutes of stockholders and directors meetings. These minutes are legal records and should be protected from tampering.

When preparing corporate minutes, use watermarked paper and place the finalized minutes in binders. Any corrections resulting from a subsequent meeting should be written. Incorrect portions should be ruled out in ink and initialed in the margin. The official assistant of the corporate officer takes responsibility for the completeness and accuracy of corporate minutes, but the office professional is the one who will prepare and type them.

Format of Minutes

Follow these suggestions in preparing minutes:

1. Use plain white paper. For official corporate minutes, don't use letterhead, but do use watermarked second sheets.

2. Center and capitalize the title.

Meeting of the Executive Committee

April 2, 200_

ATTENDANCE

The weekly meeting of the executive committee was held in the office of Cortez Diaz, first Vice-President of Operations, at 10:00 a.m. on April 2, 2001. Mr. Diaz presided. Present were James Madison, Frederick McAllison, Yolanda Smith, Anne Marie Johnson, and Lewis Smith. Paricia Mendea was absent.

ITEMS COVERED

1. Contract No. 23-a.1 was approved in the amount of $125,000,000.

2. Yolanda Smith gave an update report on Contract No. 24. Further information is to be presented at the May 21 meeting.

3. Ann Marie Johnson reviewed the service budget for the first quarter. Recommendations were made. A feasibility study is to be conducted for implementation of an improved MIS.

4. Lewis Smith presented the proposed budget for the Xavius Project, a government grant. A draft copy of his recommendations will be distributed before the May 21 meeting. This item will be discussed and voted upon at the May 21 meeting.

ADJOURNMENT

The meeting was adjourned at 12:00 p.m.

James Madison
_____
James Madison, Recorder

Sample Minutes of a Weekly Committee Meeting

3. Double-space the text to allow for official corrections, if necessary. Allow a $1\frac{1}{2}$-inch left margin, a 1-inch right margin, and a generous top margin. The left margin should allow for hole-punching or binding. Be consistent.

4. Indent five to ten spaces.

5. List the name of the presiding officer and the recorder. The recorder should sign the minutes.

6. Follow the agenda's subject headings as closely as possible.

7. List absences and indicate quorums.

8. Follow the company's policy on capitalization of words such as "committee," "department," and so on.

9. Paginate at the bottom consecutively.

10. If a formal resolution, motion, or vote is passed, record it word for word.

11. Record the time of adjournment.

12. Use businesslike language. Avoid descriptive adjectives such as "outstanding."

13. List and summarize the gist of what was said, making a new bullet or paragraph for each point.

14. Transcribe minutes while they are still fresh in your mind.

15. Prepare a rough draft for approval before finalizing. To avoid confusion, make sure you name the electronic file in an organized way.

16. File a hard copy, just in case.

CORRESPONDENCE

We tend to think of correspondence in terms of letters. Not so—today, correspondence also includes electronic communications, including e-mail and faxed documents. The latter can be a problem if a hard copy is needed. For instance, most courts still do not accept faxed copies of contracts.

LETTERS

The task of typing letters has evolved radically with the proliferation of computers in the workplace. Still, the form that letters take and even some of the keyboarding terms associated with the day of the typewritten letter still hold sway. Why? Because the fundamental purpose of a business letter remains unchanged.

BASIC PRINCIPLES OF WRITING LETTERS

The biggest stumbling block to clear writing isn't a matter of technique or writing ability; it's a matter of mental attitude. The reason more people don't write better is because they are too self-centered.

In good writing, one person—and one person alone—is important: the reader. Yet, what happens when the average businessperson sits down to write a letter or report? Somewhere inside, an insidious thought occurs: "What will the reader think of me?"

The more that thought interferes with concentrating on the reader, the poorer the writing will be. In writing of any kind, the important thing is to plant an idea in the reader's mind, or to stimulate feelings or emotions.

Write to express, not to impress. Write in the same language you would use if you were carrying on a conversation across your desk. Keep it simple. Write from a "you" perspective. ("Your letter of January 15 was very much appreciated, Ms. Jones," not "I appreciated your letter.") If possible, keep the tone pleasant and friendly. Get politely to the point, wrap it up, and wish your correspondent well.

In a very real sense, letters that leave a business office are ambassadors of goodwill. The impression that an individual letter creates could mean the difference between the gain or loss of a prospective client or an influential friend for your company. This impression depends as much on the appearance of the letter as on its tone or contents.

Letter Styles

It has often been said that an ideal letter should resemble a picture in an appropriate frame. That still holds true today, especially given the use of stylish letterhead paper that includes more than the firm's logo and address. Some letterhead includes the names of the company officers in the left margin; others list product lines in the right margin. Some have a watermark mid-center.

Some organizations have different letterhead for different divisions of the organization. Access to these variations might come through the company network, or you might be able to requisition the paper stock you need from the company supply closet. Letters must be arranged and then typed or keyboarded according to the style of the letterhead as well as the letter style that the company has chosen. Most organizations have a procedural manual for their employees, illustrating the letter style and explaining how they want the various parts of the business letter to appear.

Given office technology, letters should not contain misspellings or other errors—check every piece of correspondence. Some software programs

Letter 1: Block Style with Open Punctuation

require spellchecking; others use a color to raise a question about a spelling or other error.

After you have finished typing your letter, use the print preview function to view it before printing. This also will help you center your letter on the paper when it is printed. Does the finished product look professional?

Regardless of the technology you're using, you still should follow one of the accepted modern letter styles. Each is addressed in the following sections.

Block Style (Letter 1)
The block style letter, also called a full block style letter, aligns all lines at the left margin. Paragraphs are not indented.

Modified Block Style (Letters 2 and 3)
The modified block style letter places the dateline, the complimentary close, and the sender's name and title in the center of the page. Paragraphs may be

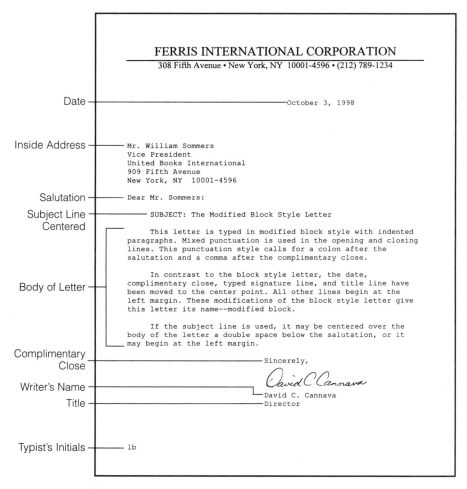

FERRIS INTERNATIONAL CORPORATION
308 Fifth Avenue • New York, NY 10001-4596 • (212) 789-1234

Date —————— October 3, 1998

Inside Address —————— Mr. William Sommers
Vice President
United Books International
909 Fifth Avenue
New York, NY 10001-4596

Salutation —————— Dear Mr. Sommers:

Subject Line Centered —————— SUBJECT: The Modified Block Style Letter

Body of Letter —

    This letter is typed in modified block style with indented paragraphs. Mixed punctuation is used in the opening and closing lines. This punctuation style calls for a colon after the salutation and a comma after the complimentary close.

    In contrast to the block style letter, the date, complimentary close, typed signature line, and title line have been moved to the center point. All other lines begin at the left margin. These modifications of the block style letter give this letter its name--modified block.

    If the subject line is used, it may be centered over the body of the letter a double space below the salutation, or it may begin at the left margin.

Complimentary Close —————— Sincerely,

David C. Cannava

Writer's Name —————— David C. Cannava
Title —————— Director

Typist's Initials —————— lb

Letter 2: Modified Block Style, with Indented Paragraphs and Mixed Punctuation

indented, or they may begin at the left margin. On computers, the trend is not to indent unless a very short letter is double-spaced.

Simplified Letter Style (Letter 4)

The simplified letter style, traditionally known as the AMS (Administrative Management Society) letter, is the most modern letter style. This style eliminates the salutation and the complimentary close. A subject line typed on the third line below the inside address in all capital letters replaces the salutation. All lines begin at the left margin. The sender's name and title are typed in all capital letters three or four lines below the body of the letter. This style of letter eliminates salutation problems (whether to use Ms., Gentlemen, or Ladies and Gentlemen).

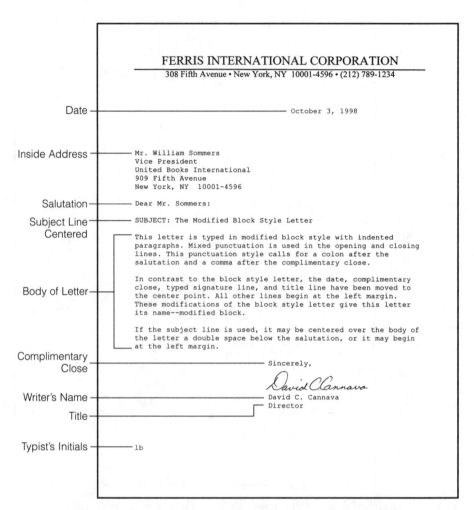

Letter 3: Modified Block Style, with Blocked Paragraphs and Mixed Punctuation

Business Letter Punctuation

Two punctuation styles exist for business letters. In *mixed punctuation style,* a colon is placed after the salutation and a comma is placed after the complimentary close. In *open punctuation style,* no punctuation is used after the salutation or the complimentary close.

Basic Parts of a Business Letter

Although companies use different looks in their letters, the letters themselves have the following elements in common:

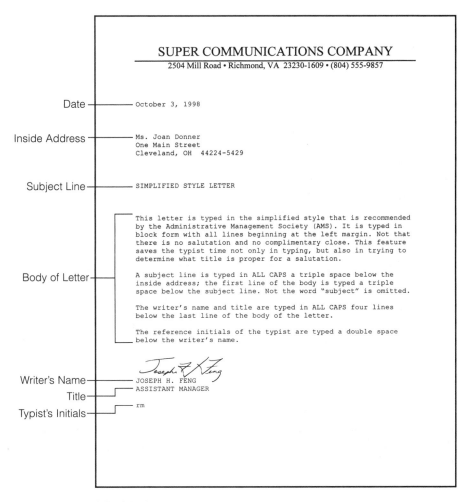

Date — October 3, 1998

Inside Address —
Ms. Joan Donner
One Main Street
Cleveland, OH 44224-5429

Subject Line — SIMPLIFIED STYLE LETTER

Body of Letter —
This letter is typed in the simplified style that is recommended by the Administrative Management Society (AMS). It is typed in block form with all lines beginning at the left margin. Not that there is no salutation and no complimentary close. This feature saves the typist time not only in typing, but also in trying to determine what title is proper for a salutation.

A subject line is typed in ALL CAPS a triple space below the inside address; the first line of the body is typed a triple space below the subject line. Not the word "subject" is omitted.

The writer's name and title are typed in ALL CAPS four lines below the last line of the body of the letter.

The reference initials of the typist are typed a double space below the writer's name.

Writer's Name — JOSEPH H. FENG
Title — ASSISTANT MANAGER
Typist's Initials — rm

Letter 4: Simplified Style

Letterhead

Most business letters still go on preprinted letterhead. The format of the letterhead differs with each firm, but the contents of the letterhead remain fairly standard: the company name, the street address, the name of the city and state, and the ZIP code. Other elements that might appear in the letterhead are the telephone number (with area code) of the firm, and the names and titles of the corporate officers.

Dateline

The dateline begins on about the third line below the company letterhead, or on line 14 (counting down from the top of the page), whichever is more eye-appealing for letter placement. The dateline consists of the month, the day, and the year. The month is always spelled in full, the date and the year are given as numerals, and the date is followed by a comma.

Preferred style	October 3, 2001
Military style	3 October 2001
Unacceptable styles	October 3rd, 2001
	Oct. 3, 2001

A letter from a foreign country more likely will follow the military style, with the day of the month first, followed by the month, and finally the year.

Inside Address

A complete inside address is very important to ensure not only that the letter is directed to the correct person, but also that accurate files can be established. The inside address may be typed anywhere from three to twelve lines below the date line, depending on the length of the letter; it aligns with the left margin for all letter styles.

The inside address should include the following elements: person's name, person's title, name of company or organization, street address, city name, state name, and ZIP code. If the letter addresses a company or organization, or a person at a company or organization, the inside address should be typed exactly as it appears in the addressee's letterhead.

If you are unable to determine a specific person's name, then you may use an *attention line* with a business title. In this way, the letter will be directed to the proper person. The attention line is the second line of the inside address.

If the address includes an apartment number or room number, type these elements on the same line as the street. State names should be abbreviated in the address according to the two-letter state abbreviations. The nine-digit ZIP code is typed one or two spaces after the state abbreviation.

Mr. John Alexander, President
ABZ Company
1234 East Sixth Street, Room 1410
Buffalo, NY 14222-5147

The ABZ Company
Attention Sales Manager
1234 East Sixth Street
Buffalo, NY 14222-5147

Mr. John Alexander
National Sales Manager
ABZ Company
P.O. Box 1614
Buffalo, NY 14222-5147

Mr. John Alexander
666 Fifth Avenue, Apt. 4D
Buffalo, NY 14222-5147

Follow these general guidelines when typing the inside address:

- Type names as they appear in the letterhead; always check the spelling of proper names by referring to your files.

- The number (#) symbol is not necessary when typing the house number, room number, or post office box number. House numbers (with the exception of "one") are typed in figures.

    One East Sixth Street

    2 East Sixth Street

- When street names are numbers, write out names below ten, and use figures for names above ten.

- When figures are used in street addresses, it is not necessary to use endings such as *st, d, nd,* or *rd* after the numbered street name.

    1234 East 12 Street

- Type the city name, state name, and ZIP code on the same line.

- Type the city name in full, followed by a comma and then the two-letter state abbreviation.

- Type the ZIP code one or two spaces after the two-letter state abbreviation. No punctuation follows the state abbreviation.

Salutation

The salutation is typed two lines below the last line of the inside address. The salutation is omitted in the simplified letter. In all other letter styles, the salutation is typed, starting at the left margin and followed by a colon if mixed punctuation is used.

Capitalization of salutations. Capitalize the first word, the title, and any noun in the salutation:

    Dear Mr. Jones

    My dear Professor Clark

    Dear Ms. Morgan

    Your Excellency

Abbreviations in salutations. Abbreviate Mr., Ms., Messrs., and Dr.. Write out other titles, such as Captain, Professor, Father, Reverend, and so on.

Forms of salutations. For the forms of salutations to use in addressing church or government officials, judges, doctors, and so on, see the Grammar and Punctuation Guide at the back of this book.

When an organization is comprised of men and women, the salutation used is still "Gentlemen" if the correspondence is addressed to a company.

Although some groups frown upon this style, it is still used simply because a more acceptable salutation has not yet evolved. Alternative salutations that are becoming more popular include "Ladies and Gentlemen," or the appropriate title or function: Dear Treasurer, Dear Review Committee, and so on.

Guidelines for Salutations

Addressee	Salutation
Firm's name	Gentlemen
Firm's name, with an attention line	Gentlemen
Married woman, a widow, or a divorced woman who uses the title Mrs.	Dear Mrs. Jones
Unmarried woman	Dear Ms. Jones
Unknown whether a woman is married or single	Dear Ms. Jones
Group comprised of men and women	Ladies and Gentlemen
Married couple	Dear Mr. and Mrs. Jones
Man and a woman	Dear Mr. Jones and Ms. Black
	Dear Sir and Madam

Body of the Letter

The part of the letter containing the message is known as the *body*. The body is typed a double space below the salutation, or a double space below the subject line. The paragraphs should be blocked or indented, depending upon the letter style used. Paragraphs are single-spaced. Occasionally, short letters are typed in double space.

Whether the lines are single-spaced or double-spaced, use only double spacing between paragraphs.

Tabulated matter in body of the letter. Tabulated matter in the body of a letter is indented at least five spaces from both the left and right margins.

Enumerated paragraphs. Enumerated paragraphs are also indented five spaces from both the right and left margins. These paragraphs begin with a number followed by a period. Two spaces after the period, begin typing the paragraph. Single-space each enumerated paragraph, but double-space between the enumerated paragraphs. (If each enumerated paragraph contains only one line, you may single-space between paragraphs.)

1.

2.

Complimentary Closing

The complimentary closing is typed two lines below the last line of the body of the letter.

Capitalize only the first word in the complimentary closing. Follow the complimentary closing with a comma, unless open punctuation is used; in that case, no punctuation is needed.

Placement of complimentary closing. The placement of the complimentary closing depends upon which letter style is used (see Letters 1–3 and 5).

Degrees of formality. As with the salutation, degrees of formality also are recognized in complimentary closings.

- *Formal tone:* Yours truly, Yours very truly, Very truly yours

- *More formal tone:* Respectfully yours, Yours respectfully, Very respectfully yours, Yours very respectfully

- *Less formal and more personal tone:* Sincerely, Cordially, Sincerely yours, Cordially yours, Yours sincerely

Signature and Title

When a company name appears as part of the signature, it is typed in all capitals a double space below the complimentary closing. The typewritten signature then is typed on the fourth line below the company name or the complimentary closing. Place the penned signature in the intervening space. If a letter is unusually short, place the typed signature on the sixth or eighth line below the company name or the complimentary closing. If the signer's handwriting is unusually large, the signature may be typed from five to eight lines below the company name or complimentary closing.

The writer's title may appear on the same line with the typed signature, or on the line below the typed signature, whichever gives a better balance to the page.

Yours very truly,

Clarence Brown

Clarence Brown, Manager

Yours very truly,

Clarence Brown

Clarence Brown
Manager

In the simplified letter style, beginning at the left margin, type the writer's name and title on the fifth line below the body of the letter in all capital letters, or type the name on the fifth line and the title on the sixth line (see Letter 4).

Joseph H. Feng

JOSEPH H. FENG
ASSISTANT MANAGER

Division or department. Frequently, a division or department is used in the closing lines of a letter; it is typed below the typed signature and title, as follows:

Very truly yours,

R. M. Brown, Supervisor
Plastics Division

More than one signature. When a letter requires two signatures, use either of the following forms:

Sincerely yours,

Ms. Jane R. Jones   Milton Trout
District Manager   General Manager

Sincerely yours,

Ms. Jane R. Jones
District Manager

Milton Trout
General Manager

Signature for the employer. If, as an assistant, you are required to sign a letter for your employer, you may use either one of the following forms:

Sincerely yours,   Sincerely yours,

Secretary to Ms. Jones   Ms. Kristi Hart
                                    Secretary to Ms. Jones

Signing someone else's name. When signing someone else's name, it is not necessary to write "per" or "by." Simply sign the individual's name, and then write your initials. If your employer has a facsimile signature, use it.

When the individual signing a letter for another person is not the person's assistant, use either one of these forms:

Sincerely yours,   Sincerely yours,

For Milton Trout   Milton Trout
General Manager   General Manager

Academic, military, and professional titles. These titles should appear in the typewritten signatures, as follows:

Yours truly,

Grace Johnson

Ms. Grace Johnson, C.P.S.

Yours truly,

James Simpson

James Simpson, M.D.

Yours truly,

Laura Wilson

Laura Wilson, Ph.D.
Professor of Humanities

Yours truly,

Leonard J. Richardson

Leonard J. Richardson
Colonel, USAF

The salutations in replies to each of these would be, respectively, Dear Ms. Johnson, Dear Dr. Simpson, Dear Professor Wilson, and Dear Colonel Richardson.

Courtesy titles. When a first name could be a man's or a woman's name, or if initials are used, call ahead to clarify or omit the use the courtesy title.

Sincerely,

Dale Harrington

Mr. Dale Harrington

Sincerely yours,

Dale Harrington

Mr. D. K. Harrington

If the letter requires the addressee to sign and return it, the name of the addressee will be at the end of the letter with space above for his or her signature. Below this will be space set aside for the date of signature. On the other side of the letter, the sender will have signed his or her name on another line; beneath will be the typed name. Beneath this will be a line under which the word "Date" appears.

> **TIP:** If you have a name that is common in either gender, you might try a courtesy title in the signature line of letters, (Ms. or Mr.). This helps in the reply and any follow-up calls.

Reference Initials

Today, most firms prefer only the typist's reference initials. Occasionally, two sets of initials appear: The first set represents the author of the written document and the second set is that of the typist. If both sets of initials are used, the first set is typed in capital letters and the second set in lowercase with either a slash or a colon separating the sets.

As middle managers increasingly prepare their own letters, reference initials are disappearing. However, if you are preparing a letter for your manager or another person, it is important that you use reference initials.

Reference initials are typed at the left margin a double space below the typewritten signature and title. Illustrations are as follows:

JRJ:lm   JRJ (author of document) and lm (typist)

JRJ/lm   JRJ (author of document) and lm (typist)

lm   (typist's initials only)

File Name Notation

With most letters being prepared on computers and stored in a computer record for future reference, you might want to actually put the file name on the correspondence. (Because it's computer-generated, use a smaller type size to make it less apparent, if possible.) Put the file name on a line of its own below the reference initials.

Before you do this, make sure that your computer can handle file names of more than eight characters. Furthermore, be aware that the letters after the dot represent the application extension, not the place to show it's a letter (for instance, you would name a file letter.doc, not jones.let). If you must e-mail files back and forth, this is doubly important.

Avoid emoticons (little smilies common in e-mail communication to show humor or emotion) in your business memos, as tempting as it may be to use them. Save these for your personal correspondence on the Net.

Other Elements in a Business Letter

In addition to the standard parts in all business letters, other elements sometimes are included.

Attention Line

The writer might want to direct the letter to a particular person or department within the firm. When the inside address is directed to a firm name and the writer wants a certain person or specific department also to be aware of the contents of the letter, an attention line should be used.

The post office recommends putting the attention line first in an address. For consistency, use that form in the letter as well. The word "attention" must appear; however, no punctuation is necessary after it.

ACE Recruitment International
Attention Mr. Samuel Jones
8225 Dunwoody Place
Atlanta, GA 30339-7329

Subject Line

When a subject line is used, it should be typed a double space below the salutation.

The subject line may be typed starting at the left margin, centered, or indented five spaces, depending on the style of the letter. The word "Subject" may precede the subject line, typed in all uppercase or typed in initial caps. Today, many businesses prefer to type the subject line in all uppercase, without the word "Subject" preceding it.

If the simplified letter style is used, the subject line should replace the salutation and be typed on the third line below the last line of the inside address. The subject line should be typed at the left margin in all uppercase. The word "Subject" does not precede the subject line.

Reply Reference Notation

Place the notation as you would a subject line. The word "Reference" (or "Re"), followed by a colon and two spaces, may be shown before the notation.

Enclosure Notation

Whenever an item is to be enclosed with a letter, this should be indicated on the letter by typing an enclosure notation two lines below the reference initials at the left margin. This tells the recipient to check the envelope or package for additional items.

When more than one item is enclosed, any one of the following forms may be used:

Enclosures 2   Enc. 2

Enclosures (2)

Important enclosures should be listed:

Enclosure: check   Enclosures:
                               1. check
Enclosures: check contract   2. contract

Copy Notation

When a copy is prepared for the information of a person other than the addressee of the letter, a notation followed by the name of the person receiving the copy is typed at the left margin, a double space below the reference initials or enclosure notation. If more than one person is to receive a copy, the names should be listed either in order of importance in the company or in alphabetical order. Common examples follow:

ms	ms
Enclosure	cc Raymond Smith
cc: Raymond Smith	
Albert Wayne	

Some organizations keep a record of their correspondence by preparing a photocopy of outgoing communications. The following notations may be used:

pc: Rosemarie Sweeting	pc Rosemarie Sweeting

Other organizations make no distinction as to the type of copy made and use the following notations:

c: Sandra Delgado	c Sandra Delgado

Blind Copies
In some instances, it is necessary to send a copy of a letter to one or more persons without the knowledge of the addressee. This is known as a blind copy *(bcc,* for *blind carbon copy).* To make this special notation, type the bcc notation for only the blind copy recipients at the bottom of the letter at the left margin. Make sure the firm's file copy shows all the bcc notations.

Postscript
A postscript often is used to emphasize a special point by setting it apart from the rest of the letter, or to relay a personal message to the recipient of the letter.

A postscript should be typed as a single-spaced paragraph a double space below the last notation. Acceptable forms include PS:, P.S., or neither. Indent the paragraph if the paragraphs of the letter are indented.

Mailing Notation
Any special mailing delivery (airmail, special delivery, registered, certified, express mail, by fax) should be typed midway between the date and the inside address. This should appear in all uppercase at the left margin.

Multiple Page Letters
When a letter consists of more than one page, the second sheets or successive pages are typed on paper of the same size, color, and quality as the letterhead. If possible, leave at least two lines of a paragraph at the bottom of the page, and carry at least two lines to the next page. Do not end a page with a divided word.

Each successive page requires a *heading.* The heading consists of the name of the addressee, the page number of the letter, and the date, typed on the

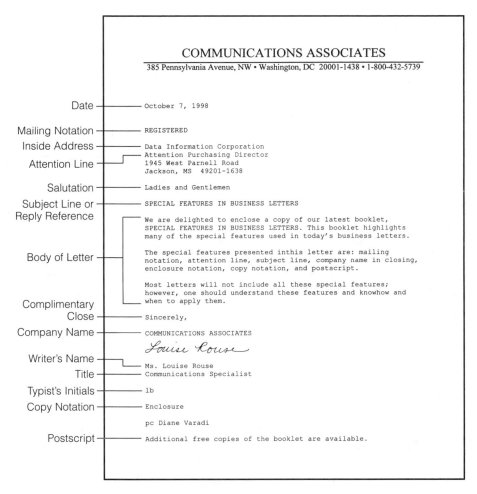

Letter 5: Block Style, with Open Punctuation Special Features

seventh line from the top edge of the paper. Triple-space after the heading and continue typing the remainder of the letter. Use the same-side margins as for the first page.

Two formats exist for headings for the second and subsequent pages of multiple-page letters: block style and horizontal style. The block style heading is typed at the left margin:

Ms. Jane R. Smith
Page 2
October 7, xxxx

In the horizontal style, the name of the addressee is typed at the left margin, the page number is centered, and the dateline ends at the right margin:

Ms. Jane R. Smith   2   October 7, xxxx

This all can be done automatically by using headers and footers. Just prepare the headers to contain the date and correct page numbers automatically.

> **TIP:** If you want to be sure that a letter will look good on letterhead, print it first on plain paper. Then hold the letter up to the light against a blank sheet of letterhead. You'll be able to see how well the margins work—in particular, the top and bottom margins, depending on letterhead style. Some letterhead pages have deep top margins; others include corporate information on the bottom.

Using Templates

When you use templates, set them up so they contain all the standard parts and margins. Then all you do is type your letters. If you use more than one template with different margins or spacing, you will want to set up style sheets and template files to hold the various templates.

Doing Mass Mailings

Among your responsibilities might be conducting mass mailings for your company. For example, your task might be to handle a list of 100 names. Here's how to set up a mail merge. You key the letter, replacing areas that would be personalized (such as the inside address, greeting, and even text in the body of the letter) with codes that tell the program what to put there. Then you compile a file of addresses, greetings, and other information that fits the required codes for the master letter. When you merge the two, the program automatically creates each individual letter with the information from the address file. You often can create these address files from databases from the start.

> **TIP:** Not every software program calls the combining of a list of addresses into their respective letters a *mail merge*. To see if your software program has the function, check the help menu for keywords such as *personalized mailings*.

Mail-merge letters are pretty standard. Most people recognize that they were on a large list, even if their letter was personalized. Still, any attempt to personalize these letters is a nice touch.

One way to add a personal touch is to have the person sending the letter sign each one—and sometimes even add a little note in his or her own handwriting.

If you are talking about 200 letters, however, you might want to scan in a signature—most word processing programs will let you set a signature as an image. Alternatively, you can use a stamp with the person's signature.

Envelopes

When preparing business envelopes, you must observe several guidelines because the post office optical character readers (OCRs) are programmed to scan a specific area of the envelope. The address must be completely within the read zone, blocked, and single-spaced. Two-letter state abbreviations must be used. Nine-digit ZIP codes should be used, if available. Apartment and room numbers should follow the street address on the same line. The U.S. Postal Service prefers, but does not require, the use of all capital letters and no punctuation in envelope addresses.

The OCR will be happy to direct your mail to its proper destination, but it first must locate the delivery address and read it. The "eye" of the OCR looks for the address within an imaginary rectangle on each piece of mail. Make some quick measurements—if the delivery address is located within the following boundaries, the OCR won't have any trouble finding it:

Sides of rectangle	$^1/_2$ inch from the right and left edge
Bottom of rectangle	$^5/_8$ inch up from the bottom edge
Top of rectangle	$2^3/_4$ inches up from bottom edge

Non-Address Information

Because the OCR looks for the address in a particular area, extraneous printing can confuse it. Thus, the space below and on either side of the delivery address line, within the OCR read area, should be clear of all printing and other markings that are not actually part of the address (such as the return address, special notations, advertising copy, company logos, and so on). Positioning such information as far away from the address as possible helps.

Bar Code Clear Area

After reading an address, the OCR prints the appropriate bar code on the bottom of the mail piece for other postal scanners to use to direct the mail. The OCR rejects the mail and delays delivery if it sees some other type of printing where the bar code goes. Leave blank an area measuring $^5/_8$ inch high and $4^3/_4$ inches wide from the right corner of the mail piece.

The two standard-size envelopes are as follows:

- No. 6$^3/_4$ envelope measures 6$^1/_2$ × 3$^5/_8$ inches

- No. 10 envelope measures $^9/_{12}$ × 4$^1/_8$ inches

Special notations to the addressee (confidential, hold for arrival, personal) should be typed in all uppercase about three lines below the return address.

Special mailing notations (airmail, special delivery, registered, certified) should be typed below the stamp (about line nine) to end five to six spaces from the right edge of the envelope; these notations also should be typed in all uppercase.

```
Mr. L.M. Smith
245 Main Street
Glendale, NY 11385-7342


                                        REGISTERED

                Data Information Center
                Attention Purchasing Director
                1945 W. Parnell Road
                Jackson, MS 49201-1638
```

Traditional Method for Addressing a No. 10 Envelope

```
  Mr. L.M. Smith
  245 Main Street
  Glendale, NY 11385-7342

  HOLD FOR ARRIVAL


                Ms. Roberta Rogers
                987 Kingston Drive, Apt. 7
                Des Moines, IA 50310-3636
```

Traditional Method for Addressing a No. 6³/₄ Envelope

Although most assistants use a computer for their correspondence, they often keep their old reliable typewriter to type addresses on letters. Still, it's possible to do envelopes with your printer if you use print labels. Many brands that fit into laser printers come in white, colored, and clear versions.

FAXES

Faxes have made a tremendous difference in the way in which we do business—in particular, the tempo of communications. A letter that might take several days to reach us can be in our hands in a few minutes. If a negative side exists to faxes, it is that this convenience is often used when there is no need for urgency.

If you are to be successful in your position, you must be familiar with your firm's fax machine. If your computer has the capability, you also must be able to fax directly from your computer. Suppose that your boss must call an emergency directors meeting. You know that many of your firm's trustees don't check their e-mail regularly. Rather than e-mail, you might want to fax them, either from your computer or from your company's fax machine.

Given the importance of faxes, you should get the fax number—as well as e-mail address—for everyone with whom your boss does business.

Fax Protocol

Part of faxing is knowing what is appropriate to fax. Letters, agendas, messages, and other business-related faxing are always appropriate, depending on the receiver and the topic. However, with the proliferation of fax machines, the unsolicited fax has become an unwelcome intruder. Unsolicited faxes often include business-related messages, discounts, special offers, announcements, and so on. Even if these must be sent out to a group of clients or customers, they are not always welcome or appropriate.

Junk faxes tie up lines, use supplies, run up phone bills, and sidetrack the fax's very purpose—getting important messages in a timely fashion.

Junk faxes can range from an unasked-for cartoon from a colleague on another floor of your office to a copy of a chain letter, to a corporate advertisement about special discount pricing. What distinguishes junk faxes from worthwhile documents isn't their quantity, but their worth. A fax from your CEO or a client firm about a new product would not be junk mail because it would have an impact on your work.

> **TIP:** Be guided by this rule proffered by the *New York Times:* "Fax unto others as you would have others fax unto you."

State and federal laws on junk faxes are still in development, but you still can fight junk faxes. Send back a message to the senders of the junk faxes to cease and desist; tell them that their messages are tying up your machine and not building goodwill.

Dealing with the Fax Machine

Some assistants take on the responsibility for their department's fax machine; other machines are serviced by a supplier. Even if you have an outside supplier, you should know some basics about the machine: how to insert paper, how to program autodial lists for common groups (such as a board or a group of remote employees), and the like.

> **TIP:** If you have an older fax machine, it will use rolls of thermal paper. When the faxes come off, they often curl. Don't send these rolls of thermal fax paper originals back through the fax machine. They can cause jams, and the treated paper can damage scanners. Photocopy the fax, and then fax the copy.

Want to fax faster? A fax moves quickly over lighter portions of the document and more slowly over darker portions. To fax faster, make sure that whatever you're transmitting has no unnecessary large portions of solid black (such as letterhead or a fax cover sheet with large black or colored portions). Sometimes, copiers can leave black edges, as can fax machines. Trim these off if they'll cause problems.

Fax-photocopier teamwork. Does your photocopier have a feature that enables you to reduce/enlarge images? Reduce airy and easy-to-read documents before faxing. A tighter original can cut transmission time. Teach others to do the same when faxing to you, and you'll save paper.

On the cover sheet, note the percentage that the document has been reduced. This allows easier re-enlarging if the recipient desires.

Incoming fax jam? If you're deluged with faxes and plan to put a second machine to work fielding calls, don't publicize the new number. Instead, arrange with the phone company to have the existing fax line roll or automatically switch to the new line when the established number's busy. When you order the new lines from the phone company, make sure you let the company know how and in what order you want multiple lines to roll.

Efficient Faxing

Let's face it, faxing can be a real time drain. Numbers don't connect, machines jam, machines on the other end are busy, and, even when everything seems normal, your boss calls from the business trip furious that she didn't receive anything. Or, she received three pages and went to the meeting to discover that pages four and five were missing. Or, she asked at the hotel front desk and was sent to the business center where you faxed it—and it was closed. By the time you call and resend, and resend and call, it's lunchtime! If you plan ahead and establish a routine, you can easily fax and verify, making both your boss and yourself look like stars.

Use cover sheets. Use a cover sheet for all fax transmissions. Identify all relevant information from your end: your company and mailing address, the individual sender, fax and voice line numbers, date of transmission, and total number of pages (including the cover sheet). If you have a long fax, it's useful to number each page as 1 of 10, 2 of 10, and so forth—especially if you're faxing something important and need to easily verify that it arrived. For example, if you are faxing a report to your boss at a hotel in England, you want to verify that it arrived (if it didn't, you could be in trouble), and you want to easily and quickly verify if any pages are missing. With a numbering system, the person on the other end can easily determine what, if anything, needs to be re-sent.

When you address your cover sheet, make sure that you address it to a specific person, not just a department or a company. If you are sending to a hotel, identify whether the person is a guest or on staff. You should note "hold for arrival" if the person is checking in later that day.

Often, if you are sending a letter or written message with your fax, you can combine the fax cover and letter into one document. Office supply companies also stock the sticky fax notes that can be placed directly on the first page of the fax. These are useful but sometimes can jam the machine, so be careful.

Verify the receipt. Be proactive in making sure that your fax has arrived. Call to confirm its receipt so you can quickly right any wrongs from your end. In larger organizations in which the fax goes to a central location and then must be distributed, the intended recipient can hustle things along from that end.

Actually look at the transmission-confirmation report that you get from your machine (and review the autodial log you get if you do the paper check). Keep in mind, though, that the transmission log isn't gospel. If it's really important, check on the receiving end. The transmission log might show that the other fax machine received it, but the other fax machine could have stored but not printed it, run out of paper, or experienced some other malfunction.

As fax numbers proliferate, a misdialed eleven-number string is more likely to connect to another fax machine and send your document to a total stranger. One-touch speed dialing also might send material rocketing off to J while K waits impatiently for the material you promised to send immediately.

> **TIP:** Remember, faxes aren't confidential! If you need to fax a confidential document, the best thing to do is phone the receiver or the assistant or other office professional picking it up on the other end. Have this person pick up the document directly from the fax machine. If you are faxing to a hotel and security is important, phone ahead and make sure the person who receives it immediately seals it in envelope. In special circumstances, you can always ask the hotel to hand-deliver the fax to the recipient's office or room.

Sending Large or Multiple Faxes

On occasions, you will do a mass faxing yourself. Suppose that you are organizing a meeting of customers for your manager. You want to remind them to make their reservations in time to get rooms at the hotel where the meeting will be held. The reminder note has a registration form attached that you've taken from the conference brochure.

TIPS FOR EFFICIENT FAXES

- Keep faxes short.

- Use a cover sheet when faxing to a large organization.

- Do not use a cover sheet when faxing to a small organization.

- As a cover sheet or not, the first page should include the following, typed or written clearly at the top of the page: addressee's name, your own name, and the total number of pages being faxed.

- Always use 1-inch margins.

- Reduce oversized documents (including those that do not have 1-inch margins) on a copy machine before faxing them.

- Number the pages being faxed, even if the document is already paginated—this is especially important if you're faxing only a portion of a document.

- Do not put folded, stapled, or otherwise mutilated documents through the fax machine. Make a copy, and then run the copy through the fax machine.

- Do not exceed your machine's paper feeder capacity.

- Check for incoming faxes frequently.

- Clear incoming faxes from the machine as they are delivered to prevent paper jams.

- Make sure you have enough paper in the machine to last the entire work day.

Here are some points to remember:

- If you are using the registration form from the brochure, check to see whether it has fax-back information if you want the customers to fax it back.

- Check your machine's instruction manual for how to set up phone lists for multiple mailings on the machine.

- Find out whether your machine has automatic transmission. By timing transmissions for hours when rates are lower, senders can gain substantial savings. If your machine includes a polling feature, this also represents a more efficient way to send the same document to multiple locations when measured by staff time and cost.

- If you have lots of faxes, use an automatic dialing system, and fax before or after regular business hours to avoid busy-signal delays. You also might snag the company some savings in off-peak phone rates.

- Faxing the wrong kind of document can be ineffective and costly. For example, computer printouts, which are difficult to read in the original, become almost impossible to understand when faxed. Often, blueprints or architectural renderings and other artwork lose necessary clarity when faxed. Odd-sized originals that reduce disproportionately when faxed can lose important details.

- Lengthy documents (five or more pages) not needed in a rush often are better sent through the mail, especially over long distances. The pages of multipage documents can get mixed up or lost easily, which can hurt rather than help communication.

Choosing Fax Over Regular Mail

Faxes are more public than postal correspondence, and many people prefer the privacy of a letter received in the mail. Find out before you fax.

Timing is the key issue when choosing between mail and fax, however. If someone needs something right away, fax it. Cost isn't an issue because a fax costs no more than a long-distance phone call.

Remember the intangibles. The big-production, super-sales brochure or extra-elegant report quickly turns into just more sheets of fax paper when it's printed out at the recipients' end. And the impression they get turns out to be much less than you meant to make. The advantages of rushing the real thing by mail might outweigh its cost and the immediacy of a fax.

Also remember that sometimes you can get better impact by faxing something that otherwise would be mailed. A faxed thank-you for the sale, the appointment, or the information might be appropriate. This can be a real attention-getter, and it allows for a degree of informality that a letter doesn't. Likewise, consider faxing birthday and company anniversary greetings, congrats on a promotion, or celebratory greetings. Just remember, as in any other situation, use a little judgment. The medium depends on the recipient, the sender, and the occasion.

ARE FAXES LEGALLY BINDING?

Many courts have refused to accept faxed documents as evidence. Thermal paper faxes are least likely to be accepted in a court of law because of the poor quality of reproduction. But with plain-resolution paper, faxes might look as clean and clear as a typed document and stand up to the legal test.

Fax Formatting

What kinds of faxes are reader-friendly? Unfortunately, fewer than you might think. Clarity is not everything with faxes; it's virtually the only thing. Here are some tips for creating reader-friendly faxes.

- *Plain Jane wins the day.* Numbers are often the very reason for a fax, but whether you fax words or numbers, choose a plain, clean typeface that leaves little chance for misreading. Sans-serif typefaces such as Helvetica and Courier hold up very well when faxed, but serif typefaces such as Times Roman do not.

- *Don't be bold.* The process of faxing alone makes the print on the end product appear bolder. Additional boldface type sometimes can turn the print into unreadable black blobs. Stick to regular or lightface type.

- *No italics for emphasis.* Italic type comes out even more ragged in fax than regular type. To emphasize key lines, apply underscore.

- *Get the points.* What's legible on this end might not be legible on the receiving end. This is just as true for point size as for other elements of design. Try for a minimum of 12-point type when faxing. The 10-point type, usually quite legible in the original, gets hard to read on the other end of the transmission.

- *The acid test.* Still not sure that what you've created is readable? Then fax filled-in copies of the suspicious form or document to yourself. Or, at least run them through the fax machine on copy mode. Can you read everything clearly? If not, then the recipient won't either—it's time to redesign.

E-MAIL

E-mail has rapidly become an indispensable tool in business communications. Because technology is constantly advancing—and because the Internet is currently the red-hot communication highway—this growth will doubtless continue.

As the use of e-mail grows, it will continue to affect the way business is done—and certainly the way communications are handled. In many organizations, e-mail has replaced interoffice memos and traditional mail. Not only does it enable us to communicate swiftly, but we can send it with attachments to support our communications, from spreadsheets to graphics.

Even in offices such as consulting firms or investment banks (which don't use lots of technology or e-mail), some individuals are using e-mail as the new way of corresponding. It has replaced letters in many areas and is replacing faxes as well because you can easily attach and send spreadsheets and other documents. E-mail also is much more confidential (although many companies have policies allowing them to monitor employee e-mail). When you get into e-mail etiquette, approach it from the correspondence angle: E-mail enables you to bcc, cc, and send out multiple copies.

In a nutshell, e-mail in offices uses computers and networks hooked to the Internet (or, in some cases, to individual modems and phone lines) to transmit messages from one computer to another; this turns the computer into an electronic mailbox. The transmittals do not require paper. Systems operate 24 hours a day, so time differences do not cause any difficulty. Messages can be sent to multiple destinations simultaneously and can be stored, retrieved, and often printed out virtually at will. Messages travel over the Internet; depending on the traffic and the speed of your connection, they can arrive almost simultaneously.

Most offices have dedicated e-mail systems that run on internal networks. With this system, each user gets an individual mail account or mailbox to send and receive mail both internally and, if set up over the Internet, to anyone else with an e-mail address. Companies use e-mail for in-house communications but also for many customers, prospects, and employees who can be contacted via computer workstations and terminals in their places of business or their homes.

As with any new technology, the etiquette, rules, procedures, legal issues, and such surrounding e-mail messaging are still in transition. Beyond that, here's a roundup of simple guidelines that have evolved so far.

You will use e-mail in many ways, from short memos to remind people about the date for the next team meeting, to the distribution of a report (as an attachment) for the meeting's attendees, to an announcement to potential customers about the product that the team has developed. You or your boss might e-mail someone down the hall or across the ocean. Rather than call someone with a question and risk telephone tag, it's so much easier to send your question as e-mail.

As you use e-mail, keep some points in mind. First and foremost, e-mail messages are still very public and are best kept straightforward. Further, e-mail is a form of professional communication and, as such, should be treated professionally. Avoid jargon and the cute stuff. E-mail has fostered a shorthand of its own (such as LOL = Laughing Out Loud) and visual representations, called *emoticons* (the little sideways happy or sad faces made up of punctuation marks are the best known). These are out of place in most business communications.

Don't abuse e-mail. Don't rehash a previously sent message. Keep your e-mail messages brief, ideally to one page or screen.

To grab the reader's attention, use the subject line wisely. E-mail scammers and junk e-mailers do this to tempt you. For your business e-mail correspondence, be as specific as you can in the subject line to involve your reader(s). For example, "Per Diem Allowance Increase" is better than "Travel Changes."

Divide your message into paragraphs: Don't force everything into one big run-on paragraph. If bullets, indents, or spaces between ideas will increase clarity, use them. Finally, organize your e-mail files.

Just as with paper files, dump, "deadfile," or otherwise deal with e-mail that has been on the system too long. How long is too long? In the ethereal world of electronic communication, thirty to sixty days probably represents the outside limit. Anything on the system longer should be archived in some other way: paper, disk, or another electronic backup format.

FOR MORE INFORMATION

If you can't find what you need from the phone numbers and Web sites listed in this chapter, you may need to expand your search.

- For more information on communications, business etiquette, or face-to-face skills, check your local library in the business communications or self help sections.

- For more information on formal letters, see the CD-ROM that accompanies this book. "1001 Essential Letters" gives examples, templates, and other valuable information for letter-writing help.

- For more information on dialing international calls, check your telephone directory. It will provide specific instructions.

- For more information on conducting formal meetings, including parliamentary procedure and formal minutes, check your local library or bookstore in the reference book section.

2

OTHER OFFICE DOCUMENTS

◆

Although a great number of office communications happen via phone, fax, and e-mail, today's office professional must be familiar with many other kinds of documents in order to function. These communications include everything from spreadsheets to reports to slides. The office professional might be supporting a corporate executive who gives presentations or a team that needs materials for training. Whatever the duties, they should have an idea of the technology available and its capabilities for creating the most effective work in the most efficient manner.

Today's office environment is more electronic and more technology-based than ever. Yet it's also true that there are more and more reports generated in the traditional format of words on paper. That means professional documents, including reports, letters, and spreadsheets, are prepared with the aid of computers, but executed or produced by the "brain-sweat" and talent of the office professionals.

In this chapter, we will discuss the preparation of reports: annual reports, business presentations, newsletters, sales reports, and other business documents.

BUSINESS REPORTS

A business report is a lengthy, in-depth communication, containing facts and ideas, that is usually prepared internally for co-workers, a superior, a committee, or a team. Reports can appear in several forms, and there is no authoritative list of all types of reports. Reports may be analytical, compartmentalized, or in the form of a catalog. The procedures here put the elements together to produce an effective, quality report. Reports may be produced by an outside printer or publisher (such as a corporation's annual report), produced internally on desktop publishing systems (such as an employee newsletter or committee report), or produced internally in regular word processing software (such as a white paper or another special report for a superior). The office professional might be responsible for anything from typing the information to simply having the files prepared to send out.

TYPES OF BUSINESS REPORTS

There are many types of business reports—here are just a few types you'll see in use in today's offices:

- *Corporate Report.* This category includes memorandum reports, letter reports, and mega-reports (very lengthy, complex reports, containing hundreds of pages). A corporate report might introduce and analyze a specific problem (the company's exposure to Y2K liability, for example), discuss it, and provide impetus for its resolution. The content may be technical or general. One office support person may have responsibility for the production of the entire report, including careful proofreading, checking for accuracy, duplication, binding, collating, and distribution.

■ *White Paper.* A white paper often refers to a government report. Examples include Health Maintenance Organizations (HMOs), privatizing Social Security funds, or a detailed authoritative report on any single subject (process re-engineering or corporate environmental responsibility, for example). White papers usually involve citations to outside sources, and may contain a bibliography and footnotes as well.

■ *Project or Committee Report.* This report is usually the collective or collaborative work of a team of people. One person is typically assigned the responsibility for integrating the material, seeing that it has a single voice or sound (as if one person wrote the text), and preparing it to look like a formally prepared document. A typical report might deal with safety issues in the workplace, proposed locations for a new plant, or entry of the company's products into the Euromarket.

■ *Executive Summary.* An executive summary is a brief description and summation of a report's contents. Significant data are summarized. A summary of this type is used for problem-solving and defines the problem, determines how it should be solved, and what the benefits are. Usually, detailed data are not given. The summary may be part of a longer report. An example of an executive summary is one seen in a research report recommending investment in a particular company. Another might be a one-page review of sales that precedes a consolidated financial report in which the details on the operating results or revenues of the company's divisions or domestic and international operations are given. Executive summaries digest the contents of the larger report, telling the reader the key facts in a concise way. Their purpose is to give the reader the gist of the entire document or report at a glance. So, the executive summary is quite often one of the most important elements of the report and is carefully prepared to communicate the facts of the report in a terse style.

■ *Abstract.* An abstract, like an executive summary, is a brief description or overview of the contents of a report. There are two types of abstracts: informative and descriptive. An *informative abstract* is a summary, an internal discussion. A *descriptive abstract* lists the elements covered in a complete report without stating the supporting data; it is an external discussion or framework.

FORMAT AND PREPARATION

Careful formatting and preparation of a business report are musts. Fortunately, the software bundled with office computers make report preparation much easier than it used to be. However, it's also true that software allows the user to include so many bells and whistles in a report that it can look "amateurish" and be difficult to read. You must be consistent in form, type style (e.g., italics, bold), and fonts to produce a quality document.

Even with computer software capability, it's often best to think about the report before beginning its preparation at the keyboard. Should the document contain headers and footers, with the title of the report on the right-hand header and the section head on the left-hand header? Do you want automatic page numbering to appear; if so, where on the page? All of this preparation is fairly manageable with today's word processing programs. In fact, inserting charts, checklists, and graphics is easy as well. You can even import spreadsheets or illustrations with a simple click of the mouse. Moving text is the same simple maneuver of highlight, edit, cut, and paste. Remember, too, that there are templates available in most word processing programs for reports, memos, newsletters, and brochures.

Today's wide range of business services also helps the office professional think of how the report will be presented. Will it be spiral-bound or presented in a folder? Give thought to the paper, type style and font, format, and presentation, as well as the special features of the report and the care and use of the equipment to be used in preparing the report.

Paper

Reports should use a good quality of paper, usually $8\frac{1}{2}" \times 11"$ white paper with 24 percent rag content. This is a better quality paper than copier paper or regular printer paper—it is closer to letterhead-quality paper. The higher the rag content of paper, the longer its life.

A watermark imprinted on rag-content paper tells the brand of paper and the percentage of cotton fiber in it. To read the watermark, hold a blank piece of paper up to a light source. The right side of the paper shows a readable watermark. Use either 16-, 20-, or 24-pound paper. Print on the face of the paper showing the readable watermark.

If you are looking for a higher quality paper to print a report on, check with an office supply expert. They can recommend papers that will not only look good, but also will run through a laser printer or copier without jamming. Multiple originals can be generated by computers, and many offices use photocopiers to produce quality copies.

Here are some rules of thumb for selecting paper. Is it a throwaway report for the sales force? If so, you might simply use a photocopy machine to make duplicates of the original. If it is a report that will be read by everyone in management, letterhead may be needed. If you use letterhead for the first sheet in lengthy reports, you can use blank letterhead for the additional pages. If the report is for the Board of Directors, the CEO, or other shareholders, you might want to have the whole thing handled outside by a commercial print shop. It can be printed on expensive paper and bound in a report cover, which is a good idea for reports that contain graphics and other color charts that look best on coated papers.

Of course, you must consider budgets, there are hybrid methods of combining inside and outside work to save on costs. For example, you could have the local print shop handle the printing of color graphs and charts for the report, collate them into the text portion you prepared in the office, and bind the whole thing for you. You wouldn't want to do this for the annual report unless instructed to do so because here is where the company usually puts its best efforts into presentation.

Choosing Type

A 10-point font is preferred for reports because its large size makes it easier to read. As for design, the conventional roman typeface is still the most widely acceptable. A sturdy, modern sans-serif design is clean, easy to read, and makes single-spaced or tightly packed data appear less crowded. It's often used for report titles, headings, and captions for figures and tables. Italic type or underscoring may be used to highlight certain words in the text of a report. The underscoring equals and should be interpreted as the word(s) being in italics. In all cases, the style must be good letter quality. The format must be consistent throughout the report.

Of course, these are guidelines; you should be guided by the application and use of the material. A short sales report that contains numbers that are to be scanned quickly (for example, a weekly sales report), could be done in 12- or even 14-point type. If you plan to use callouts (marginal notations or excerpts that summarize key points in the text), drop to a smaller font, usually 8-point type, or 2 points below the body type.

Remember that while you may be creative with the use of fonts and want to try something different once in awhile, the best way to go is clean, crisp, and uncluttered. No more than three fonts on a page is a good rule. If you are working in a funky organization, then the rules may not apply. Also, the corporate culture may be avant-garde. Consider the in-your-face style of *Wired* magazine and some of its more recent imitators. Just remember that those pioneers employ professional graphic artists who have a lot of experience under their belts. It may look easy to create at the cutting edge of design, but the best designs for most of us in business are clean, crisp, and simple with a lot of white space.

PARTS OF A BUSINESS REPORT

The business report may include all or some of the following formal sections, along with the main body: letter or memorandum of transmittal, title page, preface, table of contents, list of tables and/or figures, bibliography, appendices, and index.

Although the report itself may contain no words authored by you, the way it looks is directly influenced by your hand. The look reflects on you as the report designer—your efforts make the information or data look good, not only to the readers but to the people who wrote the text.

A word here about writing. Although usually not necessary, if you notice some erroneous data, bad grammar, or spelling, it's a good idea to call it to the boss's attention and explain how you will fix it. Another opportunity exists with the collaborative report, written by several writers. You can see whether everything reads as if it were one voice or author. If not, then some tweaking or copy editing will often improve the way it reads, to everyone's delight. You make the authors look better, the readers are impressed, and most folks appreciate the wordsmithing.

Parts of the business report are discussed in the following paragraphs.

Letter of transmittal. A letter of transmittal is used to introduce the reader to the report. The content of the letter should tell the reader what the topic of the report is, why it was written, how it was compiled, who worked on it, and what major findings or conclusions resulted from the research. The letter of transmittal appears directly after the title page, and it may be typed in any acceptable business letter or memorandum format.

Title page. The title page usually contains the name or title of the report, the name and title of the person or organization for whom it was written, the name and title of the person or group who wrote it, and the date it was submitted. The title page may also include more information, if necessary. As a general rule, place the main title in all uppercase letters, approximately 2 inches from the top of the page. Put the date 2 inches from the bottom of the page. Space the other information equally between the top and bottom margins, typed in lowercase letters, with the first letter of each main word capitalized. Center each line horizontally. There are various formats for title pages. For an acceptable style, see the following figure.

Preface. The preface, also called the *foreword,* is optional. It allows the writer to give a personal message to the reader. The author may, for example, provide special information that may not appear in the body of the report, such as the methods used, points of emphasis, pragmatic considerations, or reasons for treatment of content.

Table of contents. The table of contents (TOC) is one of the last things prepared, after all pages of the report are completed and numbered. The table of contents lists, in chronological order, the numbers and titles of the sections or chapters in the report, and the pages on which they begin. It should not be confused with the index, which is arranged alphabetically and includes more items. If your computer software has a table-of-contents feature, generate the TOC that way.

To format the table of contents, type the heading "TABLE OF CONTENTS" in all uppercase, centered 2 inches from the top edge of the paper.

```
        INTRODUCING INFORMATION PROCESSING INTO THE BUSINESS CURRICULUM AT
                        ST. ANN'S TECHNICAL COLLEGE




                            The Effect of Change
        The State University of New York Program in Office Management
                                    by
                        Technical Consultants, Inc.








                             August 16, 200_
```

Example of a Title Page

Type "Page" a triple space below the heading. Begin typing the contents a double space below "Page" at the left margin. Use the same margins that you use in typing the body of the report. A good style is to use all uppercase letters when typing those entries of the contents page that refer to the major sections of the report. The sections of lesser importance should be indented under their main headings and listed in the same sequence as they appear in the report.

Example of a Table of Contents

Only the initial letters of main words should be uppercase. Leaders should be used to guide the reader's eye across the page from a content's entry to the page number. See the above figure for an example.

  List of illustrations. When a report contains several tables, charts, and/or other figures by way of illustration, separate lists of these should be included after the table of contents. Number each title or figure, and give the full caption or title of each. A computer spreadsheet or word processing program with a table-numbering feature may aid you here. If the number of illustrations is not significant, they can be listed in, or simply added to the end of, the table of contents. Conversely, should the report contain both tables and figures (and many of each), individual lists may make sense. The list of tables would precede the list of figures, each list on its own page.

Body of the Report

Whether you design it yourself or use a template from your word processing application, organization and presentation of the information is key. Here are some guidelines rooted in the classic style of setting up reports.

Margins. Margins for reports and manuscripts are a minimum of 1 inch; however, many authors prefer margins of 1¼ inches. When the report is to be bound on the left side, allow for the binding by making the left margin 1½ inches wide and reducing the right margin accordingly.

The top margin on the first page should be at least 2 inches; on the other pages, it should be 1 inch. If the report is to be bound at the top, allow an additional one-half inch for this. Keep the bottom margins at least 1 inch deep; in some cases, you may want to make them as much as 1½ inches deep.

Spacing. Usually, reports are double-spaced and the first line of each paragraph is indented. The following figure presents a page from a report.

In the text itself, when a long quote (of three lines or more) is set apart from the rest of the text as a separate paragraph, it should be single spaced, the quote marks should be dropped, and the paragraph should be indented an extra five spaces inside the right and left margins. Further indent the first line of the quotation to show a paragraph indention. Copy the indented quotation in single spacing, and omit the quotation marks. The indention tells the reader that the material is a quote.

If listings are included in your report, single-space them. Center the items on the page. If listings contain widely separated columns, use leaders to assist the eye in reading the material.

Allow at least two lines of a paragraph to appear at the bottom and top of each page, adjusting the bottom margin, if necessary, to make sure that one line doesn't end up standing alone at the bottom or top of a page. Make sure, too, that words aren't divided across pages.

White space. When preparing each page of the business report, avoid leaving excessive space without type. This space distracts the reader and takes away from the appearance, organization, and format of the page. If white space is necessary before and after an illustration, artwork, or visual, leave not more than 2 inches.

Tables, figures, and illustrations. The placement of tables, figures, and illustrations in the body of the business report is very important and must be carefully done. Each visual (whether a table, figure, or other type of illustration) must have its own identification number (Table 1, Table 2, and so forth;

<u>Population Under Investigation</u>

　　The population under investigation for this study is the administration of the College, the Business and Economics Division, the Secretarial Administration Department, the students enrolled in the secretarial program, the surrounding business community, and the certificated and classified staff of San Bernardino Valley College.

<u>Definition of Terms</u>

　　<u>Mag Card II Typewriter.</u> Paula Cecil states in her word processing textbook:

　　　　In April 1973 IBM introduced the use of "memory" in word processing typewriters with its new Mag Card II. Previously, recording of typing had been made directly onto the magnetic tape. But on the Mag Card II the recording is made "in memory" from which it can be played back. If the operator wants to store the recording on a card, a button is depressed which records all information that was typed into memory.[4]

　　<u>Memory Typewriter.</u> In the same textbook Ms. Cecil describes the Memory Typewriter:

　　　　In March 1974, another member of the IBM family was introduced: the Memory Typewriter. This unit has all the features of the Mag Card II except the use of cards, thereby eliminating long storage and merging applications. The Memory Typewriter has a 50-page memory storage and a 4000-character-per-page capacity for revising, which means a total memory capacity of 200,000 characters. This unit is sold mainly to small offices for production of regular correspondence, some stored letters or paragraphs, and short-turnaround revisions.[5]

---

　　[4]Paula B. Cecil. *Word Processing in the Modern Office* (Menlo Park, California: Cummings Publishing Co., 1976), pp. 85-86.

　　[5]*Ibid.*, p. 87.

Example Page from the Body of a Report

Figure 1, Figure 2, and so forth). Tables may present quantitative or qualitative data, and the data should be arranged so that the significance of different items is obvious at a glance. Allow ample spacing between rows and columns; white space helps lend order to the data being displayed. Turning a report sideways to read a table or study a figure is often an inconvenience to the reader. If possible, reduce the visual enough so that it conforms to the margins but retains its readability. Again, computer software may do much of the work for you.

Headings. The main heading is centered in uppercase letters at the beginning of the report. As a rule, no other heading should be typed in uppercase letters. If the report has a subheading (a secondary heading that explains or amplifies the main heading), separate it from the main heading with a double space, and then use a triple space between the subheading and the body of the report. The subheading should be centered, and the initial letter of the main word or words should be uppercase.

First-order subheadings are preceded by a triple space and followed by a double space. Side headings should be placed flush left, underlined with main words capitalized, and have no terminal period (or other terminal punctuation).

Second-order subheadings or paragraph headings are preceded by a double space. They are indented to the paragraph point (usually only the first word is capitalized), underlined, and followed by a period. Begin typing the paragraph on the same line as the heading.

Footnotes/Endnotes. Footnotes have a number of purposes: They may confirm or add meaning to the author's statements; they may refer to other parts of the report that have a bearing on the topic discussed; they may make acknowledgments; or they sometimes make additional explanations of the content or terms used.

Footnotes are marked in the text by figures called *superscripts.* The superscript is typed one-half space above the line of writing where it occurs and immediately follows the word or statement to which the footnote applies.

Most software packages have a footnote feature that makes the spacing and arrangement of footnotes fast and easy.

Footnotes may be numbered in one of two ways: consecutively throughout the article or chapter; or consecutively on each page, beginning with the number 1 for each new page. Be uniform in numbering the references. In rough-draft work and thesis work, numbering footnotes consecutively on each page simplifies the typing. Then, if there is an addition, deletion, or correction, subsequent footnotes need not be renumbered.

When using footnotes, put the reference figure in the text following the passage to which the footnote refers.

Most word processing software will automatically position the footnote on the page in the appropriate place with the superscript number. Single-space footnotes, using a slightly smaller typeface than the text size, if possible.

Double-space between two footnotes that appear on one page. If there are many footnote references throughout the report, consider having them appear as endnotes that go (no surprise) at the end of the document or at the end of a section. Endnotes can make the report more readable, although they force the reader to flip back and forth to use the references.

For a footnote that refers to published material, give the same information that is given in a bibliographical reference plus the page number of the cited material. The following two examples follow the *Chicago Manual of Style.*

[3]Rosemary T. Fruehling and Constance K. Weaver, *Electronic Office Procedures* (New York: McGraw-Hill Book Company, 1987), p. 29.

Example of a Footnote: Book with Two Authors

[4]Stephen McMillen, "Secretarial Development: The Other Side of the Coin," *The Secretary* (June/July, 1987), p. 26.

Example of a Footnote: Magazine Article

If two or more footnotes are identical, you do not need to retype the details. Use one of the following abbreviations for Latin phrases:

Ibid., meaning "in the same place." Use *Ibid.* when referring to the work cited in the immediately preceding footnote, without an intervening footnote. This abbreviation may be used several times in succession. Here is an example:

[5]*Ibid.* (Use when the reference is identical to the one in the preceding footnote.)

[6]*Ibid., p.* 35. (Use when the reference is identical to the one in the preceding footnote but on a different page.)

Example of an "Ibid." Footnote

Loc. cit., meaning "in the place cited." Use *loc. cit.* with nonconsecutive footnotes that refer to the same material, the same work, and the same page or pages. Repeat the author's name before *loc. cit.*

Op. cit., meaning "in the work cited." Use *op. cit.* with nonconsecutive footnotes that refer to the same work, but to different pages. Repeat the author's last name. Here is an example:

```
 _____
 ⁸Walshe, loc. cit.

 ⁹Baker, op. cit., p. 77.
```

Example of an "Op. cit." Footnote

Sometimes, footnotes appear at the end of a report on a separate sheet titled "Works Cited."

Header/footer. Once again, computers make this element easier to execute. A *header* is a line or two at the top of each page in the report or at the top of the first page of the report that contains identifying information. Usually, the header contains the topic or subtopic in that particular section of the report. It may also identify a specific section of the report by number. Following is an example of a header:

```
                    TypeRight Software Version 4.0
                    Chapter 1.3: Compatibility

        The program design of major software is copyrighted.
   Moreover, some programs are compatible with major manufacturer's
   equipment. However, caution must be taken as to […]
```

Example of a Header

A *footer,* located at the bottom of a page, also has identifying information. Generally, it contains the date of the report, page number, and other data. Following is an example of a footer:

```
   Recommendation:      Specifications must be drafted by the end of
                        the third quarter. The feasibilitiy study will
                        cost $30,000.

   September 1, 200_                              Confidential
```

Example of a Footer

Bibliography and Appendices

A *bibliography* includes the references used in the preparation of the report. Arrange it alphabetically by authors' last names. When listing books, copy the information from the title page, rather than from the outside cover. When listing references from periodicals, take the title from the article itself.

Depending on the content of some reports and the company's policy, items in the bibliography may be numbered in order of their appearance in the report. Sometimes, you may be asked to use abbreviated (shortened) forms of citations in your draft copy and complete forms in the final copy.

Each reference lists the surname of the author, followed by given name or initials, the title of the work, the publisher, the place of publication, and the date of publication. When using references from periodicals, you may include such identifying information as volume and page numbers. Observe these rules:

- Use italics for the titles of books and magazines.

- Enclose the titles of magazine articles in quotation marks.

- Type the author's initials after the surname. If some references use a full name and others only initials, be consistent, particularly when the references come close together. Usually, it is better to use the full name.

- If the author has written some books alone and collaborated with other authors on other projects, list first those books the author wrote alone.

- If the publication has more than three authors, list the publication under the name of the first mentioned author and then use the words "and others" or *et al.*

- If the publication is out of print, indicate this in parentheses following the reference.

- Volume numbers of periodicals are written with Arabic numerals.

- To make the author's name stand out, type the first line of the entry at the left margin and indent all other lines.

- If there are many sources of reference material, classify them according to books, periodicals, pamphlets, or other media.

- When two or more books by the same author are listed in succession, instead of retyping the author's name each time, simply use a solid line of five underscores followed by a comma. See the example on the opposite page.

References. Only citations used or referred to in the report are listed in the bibliography. Some reports provide a listing of suggested or recommended readings. These are separate from the bibliography and should be noted as

Popyk, Marilyn K., *Word Processing: Essential Concepts,* New York: McGraw-Hill Book Company, 1983.

_____, *Word Processing and Information Systems: A Practical Approach to Concepts,* New York: McGraw-Hill Book Company, 1986.

Example of Two Sequential Books by the Same Author in a Bibliography

such. In other words, the suggested or recommended readings (books, magazines, films, and so on) are neither cited nor used in the preparation of the report; they are intended for further study or review only.

There are a number of style manuals that can be used in preparing a bibliography (or other parts of a report). Whatever manual you choose, use it properly: consistency, clarity, and common sense must prevail. See the example of one type of bibliography on the next page.

Appendix. Material supportive to the report should be placed in a supplementary section called an appendix. It should follow the bibliography. Examples of items placed in the appendix are copies of questionnaires, maps, lists, tables, sample forms and letters, and detailed summaries of data, notes, tables, a glossary of terms, and any other material that might be considered supplementary to the text itself.

The appendix may be preceded by an introductory page entitled APPENDIX, typed in all uppercase letters, and centered both horizontally and vertically. This page may also include a list of the items included in the appendix. If a list is included, both the title and the list are centered vertically, or the title may be placed two inches from the top of the paper with the listing beginning a triple space below the title. When more than one item is appended, each item should be numbered or lettered and placed under a separate heading, such as Appendix A, Appendix B, and so on. If you have more than 26 appendices, begin the 27th by doubling the letter as AA, BB, CC, and so forth.

If an appendix is rather lengthy and bulky, label it "Enclosure" and attach it after the last appendix. If there is only one appendix, no letter or number is necessary. The word "Appendix" is sufficient. Triple-space and begin the text of that single appendix.

In cases in which there are only one or two items to follow the end of a report, they may be labeled as "attachments." A sample questionnaire at the end of a survey is a good example of an item that could be called an attachment. Although there are no formal rules for naming attachments, the term may be considered appropriate for material supplementary to the text in a letter or report. It is not appropriate for anything more formal, such as a monograph or book.

B I B L I O G R A P H Y

Books

Fruehling, Rosemary T., and Weaver, Constance K. *Electronic Office Procedures.* New York: McGraw-Hill Book Co., 1987. 544 pp.

Keene, Michael L. *Effective Professional Writing.* Lexington, MA: D.C. Heath and Co., 1987. 450 pp.

Popyk, Marilyn K. *Word Processing and Information Systems: A Practical Approach to Concepts.* New York: McGraw-Hill Book Co., 1983. 336 pp.

Journals

Hart, M.B. "Status of OS in 29 Texas Companies (With Implications for OS Curricula)," *Office Systems Research Journal.* (1986).

McEntee, A. "Determining Core Competencies Necessary for Success in the Automated Office," *Journal of the Business Education Association of New York.* (1985).

Munter, M. "Using the Computer in Business Communication Courses," *The Journal of Business Communication.* (1986).

Unpublished Work

Xavier, Chris. "Office Needs" (Assessment Criteria, Star Associations, 1988), "Mimeographed."

Example of a Bibliography

Short Reports

Somewhere between the informality of a memo and the large-scale business or technical report described earlier lies a document commonly referred to as a *short report*. Very often an update between fewer people than might receive a full-blown business report, a short report has an objective to convey certain information less formally, and in fewer than four or five pages.

TECHNICAL REPORTS

Preparing reports for engineers, chemists, mathematicians, scientists, and other professionals often involves what used to be called "technical typing."

Today's word processing software has eased the burden of preparing such reports a bit, but the task still requires a mastery of such seldom-used skills as equation typing. And because the various disciplines demand an understanding of uncommon symbols and terminology, accuracy in report preparation becomes more important than speed.

Check the help manual for your word processing software. It will tell you what special typing rules you can set up to help you prepare technical documents. Even if you aren't a word processing whiz, here are a few guidelines that may help you make some headway:

- It is essential to double-space a technical report to accommodate the superscripts and subscripts required by many equations. Most word processing software can let even the casual keyboarder enter these symbols.

- Check your computer application's help menu to find out where to find mathematical symbols or Greek letters that are often necessary in a technical document.

- As a rule, leave a space before and after the arithmetical operational symbols: $=$, $+$, $-$, $\div$, $\times$. However, if the symbol is used adjectivally (-3, for example), there should be no space between the minus sign and the 3.

- Multiplication is expressed by using the "$\times$" or a centered period ($4 \cdot 6$), or by parentheses enclosing an expression to be multiplied. Often, the multiplication sign is omitted and the letters are typed together, as *ab*. Thus, in the equation $7ad(s - y) = mx$, there is no space between d and the opening parenthesis, but there is a space before and after the equal sign and the minus sign.

- Type fractions as follows: If the equation is short, the fraction may be part of the running text and is typed in the shilling style, which looks like this: 4/5. If you use mixed numbers, put a space between the whole number and the shilling fraction (for example, 43 5/6).

continues

TECHNICAL REPORTS *continued*

■ Equations are numbered consecutively throughout a report to make it easy to refer to any equation in the text. Each equation number is put in parentheses at the right margin. When making reference to these equation numbers, abbreviate equation to "Eq." Your reference will look like this: (Eq. 5).

Usually punctuation is not used with equations. If your author requests punctuation in equations, observe these rules:

■ Consider each equation as a clause of a complex sentence, and follow it with either a comma or semicolon.

■ If the equation concludes the sentence, a period follows it.

■ If you have a series of equations, introduce them by a colon in the line preceding the equations.

Sometimes, equations are too long for one line and must be placed on several lines. Break them before the equal sign when possible. Another good place to divide an equation is before any one of the operational signs ($+$, $-$, $\times$, $\div$). You may also divide it between fractions, or after brackets and parentheses. Do not put part of an equation on one page and the rest of it on the next page.

Some authors help their typists to read the symbols in an equation by writing all lowercase symbols and printing uppercase symbols. It may also be helpful to draft all the equations in the report before typing. Let the author check your arrangement of the equations. If the author has no objection, then you are ready to do the finished report and can proceed with confidence that the material is arranged in the very best form.

Very often, the structure of the short report is determined by the needs of the recipient. It might be delivered with some regularity (monthly, for example), and always follow a prescribed format.

In the content, there's less reliance on providing every detail and more action orientation. Some recipients prefer that the short reports they receive begin with the conclusion, and then paint the supporting background with broad strokes. Typically, the short or informal report answers the classic five Ws (who, what, when, where, why), and also tells how. If charts, figures, or other data are required, they are typically handled as attachments—referred to less formally in the body of the report.

VISUAL AIDS

Visual aids are any display materials in business reports, formal presentations, or other documents circulated to people both in and out of the company. They often present an easy way to communicate complicated sales data or growth numbers. Today's software programs make it much easier to not only create relevant and attractive graphs and charts, but to also share them between programs. It is easier to create a graph or chart in a spreadsheet program, include it in the written report, add captions and text, and then include the new graphic in the slide presentation that will accompany the report. With a little judicious use of color printing or copying—maybe a page or two—visuals can greatly increase the professional appearance of information. From photos scanned in and added to reports, to animated bullet points in a slide presentation, the office professional can help create effective visuals for reports or presentations.

One of the easiest ways to manipulate data or information is in spreadsheet or database programs, such as Microsoft Excel or Access. Using features like graphs, charts, and pivot tables gives you many ways to present the same data in different formats.

For example, let's say you have a spreadsheet in Microsoft Excel 97 with the following data in four different columns:

Customer	Product	Order Date	Amount of Order

From this data, you could reorganize information by using pivot tables to display a table organized by product, by ascending or descending dollar amounts, or by order dates. Simply go to the data menu and click on the pivot table feature.

Some guidelines for pivot table creation are as follows:

- Label the columns. Because pivot tables use column labels to cross-tabulate data, you can summarize data by customer, product, or amount of order.

- Use one worksheet row for each record. Pivot tables summarize data stored in rows.

- Use date format for any column with dates. See the format menu and date category to select the type of date display you want.

In addition, you can display the data graphically as either a bar chart, column, pie chart, or scatter diagram by clicking on the Excel Chart Wizard. Even stock charts are easy to create.

Other business-strength features worth exploring are sales forecasts created by predicting future sales based on the results of recent months, determining sales trends and predicting sales trends when you have a certain number of months of known years, and future assumptions you build into a formula. Again, you can chart a trend line by using the Excel Chart Wizard. One of the secrets of being a valued office professional is to get comfortable with the advanced features of the word processing and database programs in your office.

Tables and charts aren't static illustrations any more, either. If your team is giving a report in a formal presentation, you can take the same tables and charts used in the report, import them into the PowerPoint program, and create color slides with several clicks of the mouse or keyboard commands. Learning how to do this adds value to your skills in any professional setting. And it's fairly easy to accomplish: All it takes is time and effort. But the payoff is worth it.

In general, visuals are used to enhance the aesthetics of the page, clarify a key point in the text, add emphasis to the subject, arouse the reader's interest, simplify the explanation of technical or other complex subjects, and make the treatment of the subject stand out from similar materials. For example, if you are preparing a divisional report for a headquarters presentation with many other division heads, or if you are preparing a request for funds for a group of investors with other entrepreneurs, visual aids can add a lot to the absorption and interest level of the audience.

TYPES OF VISUALS

The type of visual to use depends on the intended purpose of the visual, the audience, the subject, the type of paper to be used, and the printing process to be used for reproduction.

Basically, there are two types of visuals: pictorial, and numerical or other data. Pictorials include photographs, figures, and illustrations. Numerical data include tables, charts, and graphs.

Choosing a Chart Style

Today's software programs do everything from basic pie charts to full-blown 3-D animated slide shows. We may not all be professional designers, but by following a few guidelines, we all can produce a professional-looking presentation.

As you look at a set of raw numbers and wonder whether they'd be best shown as a pie chart, line graph, or stacked bar chart, remember that choosing the appropriate style is probably the single hardest part of creating a chart.

The three basic styles for charts are Pie, Bar, and Line. More sophisticated styles—such as Histogram, Dual Y-Axis, or High/Low/Close—are just hybrids of the basics. When selecting a chart style, ask yourself what message you are trying to convey and to whom. Then, choose the simplest style that will most effectively communicate this message.

The good news is that most software programs allow you to change styles after you have created the chart without having to re-key the data. For example, the Chart Wizard feature of Microsoft Word allows you to create many different looks at the same data, as mentioned previously. In addition, you can reorganize the data in a spreadsheet by columns. Take advantage of this feature to "try on" different styles; just be sure to save the chart "as is" before moving to the next style. Most programs also allow you to save the chart and import it into another program such as a word processing program.

Pie Charts

Pie charts are the simplest of all. From fourth grade on, most of us can easily "read" a pie chart. Therefore, it's most effective when illustrating a simple concept.

Pie charts are used to compare parts to a whole or percentages of a whole. The pieces of pie, or wedges, are the parts; the entire pie is the whole. You can compare the pieces to each other, and to the sum of the pieces.

Use a pie chart when your data sets add up to a meaningful number or whole—to compare regional sales to each other and to the national total, for example.

When choosing pie charts, be sure that the color selection has enough contrast so that the different colored segments are readable. Also be careful about contrasting type to the colors selected if the type will appear beside the segments on anything other than white paper, or if the legends will appear on top of the colors in the segments themselves.

If the pie chart is in black and white, then check to make sure that the shading, textures, or crosshatching (or whatever you have available in your individual software bundle) are readable. The best way to check for readability is to print the chart because what you see on the screen is not necessarily the same thing you get on paper.

Bar Charts

Bar charts are the most popular chart style in business use, perhaps because the bar has a substantial feel, lending a sense of weight or importance to the presentation.

Single bar charts show single factors, such as sales or expenses, changing over equal time periods such as months, quarters, or years. As a variation, cluster bar charts can display multiple factors side by side, also over equal time periods.

Stacked bar charts, in which the multiple factors are placed on top of each other, are best used to show how parts of a whole change over equal time periods, such as quarterly sales broken out by region. Like the pie chart, use the stacked bar chart only when your parts add up to a meaningful whole.

Here's a little practical advice about bar charts: Stacked charts are a simple device for overlaying multiple factors in a single illustration, but they can be hard to read when using different colors. In black and white, the various shadings must be high-contrast to show up well. Also, if the differences in the factors are not significant they might be almost imperceptible to the reader and can minimize the impact of your information. Pie charts are often a better choice in this situation.

Line Charts

Line charts are useful to compare trends over time, particularly when dramatic changes have taken place. If your data turns out to be a boring flat line, adjust the scaling of the Y-axis by reducing the minimum or maximum value settings, or choose a completely different chart style.

You may choose a straight line to connect each data point (also known as a "zigzag" or "Alpine" line); a trend line, which is drawn straight through the average of data points; or a curved line, which draws a smooth curving line through the average of the data points.

THE FOUR Cs OF CHART DESIGN

Once you've chosen the style that best conveys your message, your next consideration is designing the chart itself. Keep the chart as simple as possible. If a design element, such as a grid or 3-D effect, does not enhance the message, get rid of it!

The following guidelines, which we call the "Four Cs of Chart Design," will help you make design decisions. You should be concise, conservative, consistent, and careful!

Be Concise

Keep your data and text simple and clear. Avoid using more than five sets of data in any chart. To reduce the number of data sets, look for ways to consolidate: Instead of 12 months, try four quarters; instead of 50 states, try four geographical regions.

In a text chart, pretend that each word costs $50 and edit accordingly. Eliminate articles and prepositions whenever possible.

Be Conservative

Use colors, fonts, and special effects sparingly. Just because you can use 12 different fonts in a single chart doesn't mean you should; you want to avoid the appearance of a "ransom note" or an explosion in a font factory.

When choosing colors and patterns, aim for strong contrast between colors and patterns so that viewers can readily distinguish one series from the next. Watch out for colors or patterns that conflict or create optical illusions.

Be Consistent

Use uniform patterns, colors, formats, and fonts throughout an entire presentation. You may even want to unify the look of all corporate presentations across departments.

In text charts, particularly in bulleted lists, check that grammar and phrasing are consistent. For example, don't put "Running," "Jumping," and "Swim" at the start of three bullets. The parallel structure of bulleted lists emphasizes any discrepancies in verb tense and voice or in noun pluralization.

A consistent format helps viewers to understand more quickly and easily; they don't have to waste time trying to figure out different chart formats.

If you are designing charts that will go into a slide or other presentation program, think about which colors will look best and be most readable and professional looking. Don't make the callouts yellow or pink.

Be Careful

Nothing is more embarrassing than to see a mistake magnified 100 times on the boardroom projection screen! Check your work carefully. Use your spell checker, then proofread a hard copy as well. Make sure that all data points are labeled correctly. Verify that percentage amounts add up to 100; sometimes, due to mathematical rounding, the percentages may be slightly off, adding up to 99 or 101. If this is the case, simply "nudge" your data a bit so that it adds up to 100—or use an asterisk to explain at the bottom.

PRESENTATIONS

Chances are that, as an office professional, you won't often have to get up in front of the board of executives and make a formal presentation. However, there are times when it might be necessary for you to address a group or other members of your team or office. Whatever the circumstances, whether explaining that your boss will be delayed and the agenda has been rearranged, or expressing your opinion in a staff meeting, it is always best to present yourself in the most organized and professional manner possible.

What are the secrets of speaking effectively before a group, whether delivering a formal speech or just standing up in a committee meeting "to say a few words"? Dale Carnegie, who founded an entire school of public speaking, thought the secrets involved making our listeners like us. He offered 12 specific points on ways to achieve this end.

- *If you're honored to speak before an audience, say so.* And say why. Even if a group is unimportant, the mere invitation to speak before it is a compliment. If the group is large or in some way important to you, the compliment and the honor are that much greater.

- *Compliment your listeners in turn.* Talk about the good works the group does or the fascinating reason that brings its members together. If you're new to the group and to the area, find out a few facts about both and work these into your speech. Personalizing your speech shows your listeners you know who they are—and you like them. They'll be ready to like you back.

- *Mention a few listeners by name.* This further personalization is a highly effective move, but to be successful it must be worked into your speech at logical and sincere moments. "When Mr. Jones first asked me to speak . . ."; "When Mrs. Rivera was showing me the grounds this morning. . . ." The technique also must be used sparingly because it would be awkward to try to mention every single member of the audience.

- *Be humble.* Your listeners already know your abilities—that's why they asked you to speak. If you downplay these abilities, your listeners will eagerly build you up in their own minds.

- *Say "we" instead of "you."* To get listeners on your side, it's better to join them rather than to preach or to be condescending. "If we could all pull together on this project" sounds more inviting than "If you could all pull together on this project."

- *Let both your face and your voice smile and be friendly.* Too harsh or scolding an expression—even if you have some bad news to impart during the speech—will turn listeners off. Keep your tone mild.

- *Appeal to your listeners' self-interests.* What are their problems? How can you help their work be easier, faster, or cheaper? How can you help them stop worrying or expand their business? What do they want to hear? If you have a set subject on which you're going to talk, meet a few group members ahead of time to see where their concerns are. With a little juggling, you can connect their interests to your own so that your topic will appeal to their self-interests.

- *Have a good time talking.* Be enthusiastic about your subject and you will sweep your listeners up into the emotion. When you enjoy yourself, they will enjoy themselves and will count your speech a great success.

- *Don't apologize.* Apologize for nothing except being late, which is common courtesy. If you're not ready for your speech, for example, apologizing will only antagonize your audience, making it seem as if you thought little enough of them not to prepare ahead of time. It's better to simply forge ahead. Even when apologies don't antagonize the listeners, they make you seem unsure of yourself. You may be, in truth, but why make it more noticeable by pointing it out?

- *Appeal to your listeners' better emotions.* Even supposedly cynical people respond to what's good in the world: it's what they want for themselves and their families. You needn't try to gush emotion at every turn of phrase. Just remember that what moves and inspires you will probably move and inspire your audience.

- *Welcome criticism.* If your message is controversial or apt to upset people, in your speech invite possible critics to later offer you suggestions. If you think you're ill-spoken, acknowledge it, then say, "But it's my message, not my style, that's important."

- *Speak with sincerity and honesty.* An eloquent speaking ability only impresses listeners in the very beginning. What they'll take home with them is your character, your integrity, and your own belief in the subject.

PRESENTATION AND GRAPHICS SOFTWARE

Chances are that if your boss or team has been preparing a lengthy report or document, someone is going to have to give a formal presentation. Given the data that needs to be explained, and given the fact that nothing is more boring than a person standing motionless at the podium while he or she reads, you will probably want to prepare visual aids.

Computers to the rescue again. Presentation software gives most computer-literate offices the capability to create at least passable charts and graphics. These can be output as paper documents, of course, but they also can be made into projectable slides or overheads, saved for display on other computer screens, or transmitted electronically to other sites.

Resist temptation. Relatively easy to master presentation desktopping skills, coupled with clip art packages loaded with tens of thousands of illustrations and a palette more colorful than any rainbow, provide a strong temptation to create presentation graphics that rival the ceiling of the Sistine Chapel. But even if you have the skill of Michelangelo, do not use it here.

Here are some rules of thumb:

- A good highway billboard has no more than six words. Present one idea on each visual and choose your words carefully. It's easier to read short bullet points than long lines of text.

- Keep the text of a slide or screen to a maximum of six lines of text, with no more than six words per line.

- Use graphics to support main ideas and crucial facts. Choose a graphic theme. Use it consistently. Try using charts for comparison information.

- Adjust your type. Choose one or two classic faces that are easy to read. All uppercase can be difficult to read; use uppercase and lowercase. Save the all uppercase to emphasize one word or concept.

■ Don't sweat the punctuation. You're grouping information visually, so let good design serve as punctuation. Bullet points can help.

WEB PAGES

Although you can learn more about the World Wide Web in Chapter 5, for the purposes of office documents, you should know that the Web is a computer network that allows you to view documents by using a browser such as Internet Explorer or Netscape Communicator. A Web page is simply a document that may contain text and graphics.

Nowadays, the Internet, and intranets or internal Web sites are fairly common. Although most companies today have at least a rudimentary site up and running, many companies have e-commerce or actual business transactions taking place on their sites. As we move into the next decade, more and more companies will disseminate more and more information—such as regular company updates, bulletins, and HR-type messages over their intranets. In some areas like sales, the regular output of the department will be put up on the company intranet for distribution to all departments. As the office professional, you may be the one preparing this information for the Web or even posting the document. Very active companies post Web pages daily (customer service, warehouse). Some departments may post weekly (human resources), monthly (sales), or quarterly (finance).

While building a simple Web page may seem like an intimidating task, it's incredibly simple to prepare a document to go on the Web—usually it's as simple as changing the way you save it. In Microsoft Word, for example, click the File menu and you'll see the command Save as HTML. (HTML is the language that browsers use to "read" the document on the Web.) In the Edit menu, you can place a portion of a document (or all of it) as a hyperlink in another document, so the reader can refer to it by simply clicking on the link retrieving the related text. This helps readers who may want more information about a particular term or concept they are reading about in a Web document. They simply click on the term or hyperlinked word, and jump to another hyperlinked document with more detailed information.

Many word processing programs, such as Microsoft Word, give users the option to save a document as a Web page. Most office packages now offer a Web page building program such as FrontPage or Publisher. Many companies that use the Web for internal documents might have an internal application for converting the file. The important thing is not to be mystified or afraid of using technology to save, convert, and work with documents. Take the time to learn a technique that works for you, the office pro, on your computer with the software at hand. If your company is just launching a Web site or a Web page, be sure to recommend that you and your department (the whole company, for that matter) get upgraded software to handle Web documents easily.

COMPANY NEWSLETTERS

Newsletters are an ideal way to establish your company as an expert in its field, remind clients of various products or services, and introduce the company to potential new clients. Newsletters are very useful within large companies to keep employees informed about what's going on inside the company, to improve morale, and to pass along things like motivational messages or recognition for a job well done.

Service businesses are a natural for newsletters, especially businesses that may be visited only once or twice a year. Lawyers and accountants can spotlight tax and legal issues that clients may not otherwise be aware of. Physicians can distribute a profile of a new medicine or describe an illness, such as the symptoms of a stroke. Dentists can report new advancements in "painless" or cosmetic dentistry.

No matter what the focus of your company—services or products—a newsletter should also contain personalized news about employees or community announcements that may affect workers. Maybe one of the company sales reps is involved in community service or has qualified for a national award, or the municipality may have instituted special emergency regulations to take effect in the event of a snowstorm. These are little extras that give the "house organ," as organizational newsletters are called, a unique look. It gives employees a reason to read the newsletters and increases the editor's visibility inside the company.

The editor of the newsletter will decide what the newsletter should cover, the frequency of publication, and the distribution list. However, the office professionals will most likely be in charge of producing it. As such, they have many duties and responsibilities. Here are some general tips and suggestions for handling newsletter production like a seasoned hand:

- Verify all grammar and spelling. Although this sounds simple, even the best spelling and grammar features of software programs won't cover such things as misuse of properly spelled words like "there" for "their," completely wrong words spelled right in the middle of a sentence, floating letters, and other chaff that just won't be picked up unless you proofread the material yourself.

- Don't use too many fancy fonts or clip art. If your business has a formal, all-business atmosphere, keep it professional, clean, and simple. Use a roman typeface for text and a sans-serif or display type for headings and callouts. If you work at a funky new age or neo-tech company, you can pull out all the stops and experiment. But this is generally better left to professional graphics people. Try getting friendly with them and you'll get some good advice based on experience. Resist the temptation to use more than a couple or three fonts per page or document.

- Use a standard paper size that can be folded into a business envelope. Legal-size paper may be an attractive size to use when you want the newsletter to stand out in a pile on someone's desk, but it requires a custom fold or a larger size envelope to stuff and mail.

- Provide room for an address label if you don't plan to mail the issues in an envelope. Check with the post office regarding requirements. By using heavier paper stock, such as 50-pound bright white, a simple fold in half once and then in half again, and the application of a stamp gets the newsletter in the mail as a self-mailer. This saves the company money in envelopes and insertion charges. And for small mailings you do yourself, it saves you time and labor.

- Keep a stack of current issues in your waiting room or reception lobby. It's a good public relations vehicle for new employees and applicants.

- Make sure that copies of back issues with articles by the boss or on topics relevant to the client are handed to the client or are on the reception area table.

- Find out who will receive the newsletter. Will it be employees only? Current and former clients and customers? Members of boards, committees, and organizations you and the boss attend? Referral sources? Suggest to the editor that topics of interest to the constituent readers be featured in future issues.

- Keep a file of sample publications from other companies. Identify what you like about them, and see if it's possible to incorporate some of their best features into your own newsletter.

You get what you pay for. Simply put, professionals get the most professional results. True, desktop publishing makes attractive documents possible, but it's no substitute for the polished skills of a graphic artist. You may find that an amateur design doesn't look as good or pack the wallop you expect or need.

Most of what's provided here is a quick and proven formula for producing a professional looking standard newsletter for the business. If you are trying to produce a one-of-a-kind look or using more than two colors it's a good idea to get some advice from a graphics professional. Do not be tempted to spend thousands of dollars on fancy hardware and software that you have no familiarity with unless you are the intrepid tinkerer who likes to go it alone and you have the time to do so.

FOR MORE INFORMATION

If you can't find what you need in this chapter, you may need to expand your search.

- For more information on preparing formal business reports, check your local library or bookstore in the reference section for resources.

- For more information on creating visuals using software applications, check your local library or bookstore in the computer book section. Books are available for any user level.

- For more information on style specifics, consult the Grammar and Punctuation Guide at the back of this book.

- For more information on formal presentations, check the library or bookstore in the business communications section.

3

OFFICE EQUIPMENT AND SUPPLIES

◆

- **Equipment selection**

  Needs Analysis

  Office Equipment Leases

- **Equipment Basics**

  Telephones and Telephone Systems

  Fax Machines

  Copiers

  Electronic Typewriters

  Recording and Dictation Equipment

  VCRs and Projectors

  Shredders

- **Equipment Maintenance and Ordering Office Supplies**

  Equipment Maintenance

  Ordering Office Supplies

  Storage

  References and Publications for Offices

  Letterhead and Business Cards

- **For More Information**

Equipment and supplies encompass the wide variety of items needed in the day-to-day running of an office—items that the office professional is often responsible for choosing, buying, and keeping in stock. The umbrella term "equipment and supplies" includes everything: the pencils and scratch pads at everyone's desk, the business cards a salesperson hands out at a trade exhibit, and the phone system that links your company with customers halfway around the world.

The selection of equipment and supplies involves a great deal more than product demonstrations and price comparisons, especially at the high-tech, high-cost end of the spectrum. In a large organization, the office professional's involvement in assessing the organization's needs likely will include determining the type of work done, assessing the ease of use of equipment or software, listing any special features required, recording functions currently being used, and identifying desired functions. On the other hand, the office professional in a small company might participate directly in the processes of equipment selection, purchasing, and maintenance because he or she is probably the person most knowledgeable about what is needed.

EQUIPMENT SELECTION

Before selecting high-end office equipment (such as phone systems, computers, copiers, and so on), a careful analysis of the company's needs should be performed: What does the company want to do? Who will be doing it? How easy will it be to do? What technical and informational support will the user have? After this analysis is reviewed and a piece of equipment is selected, there's another question to address: Should the piece be leased or bought outright? This section discusses advantages and disadvantages of each option.

This overview concludes with a look at the equipment basics found in most offices and those pieces that are most likely to fall under the responsibility of the office professional when a new item must be selected.

NEEDS ANALYSIS

Before any piece of equipment is purchased, an analysis of the office or company needs should consider the expected applications of the new equipment, its users, and its ease of use. For the users' sake, a demonstration is crucial, as is an assurance of the level of documentation, instruction, and support services that come with the equipment. With today's constantly changing technology, it is also important to know whether a piece of equipment is versatile and whether it can be upgraded.

Using a high-end copier as an example, each of these elements will be considered in the following sections.

Applications

When considering the purchase, first address the equipment's applications. Put simply, what do you want the copier to do? Of course, you want it to make multiple-page copies for individual employee use, but what else? To make copies of a special fifty-page report for internal distribution? To provide an alternative to an outside printer for a small-run customer newsletter? Consider these special uses as well as the more frequent ones.

After determining the general applications, examine specific needs. What features are required? Just black-and-white copying? Photographic color copying? Two-sided enlarged or reduced copies? Simple collating? Folding, inserting into covers, and stapling? What level of monthly volume is the copier designed for? Can the machine be programmed to do lengthy jobs after-hours to prevent tie-ups during the day? Can it be linked to PCs for remote programming? Samples of actual or anticipated applications should be carefully analyzed to determine the features needed.

Still other considerations must be addressed. Does it make sense to have a multifunction machine that incorporates scanning, faxing, and so on besides its copying capability? If the copier has fax capability, does it have an anti-junk-mail filter for incoming faxes? Does it have storage memory? Can it physically manipulate the image?

Is security an issue? What about expensive unauthorized use? Can the copier be programmed to accept passwords? Can it diagnose its own problems? Can it be fixed from the manufacturer's remote location via modem?

Users

Think about who will use the equipment (in this case, the copier). How many individual users will share it? How many departments? Can it be shared by departments, or will each department require its own? Does one department have less need for a special features machine? Would that department be better served by buying a second small machine that handles only basic black-and-white copies?

Ease of Use

Many copiers use icons or pictures to represent the task to be performed. Users make choices by touching a control panel to change the number of copies, the size of the reproduced image, the darkness or lightness, and so on. Similarly, multifunction machines should quickly switch from one use to another, and each function's special features should be clearly labeled.

Loading paper trays and clearing jams also should be easily accomplished by all users, reducing the need to call on the office professional for help. Additional tasks that are usually performed by the office professional, such as changing toner cartridges, should be simply and neatly accomplished.

Demonstration

Although a vendor demonstration will highlight the good features of the piece of equipment being sold, there are a few points to remember. Because demonstrations are done by experienced personnel who know the product well, features that may be difficult to use sometimes only *look* as if they are very simple. Also, features that are important to you might not even be part of the demonstration. Make sure that the product demonstration is done with the application of the user in mind.

Again, let's use the example of the copier. Actual jobs should be performed—on both the copiers and the multifunction machines. Be sure to include the most complex combinations of functions. These functions should be tried by one or more people other than the office professionals who are familiar with the department or company's copying needs. Some vendors also might arrange for an in-house trial period of a piece of equipment—a "free trial" or a brief rental period. This tryout provides the best test because it happens under actual user conditions.

For both demonstrations and trial periods, the machine should be the exact make and model as the one being considered for purchase.

Documentation and Support

Documentation and support are primary areas of concern, especially for novice users and for users of more sophisticated pieces of equipment such as telephone systems, multifunction copiers, and computers. Equipment should come with detailed setup instructions, as in a tutorial disk. No matter which pieces are selected, the instruction manuals should be well organized and clearly written for beginners, not veteran users or technicians.

For computer users, templates that fit over the keyboard and list the functions performed by various keys or combinations can offer great help. An extensive selection of "how-to" books on PCs, operating systems, and software packages also can help simplify use.

For all kinds of equipment and software, ask if the company has a toll-free number to call with questions, at least for an initial period. In general, the level of support provided is greater with larger purchases; a desktop shredder, for example, comes with less support than an industrial-quality shredder. The level of support is also greater for a large company buying in quantity. Often a computer or office superstore also can provide more guidance than a mail-order house.

Vendors who provide training on the higher-end pieces generally train a certain number of employees to use the equipment. After the initial training, vendors usually charge a fee for each additional person trained. Some types of training—particularly for PCs on large systems—must be provided for newly hired, upgraded, and transferred personnel. Although an in-house training department might be appropriate for a large corporation, a smaller company might bring a trainer in-house. Individual users then might have to attend a seminar or course, or purchase an audiovisual training package.

Versatility and Upgradability

A major concern when purchasing equipment and software is the continual advances in technology. While purchases should include the needs of the foreseeable future, overbuying now can be much more expensive than upgrading later, especially as the cost of technology keeps dropping. Upgrades for computer hardware and software are familiar to everyone, but these are not the only products that can be upgraded. In analyzing the copier, for example, do you foresee the possibility that the company computers might become networked? In that case, can the copier be upgraded later to add network printing? Or can it be upgraded to scan to the network, individual PC, or e-mail? Ask about a machine's future capabilities as well as its current ones.

Other Considerations

Other important considerations exist for all types of equipment: guaranties, warranties, responsibility for repairs, extended warranties, and so on. In short, what happens when a problem occurs with the functioning of the equipment? What is covered under the original guaranty, by whom, and for how long a period? Is a maintenance contract available through the vendor? Is the repair provided by the vendor, or is it contracted to a third party? If the equipment is purchased from a computer store, does it have to be brought in for repair? Is on-site service available? Is a substitute available while the equipment is being repaired? All questions should be answered before any purchase takes place.

OFFICE EQUIPMENT LEASES

Years ago, most office equipment was bought as a matter of routine. Now, the office professional with purchasing duties faces an additional choice: to buy or lease? Basically, a lease is a rental agreement for a limited period of time. An estimated 80 percent of all companies now lease some, if not all, of their equipment because a lease offers the following distinct advantages:

- *A short-term lease is ideal for ever-changing technology.* This is perhaps the single most important reason for leasing pieces of equipment such as computers, which quickly become obsolete.

- *Repairs and servicing are usually covered by the agreement.* Except for routine wear and tear, major problems are not the company's responsibility. What constitutes wear and tear, however, should be spelled out.

- *Tax advantages make leasing very attractive.* Instead of averaging tax deductions for the cost of the item over what current tax law says is the life of the item, the company can deduct the lease payments in full as they are made.

On the other hand, leasing carries the following *disadvantages:*

- *Poor terms.* The company could get locked into a lease with unfavorable terms, or one that is too long for what the company later discovers is its true needs.

- *More costly than buying.* The lease could end up being as or more expensive than ownership over the full term of the lease. If the company decides to buy the item at the end of the term, the total of all lease payments plus the final purchase price almost always costs more than buying the piece in the beginning.

- *No extras.* The lease may not include such expected items as maintenance, repairs, insurance, and so on.

- *Too long.* If the lease extends beyond the life of the item, the company is forced to essentially pay rental money on outdated equipment. If the company breaks the lease to update its equipment, it may have to pay an early-termination penalty.

- *Poor quality.* The rental equipment is not brand-new, as expected. Although these disadvantages do not apply to the best leases (which is why lease arrangements are so popular), the office professional should approach leasing with the idea that it has as many, if not more, risks as buying.

As with all purchasing deals, the office professional should specify to the vendors what the company wants: Be sure to establish the type and frequency of equipment servicing, get written bids from several vendors, make sure that contracts spell out details of maintenance and repair, try to ensure that equipment can be upgraded without breaking the old lease (upgrading won't be necessary for many items), and hand over the final negotiated contract for legal approval.

EQUIPMENT BASICS

Whether a company is a five-person ad agency, a factory employing hundreds of shift workers, or a national financial firm with thousands of stockbrokers, certain pieces of equipment are basic to every office.

TELEPHONES AND TELEPHONE SYSTEMS

Telephones have always been critical to a company's profitability because they are major sources of client contact. Now, those same lines are the heart of most of today's business communications systems because they send and receive voice, video, and data—both within a company's own boundaries and out to the world. The lone telecommuter working at midnight, the company's internal network, faxes to customers, and the company Web site handling hundreds of hits a day are all part of what was once the plain old telephone.

Features and Accessories

The telephone itself may have several features: speed dialing, last number recall, memory keys for frequently called numbers, caller ID, a built-in modem jack, a speakerphone, and an indicator light to show that a message is waiting. In a standard telephone, the message is transmitted through underground and above-ground phone wires.

Headsets. If the office professional or other employees spend long periods of time on the phone (especially while doing other tasks), a telephone headset is a smart investment. The newest models are very small and lightweight, help ease neck cramps, and leave hands free to use the keyboard, search files, and so on. Headsets must be compatible with the company's current phone system.

Cellular phones. Though once reserved for the salesperson on the road, cell phones are now in use everywhere and by everyone, from the busy manager who's in touch with the office while roaming the plant floor, to the technician who returns calls while on another job site.

When trying to decide on a cell phone, the confusing terminology may appear to be written by the same demons who write the tax laws. Part of the problem is common usage of the terms *cell phone* and *wireless phone* to refer to the same thing, as well as advancing and overlapping technology. Basically, cellular phones operate like a radio station, sending and receiving signals from a transmitter that covers a certain geographic location called a *cell*. The signal is transferred from cell to cell as the caller moves. Wireless phones operate like cellular phones, but instead of using radio signals and analog technology, they use high-frequency microwaves and digital technology. Although they can be cheaper to use, wireless phones are subject to interference from weather and terrain (in flat-lying regions, interference is not a problem). Some phones combine the two technologies and use both radio and microwaves.

Because the term *cell phone* has become almost generic, this book uses that term. The important thing in selecting a cell phone is to look for digital technology. The analog technology of most existing cell phones is subject to interference or "cross-talk" from radios and other phone users. Thus, an analog cell phone poses a security risk in two ways: The phone number and sometimes the PIN number can be scanned and cloned by phone thieves monitoring the air; and the conversation itself sometimes can be overheard, making cell phones a poor choice for discussing confidential business matters. Digital technology is much less subject to these security problems, plus it provides better sound and a stronger resistance to interference. Not all areas are equipped with digital technology yet, but the number of cities offering it is constantly increasing. In the meantime, if a caller is in such an area, the digital phones automatically switch to analog (they are subject to the same vulnerabilities as analog phones during that time).

Cell phones can be purchased with the monthly phone service, or sometimes are even given away. Rates are continually dropping, but other important considerations exist when pricing phones and service. Telecommunications providers offer a bewildering number of package deals, with so many free minutes, free weekends, peak hours, off hours, and so on. Be sure to compare a package deal against actual usage patterns and costs. In addition, check out the issue of roaming charges—fees for traveling outside the caller's local area. Cell phones using analog technology may impose roaming charges of as much as $1.50 per minute in addition to the cost of the call itself, as well as a daily fee just for roaming. Obviously, these telephone charges can mean enormous company expense for its employees on the road. Many digital phones have dropped roaming charges or include them in a cheaper flat rate within a package that includes a certain geographical area. Again, check actual usage against package costs.

Beepers and pagers. Before everyone had a phone in their pocket, beepers were the most common way to stay in touch while away from the office. Beepers are essentially tiny radio receivers that are always tuned to one station. When someone calls the beeper number, the call is picked up by the beeper service and transmitted to the beeper, the tiny machine chirps, and the individual knows it is time to phone in. Though just a multifunction version of the same thing, *pager* is now the preferred term—*beeper* is considered to be less upscale. A pager still beeps, but it may also silently vibrate. And instead of simply offering a way to say "Call in now," a pager can show the individual caller's number, his or her name, and printed text. Depending on the model, pagers can even supply a voice message.

Prices vary, depending on what features are wanted. Many paging companies offer the pager itself at low or no cost because the monthly service must be purchased at the same time. The price of this service depends on whether the individual wants to be paged within a local area only, within a wider geographical region, or nationwide. Currently, a pager is less expensive than a cell phone, but as pagers add features and raise their costs, and as telephone technology improves its quality and reduces cost, the cell phone eventually could win out entirely as the more useful of the two because of its immediacy.

Telephone Systems

The kind of phone system that the office professional recommends depends on the size of the company and the type of features wanted or needed. It's important to find the right balance between a system size that will accommodate growth (because phone systems are estimated to last seven to ten years) and one that is needlessly big (and usually needlessly expensive). A general rule of thumb is to purchase a capability of 50 percent more lines than currently used. For example, if a company now has 200 lines, its new system should rewire for 300 lines. Of course, if a company has a pattern of exceptionally rapid growth, that 50 percent figure should be adjusted upward accordingly.

The appropriateness of the following systems is based on the employee number, as well as the features desired. (*Employee number* refers to the number of employees who actually use the phones. The number of phone lines needed for a factory, for example, would not be based on the number of plant workers.)

Intercom. If a company has fewer than ten employees and most of them work in the same room, the company might want to use an intercom system. This is basically a single phone number, answered by a receptionist, with extension lines on each desk. The call comes into one of the available lines, and the receptionist announces the call over an overhead intercom: "Pat, call on Line 3." An intercom system involves buying only the receptionist's main phone and the intercom, and the individual phones with buttons to show which lines are open. The system uses the existing wiring and works through the usual service from the phone company, but it is very limited as far as expanding for employee growth or for adding features such as voice mail.

Centrex. Another option for small companies with twenty or fewer employees is a Centrex system. Basically, the local phone company acts as the business' phone system. Each employee has his or her own touch-tone phone and phone number. A company's existing phones can be used, and no rewiring is necessary. Unlike installing a larger system, Centrex involves no upfront capital costs, service contracts, or ongoing hassles with vendors. Features such as voice mail, call forwarding, three-way calling, and call transfer can be arranged for each number through the phone company.

Besides the simplicity of operation, another benefit of Centrex is that it makes small companies appear—by phone—to be much larger than they are. For example, with a single regular phone, the office professional of the one-room, start-up accounting firm might say, "She's not here," when a call comes in for the boss. The absence is obvious because the boss's empty desk is a cramped 6 inches away. With Centrex, the office professional can say, "She's in a meeting right now. May I connect you to her voice mail?" The caller is now imagining that the boss is down the hall in the conference room with all those junior partners.

Because each line is charged individually, Centrex price-per-minute charges on some features can mount up. Although this is the only major drawback of the system, it may be a sizable one for some smaller companies.

"Keyless" systems. Another system for small companies (with less than thirty employees) is called a "keyless" system, which also works on standard wiring. The company buys special phones that are plugged into current telephone jacks that provide up to three separate phone lines, with several more extensions for each line. That's all the equipment that must be purchased. Within the office, the phones can transfer calls, handle standard teleconferencing, and handle station-to-station intercom calls. Other features require a more sophisticated system, however.

"Key" systems. Larger companies (with up to 200 employees) or smaller companies with special needs (such as music-on-hold) must be connected to a "key" system, a central processing unit that organizes and routes calls automatically. Existing phones can be used, but the central processing unit must be purchased. Every company phone then must be wired to it. Although key systems used to be limited to basics such as voice mail and automated answering, they are now actually hybrids and are beginning to pick up many of the additional features of the PBX (discussed next).

PBX (Private Branch Exchange). A PBX system fills the needs of the largest companies (with up to thousands of employees) and those that want maximum phone features. Some smaller companies also might opt for a PBX if their phone demands are extensive because a PBX provides features less expensively than Centrex. PBX features include multiparty conferencing, automatic call distribution ("Please wait and the next available representative will answer your call"), voice mail, automated answering, and other standard features (call forwarding, call waiting, and so on). Special equipment and wiring are necessary; the company buys these and installs them on company property. Because of the complexity of the setup, however, the vendor or outside firm must supply ongoing maintenance. A market for used equipment does exist, so buying certain used components is a way to reduce costs; still, an expert's guidance is needed for the selection. By the same token, this serves as a way for unscrupulous vendors to raise profits by charging new-equipment prices, so be sure of the vendor's reputation for integrity.

T-1 lines. For even higher-volume (and better sounding) calling, companies may want to investigate T-1 lines, which are dedicated lines that use a high-speed digital circuit. Each line can carry twenty-four conversations at the same time—and for less money than twenty-four separate phone lines cost. The company enjoys a discount because the T-1 lines bypass the local phone company and tie in directly to the long-distance carrier. A T-1 line can be upgraded to double its capacity to forty-eight conversations per line. (A T-3 line has the capacity of twenty-eight T-1s.)

T-1s are used by companies with substantial long-distance calling costs. Because installing the T-1 wiring and equipment is expensive, a company's long-distance bills should be at least $3,000 to $5,000 per month per location before a T-1 is considered cost-effective. In some states, however (such as in those on the two seaboards), so much competition exists between phone companies that sometimes having a T-1 offers only minimal savings. Compare carefully. A T-1 line can be divided among customers (this is called a *fractional T-1*), but the same expensive equipment and wiring must be installed.

Cost is not the only reason to consider a T-1 line. One of its major advantages is its speed. Because its bandwidth is wider, a T-1 line can transmit much more information per second than traditional phone lines. This speed becomes increasingly important when a company is online. Modems over traditional analog phone lines transmit 56Kbps (kilobytes per second), which is adequate for many business needs, including e-mail, general Web searches, and maintenance of a Web site with limited daily hits. However, when a Web site has extensive graphics, includes a multimedia presentation, or attracts (or is trying to attract) hundreds of hits a day, a company should consider a faster line. You know from your own experience how many online sites you've abandoned without ever visiting because the site simply took too much time to load. If the site is commercial—an online shopping site, for example—slowness can spell disaster.

A step up from the traditional phone line is the wider bandwidth provided by ISDN (Integrated Services Digital Network). Using the existing copper phone lines available from local phone companies, ISDN offers a speed of 128Kbps, which, depending on the application, can be more than four times faster than traditional telephone service. ISDN provides better and faster connections to the Internet, as well as between two computers, two networks, and the telecommuter and the office. Telecommuters even can split the bandwidth and use 64Kbps for voice communication and 64Kbps for online use at the same time—and on a single line.

When an ISDN is too slow to hold the amount of data per second being transmitted, a T-1 line may be the answer because it can transmit 1.544Mbps. When Web page traffic approaches 500 hits a day, at least a half T-1 should be considered.

Voice-mail systems. In theory, voice mail is a way to expand and enhance the company's telephone capabilities. Voice mail can reduce or eliminate the need for a receptionist or operator, thus freeing up that person to handle other work as well. It enables personnel to work without interruptions, and to receive messages and make calls at their convenience. It even can work as a marketing tool, providing callers with new product information and describing existing services. In practice, however, voice mail can be a message-eating nightmare from which there's no escape.

Buying a voice mail system can be almost as complicated as buying the phone system itself. The simplest units are little more than answering machines for each line. As with phone systems, the more sophisticated systems require vendor installation and maintenance and enable users to do the following:

- Listen to, erase, store, or transfer messages

- Pre-record messages to send to other mailboxes at later scheduled times

- Record and choose from multiple greetings ("I'm either away from my desk right now or on the other line . . ."; "I'm out of the office until next Tuesday. For emergencies, please call . . ."; "I'm in, but I'm working on deadline . . ."; and so on)

- Route messages

- Give the same message to multiple people, as in fax polling

- Notify the individual's pager when there's voice mail

- Be linked to e-mail and faxes

Certain systems have "automated attendants" that answer the company's main phone and route the call, eliminating busy signals, the need to put callers on hold, and so on.

Although features such as these are always attractive, the office professional should ask the following important questions before choosing a voice-mail system:

- Will the proposed voice-mail system be compatible with the existing phone system?

- Must the voice-mail system come from the vendor who sold or is selling the company its phone system? (The answer should be no.)

- Can the voice-mail system store old messages until the recipient decides to erase them?

- Does each mailbox have its own security pass code?

- Can messages be retrieved while away from the office?

- Is the caller at each prompt able to repeat the menu by pushing a certain button?

- Is the caller at each prompt always able to reach a live voice, usually by dialing "0" to get the operator?

New voice-mail systems are as dreaded by employees as by customers, so make sure that the vendor includes full training in the package by the vendor.

What does an office professional do in the face of these bewildering choices? The best course may be to determine what features the company wants or needs in its phone system. Then, armed with the answers, the office professional can seek help from a competent vendor. Because the vendor not

TELEPHONES AND THE FUTURE

Telephone systems are on the brink of a revolution. Although existing systems will continue to be used for years, new technology involving PCs and the Internet are transforming the future. For example, PC PBXs and PC-based telephony make it easy and much less expensive for smaller companies to set up PBX systems and maintain these systems themselves without an outside vendor. Computer telephony integration links the individual's PC to the phone system. For example, caller ID will send the caller's name and number to the employee's PC; if the caller is a customer, his or her account will automatically appear on the employee's screen—and the phone may not even be answered yet. Internet telephony enables companies to route calls over existing phone lines, over a private network, or over the Internet. A main advantage of this is the reduction of long-distance call costs.

only bases its profits on the size and brand of the system purchased but also often works as the administrator of the system, choose carefully. When considering recommendations for vendors, the office professional should ask these questions:

- Does the particular system leave room for growth? How much?

- Can extra features be added onto a particular system later? If so, which ones?

- Can the company use its own telephones with the system? (Being limited to the vendor's phones may indicate a way the vendor is trying to boost cost.)

- If the company must buy vendor phones, do the phones use standard dial tones, ringing, busy signals, and out-of-order signals? (If not, this again could indicate a way to boost costs because unusual signals will not respond to standard signals, thus making it impossible to buy, say, voice mail from another vendor.)

- How experienced is the vendor?

- Is the vendor licensed by the state as a contractor to do the work?

- Is the vendor insured and bonded? Ask for proof.

- Does the vendor have 24-hour technical support for the new telephone system?

- How fast is the vendor's emergency response time?

- Is the vendor factory authorized and factory-certified for the brand desired by the company?

- Will the vendor supply recommendations from other customers?

- Will the vendor supply an itemized bid (not a package deal) for better comparison?

- How much time will it take to add new lines or services?

- Is leasing the telephone equipment an option with this particular vendor, and is leasing a good option for your company?

FAX MACHINES

Just as traditional postal delivery is often replaced by priority and overnight mail, overnight mail is often replaced by the fax. "Quickly" has come to mean "instantaneously."

Fax transmission is a flexible, inexpensive, and simple method of sending information instantly in the form of image replication (facsimile). A fax transmission can be generated in two ways: (1) from a fax machine, or (2) from a computer with faxing capability.

Although fax machines are standard in offices today, faxing from computers is less common. To fax directly from your computer, you need a system with a fax modem and a phone line. After installing the required fax software, you can send a fax as if you were printing a letter. When you go to output the document, the software dials the number and faxes the document.

Many people use the fax to instantly send a single letter to a single recipient. They dial the number into the telephone keypad and press the Start button. Fax machines have many other strengths that are often overlooked.

Suppose a business must notify all its customers immediately that an error was found, or must notify the entire sales force that an important deadline has been changed. The time involved in telephoning or mailing a letter to each recipient would be prohibitive. This is where fax transmissions come in. The fax has the capability of broadcasting—that is, automatically sending a list of fax numbers with the same transmission.

A WORD OF CAUTION ABOUT BROADCASTING

Although junk mail still clogs regular postal delivery, it is illegal to send electronic junk mail—unsolicited fax transmissions that advertise or sell services or products. Check in advance to see that all recipients on a broadcast list want to be included.

Not every machine has the same capabilities. The office professional should read the user's manual in detail or contact the dealer to become familiar with the full capabilities of the machine currently in use. Following are some of its possible features, or features to look for in a new machine (certain features require being linked to a computer):

- Message confirmation and/or error printouts

- Multiple-number speed dial

- Capability of storing pages as they arrive and printing when available, so as not to tie up the phone line while printing pages

- Memory for scanning documents and sending later, for delayed sending or so the sender doesn't have to wait for each page to transmit, or for sending when rates are lower

- Capability of sending the same document to multiple locations without having to rescan the document each time

- Capability of storing incoming messages in mailboxes so that the person with the proper access code can retrieve them

- Gray-scale controls that can adjust the resolution of the graphics

- Built-in surge protector

- Upgradable memory to store hundreds of pages

- Capability of creating logos, letterheads, forms, and protected signatures

- Prioritization of faxes so that urgent ones transmit first

- Data compression that substitutes symbols for words and phrases in a process that condenses information and enables faster transmissions (similar to disk compression)

- Capability of exporting transmission histories to spreadsheets, databases, and so on

With today's lower long-distance rates and higher postage charges, it is sometimes actually less expensive to send a fax than to send a letter. Unless urgency preempts all other reasons, the office professional should use the more cost-effective method. However, he or she also should be sensitive to the contents of the fax. Confidentiality has always been a significant risk with faxes: The machines are often located in open areas, so messages are usually seen by at least one other person before they reach the recipient. Newer machines store messages for individuals and require passwords before each mailbox can be opened, but not every recipient has this feature.

Another cost factor in fax usage is the full-size cover sheet. It is estimated that billions of dollars are spent each year on this single sheet, which is immediately discarded. A small sticky note attached at the top may suffice; letters that have an address and closing signature may not need a cover sheet at all.

COPIERS

The essential reason for buying a copier is, of course, to make copies, but the added features of the newest machines often can obscure that basic fact. Once-impressive features such as two-sided copying, color copying, and size reduction or enlargement are now taken for granted because copiers have become miniprinting systems. Depending on the model, they can print as many as two copies per second, can edit and store copy, and can be programmed to work off-hours. A copier's printing capability is joined by the capability to collate, sort, staple, and add a heavy-stock cover, if desired. Other models work as multifunction machines, giving the copier scanning capability. Add a phone line, and the copier is also a phone, answering machine, and fax (with anti-junk-fax function). In addition, some copiers can be linked to the office network to work as printers, with all the instructions—down to delayed printing—programmable from the user's desktop PC.

The new generation of copiers are digital machines. Although very expensive at the moment and therefore not yet widely used, these new machines can scan a document once and store it in memory to produce other originals, not copies. Image manipulation is also possible with digital machines, as are remote diagnosis and trouble-shooting.

Because all these features add considerably to the cost, the office professional should choose with care. Salespeople or in-house employees will persuasively explain how certain features are an absolute necessity. Vendors will try to sell package deals that *seem* to throw in the extra features at no cost. But absolute necessities are often just a wish list, and each feature has a cost even within a special package. Therefore, it is better to decide beforehand exactly what is needed by the company, and then to shop for only what is needed. The savings can be significant.

In contrast with employees generating an extravagant features wish list are those employees who will *not* use the special features at all. The individual may be afraid of doing something wrong and breaking the machine, or he or she may be too reluctant (or even too lazy) to learn a new procedure. A simple example is the employee who always uses two pieces of paper rather than making a double-sided copy (clearly a waste of money and resources) or the clerk who would rather spend hours stapling a cover to a collated report rather than programming the copier to do it. If certain complicated jobs must be done by using the special features, employees who resist learning will try to turn these copying projects over to the office professional. Training these people (and retraining them, if necessary) is essential if the company is to recoup its investment in terms of greater employee efficiency and time savings.

One of the most critical aspects of buying a copier is knowing its volume-per-month capability. Don't underestimate the company's usage. Although lower-volume machines are less expensive, underestimating usage makes lines at the copier longer and also can result in frequent problems and breakdowns. Keep careful watch of the present usage before selecting a model. Plan for growth. If usage is low but the number of employees per machine is about fifty or more, a second copier is often a good idea. If one machine has features, the second can be the most basic of models.

Copier Paper

The selection of the right copy paper is crucial to the machine's performance. To prevent jamming, choose the manufacturer's recommended paper weight. Also look for paper that is evenly trimmed, that can withstand copier heat, and that doesn't have a tendency to curl.

Copier paper is generally available from any office supply store, office superstore, or catalog company. Businesses with high paper consumption may want to consider buying paper directly from paper manufacturers. For information on how to buy from these major companies directly (or through their regional representatives), see the following Web sites:

Boise Cascade, at www.bcop.com

Georgia Pacific, at www.gp.com

Hammermill, at www.hammermill.com

The company's rate of usage will help determine whether paper can be bought in money-saving bulk. If paper is kept in a low-humidity, moderate-temperature environment, it may keep for extended periods as well. So even if a company does not use paper rapidly, it may still see some savings with bulk-buying if proper storage space is available. For a beginning rule of thumb, plan on reordering when the stock falls to 25 percent of the original quantity. This should accommodate even large rush jobs while the stock is being replenished. Adjust this 25 percent figure later, when you're familiar with the company's copying needs and patterns.

ELECTRONIC TYPEWRITERS

The birth of the electronic typewriter was sandwiched somewhere between the older electric typewriter and the word processor; as a piece of equipment, it is a hybrid of the two. Electronic typewriters do not have separate monitors or printers, but they do have small electronic display screens above the keyboard that show a partial page. These machines have become more sophisticated in recent years; many have built-in spell-checkers, text-editing capabilities, spreadsheet and mail-merge capabilities, limited font selections, timer alerts, formatting functions, upgradable memory, and security passwords. Some include a 100-key buffer zone so that even the fastest typist won't end up with snarled keys, as with an electric typewriter. Some electronic typewriters can be networked to computers and used as printers.

Although the market for electronic typewriters has plummeted, a viable niche still exists for them. They are durable and easy to use, and an electronic typewriter can handle some jobs faster and better than a computer. For example, electronic typewriters are more practical than computers for printing on checks or index cards, to generate printed paper forms that have not been computerized, to type on preprinted forms, and so on.

For example, to address a single envelope by computer, the office professional must boot up the computer, pull up the word processing program, click Envelopes, type in the return and main addresses, select the font style and size, remove the paper from the paper tray, adjust the tray to accommodate the wider-width envelope, insert an envelope, and then click Print. By contrast, he or she merely needs to turn on an electronic typewriter, insert an envelope, type, and it's done. Obviously, the electronic typewriter is not a replacement for the computer, but it can be a handy accessory.

RECORDING AND DICTATION EQUIPMENT

Suppose that your boss is eating a brown-bag lunch while stuck on the freeway. Sudden inspiration hits and he wants to change the opening of his motivational speech to the Lions Club next week. He takes out his pocket recorder and creates a new opening about how to succeed despite being stuck in life's traffic jams. That afternoon, he drops the disk on your desk and asks you to make the changes to his typed speech.

Although the old phrase "Take a letter" may not have been spoken in years, executives are still dictating letters, reports, random thoughts, and more—all into tiny recorders that go wherever they travel. Today, two types of portable models exist: much smaller versions of the old tape recorder and new digital machines that use disks.

Tape machines now come with special features such as the capability to screen out background noises (angry motorists in the next lane and the rustling of sandwiches being unwrapped, for example). They also can be switched on by voice activation, prevent accidental erasing of tapes, erase tapes rapidly, go at once to the end of the dictation, stamp the time and date, and so on. Digital machines can do the same and also insert urgent items at the front of the disk without erasing the rest, allow random access to any message on the disk, use electronic indexing, provide a bigger capacity, and use access codes for security. Some models can be linked to a PC. These can send contents automatically to a word processing program or e-mail, which eliminates the office assistant's need to transcribe.

Larger table-top recorders, sometimes called *conference recorders,* have sensitive recording capabilities that can follow all the proceedings of a meeting without having to be moved as the speakers change.

Many recorders, including the smaller ones, come with a foot-pedal attachment to control the playback speed as the material is played and keyboarded. Some larger transcription models only play back, although they have many of the recorder's features that are useful for transcription, such as electronic indexing, end of dictation codes, and so on.

VCRs AND PROJECTORS

Though the technology is relatively new, people have become spoiled very quickly: They now expect presentations to be in color and contain either live action or animation, even though a sophisticated presentation used to be a slide show. Today, *low-tech* is no longer a flip chart but a VCR, and *high-tech* means an LCD projector that produces computer graphics, millions of colors, and multimedia presentations.

VCRs

Basically, the same VCRs for use at home for recording favorite programs are used by businesses today for training and presentation purposes. The office professional should not forget that videotapes also can be made from special company occasions such as picnics, parties, charitable affairs, and more. In addition, press releases to cable and network news shows are bolstered when they are accompanied by footage of a person or event, as well as general scenes of the company itself.

When choosing a VCR, many of the features that are personally attractive also are important for business use: four heads rather than two for clearer images during pauses or searches, onscreen menus for easier programming, a digital tape counter that measures in real time rather than numbers, an automatic clock set to adjust for power outages and daylight saving time, automatic picture control to adjust for lower-grade or worn tapes, automatic tracking, electronic index searching to bookmark spots for easy reference, and an automatic head cleaner.

If the company plans to record its own videotapes, look for these extra features: jog/shuttle control, which enables the user to browse a tape either quickly or frame by frame for editing; an audio/video insert, which provides for both audio dubbing and inserting new video clips while maintaining a single soundtrack; and a flying erase head, which helps smooth scene transitions and recording starts and stops.

Projectors

Computers can produce amazing presentations with colors, graphics, sounds, and animation. But only a bare handful of people can view a monitor at the same time. To display a computer-generated program to a large audience, the LCD (liquid crystal display) projector was developed.

Now, armed with a laptop and a portable LCD projector, a salesperson can present a pitch to audiences of various sizes. In the past, if any information on a product or service changed while the salesperson was on the road, he or she had to wait until new charts or slides were made up and delivered by special courier. With LCD technology, he or she can easily connect back to the company's computer via modem and receive the updated program from the office professional.

LCD panels are positioned on top of the light of an overhead projector. LCD projectors come equipped with their own light source. The panel itself hooks up to the computer—often a laptop—and as the presentation data comes up on the computer monitor, the LCD panel projects the images onto a regular projection screen or, if necessary, onto a blank wall. Some models use just one panel or matrix that produces a single image on the screen; others use multiple panels and a series of lenses, producing multiple images that are then united on the screen. Multiple panels provide a brighter image, but they may face convergence problems if all the separate images are not exactly aligned.

The future of projectors seems to lie with DLP (digital light processing) technology, although this is still in development. DLP projectors use many more panels than LCDs do, and each panel is covered by tiny mirrors that reflect light outward. The image is projected onto the screen one color at a time, but in such rapid succession that the brain fills in the gaps to create what appears to be a solid picture. The image is brighter than that from an LCD projector and presents a seamless surface, unlike the pixel-dotted surface of LCDs. But

DLPs are still being refined; at the moment, they are too large and expensive by comparison and can't yet compete with the performance of the best LCDs.

When choosing an LCD panel or projector, an office professional should come prepared with answers to the following questions, which determine the type of projector best suited to the company's needs:

- What is the typical size of the audience for whom presentations are given?

- What is the typical room size?

- What are the typical lighting conditions: complete darkness, some light, or fully lit rooms?

- How clear a picture resolution is desired?

- Will the presentation incorporate photos, video clips, or sound?

- How much travel is planned for a typical projector?

- How portable should the projector be?

- Will the company be projecting special images, such as high-resolution photography, CAD (computer-aided design) drawings, or maps?

- Are special features desired, such as a remote control, stereo Surround-sound, or simultaneous computer and video display?

When comparing projectors, check how much light reaches the screen (whether the actual screen or the room wall). This is reported in the product specifications in terms of ANSI lumens: The higher the number, the more light there is, and the better the image appears. Both LCD projectors and today's new overhead projectors use either a metal halide bulb or a halogen bulb. Although metal halide bulbs can cost ten times as much as halogen bulbs, the price usually evens out because halide bulbs last much longer. Halogen bulbs are best for projectors that see a lot of travel because the bulb is common and can be more easily replaced on the road if broken. The projector's lamp is wired for only one or the other; the choice must be made at the time of purchase because the bulbs are not interchangeable.

PURCHASING NOTE

The process of creating LCD panels is so complex that nearly every projector shows a few defective pixels—dots that are either permanently bright or permanently dark. The manufacturer tolerates a set number of these (find out specifically how many); only when this number is exceeded is the projector itself considered defective.

In general, look at the projector's focusing capability, the quality of its images, its fidelity to the original colors, and the uniformity of the brightness on the screen. Specifically, look for the type of image controls on the unit itself. What can be adjusted? In addition, some models come with a memory card if the user wants to run presentations without the laptop. Most projectors come with built-in stereo speakers; some also have a microphone jack so the presenter can speak over the same system.

SHREDDERS

Suppose that an executive has asked for a copy of a confidential report that has been sent to her before she forwards it to the next person on the routing list. You don't notice that the person ahead of you has adjusted the controls and you make a copy that, while readable, is too light. Tearing the paper into pieces is time-consuming and unreliable. That's one good reason why a small shredder should be next to every copier.

Paper shredders cannot make paper disappear, but they can make personal or confidential information disappear. Payroll lists, customer records, telephone logs, meeting minutes, personnel evaluations, pay scales, product specifications, market analyses, customer lists, design changes, and canceled checks are just a few types of sensitive materials that should remain confidential. Industrial espionage is a major concern today; many research companies not only shred top secret information but also keep the shreds. And with increasing lawsuits on all fronts, companies are less likely to put anything in the simple wastebasket.

The need for a shredder goes far beyond the business world. Law firms, medical offices, and pharmacists also regularly deal with confidential information that should be shredded. Schools should not put student and personnel files into the regular trash, even if they have expired. Anyone who has private information of any kind has a need for a shredder.

Shredders come in a wide range of styles, capabilities, prices, and shredding options. Flat paper can be shredded into long strips as wide as egg noodles or as fine as angel-hair pasta; for maximum security, it can even be cross-cut into confetti-like particles. The style selection ranges from desktop models to large free-standing units that can handle thick wads of paper and folders (including staples and paper clips)—as well as disks, cassettes, microfilm, and microfiche—and still run continuously without overheating. Popular features include an electronic eye that turns the shredder on and off, a function that stops the shredder when the waste bin beneath is full, and casters to move the shredder to the documents rather than add the extra security risk of transporting sensitive documents from their locked location.

When selecting a shredder, consider the level of security desired, the volume that the shredder must handle, and the kinds of material it is expected to shred (checks, letter-size paper, folders, computer printouts, and so on). Also consider the company's multiple shredding needs. You may want a desktop unit for you and the executive, another to put in the copy room, and a larger unit to be located in the central records department.

Shredding services are available from outside firms (look under Recycling in the Yellow Pages). However, many firms that are already concerned about privacy may be reluctant to place their confidential papers in the hands of an outside party, even for the time it takes to shred the papers. For companies with extensive files, owning one of the larger shredders may make sense.

Shredded material can be recycled or internally recycled by certain model shredding machines that turn old files and such into packing material.

No matter what the company or organization, buying a shredder is only the first step in its proper use. Employees must learn how to make the decision about what should be shredded and what should be kept. The office professional may want to draw up a memo detailing the types of documents that should be shredded, along with instructions about how it should be done—whether the material is to be left with you or brought to a central shredding location, or whether an appointment should be made for the portable shredder to be wheeled to a particular location.

EQUIPMENT MAINTENANCE AND ORDERING OFFICE SUPPLIES

Among the many duties of office professionals is the job of office management. This all-encompassing term can range from tracking lost change in the vending machine, to purchasing office supplies, to arranging maintenance and repairs of office equipment.

Although such petty duties as change-tracking might accompany the job, two office-management duties are critical to the efficient running of the department or the whole company. These responsibilities are maintaining the equipment and ordering office supplies.

EQUIPMENT MAINTENANCE

Basic equipment maintenance ranges from the scheduled visits of the copier repair team to the employees' basic understanding of how to put paper in the fax machine. When dealing with office equipment, employees must know enough about a machine's operation to understand whether it is broken when it stops working. Employees also must know that the office professional—or whoever else is maintaining the files of warranties, service contracts, and lists of repair people—should be notified immediately if there's a problem. So often a line of people will walk into the copy room, discover that the copier is out of paper, and then lazily decide that their copy was not important enough to warrant either filling the machine themselves or notifying you. Likewise, many people will attempt to use a machine, find out that it's malfunctioning, and then simply walk away from it rather than tell anyone.

When any new piece of equipment comes into the office—whether purchased by the office professional or not, whether to be used by the office professional or not—he or she should become familiar with the user's manual as soon as possible. Even if the equipment is not for the office professional's use, the actual user is likely to come to you to see how it works—and will definitely come to you when there is a problem.

For each piece of equipment, read the manual carefully. Note anything that might become difficult to operate under the company's specific conditions. Note any necessary accessories or attachments that require special ordering: cords, covers, uncommon battery sizes, and so on. Fill out the warranty card at once to register the equipment. Make two copies of the warranty card that shows the equipment's make, model, and serial number. Tape one copy of the card to a discreet location on the equipment itself (inside a hard cover, for example, or on the side of the machine). Do not give it to the user; employees come and go while equipment remains. File the other copy with the warranty itself, the service contract if any, and the manual (once the user is done with it). Following up on getting the manual will probably be necessary because in the beginning the user may not want to part with it.

Check for technical-support numbers, recommended service dealers, and so on, all of which might be listed in separate publications that come with the equipment. File these as well.

If the equipment is for general use (a copier or fax machine, for example), make a copy of the basic instructions and post it on the nearest wall. If there's no single list of instructions in the manual conveniently written up for this, condense one from your own understanding of the guide, type it up, and post it. File the copy as above with the warranty. This procedure helps prevent loss of important paperwork regarding the machines and accommodates faster servicing.

General Troubleshooting Instructions

The most important part of troubleshooting is the correct use and regular maintenance of equipment. This keeps problems to a minimum.

Scheduled maintenance. Just as a car needs regular oil changes and lube jobs even if it is running well, pieces of office equipment need regular maintenance to prevent cash- and time-consuming emergencies. In the user's manual for each piece of equipment, the manufacturer often includes a list of recommended maintenance practices. Some of these involve simple cleaning and can be performed in the office by the user. Others must be scheduled, whether through the manufacturer or through a service contract with an outside firm.

For each piece of equipment, use the same file folder that holds the warranty and user's manual. Write the basic warranty-registration information on

☎ 800 SERVICE AND SUPPORT NUMBERS FOR OFFICE EQUIPMENT MANUFACTURERS

Brother International	800-276-7746
Canon	800-652-2666
Epson America	800-289-3776
Hewlett-Packard, Co.	800-752-0900
IBM	800-426-2968
Konica	800-256-6422
Kyocera Electronics, Inc.	800-232-6797
Lexmark International, Inc.	800-358-5835
Mita Copystar America	800-222-6482
Murata Business Systems	800-543-4636
NEC America	800-632-4636
Okidata	800-654-3282
Panasonic	800-742-8086
Ricoh	800-637-4264
Sharp Electronics	800-237-4277
Toshiba	800-334-3445
Xerox	800-862-6567

the inside cover of the folder, as well as the phone numbers of the manufacturer, the place of purchase, and the service company. Note the cost of the equipment as well. When the file becomes thick, having this information right on the inside cover will save much thumbing through of papers. It is handy to have all the information in one place when calling to schedule service or a repair because the make and model will be one of the first questions asked.

If the company has a service contract, be sure to note whether the technician comes automatically or whether the service call must be scheduled.

Each time a piece of equipment is serviced or repaired, note it in the file. Include the nature of the problem, the amount of time lost, and the cost involved. Tracking the actual maintenance will help determine the machine's overall efficiency over time and its actual price to run—both details necessary for making new purchasing decisions at a later time.

Enter all recommendations for regular maintenance on a yearly calendar. This enables timely scheduling of appointments and prepares users for periods of downtime.

Trouble-shooting. Besides instructions, most manuals have a list of troubleshooting directions: "If X goes wrong, try doing Y." These directions offer quick and simple solutions to the equipment's most common problems. Both the users and the office professional should confine their activities to those on the trouble-shooting list. If the trouble-shooting list recommends something that makes either person uncomfortable—going under the hood of the computer, for example—leave that for the repair person.

Certain troubleshooting recommendations will be basic to all equipment and are the common-sense directions often forgotten when something goes wrong: Check that the batteries have life, that the machine is switched on, that extension cords are plugged in firmly at both ends, that peripherals are firmly attached at both ends, that the paper or ink supply is filled, and so on. Do not overlook the obvious. Because machines work under only a specific set of conditions, make sure that all the conditions are fulfilled. The office professional might have to try to get the machine to operate after it has been reported as broken. Often, the user might skip a step in procedure, while the office professional will automatically perform it. It may be annoying to be called away from work to fix something that wasn't broken, but this can prevent a loss of downtime while an "Out of order" sign is taped up—and it also prevents calling a repair person for a needless (and pricey) appointment.

ORDERING OFFICE SUPPLIES

Ordering office supplies is another critical responsibility of office management. Sufficient supplies always should be on hand to finish the job and to prevent idle time caused by lack of supplies. On the other hand, the inventory should not be so bloated that supplies dry up, pass critical expiration dates, or otherwise become useless.

Catalogs and Superstores

In lieu of dealing with vendors and manufacturers, catalogs and superstores may offer great convenience and sometimes significant savings. But there also can be hidden costs. For example, superstores must factor in the cost of regional and national advertising, the cost of rental space for the retail operation in addition to warehouse space for the items, and the cost of retail staff salaries. Superstores often carry mostly name brands, while lower-priced, no-name clones could be of equal quality. In addition, the office professional must figure in the time spent traveling to and shopping in superstores.

Catalogs—without a showroom—solve many of these problems. But look for reputable companies that others can recommend. When dealing with a catalog company for the first time, order cautiously to test delivery speed and the

TIPS FOR PURCHASING SUPPLIES

Purchasing involves much more than just selecting a particular brand and model of office machine. The office professional also might be responsible for choosing the vendor, shopping by store or catalog, putting in verbal orders, changing the numbers of items ordered to take advantage of quantity discounts, negotiating prices and services, approving invoices, and more. Keep these hints in mind when purchasing supplies and equipment:

- Always take several bids on major purchases; take bids on reorders from time to time to keep prices competitive.

- Negotiate prices, but know which items are not worth negotiating.

- Consider the savings of close-out items, but weigh them carefully in terms of long-term use and maintenance if they are used for constantly updated items such as computers.

- Use more than one vendor so that a backup is always available.

- Get specific delivery dates, confirm them later in writing, and follow-up quickly when they pass; if timeliness is not important to you, it will not be important to the vendor.

- Remember that small companies often can give better attention to rush jobs than larger companies.

- Make sure that the specifications provided to vendors are exact, and are checked and rechecked.

quality of the items. Be certain of return policies and return shipping. Check that equipment is new and not someone else's reconditioned lemon.

Logging and Ordering

A simple notebook or computer file begins the process of establishing a regular and efficient ordering system. For each item, record the name of the item, its place of purchase, its stock number, when it was ordered, how long the actual delivery took, and how long the supply lasted. This process will help determine when it's time to reorder. For example, if an order takes a week to be delivered, order it a month in advance, which allows for three weeks leeway. Of course, if an item must be special-ordered, or if back orders often take longer than usual or promised, include extra time.

As a safety measure, put a note on the box or container of each item (on the side that faces outward when in the supply closet). The note should read,

800 NUMBERS FOR OFFICE SUPPLY RESOURCES

Global Computer Supplies	800-845-6225
Modern Service Office Supplies	800-672-6767
Office Depot	800-685-8800
Office Max	800-788-8080
Penny Wise	800-942-3311
Staples	800-333-3330
Viking Office Products	800-421-1222

"Notify (office professional's name) when only (XX) are left." This note will help during times when an item is used up unusually quickly.

Because of the myriad supplies used in today's offices, an office professional might be placing an order each day if he or she ordered each item separately as needed. So try to look for ordering patterns, especially within the same place of purchase. For example, ten items regularly come from Catalog X. Four items are fairly slow-moving; the other six items are used up almost three times as quickly. Instead of ordering each of the ten items separately, order the six fast-moving items together; once every third time, add the four slow-moving items to the order. Or, if the company has the space, double up on the quantity for each of the six items and order only half as often. The slow-moving items might be added in every time or every other time, depending on whether their number also was doubled. Check for quantity discounts—they may make it worthwhile to find the space.

Depending on company policy, the office professional might be required to keep an individual log of personal use and a log of general use to help prevent waste and pilferage. At its strictest, this policy could involve keeping supply cabinets locked and not handing out a new item until the empty is handed in. Although the practice might garner complaints, follow it closely because maintaining and ordering supplies involves a tremendous responsibility.

What sort of products come under ordering and logging duties? The following list shows the wide variety possible in the area of consumables—items that are ordered, used up, and ordered again:

- *Paper and filing products.* Writing pads, legal pads, steno pads, memo pads, scratch pads, message pads, notebooks, index cards, business cards, sticky notes, labels, invoices, other forms, covers, portfolios, ring binders, dividers, name tags, letterhead and stationery, business envelopes, manila envelopes, shipping envelopes, printer paper, copier paper, fax machine paper, manila file folders, hanging folders, file pockets, file wallets, storage boxes.

■ *Computer supplies.* Floppy disks, ZIP disks, backup tapes, printer toner cartridges, recordable CD-ROMs, compressed air spray.

■ *Duplicating and dictating supplies.* Steno pads, tapes of all sizes, disks, batteries, fax machine toner cartridges, fax machine drum cartridges, fax cartridges, printer ribbons.

■ *Desk supplies.* Pens, pencils, highlighters, markers, correction pens, ink refills, lead refills, erasers, gluesticks, staples, clear tape, packing tape, masking tape, mailing tape, mailing tubes, paper clips, binder clips, hole reinforcements, rubber bands, rubber stamps, ink, pushpins, calendars, planners.

■ *Miscellaneous.* Light bulbs, clipboards, camera film, transparency film, videotapes, easel pads, coffee, tea, cleaning supplies, first-aid supplies, wastebasket liners, toilet paper, paper towels, tissues, lunchroom supplies, bottled water.

STORAGE

Because office supplies must be kept somewhere, storage is always a consideration when ordering. Unlike the local store that can run an inventory clearance sale when it wants to stock up on new items, the office professional works under the same strict limitations but without such a quick and easy way to make space. For every item that is brought into the company, these questions must be asked: Where will it go? If it is a replacement item, will the old item be stored, moved to another branch of the company, or thrown out? Can delivery of the new and moving of the old be timed so that two of the same aren't competing for the same space (even temporarily) or leaving users without any equipment at all?

Even ordinary items might have special storage needs. Printer cartridges, for example, come with expiration dates; if the package is opened, it should be used within a few months, regardless of expiration date. Cartridges and disks are sensitive to extreme temperatures and direct sunlight. Envelopes should be used within two years or the glue may no longer seal properly. Improperly stored paper picks up heat and humidity and begins to curl, causing jams. For every item, check with the manufacturer for the proper storage technique and shelf life.

COMMON OFFICE SUPPLIES CHECKLIST

Paper and Filing Products

☐ Typing paper

☐ Stationery (letterhead)

☐ Envelopes

☐ Correction fluid (with thinner; white and color as needed)

☐ Scratch pads and paper

☐ Manila or plastic file folders (color-coded as needed)

☐ Hanging file folders

☐ File folder tabs and labels

☐ Memo pads

☐ Dictation notebooks

☐ Alphabetized dividers

☐ Telephone message pads

☐ File baskets, trays, and stacks

☐ 3 × 5 cards

☐ 4 × 6 cards

☐ Transparent tape

☐ Bookmarks

☐ Card files

☐ Calendars

☐ Planning diaries

☐ Business envelopes

☐ Manila envelopes

☐ Padded envelopes

☐ Binders

☐ Loose-leaf covers and fillers

☐ Mailing tape

☐ Telex paper (in rolls)

☐ Address labels

☐ Paper for calculating machines

☐ Postage stamps

Computer Supplies

☐ Printer ribbons

☐ Printer cartridges

☐ Floppy disks

☐ Floppy disk trays

Duplicating and Dictating Supplies

☐ Cassette tapes

☐ Tape storage unit

☐ Tape demagnetizer

☐ Tape splicer

☐ Microfilm

☐ Microfiche film

☐ Microfiche index

☐ Copier toner

Desk Supplies

- ☐ Staplers
- ☐ Staples
- ☐ Staple removers
- ☐ Letter openers
- ☐ Pen and pencil holders
- ☐ Tape dispensers
- ☐ Rulers
- ☐ Fine-line, broad-nib, or felt-tip pens
- ☐ Paper clips
- ☐ Rubber bands
- ☐ Writing and marking pencils
- ☐ Magnifying glasses
- ☐ Erasers
- ☐ Scissors
- ☐ Rubber stamps, including date stamps
- ☐ Ink pads
- ☐ Push pins
- ☐ Book holders
- ☐ Bookends

Miscellaneous

- ☐ Postal scales
- ☐ Globe
- ☐ First-aid kit
- ☐ Maps
- ☐ Fire extinguisher
- ☐ Easels
- ☐ Keys
- ☐ Planning boards
- ☐ Batteries

Desk Reference Sources

- ☐ Desk dictionary
- ☐ International area code booklet
- ☐ Secretarial handbook
- ☐ Current office supply catalog
- ☐ Office address and/or telephone directory (booklet, sheet, or rotary file)
- ☐ Style manual
- ☐ Almanac
- ☐ Chart for current postal rates
- ☐ ZIP code directory
- ☐ Telephone directory
- ☐ Telex directory, if needed

REFERENCES AND PUBLICATIONS FOR OFFICES

A good reference library will save the office professional countless questions and searches. For correspondence needs, include a college dictionary, a thesaurus, and a grammar and usage guide. Combination books and dictionary or thesaurus programs in word processing will not provide the in-depth knowledge of separate volumes, although a good-quality dictionary on a CD-ROM may work as well. For most offices, an unabridged dictionary (which may run two or more volumes and carry a hefty price tag) provides too much information, while a pocket dictionary provides too little. A college dictionary—which will be identified as such in its title—will handle almost all your needs.

In addition to this absolute minimum, it is useful to have a desk reference—a single-volume encyclopedia on a subject (in this case, a business reference). *The New York Public Library Business Desk Reference* is one such title, as is the *Wall Street Journal Almanac*. A collection of ready-to-use business letters can be helpful, too, as can a handbook for technical writing and a book on business etiquette.

If the executive travels or clients are far-flung, include both a world atlas and a road atlas on the shelf, as well as a time-conversion table or universal clock, and an area-code/country-code chart for phone calls. If clients speak languages other than English, add foreign-language volumes, such as an English-to-Spanish/Spanish-to-English dictionary. Even if the office professional does not speak the language or is required to have client contact, these books can be invaluable because words may appear in files, letters, and so on.

If the office professional attends or chairs many meetings, a copy of the *New Roberts Rules of Order* describes ways to organize and run meetings in the parliamentary style. This resource also includes helpful hints for making meetings a success.

Phone books of major cities—at least the neighboring ones—have much valuable information.

Also look for a dictionary of business terms. If the company works in a specialized area or has frequent contact with one, specialty dictionaries are also available, such as a dictionary of legal or medical terms.

Finally, don't overlook sources of information already in your office. If the company deals in a specialized area such as technology, pharmaceuticals, or manufacturing, it's likely that it subscribes to numerous magazines, newspapers, and trade journals that relate specifically to that industry. These can be a tremendous reference, so file them after they've been routed and read. If publications are not routed but are left in a common area, allow them to remain a certain amount of time before filing (for example, two to three days for daily newspapers, two weeks for weeklies, one month for monthlies, and two months for quarterlies).

Each office has its own reference needs, and each office professional has his or her own reference preferences. The best way to decide on yours is to be familiar with what's available, with the needs of the company's employees, and with your own needs and habits of working.

LETTERHEAD AND BUSINESS CARDS

A company's letterhead stationery and business cards are more than simple paper on which to convey a message—they present a distinct image to employees, clients, and potential clients. The letterhead might be a person's first introduction to the company, and first impressions do count. Over time, the letterhead itself creates brand awareness and becomes in itself a type of publicity for the company—especially if it incorporates a logo.

When changing or choosing stationery or business cards, the office professional must be aware of three things: the quality of the paper, the type of printing, and the design of the image. The 20-pound stock paper that people are so accustomed to seeing in reports and photocopies is insufficient for stationery. A professional printer can display a variety of weights, colors, and textures.

Laid paper has a smooth surface, with very fine lines and crosslines. *Wove paper* has a thicker pattern, so that a mesh can be seen when the paper is held to the light. *Parchment* is an off-white paper treated to resemble actual parchment. A *linen finish* adds a noticeable texture to the paper's surface as if it were cloth. *Bond paper* has cotton fibers incorporated into it. In the right weight, any of these is suitable for business stationery, though some texture is preferred by many people for no other reason than that it feels substantial—and *substantial* is a word most companies like to have associated with them.

Whites, ivories, and light grays are standard colors; soft, muted pastels also can be used with care.

Different types of printing are also acceptable: Lithography provides a flat surface, and thermography has a raised surface. Stationery also can be engraved (in which the letters and design are cut into the paper) or embossed (in which the letters and design are pressed into the surface from the back, also creating a raised surface). Foil stamping involves a very thin sheet of metal pressed into the stationery as all or part of the design. Any of these is suitable for business stationery, although thermographic printing cannot tolerate the high heat of fax machines and the printing may melt inside the fax.

The design of the logo should be clear and clean. It does not matter whether the logo is a representation or an abstract image, as long as it is immediately recognizable. The letters should be large enough to be easily read without seeming egotistical or without overpowering the contents of the letter itself. As technology progresses, designers must keep in mind the extra lines of information that are needed—not only company name, address, and phone number (and perhaps an individual's name and title), but also a fax number and Web address. It's important that the design not look cluttered.

When ordering letterhead, office professionals also should order a supply of matching plain paper for those letters that are longer than one page.

Envelopes should match stationery in paper quality, color, type of printing, and font type. If a logo is used, it may be repeated in a smaller version on the envelope.

Many laser and ink jet printers now come with stationery programs to print letterhead, envelopes, and even business cards. At its best, with the purchase of quality paper, printers can simulate lithography. At its worst, the result looks like the company ran out of stationery and is copying its last blank sheet of letterhead, which creates a very poor impression. For that very reason, watch supplies carefully and reorder them with a safe margin of time.

Business cards use the same types of printing as letterhead and mimic its design and color on a heavy paper or light cardboard. Just as too-thin stationery gives a bad impression, so do lightweight business cards. Whenever possible, card stock rather than a heavy paper should be chosen. Preferably, an individual should use business cards imprinted with his or her own name and title, rather than just a company card with the name inked in. The latter makes the person seem insignificant and might prompt clients to search for someone more important. If the company does not provide the executive and/or the office professional with individual business cards, it is worth the small investment to have them made at a personal cost.

A variety of vendors will print stationery and business cards. Open the Yellow Pages under Printers, and you will see dozens of listings, from private commercial printers to nationally franchised instant printers. Weigh the company's needs of quality against price and speed when choosing. After you've decided upon a place (unless you have recommendations and have seen samples from people you know), make the initial order modest (even though it will cost more). If the first order is satisfactory, you can increase the size of later orders.

Other sources of letterheads and business cards can be found online. Note, however, that if you are using a search engine that rates its listings, this function rates the attractiveness, speed, informativeness, and usefulness only of the site itself—*not* the printer.

FOR MORE INFORMATION

If you can't find what you need from the phone numbers and Web sites listed in this chapter, you may need to expand your search.

- For more information on large office equipment such as copiers and fax machines, check in your phone directory under Office Equipment. Most stores will have sales people who will talk you through the basics.

- For more information on small office supplies and where to order, check in your phone directory under Office Supplies. Often, office "super-stores" will have catalogs and delivery services.

- For more information on telephones and office phone systems, check in your Yellow Pages under telecommunications and/or telephones. Many companies have sales reps who will help you assess your needs.

- For more information on obtaining or renting VCRs, projectors, video monitors and other equipment, check in your Yellow Pages under Audio/Visual. Many companies provide daily rental services and will pick up and deliver.

4

MAILING AND SHIPPING

◆

- ■ **The Office Mail**

  Incoming Mail

  Outgoing Mail

- ■ **Mailing and Shipping Services**

  Basic Shipping Services

  Mailing and Shipping on the Grand Scale

  Commercial Package-Delivery Services

  Air Freight

  Counter-to-Counter Shipping

  Couriers and Messengers

  Foreign Mail and Shipping

- ■ **Other Types of Office Communication**

  Telegram

  Cablegram

  Telex

  Fax

- ■ **U.S. Postal Service**

  Types and Classes of Mail

  Types of USPS Services

  International Mail

  Postage Meters

- ■ **For More Information**

Effective and efficient communication methods are essential for any business and its employees. These methods increasingly involve high-tech communication, such as e-mail and faxes. Nevertheless, some of the basic methods of communication—namely, mailing and shipping—will always remain necessary. They have also remained largely unchanged. Like most office technologies, though, mailing and shipping have become more complicated with time. In the past, office professionals only had to know how to seal a package and address a letter. Today, they must know everything from airline cargo schedules to overnight pickup times. They must have such varied skills as running postage meters for hundreds of letters and tracking packages on the Internet.

THE OFFICE MAIL

The processing and handling of the mail—U.S. Postal Service mail, express and courier deliveries, and faxes—constitutes one of the most important daily tasks in business. The office mail delivery may represent orders, contracts, inquiries, and many other transactions integral to business. And the office mail may come in several stages: overnight packages, U.S. mail, and nonpriority deliveries. The smooth operation of the office literally depends on the manner in which mail is handled before it leaves the office—or once it arrives.

INCOMING MAIL

The size of an organization has a great bearing on its system for handling mail. In a small office, one person might sort and open all mail except that marked "Personal" or "Confidential." In bigger offices, a designated person might sort the mail, placing mail in folders that are delivered to the recipients' offices, putting the folders in individual mail boxes, or giving them to a designated person. In some offices, faxes might also be delivered to the same boxes or perhaps placed in separate folders near the fax machine. Each office professional will need to work out a system that most efficiently sorts and distributes faxes.

A large organization usually has an entire department where both incoming and outgoing mail are handled according to a standardized system. Mail is sorted—but not opened—and then distributed to mail centers or boxes, or in some cases to individual employees. Either way, the key to effective mail handling is a routine that works for that office.

Courier and overnight express packages should be delivered to addressees as soon as they arrive. Packages that are shipped overnight or by courier are usually important and/or time sensitive.

No matter which system you use for handling mail, letters marked as "Personal" or "Confidential" or any mail that looks particularly personal should be delivered unopened to the addressee. Keep in mind that all mail should be treated as confidential within the office, and the office professional should take care not to repeat or share any information that he or she comes across while opening the company mail.

Picking Up the Mail

Mail will arrive at your office one of two ways: If you have a street address, it will be delivered; if you have a post office box, you will have to pick it up. Most offices have mail delivered. However, if you have a small office with few staff who are not always there, for example a small consulting office or a business that has no foot traffic, a post office box might be best for you.

If you do have a post office box, assign someone to check it every day. It's not a good idea to have someone check it at the end of the day and take the mail home with them; that could lead to problems. The best plan is to find out when the mail is usually sorted (sometimes midmorning, sometimes early afternoon, depending on your post office) and have someone check it then.

Of course, a large mail room or department will have a regular delivery of mail for the entire company from the post office. If you are an assistant for a manager, group, or executive that depends heavily on postal mail, make sure you know when the daily delivery is to the mail room and approximately how much time elapses between delivery to the mail room and delivery to your box or desk.

> **TIP:** If your company wants mail from a post office box delivered to the office, it can hire a service to pick up the mail every day. Such services will make daily deliveries for a fee.

Opening Mail

If you are employed in a small company, you might be responsible for opening and sorting the mail. In a larger company, if you are an assistant for a department or executive, you will be responsible for opening the mail delivered to you by the mail room. If you are responsible for opening the mail on a daily basis, take a minute to prepare before you begin. Use a clear space and keep items you might need close at hand. To efficiently process the mail, here are some items you will want to keep handy:

- Envelope opener
- Stapler
- Paper clips
- Date and time stamp
- Routing slips
- Transparent tape

- Pencils/pens (at least two different colors)
- Memo pad
- Mail register or log, if needed
- Staple remover

If electric equipment, such as a mail opener, stapler, or time stamp, is available, use it. It will save two-thirds of the time as compared with manual equipment, depending on the amount of mail you have to handle every day.

The mail should be opened as soon as it is delivered to your desk, and an orderly procedure should be followed to ensure that nothing is misplaced or lost. Time spent organizing your mail processing system is time saved in the long run. With a system in place, you can quickly and efficiently get important documents to the proper recipients.

Opening the envelopes. All envelopes should be opened before the contents are removed from any of them. To ensure that the contents will not be torn while the letter is being opened, tap the envelope firmly on the edge of the desk so that the contents will slip away from the top. Slit the top of the envelope with a letter opener. If the contents of a letter are cut by the opener, use transparent tape to join the parts together.

Checking the contents. After removing the contents of an envelope, check the letter for a return address. If there is none, staple or paper-clip the envelope containing the return address to the contents. The envelope should also be retained if the signature on the letter is not easily legible.

Check to determine that all enclosures stipulated in the letter are accounted for. If not, a notation should be made immediately on the face of the letter, indicating what is missing.

Even though annotating a letter is one of the procedures encouraged, some companies do not like correspondence marked up, especially legal or business firms that might have to submit a piece of correspondence as evidence in a court of law. Always follow company policy. Some companies prefer that you place a sticky note with the notation on the face of the letter. It serves the same purpose and doesn't alter the document itself.

Dating the mail. It is always wise to affix each day's date on incoming mail. The easiest procedure is to use a rubber stamp. Such a procedure is helpful if the letter has arrived too late to meet a requested deadline, has been in transit longer than it should have been, or is undated. In either of the last two cases, it is best to staple the envelope to the letter, in addition to dating the letter. This will give evidence of the date of mailing as well as the date of receipt.

Envelopes. In general you may destroy the envelope after you have ascertained that everything has been removed and that there are no problems concerning the names, addresses, or dates. However, in certain situations, especially legal matters, an envelope sometimes serves as evidence of date and time received (from the canceled postage stamp). In such situations, keep the envelope and clip or staple it to the back of the letter.

Preparing Mail

If you are an assistant for an executive or manager who receives large amounts of mail, he or she may want you to "prepare" the mail, which means that you read through it, make notes, and help prioritize. Some specifics include:

1. Read each letter or document, underlining important points that will aid you and your employer in answering the letter. Underline only those things that are of significance, such as publications, dates, and names of people.

2. Make annotations on documents, where appropriate, using removable notes. Do not write directly on any legal documents. Generally, annotations fall into four categories:

   a. Documents to be signed, such as contracts, agreements, employee documents, and expense reports. Make a separate folder for documents requiring a signature, and use multiple categories if your boss needs to prioritize the documents when there isn't time to sign them all at once.

   b. Action required by the letter—date, such as an appointment for the correspondent or reservations for a trip the employer may have to make as a result of the correspondence, and so on.

   c. Procedures to be followed. These may depend upon former correspondence with the same person or related correspondence, which will have to be sought in the files.

   d. The priority the letter should receive, symbolized by a code. In an agreement with the employer, a given place on each letter should be established for this code. For example, a red number may be written in the upper-left corner. Such codes might be:

      Code 1. Mail and reports having high priority and requiring a decision. These should be answered the same day they are received. (It is assumed that personal or confidential mail is delivered unopened to the addressee as soon as it arrives on the office professional's desk.)

      Code 2. Mail for which additional information must be procured and for which an answer may have to be deferred for a day or two while data are being collected. *All mail should be answered within 48 hours of receipt,* except under very unusual circumstances.

      Code 3. Routine mail that an office professional may be able to handle. Many employers want to see all mail; it is wise to determine an employer's preference in this regard. After the relationship is well established, many support personnel have their employers' permission to reply to routine letters. In such instances, it is usually good procedure to supply the employer with copies of the letters sent as well as the original letter.

Code 4. Letters that require notations but no reply.

This type of procedure makes it a simple matter to encode and sort the mail as you are preparing it for the employer. A fifth or even a sixth category may be added as needed. Important reports usually require a special category, while weekly, monthly, or semimonthly periodicals may require no encoding. Most employers prefer to examine the periodicals before they are made available to others in the office.

Preparing supplementary material. As the letters are being annotated, an efficient office professional will also make a list of files or pieces of correspondence and other information to be looked up before presenting the correspondence to the employer.

Some employers wish to see the mail as soon as it has been opened. In that case, bring the mail in as soon as you have annotated it. While the mail is being read, you can take the compiled list and seek the necessary files, reports, and other information for acting upon the urgent mail. To keep all papers pertaining to each piece of correspondence together, use file folders or small clips.

Arranging the mail. After the sorting process has been completed, arrange the mail either in one pile with the high-priority mail on top or in any other arrangement that has been agreed upon. Whenever the mail is placed on the desk of the employer, some provision should be made to prevent others from reading the top letter; for example, simply place the top letter face down.

Absence of the employer. When the employer is away from the office, letters requiring immediate replies may be handled in either of two ways. First, if a decision must be made immediately, give the mail to the person in charge during the employer's absence. Second, if the employer will be in the office within a day or two and the decision can wait, contact the sender immediately and explain when a reply may be expected and the reason for the delay.

The efficient assistant to whom the employer has entrusted routine correspondence will maintain a file of materials handled during the employer's absence. The folder should be readily at hand upon the employer's return.

OUTGOING MAIL

Even if your company is large enough to have a mailing and shipping department, chances are you will in some way be responsible for preparing outgoing mail. Time and expense can be saved by learning about the various postal and shipping services available and the general regulations and normal charges pertinent to these services. It is important to be alert to frequent changes. If your company is small, remember to talk with your post office representative

PREPARING A PACKAGE FOR SHIPPING

If your company doesn't have a mail room, chances are high that you will prepare packages for shipping. Whether it's a box of magazines or a laptop computer, some basic rules apply for shipping items safely. The goal is to get a package from your office to its destination without the contents breaking or the package getting lost.

- Use a sturdy box. Avoid using boxes that have worn corners or torn tops or sides, even if they are reinforced with tape.

- Use packing material all around the item. If you are shipping something fragile, remember to use packing material underneath it and all around it.

- Stuff glass and fragile hollow items like glasses or vases with newspaper or packing material.

- Remove batteries from electronic equipment such as laptops and calculators. Wrap separately.

- Use tape that is designed for shipping, such as pressure-sensitive tape, nylon-reinforced paper tape, or glass-reinforced pressure-sensitive tape.

- Tape the bottom and sides of the package, especially if it is heavy.

- Don't use wrapping paper, string, masking tape, or cellophane tape.

- Type or print the label clearly; then place it in the center of the top of the box. Tape over the label with clear tape to keep it in place and to keep it from smearing. Make sure you put the delivery and return addresses on one side of the package only.

- Make sure you include a clear return address for the package.

- If shipping by UPS or other commercial shipper, make sure you affix all the proper stamps, weight notations, and tracking documents.

- If shipping internationally, make sure you have included all the appropriate customs documents.

before preparing a large mailing. There may be certain size and weight restrictions that you'll want to know about before you start a large project.

For preparing outgoing mail, keep a few supplies at your desk to save time. For overnight delivery, have some overnight folders or packages handy. Keep the name of the courier service (and the contact's name), along with the account information, in your card file or in another list of contacts. For regular mailings, keep these items handy:

- Number 10 and Number 6³/₄ envelopes

- Preprinted labels and/or return address stickers

- Water bottle for moistening envelopes

For larger mail rooms or mail spaces in offices, have on hand:

- Clear or reinforced packing tape

- Packing material (used computer print-out paper works well, or styrofoam "peanuts" available from any shipping store)

- Large labels for boxes

- Small postage scale for letters

- Large scale for packages (make sure it's calibrated)

- Postage meter for letters (larger meters will both seal and stamp envelopes)

- Assorted stamps

- Tracking book for overnight shipping

Getting Mail Out

With today's services, there are a multitude of ways to send packages and documents. In a large company, make sure you know where to drop off mail and packages for pickup—and when the last pickup of the day is. Also make sure you note the cutoff for overnight deliveries and shipping other packages. Each mail department will have a slightly different policy. For smaller offices, make sure someone is responsible every day for dropping the mail at the post office before the last pickup of the day. If packages need to be shipped or must go overnight, someone should be responsible for calling UPS, FedEx, or any other shipping or overnight delivery service for pickup. If your shipping person makes a daily stop at your office, make sure everyone is aware what time the cutoff is for having packages fully prepared. The pickup person is usually on a tight schedule, so don't keep him or her waiting while you add labels, re-tape, or otherwise prepare your package for shipping.

MINIMUM AND NONSTANDARD MAIL SIZES

Minimum Size Standards

Pieces ¼-inch thick or less are mailable if they are rectangular and:

- At least 3½ inches high
- At least 5 inches long (items sent to foreign countries must be at least 5½ inches long)
- At least .007 inch thick (about the thickness of a postcard)

Mail not meeting these standards is returned to sender.

Nonstandard Size Mail

Nonstandard size mail is more costly to handle because it usually cannot be mechanically processed. First-Class Mail, single-piece Standard Mail (A), and international letters are nonstandard if they weigh 1 ounce or less and if they exceed any of these size limits:

- Height exceeds 6⅛ inches
- Length exceeds 11½ inches
- Thickness exceeds ¼ inch
- Length divided by height is less than 1.3 or more than 2.5 inches

A surcharge, in addition to the applicable postage and fees, is applied to each piece of nonstandard size mail for two reasons: It compensates the U.S. Postal Service for the added cost of manually handling nonstandard mail, and it promotes the design and use of mail that can be processed mechanically.

TIP: Make sure everyone in the office knows the regular pickup schedule for packages and letters. If the mail room is closing early, send out an e-mail so employees can get any critical mail or overnight packages out.

MAILING AND SHIPPING SERVICES

Sometimes, for any of a variety of reasons, an office professional needs help with mailing and shipping. Whether it's the odd-shaped office chair that needs to be shipped to an employee who works from home, or 100,000 brochures that need to go to customers, the task can be daunting. Often, it is worth the money to have an outside, professional service tackle the job.

BASIC SHIPPING SERVICES

For the packages and large items that need to be shipped, commercial mail and parcel centers have sprung up as retail businesses. These centers can handle many of the office functions that you might have to tackle, for a fee, naturally. Typical services include making photocopies, wrapping and shipping packages, and providing private postal boxes.

If your business is willing to pay the premium for the convenience these services offer, this can be a time- and effort-saving way to go, especially for the small office or home office that doesn't warrant the investment in, say, higher-volume, higher-speed copiers. It can pay to shop for service, price, and convenience.

Some operations are linked as part of large franchises, some may operate as semiautonomous "departments" in office supply stores, and still others are independently owned and operated. Typically they're located for convenience in downtown centers or easy-to-reach malls. Look for them in the advertising pages of the phone book under "Mailing Services" or in the white pages under their franchise name.

> **TIP:** Retail shipping centers are great places to pack and ship odd-size packages safely, but you should keep close track of your expenses if you use them to send overnight mail or to rent a postal box. If you work at home in a small office, it is probably worth your while to get your own company account with a shipping company—and the company will usually come to your office for a pickup when you call.

MAILING AND SHIPPING ON THE GRAND SCALE

The large-scale direct mail campaign or shipping effort requires proportionately greater planning. There are, for example, significant postal economies to be gained by doing a number of things in a very deliberate and specific way. But managing the requisite elements is usually beyond the scope of the daily routine in most office settings.

Examples of such large-scale efforts include designing direct mail promotional pieces for your company that qualify for significant "bulk" postal discounts; placing logos and advertising copy; and ZIP-sequencing a significant quantity of letter-type mail, delivering it to the post office in order, and arranging for reply mail. The preceding are just a few elements of a very complicated and sophisticated business. If these tasks are not a big part of your company's primary business, you should probably not tackle a large-scale mailing or shipping effort alone.

In advertising agencies, commercial printing companies, and full-time mailing services, you'll find people who make it their business to execute direct marketing campaigns professionally. Get them to work for you when the mailing/shipping stakes are high.

COMMERCIAL PACKAGE-DELIVERY SERVICES

Beyond the U.S. Postal Service, there are any number of commercial package-delivery services. Currently they are used most often to ship larger packages than what the U.S. Postal Service (USPS) handles easily or conveniently, or when extra-speedy service is worth the extra cost that such shippers typically charge.

> **TIP:** Often, when working on big projects and tight schedules, a package or document will need to be shipped or scheduled for overnight delivery after the appointed pickup time. Keep a list available for everyone in the office giving the deadlines and drop-offs for other shipping services or stations. For example, in California, UPS makes office pickups for overnight shipping around 4:00 P.M.; even if you drive to the UPS office at the airport, the latest you can ship a package overnight might be 6:45 P.M. On the East Coast, packages can be shipped overnight often as late as 9:00 P.M. All of these times change often, so always check before sending someone out.

Several high-profile companies, such as United Parcel Service (UPS), FedEx, Airborne Express, and DHL are synonymous with "overnight" delivery.

There are, it should be noted, numerous alternatives to these high-profile shippers. To find shippers, check your telephone directory under "Delivery Services" or "Package Express Service."

Commercial package shippers typically offer overnight service with multiple levels: usually, early morning next day, midday or early afternoon, and next day delivery. Other services might include two- to three-day service for a discounted rate, package tracking, door-to-door pickup and delivery, etc. Some shipping companies also offer "ground" service as a regular package shipping option. Picking the best service for the package is key. If you are shipping important documents for an early morning meeting, then priority next day is what you'll need. If morning delivery isn't necessary, then the less-expensive next day or two-day service will suffice. Ground or overland shipping is usually best for large packages that don't need to arrive right away.

The type of service, costs, and speed of delivery vary from service to service. Individual companies can provide comparative information on rates and limitations on items transported. Just remember, the needs of the business should drive the decision making process. Volume discounts can be negotiated. Electronic connection to the shipper might speed the process and cut your paperwork.

COMMERCIAL PACKAGE-DELIVERY SERVICES				
Company	Same Day	Next Morning	Next Afternoon	2–3 Day	Door-to-Door Delivery
Airborne Express		X	X	X	X
American Airlines	X	X	X	X	X^1
Associated Global Systems	X	X	X	X	X
Burlington Air Express	X	X^1	X	X	X
Continental Airlines	X	X	X	X	X^1
Delta Airlines DASH	X^1	X^1	X^1	X^1	X^1
DHL Worldwide	X	X			X
Emery Worldwide		X	X	X	X
FedEx		X	X	X	X
Roadway Express	X	X	X	X	X^1
Roadway Package Service				X	X^1
Sky Courier	X^1	X^1	X^1		X^1
Sonic Air	X	X	X	X	X
TNT Express Worldwide	X	X	X	X	X
TWA	X	X	X	X	X
United Airlines	X	X	X	X	X^1
UPS		X^1	X^1	X^1	X^1
US Airways	X	X	X	X	X^1
USPS Express Mail		X^1	X	X	X

[1] Domestic shipments only.

> **TIP:** Always record the tracking number! Most overnight shipping companies now offer Web sites that let you instantly find out where your package is, if it's been delivered, and who signed for it. Don't hesitate to track it down if it hasn't arrived on time. Often you can get credit back to your account if your package doesn't arrive on time.

Don't buy more service than you need. If the volume of any one kind of shipment does not warrant using a special shipper, then consolidating your mixed bag of shipping with a single service source may be the most sensible course, even though it may not be the most economical for all types of shipments.

AIR FREIGHT

Air freight, also known as air cargo shipping, is a service typically offered by airline companies for shipping packages on passenger airline flights. The cargo is loaded on the plane and rides in the cargo hold with passenger luggage. It can be used for any size package, as long as it doesn't exceed the airline size and weight requirements. The service is timely, but packages need to be delivered and picked up to and from the airport. However, air freight services will often deliver the cargo on the other end as part of the service. Such service is only a bit more costly and works best for large and awkward packages, but make sure you call ahead to package the cargo correctly. Often there is also a weight limit.

> **TIP:** Air freight terminals are located at major airports, away from the main passenger terminal buildings. If you are picking up or dropping off a package for air freight, make sure you get directions to the building. Also make sure you get a price and find out the method of payment. It's frustrating to make a long trek to the freight terminal only to find out that the company check you brought is unacceptable and they take only credit cards.

COUNTER-TO-COUNTER SHIPPING

Counter-to-counter shipping is another type of shipping service offered by airline companies. It varies from air freight in several important ways. Packages shipped counter-to-counter travel in the cargo hold of an aircraft with passenger luggage, the same as air freight, but they are processsed in the main passenger terminal as if they were luggage—unlike air freight which goes to and

---

TIPS FOR RETAINING A COURIER SERVICE

- There are more than 10,000 courier services in the United States.
- Most are dedicated to servicing a particular region.
- Some operate 24 hours a day.
- Most require you to set up an account in advance.
- Ask for references in advance.
- Compare reliability and variety of services offered, as well as cost.
- Most offer regular and rush services.

---

from a separate airline freight terminal. When packages are shipped counter-to-counter, you drop them off in the baggage office at the airline terminal and they come off the conveyer belt in baggage claim with passenger baggage.

While air freight is good for large or awkward packages, counter-to-counter is better for small packages that must arrive faster than overnight in another city. Suppose you are supporting staff who are running an important conference in Washington, D.C., and you are in the home office in San Francisco; you can get those brochures to them that they need for an 8:00 A.M. meeting. Just call the airline and specify when you want the packages to arrive. They'll give you the flight info, and you drive the package to the airport just as if you were dropping off a passenger. Payment is made at the drop-off. It's a bit more expensive than standard air freight, but worth it when the situation is time critical. There are weight limits and time limits, so call ahead. And make sure you forward the flight arrival info to the recipients—someone will have to go to the airport to pick up the package.

COURIERS AND MESSENGERS

Here's a service that is, by and large, truly local. Need to get a packet of information across town in a hurry? Well, if you've ever been downtown in a large city and almost run over by a bicycle or, in a smaller city or town, seen delivery vehicles zipping between offices, you've seen the couriers and messengers that are largely relied upon in many cities for door-to-door communications.

If you will be using a service in the near future, call ahead to set up an account. If you wait to call until the first time you need them, it could take longer. Often, to set up an account, courier services will check credit worthiness. You should do a similar degree of reference checking, especially about punctuality of such services and the company's reputation for courteous and professional service.

Make sure you brief office staff on the delivery windows and costs. Usually courier services are set up so that anyone can schedule a pickup. Make sure anyone who schedules a pickup is aware that there is usually a significant cost difference between, say, one- to two-hour service and three- to four-hour service.

FOREIGN MAIL AND SHIPPING

Most of today's commercial shipping services can deliver packages internationally. Even though they may not guarantee overnight service to some areas, they are often the fastest way to ship overseas. Documents are usually required for packages that are shipped internationally, whether by airlines or by commercial shipping services like UPS. However, some shipping companies do not require documentation for letter-size envelopes. If you have a mail or shipping department, they will usually take care of this for you. If you prepare your own packages, however, call ahead to verify what will be required and to find out size, weight limits, documentation required, which items you can and cannot ship, etc.

OTHER TYPES OF OFFICE COMMUNICATION

Long before faxing was a common occurrence and e-mail deluged office and home computers everywhere, there were other "electronic" forms of communication. Cables and telegrams were the primary way urgent messages were communicated between businesses for much of this century. In the 1970s and 1980s, telex was popular, especially among international business, but as the facsimile machine came on the scene and more companies were able to communicate via computer networks and the Internet, many of these once popular forms of office communication fell by the wayside. Most are still available today, although it may take some research to find a service. Try the local phone directory or the Post Office.

Note that these services are still utilized in many foreign countries. Even though they are not frequently used in the United States, a good office professional should at least know what the service is and where to find it.

TELEGRAM

A telegram is still a valid method for sending messages anywhere in the continental United States. A *telegram* is a message transmitted through a company called Western Union, and the message typically is phoned to the recipient. If the sender wants a printed message delivered as well, that must be

WEB SITES FOR SHIPPING SERVICES	
FedEx	http://www.fedex.com
Institute of Management and Administration's Mail Center Management Report Site	http://www.ioma.com/ioma/mcmr
Mail Boxes, Etc.	http://www.mbe.com
United Parcel Service	http://www.ups.com
United States Postal Service	http://www.usps.gov

indicated. Many offices require a typed copy for their files. The typed telegram is spaced to fit printed lines on a form. The cost of a telegram may be charged to the sender's phone number. The message is usually brief because the number of words determines the cost.

Telegrams are accepted for immediate transmission for delivery within two hours by telephone and five hours by messenger, subject to the open hours of the delivery office and special holiday concerns.

CABLEGRAM

A *cablegram* is essentially an international telegram that can be sent to almost every country in the world in the language of the recipient. A cablegram is also sent by Western Union and is usually delivered within 24 hours. It is most often printed out and hand delivered, but in some areas of the world it may be mailed or phoned to the recipient.

TELEX

Most telexes today are international and are used where e-mail or fax aren't available. *Telexes* are basically connected-by-phone typewriters that only handle numbers and letters, and cannot transmit graphic images. Some companies maintain their own networks. Others use Western Union's teletypewriter network. Either way, telexes offer the timeliness of a phone call and the convenience of a paper copy.

FAX

Once called by its full name "facsimile transmission" and requiring sizeable pieces of equipment that used chemically coated thermal paper, technological advances have made the *fax* another must-have piece of communications equipment for most modern offices. Today's machines send instantly and receive on regular copy paper.

Virtually any type of document—photographs, diagrams, statistical information, handwritten or typewritten messages—can be faxed within a matter of minutes. And the received document looks substantially like the original.

☎ **800 NUMBERS FOR COMMERCIAL PACKAGE-DELIVERY SERVICES**

Airborne Express	800-247-2676
American Airlines	800-443-7300
Associated Global Systems	800-645-8300
Burlington Air Express	800-225-5229
Continental Airlines	800-421-2456
Delta Airlines DASH	800-638-7333
DHL Worldwide	800-272-7345
Emery Worldwide	800-443-6379
FedEx	800-238-5355
Roadway Express	800-257-2837
Roadway Package Service	800-762-3725
Sky Courier	800-336-3344
Sonic Air	800-782-7892
TNT Express Worldwide	800-368-3400
TWA	800-892-2746
United Airlines	800-825-3788
United Parcel Service	800-742-5877
US Airways	800-428-4322
U.S. Postal Service Express Mail	800-222-1811

U.S. POSTAL SERVICE

Despite the number of commercial package delivery services, the U.S. Postal Service still carries the bulk of all mail that is delivered in this country every day. If your company does a large amount of bulk or commercial mailing, chances are you already have talked to an agent at the post office who works with companies having bulk mail accounts. To get a bulk mail permit, you need an account with the post office. They will coordinate with you the postage amounts and payments to ensure that your business mail is delivered on time.

Sometimes the policies can be so confusing for different weights, sizes, ZIP codes, etc., that it's best to talk to the post office before you plan your marketing piece or brochure. That way you can design your piece around the most cost effective mode of delivery. It also saves surprises when you're all finished with your mailing and find out you have made it too large, too small, or too heavy to fit in a price range.

For updates and changes, check the USPS Web site for the latest pricing and addressing information. Electronic tools such as the Postal Explorer CD-ROM from USPS provide a minimally priced desktop toolbox of information. And finally, if your shipping and mailing volumes are sizeable, membership in organizations such as local Mail Councils may be useful, as well as training by, or subscriptions from, nonprofit or for-profit third parties. Check out the Web site.

There are several primary sources of authoritative information about services offered by the U.S. Postal Service. A comprehensive, yet understandable, overview source that is good for office reference is the *Quick Service Guide,* available from your local post office, from a Postal Business Center, or directly from the Postal Service, National Customer Support Center, 6060 Primacy Parkway, Memphis, TN 38188-0001; telephone: 800-238-3150. Or you can find it easily at the USPS Web site.

TYPES AND CLASSES OF MAIL

From personal letters to business correspondence and from advertisements to magazines and packages, the U.S. Postal Service (USPS) handles a huge volume of mail. It also offers a wide range of services, many of which are not provided by any other mail delivery entity. Although the USPS does offer overnight shipping, it really specializes in handling bulk and commercial mail at a reasonable rate—and in a timely manner. Before you choose a rate or service, make sure you call the Post Office for additional information on special mailing rates for books, catalogs, and international mailings.

First-Class Mail

Use *First-Class Mail* for sending letters, postcards, stamped cards, greeting cards, personal notes, checks, and money orders. If you have mail that weighs over 13 ounces, such as a package or large letter packet, you must send it Priority Mail. The post office can tell you how much the postage will be, or if you have a postage meter at the office, it will automatically calculate the rate.

All First-Class Mail receives prompt handling and transportation. If your First-Class Mail is not letter size, make sure to mark it "First Class." First-Class Mail moves fairly well, but expect delivery domestically to take three to seven days depending on the distance.

Express Mail

Express Mail is the USPS overnight delivery service. It is also offered internationally. Important letters, documents, and merchandise may be sent Express Mail. A full postage refund is made for all domestic shipments delivered later than the guaranteed commitment for that particular service.

To use Express Mail Next Day Service, take your shipment to a post office that offers the service, generally by 5:00 P.M.; deposit it in the Express Mail collection box or call for on-demand pickup or hand it to your letter carrier. Your local post office can give you specific Express Mail acceptance times for your area. Depending on the destination, your mailing will be delivered to the addressee either by noon or by 3:00 P.M. the next day. Express Mail Post Office to Post Office service can also be picked up at the destination post office by 10:00 A.M. the next day.

Priority Mail

Priority Mail offers expedited delivery, usually two to three days, but not overnight service. The rate is slightly higher than regular mail but significantly lower than overnight delivery. Priority Mail should be stickered and can be used for packages up to 70 pounds.

Periodicals

Only publishers and registered news agents approved for Periodicals mailing privileges may mail at the *Periodicals* rates. For magazines and newspapers mailed by the general public, other rates such as First-Class or Standard Mail (A) must be paid.

Standard Mail (A)

Standard Mail (A) is used primarily by retailers, catalogers, and other advertisers to promote their products and services. Churches and other eligible nonprofit organizations may apply to take advantage of nonprofit rates for their large mailings.

Currently, the minimum volume needed for using either the Standard Mail (A) rates or the Nonprofit Standard Mail rate is 200 pieces or 50 pounds per mailing. The pieces must each weigh less than 16 ounces and be prepared in a manner that allows for efficient handling. Standard Mail (A) also includes rates that anyone may use to send individual parcels weighing less than 1 pound.

Standard Mail (B)

Standard Mail (B) is a parcel rate for packages weighing more than 1 pound. (The rate varies if First-Class Mail is attached or enclosed.) Insurance is not included in this rate but is easily purchasable.

TYPES OF USPS SERVICES

There are several services offered by the United States Postal Service not offered by any other company or organization.

General Delivery

General delivery is used primarily at post offices without carrier delivery or those serving travelers and other customers who do not have a permanent mailing address. Mail endorsed "General Delivery" is placed in a general delivery case. The mail can be picked up by the addressee on request at a retail window. Proper identification is required.

Mail Forwarding

If your office is moving, your mail will follow you! By filling out the proper forms—Form 3575, *Change of Address Order*—your service will be uninterrupted. You must include the effective date of the change on all notification forms. Your complete new address should be included. All Express Mail, Priority Mail, and First-Class Mail such as cards and letters are forwarded for one year. There is no charge for this service.

Periodicals mail, including magazines and newspapers, is forwarded at no charge for 60 days from the effective date of your change of address order. Publishers are required to subscribe to the USPS address correction service. Normally, magazines will not need to be forwarded for longer than 60 days.

Certificate of Mailing

A *certificate of mailing* is a receipt showing evidence of mailing. It can be purchased only at the time of mailing. The certificate does not provide insurance coverage for loss or damage, nor does it provide proof of delivery. No record is kept at the mailing office, and a receipt is not obtained when mail is delivered to the addressee.

Certified Mail

Certified mail provides proof of mailing and delivery of mail. The sender receives a mailing receipt at the time of mailing, and a record of delivery is kept at the recipient's post office. A return receipt to provide the sender with proof of delivery can also be purchased for an additional fee. Certified mail service is available only for First-Class Mail or Priority Mail. Certified mail is not available for international mail, nor does it offer insurance protection.

Collect on Delivery

Collect on Delivery, COD, service is used when the mailer wants to collect payment for the merchandise and/or postage when the merchandise is delivered. COD service can be used for merchandise sent by First-Class Mail, registered mail, Express Mail, Priority Mail, or Standard Mail. The addressee has the choice of paying for the COD at the time of delivery, either by cash or by personal check, and the merchandise must have been ordered by the addressee.

Fees charged for this service include insurance protection against loss or damage.

Merchandise Return Service

Merchandise return service allows permit holders to pay the postage and fees for merchandise returned to them. The service enables the recipient to return a parcel and have the postage paid by the sender. Under this arrangement, the shipper provides a special label with instructions to attach it to the returning parcel. Apply this label to the parcel and deposit the parcel at a post office or, if it is under 16 ounces, place it in a mailbox.

POST OFFICE BOXES

Post office box service is available for businesses and individuals at most post offices for a small semiannual or annual fee. There are five post office box sizes from which to choose. The fee varies with the size of the box and the classification category of the post office. Post office box delivery is a secure and private means of getting your mail anytime the lobby of the post office is open. With post offices conveniently located near most businesses, you can get a jump on your day by receiving your mail at a post office box near where you work.

Registered Mail

Registered mail is the most secure service option offered by the Postal Service. It provides added protection for valuable and important mail. Registered articles are placed under tight security from the point of mailing to the point of delivery. First-Class Mail or Priority Mail postage is required on domestic registered mail. Return receipt and restricted delivery services are available for additional fees, and insurance up to $25,000 can be purchased on domestic registered mail at the mailer's option. Registered mail to Canada is subject to $1,000 indemnity limit. For all other countries the indemnity limit is currently $42.30.

Restricted Delivery

Restricted delivery means that the sender's mail is delivered only to a specific addressee or to someone authorized in writing to receive mail for the addressee. Restricted delivery mail addressed to officials of government agencies, members of the legislative and judicial branches of federal and state governments, members of the diplomatic corps, minors, and individuals under guardianship can be delivered to an agent without the addressee's written authorization. Restricted delivery is available only for registered mail, certified mail, COD mail, and mail insured for more than $50.

Return Receipt

A *return receipt* can be purchased for COD mail, Express Mail, mail insured for more than $50, and registered or certified mail. The return receipt shows who signed for the item and the date that it was delivered. Unless prohibited by law, the return receipt also provides the delivery address if the address on the mailpiece is no longer correct. Return receipt service can be purchased in conjunction with restricted delivery service. It can also be requested before or after mailing.

Return Receipt for Merchandise

This form of *return receipt* service provides a mailing receipt, return receipt, and record of delivery. It is available for merchandise sent at the First-Class Mail, Priority Mail, and Standard Mail postage rates.

Special Handling

Special handling service is required for parcels whose unusual contents require additional care in transit and handling.

Special handling is not required for those parcels sent by First-Class Mail, Express Mail, or Priority Mail. Examples of such contents include live poultry or bees. Special handling is available for Standard Mail only, including insured and COD mail. This service provides preferential handling to the extent practical in dispatch and transportation.

INTERNATIONAL MAIL

All mail originating in foreign countries and U.S. overseas territories, other than the Commonwealth of Puerto Rico, is subject to U.S. Customs Service examination upon entering the United States. Many imported goods are subject to the payment of U.S. Customs duty. When dutiable merchandise enters the United States by mail, the amount due is determined by the Customs Service but is collected by the Postal Service. When the duty is collected on behalf of the Customs Service, the Postal Service also collects a customs clearance and delivery fee on each dutiable item.

Types of International Mail

LC Mail—lettres et cartes—includes aerograms, letters, postcards, and postal cards. LC Mail is defined as "personal handwritten or typewritten communications having the character of current correspondence." The weight limit for LC Mail is 4 pounds. Type the word *letter* or *lettre* on the envelope. If the contents are not duty-free, you must attach *Customs Douane C-1* (Form 2976) or *Customs Declaration C-2* (Form 2976A) for packages valued above $400.

AO Mail—autre objets—includes printed matter, books, sheet music, small packets, periodicals, and audio and videotapes. The weight limit for AO Mail varies. Printed matter weighing between 11 and 66 pounds that is to go to a single address can be packaged in a *direct sack* or *M-bag.* Type the words "Printed Matter," or "Printed Matter—Periodicals," or "Printed Matter—Videotapes" on the package. If the contents are not duty-free, you must attach *Customs Douane C-1* (Form 2976) or *Customs Declaration C-2* (Form 2976A) for packages valued above $400.

Small Packet Mail covers gifts, merchandise, and commercial documents that don't fall under the definition of LC Mail can be shipped as AO Mail. Type the words "Small Packet" on the package. You must attach *Customs Douane C-1* (Form 2976) or *Customs Declaration C-2* (Form 2976A) for packages valued above $400. Cambodia, Cuba, and North Korea do not accept these Small Packets.

TIPS FOR OVERSEAS SHIPPING AND MAILING

Follow USPS address quality standards when addressing international packages. On the last line, include only the name of the destination country in capital letters. The same is true for the return address.

Include the destination country's postal codes if known. These should go on the second to last line after the city, state, or province name.

The U.S. Customs Service requires you to declare the content and value of mail shipped internationally.

*CP International Mail—colis postaux—*is very similar to USPS parcel post. It includes merchandise and nonletter mail. The weight limit for CP International Mail is 22 to 44 pounds. You must attach *Parcel Post Customs Declaration* (Form 2966-A) or *Parcel Post Customs Declaration and Dispatch Note* (Form 2966-B).

*EMS Mail—Express Mail International Service—*is very similar to USPS Express Mail; however, the service is not guaranteed. Packages can be insured. Corporate accounts can be established. Not all countries worldwide provide this service—check with the USPS. You must attach *Customs Douane C-1* (Form 2976) or *Parcel Post Customs Declaration* (Form 2966-A).

*IPA Mail—International Priority Airmail—*includes all LC and AP Mail. Volume and sorting requirements must be met. IPA Mail is designed to provide an international fast delivery alternative—check with the USPS for rates and requirements.

*ISAL Mail—International Surface Air Lift—*includes printed matter and is designed to provide faster service than surface mail at less cost than airmail. Drop-off sites are specified by the USPS—check with the USPS for rates and sites.

*WPL Mail—Worldpost Priority Letter—*is available in two flat-rate sizes: $9 \times 11^1/_2$ and 5×9. WPL Mail is delivered within four days on average.

All printed matter items, small packets, and parcel post packages may be sent either airmail or surface mail. Check with your local post office for specific information about the mail service in the country to which you are mailing.

Customs Forms

Customs forms are required when you send dutiable letter packages, small packets, printed matter, and parcels to international destinations. The specific customs form is governed by the type of mail, the weight of the item, and the regulations of the destination country.

Individual countries may restrict or prohibit certain articles, which makes them nonmailable. Articles that are restricted are subject to the import requirements of that country. The *International Mail Manual,* available at your local post office, gives specific information about restrictions and prohibitions for individual countries and about the forms required for mailing.

POSTAGE METERS

When a mailer uses a postage meter, the postage, place of mailing, and date are imprinted at the mailer's place of business. Many mailers, including those mailing a relatively small volume of mail, have found that this convenience more than offsets the costs of maintaining an account and leasing the machine.

POSTAGE METER VENDORS

Ascom Hasler Mailing Systems
19 Forest Parkway
Shelton, CT 06484-0903
203-926-1087

Friden Neopost
30955 Huntwood Avenue
Hayward, CA 94544-7085
800-624-7892

Pitney-Bowes, Inc.
Walter H. Wheeler Jr. Drive
Stamford, CT 06926-0001
203-356-5000

Postalia, Inc.
1980 University Lane
Lisle, IL 60532-2152
708-241-9090

Currently four companies are authorized by the USPS to manufacture and rent you postage meters. They are: Pitney-Bowes, Inc., Postalia, Friden Neopost, and Ascom Hasler Mailing Systems. Your phone book should reveal dealers in your area who will help you assess the costs and benefits, help complete the necessary paperwork, show you how to operate the equipment, and get you started with the USPS.

What do postage meters do? How do they work?

- Postage meters help monitor shipping costs.

- Metered mail is processed more quickly.

- Use fluorescent ink to ensure speedy processing.

- Postage meters can only be rented, not purchased.

- A license from the U.S. Postal Service is required.

- Postage meters must be reset every three months.

- Older model meters must be taken to a post office to be reset.

- Newer models can often be reset by calling the manufacturer, sometimes even via a modem.

- Most models can hold enough postage ($100 to $10,000) for the entire quarter.

- Payment for postage must be received by the U.S. Postal Service before a meter can be reset (except for Neopost machines).

FOR MORE INFORMATION

If you can't find what you need from the phone numbers and Web sites listed in this chapter, you may need to expand your search.

- For more information on mailing: Try the United States Postal Service Web Site (www.usps.gov). For more specific information, call your local post office.

- For more information on shipping: Check Web sites for individual shipping companies. Call airlines directly for all information on air cargo and air freight shipping. Most Web sites for individual shipping companies can now process tracking numbers for packages.

- For more information on other forms of office communication: Check your Yellow Pages for information on Telex, Telegram, and other services. Call Western Union directly if you have questions about types of service or costs.

5

COMPUTERS

◆

■ **Personal Computers**

> Parts of the PC
> Peripherals
> Types of PCs

■ **Networks**

> Two Kinds of Networks
> Network and Internet Communications

■ **Operating Systems**

■ **Software Applications**

> Word Processing Software
> Spreadsheet Software
> Database Management (DBM)
> Presentation Software
> Desktop Publishing
> Communications Software
> Other Applications

■ **Basic Guidelines for Selecting Software**

> Understanding Upgrades
> Software Bundles

■ **For More Information**

The impact of the computer on the office and personal environment grown exponentially since the first computer was introduced just after World War II. The first-generation machines were expensive, often room-sized mainframes capable of processing a few millions of instructions per minute. Next came smaller, general-purpose minicomputers tailored to meet the needs of small to medium-sized businesses. In the early 1980s, the smallest and fastest-growing category of computers evolved: personal computers (PCs). Originally known as microcomputers, these computers earned their names from the microprocessor chips that function as the brain.

Today's desktop computers, or PCs, are faster and more powerful than earlier mainframes and can process many millions of instructions per second. Chip-processing speed is measured in Hertz (Hz). One Hertz equals a million instructions per second. That means that a Pentium processor with a speed of 450 megahertz (MHz) is capable of processing 450 million instructions per second. PCs have grown in speed, memory, and capability; they are used in businesses, schools, and homes and now make up the largest and fastest-growing category of computers.

PERSONAL COMPUTERS

Most of the processing parts of the computer are invisible to the eye. As a user, you mainly are concerned with the applications of the PC and the most popular software packages to run those applications. Today's PCs most commonly are used for the following functions: word processing of letters and all forms of written communications (Word, WordPerfect); spreadsheets (Excel, Lotus); accounting and bookkeeping (Quicken, QuickBooks); presentation graphics (PowerPoint); database applications (Access, Approach, FileMaker, Oracle, Paradox); networking and e-mail (Outlook, Outlook Express, Lotus Notes, cc:Mail, Lotus Domino, HotMail, Juno); desktop publishing and multimedia graphics (Adobe Illustrator, AutoCAD, CorelDraw, Macromedia Director, Microsoft Publisher, Pagemaker, QuarkExpress); project management (Microsoft Project); and image creation and management (CorelDraw, Photoshop, Adobe PhotoMagic, Freehand). Many new office installations with late-model computers come with popular multiple software applications (word processing, spreadsheets, database, and so on) bundled into suites (Office, Works). These are the names of the applications you are likely to see when you boot up the computer and look at your desktop onscreen display.

PARTS OF THE PC

The basic desktop computer system consists of a monitor, a central processing unit (CPU), disk drives, a keyboard, a printer, and a mouse. This equipment is known as the *hardware;* the various programs are called the *software.*

Typical Computer Setup

Monitors

The monitor is a television-like viewscreen, also called the screen or cathode ray tube (CRT). Many monitors have tilt-and-swivel bases so the user can position them for comfortable viewing. The sharpness of the image depends on the resolution, which is the number of pixels (dots) that make up the monitor's image. More pixels on the screen mean a higher resolution and, therefore, a sharper image. So, if resolution is expressed as 640 × 480 (which is standard VGA resolution), that means there are 640 pixels per line on the horizontal axis and 480 pixels per line on the vertical axis. This is okay for word processing applications but is not as good for multiple windows, graphics, or complex images. That's where SVGA comes in. Here the standard is 800 × 600, up to 1600 × 1280 pixels per line. Super VGA standards enable users to see additional rows of spreadsheets and to see as many as two full pages simultaneously.

The choice of a monitor depends on how the PC will be used. Is it for calculations and spreadsheets? Graphics? Desktop publishing? Multiple uses? Also consider interlaced versus non-interlaced display. (Interlaced versions display odd lines and then even lines, every other line first, and then fill in the gaps by generating a refreshed image at every other pass.) Users who sit in front of a monitor for several hours a day will prefer the non-interlaced monitors, which refresh every line on every pass—the result is less annoying flickering and jumping of horizontal lines. BuyersZone recommends a dot pitch of 0.28mm or better and a 72Hz vertical refresh rate in every resolution you expect to use. For larger 20- or 21-inch monitors, a dot pitch of 0.30 or 0.31 is acceptable.

If you don't know what kind of monitor you have or its age, check the model number and manufacturer's name (usually found on the back or bottom of the unit), call the manufacturer's help line, ask for customer service, and give the technical support staff the information. The staff should be able to help you determine the type of monitor and its age. To determine the size of the screen display, just measure diagonally across the screen with a ruler.

PC vs. Mac

The vast majority of the market share in personal computers that sit on desktops belongs to IBM-compatible machines running the Windows operating system. Apple or Macintosh users represent a smaller part of the installed computer population, but these are very loyal fans of the company and its operating system. A simple way to determine whether to go with either the Windows-based PC or an Apple/Macintosh computer is to think about the applications you plan for the equipment. In a standard office environment with professional services (accounting, legal, medical) and business services (landscaping, equipment repair, contracting), and one whose main functions and outputs include word processing, accounting, financial spreadsheets, and database management (with some creative or graphics communications applications thrown in), the Windows-compatible computer is the usual choice (although you could choose either one, depending upon price and your willingness to tinker with programs). PCs have the largest installed based in business and usually cost less than comparable Macintosh units.

If your desired applications include heavy graphics creation (such as brochures, display ads, newsletters, desktop publishing, and print production), the Apple computer still is considered by many professionals to be the best choice for businesses in advertising, graphic arts services, Web site development, and video game creation. However, most home-office workers, small-computer users, and entrepreneurs will use PCs.

Both Apple and Microsoft, the maker of the Windows operating system, constantly are creating new versions of their software to be more compatible. As to whether the current Apple users will have to change over to PCs due to the eventual disappearance of Mac machines, that's no longer an issue. For a variety of reasons, including competitive considerations, Apple's Mac machines are likely to be around for the foreseeable future.

Central Processing Unit (CPU)

The operation of the PC takes place in the central processing unit (CPU); it's the computer's brain. In PCs, the CPU is a single processing chip; in mini-computers, it can be contained in one or more printed circuit boards. In mainframes, the CPU is contained in several boards.

The CPU of the PC is housed in a rectangular case or box that sits on your desktop, which might be under or beside the monitor. Sometimes it sits under the desk in a tower arrangement that is a taller, narrower, and free-standing array for the CPU. The CPU houses the following: the motherboard, the processing chip, the processor memory (RAM), input/output devices that transfer data between the CPU and any peripheral devices, the hard drive or permanent storage memory device, a floppy disk drive, the CD-ROM drive, and any fixed disk drive (such as a ZIP, Syquest, or Inmation drive).

CPU Components

Memory

The computer has two kinds of memory: read-only memory (ROM) and random access memory (RAM).

ROM is the permanent memory that contains the information to make the computer run. Even when the computer is turned off, ROM is not affected. RAM is the memory discussed when buying a computer: It is a temporary workspace in which the computer runs and stores the information on which the user is working. RAM is wiped out as soon as the computer is turned off. RAM capacity is measured in kilobytes (K or KB, meaning thousands of bytes) and megabytes (M or MB, meaning millions of bytes). Early computers had RAM capacities of 64K, which expanded to 640K. Today, computers have RAM capacities of 256M, and RAM can be added to computers by placing an additional RAM chip on the motherboard. This is an effective way of increasing the working speed of the computer because it decreases the need for the processor to access data from the hard drive.

As with RAM, ROM also can be increased. One way is to have a technician install a new higher-capacity hard drive for you (hard drives are relatively inexpensive and the process is not difficult). But an integral part of the process involves transferring the data from your old drive to your new drive. Software programs can make this process easier if you prefer to do it yourself,

WEB SITES FOR COMPUTER HARDWARE AND SOFTWARE SUPPORT

Acer	www.acer.com
AST	www.ast.com
Brother	www.brother.com
Canon	www.ccsi.canon.com
Casio	www.casio.com
Compaq	www.compaq.com
CTX	www.ctxintl.com
Dell	www.dell.com
Digital	www.digital.com
Epson	www.epson.com
Hewlett Packard	www.hp.com
IBM	www.ibm.com
Info Peripherals	www.infoconnection.com
Inteva	www.inteva.com
KLH	www.sierrainc.com
Logitech	www.logitech.com
Mustek	www.mustek.com
Packard Bell	www.packardbell.com
Panasonic	www.panasonic.com
PC Brand	www.sierrainc.com
Pionex	www.pionex.com
Positive	www.sierrainc.com
Premier	www.sierrainc.com
Sharp	www.sharp-usa.com
Toshiba	www.toshiba.com

but the technician can perform this task for you when installing the new drive. Also be sure to ask the technician to partition the drive that divides large drives into smaller segments. This makes file storage less cumbersome and enables you to store different programs on different parts of the drive. Another way of adding storage is to add a second hard drive. Newer computers have additional ports into which the new drive can plug, much like the auxiliary input/output ports on a stereo system.

Hard Disk Drives

The early PCs used floppy disks only, but as the amount of information and the size of programs grew, storage capacity needs increased. The hard disk drive then became available. This type of drive is built into the computer and stores data and programs. Information can be transferred to and from disks for portability. A hard disk can store much more information than a floppy disk, typically from 500M to more than 17 gigabytes (GB, meaning 1000M of data, or 1 billion bytes). Information retrieval also works much faster on hard disk drives.

Floppy Disks

Floppy disks are 3½-inch hard plastic disks, formerly called *diskettes*. The disks are inserted into slots called disk drives, which copy and record information. Floppies are portable and can be interchanged from one computer to another. Disk capacity equals sides plus density: The *density* of the disk refers to the spacing of the magnetic storage units used in recording data. Double-sided (DS) double-density disks can record information on the top and bottom. In general, a high-density drive can accommodate either a low-density or a high-density disk; a low-density drive can accommodate only a low-density disk. Today's computers come with only high-density drives.

Disks must be formatted before they can store information. When you buy a box of disks, you can buy them preformatted to run on most IBM computers, or you can format them yourself on your own machine.

TIP: A floppy disk drive—usually the A drive—is subject to a lot of use and sometimes will fail to read a disk. Before calling in a computer repair service, try a disk drive cleaner system available from the local computer store. That and a shot of compressed air (available in spray cans) often will restore the drive to working order.

Another obvious but sometimes overlooked reason that a computer fails to read the disk is that sometimes disks are damaged or faulty right out of the box. Be sure to try another disk in the drive to verify that a problem exists with the drive and not the disk. If time permits, and if you don't have a lot of extra disks on hand, you also might try reformatting the disk in an attempt to get rid of the error or fault that caused it to fail the first time.

CD-ROMs

A CD-ROM (compact disc, read-only memory) is a plastic permanent storage compact disc that is read by an optical laser. A CD-ROM is capable of storing more than 600M of data, up to 300,000 pages of text, tens of thousands of images, and stereo sound. A CD-ROM drive can be either internal or external, and it connects to the computer through a controller card. The transfer rate for data is 150K per second. Current speeds are measured in multiples of that rate (32X = 32 × 150K).

CD-ROMs are helpful for holding vast amounts of data, such as encyclopedias, which would take up a lot of room on a hard drive. The computer CD-ROM also can play stereo music, but audio CD players cannot read computer CD-ROMs. Although originally a read-only drive, a recordable CD-ROM (CD-R) drive now permits you to record data that can be played on any CD-ROM player. Rewritable drives (CD-RW) accommodate updating and deleting of files, as needed. If your computer doesn't have a CD-ROM drive, you can purchase an external one to hook up to your machine.

Keyboard

The letters on the keyboard are laid out like a typewriter. In addition, the keyboard contains cursor control keys (arrows pointing up, down, left, and right) that are used to move the cursor around the screen, function keys (labeled F1 through F12) that act as shortcuts to performing certain operations, and a numeric keypad that looks like a calculator for computational input.

A Standard Keyboard

Redesign of keyboards is inviting a lot of attention as more people spend a large part of their time in front of the PC. Some of the more ergonomic designs include keyboards with built-in wrist pads and a more user-friendly design that optimizes the way the user positions the hands when typing to counteract repetitive stress syndrome (RSS) problems such as carpal tunnel syndrome. But here's an old-fashioned tip that, although not medically endorsed or guaranteed, can help save you needless pain: In the days before flat keyboards and even electric typewriters, carpal tunnel syndrome was almost unheard of because of the placement of the hands at the typewriter and the attitude of the typist. To get the old typewriter keys to strike the paper, it took some effort and strength—the hands had to be placed so that the user could strike the keys with some authority.

Quite simply, this involves keeping your wrists straight while typing and keeping your hands elevated above the keys. Take a look around the office today and you'll find many people with their hands flat on the keyboards and many wrists resting flat on the desk surface behind the keyboard, which is like heavy lifting without using your legs. Although recent developments in keyboards have tried to compensate for this tendency, try this simple old-fashioned approach and see whether it helps.

An Ergonomic Keyboard

Mouse

The mouse is a hand-held pointing device that takes the place of the cursor control keys and many function keys in performing routine computing tasks. When the cursor moves, a small arrow or bar-shaped pointer moves on the screen. The mouse can be used to select words, sentences, or paragraphs from the text that must be manipulated. Although some people find the mouse difficult to get used to at first, it is an indispensable tool for certain tasks and is easy to use once you become familiar with it.

Mouse users are also subject to wrist injury, but because of the way the mouse is used, the old-fashioned tip described previously is not likely to solve the problem. Here, a wrist support pad (available at your local computer supply store) comes in handy. Other innovative mouse designs incorporate wrist support, but these are available only from specialty suppliers.

COMPUTER BACKUPS

Backing up systems regularly helps businesses avoid the catastrophes that can happen at any time, such as fires, floods, or burglary. Many companies experience smaller losses, such as system crashes, accidental erasures, and computer viruses. It's rare for a company not to have experienced any of these problems, so a computer backup system and a regular policy of backing up valuable data makes for a good business practice.

Although different types exist, a backup generally involves the creation of a duplicate copy of certain files stored separately and used to restore data to the computer in the event of either a hard drive crash (a hard disk failure), corruption of files by viruses, or software failure. In a complete system backup, a copy is made of all installed software, as well as all files stored on the computer's hard drive. This backup usually requires a lot of floppy disks—and with today's memory-hungry programs, it is more likely to require a heavier-duty storage medium such as a ZIP, Syquest, or Inmation drive; a tape drive; or a separate tape storage device. In a data-only backup, copies are made of all files stored in the computer; if need be, the software is reloaded from the original CD-ROMs or disks.

After performing a complete system backup and complete file backup, subsequent backups might be incremental (in which case, the files that have been changed or added since the last backup are copied and all other files are left alone). This takes a lot less time than another complete backup.

Make sure that the data is stored in a safe and secure place, preferably at a completely different location than the primary site. In a small office, this process might mean having someone take home the disks on a regular basis. Why is this so important? Two reasons: Fires and floods can destroy not only the primary computer and storage medium, but also the entire site where backups are contained.

PERIPHERALS

Peripherals are the devices that hook up to a computer to help it—and you—do the job better. Peripherals include everything from additional drives to printers and speakers.

TIP: When you do backups and/or make copies of files, check the disk to make sure that the data you think you backed up or copied is actually there. Sometimes, backups are made and files copied on disks that, when needed for purposes of restoring data, are found to contain no data. To cover yourself when making a copy of a file on a disk, simply use the File Open command to determine whether the file does in fact exist on the disk.

Mei-Yun Lee, president of BuyersZone, adds the following special tips on data recovery or computer backup systems:

- Clean drives often. If you are using a tape drive to back up your data, remember that tape drives require frequent cleaning to remain in good working condition. Buy a tape head cleaner, and set a regular schedule for cleaning the drive to prolong its life.

- Frequently used tapes should be retired after one year of use.

- Store offsite. Businesses should keep one complete set of data offsite at all times. In small offices, one person can collect all copies of files and literally take them home each day. In larger offices, a backup to a network is a good approach. The network itself usually is backed up regularly with an offsite location. In highly sensitive environments, a multiple backup should be made with three copies of data. If a backup does not go as planned, two recent copies of the data are still available.

- A final word of advice: Even small businesses can afford the services of an outside vendor to perform needed backups of sensitive or valuable data and then store it offsite.

Modems

The modem (modulator-demodulator) is the device that enables a computer to connect to a telephone line or another computer network. The modem translates digital signals into analog signals so they can travel over a telephone line, and then translates them back into digital signals that can be read by the receiving computer. Modems communicate at various speeds; the more that computer communications grow, the more the need for speed grows also. Current modems are rated at 56K, or 56,000 bits per second (bps), but most functional transmission speeds are limited to 33.6Kbps—especially over the Internet, where an Internet service provider (ISP) works as an intermediary.

You need a modem for a lot of reasons, such as to telecommute or work from home (and dial up the office or corporate computer network), to dial into your ISP, and to retrieve your e-mail.

Personal and small-business computer users can manage with the current crop of modems as long as they comply with the v90 Standards set by the International Telecommunications Union (ITU). However, the number of smaller businesses using the Internet is increasing enormously, with an estimated 41 percent currently. There will be an estimated 4.3 million businesses by 2001, according to a study by the International Data Group (IDG). This surge in growth will drive the industry to provide newer, higher-speed technology for accessing the Internet at more affordable prices. The following sections discuss current choices for businesses and entrepreneurs to consider.

Removable Cartridge Drives

Cartridge drives (such as ZIP, JAZ, and SyQuest) hold around 2GB of data—double the amount with compression—making them a good method for backing up individual computers. Data-access rates are fast, but the disks are expensive, so backing up many gigabytes of data is impractical. Networked computers usually are backed up to a remote site, either inside the office or an outside site via the network or the Internet.

Printers

Given the amount of documentation created in business, a printer is the most necessary piece of equipment needed next to the computer. The most common printers today are laser printers, inkjet printers, and dot-matrix printers. All three might be found in an office if connected output can be directed to any one of them for desired purpose.

Laser printers offer the fastest, most efficient way to produce text and images, offering high speeds and good resolution at relatively low cost. The laser printer uses a technology similar to a dry copy machine, electrostatically charging a photosensitive image drum. Toner particles are attracted to those areas of the drum that are charged; when paper passes over the drum, the particles are deposited onto the paper. Heat then fuses the toner particles to the paper.

TIP: In offices with PCs, look for printers that support PCL5 printer language—anything less will not support complex document printing. If the business outputs to service bureaus or has Macintosh computers in its network, it needs a printer that uses the Postscript language. This is universally accepted printer language that prints documents the same way, no matter what equipment exists on the other end. However, because Postscript printers are more expensive than PCL printers, PCL types might be just fine for a small office application. Although laser printers are most popular because they are quiet and fast, they have a few drawbacks: They cannot handle multiple forms, and they usually cannot accept anything larger than legal-size paper.

Inkjet printers use tiny jets to spray droplets of ink onto the page, and the refinement in the ink compound has made this technology attractive and highly affordable. To the untrained eye, little difference exists between the quality of an inkjet printer and a laser printer. Most offices can get by with 300dpi (dots per inch) printing, especially for text and black-and-white work. 600dpi is becoming the norm on many printers (it offers four times the clarity of 300dpi), but the naked eye can scarcely tell the difference, especially on text. A major advantage of the inkjet is its portability—it can be taken on the road and used with either a laptop or a portable computer.

Dot-matrix printers are impact printers that use a row of small pins, wires, and hammers that shoot up to make dots on the paper, creating text and graphics. Their most common use is for printing invoices, purchase orders, shipping forms, labels, and other multipart forms. Dot-matrix printers can print through multipart forms in a single pass, allowing them to produce more pages than even high-speed laser printers. Two types of printers exist: 9-pin and 24-pin. At one time, the trend was moving from 9- to 24-pin but recently has moved back to 9-pin. In the applications for dot-matrix printing, 9-pin is fine—in most cases, it is faster and less expensive. These printers can print in letter-quality mode for correspondence-quality output, or draft mode or near letter quality for forms applications.

The only other important consideration involves the number of parts you might have in a printing application for forms (invoices, purchase orders, and shipping labels). Dot-matrix printers use continuous-form paper, which runs through a tractor mechanism. The paper attaches to the tractor with holes that are part of a perforated strip that can be pulled away. Continuous-form envelopes, labels, and forms are also available. Although laser printers have become the office standard for letters and proposals, dot-matrix printers remain an important part of back-office operations in many firms.

Color printers are now within the reach of most users and have a lot to offer to low- to high-end users. Five types of color printers exist: inkjet, laser, solid ink, dry wax, and dye sublimation. The laser printers work ideally for high-end graphics and commercial presentations, for which precise imaging and reproduction are important. For home and small office use, the color inkjet printer will do the job adequately for a fraction of the cost of a color laser machine. Inkjet printers are more than sufficient when printing a color proof of a job to check the overall look before sending it to the printer. The drawback of an inkjet, however, is dealing with smudgy, wet-looking paper when heavily inked images are laid down.

Color printers also can function as black-and-white printers. In busy offices, however, most inkjets are too slow. If speed is important, a laser printer offers the best option. For advertising, marketing, and high-end graphics printing and presentation needs, one of the other top-of-the-line laser printers might serve as a better choice. A visit to online buying/advisory services such as BuyersZone (www.buyerszone.com) or the local professional vendor in your area can point you in the right direction.

CHOOSING A PRINTER

Printers are pretty much a commodity product, so pricing is very competitive among the major brands. You might ask your colleagues and friends what their experiences have been with various brands, and what potential problems exist in interactions with your software programs. For example, I once purchased a brand-new printer that wasn't listed on the setup menu in my computer, so I used a default setting. The printer gave me problems for more than two years, even after replacing the printer drivers and spending hours with tech support. I finally had to replace it.

Another item is cartridges: If you use the printer heavily, you might want to go for a laser printer because its cartridges can last for several thousand copies before being replaced. Inkjets that use separate ink cartridges for black ink and three different colors must be replaced much more often. Some low-end models have combined the various color inks into one cartridge, so you have to replace all colors whenever one of them runs out. If your main application involves printing word processing documents, you need not bother with the extra added expense of a color printer.

- *Printing speed.* This is the number of pages per minute that the printer can spit out. (In actual use, however, the speeds are slower.) Speed is determined by the processor in the printer; higher-speed printers cost more. Determine what your needs are and buy accordingly. Also ask whether the printing speed refers to regular letter-quality mode or draft mode (which can be almost twice as fast as letter quality, but is not suitable for either copying or printing).

- *Paper tray capacity.* This factor is important even for small offices. A capacity of up to 250 pages in one tray is adequate for some and not for others. Some printers offer more than one tray, which is a valuable feature if you switch from plain paper to letterhead and also handle envelopes and documents with the same printer. For heavy envelope work, consider a dedicated envelope printer.

- *Toner cartridges, drums, corona wires, and ozone filters.* It's a good idea to figure these costs into the buying process.

- *Black-and-white versus color.* Word processors and most communications-only functions in the firm, as well as accounting and finance users, don't need color printers. Graphic artists and people involved in marketing communications probably have a regular need for color printing. So, too, do the folks who produce your newsletters in-house. If the need is only occasional, it's a good idea to price having color jobs printed at the office supply superstore or copy places. If you work from home and share the printer with other family members—and, yes, that includes kids—a color printer is a no-brainer decision.

Plotter

A plotter is a type of printer used to print certain graphs and charts. Many types of plotters produce pages or transparencies and also draw curved lines, three-dimensional figures, bar charts, graphs, and so on with computer-based instruction. Some plotters even add text labels to the charts or transparencies. Engineering applications can include blueprints and schematics; business applications can include sales projections and presentation graphics. Few differences in quality exist between the low-end and high-end plotters—mainly, these involve ease of use, features, and budget.

Scanner

A scanner is a device that can "read" text and graphics. A copy of the scanned image is stored on magnetic media as it simultaneously reproduces on a monitor. Text, photographs, drawings, and charts can be scanned and used in desktop publishing or electronic filing. Accuracy depends on the quality of the document being scanned, so the smart user should review the scanned image for the occasional error resulting from the scanner misreading data. Most scanners come bundled with Optical Character Recognition (OCR) capability that can convert images into computer-editable format.

Scanners are available at affordable prices for every level of user. They range from hand-held portable models costing less than a couple hundred dollars, to moderately priced flatbed scanners, to sophisticated drum scanners costing much more. High-end multi-function devices also offer the capability of printing, copying, and collating right from your desk via the print and processing options menu. Many national office equipment dealers offer a huge variety of brand-name models. Office products superstores also can be a good place to shop locally. Online shoppers can consult a number of good Internet Office buying services, such as BuyersZone (www.buyers.zone.com).

Uninterruptible Power Supplies (UPS)

Although not technically a peripheral, the most useful additional item you can add to your computer is an uninterruptible power supply (UPS). Depending on the integrity of local electrical lines—how often you experience surges or spikes, such as when light bulbs flicker suddenly or how often your power goes off—you should consider a UPS. Even if your power goes off only once a year, a UPS can save you valuable time and work. This device contains a large battery and circuitry. When the circuitry detects a surge or spike, it switches the computer from AC to DC power. The battery in the UPS gives you enough time to stop working, save your work on a disk, and conduct an orderly shutdown of your system. Normally, you get about a 10-minute window to safely save and close down your system. If this is not enough time, some units can provide alternative power for a day or more, but these are expensive. Many manufacturers sell power-management systems that can be integrated with your computer equipment. These systems are outlet strips with surge protection; each outlet is designed for a specific piece of equipment or peripheral. For more information on other consumer electronics products and accessories, see the Consumer Electronics Manufacturers Association Web site (www.eia.org/cema).

The cost of UPSs vary from very inexpensive to expensive, depending on how much capacity you need—how many machines are hooked up—and how much time you need in reserve power to safely save open or working files and then shut down all systems. These devices are now available wherever computer and computer peripherals are sold.

Video Equipment

The growth of home-based businesses and entrepreneurs has pushed technology into accommodating independent business people to reach out and touch customers while running their businesses from home. Desktop videoconferencing systems typically include the following equipment you'll have to add to your computer: a video camera, a video capture card (installed internally), a modem (you may already have this, but check to see if the one with the video system is faster or is a later model with newer software), speakers (already standard equipment on most PCs), a microphone, and a software bundle. You can use videoconferencing to connect business owners, to customers, to remote employees, and to suppliers around the world without having to leave home.

The biggest barrier to quality so far is the use of old copper wire telephone cable to broadcast images. Television broadcasts 30 frames per second, whereas copper phone lines broadcast 3 to 13 frames per second. Two new standards developed by the International Telecommunications Union (ITU) have emerged, however: H.324, which improves video quality; and H.323, which improves communication in Internet, intranet, and local area network (LAN) environments. Digital Video Systems are available from 3Com Corp. (www.3com.com/bigpicture), Connectix Corp. (www.quickcam.com), Cubic VideoComm (www.cvideomail.com), and Intel Corp. (www.intel.com).

TYPES OF PCs

Offices today have many different types of PCs. You are likely to encounter familiar names such as IBM, as well as Compaq, NEC, Micron, Dell, Gateway, and many others—all are PCs or IBM-compatibles. With Macs, it's pretty much a Macintosh computer—although some clones were made for a few years, the clone population is small. Different types of PCs also exist in terms of function. Some high-end workstation computers serve a single user application, such as graphics or simulation, or a database application. These might have brand names such as Digital or Sun if they are running a UNIX operating system. They also might run Windows NT and look like any other PC or PC-compatible; or they might be a workstation or terminal connected to a network and referred to as a client (same as user), running routine applications such as word processing and spreadsheets.

Desktop Systems

Any computer that sits on a desktop is referred to as a desktop computer, whether it is a PC or a Mac. If it is networked to other computers, the computer is part of a desktop system. Desktop equipment also includes workstations or personal computer look-alikes in a graphics, computer-aided design (CAD), computer-aided manufacturing (CAM), or other high-end application. These might be made by Sun Microsystems, Hewlett Packard, Digital, Silicon Graphics, IBM, Dell, Gateway, or Compaq.

Laptop or Notebook Computers

Laptop, or *notebook,* refers to computers that can easily be carried around. These terms have given way to a newer term, *mobile computing,* which includes portables, laptops, palm computing devices, and personal digital assistants.

Laptops or notebook computers are highly functional for individuals on the go, such as executives or salespeople. They double as desktops because they have the capability of connecting to peripherals such as monitors, keyboards, CD-ROM drives, and printers. They also can connect to mainframes and other networked computers through communications ports, enabling telecommuters to keep in touch with the office and salespeople to demonstrate online services. Laptops or portables are typically more expensive than comparably equipped desktop PCs, but their advantages for the mobile professional or person who needs a virtual office usually make the extra cost worthwhile. Consider the following when buying a portable computer:

- *Size of the screen display.* Go for the largest available viewing area. Even an inch can make a big difference if you spend quite a bit of time at the machine or are doing demos for clients. After all, not every client's computer will be capable of running your applications on a PC. In fact, a recent survey shows that the largest installed operating system is still Windows 3.1. To sidestep problems with the client's equipment, bring your own.

■ *Battery life.* If you work frequently in places where electric power isn't available—such as on airplanes, buses, and trains—you'll appreciate batteries that have a life longer than that of a May fly. Batteries can last up to several hours, and many laptops have extra slots where you can add extra battery capacity. Some also have removable batteries that you can charge and bring along as extras.

■ *Storage capacity.* Hard drive sizes have increased to meet the needs of the new software applications. If you have the option of purchasing more hard drive capacity, it's a worthwhile option if you want to add after-market software or other applications that didn't come with the computer originally. The better purchase option is RAM because it increases your computer's capability of handling any industrial-strength graphics or presentation software you might add after the purchase.

■ *Navigation type.* Most portable keyboards incorporate a mouse-type device that enables you to navigate without tabbing and shifting. Often you can use attachable rollerballs (similar to a mouse) and pointers that are little nubs (not quite like a joystick) to move around on the screen.

■ *Docking station capability.* This worthwhile feature in a virtual office setup (that's an office where a desk might exist for any visiting employee who needs it at the time) enables you to hook up a laptop to a base station with a power supply, keyboard, and monitor. Multiple location setups have a network and network storage. When in the office, the user inserts the portable into the docking station, which functions with the ease of a desktop unit. When the user leaves, he or she simply takes the portables.

On a smaller scale, you can purchase a computer with a docking station configuration so that when you are at home base, you sit in front of a standard size monitor, with a regular power supply and other stationary peripherals such as a high-speed printer or scanner. When you leave the office, you simply pull the portable out of the docking station and your office, taking necessary files and portable computing power with you. This is an especially useful feature for people who travel regularly. If you have several associates in different locations, each can use a docking mechanism with a networked hard drive and then remove his or her laptop with any files needed for travel; use the home base for printing, e-mailing messages, faxing, and perhaps providing workgroup file access.

☎ **800 SERVICE AND SUPPORT NUMBERS FOR HARDWARE AND SOFTWARE MANUFACTURERS**

Acer	800-445-6495
Adobe Systems	800-833-6687
Apple Computer, Inc.	800-538-9696
AST Computer, Inc.	800-758-0278
Brother International	800-276-7746
Canon	800-423-2366
Casio	800-634-1895
Citizen America	800-477-4683
Claris Corporation	800-325-2747
Compaq	800-652-6672
Consumer Technology Northwest	800-356-3983
CTX	
Desktops	800-367-0533
Monitors	800-888-2120
Notebooks	800-285-1889
Corel	800-772-6735
Dell Computer Corporation	800-247-9362
Digital	
Computers	800-354-9000
Printers	800-365-0696
Epson America	800-922-8911
Gateway 2000	800-846-2000
Hewlett-Packard, Co.	800-243-9816
IBM	800-772-2227
Info Peripherals	800-777-3280
Inteva	800-480-4519
Intuit	800-816-8025
Iomega	800-697-8833

continues

800 SERVICE AND SUPPORT NUMBERS FOR HARDWARE AND SOFTWARE MANUFACTURERS *continued*

JASC	800-622-2793
KLH	800-347-1222
Konica	800-256-6422
Kyocera Electronics, Inc.	800-232-6797
Lanier Information Services	800-708-7088
Lexmark International, Inc.	800-891-0331
Logitech	800-231-7717
Microsoft	800-426-9400
NEC America	800-632-4636
Netscape	800-320-2099
Novell	800-451-5151
Okidata	800-654-3282
Packard Bell	800-244-0049
Panasonic	800-222-0584
PC Brand	800-255-5245
Peachtree Software	800-247-3224
Pionex	800-313-1995
Positive	800-452-6345
Premier	800-347-1222
Quark	800-788-7835
Sharp Electronics	800-237-4277
Sony	800-352-7669
Symantec	800-441-7234
Tektronix	800-835-6100
Texas Instruments	800-527-3500
Toshiba	800-334-3445
Visio Corporation	800-248-4746
Zenith Data Systems	800-533-0331

Personal Digital Assistants

Personal digital assistants (or PDAs) are computers that literally fit in the palm of your hand. Although limited in storage and applications capability, these machines are very convenient when traveling light and in situations when a simpler hand-held device is preferable. Some hand-held PCs run a scaled-down operating system called Window CE, which is a version of Windows 95 that includes many programs and applications. Other PDAs offer the capability of handwriting notes with a stylus right on the screen of the machine and later backing it up into a PC. With many hand-held computers, you can plug in desktop-size peripherals, such as keyboards or modems, and access the Internet, get your e-mail, or type long documents. Some enable you to download data, schedules, and documents directly from your desktop system using docking capabilities.

Some popular uses of PDAs include the following:

- Taking notes at an offsite meeting with a client when a laptop is unavailable or inconvenient to use.

- Jotting down memos and scheduling meetings or appointments on the spot with a device you can keep in your breast pocket. You can later update your scheduling on the PC or laptop.

- Replacing spiral notebooks and other memo pads. Instead of writing cramped handwritten notes that you have to type into the PC, you can jot down thoughts, digest a meeting on the spot, and then transfer the notes into a word processing document on your PC without rekeying by using a synchronizing device.

NETWORKS

Technology has brought the network up to the speed of light, at least figuratively. Formerly, networks of individuals, professionals, or companies used to communicate or get together via phone, association meetings, mail, and newsletters. In the office, documents used to be routed in hard copy. Now affinity groups, business partners, employees, stockholders, and even team members working on the same project can connect via computer. People in offices even at the most basic levels share applications, documents, and files.

TWO KINDS OF NETWORKS

Computer networks can be constructed in two basic ways: All the computers can be connected to a central host computer or server (a large computer containing data and shared programs); or all the computers can be hooked up to each other, enabling users to access certain files and data on other users' hard drives. In networking terminology, a user (called an "end user") works on a computer or workstation (also called a "client"). When the client works with the central host computer (the "server"), it creates a client-server relationship.

Networks communicate by using a network operating system (such as Novell NetWare, UNIX, Windows NT, or Apple Talk) and some form of communications medium. Each computer in the network is connected via a twisted cable—copper, fiber optic, or coaxial—and a network adapter card that is installed in each computer on the network. In a simple or local area network configuration (called a peer-to-peer network) in which all the computers exist in the same location, computers are linked directly via wires with no central server or host computer. Each computer has its own data, files, and storage. This creates a simple but effective—and relatively inexpensive—network on a small scale. In this configuration, each of the computers in the network can function as a server, and all members in the network can share or access their data files.

At the next level, all computers connect to a central server that manages the network. Each computer might or might not have hard disks with data files, but the network data is stored in a host computer. If the computer is just a workstation, it accesses its information, files, and data from a central computer and might have only floppy disk storage.

Either of these two types of networks, implemented in a single office or location, is called a local area network (LAN). Most LANs connect or share data using Ethernet, Token Ring, FDDI, or ATM technology.

Wide area networks (WANs) connect computers that might exist in a number of different locations, through a communications service provider such as a phone company, a satellite broadcaster, or a cable company. WANs can be used for hooking branch offices of a company together. Within each company office might be a LAN, and the LANs connect to the WAN to function as a single network. The Internet serves as a good example of a WAN in which a single or server computer connects via modem over the phone line to the Internet, which in turn connects to one of the networked computer databases anywhere in the world.

Advantages and Disadvantages of a LAN

Because a LAN is a multiuser computer system, administrators face pros and cons in deciding what kind of LAN is right for the office. Some LANs enable PCs to share software programs as well as hardware, such as printers and storage devices. What are the advantages and the disadvantages of these kinds of networks? What kind of questions do you need to ask before you decide which is right for you? Let's take a look at some of the advantages and disadvantages of both to help your organization make the right choice.

LAN Advantages

- *Shared software.* Some companies computerize their operations on a piecemeal basis, adding PCs and software as needed. Over time, this practice can lead to a lot of software proliferating in the organization, which might or might not be compatible with all users. From an internal viewpoint, this complicates technical support and also makes the installation process complicated for less-sophisticated users. The advantages of everyone using the same software are obvious, yet copying programs to share among separate users is illegal. A LAN solves that problem. The preferred or company-specified standard software for generalized applications (spreadsheets, word processing, presentations, and contact management) resides on the company server and easily can be downloaded for new or added users as needed. In workgroups where many people on different PCs must get into their copy of the same file to provide editing or other inputs, a LAN automatically keeps the file updated for all users.

- *Shared hardware.* One printer per PC might suit individuals but might not be cost-effective when printers sit idle for blocks of time. A LAN enables users to share printers and other peripherals.

- *Shared file storage.* By storing company files and workgroup documents on a communal server in a LAN setup, less need exists for upgrading the hard drives on each computer desktop. You can add large central storage devices for less cost per gigabyte of storage in a central server location than you can on each individual desktop.

- *Centralized backup.* If backing up on individual PCs occurs only occasionally, a LAN is ideal. Regularly accessed files are maintained on the network server and stored in a central location. If an individual PC goes down, the files still can be accessed by another computer; if your computer has a terminal crash and a new computer must be installed, the latest version of the files can be downloaded, along with the application software, right from the network server.

- *Support for flexible needs.* A LAN can be "hard-wired," with cables connecting each individual workstation to the central computer. Or, it can be wireless, with ranges of 5 miles and more possible. This provides excellent support for companies that have shifting staff need; that are changing to the fluidity of virtual offices; that use mobile sites; or that are subject to frequent flooding, hurricanes, and the like.

LAN Disadvantages

- *Cost.* The cost of installing a LAN can seem prohibitive and must be spread among the system's workstations. For maximum results, you must find the break-even point for your company: Determine how many workstations are needed before costs are lower than the combined costs of separate PCs. The number of printers on a LAN and how much they're shared is also a key to costs.

■ *Downtime.* Depending on your network configuration, PCs, or certain applications (such as e-mail or Internet access) can be unavailable when the LAN is down. Extra care in the selection of your network configuration and installation process can help reduce downtime. In any case, take certain precautions, such as duplicating certain emergency files as a matter of routine to a separate hard drive.

■ *Administration.* After you commit to a LAN, depending on the size, you might need a specific person to oversee the system. The duties of this administrator include providing new and ongoing training on LAN use,

---

CHOOSING A LAN SYSTEM

■ *Consider users first.* Talk to the people who will be on the network. What do they do on their current PCs? What would they like to do? What software do they use now? What specific applications are they running?

■ *Overestimate needs.* Most offices find that the actual use of their LAN is much greater than what they projected. If growth hasn't been built into the system, the LAN will quickly become obsolete. A professional guideline is to plan for 50 percent growth in LAN usage each year.

■ *Inventory hardware.* Take an inventory of all existing hardware to see how much of it can be incorporated into the new LAN.

■ *Piece it together.* Arranging the location of workstations and printers is like piecing together a jigsaw puzzle. Consider the personalities as you draw up floor plans and decide who will share equipment.

■ *Let vendors help.* LANs are more complex that PCs. Consequently, vendors offer more assistance in deciding whether a LAN makes sense and what equipment might be needed.

■ *Allow for training.* With any new technology-based system, you must build in time and cost for training key individuals. If no individual has been named as network administrator, you can look initially to the vendor for support and training. Although training is expensive in both time and money, you might see long-term returns.

adding and deleting users on the network, backing up data, maintaining security, and performing a host of computer housekeeping chores. With a small LAN of about twenty users, the duties likely will fall to a current employee who is computer-literate. If your company has some technical types on board, these people are perfect for the work. If not, the job could fall to you, which will even seem natural if you've been involved in selecting the system. A larger LAN needs a full-time employee to oversee its operations. Many companies make the mistake of buying the system without being willing to hire the needed administrator.

- *LAN security.* Security on a network starts at the very beginning. A well-designed system can without a doubt provide more security than that available from a PC. On the other hand, poorly designed security turns each separate workstation into a possible information leak.

NETWORK AND INTERNET COMMUNICATIONS

Computers on a network might be Macintosh, IBM PCs, or clones. To facilitate communication, computers need a common standard for communicating, as well as certain protocols or a universal set of rules about how to do certain things, from sending messages, to downloading files or programs. Computers on a LAN communicate with a protocol such as Ethernet. However, when computers from different networks work together to create or communicate on a WAN, they must communicate with a common protocol.

To connect to a WAN, computers usually communicate one-to-one over a phone line via a modem, which transfers digital information from the computer into analog information that can travel over the phone line. At the receiving end, the analog data is translated back into digital data that the receiving computer understands. Modems use communication software, containing additional rules such as file transfer protocols, which accommodate the transfer of files between two computers that are directly hooked together.

Internet Protocols

Computers connecting over the Internet use a universal protocol, called Transmission Control Protocol/Internet Protocol (TCP/IP). This is the standard for communication between computers and servers that was developed in the early days of the Internet. At that time, it was known as the ARPANET and fell under the control of the Department of Defense. TCP/IP enables computers and servers of all types (PCs or Macs) that use different forms of operating systems and hardware configurations to directly get in touch with one another. TCP, the transmission control protocol part of TCP/IP, enables computers to connect and exchange data, and ensures that the data is delivered in the order sent. The IP protocol contains the format of the data and the address or unique mailbox of the computer to which the data is to be sent.

TOPICS YOU CAN FIND ON THE INTERNET

You can find almost anything on the Internet, whether it be information on your favorite hobby or much-needed research for that business presentation. These are a few examples of what you can do on the Internet:

- *Hobbies and entertainment.* You can play online games, get movie reviews, be privy to hobbyist discussions, obtain travel information, and make travel arrangements.

- *Databases and research.* Virtually every important trade journal and reference publication is offered online. Access government, academic, and business information via online encyclopedias, magazines, textbooks, and newspapers.

- *News and finance.* Get up-to-the-minute news from the newswire services the newspapers use. Stay informed about local and international weather forecasts, stock quotations, brokerage services, company information, Dun & Bradstreet's profiles, Standard & Poor's profiles, and treasury fund rates.

After your computer connects to the Internet, it continues to communicate using TCP/IP. However, when it begins to load and run programs from certain parts of the Internet, such as the World Wide Web, it uses other computer and scripting languages to accomplish its goals.

The Internet is a large network in which your computer acts as a client. Through the Internet, you now can do just about everything, including watching the stock market ticker-tape, checking fast-breaking industry news, getting PC support services, conducting industrial research, making travel arrangements, getting detailed driving maps and directions, playing interactive games, finding medical advice, and much more.

To access information, your computer must use several client applications. Some applications, such as Telnet, Gopher, and FTP, help you transfer files and text data between other computers on the network. Two of the most well-known clients, Netscape Navigator and Internet Explorer, are browsers that give you access to the World Wide Web.

The Web is a graphical interface to the Internet. Using a markup language called HTML, anyone can post text, pictures, movies, or sound on the Web. To view these pages, you need the client, or browser.

One of several programming languages that have facilitated communications on the World Wide Web is Java, which is similar to the C++ language but easier to use. Java enables programmers to write applications that run on Web-capable browsers such as Netscape Navigator and Internet Explorer. The appeal of Java is that it is designed for writing programs that can safely be downloaded from the Internet and immediately run by the receiving computers without having to worry about the infection of a virus. Using a mini-Java application called an *applet,* programmers can create stand-alone applications such as spreadsheets, animation, or other functions that can be run on any computer.

Hypertext Markup Language (HTML) is the Web's programming language or source code used to create documents and forms on the Web. HTML displays information easily and has interactive forms capability. It explains to the browser how to display the various documents on the Web; documents created in HTML can support graphics, video, and audio. Javascript, the independent and open language developed by Netscape, interfaces well with HTML and enables Web authors to develop interactive sites rich with features.

Intranets

An intranet is a network based on Internet protocols (TCP/IP) that contains information internal to the organization. This information can be shared by members, employees, and others in such areas as operations, inventory, job postings, logistics, approved vendors, and more. Because this information is considered to be proprietary, access is restricted; the network is protected by a firewall or security screen to prevent unauthorized access. An intranet works like a company's own private Internet—it is a very inexpensive way for a company to connect its employees to needed information about the company. No customized software development is required, nor does a private network have to be developed. Intranets use the language of the Internet and can be read by anyone who has a browser and the proper authorization. The intranet uses the same programming languages and browsers that computers need to access the Internet.

Extranets

As with intranets, an extranet is a small, private Internet. This is a network that contains information about the organization that it then shares with certain people outside the company, such as vendors, customers, and other business partners. The extranet is a secure network that is protected by a firewall to prevent unauthorized access; registered users access it via a password. An extranet can have different levels of access built into it, and it often connects information contained on more than one intranet. For example, an extranet can permit vendors or suppliers to obtain inventory and shipping status (as FedEx and UPS have with their customer tracking systems), and it can enable investors and customers to access financial and corporate news information. Because extranets are relatively new, innovative uses for them are still developing. Extranets have great potential appeal to joint venture partners and project developers who can use extranets to hold virtual meetings.

Connecting to the Internet

Consumers and businesses have quickly taken to using the Internet. In fact, the popularity of the Internet is its own worst enemy in the short term because the network is nearly collapsing from its own weight. The main problem is traffic, or the number of people trying to access the Internet and the amount of information being requested or transferred at any given time at a single location.

SOME ONLINE SERVICE AND INTERNET SERVICE PROVIDERS

Online services: America Online, CompuServe, Dow Jones News/ Retrieval Service, and Genie

National ISPs: Microsoft News, MCI Worldcomm, AT&T Worldnet, NewsNet, Prodigy, Netcom, Spry, PSINET, IDT, and GTE Internet, to name a few

---

As a single user, you can connect to the Internet right from your own personal computer. (A good computer will have at least a Pentium processor, at least 32M of RAM and a run speed of more than 200MHz.) You need a browser (the piece of software that gets you to the online universe), a modem (what connects you over the phone line), a plain copper telephone line, and an Internet service provider (ISP), which provides your gateway to the Internet. Your modem should have a speed of at least 56Kbps, although many service providers still do not support that speed. If you are a business user who need to be online most of the time, you'll want a dedicated separate phone line to connect you to the Internet. With more than one employee, a single phone line can be a problem. If you are at a business site, you should consider how many people will seek access and how many times per day they will need to connect.

Connection Speed

With a standard connection to the Internet via a computer, modem, and phone line, your transmission speed is limited by the speed of your modem and the speed that your local or national service provider supports. In addition, you might be limited by the capacity of your particular phone line. Limitations such as old lines, faulty connections, and line leaks can seriously affect your connection speed. For example, I have a 56Kbps modem and a regular but dedicated copper phone line to connect to my national service provider. My download speeds, however, never exceed 33Kbps; most of the time, I connect at 26.4Kbps or 24Kbps. An optional connection line will get me in at 56Kbps, but this fee-based line costs around 10 cents per minute.

For a business, consider other options. One alternative is to connect several of your organization's computers to a network, and then connect the network to a faster T-1 line that gets you to the Internet at 1.5Mbps—or nearly 50 times faster than the 33Kbps mentioned previously. This is especially valuable if you download Web pages with graphics, which slow page-capture time considerably. Other alternatives range from cheap to expensive. A good ISP or local Net services firm can provide guidance in this area. Of course, if you plan to conduct commerce on the Net, you will need a computer and your own server online 24 hours a day. In that case, a high-speed connection to the Net is crucial for you and your customers. Here again, alternatives exist, such as leasing space on a server at your ISP or Web-hosting firm.

- *Integrated Services Digital Network (ISDN).* An ISDN line accommodates voice and data over a single line provided by local phone companies. It uses two bearer channels (B-channels) that enable data and voice to synchronously download and upload at rates up to 64Kbps, or a total data rate of 128Kbps—this is twice the speed of the fastest current v.90 standard modem. Connecting an ISDN line to a computer requires special equipment: an ISDN terminal adapter (sometimes called an ISDN modem) that plugs into the computer, and an NT-1 (or network terminator) that plugs into the ISDN line itself.

- *T-1.* T-1 is a direct cable connection from point to point over a copper wire line, with a total capability of 1.5Mbps (million bits per second). Ideal for entrepreneurs, Web sites, and companies with moderate-to-heavy Internet needs, the T-1 line offers the advantage of fast continual Internet access for a host of computers at an office. Each connection supports up to 24 channels of 64Kbps communication. Other advantages include supersonic file transfer (FTP) and downloads. Requirements include special hardware, setup costs, and monthly rates in the range of $1,000.

- *Digital subscriber line (DSL).* A cost-effective and speedy alternative to T-1, digital subscriber line technology is fairly new and somewhat unproved, but it is catching on rapidly because of its promise. The DSL provides ultrafast information pull from the Internet at 1.5Mbps and speedy 64Kbps transmission uploads to the Internet. This option is ideal for businesses in which the greatest need is to download or receive information instead of uploading or sending information over the Internet. Bell Atlantic recently launched a version of DSL called ASDL that works over copper lines and is considerably more affordable than T-1.

Connection Method

Depending on the size of your office, the number of employees, and how many e-mail accounts you'll need, your office will have a variety of options for Internet service. Although from home you can connect through an online service, for the office you should look at an Internet service provider. Some ISPs specialize in providing Internet services to businesses—your local phone company might be a good place to start. Ultimately, you'll want a cost-effective service provider to which your corporate LAN will connect directly. You'll probably want your own domain name for e-mail accounts, and maybe a Web site, too. Most full-service Internet access providers offer services that will get your domain, set up your individual e-mail accounts, and even design your Web page. Consider all these factors and more when you determine your company's Internet needs.

Online Services. Online services are commercial communications networks that grant subscribers access to their data. Online services include anything from Lexis-Nexis databases, to law libraries, to America Online—anything that charges you a fee to access just their data and network is an online service. To retrieve their information, you must access the provider, either through another Internet link or via a direct dial-up connection from your computer. Online services either charge flat monthly rates, charge by the hour, or charge by the document accessed.

ONLINE SERVICES

The following represent just a few of the online features that are available from the major ISPs. Make sure you check the availability of these features before you join.

- *Bulletin board systems (BBSs) (also called message boards).* With BBSs, you can retrieve messages and reply to other people's messages, get answers to technical questions, obtain driving and weather updates, get information on shareware (public-domain software), improve vendor responsiveness, and so on. BBSs also enable you to post a message and see a posted response from another user.

- *Chat rooms.* Chat rooms are real-time message boards. These are useful for online interviews and press conferences, as well as other collaborative events. They are also heavily featured for everything from fans gathering to discuss their favorite TV show to real-time news updates.

- *Instant messaging.* When you are online and want to know who else in your community of interest is online, you can sign on to the instant messaging board by using one of several versions of software that can be downloaded. You'll then be in real-time chat with them, no matter which ISP the other person uses.

- *Access to the other Internet services.* Getting to the Internet and to search engines or bulletin boards can be a snap because most online services provide basic Internet access.

CHOOSING AN ISP

This list of questions can help you decide on the right service provider:

- *Monthly charges.* Some ISPs provide unlimited service; others provide service for a flat fee for a certain number of hours, currently around 150 hours per month.

- *Local access numbers.* If you plan to spend a lot of time online, then you'll want a local access number to avoid long-distance charges.

- *Connection.* Find out if your service has a T-1 or a T-3 connection. Depending on how many customers they have, it could make a difference.

- *Backup connection.* Does the ISP provide an alternative connection through another carrier if its connection is down?

- *Number of subscribers per modem.* If too many users exist per modem connection, you will encounter a lot of busy signals during peak load time.

- *Web space.* Do you get free Web space of your own for setting up your own business or personal site?

- *Backups.* Does the provider back up the system regularly?

- *E-mail auto responders.* Does the ISP provide a way to automatically respond to inquirers?

- *Rating.* Regularly published reliability ratings exist; ask for this number.

- *High bandwidth connection options.* Can you connect directly to their network?

Internet service providers (ISPs). The Internet is simply a huge global network that connects millions of computers, most of which host a database of specific information. To get a connection to the Internet, you need an Internet service provider. Both local and national service providers exist. Although both provide comparable service, the local provider can be a good choice for a home office business or sole proprietor because it is usually available if you run into trouble. (On the other hand, most national service providers provide 24-hour technical support.) To find a good local provider, the best bet is to ask colleagues and area users for a reference. Among the national providers, the universe is expanding rapidly as the number of users expands. You might want to investigate an ISP that offers free server space for Web pages or an ISP connected with your long-distance service for combined billing. Most ISPs bill a flat monthly rate for unlimited usage.

OPERATING SYSTEMS

The operating system (OS) is the underlying program that runs the computer and all its applications. This is the first program that loads when the computer is turned on, and it tells the computer what to do in language and instructions that the machine understands. Operating systems have names that often depend on the type of computer or when the system was released. When you select an application to run on your computer (such as a word processing or spreadsheet program), you must make sure it runs on the operating system you have.

The original operating system for PCs was called DOS, which stands for disk operating system. DOS had limitations, however, because it accommodated only one program at a time and required a lot of commands to properly instruct the computer. DOS was followed by Microsoft's Windows program, which mimicked the Macintosh graphics-based operating system developed by Apple Computer. As a shell program with DOS running in the background, the first Windows program was not a true operating system; it was an improvement that allowed more than one program to run at a time. Windows 95 and Windows 98 are true operating systems that represent major improvements over each preceding system.

These newer OSs also require a lot more computer horsepower to run applications and multiple software programs. Each new Windows version comes closer to making computer instruction invisible to the user. All that's required is to click on a broad-based menu of icons to run software programs for the Windows platform. All programs run inside their own window on the computer. Microsoft worked with the developers of most programs for Windows, so they operate pretty much the same way. For example, instructions such as printing setups; printing, copying, and merging; filing; and saving are very similar and often use the same keystrokes.

As with DOS, Windows was meant for a single computer user. Other types of operating systems work better for some types of offices. Offices with many networked computers, workgroups, and other networked multiuser environments run Windows NT and UNIX. Other PC operating systems include OS/2, SCO, Xenix, and AIX. Macintosh computers from Apple run System 7 or 8 and A/UX (Apple's UNIX-based system). Digital's VAX computers (now part of Compaq Computer) use VMS and ULTRIX (UNIX). IBM mainframes use MVS VM and VSE.

Common Operating Systems

System	Description
DOS and Windows 3.*x*	The most popular operating systems in business today
Windows 95	Popular 16-bit operating system that succeeded Windows 3.*x*, adding a graphical user interface (GUI) like the Apple OSs
Windows 98	The current version and last 16-bit Windows OS from Microsoft
System 7	Apple's Macintosh operating system
Mac OS	System 8*x* for the Macintosh
AIX	IBM variant of UNIX for workstations
OS/2	IBM's multitasking operating systems with a GUI that runs DOS, OS/2, and Windows applications
Windows NT.*x*	A 32-bit system from Microsoft that runs DOS and Windows applications
BeOS	Multitasking operating system for the Power Mac
Solaris	Sunsoft variant of UNIX for PCs, the Power PC, and SPARC computers
VMS	Digital's multitasking, multiuser virtual memory operating system
Ultrix	Digital's variant of the UNIX OS for the VAX and PDP-11 series
Windows CE	A limited-application Windows operating system from Microsoft that runs hand-held PCs such as the Palm Pilot

SOFTWARE APPLICATIONS

Computer software falls into two major categories: system software and software applications. System software includes the control programs for the operating system, the communications system, and database management. Applications software packages process data in specific ways, such as word processing, spreadsheets, inventory, and packages available for business in several categories. The following table contains just a few relevant categories and subcategories (courtesy of Beyond.com, www.beyond.com, an Internet software superstore):

Common Types of Software

Category	Application
Business	Presentation graphics
	Legal
	Database/statistics
	Project/time management
	Finance
	General business
	Writing/spreadsheet tools
Communications	E-mail
	Communication
	Fax and document imaging
	Palm Pilot accessories
	Macintosh software
	Windows software—Palm Pilot/Win CE
Graphics	Clip art and fonts
	CAD
	Desktop publishing
	Graphics and presentations
	Multimedia
	Adobe typefaces
Utilities	Antivirus
	Backup and security
	File conversion and transfer
	Operating systems
Reference	Legal
	Encyclopedia
	Dictionary and thesaurus
	Atlas and mapping
	Directories
	Medical
	Career
	Foreign language

WORD PROCESSING SOFTWARE

In the early days of computers, a major distinction arose among people who were word processing experts, people who created graphics, and people who designed page layout. With the new software currently on the market, those lines are becoming blurred. Today, virtually anyone who can type, write clearly, and develop an eye for design can produce all kinds of documents. In the past, you had to use several pieces of software to design a document that would require a layout function: one for word processing and one for desktop publishing. Today, most word processing software applications offer more robust options for users who want to do a little more.

Most of the software packages on the market have the basic functions: text editing tools, cut and paste tools, print preview capability, search and replace tools, file management capability, a spell checker, a thesaurus, an electronic clipboard, font manipulation tools, and so on. The following are some of the special features that you should look for in word processing and/or desktop publishing (WP/DTP) software, if a combination is needed. Not all positions in offices require desktop publishing skills, so analyze the situation realistically. Desktop publishing software can be expensive and time-consuming to learn and use.

- *Styles.* Can the software apply multiple formats to words, phrases, headers, footers, paragraphs, and documents? For example, if you are preparing a newsletter and need assorted fonts, is there an option for creating a style sheet?

- *Columnization.* Does the software set up a page for multiple columns that can automatically wrap?

- *Importing graphics.* Can graphics be created in another source—chart, paint or draw program, clip art, or spreadsheet—and be imported? Once imported, is the image static, or can it be adjusted for size and shape?

- *Boxes and lines.* Can boxes and horizontal and vertical lines be created without using a line draw feature? Can the inside of a box be shaded to emphasize the text?

- *Leading and kerning. Leading* adjusts the spacing between lines and paragraphs; *kerning* adjusts the spacing between characters. Can leading and kerning be adjusted to make the page more readable?

- *Headers and footers.* A *header* is information repeated at the top of several or all pages; and a *footer* is information repeated at the bottom of several or all pages. Does the software handle headers and footers with the versatility of odd and even pages?

- *Large document handling.* Can the software separate files for sections of a large document, keep track of their order, and paginate for internal numbering (1-1, 1-2, 2-1, 2-2)?

- *Index and table of contents generation.* Can the software generate an index and/or table of contents electronically? Does it perform automatic updates when changes are made to the document?

- *WYSIWYG (what you see is what you get).* Does the software display on the screen what the printed page will look like?

Electronic Clip Art

Electronic clip art is a variety of ready-made graphics that can be used to improve the appearance of presentations, reports, newsletters, and so on. It can be electronically cut and pasted into documents, and it can be imported into most WP/DTP software. Electronic clip art is available for a wide variety of businesses and industries, educational institutions, and personal uses.

BASIC SOFTWARE NEEDS ASSESSMENT QUESTIONS

1. What are the required tasks?

2. What are the current software applications in use?

3. Do the current applications perform the required tasks adequately?

4. What software applications are needed to perform required tasks that are not currently being addressed?

5. How often will the software be used?

6. Who will be using the software?

7. What is the users' level of computer expertise?

8. What kind of training programs are currently in place?

9. What is the budget for new training programs?

10. What types of documents are currently produced?

11. What types of documents will a new software application produce?

12. Will these new documents require a change in printers?

13. What type of computer hardware is currently in use?

14. What is the budget if different hardware is needed?

15. What is the current operating system?

16. What is the budget if a different operating system is needed?

SPREADSHEET SOFTWARE

The development of the electronic spreadsheet was the fuel that sent PC sales skyrocketing in the early years. Spreadsheets are arranged in a grid, with columns (vertical) and rows (horizontal). The intersection of a column and a row is called a *cell*. Cells can be assigned a number or a formula, or can be identified in a special way. Text, mathematical formulas, and values are entered in the cells. The beauty of the spreadsheet is that if a value or formula is changed, everything affected by the change can be automatically recalculated. The format can be saved so that only new information need be entered. A year-to-date report, for example, requires simply calling up the last report and adding the current month's figures. The spreadsheet recalculates the year-to-date numbers automatically.

Add-on packages have been developed to give additional functions to spreadsheet information. For example, a word processing add-on that links a table to a spreadsheet updates the information in the document to reflect the changes made in the spreadsheet. Graphic add-ons enable the user to display the spreadsheet information by using a variety of graphs. The benefit is that the user does not have to exit the spreadsheet to utilize the add-on. The following is an example of an electronic spreadsheet:

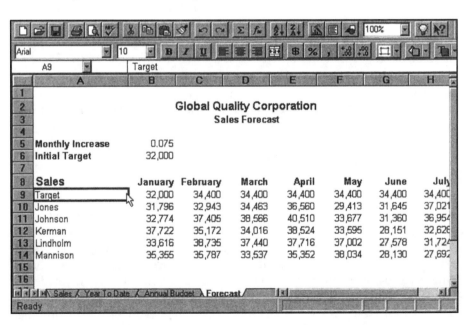

Sample Electronic Spreadsheet

DATABASE MANAGEMENT (DBM)

Database management software (DBMS) enters, organizes, stores, and retrieves data. These programs organize data in a manner similar to a filing cabinet. Data first is organized into files relating to a particular subject, such as customer lists, accounts receivable, employees, and inventory. Within the files are individual records, which can be compared to the folders in the file cabinet. Specific information in each record is broken down and contained in fields. For example, an employee record might have fields such as Last Name, First Name, Date of Birth, Address, Department, Date of Hire, and Position.

DBM software directs the computer to search the files and assemble specific information from the records into a report form that can be used to make informed decisions. Knowing what type of information will be needed aids the structure of the database so that retrieval is efficient.

Databases come in all shapes and sizes. For example, a database for contact names and addresses is a familiar one in offices. Customer names, addresses, phone numbers, and particles purchased, for example, all can be documented in a database. You can access that database to do a mailing, contact the customers, get a history of their purchases, or find out how many socks were sold on any given day. The most common example of a database is a spreadsheet application such as Microsoft Excel or Lotus 1-2-3. The database holds the data in a predefined format (dollar, general, or scientific), organized the way you defined it—by the rows (type of expense) and columns (date). The data can be stored either as inputted or as derived from a calculation. To access the information, start the application package (Excel) and open a spreadsheet (database).

A step up from a spreadsheet, you can create a database of items and information about items and then link them together.

Types of Databases

Two types of databases exist: flat file and relational. In a flat file database, each record is contained in a single table. You can page through each table to find data, but the individual tables have no relational capability with any other table. In a relational database, records are maintained in a collection of tables, each containing information about one subject. However, the tables are related so that you can use or collect information from more than one table at a time. Access is the most common example. In Microsoft Access, you define the items in which you are interested (Customer and Past Orders, for instance) and what you want to know about the items of interest (Customer: Customer Address, Customer Telephone; Past Orders: What was ordered, quality, when). Your access mechanism (MS Access) enables you to ask questions that would link the items of interest (which customers who live in New York City ordered more than one regular pizza in June).

Access and most other Windows-based databases are relational, but some offices still run other UNIX or DOS flat-file databases that are not relational.

Again, databases come in all different sizes. Many technologies exist today to assist you in obtaining answers to questions. One of the primary technology areas on everyone's mind is the Internet. Though extremely important, this offers a communication mechanism to information. The Internet provides access to more information for the corporation and provides a communication facility to reach a wider audience.

The key words in the above paragraph are *access* and *communication of information*. The Internet is *not* the information nor the data that provides information. It is *not* the storage of data. It is *not* the completeness or consistency of data. To be complete, consistent, and accessible in a timely manner, data must be kept in a well-designed database.

This is the purpose of a database: to store clear, concise, and consistent data in a format that is easily and quickly accessible. A database is the automated filing cabinet of all data. It comes or can be built in all shapes and sizes.

Today's businesses capture crucial information in databases, such as customer lists, product inventory, payroll schedules, employee history, sales by territory, and so forth. Many corporations separate operational data from informational data: Operational data is data gathered from business transaction-oriented information systems. Examples are order-entry type systems, online banking systems, or billing systems.

PRESENTATION SOFTWARE

Increasingly, sales, marketing, and communications employees (as well as company executives) are conducting their own presentations in a professional manner by using easy-to-learn, easy-to-use software. Although many presentation programs are available, you probably have the software bundled with the most popular office suite of software products out there: That's PowerPoint. With PowerPoint, you have the option of creating the following:

- A slide presentation for overheads

- An electronic presentation from your computer or laptop

- Audience handouts

- Speaker notes that the presenter can use at the lectern

PowerPoint is easy to use, and with a feature called the AutoContent Wizard, you can get step-by-step guidance in creating any number of reports or presentation formats, such as the following:

- Progress reports

- Financial overviews

- Strategy recommendations
- Business plans
- Marketing plans
- Status reports

The AutoContent Wizard has templates for the structure and organization of the material, as well as several different styles of presentation graphics. In short, even the most timid of new software users will want to try this easy-to use program.

For example, the Business Plan Wizard tiles the outline for the following slides or presentation windows:

- Mission Statement
- The Management Team
- Market Summary
- Opportunities
- Business Concept
- Competition
- Goals and Objectives
- Financial Plans
- Resource Requirements
- Risks & Rewards
- Key Issues

By following this template, all you need to do is state the information in the areas provided—and voila! You have a complete and professional looking business plan. This is just one of PowerPoint's more than 50 prebuilt content templates that give you a head start on creating top-notch presentations.

Corel Presentations 8, which is packaged with its WordPerfect suite, also comes with predesigned slide shows that you can customize, as well as tools to help you create and move through the presentation. These programs make it easier than ever for even the first-time user to develop quality presentations.

DESKTOP PUBLISHING

Desktop publishing (DTP) systems are becoming extremely popular as prices come down, and software programs come with an increasing number of user-friendly features. DTP eliminates many time-consuming steps in creating

TIPS FOR BUYING THE RIGHT SOFTWARE

- Start your search at least 90 days before you need the software.

- Conduct a needs assessment.

- Identify the tasks the software must perform.

- Make a list of the available software packages that meet your needs.

- Determine the features and benefits that differentiate one package from another.

- Create a grid to help compare the packages.

- Consult current users of the different packages for references.

- Determine how easy the packages' features will be to learn.

- Research the packages' general availability.

- Determine which packages will be compatible with hardware already in use.

- Determine which packages will be compatible with other software already in use.

- Determine the kind of training available.

- Verify that support is available after the sale.

- Make sure that support is provided by a reputable and well-established company.

- Make sure a toll-free number is available for technical support.

- Determine whether you can join a user group.

- Make sure you understand what kind of maintenance, if any, will be required.

- Determine whether the software package is easily upgradable.

- Determine whether the software company will provide upgrades for free or at a discount.

- Identify which add-on packages, if any, are available for the software.

- Request a demonstration or trial use.

camera-ready art. The layout occurs directly on the computer screen, with changes in type size and style made with a click of the mouse or a key. Headlines, graphics, and text can be moved easily. When you're finally satisfied with the result of your creative efforts, your computer printer produces camera-ready art for the printer. No more paste-ups—just neat, clean, simple, and fast. You also can save on typesetting and printing costs through desktop publishing.

You can learn to do many tasks in-house with a little DTP experience and the easy-to-learn software programs currently available:

- Newsletters
- Stationery
- Calendars
- Banners
- Awards
- Flyers
- Holiday greeting cards
- Awards
- Brochures
- Business cards
- Ads
- Marketing brochures
- Mailers
- Catalogs

Another convenient feature in DTP is the capability of creating a file on disk that is ready for the printer. This feature tells the printer what it needs to know to print without any further design specifications from you. With DTP becoming the next logical step up from word processing—and given the potentially significant savings to be realized from the output—the only remaining question becomes whether to do it. Here are some things to ponder before pushing forward:

- *Planning ahead.* How much time is there to devote to the effort? Getting the same kind of results as a professional printer and typesetter doesn't happen quickly (or maybe ever). If time is valuable and limited, desktop publishing might not be a bargain in the short term.

- *Equipment needs.* Although feature-rich programs make DTP appealing, they also require a lot of memory and fast processors to work well. This could mean upgrading to a faster processor and a more expensive laser printer to get the quality output desired. The laser also might not have a sufficient selection of typeface fonts to meet your needs.

- *Proficiency.* Even if you are a successful do-it-yourselfer, very few people can get professional results from DTP if it's a "sometime" thing. Professionals get the most professional results. Although acceptable and attractive documents can be obtained, don't expect to outproduce a graphic artist.

- *Learning curves.* DTP software can be very friendly, with all kinds of help screens and pull-down menus. However, there is no substitute for formal training. You almost certainly will invest a significant amount of money in new equipment. It's a good idea to back up that investment with the kind of basic training that will help get you up to speed in a hurry. Look for formalized classes in your area, particularly those given by national training centers and sometimes local colleges. This training certainly won't turn a novice into a DTP professional overnight, but at least it might keep you from the maddening tinkering that chews up hours of precious time. If you want to be able to keep working at the business full-time while learning, search for evening training classes.

TIP: Don't take training classes before you have your own equipment to work with. DTP is a hands-on experience; if you take classes, you need to use the newfound skills you've gained as quickly as possible—or risk losing them.

COMMUNICATIONS SOFTWARE

Communications packages enable PCs to "talk" to each other. Such software requires a modem and a connection to telephone lines. The communications software handles logging on and off the communications network, dialing, saving messages, and sending or receiving information from a central computer.

E-mail

E-mail is becoming a necessity for many of today's businesses. Although the adoption rate has been slower in some professions than others, executives and office professionals alike are integrating e-mail into their work life. When you set up your system or log on in the morning to your network, you access your e-mail account, which probably has a password to safeguard your privacy.

After you log on to your e-mail application, you can compose, send, receive, and reply to messages. Depending on the application, you can file, archive, automatically reply to, and sort your messages. The application you use depends on your network because the same application will be deployed for every user.

Fax Software

You can take advantage of creating and sending a fax without leaving the desk if you have a fax program on your computer. Daily faxing in quantity costs a lot of money over the phone lines, especially at peak hourly rates (the phone companies have carefully calculated peak hours to take advantage of this business activity). With fax software comes store and forward options that enable you to send during off-peak hours—and save money, too.

If you do not have fax software, it's inexpensive and easy to install in Windows or Mac machines. You need a modem on your machine with fax capability, however. If you have no modem, the simple solution is to purchase one with fax and modem capability. The software will come bundled with the product. The third option is to use a fax-forwarding service that operates off your e-mail by way of your Internet service provider: You create a fax document in your e-mail program, add the appropriate names to the fax header, and then e-mail the whole thing to your ISP, where it is routed to all the appropriate addresses at Internet calling rates.

Electronic Data Interchange (EDI)

Electronic data exchange (EDI), which is a worldwide movement, is the computer-to-computer exchange of business information. EDI is rapidly changing the way companies do business because any company that sells goods and/or services can benefit from EDI. A company can send purchase orders, invoices, confirmations, shipping papers, inquiries, financial reports, and so on directly from its computer to the computer of the trading partner. The information is keyed in a standardized, structured format. The information must be keyed in only once and then can be processed for all related transactions. The following are just some of the industries using EDI: manufacturers, government offices, health care agencies, grocery retailers, transportation branches, publishing companies, and retail businesses.

The American National Standards Institute (ANSI) is the recognized coordinator for national and international standards information. For detailed information about EDI standards, contact the Publications Department, Data Interchange Standards Association, Inc., 1800 Diagonal Road, Suite 355, Alexandria, VA 22314-2852; 703-548-7005.

OTHER APPLICATIONS

Although the following list of applications barely begins to skim the surface, it will give you an idea of the variety of software that is on the market.

Project planning. Project planning is essential for the success of an office professional. Look for software that helps with scheduling calendars, planning projects, writing reports, and preparing Gantt and PERT charts.

Employee handbooks. If you must create an office or employee handbook, find a software application that can help. Such software includes information on how to find good employees, employment application forms, interview questions, a new employee orientation guide, performance evaluations, and so on.

Bookkeeping and accounting. Available programs range from entry-level bookkeeping to advanced accounting "what-if" scenarios, cash control, credit card tracking, job costing, a general ledger, accounts receivable and payable, payroll, inventory control, invoicing, income tax preparation, and much more. Packages are available for companies of all sizes, from those with one employee to those with hundreds.

Money management. Some programs help take control of finances. Use these programs to set budgets, write checks, track investments and expenses, collect financial data, set and modify financial goals, judge whether investments are performing as they should, learn how loans are front-loaded with interest, calculate interest rates, and much more.

Starting a business. For those entrepreneurs who want to start their own businesses, software can lead you to sources for business loans, grants, venture capital, and government contracts.

Maps. Get instant route planning and maps of major national and international cities.

BASIC GUIDELINES FOR SELECTING SOFTWARE

Buying computer software is like buying a plane ticket: Purchase on impulse or at the full retail rate, and you are wasting possibly hundreds of dollars per unit. On the other hand, if you're prepared to do some homework, planning, and comparison shopping, you can find real bargains. If you're buying for other employees besides yourself, the company savings can add up fast.

To begin saving money on software, you need to know your options in upgrades, software bundles, and integrated packages.

UNDERSTANDING UPGRADES

Software manufacturers realize that it's easier to sell their new products to a user already committed to its old products. Because of this, upgrades now account for an estimated one in every six software units sold. Upgrades offer registered computer users a great opportunity to save money.

Software vendors offer two kinds of upgrade pricing plans: a standard or traditional upgrade, and a competitive upgrade. In a standard upgrade purchase, you pay a reduced price for the latest edition of a software product because you already own an older version of the same product. Most software upgrades are mailed directly to registered users by the manufacturers (and it is a good reason for returning those registration cards to the manufacturers). When you receive vendor upgrade notifications, compare the upgrade price offered directly from the manufacturer to other special offers from software resellers. Sometimes, high-volume resellers can beat the vendor's price.

Competitive upgrades are designed to lure you away from one product to a similar product by a competing vendor. Competitive upgrade offers might arrive in the mail, and also can be found on specially marked software boxes on reseller shelves and in the pages of mail-order catalogs and PC magazines. To take advantage of a competitive upgrade, you usually must provide the original title page from the manual for the software you currently are using as proof of ownership.

Besides the new versions of software that are changing to incorporate more bells and whistles, existing software is subject to frequent minor revisions. Some of these changes come in response to consumer demand; others are a result of companies finding and fixing little bugs that the original developers didn't notice before the software was released. These are usually fixed with patches.

Next are device drivers, the program routines that enable the operating system to communicate with the device in question to get it to perform requested functions such as printing or displaying a graphic onscreen. Manufacturers release new drivers in response to complaints that the original drivers didn't work that well. Many troubles that users have with new software can be traced back to inadequate drivers. Although patches are nice-to-have fixes, they aren't necessary. Device drivers are often a necessity for users who want to use their hardware with the latest software, however.

Most popular software can be updated for new patches and device drivers via the World Wide Web, including the following:

- Windows 95 (www.microsoft.com/windows95/info/updates.htm)

- Windows 98 (www.microsoft.com/windows98/info/updates.htm)

- Microsoft Internet Explorer (www.microsoft.com/ie4)

- Netscape Navigator (www.netscape.com)

- Lotus (www.lotus.com)

- Corel (www.corel.com)

- Microsoft Office (www.microsoft.com/office)

- Quicken (www.intuit.com/support/updates)

If it sounds like a time-consuming hassle to update software, it certainly can be. A couple of software packages have taken the mystery out of updating your favorite programs by searching the Internet for the updates and automatically downloading them: Cybermedia's Oil Change and Symantec's Norton Live Update are two of these.

Watch for the availability of updates for your software because no matter how carefully designed the new software bundles are (and even if you are getting one of the newest releases out there at the time you read this book), responsible software companies fix user-discovered glitches as they are reported. You might even discover a fix for a problem you think you have discovered. For example, when Office 97 first shipped, the new versions of Word and Excel that were included could not read files saved in earlier versions. As soon as Microsoft discovered the problem, the company posted a downloadable patch or fix for the problem.

SOFTWARE BUNDLES

Software bundling is a marketing tactic: A manufacturer groups several of its own products into a unit or *bundle,* usually a group of popular software programs that perform functions necessary for most office and home users. The price on the bundles is reduced so that it is significantly less than if each product were purchased separately. Manufacturers' bundles are usually made up of high-end, expensive products that offer industrial-strength features. You'll also find bundles assembled by major resellers and mail-order outfits that combine products from assorted vendors. The resellers can purchase programs directly from the manufacturers at a discount because of their volume. These programs are packaged with rebates, coupons, or smaller inexpensive products to make an attractively priced group.

In choosing any bundle, evaluate each program individually. Make sure that you actually need each one of them. If not, add up the cost of the ones you really will use and compare this to the bundle price. Bundles are often a good deal for users or small businesses that are starting from scratch with new computers, or for anyone moving all at once to a new operating environment, such as from Windows 3.*x* to Windows 95 or 98. Less can be more if you don't

PURCHASING APPLICATIONS

Purchasing the right applications program can be easy if you follow a few simple steps:

■ *Determine how involved your business needs are.* Will you be writing vanilla letters, interoffice memos, fax transmittals, and routine office correspondence; or creating reports, graphics, and slick presentations?

■ *Decide what features you want to have.* Do you like to create from scratch, and are you very experienced at building fancy documents? Do you like applying factory features? Simple test: Are you a point-and-shoot photographer, or do you like to go to manual programming? If point-and-shoot is your response, one of the full-featured professional office suites will satisfy most of your needs.

■ *Check PC magazines.* Publications such as *PC World* and *PC Magazine* print reviews of the latest and best-selling programs in the category you seek.

■ *Look for references.* Ask fellow users or colleagues about their likes and dislikes about various programs.

The software recommendations in the table on pages 214-215 were compiled from a general listing of the best of the 1997 software. This list appeared in the January 1998 issue of *PC Magazine,* published by Ziff-Davis and is available online at www.zdnet.com/pcmag/special/bestof97/software.htm.

really need an industrial-strength product. Often, a single, simpler product that combines several functions is a better solution.

Integrated packages, or suites, often combine several functions and have improved greatly (they frequently appear on the top-ten software sales lists). Generally, suites include a word processor, a spreadsheet, and a database application. Software developers trim some of the features of their flagship product for the "lite" version. For example, the word processor might not handle snake or newspaper-style columns, or the spreadsheet might contain 70 built-in mathematical functions instead of 750. Despite the reduction in features, the programs are streamlined to work well together. As a result, incorporating a chart into a document (for example, an Excel spreadsheet into a Word document) takes a couple of keystrokes instead of 20 and involves no translation at all. Look for bargains by comparison shopping at local computer supply stores, national chains, and mail-order catalogs. Also consider shopping direct from your office through companies such as Beyond.com.

No discussion of software bundles would be complete without mentioning Microsoft Office. This package has an installed base of more than 22 million licensed users and can be found at the sites of more than 90 percent of Fortune 500 companies. A new version (Microsoft Office 2000) currently is planned for 1999.

Office 2000 probably will come in more versions, but the flavors listed here show how Microsoft bundles different applications to target different segments of the market.

Office 97 comes in three versions:

- *Office 97 Regular Edition.* All Office bundles include Word 97, Excel 97, and Outlook 97. The standard edition of the bundle adds PowerPoint 97. This edition is perfectly adequate for most home users and small offices.

- *Office 97 Professional Edition.* In addition to the standard package, the professional edition adds Access 97 (a database program), PowerPoint presentation software, Binder 97 document-management software, and Bookshelf Basics (a reference program). This is a good package for most professional and larger offices.

- *Office 97 Small Business Edition.* This package has the standard three programs as well as Publisher 97, Financial Manager 97, and AutoMap Streets Plus. This o.ne is a good choice for business people on the go who typically work with laptops. If you purchase a PC today, it most likely comes with Microsoft's Office suite as well as its operating system. Your choice of versions depends upon your planned use. One universal feature of all Office bundles is that they are designed to create Web pages from Word and Excel documents. This is done by saving the document or worksheet in HTML format.

Although Office was designed to offer a broad package for a large constituency of users, at times you might want to choose a version without some features, and to get an industrial-strength, dedicated program that has options such as desktop publishing (such as Adobe PageMaker, if you are a professional publisher) or Web page design (such as Microsoft Front Page, if you plan to run a commercial business that generates a lot of activity or visits).

Software Recommendations

Category	Product	Comments
Application suite	Microsoft Office 97 Redmond, Washington Microsoft Corp. 800-426-9400 www.microsoft.com	Available in a standard edition including Word, Excel, and PowerPoint. A Professional Edition adds Access (a database program), Outlook (a new information manager and e-mail client), an animated Office Assistant, and new Internet tools.
Graphics: Professional Desktop Publishing	Adobe Pagemaker 6.5 Adobe Systems Inc. San Jose, California 800-843-7263 www.adobe.com	Offers nearly all the features that print designers require, combined with new, innovative Web-publishing tools.
Graphics: Personal Desktop Publishing	Microsoft Publisher 97	Fit for the novice desktop publisher, this program is capable of designing projects for both print and the Web.
Graphics: Professional Image Editing	Corel Photo-Pain 7 Plus Corel Corp. Ottowa, Ontario 800-772-6735 www.corel.com	A rival of Adobe Photoshop. Contains new editing tools: object-editing modes, transparency tools, and lens objects that allow preview of color and tonal adjustments without affecting the image. Can export client- or server-side maps.
Graphics: Personal Image Editing	Microsoft Picture It! 2.0	Powerful and easy-to-use image editor for the consumer market. Enables novices to work with images easily.

Category	Product	Comments
Graphics: Illustration	Macromedia FreeHand 7 Macromedia Inc. San Francisco, California 800-288-4797 www.macromedia.com	Illustration package for both artists and Webmasters. Has WYSIWYG features and Web format support.
Video Editing: Professional Video Editing	Adobe Premiere 4.2	The pioneer tool of choice for desktop video editing.
Video Editing: Personal Video Editing	MGI Video Wave. MGI Software Corp. Richmond Hill, Ontario 888-644-7638 www.mgisoft.com	Makes video editing understandable for beginners.
Business Diagramming	Visio Professional 5.0 Visio Corp. Seattle, Washington 800-246-4746 www.visio.com	Visio pioneered business graphics programs, enabling those who can't draw a straight line to create professional-looking charts.
Personal Finance	Quicken Deluxe 6.0 Intuit Inc. Mountain View, California 800-446-8848 www.quicken.com	A popular personal finance program with many new features.
Applications Development	Microsoft Visual Basic 5.0	The clear choice for powerful, yet easy-to-use programming development. Available in three versions: Professional, a high-end Enterprise, and a low-end Learners Edition.

FOR MORE INFORMATION

If you can't find what you need from the phone numbers and Web sites listed in this chapter, you may need to expand your search.

■ For more information and definitions of computer terminology, see *Webster's New World Dictionary of Computer Terms* from Que or check with your local bookstore in the computer or reference section.

■ For more information on the parts of computers and how they work, see *How Computers Work* by Ron White, published by Que. Its detailed full-color drawings explain the intricate details of computers and their peripherals allowing you to select what's best for you.

■ For more information on the Internet, intranets and how they work, see *How the Internet Works,* published by Que. It contains color illustrations showing how e-mail, the Web, and other aspects of the Internet work.

■ For more information on purchasing computer equipment, the Internet is the best place to start. See the Web sites in the chapter and ask lots of questions.

6

OFFICE ENVIRONMENTS AND WORKSTATIONS

◆

■ **Selecting and Optimizing Workspace**

    Using a Floor Plan

    Office Lighting

    Office Furniture

    Computers in the Office

■ **Workstations in the Office**

    Components of Workstations

    Workstation Adjustment Ergonomics

    Organization of the Workstation

■ **Office Safety, Health, and Security**

    Office Health and Safety

    Disaster Planning

    Security

    Office Maintenance

    Policies and Procedures Manuals

■ **Moving Without Headaches**

■ **For More Information**

Nothing affects an office as much as its environment. The image of the office, its productivity, and the contentment of its employees and clients are all directly affected by the design of the office. An office must be functional, aesthetic, and comfortable while still remaining efficient and cost-effective. This is a lot to juggle, but decisions made regarding the office environment have ramifications that will determine even the success or failure of the business. Therefore, it is imperative to ensure that any decision made regarding furniture, equipment, and standards is the right one.

SELECTING AND OPTIMIZING WORKSPACE

The optimal workspace varies from office to office. However, several factors remain constant when determining what is best suited for your business. The optimal workspace will be one that lends itself to the needs of your office, that contributes to efficiency, and that promotes employee contentment. The optimal workspace also will be determined by the constraints of the building and what is cost-effective. Pre-planning is essential to accomplishing these goals—the more time spent planning before implementing, the greater your chances of reducing the probability of error afterward.

USING A FLOOR PLAN

The most popular method by which to decide the layout of the office is certainly trial and error. This is unfortunate, however, because a significant amount of time and expense is dedicated to the error portion of the equation. With a small amount of effort and foresight, office workspace can be planned to be efficient and cost-effective.

A thoroughly developed floor plan represents the first, biggest, and most important step in workspace planning. To start, obtain documentation of the available space; the building manager generally can provide a copy of the design or architectural plans of the building. If this is not available, simply measure the space and transfer the measurements to grid paper. Each grid should represent a set distance, such as one box representing one foot. Include the measurements of any obstructions or permanent fixtures, such as columns or divider walls, and ensure that they are accurately represented on the page. In addition, include items such as doors, hallways, windows, and other structures that will affect the workflow. Finally, mark the position and location of all electrical outlets.

In addition to grid paper, office supply stores carry kits designed to aid in effective space planning. These kits usually contain generic cutouts of office furniture and equipment, as well as detailed instructions on their applications. When using these kits, ensure that the size and shape of all items directly reflect your own space and equipment. A recent innovation growing in popularity is the space planner software kit for the computer. These software kits enable users to try different arrangements and resize all items with the touch of a button.

After the floor plan has been laid out, it can be used to determine the size of furniture and equipment that will fit in the office. If furniture and equipment already have been purchased, measure these items, draw them to the scale established on the floor plan, and then cut out the representations. These cutouts can then be used to try out different arrangements on the floor plan so that you can avoid physically moving furniture and equipment around the office.

When designing the floor plan, consider the following issues:

- *Noise level.* Some employees need a more quiet workspace than others.

- *Privacy.* Besides quiet, some employees need a workspace where they can carry on confidential conversations.

- *Workflow.* Individuals who work together on the same kind of work should be placed together to facilitate the flow of assignments and communications.

- *Need for team discussion.* Set aside space for group discussions, with sufficient room at least for a round table and a few chairs for a team meeting.

- *Visitors.* Sometimes, a visitor will have to wait outside the workspace. Set up a quiet place, away from the flow of office traffic, where a visitor can sit until the person with whom he or she has an appointment is available.

- *Flow of traffic.* Consider the comings and goings not only of visitors but also of staff members, to minimize disruptions from co-workers as they go from one area of the office to another.

- *Key resources.* Consider where to place the network printer, office supply cabinets, and other resources used by all within the office so everything is accessible.

Many computer software programs offer planning tools to help create a floor plan. Visit your local software supplier to discuss the pros and cons of various offerings.

The final floor plan should be made up of large and small boxes—the larger boxes illustrate offices or cubicles, and the smaller boxes inside or outside these larger boxes illustrate desks and other office furniture.

OFFICE LIGHTING

Lighting is essential for productivity. Whenever possible, natural light should be used in the office because it provides a sense of openness and is the most familiar for human eyes. Artificial lighting will still be required, however, because natural lighting is not always possible and because detailed work such as graphic design requires stronger illumination than can be provided by natural light. Although specialized lighting exists for every function, three basic choices work for general purposes, as discussed in the following sections.

Incandescent Lighting

Incandescent lights are the standard light bulbs used in the home. Incandescent lighting is popular because of its availability, its capability to be easily directed, and the low cost of the bulbs. In addition, the illumination quality of an incandescent bulb is very warm. On the downside, however, incandescent bulbs require frequent replacement and burn substantially more electricity than other bulbs, thereby lowering their cost-effectiveness.

Fluorescent Lighting

Fluorescent lights are long tubes most often used in businesses and offices. Although the most expensive to purchase initially, fluorescent bulbs last significantly longer than incandescent bulbs and burn the least electricity, making them the most cost-effective and thereby contributing to their popularity. Fluorescent lighting is strongly artificial and not easily directed, however, so it works primarily for general-purpose overall lighting.

Halogen Lighting

On the rise in popularity, halogen lights come in a variety of shapes, produce a more natural and warm light than that of fluorescent bulbs, and can easily be directed. Halogen lights burn more electricity than fluorescents, but not as much as incandescents. Also, although they cost much more initially than fluorescents, you don't have to replace them as often, which makes them more cost-efficient in the long run.

The Best Light for the Workspace

Besides cost, consider the most appropriate lighting for your workspace. Halogen bulbs are used often in restaurants and other public places, but fluorescents don't create the tiring glare that halogens can.

The best-lit office is one that offers various degrees of lighting required for each area or task yet blends the different illumination levels harmoniously. To accomplish this, install general lighting, such as fluorescents, overhead so that all areas of the room are evenly lit. As much as possible, ensure that furniture, walls, and other obstructions don't create shadows. In addition, position overhead lights in relation to windows and computers to minimize glare. General lighting should mimic the illumination of natural light to avoid eye strain.

After establishing the overhead lighting levels and positions, determine which areas require more specific lighting. Desks, credenzas, and audiovisual rooms all require different types of lighting and should be addressed individually. Desk lamps, spotlights, and sconces provide varying degrees of illumination and can be placed to correspond to the varying light requirements. Don't limit the types and styles of lighting—mixing and matching can yield great results. An incandescent floor lamp can add a homey feel in a reception area, while halogen track lighting along hallways may add a sense of style. Above all, ensure that sufficient lighting exists. Although excessive lighting can always be reduced or dimmed, insufficient lighting may be difficult to address later, can lead to accidents, and can create eye strain and headaches.

Natural light or soft light generally works better than high-intensity lighting. But those who do close work, such as proofreading spreadsheets, manuscripts, or reports, need high-intensity lighting. If you get complaints about eye strain, headaches, fatigue—and, yes, mistakes—you probably have a lighting problem.

OFFICE FURNITURE

The selection of office furniture is a subjective decision based almost entirely on the taste of the individual. Rich woods, antiques, and leather-upholstered furniture once were the domain of executive offices, while computers and other technology were confined to minimalist styles composed of steel and plastic. Happily, furniture is being created today in all styles and price ranges that also accommodate technology and adhere to a predetermined sense of style. Therefore, selection of furniture can include functionality, size, and comfort.

Desks and Other Furnishings

In addition to simply providing a workspace, a desk can portray the success of the office, the level of the employee, and the style of both. Aesthetics, then, certainly are an important component of desk selection. The primary purpose of the desk is to be functional, however, so take care to ensure that the desk is comfortable and sufficiently meets the requirements of the job. A receptionist may need a counter, or a draftsperson may need a canted surface. Fortunately, no shortage of styles, colors, shapes, and models of desks exists—most can address even the most demanding needs.

Much of the new furniture today is modular, which means that it is capable of fitting together in various arrangements. As you develop the floor plans for individual workspaces, consider not only the size of desk needed, but also other furnishings that the employee will need—from file cabinets that can attach to the desk to overhead storage bins. Some individuals will want a

LEASING VS. BUYING FURNITURE AND EQUIPMENT

Carefully think through the decision to buy or lease office furniture and equipment by weighing all options and the circumstances of your business.

The most obvious benefit of leasing is the capability to fully furnish an office with the necessary furniture and equipment without tying up a significant amount of capital. Leasing generally doesn't require a down payment, and the monthly payments are almost always lower than finance payments for furniture or equipment that is purchased over time. This demands significant consideration for a start-up business or a business with little capital. In addition, because of the rapid pace of technological advances, leasing office equipment such as computers, printers, and copiers enables a company to return the equipment for more state-of-the-art models later. For companies that need the furniture or equipment for a limited time, leasing also makes a particularly viable option. However, monthly payments for leased equipment include charges to cover the leasing company's overhead and profit, which creates an unnecessary business expense that adds no value to your company.

Companies are better advised to purchase furniture and equipment whenever possible because buying creates an asset for the company. Furniture will be around for a long time and portray an image, so companies also should buy the best quality possible. This raises the cost, but remember that the best does not always mean the most expensive. When cost is an issue, this can be minimized by several methods, such as purchasing wholesale for larger offices or negotiating better deals from retailers. Purchasing used or slightly damaged furniture is also an option, as is buying equipment that is less than top-of-the-line, such as discontinued or demonstration models and floor models. The exception to this is computers, which never should be purchased damaged or after they are obsolete. Businesses also should check out overlooked retail channels such as auctions, estate sales, and business liquidation sales, as well as the classified section of the local newspaper.

counter on which they can store magazines or stacks of folders they are currently completing. Others prefer overhead cabinets, in which they can put these same materials. The more suitable the furnishings are to the employees' work styles or personal needs, the more productive those people will be. For instance, an employee may prefer a desk at standing height if he or she dislikes constantly sitting, whereas another might want a table rather than traditional desk, with side cabinets to store materials traditionally kept in a desk.

Ensure that your desk is the appropriate height. A height of 30 inches is recommended for most writing tasks; desks for typing and keyboard carrels should average about 26 inches from the floor. Desks also should be high enough to provide sufficient space for leg and knee comfort. Desks that are high enough might offer sufficient space for small file cabinets or other case goods to be placed under them, thereby preserving office space and providing a spot for files and paperwork that is used regularly.

In the past, desks were placed in the center of rooms, with a minimum of 4 feet of open space around the sides. Today's offices are considerably smaller than those of the past, given rental costs for office space. As a result, most desks are positioned against a wall, and other furnishings are placed on either side of the desk and/or opposite the desk.

If you will be interacting often with clients or other employees across your desk, you may want to consider a separate meeting table. Meeting tables are less formal and provide a more open feel, making others feel more comfortable and less confined.

Even if your desk is in a small cubicle, adding a chair next to it makes your workspace more inviting.

Computer Furniture

The proliferation of computers in the workplace has caused a similar proliferation of computer furniture. *Computer furniture* is a generic term that encompasses any furniture related to computers, from an adjustable stand for a monitor or printer, to an entire office system. As a general rule, referring to computer furniture also takes into account individual pieces. This type of furniture is the optimal choice for anyone who works with a computer because it is specifically designed to accommodate the needs raised by computers and their use. Due to its relatively recent invention, computer furniture also can encompass recent innovations and new discoveries in such areas as ergonomics, acoustics, and lighting. Although early offerings were over-engineered and often prohibitively expensive, most computer furniture today is relatively inexpensive and better designed. As a result, its popularity continues to increase. The National Products Association reports that one-fourth of all office furniture purchased today is computer-related.

File Storage

Today's paperless society is anything but paperless. Not only are offices generating increasing amounts of paper, but their storage space requirements also are growing in proportion. File cabinets can provide the necessary storage for this mass of paper generated by all offices. Fortunately, file cabinets are no longer solely utilitarian and are available in rich woods, jazzy plastics, and even padded fabric covers. This type of storage is not limited to file cabinets, however, so you should determine whether your needs might not be better met with rolling file racks, disposable cardboard file cabinets, or the services of a file archive firm.

Two basic types of file cabinets exist: vertical and lateral.

Vertical. When opened, vertical file cabinets position files to face the person. These cabinets are the most common, possibly because of their minimal space requirements. Most come with two drawers, which stand about 3 feet high; or four drawers, which stand about 5½ feet high. Because of its low height, the two-drawer style is particularly useful in offices with limited space because it can be placed under desks or tables. Always take care when opening the drawers; the stacking design and the unevenly distributed weight caused by open drawers can cause the unit to tip.

Lateral. Lateral file cabinets position files so that their side faces the person opening the drawer. These files are much more stable and therefore often are used as space dividers or credenzas. Lateral files come primarily with two drawers that stand about 3 feet high, four drawers that stand about 4 feet high, and five drawers that stand about 5½ feet high. Lateral file cabinets are particularly popular for legal files because the depth of these cabinets easily accommodates the additional length of these files. When both legal (8½ inches × 14 inches) and letter (8½ inches × 11 inches) files are used, lateral files are the best choice because most are built with moveable tracks to accommodate both sizes.

Storage needs should determine the kind of file cabinets selected. Some cabinets have two drawers; others have three; still others have five. The amount of materials with which you work and must maintain in your work area should determine the kinds of cabinets you choose.

COMPUTERS IN THE OFFICE

The computer revolution has arrived, changing the way we conduct business. Computers are now an integral part of the office (see chapter 5). Computers represent a large investment and come in a dizzying assortment of sizes, types, and capabilities.

There's more to purchasing computers than selecting a vendor and comparing prices. For instance, computers draw considerable power, so you must be sure that your facility is wired to accommodate the equipment you purchase. Review information on computers you are considering, and compare that information with the information contained in your lease or discuss this issue with potential vendors. Besides purchasing hardware within the limits set forth on your building blueprints, you should use power strips for each computer. A *power strip* is a heavy-duty extension cord with enough outlets to accommodate all the plugs in your system. The power strip has an on-off switch that enables you to control all the outlets at once; you can leave your computer, monitor, and printer permanently switched on and control them through the strip. More importantly, you can keep power surges or spikes from damaging your computers and other electronic equipment in use in your office.

A loss of power, on the other hand, can be prevented by a power-backup system, which provides emergency power for as little as ten minutes or up to an hour or more. Because even a brief power outage can wipe out considerable work, be sure to discuss a power-backup system with systems personnel. These systems cost considerably more than a power strip, so you may have to obtain written authorization from senior management.

WORKSTATIONS IN THE OFFICE

Workstations evolved from the open-office concept in Germany after World War II. Attempts to absorb excessive noise through the use of fabric-covered screens eventually developed into the construction of systems furniture that, in turn, evolved into today's workstations.

As you walk through an office of this type, you can see row after row of small cubicles in which employees work. In marketing firms, for instance, each cubicle might house telemarketers on the phone with potential customers. In open-landscaped offices, such as those found in insurance agencies or government offices, you can see desks lined up in rows, with filing cabinets on a side wall. These setups have become more popular because of their rental space savings.

As the workplace continues to evolve, workstations have secured a place for themselves through their adaptability to changing needs, space, and technology. It is this same adaptability that accounts for the millions of possible types of workstations through the use of interchangeable components and styles. It's virtually impossible not to find a workstation that addresses the specific needs of the individual as well as the dictates of the office: Determining *which* one to choose is the task.

COMPONENTS OF WORKSTATIONS

The use of computers has made the workstation a frequent site in offices. Depending on the work in the office, these workstations now are the standard for employees. Managers have a modified version, with space for a more traditional desk in the center of their offices and modularized furnishings for storage purposes. Workstations appear in insurance companies, telemarketing organizations, purchasing departments, and advertising agencies, to name a few organizations.

Most workstations are designed specifically for computers, as well as for peripherals such as printers, cables, and necessary electrical outlets. In addition to more effectively handling modern technology, many models are better designed ergonomically and look more aesthetically pleasing. Workstations can come predesigned or can be standardized for an entire corporation or building. The current trend, however, is to create a customized workstation from a variety of modularized components that is specific to the needs of the individual. Typically, these workstations include a minimum of desktop space, computer accommodations, file space, and bookshelves. However, they also can mix and match the following components:

- Desktops

- Meeting tables

- Printer stands

- Credenzas

- Shelves or bookcases

- Electrical strips or raceways

- Chairs

- Dividers or wall panels

- Keyboard carrels

- Filing cabinets

WORKSTATION ADJUSTMENT ERGONOMICS

Ergonomics is the study of the effects of physical design of equipment on the physical and emotional well-being of its users. In considering the ergonomics of a workstation, for instance, you would be concerned about how far the user must stretch to reach the phone on his or her desk, as well as how much the chair can adjust to minimize stress on the user's neck or back muscles. Ergonomics also deals with the size and shape of armrests on the chair, and whether the on/off switch is labeled so it can be read from a comfortable position.

Specifically, ergonomics is defined by *Webster's New World Dictionary* as "the science that seeks to adapt work or working conditions to suit the worker."

In practice, ergonomics is concerned with adapting the work environment to fit your body and to reduce and eliminate pain, discomfort, and strain. Ergonomics affects more than just your body, however, because physical discomfort contributes to mental fatigue, irritability, and an inability to concentrate. All this leads to reduced productivity. Almost half of all workers' compensation claims are based on repetitive stress injuries brought about by bad ergonomic design or adjustment. Employers are well advised, therefore, to provide ergonomically correct and adjustable furniture, while employees should ensure they are adjusted optimally.

Increasingly, as employees spend more time on their computers, the issue of ergonomics has become important. Often, employees will petition for ergonomically designed equipment when organizations undertake redesign. The issue can become a subject of employee-organized wellness programs and have prompted many organizations to invest in ergonomically designed equipment to increase employee satisfaction.

The Chair

Proper seating is the single most important aspect of any workstation because the average office worker spends 75 percent of his or her time seated. A good chair should adjust for height, back support, and tilt. In addition, the upholstery should absorb moisture and not permit sliding. The back of the chair should come up to the shoulder blades and support the lower spine. If necessary, a back support cushion can be added to provide additional support. The seat should tip slightly forward so as not to restrict blood flow to the legs. The height of the chair should place hands and wrists level with the keyboard, yet keep feet flat on the floor. If feet dangle, use a foot rest. Armrests, if provided, should not interfere with movement.

Most of this equipment can be purchased at office supply firms or orthopedic suppliers.

The Monitor

The computer monitor should be from one arm's length to 28 inches away. The top of the screen should be level with your forehead or slightly lower. The monitor should be placed directly in front of you or in the opposite direction of your predominant hand and tilted slightly upward. Use an anti-glare screen or computer filter to minimize eye fatigue caused by glare and reduce radiation emissions. Adjust the brightness and contrast controls until you find a display that is comfortable. If you use a copy stand, it should be at the same height and distance from you as the monitor. Take frequent breaks, and focus your eyes at distant objects often. Again, necessary items are available at office supply firms.

The Keyboard

Keyboard carrels or platforms should place your forearms parallel to the floor and place your hands comfortably in front of you. Mouse pads or trackballs should be immediately next to the keyboard and at the same height. When typing, use a light touch; use your entire arm when moving the mouse or trackball. A padded wrist rest should be placed in front of the keyboard to reduce the chances of developing carpal tunnel syndrome.

The latest keyboards come in a curved shape or in two parts. The keyboard has been redesigned so the arms and elbows are positioned ergonomically, to reduce stress on shoulders. These newer designs can be purchased in a computer equipment supplier or office supply firm, along with wrist pads or wrist/mouse pads.

Shelves and Bookcases

Shelves and bookcases should be designed and adjusted to be reached without having to get up from your chair. Therefore, shelves and bookcases that stand on the floor are the best, ergonomically speaking. Shelves and bookcases installed above you should be placed in the direction of your predominant hand. Never stuff or force anything into these shelves or bookcases because the items may fall out when the case is opened and cause injury.

Other Accessories

New computer accessories are being released almost every day, and each comes with an ergonomic promise. Whether you want the larger-sized mouse or the bigger trackball, visit a supply store before purchasing one of the new goodies on sale. Be sure that they do for you what the ads promise before buying them.

ORGANIZATION OF THE WORKSTATION

Workstations should be organized with several factors in mind: ergonomics, the frequency of use of the various pieces, and the design of the workstation itself. The most predominant feature of the workstation is likely to be the placement of the computer because this is almost certainly the equipment that will be used most during the workday. Most workstations are designed with this in mind, and holes and raceways for the necessary cords are positioned to correspond accordingly.

> **TIP:** The placement of electrical equipment should never necessitate the use of extension cords. If optimal positioning of these items is contradicted by the design of the workstation, consult an electrician about possible solutions, or consider replacing the workstation with a more appropriate design.

Especially with modular units, however, the decision of where to place other components is often left up to the individual. A good method to determine the correct placement of each item is to make a list of all items that are used throughout the workday, and then to divide this list into constantly used items, frequently used items, and seldom used items. Compare this list with a list of the components, and a trend will begin to appear. For example, if you frequently meet with clients or other employees, it might be a good idea to place a small meeting table at the end of the workstation close to the working area. If you seldom use certain files and records, place them in file cabinets in a different location. Files and records you constantly use should be placed in file cabinets under the desk.

In addition, it is a good idea to determine your position in the office and its consequences. If you are near a high-traffic area, for example, your workstation should be organized to minimize disruption and avoid injuries. As another example, being close to a window might dictate the placement of your monitor to reduce glare.

Workstation Accessories

Accessories such as Rolodexes, office supply caddies, and desk mats are the most individual and frequently used items in the workplace. The selection of these items should be left to the discretion of the individual employee, whenever possible, because he or she is best qualified to determine individual work habits and personal taste. A common method is to provide a catalog from which employees can choose individual items. Another method is to purchase items in several different styles, and allow the employee to take what he or she wants or needs from a centralized supply location. Some offices even enable employees to purchase items from any source, and then later reimburse them for the cost.

Many offices require a more uniform look, however. If this is the case, a clearly worded policy is essential for maintaining office standards. Employees also should be informed of the reasons for these decisions. Explaining to employees that standardization is required because of cost-effectiveness, safety factors, or the desire to portray a certain image for the office will make such measures more palatable and increase compliance.

In either case, the positioning of these items on the workstation always should be left to the employee, who should place these items in relation to what is most comfortable and effective for his or her work habits. This will increase productivity and reduce the likelihood of injury or discomfort.

Reducing Paper Waste and Recycling

Awareness of our responsibility to our planet continues to grow. Natural resources are being depleted at an alarming rate, and finding space for our increasing production of garbage is a monumental problem. In response, a variety of environmentally superior products are being produced and initiatives are being implemented to address this situation. Most buildings and offices, for example, are required to recycle and separate recyclable waste from other garbage. As an added bonus to the company, this policy also reduces costs, clutter, accidents, and the likelihood of fire.

Employees should be encouraged to participate in recycling initiatives; seek their input to find new ways to reduce the use of paper. Environmental groups, such as Earth Now and Greenpeace, are also excellent sources of information on how to promote recycling in the office and reduce the excessive use of paper. Before taking too much time and energy to set up a recycling program, however, check with the facilities or building management to determine the policy for recycling. Sometimes recycled trash is automatically removed with regular trash; you may, however, need to contract with an outside firm. Make

WORKSTATION EVALUATION CHECKLIST

Chairs

Yes No

☐ ☐ Is the chair comfortable?

☐ ☐ Can the chair be easily cleaned and maintained?

☐ ☐ Does the chair swivel?

☐ ☐ Can the seat height be adjusted to a height equal to the distance from the crease at the back of your knee to the floor?

☐ ☐ Can the seat height be adjusted so that your arms stay at the correct angle for keyboard use?

☐ ☐ Can height adjustments be made easily?

☐ ☐ If you are a short person, are footrests available?

☐ ☐ Does the lumbar support maintain the proper curvature of you back (as if you were standing)?

☐ ☐ Can the backrest recline and lock in at least two positions?

☐ ☐ Can you adjust the backrest to tilt forward for extended work periods in front of a computer monitor?

☐ ☐ Do the armrests interfere with movement?

☐ ☐ Do the armrests take enough pressure off your wrists when keyboarding?

☐ ☐ Do the armrests support leaning positions?

☐ ☐ Does the seat have a rounded front edge that maintains good circulation?

☐ ☐ Can the seat tilt and lock in a forward position for prolonged keyboarding?

☐ ☐ Does the chair have a five-leg base to prevent tipping?

☐ ☐ Are casters dual-wheeled to enable easy rolling?

Work Surfaces

Yes No

☐ ☐ Is the work surface at least 30 inches deep to accommodate all necessary equipment?

☐ ☐ Is the work surface between 26 and 29 inches high, or at least slightly above elbow height when seated?

☐ ☐ Can the workspace be adjusted to accommodate you if you are either right- or left-handed?

☐ ☐ Is all equipment within your arm's normal reach?

☐ ☐ Is adequate storage available for handbooks, documents, personal belongings, and other items?

☐ ☐ Are different work surface heights and angles necessary and available for different tasks?

☐ ☐ Does the area under the work surface provide adequate leg room, and is it free of obstacles?

Computers

Yes No

☐ ☐ Can you position the center line of the monitor screen slightly below eye level?

☐ ☐ Is the keyboard position adjustable to ensure that your lower arm and hand form a straight line parallel to the keycaps?

☐ ☐ Does your copy holder maintain the proper alignment with the monitor level?

☐ ☐ Can the mouse and its pad be positioned within your elbow's free movement range to avoid shoulder strain?

☐ ☐ Is your seating position a minimum of 30 inches (or arm's length) away from the monitor to minimize any electronic or radiation emissions?

Lighting

Yes No

☐ ☐ Can workstation overhead lighting be dimmed?

☐ ☐ Is task lighting available?

☐ ☐ Is the lighting level appropriate for hard-copy tasks?

☐ ☐ Is the lighting level appropriate for computer monitor use?

☐ ☐ Is the fluorescent lighting flicker-free?

☐ ☐ Is the workstation free from glare and reflection?

☐ ☐ Are workstations positioned in relation to windows to avoid glare and reflections?

☐ ☐ Do window treatments provide an adequate means of controlling incoming light?

☐ ☐ Are filters available to reduce reflections on monitor screens?

TIPS FOR RECYCLING AND REDUCING PAPER WASTE

- Review and change documents on the computer screen.
- Print only the number of copies you need.
- Use the print preview feature of your word processing program, if it has one.
- Use e-mail whenever appropriate.
- Archive e-mail messages on your computer instead of printing and filing hard copies.
- Reuse paper that has already been printed on one side for printing drafts.
- Make double-sided photocopies whenever feasible.
- Use bulletin boards (electronic or otherwise).
- Use white legal pads instead of colored ones; they are easier to recycle.
- Adopt a white-paper recycling program; many waste-management companies can help you set this up.
- Reuse shipping boxes and packing whenever possible.
- Use bad photocopies and obsolete stationery for drafts, internal memos, and notepads.
- Have clear plans about how recyclables will be delivered to recycling facilities.
- Coordinate with the building management's recycling plans to ensure their support.
- Post memos in a central location rather than providing individual copies.
- Consolidate files to one location.
- Edit documents onscreen rather than printing drafts.
- Provide separate wastebaskets for paper and other garbage.
- Limit the amount of file space in individual offices.
- Provide documents on disk rather than hard copy.
- Provide one copy and route it with a circulation list rather than a distributing multiple copies.

sure that processes are in place to get the recycled material to the recycling plant—instead of sorting paper to have it all go back in the building trash again.

OFFICE SAFETY, HEALTH, AND SECURITY

Organizations have a responsibility to their employees to ensure that facilities are safe and secure. It's to their advantage to create an environment in which employees are safe from accidents, illnesses, theft, or the violent acts of visitors or coworkers. Employees are more productive when they believe their companies are concerned for their well-being.

OFFICE HEALTH AND SAFETY

No one likes to think about the chances of injury or illness in the office. However, we probably spend more time in the office than anywhere else except our homes. It is in all of our best interests, therefore, to ensure that the conditions for injury or illness are minimized as much as possible, and that we are suitably prepared to deal with any situation before it arises. This responsibility is set forth in the Occupational Safety and Health Act.

The Occupational Safety and Health Administration

The Occupational Safety and Health Administration (OSHA) was created in 1970, when Congress passed the Occupational Safety and Health Act to establish minimum standards for worker health and safety, and to provide protection for employees from hazardous working conditions. OSHA regulations cover a variety of areas, including first aid, protective equipment, fire protection, workplace ventilation, and exposure to dangerous chemicals or conditions.

OSHA requires that companies with a minimum of eleven employees maintain documentation logs of job injuries that required medical attention, and make these logs available to all employees. These logs, which are known as 101 and 200 reports, are submitted to and reviewed by OSHA investigators, who may determine that an inspection of the work site is in order. Inspections also can be called in response to an accident or a complaint filed by an employee, can be regularly scheduled, or can occur unannounced at random.

Accidents take various forms. We all know it's bad luck to walk under ladders, but employees who are preoccupied with their work may still do so and be hit by some object that slips from the hands of the person on the ladder. If the top drawer in a file cabinet is filled first, the cabinet may topple on the worker who did not think to fill the cabinet from the bottom drawer. Employees might slip or trip, and break a leg or arm. More serious accidents could maim, even kill. If an accident occurs in the workplace, it must be investigated by the

---

BASIC OFFICE SAFETY

A few tips to avoid frequent problems follow:

- Keep floors clean and clear to avoid slips and falls.

- Spills and litter should be dealt with immediately, not left for the janitorial crew.

- Frayed carpets and loose tiles should be replaced or repaired immediately, and the area should be blocked off until action is taken.

- Desk and file drawers should be closed when not in use to prevent tripping.

- File cabinet tops should not be used for storage because items may fall off by the vibrations of opening and closing drawers.

- Avoid the use of extension cords whenever possible because they can cause tripping and are a fire hazard.

- Ensure that all areas of the office are adequately lit at all times.

- Employees should never run or engage in horseplay in the office.

---

person responsible for the facility's safety; this might be the safety director, a manager, or a floor monitor. OSHA demands a report on all accidents that occur—even those that seem to occur from personal clumsiness. Sometimes accidents credited to the accident-prone are due to individuals who may be overworked or tired from long shifts; such incidents must be investigated to identify and eliminate the cause.

If unsafe conditions or discrepancies are discovered during the inspection, the investigator will issue a citation that establishes a timeframe within which the condition must be rectified. A fine, penalty, or (in extreme situations) prison sentence also might be levied, depending on the circumstances or severity of the problem. Employers can challenge these citations and present the case to a judge in a court of law. It's a much better idea to avoid these situations by ensuring that the office complies with the standards set by OSHA. The free *OSHA Handbook for Small Business* can be obtained at the following address:

Occupational Safety and Health Administration
Department of Labor
200 Constitution Avenue NW
Room N3700
Washington, DC 20210
202-219-7266

SMOKING IN THE WORKPLACE

Smoking in the workplace is now rare in any form. Recent legislation has effectively banned smoking in public places, and Corporate America has eagerly followed suit with policies that further restrict smoking in the office. In spite of this trend and the general public's growing intolerance, odds are that at least a couple of employees in any company will be affirmed smokers. This doesn't usually lead to problems with the implementation of a clear and complete policy (for example, "Absolutely no smoking anywhere in the building") that all employees know is uniformly enforced.

If your office has several smokers, you may want to consider providing a smoking room. The time saved by employees not having to leave the building will increase productivity as well as increase smokers' morale. Smoking rooms should be as far away from the general areas of the building as possible and should have airtight doors. An independent ventilation system, or "smoke-eater," will keep the room bearable if there are many smokers and will help to keep the smell of smoke from traveling outside the room. It is also a good idea to check with your local fire department regarding pertinent regulations, as well as tips to avoid fire accidents.

Your best bet, however, is the arrangement of programs to help your smokers quit. Most smokers don't want to smoke, but they are unsure of how to go about giving up the addiction. The American Lung Association is a good source of programs and referrals to outside programs designed to help people kick the habit. Hypnotherapists, nicotine patches, and drug programs are effective and easily available, and new methods are being developed every day. Ensure that your smokers know these programs are available whenever they want them—and it's a good idea to offer them more than once. Research indicates that almost no one successfully quits on the first try, so it's important that office smokers know that they haven't failed if they don't quit on the first, second, or even third attempt. It's far more important that they continue to try.

Employees who are injured on the job or who suffer from illnesses related to their work are covered by workers' compensation. This compensation replaces their salary until they have recovered and can return to work. State statutes vary about workers' compensation: The trend is to reduce the time employees stay away from work by identifying alternative jobs that they can do while they recover.

REPETITIVE STRESS INJURIES

General Symptoms

Most repetitive stress injuries are localized in the areas of the fingers, hands, wrists, forearms, shoulders, and neck. The most common include these:

- Stiffness
- Inflammation
- Persistent tingling
- Persistent numbness
- Being awakened at night by this tingling and/or numbness
- Chronic change in hand temperature
- Generalized weakness
- Shooting pains
- Tendency to drop small, lightweight objects

Tips for Prevention

Here are several tips for preventing repetitive stress injuries:

- Exercise regularly outside of the office.
- Include aerobic exercise for better circulation.
- Include resistance training to build muscle mass.
- Practice yoga, tai chi, or other relaxation exercises.
- Use basic ergonomic principles when setting up (or changing) your workstation.
- Stretch at your desk frequently.
- Take frequent short breaks away from your desk at approximately half-hour intervals; use these breaks to move around and stretch your entire body.
- If keyboarding, keep wrists in a relaxed, comfortable position.
- At the first signs of an injury, use ice, braces, and anti-inflammatory medications, and consult your doctor.

Preventing Accidents and Work-Related Injuries

More than six million job-related accidents occur annually, costing companies fifty-seven million lost work days, $420 per worker, and more than $50 billion in workers' compensation programs. To prevent accidents, offices should implement a safety incentive program. This type of program should enlist the participation of all employees to pinpoint problems, determine solutions, and provide insight into the circumstances surrounding past accidents.

In addition to formalized safety incentive programs, however, employees should be reminded that they are responsible for their own safety and should be encouraged to bring to the attention of management anything they believe could threaten the safety of themselves or their co-workers. Employee-run wellness programs have developed from exactly this kind of initiative.

Employees are increasingly coming together to put on programs in which authorities on a variety of health-related issues address staff members. Relevant issues include health-related (as in weight control, diabetes, high blood pressure) or ergonomic ones, such as repetitive stress injuries from excessive typing or eyestrain from staring for long periods at the computer screen. Companies also sponsor memberships in health clubs or pay a portion of the costs. Organizations have found that healthy employees mean higher productivity. Furthermore, such initiatives demonstrate concern for the workers, which translates into motivated employees.

First Aid

Many injuries and illnesses can be addressed directly in the office with a minimum of care and fuss. A few preparations can help you effectively deal with them when they occur. First, ensure that your office has a first-aid kit. Determine the most probable incidents for your office, and consult appropriate salespersons or office supply distributors about which first-aid kit is most appropriate. As a minimum, however, the kid should contain bandages, hot and cold compresses, eyewashes, and minor pain relievers. In addition, place the phone numbers of the nearest hospital and emergency services in the kit for immediate access.

Keep on hand a list of anyone in the office who has any type of medical training: These include Emergency Medical Technicians (EMTs), nurses, and physicians. Don't hesitate to consult these individuals in any situation that requires medical attention. If no one in the office has any type of medical training, contact your local office of the American Red Cross. This organization runs first-aid training sessions on a regular basis, covering areas such as choking, CPR, and basic first aid for a variety of situations. A training session for the entire office can be arranged onsite, but as a minimum, several representatives of the office should be sent for training.

CHECKLIST FOR OFFICE FIRST-AID KIT

☐ 100 assorted adhesive bandages

☐ 1 roll 2-inch elastic-wrap bandage

☐ 1 roll 3-inch elastic-wrap bandage

☐ 2 rolls soft gauze bandages

☐ 3 gauze pads, 2×2, 3×3, 4×4

☐ 4 butterfly bandages

☐ 2 sterile eye pads

☐ 2 large triangular bandages, $40 \times 40 \times 55$

☐ 1 roll $\frac{1}{2}$-inch hypoallergenic first-aid tape

☐ 10 cotton swabs

☐ 10 antiseptic wipes

☐ 1 container antiseptic soap

☐ 1 tube antimicrobial skin ointment (mycin family or triple antibiotic)

☐ 1 tube burn cream

☐ 1 bottle of aspirin or other analgesic pain reliever

☐ 1 container activated charcoal

☐ 3 cylinders of smelling salts

☐ 1 over-the-counter antihistamine

☐ 1 insect-sting kit

☐ 1 eyewash cup and solution

☐ 1 instant ice pack

☐ 1 pair blunt-nosed scissors

☐ 1 pair tweezers

☐ 1 thermometer

☐ 10 assorted safety pins

☐ 5 assorted splints

☐ 5 pair disposable rubber/latex gloves

☐ 1 sterile mouth protector for CPR

☐ 1 small flashlight

☐ 1 first-aid handbook

DISASTER PLANNING

Major disasters such as fire and flood in the office are rare. When they do occur, however, they are usually debilitating enough to completely suspend all work activity and, in many cases, cause the office to go out of business altogether. In spite of this, little thought is given to the office's response to a disaster even though the amount of preparation before a disaster is directly proportional to the office's capability to survive and recover in the event of an emergency. This poor planning is unfortunate; once established, disaster plans require little attention and yield positive results.

Most offices deal in the commodity of information. In addition, as most offices are computerized, it is relatively easy to minimize the disruption of work by ensuring that computerized information is available from another source. This can be done in several ways. Offices can secure the services of an outside disaster recovery firm that will download all computerized information on a regular basis, as well as provide office space in the event of a disaster. In addition, companies can connect their internal computer networks to a mainframe outside the office that is reserved specifically for this purpose. Companies also can download all information once a week to a tape, which is then stored off-premises. Files and information such as personnel files, client lists, and financial records that will be necessary to resume business also should be duplicated and stored offsite. Remember to update these files periodically.

Most organizations practice risk management to ensure that an accident or other disaster will not keep them from immediately resuming business. Insurance advisors can come into the facility and review operating procedures to minimize risks. These procedures might include ensuring that critical paper files are copied and stored elsewhere, reviewing hiring procedures to avoid negligent hiring or bringing individuals onboard with criminal records, or reviewing warehousing or manufacturing processes to avoid hazardous conditions.

To keep employees working, employers should consider providing temporary at-home computers for their employees, or purchasing software that will enable employees to connect their personal computers to the office network or mainframe. If the cost is prohibitive, a contract can be established to rent or lease computers for employees to use at home until the situation is resolved. When cost is an issue, companies can create innovative solutions. For example, consider a buddy system with another company, in which each company provides space and equipment for the other in the case of a disaster. These types of solutions require minimum expense and can be equally effective.

On an individual level, you can take actions to personally safeguard yourself and help your co-workers in a crisis such as a major fire.

Fire

The hazard of fire is a very real concern in the office. The biggest problem with fire safety is that it is rarely an issue until after the fact.

- Create a written plan for fire safety that specifies the actions to be taken by all employees to reduce the likelihood of a fire in the office. Also specify actions to be taken in the event of a fire. This plan should consider the office layout, available exits, and routes for evacuation. For instance, most organizational plans note that evacuation of the building should be by stairway, not elevators, unless instructed by a firefighter. Besides health reasons, smoking by employees should be discouraged because smoking is a major cause of fire in offices (second only to electrical fires). The plan should be shared with all employees, and fire drills should be held at least twice a year to ensure that new employees are familiar with the steps to take in the event of a fire. Your local fire department will be happy to work with you to devise and evaluate your plan. Experts want to come to your office *before* there is a need—they will review the procedures you have set, identify better actions if they exist, and answer employees' questions so they are clear not only about how to ensure their safety but also how to avoid endangering their co-workers.

- Establish a date once every six months to ensure that smoke detectors and fire extinguishers are in good working order. Use this same date, at a minimum, to conduct a fire drill. Predetermine a location outside the building where employees are to gather, and charge one employee with headcount responsibility. Remind all employees that elevators are not to be used in a fire.

- Ensure that office fire extinguishers have an ABC rating, which indicates that they can be used on all types of fires. Periodically demonstrate their proper use to all staff.

- The fire department provides free stickers that display an emergency fire telephone number—these should be attached to every office telephone. When possible, the company's alarm system should be linked directly to the local fire department.

- Electrical-code violations are the leading cause of fires in the office. Check the office for overloaded sockets; frayed electrical cords; light bulbs that exceed wattage recommendations; and wires under or near rugs, upholstery, or drapes. Rectify any violations immediately.

If you must evacuate a building because of a fire, walk calmly down the stairwell; don't push or shove. Follow instructions given by fire personnel, which often means that you should exit the building, although occasionally it may be sufficient to exit to a floor beneath the fire.

Most organizations have a fire monitor on each floor of their buildings. When you hear the fire alarm, don't worry about personal possessions. Go immediately to the area designated by your fire plan, which is usually near a fire exit.

> **TIP:** Because some stairwells aren't well-lit, you may want to keep a flashlight in your workspace in case of a fire or other emergency that requires you to walk down the stairs.

SECURITY

Employees have a right to office security. Legislation constantly verifies that employees must be provided a work environment that is safe and that offers no threat to their well-being. As a result, offices are liable for almost any incident or situation that brings harm to an employee. Therefore, reasonable safety precautions should be taken to provide employee security and reduce incidents such as theft.

Beyond those concerning human life, establish security procedures to safeguard equipment or other items of worth within the organization, including proprietary information. Whatever your business—from software production, to publishing to manufacturing—you have records that should be protected by security systems and security personnel.

Access to the workplace should always be limited and, if possible, guarded. Receptionists and entrance guards can successfully limit access by unauthorized personnel. In larger offices, employees should be issued badges or other forms of identification for access whenever possible. In addition, internal phones or intercoms should be provided to identify visitors before they enter the premises.

In addition, doors and windows should automatically lock from the outside upon closing. Employees should be reminded never to prop open windows or doors because this could endanger their security. Delivery personnel and suppliers should have a centralized location to deposit their items, and the receiving employee should be contacted to retrieve the items from this location. Delivery personnel should never be allowed to freely roam through the workplace.

Finally, visitors and clients should be provided with a waiting area in the front of the office. Employees should meet them there and stay with them the entire time they are in the office. Employees should be reminded to question strangers who are unaccompanied in the workplace and never to provide access to the office to unknown people.

The treatment of visitors will vary with the size of the office. Most organizations have a waiting area—on every floor or on only one floor. In any case, ask visitors to come to the nearest visitors' area and identify themselves to the receptionist. Then you can go and get them.

Some organizations don't have receptionists. Instead, there is a phone for visitors to use to alert the party they have come to visit. Be sure that your visitor has your extension. Periodically check to see that the phone is indeed working. You also might want to list the names and extensions of all those on that floor.

Smaller organizations depend on the building's security system. At the very least, the system might include a sign-in system with careful control of the comings and goings of visitors and those with packages.

Within your organization, distribute rules about the treatment of visitors. For instance, they should not be allowed to wander around the office, no matter who they are. Furthermore, you should not allow strangers to follow you through office doors that lead to the work area. If you feel unsure about confronting them yourself, you should have the number of security or another person designated for security handy.

It is also unwise to stay in a building alone late into the night. Plan with co-workers to work together either in the evening or on a weekend.

Terrorism and Disgruntled Employees

Fortunately, the number of incidents of terrorism and sabotage from disgruntled employees and former employees is low. A situation is unlikely to occur in your own organization, but it is better to be prepared. The consequences and repercussions are severe enough to warrant attention and action.

The office is most susceptible to sabotage from current employees because they have access to the workplace. Obviously, no one wants to institute a police state within the office because this would only increase feelings of ill will and make for an uncomfortable work environment. However, if circumstances predict the possibility of sabotage, this can be minimized by limiting employee access to areas that directly pertain to their job, as well as requiring that employees leave at a certain time and not work unaccompanied after hours. A better method of addressing this danger, however, is by ensuring that the lines of communication in the office remain open and honest. Employees who feel empowered to express their concerns and feelings and who are given the truth regarding unpleasant situations are far less likely to react with violence, hostility, or sabotage. Not only will they feel safer, but they also will feel that their organization truly understands its responsibility for their well-being.

A bigger danger is the threat of attack by former disgruntled employees. Terminations and layoffs are always unpleasant situations and often are accompanied by enormous hostility and anger. Employees who are let go always should be accompanied while they clear their desk and should be escorted out of the building immediately. Ensure that all keys, passes, and office identification are collected at this time, and withhold final checks until these items are returned. Although re-entry is sometimes inevitable, former employees should have restricted access to the office as any stranger would, and they should be accompanied at all times while on the premises. In any situation in which the threat of violence is present, contact your local police station immediately.

OFFICE MAINTENANCE

A clean office is an effective office. Although your firm probably pays for janitorial services, you should work to keep your office neat. Cleanliness promotes productivity, increases employee morale, and projects a good image. Sadly, the issue of cleanliness in the office often is relegated solely to contracted cleaning staff and building maintenance. This is unfortunate because a cluttered and dirty office can be a safety hazard, contributing to illness and possible injury, as well as making the office an unpleasant place to work.

Janitorial Services

Most organizations contract for cleaning services, which include vacuuming, dusting, and emptying waste cans. Some services take on the responsibility for taking recycled paper to a recycling center, and some shred documents for firms whose tossed paperwork may contain proprietary information.

Some businesses contract for this service. Sometimes the landlord of a building leases the service for all corporate tenants. Janitorial services will clean kitchens or break areas but won't deal with personal items. They also won't deal with messy offices, cluttered workspaces, and other barriers to an office. Even though your office has janitorial service, there are a few basic ways to keep the office tidy and make it better for everyone.

- *Post signs.* This is the single best way to remind employees throughout the workday. Create signs for common areas such as kitchens, copier areas, and meeting rooms. Signs might read, "The refrigerator is cleaned Friday at 5 p.m. Take home any containers." Post whatever is appropriate for the work area.

- *Establish cleaning days.* As warranted by the condition of your office, periodically reserve workdays for the purpose of cleaning. Allow employees to dress casually and, if possible, provide things that will make the day enjoyable, such as a company-sponsored lunch, music, or contests for the cleanest office.

- *Develop a written policy.* Circulate a written policy with the office's expectations and standards for cleanliness. Remind employees to dispose of old files, keep food in the appropriate areas, and reduce clutter in common areas. Be careful not to lecture, however, because this may put off employees and create feelings of resentment.

■ *Set an example for others.* If you want others to keep their work areas and common areas neat, you should do so yourself.

POLICIES AND PROCEDURES MANUALS

It is easier to run an office if employees have a clear sense of their responsibilities, how the company expects to achieve its mission, and the rules that the organization expects its employees to follow as they carry out their responsibilities and work toward accomplishing that mission.

That's where policies and procedures manuals come in handy. These are particularly valued by new and part-time workers because they can fill in the gaps left from orientation efforts or remind them about specific rules or activities. Policy manuals cover general guidelines governing how the company will operate. Procedures manuals—or employee manuals, as they are sometimes called—provide instructions for performing specific activities or tasks. A procedures manual might contain a variety of information: job descriptions of every employee, and advice on developing new ones or updating one's own; job aids to ensure that an employee does his or her work correctly; software and other operating tips to maximize productivity; instruction about such details as the preferred corporate format for memos, reports, and e-mail; and correct letterhead paper and style for correspondence. Alternatively, an organization might create separate manuals to cover each of these issues.

As companies install corporate intranets, materials that previously appeared in policies and procedures manuals are posted to the intranet. Many companies also maintain hard copies of these rules and instructions.

Usually, the manuals themselves come in the form of loose-leaf binders so that sheets can be added or updated as the need arises. The following section examines the kinds of content that should be covered in policy and procedures manuals. (In the case of procedures manuals, note that the text might refer to a single book or the beginnings of a manager's personal library.)

Office professionals sometimes might be called upon to help assemble or create a policy manual. Keep in mind a few simple ways to make it usable:

■ Outline the contents if you are producing your first policies and procedures manual. Your outline should include the kinds of information you want to include in the manual, such as department job descriptions, phone etiquette, filing, business travel, memos and letters, supplies, procedures for handling complaints, and grievance procedures.

■ Use a brightly colored binder, and give a title to the manual so that its purpose is obvious. A manager should provide a manual for each employee who reports to him or her, and should encourage each individual to place the manual in a prominent place on or near the desk, where it is easily accessible to those who may need it in the employee's absence.

- Number all the pages. Because there may be changes to the contents, number each page by tab (if you separate multiple parts with tabbed pages) instead of numbering pages continuously throughout the manual Starting with page 1, number all pages consecutively for all material within that part.

- Include a table of contents and an index so that someone new to the organization can easily find the information he or she needs.

- Be complete but brief. The manual shouldn't go overboard in its explanations, but critical points should not be left out. For instance, if a computer problem occurs, the worker should know not only to call technical support, but he or she also should also know the name of the individual and any extension numbers.

What to Include

Policies manuals reflect the governance of the company, contain policy statements that reflect the basis of management decision making, and spell out the rules that everyone within the organization is expected to follow. Most policies manuals are divided into two categories: corporate information and general personnel policies.

Corporate information includes the organization's values or basic beliefs (including commitments to shareholders, customers, and employees), the corporate structure as a whole (for instance, subsidiaries or branch offices, and their locations and functions), and operations within each facility (with special attention to departments at headquarters and their responsibilities). If the organization takes a strong stand on a specific issue, such as diversity or the environment, this is also noted in this section of the manual.

The remainder of the manual is made up of general personnel policies: the organization's adherence to federal and state laws and regulations (such as Title VII); personnel issues such as recruiting, interviewing, hiring, termination, and the privacy guaranteed to employee personnel files; issues of attendance and punctuality; dress code; payroll provisions (including exempt and non-exempt qualifications); business travel; and grievance, safety, sexual harassment, and other corporate programs designed to ensure the rights of employees.

Policies should be organized by categories and should be cross-referenced when an issue pertains to more than a single policy. Policies increasingly are being placed on corporate intranets in addition to being stored in policies manuals. A numbering system should be used that includes both numbers and letters to permit the addition of new policies when the need arises. Pages can be printed on both sides or on one side only, but a manager should keep each policy separate to allow for changes. All policy statements should begin on a right-hand page (if you print on both sides of the page). As mentioned earlier, do not number policy manual pages consecutively. Instead, number the pages by policy (as in, page 1 of 3).

Job Descriptions

Job descriptions provide valuable information for managers so they can make the best hiring, placement, and promotion decisions. In today's workplace, as organizations realign and then realign once more, the information also can be useful for restructuring or eliminating jobs. Certainly, screening applicants for job openings is simpler if the interviewer has a clear idea of the tasks required and knows the specific educational and experiential requirements for job candidates.

POSITION DESCRIPTION

Position: Manager, Purchasing

Div/Department: Office of the President

Location: Corporate Headquarters

Grade: 19

Complement: Budget 79.53.100

Exempt: X   **Non-exempt:**

Purpose: To oversee corporate-wide purchasing program to ensure that quality products are purchased at the least cost to the organization. Responsible for the staff and staffing needs necessary to execute various purchasing programs in branch offices.

Essential Functions:

- Develop annual purchasing budget for office supplies, coordinating with branch office managers to maximize savings from corporatewide purchases.

- Inaugurate programs to control office supply inventory.

- Conduct annual audit of existing suppliers to determine if new suppliers should be sought, either to provide better quality or cost savings.

- Monitor operating budgets and initiate programs to address negative variances and communicate to appropriate staff positive variances.

Qualifications:

- Five to ten years as purchasing manager in company in similar field.

- Business degree.

- Knowledge of Excel and Lotus.

Measurements:

- Cost savings during the year.

- Variances from budget.

- Identification of better quality and less expensive sources for supplies.

Sample Job Description

Verbs for Describing the Job

These verbs can help an entrepreneur, a manager, or an office professional write a job description:

accelerate	deliver	identify	plan
achieve	design	implement	prepare
administer	develop	improve	prioritize
advise	devise	incorporate	process
analyze	direct	increase	produce
apply	draft	initiative	program
arrange	enhance	institute	promote
assess	establish	instruct	provide
author	evaluate	interface	recommend
automate	exceed	launch	reconcile
brief	excel	maintain	recruit
catalog	execute	manage	represent
collaborate	exhibit	maximize	research
communicate	expand	mentor	revise
compile	expedite	monitor	schedule
compose	facilitate	negotiate	streamline
computerize	fashion	operate	supervise
conceptualize	formulate	orchestrate	support
conduct	furnish	organize	train
coordinate	generate	originate	upgrade
create	handle	oversee	utilize
delegate	head	perform	

Procedures manuals can include a section that includes the job descriptions for all employees and managers, or a separate manual can be created solely for job descriptions. Most management experts recommend that job descriptions be updated annually to reflect the ongoing changes in a person's job. An up-to-date job description clarifies expectations between managers and their employees, and eliminates any problems at appraisal time. The best descriptions use active verbs to describe the work that is expected. When updated, the revisions usually are best handled by a manager and employee working together.

Each job description should list the job title, organizational department, classification (whether exempt from provisions of the Fair Labor Standards Act or non-exempt from those provisions), grade (which reflects the worth of the job and subsequent salary an occupant in the job will receive), work area location, budget from which money to pay the individual comes, and supervisor's title. If the organization is a startup and the owner needs to create job titles, he or she can contact the U.S. Department of Labor, Employment, and Training Administration (200 Constitution Avenue NW, Washington, DC 20001) for an up-to-date copy of *The Dictionary of Occupational Titles.* Trade associations also might have publications that include work characteristics, education, training requirements, and earnings and benefits within specific industries.

The first section of the job description should provide an overview of the job or a brief description. Below that usually comes a list of the duties that the job entails. Duties should be listed in order of priority. Write the primary or most frequently performed duty first, followed by the second most frequent duty, and then the third, and so on. Keep in mind that duties, rather than specific tasks, should be listed. For example, "conducts department planning sessions" is preferred over "develops agendas for department planning meetings."

In addition to the essential functions associated with the job, a manager or other person developing a job description should identify the level of supervision the position demands, as well as the job-holder's supervisory responsibilities, if any, and intercompany contacts. Finally, devote a section to the minimum qualifications for a candidate for the job and the general standards by which a holder of the job is measured.

Workstation Manual

Many organizations now place the following types of forms on their intranets: supply requisitions, customer invoices, travel information and expenses requests for petty-cash compensation, attendance, travel arrangements and expenditures, and so forth. Each form also should include samples either in the section of the procedures manual dedicated to workstation issues or in a separate binder for the workstation manual. Besides clean forms, the manual should contain a correctly filled-out copy of each form to help first-time users fill them out appropriately. The manual should include directions about accessing them on the intranet and to whom completed forms should be e-mailed.

If an organization still uses paper forms, information on who provides specific forms should be a part of the workstation manual.

Managers who operate in organizations with sophisticated intranets should include information on accessing and utilizing the intranet in their own workstation manuals, and in the manuals of those who report to them. An index of work activities that can be done on the intranet, such as requests for travel advances and hotel and plane reservations, also should be part of the workstation manual.

A directory of company personnel should be present at every workstation, with both telephone numbers and e-mail addresses. This information already might be part of a corporate intranet, but a manager might want to reproduce the directory and insert the information into a workstation manual after highlighting key contacts for the person at the workstation with a red or yellow magic marker. The names, addresses, telephone numbers, and e-mail addresses of outside contacts also should be kept up-to-date in the manual.

Be sure to include an up-to-date organization chart that includes accurate job titles and the names of the job holders (spelled correctly).

If the occupant of the workstation is involved in projects, the workstation manual should include a client list and projects done by the firm, with some file reference (either paper or computer) to enable the occupant to quickly access finished project reports.

Finally, a workstation manual should have an abbreviated version of user instructions for the software program(s) required in the workstation. Instructions for voice-mail systems also belong in the manual, including guidelines for updating messages when employees are away for extended periods from the workstation.

Job Instructions

Within the workstation manual or the larger and more encompassing procedures manual, a manager should include job instructions for performing specific tasks. The nature of the tasks determines the need for those instructions.

Some tasks must be done exactly as instructed; others can be revised based on ingenuity and creativity. For the former, a manager, entrepreneur, or office professional should detail in writing the steps to do the work. Also identify the work's purpose in terms of corporate and department objectives. This sometimes can clarify the reason behind some step that will ensure the likelihood it will be followed. Hard skills or infrequent tasks, such as processing an invoice or preparing a spreadsheet, more often need such job aids than do soft skills (such as putting together a team meeting or delegating a task).

Written job instructions, sometimes called *job aides,* begin with a description of the purpose of the task. In discussing office safety, for example, the introduction might explain what kinds of safety issues the office might encounter and then provide direction in adhering to local, state, and federal regulations on workplace safety. With project management, this could include a to-do list to ensure that the project leader has clearly identified the project's purpose, has adequate resources to accomplish the objective, and uses appropriate problem-solving and critical-thinking techniques.

When preparing the instructions for a task, a manager should visualize how the work is done and then write down each step. An entrepreneur should explain and train new office help to do this work; the job instructions serve as a reminder. Consequently, a manager wants to be sure that no aspect of a job is forgotten when recording the instructions.

The job aide should be typed as double-spaced or with large margins. During training, the manager should refer the employee to the job aide in the policies and procedures manual or workstation manual, and allow him or her to take notes in the margins.

A manager should devote a single page or group of pages to each procedure. This way, he or she won't have to redo the entire manual just to update a procedure. Just remove and replace the outdated pages.

Besides the "dos," a policies and procedures manual should include the "don'ts," such as policies limiting expenditures for meals while on business travel or the authority for signing off (approving) such expenditures (specifying those requests that demand a second signature).

Corporate Style

The policies and procedures manual might include a section devoted to preferred methods of correspondence, including the how and when of e-mail, and how to handle correspondence and printed internal memos and reports.

Increasingly, companies are looking for timesaving correspondence methods. A manager should consider how he or she wants to handle brief messages. For instance, is a letter preferable, or will a brief message on a standard-size postal card suffice? Should each piece of correspondence and each memo get a formal reply, or is it acceptable to respond by returning the original document with marginal notations after copying it? Brief notes at the bottom of a letter or report save time and cut costs, and they also reduce the number of file copies. Likewise, rather than instruct the recipient of a report or letter to respond with a written note, a manager might use a stamp that asks the recipient of the document to "Reply here to save time. Photocopy for your files."

These techniques may not be suitable for handling every report, memo, or piece of correspondence, and the policies and procedures manual or workstation manual should specify when such informality is acceptable.

Various letter styles also exist. The corporate style may be the simplified letter form (without a salutation, but containing a subject line in all capital letters); the block format (in which all elements are flush left and a salutation exists); a modified block format (with dateline, complimentary close, and signature block all aligned at the center, toward the right margin, or at the right margin); and the modified semi-block letter format (in which the dateline may appear either to the right of dead center or flush right, and the inside address and salutation are aligned flush left while the paragraphs are indented).

The preferred formats to follow in e-mail, status reports, meeting minutes, and memos should be covered in the policies and procedures manual, too. For instance, does the manager want the list of attendees at the top of meeting minutes, or does he or she prefer to focus on the substance of the minutes and put the names of attendees at the end of the minutes?

If the job holder must develop handouts as part of the job, the manual might indicate the specific color of paper stock for various handouts (for instance, yellow for computer procedures, pink for access codes, blue for client lists, and so on). Restrictions about the use of the corporate logo and changes (even small ones) that can be made to the logo also should be included in a policies and procedures manual.

Corporate style governs the letterhead and other stationery used. Department guidelines might govern the color for interoffice correspondence.

Different colors for each department will help recipients distinguish between memos and reports from accounting and those from marketing or another department more easily. Or, bright colors might be used to signify documents that need immediate attention. Corporate style, as described in the policies and procedures manual, should address these issues.

Chapter 2 contains further details as well as examples of these different types of correspondence.

Office Library

In many offices, reference materials are not kept in a central location. However, a better setup organizes these materials in one centralized place, where they are accessible to everyone in the office, from its managers to office professionals. You will want to have several reference books in your "library," but you also might want to store at least one copy of a complete procedural manual, with or without all job descriptions for the office; recent issues of management and trade magazines received by the office; and copies of each finished report, or reports on projects-in-progress, so everything is accessible to all in the workspace.

These reference books should be on hand in the department or corporate library:

- *Dictionaries.* Standard unabridged dictionaries (or even abridged dictionaries) are helpful for spelling, definitions, word divisions, and pronunciations. Some dictionaries also contain grammar rules, abbreviations, forms of address, directories of colleges and universities, signs and symbols, and common English names and their sources. Specialized dictionaries exist for such areas as law, medicine, electronics ("computerese"), and accounting.

- *Thesauruses.* A thesaurus can be helpful for editing documents because it provides alternatives for words that are used frequently. Ideally, within the same paragraph a word should not be repeated; a thesaurus can provide a synonym.

- *Directories.* Trade directories list the names, addresses, and special data about companies. Telephone companies have business-to-business directories, and a corporate library should include one for its area in addition to the more traditional Yellow and White Pages.

An office library also should have a book of business quotations, corporate manners, state and federal government agencies, and parliamentary procedure manuals. To facilitate editing and printing, include a style book such as *The Chicago Manual of Style.*

To ensure that books aren't borrowed and then never returned, managers should institute a policy that requires those who borrow a book from the reference library to sign out when they borrow the book and sign in when they return it.

MOVING WITHOUT HEADACHES

Offices move for a variety of reasons. They outgrow their space, lose their lease, downsize staff, consolidate, and so on. Moving to a new location can be a positive experience and can be done with minimal disruption if there is sufficient time and effective planning beforehand.

Moving plans depend on the size of the office and location to which it is moving. A move down the street takes considerably less work than a move out of state. Generally, offices begin to pack about a week before the actual move. The best way to pack is to number cartons so the material that needs to be unpacked first is placed in carton 1, the next-important office supplies and papers are placed in carton 2, and so on. Each employee should have his or her own set of numbered boxes that include the employee's name or location. Actual packing should be in reverse of the carton numbers, with the least important materials packaged first. This allows the office to continue to operate up until the last day or so of the move.

The move itself is likely to occur over a weekend. Individuals can tour the new facility prior to the move. Ideally, they have input into the arrangement of their furnishings in their new workspace. To speed unpacking, it is helpful to allow employees access to the new quarters once all the cartons have been moved to the new location.

If several floors of an organization are moving to a new location, identify one individual on each floor to act as the move monitor and see that the staff is kept informed of developments associated with the move. Many organizations find it helpful to set up a team made up of individuals from different parts of the organization to work together to plan the relocation.

Ideally, cartons are requisitioned and left on various floors for employees to begin packing. Prior to packing, a day may be set aside for housekeeping to ensure that materials that might rightfully be tossed aren't unnecessarily relocated. After unpacking the cartons, stack them at a single location in the new facility, where they can be picked up and either thrown out or sent for recycling each evening.

The move itself may take only a day or two, but don't underestimate the full time line, which can take from four weeks to two months in planning (or even longer if the office is moving into newly built facilities with brand-new furnishings).

To begin, take a full inventory of every item in the office, and encourage employees to do the same for their individual work areas. Depending on the size of the office, you may want to assign individuals responsibility for common areas. Determine which items should be discarded, and provide a clean-up day to accomplish this. Take measurements of all equipment and furniture that will be moving with you—you will need them for the new space. In addition, make notes on any items such as artwork, plants, and antiques that will require special handling. Take this list, the measurements, and your notes to the company contracted to perform the actual moving. With this information, you will be better equipped to intelligently discuss any concerns or questions you may have.

Obtain a floor plan of the new space you will be occupying. Post it or distribute copies to each employee with specifics about available space, restrooms, and assigned work areas. Include information about the new neighborhood and surrounding amenities such as restaurants and public transportation. This information is usually available from the building manager or the local chamber of commerce. When possible, set up a day before the move for employees to tour and become familiar with the new space. Keep a list of questions they may have and ensure that they receive thorough answers to minimize concerns about the new location.

If everyone numbered cartons not only in the order in which they should be emptied, but also by his or her name and/or new room number, employees should find their cartons at their specific workstation for unpacking.

Notify all clients and suppliers of your move. Your local post office will provide change-of-address kits free of charge. In addition, it's a good idea to create stickers to announce the move, complete with the effective date and the address and telephone number of the new location. Place these stickers on all correspondence that leaves the office. Draw up another list of everyone who should be notified to ensure that no one is accidentally overlooked. In addition to clients and suppliers, the list should include magazine subscriptions, independent contractors, and anything or anyone else associated with your office.

Systems personnel will handle moving the computers and printers. The duration in which computers are unavailable will depend on the size of the office and the changes that the new facility demands. In some instances, a company might decide to make systems changes at the same time it moves, such as updating its current network.

The switchboard will coordinate telephone systems. Ideally, employees should retain their old telephone numbers, assuming that the move is a short one. All extensions should provide a message to callers during the move to alert them that they will be unable to reach their party until the move is completed.

Although a move can be a major endeavor, there is a sense of accomplishment when it is completed.

FOR MORE INFORMATION

If you can't find what you need from the phone numbers and Web sites listed in this chapter, you may need to expand your search.

- For more information on workstations, workstation design, and office layout, check your local library or bookstore in the architecture sections. Also, look for books on occupational design.

- For more information on workstation furniture and help in planning a workable design or structure, check in the Yellow Pages under office furniture. Most large office furniture showrooms will have sales reps who can walk you through the basics of modular workspace.

- For more information on office lighting, look in the Yellow Pages under lighting or office furniture. Many office lighting products are modular and come as part of office workstations.

- For more information on first aid, check with your companies' health insurance provider. Also, check with your local hospital. First-aid classes may be available.

- For more information on federal and state government regulations and for occupational safety and health, check the government listings in your telephone directory.

- For more information on office fire safety, check with your local fire department. They may be available to help plan escape routes, evaluate office fire safety, or conduct a drill.

- For more information on office reference books, check your local bookstore or library in the reference section.

- For more information on moving, check the Yellow Pages under moving or relocation.

7

OFFICE OPERATIONS

◆

- **Forms Management**
  Generic Forms
- **Filing Systems**
  Traditional Filing Systems
  Electronic Filing Systems
  Physical Setup of Files
  Preparation of Material for Filing
  Finding and Using Files
  Indexing and Alphabetizing
  Long-Term File Maintenance
- **Managing Money**
  Managing Cash Transactions
  Handling the Bank Account
  Handling Cash Payments
  Bookkeeping
  Payroll
- **For More Information**

Increasingly, office professionals are finding themselves involved in continuous improvement projects concerned with office operations. Because of their familiarity with the various aspects of office operations, they are valued additions to these planning teams. Not only are they familiar with the work done in general, but they can suggest ways to minimize the many steps in processing paper, whether the paper is a simple form, a letter, a complex report, or another document. A team's objective may be to computerize some forms currently on paper, or it may be to do away with any forms at all by eliminating unnecessary steps.

This involvement of office professionals in restructuring office operations has grown. In fact, some organizations have given support to project teams that are made up exclusively of office professionals who meet to recommend processes or other procedures to help run the office more efficiently. The savings have been substantial in both time and money.

How broad are these teams' charters? As broad as office operations themselves, which means that office professionals increasingly are having a voice in record maintenance, recordkeeping, and much more—including bookkeeping, the processing of payroll, handling of bank deposits, and maintenance of tax records. The extent of their involvement in the planning of office operations is a reflection of their job descriptions and the needs of the offices in which they work.

One of the first places in which office professionals, either individually or in continuous improvement teams, can have an impact is in forms management.

FORMS MANAGEMENT

Forms today are very different from the forms of the past. Many companies are now putting their forms—from personnel descriptions to travel expenditure forms and requisition forms—on company intranets. Departments that maintain their own intranet, and have forms specific to their function, may also have computerized their most frequently used forms. Certainly, most companies use spreadsheets for budgeting, and still others use variations of spreadsheets for project management. Forms have gone way beyond the simple, single-page format that could be filled out on an electric typewriter.

Many forms with which office professionals work are developed by others, but forms are also developed by the office professionals themselves to minimize repetition of a memo or letter. Rather than write a memo requesting supplies, for instance, it is much simpler to have a form to send to purchasing. If the professional also coordinates supply needs for the department, he or she might create a form that lists those office supplies most frequently requested. Each staff member has copies of the form and periodically gives a copy to the office professional, who collates all requests onto a single form that is submitted to purchasing.

The secret to creating a worthwhile form for yourself and others is to think ahead about the information it will contain. To make sure that your form deals with all the issues that might arise, put yourself in the shoes not only of those who will fill out the form, but also of those who will use it.

Think about the format of the form. A factor in choosing the format—paper or electronic—is the number of individuals who will be using the form. Some forms lend themselves to paper (for example, attendance sheets, which require managerial signoff); others, which might be needed by every member of the department or corporation, may be better installed on the department or corporate computer network (for example, meeting room allocations, including audiovisual needs).

Another factor that influences the format of a form is the technological level of its user. Although most organizations are moving quickly to computerized forms, there are still occasions when it is simpler to have a form that can be kept in a manila folder and handed out to staff members as needed, usually when the need is infrequent. A case in point would be a form used by staff members to order business cards. The form would contain all the pertinent information needed by the organization to produce the cards. This would include name and title of the staff member, company address and telephone number, fax number and e-mail address, and, if there is one, the corporate Web site address.

GENERIC FORMS

In the course of your job, you will undoubtedly work with many different forms used by your department or company. You probably will even be called upon to create or implement some. Although it can seem like a fairly simple task, there are a few factors to take into account. Consider whether the form should be created from scratch or whether a preprinted form already exists that will work, whether duplicate copies will be needed, whether the form has to be printed or can be copied, what information is required, and so on. Also, don't overlook forms that were already created by a predecessor; they may be just what you need.

Before simply reordering a form that you currently use, consider whether the form is still practical. It may be time to update the form to reflect changes in office processes.

If you decide to create a form or update an existing one, first determine the information that your finished form should contain. For instance, a request for office supplies will need a requisition or budget number, but should it also have the extension number of the person making the request? What about the date when the supplies are needed? How about the date when the form is submitted?

Besides the information itself, you next need to consider the order of the information that you are requesting on the form. Does it make sense? You wouldn't ask for someone's address before asking for that person's name, for instance. Neither would you ask a manager to sign off on a new software program before he or she had specified the program. Finally, you want to think about who, besides the person for whom the form is intended, will need a copy, or even who needs to sign off on the form to get it processed.

Now sit down and type your form. Once you have created your form or chosen an existing one, take a look. Is it:

- Properly spaced, with sufficient room to be filled out either by a typewriter or by hand?

- Logical and arranged in a sequential order, according to its intended use?

- Free from obscure jargon?

- Free from the clutter of unnecessary information?

Before committing yourself to numerous printed forms or copies, ask for suggestions from the people who actually use the form. Also, check filed copies of the current form to see whether people are routinely adding information not accounted for in the form itself. Make sure all the information needed is included.

Make sure that the form is convenient for the user. The purpose of any form is efficiency. Completing a form is supposed to be easier and faster than writing all the information from scratch on a blank sheet of paper. But proper design and regular periodic review are essential for maintaining this efficiency.

Experts suggest these additional tips:

- Look for opportunities to construct multipurpose forms.

- Test your new form before your final printing. This will help you work out any bugs that you may have missed. Make sure that you proofread and run a spell checker!

- Be sure to check spacing. Too much or too little makes the form inefficient.

- Note the forms from other businesses as they cross your desk. They may provide ideas for your revisions.

- Be aware that elements on certain technical forms are essential. Before revising, have the company's legal staff review them.

FILING SYSTEMS

An efficient filing system is one that reduces clutter, separates information into recognizable categories, and makes possible the rapid and accurate retrieval of documents. There are several standard methods, and each has its advantages and disadvantages. Nevertheless, it is not the system but the use of it that determines its effectiveness. Documents need to be filed so they can be found. This applies especially to information needed for making day-to-day management decisions. Given the system, the professional should be able to pull a document from a file within five minutes of a request. What if you had to wait for more than a few minutes for professionals in a doctor's office to retrieve your file? Or a financial advisor, an insurance agent, or your family lawyer? Each of these individuals has information that is critical to your situation, and you depend on them to keep good records about you.

A large organization may employ a number of office professionals who are responsible for maintaining all the company's records in a central area. In a small office, there may be only a few file cabinets, or assistants may each keep their own. In either case, you should be familiar with all the filing systems commonly used because every office depends on one or another of them.

Of course, in today's offices, chances are that the office professional will be dealing with both paper and electronic files and filing systems. Individual desktops may be tied into a central file server or other system. Even with this proliferation of technology, the "paperless office" is still not a reality. Office professionals today must be prepared to deal with both hard copy and electronic files, and be able to access both types of documents quickly and efficiently.

TRADITIONAL FILING SYSTEMS

The basic hard-copy filing systems in use in the modern office are alphabetic, combination subject, numeric, and phonetic. *Alphabetic filing* entails filing papers by name, subject, or geographic location in alphabetical order. *Combination subject* systems use both numbers and words, or numbers and letters arranged in alphabetical order. Such names as alphanumeric, subject-numeric, and duplex-numeric are used to describe systems in this category. *Numeric,* or *nonalphabetic, filing* exercises the use of numbers for filing purposes; and such names as numeric, decimal, terminal digit, triple digit, and middle digit are used to describe systems in this category. The *phonetic filing* system involves using letters and sounds in code number form.

Filing systems may be direct or indirect. In a *direct* method of filing, a person can locate a file immediately without first having to refer to a cross-index file to find out where to look. In an *indirect* filing system, a person cannot immediately locate the file but must refer to a cross-index file to determine where to locate it. For example, if the basic filing system is a subject system and the professional wishes to locate the file for a specific firm, he or she must either know the subject under which the firm is filed or refer to an alphabetical cross-index, looking up the firm name and finding out in which subject file the file is located.

Alphabetic Systems

Almost 90 percent of all filing that is done in the office is alphabetical. In an alphabetic system, office correspondence and other papers are filed alphabetically according to name, geographic location, or subject.

Name

In a *name file,* all papers are filed alphabetically according to the last name of the person or the name of a company. It is a direct method of filing and very simple to expand because any new name is filed alphabetically without disturbing the name before or after it.

Geographic Location

In the *geographic system,* the papers are filed alphabetically according to the name of the state; then alphabetically according to the town or city within that state; then alphabetically according to the name of the correspondent within the town or city. Mail-order houses, public-utility companies, publishing houses, and organizations that serve a geographic district or have branch offices in different areas use this system of filing.

The geographic system of filing is an indirect system. It is not possible to locate the file for a specific firm without first referring to a cross-index that lists the names of all the firms in alphabetical order and gives the location of each firm. In other words, if you do not know the location of the firm, you must refer to the cross-index under the firm name and determine under what geographic location to find the file.

Subject

When a company deals with products, supplies, materials, advertising, and so forth, the *subject system* is used. It is an indirect system because a cross-index file is used in order to save time in filing and finding material, and to locate correspondence by firm name when the subject is in doubt. The folders in the subject file are arranged alphabetically by the name of the product. The material within the folders is arranged by date, with the latest date in the front of the folder.

Often, a combination of subject filing and name filing is used. If there is not enough material to set up a separate subject file, the subject captions can be set up in a name file.

Combination Subject Systems

Some companies that use the subject filing system have found it necessary to use major subject titles, with separate subcategories relating to that major topic, to more quickly locate specific information. A major subject outline containing the most important titles is set up in alphabetical order. Next, subcategory subject titles within each area are placed beneath the major subject titles. Then, numbers are used in combination with the subjects in the outline to make up the *combination subject filing system.*

When a company uses the combination subject filing system, it is extremely important that an up-to-date list be kept of all subjects and their code letters and numbers. This list should be circulated to all persons and departments needing access to the files. Likewise, a *relative index* should be made, listing all possible subjects and the location of all pertinent information pertaining to each subject. This list, too, should be updated frequently and distributed to those using the files.

Subject-Numeric

The *subject-numeric system* uses the major subject title with numbers assigned to the subcategories underneath it. For example, the subject heading "Automobile Accessories" would be treated in this manner:

AUTOMOBILE ACCESSORIES

1 Automobile Accessories: Tires

1-1 Standard Black

1-2 Whitewall

Duplex-Numeric

The *duplex-numeric system* makes use of both numbers and letters of the alphabet. A digit is selected for the subject; this is followed by a dash and another digit for a division of the subject, plus a letter for further subdivision. For example, the subject heading "Automobile Accessories" might be given the number 13, the division "Automobile Accessories: Tires" would be numbered 13-1; a further subdivision, "Automobile Accessories: Tires, Standard Black," would be numbered 13-1a; "Automobile Accessories: Tires, Whitewall" would be numbered 13-1b. The outline would look like this:

13 AUTOMOBILE ACCESSORIES

13-1 Automobile Accessories: Tires

13-1a Standard Black

13-1b Whitewall

Alphanumeric

The *alphanumeric system* uses letters of the alphabet for the major subject titles, along with letters and numbers for subtopics:

A	ADMINISTRATION
A 1	Long-Range Planning
A 1 - 1	Guidelines and Schedules
A:	Competition
A2-1	Survey Reports
A3	Public Relations
G	GOVERNMENT RELATIONS
G1	Air Pollution Control
G1-1	Vehicle Emissions
G1-1-1	Health Hazards

Numeric Systems

Numeric filing systems are nonalphabetical. All records are filed solely by numbers. Numeric systems tend to be used in highly specialized businesses.

When the numeric system is used, an *accession register* must be kept so that a particular file can be retrieved quickly. The accession register is a book or card file that contains each file number, beginning with the first number, as well as the correspondent's name on that file. The correspondents' names should be alphabetized so that you can get the file quickly if a correspondent's file number has been forgotten.

Straight Numeric

In the *straight-numeric system,* records are filed according to strict numeric sequence. Folder number 1 is given to the first client or account, folder number 2 is given to the second, and so forth, in strict numeric order. Often, these file numbers correspond to order numbers or invoices. Consequently, you might find such a system in offices of manufacturers or wholesalers.

Terminal Digit

In the *terminal-digit system,* numbers on a file are read from right to left. Usually, the last (or terminal) two digits are the drawer number, the next two digits are the folder number, and any other numbers indicate the sequence within the folders. For example, an insurance policy numbered 567,123 would be stored in drawer 23, folder 71; and the 56 would refer to its sequence in the folder. This kind of system might be found in hospitals or insurance companies.

Triple Digit

The *triple-digit system* is similar to the terminal-digit system, except that the numbers are read in three-digit units instead of two. The terminal three digits of a number are called the *primary* numbers, and the remaining digits refer to the sequence of the papers in the folders bearing the primary numbers. For example, the insurance policy numbered 567,123 would be found in folder 123, and 567 would refer to its sequence in the folder.

Middle Digit

In the *middle-digit system,* the third and fourth digits from the right are separated from the last two digits on the right. For example, in the insurance policy number 567,123, the policy would be filed in folder 71, and 23 would refer to its sequence in the folder.

Decimal System

The *decimal system* is used only in highly specialized businesses. The system may be based on the Dewey decimal system, which is the system commonly used by public libraries, although many are switching to the Library of Congress Catalog cataloging system.

Phonetic Systems

The *phonetic filing system* is a filing method based on the use of letters and sounds. Organizations that file records by individuals' surnames encounter the problem of filing names that sound alike but are spelled differently, such as Smith and Smyth, or Schmidt and Schmitt. To eliminate this problem, the Remington Rand Office Systems Division of the Sperry Rand Corporation developed the Soundex Phonetic Filing System.

Soundex is a combination of spelling, or sounds and numbers. Basic sounds are represented by six fundamental letters: the consonants *B, C, D, L, M,* and *R,* which make up the entire Soundex alphabet. Each of these consonants is given a separate code number: *B* is 1, *C* is 2, *D* is 3, *L* is 4, *M* is 5, and *R* is 6. The remaining consonants in the alphabet have the same relative sounds as the six basic Soundex consonants and are grouped with the *basic* consonant. All vowels and the letters *W, H,* and *Y* have no number and are not coded. To use this system, look at the *first* letter of the *surname* and sort by *that letter* first. Then code the *remaining* letters in the surname by looking at the following chart.

The phonetic system is used in large hospitals, police departments, and the Social Security office. It is used where there are lots of records, where requests for information come over the phone, and where retrieval must be done quickly. You'll also find such systems in mail-order firms that take orders over the phone.

Code	Key Letters and Equivalents
1	BFPV
2	CGJKQSXZ
3	DT
4	L
5	MN
6	R

To file the surname "Snyder," the first letter, *S*, is recorded. The next letter to be coded is *N*, which is code 5. *Y* is disregarded, *D* is code 3, *E* is disregarded, and *R* is code 6. The surname "Snyder" is thus coded S536.

To file the surname "Day," code the letter *D* and three zeros to show that only vowels follow the first consonant, *D*. When no consonants or not enough consonants follow the first letter in the surname, use one, two, or three zeros to give the name a three-digit code. The code for "Day" is D000. The surname "Straw" is S360, "Levy" is L100, and "Kelly" is K400.

ELECTRONIC FILING SYSTEMS

As computers spread throughout businesses and offices, the problems of locating computer files spread as well. Often the "storage" of computer files is far from the control of any one individual. Central file servers, floppy disk storage, hard drives, networked computers, tape drives, cartridge drives, writeable CDs, and who-knows-what tomorrow, mean that a "file" can be virtually anywhere. So, for starters, an office or an enterprise must come to some consensus about who is responsible for what when it comes to recordkeeping and file maintenance.

The good news for the already-burdened office professional is that, as computer-related filing tasks grow, the information technology specialist assumes some of the burden for establishing company-wide standards for what would be the equivalent of filing electronic documents.

Assuming that your company lacks someone with that assignment in your company—and simply as a matter of personal convenience for you and those you influence—here are some broad guidelines for managing electronic files. They apply, no matter what commercial software you may be using or which internal systems have been established.

Be consistent. Use a file-naming methodology that makes it easy for you and others to identify the electronic files you may end up searching for.

Remember file extensions. Missing electronic documents may not be appearing on your search screen because the search is underway for a *.DOC* file that's been inadvertently tagged as *.TXT*.

Expand your horizons. Encourage computer file users to agree to major categories of items that will be retained in the system and to make their entries consistent. A filing system is no good if only one person can discern what's in a computer record by its name alone (even though some programs allow a preview of the document).

Watch your folders and subdirectories. Get agreement from all likely file users about how certain types of material will be grouped: for example, by territory, customer name, customer number, salesperson, product, project, order date—whatever.

Tag paper documents with electronic file names. Even the so-called paperless office generates a great deal of paper, especially hard copies because the file user is afraid something may happen to the electronic file. Simply recording the file name on the paper copies of the document can save much time hunting for a "lost" electronic file.

Divide and conquer. Saving multipage material as a single file may not be efficient. A year's worth of correspondence packed into a single file and added to week after week results in a long document that must be opened and scanned to find a particular bit of old info. Unique document files may be easier to handle.

Print appropriate directories. From time to time, make a hard copy record of what's on a disk or what's in a particular area of the network. Eyeballing the list may be a faster way to search for what you seek than chugging through the listing on the screen.

Back up files. Making backup files always was worthwhile. It still is. Lost files can be recovered from the backup only if the backup has been made.

Clean up files. What's valid for file cabinets is valid for computer records. On some periodic schedule, purge the system of stuff you no longer need. Dump it or store it to a medium such as disk or tape. Less clutter on a computer or in a system server leaves fewer places for "lost" files to hide and can speed the search process.

PHYSICAL SETUP OF FILES

Several kinds of file cabinets are standard in offices today. One is the *traditional vertical filing cabinet,* which has four drawers that hold file folders enclosing material on the regulation 8½-by-11-inch typing paper. A law office or a company with many legal papers will need a wider cabinet to accommodate the longer legal paper. The standard drawer will carry a load of from 60 to 70 pounds. For efficient filing, the file drawers should not be overcrowded.

Also standard in offices today is the *lateral or horizontal file cabinet.* These cabinets can hold either letter- or legal-size folders in much larger drawers. Lateral filing is particularly useful for active files in which papers are inserted and withdrawn constantly and which are not to be retained for a long period of time. Proponents of lateral filing claim much time is saved by having the files immediately at hand and in sight.

Another option is the *open-shelf method.* It is popular in medical offices, where files are color coded and need to be viewed. Lateral or open shelf filing can result in a savings of as much as 40 percent of office floor space. The aisles between the shelves can be considerably narrower than those needed between cabinets with drawers because the additional space for pulling out drawers is not needed. Also, files can be stacked higher than drawers—in many instances, stacked to the ceiling.

Arranging Files

Files should be arranged to minimize the amount of walking required to and from the files. The file drawers may be labeled in either vertical (top to bottom) or horizontal (left to right) order. Space may be saved if the file cabinets are backed up against a wall. If there are many cabinets, it may be more efficient to arrange them in a cluster in the center of a room. Floor space is expensive; therefore, some consideration should be given to arranging cabinets economically. Adequate aisle space between cabinets must be allowed. At least 28 inches must be allowed for a file drawer when it is opened into the aisle. Long rows of cabinets should have gaps between them to save time in getting from one row to another.

To make the most productive use of your time, you may want to keep your active project files in your desk until you have completed the work. Most desks, or tables in office cubicles, have at least two drawers that are deep enough to maintain files.

Setting Up the File Drawer

The basic file drawer is divided into alphabetic sections or numeric sections. The first division consists of metal or plastic dividers that you can purchase from an office supply catalog. These fit snugly into the drawer, hanging on the drawer framework. Guides are sold in sets, based on file size. The tabs may be on the left side or in the middle of the file drawer. Behind these dividers are hanging files that subdivide sections or that call attention to important names or numbers. Individual folders, arranged alphabetically, chronologically, or numerically, are placed directly within the hanging files. These folders are used for correspondents who communicate frequently with the firm.

When five to eight pieces of correspondence from the same source have accumulated, an individual folder is set up. The full name of the correspondent is on the tab. Tabs are usually alternated in position so that one does not come directly behind another. When material is arranged in an individual folder, the latest date is always in the front of the folder.

File drawers, incidentally, come in two sizes: letter size and legal size. If your filing cabinet doesn't have legal-sized drawers, you can still accommodate legal-sized documents by filing them sideways in the drawer.

When material is placed in a miscellaneous folder, it should be arranged alphabetically, with the latest date in front for each person or subject.

Miscellaneous folders follow the individual folders at the end of each major division. They are used for correspondence that does not warrant individual folders. The tab on the miscellaneous folder may be a different size or be marked with a distinctive color so that it can easily located.

When preparing index tabs and labels for guides and folders, type the letter of the alphabet or the name. Use the first typing space below the fold of the file drawer label, and start typing two spaces from the left of the label.

Use initial capitals, and indent the second line two spaces, so that the first word on the top line will stand out. Use abbreviations if the name or subject is long. Tabs are best created on a typewriter.

Sometimes, you will want to include more than a name or number on the folder. In that case, use a label for the cuts of file folders. Cuts come left, right, and center, and you can purchase boxes of either. Most boxes contain an assortment with tabs at the left, right, and center, allowing you to stagger the folders for maximum visibility. Labels for cuts can be typed or printed. If you print them, besides measuring carefully for fit, you will want to purchase the right kind of paper so your sheet doesn't get caught in your printer.

PREPARATION OF MATERIAL FOR FILING

So, you've decided which system you're going to use, how you will divide your files, and where they're going to go. Now you're ready to begin filing. Before you start, check all papers to see whether they are to be filed and have been released for filing. Sort the material into relevant groupings. For example, if you were filing correspondence, you might want to separate it into personal, business, or contracts, etc. Remove all staples, paper clips, or other paper holders.

As you file, it's helpful to highlight or underline the name in colored pencil to indicate where the letter is to be filed. If you are using a numerical system, indicate the guide number in the upper right corner. It's also helpful to use a highlighter or colored pencil to circle important words that will help you locate a particular paper when it is needed. Make any cross-reference sheets that are required.

> **TIP:** When a letter or a record may be filed in one of two places, make out a *cross-reference sheet.* File the letter or record under the more important name, and cross-refer the second name or subject. For example, suppose you are filing a letter using the alphabetic system based on an individual account. A letter is received from Sam Crawford at Jordan Marsh Company. It would be filed under Sam Crawford. The cross-reference would be under *J* for the Marsh Jordan Company.
>
> Crawford, Sam
>
> SEE
>
> Jordan Marsh Company

Based on whichever filing system you'll be using, the following is a simple step-by-step checklist to use when you are getting ready to file material:

1. *Inspection.* Read or scan the material. Put a check mark in the upper left corner to signal that this material should be filed.

2. *Indexing.* Determine which name or subject to use for filing the material. This is vital because poor indexing means "poor finding" and a loss of time.

3. *Coding.* Coding is the physical act of marking the name, subject, and so on under which the material is to be filed. Put the code in the upper right corner. Make cross-reference sheets at this point.

4. *Sorting.* Sort the material in a rough, superficial manner: all *As* together, all *Bs* together, and so on in alphabetical order. Put all *10s* together, all *20s* together, and so on for numeric filing. Then sort each stack according to "strict sorting," using the standard filing rules that your firm uses.

5. *Filing.* Place correspondence in the folders, placing the top to the left of the folder. Put material in the miscellaneous folder alphabetically, with the latest date on top. Place material in individual folders chronologically, with the latest date on top.

FINDING AND USING FILES

The reason office professionals spend so much time deciding on, organizing, and maintaining a record-filing system is so that the information is easy to find when needed. When it is necessary to remove material from a file for use, replace the record or correspondence with an "out" guide or card. Plastic placeholders can be purchased from an office supply firm, but you can also make them yourself by using old file folders or construction paper. If you make your own, attach an index card or sheet of paper. Alternatively, you can tape an envelope inside the file folder. In this envelope, you can keep not only notes about records that have been charged out, but also new documents. The "out" folder is a good place to store new documents until the charged-out file is returned.

On the "out" card or paper, you should record the date, the name of the record taken, who has it, and the date it is to be returned. The word *Out* should be printed on the folder or sheet, or the plastic placeholder. A different color should be used, so that the guide stands out.

Be sure to record the withdrawal of any material that goes out of the office for a period of time or any material that someone is going to use away from the office. Confidential records should be used in the office and returned to the files immediately.

Card File

A card file represents an excellent way to keep track of critical files. It can be used to keep a record of files that are charged out, or used as an index for faster retrieval of documents. The cards contain the location and status of all records. It's a particularly helpful addition to your major filing system if you have a large number of documents whose location in the filing system could be forgotten. A card file (usually with 3-by-5-inch cards) is normally arranged alphabetically by name of correspondent or subject matter.

Color Coding

Color coding can be a worthwhile expedient, permitting the easier location of specific files or file sections. Before making a decision about color coding, study the various methods available and determine which would be best for the particular type of material filed in the office for which the system is intended.

Simple color coding of files can involve file folders available in a wide variety of colors, or a color tab affixed to manila folders or hanging dividers. One of the common ways to use these files is to select a new color for each year within an alphabetical file.

Different offices use color codes for different purposes. Some use colors simply to differentiate file years. Others use colors to differentiate accounts (for example, consumer versus business-to-business); others, with multiple divisions, use different colors to differentiate the in-house relationships; still others use colors to separate some accounts, customers, or other correspondents from others. For instance, some charitable organizations might use different colors to signify the level of donation.

Color coding is usually employed to identify a filing series that has been categorized by the alphabetic system or any of the several numeric systems discussed earlier in this chapter. A specific color is assigned to each number or letter. One manufacturer of filing materials (Datafile) uses twelve colors twice—the second time with a white bar that sets it apart from the first. These twenty-four colors, with white for *Y* and gray for *Z*, serve for the twenty-six letters of the alphabet.

The pattern used depends on the complexity of the material to be filed. Datafile, using its twelve colors, also has folders with two color bands for identification of the first two letters of a word or name. By identifying two letters, the file is expanded from the twenty-six letters of the alphabet to about three or four hundred segments. The possible total is 26×26, or 676, but all combinations of letters do not occur at the beginning of words or names.

All of these variations—from bars to dots to labels—can be purchased from any office supply catalog.

TIP: The key to successful use of color coding—for that matter, any filing system—is consistency. Failure just once to color code a new folder or place an "out" guide in the drawer with information on the material taken will defeat the entire purpose of having the system.

Another type of color coding, popular for use with open-shelf filing systems, involves a simpler color code. One company that keeps order files for exactly two years before discarding uses a color-coded dot on the folders holding the records for alternate years. Thus, the file at any particular time consists of folders marked in one color for one of the years represented, unmarked folders for another, and a second colored dot for the third. If, for example, the date is March 2005, the folders for April through December of 2003 (January through March having been discarded) have dots of one color, the folders for 2004 are plain, and the folders for January to date in 2005 have dots of a second color. Folders for 2006 will be plain, and then the system will repeat.

INDEXING AND ALPHABETIZING

The value of your filing system is based on your ability to quickly access files or documents within existing systems. If your system is alphabetic, it is important that you set specific rules and consistently follow them.

The following indexing rules are standard rules for filing. ARMA, the Association of Records Managers and Administrators, Inc., uses these guidelines with minor exceptions.

Individual names. Names of individuals are indexed by the last name (the surname) first, then the first name, and then the middle initial or middle name:

Name	Indexing Order
Alfred M. Amell	Amell, Alfred M.
Grace R. Gladd	Gladd, Grace R.
J. Thomas Williams	Williams, J. Thomas

Business names. The names of business establishments, institutions, and organizations are indexed as they are written, unless they embody the name of an individual. Exceptions to this rule are the names of schools. When the individual's name is part of a firm name, index by considering the last name (surname) first, and then the first name and the middle initial or middle name, if any.

Name	Indexing Order
Atlantic Service Station	Atlantic Service Station
Earl A. Stone Book Publishers	Stone, Earl A. Book Publishers
General Department Store	General Department Store
James A. Carson Company	Carson, James A. Company
J. M. Morgan Sign Company	Morgan, J. M. Sign Company
Nathan Hale Junior High School	Nathan Hale Junior High School
Rose and Peter Beauty Supplies	Rose and Peter Beauty Supplies
Rose Peter Beauty Shoppe	Peter, Rose Beauty Shoppe
Rose's Beauty Salon	Rose's Beauty Salon
Stone and Book Publishing Company	Stone and Book Publishing Company
Stone Book Publishers	Stone Book Publishers
Thomas Milford Stiles Florist Shop	Thomas Milford Stiles Florist Shop
Troy Sand and Gravel, Inc.	Troy Sand and Gravel, Inc.

Alphabetical order. Names are alphabetized by comparing each of their letters. If the first units are alike, compare the second units. If there is no second unit, the single name is filed first. The rule of "nothing before something" applies here. A surname followed by a first initial only goes before the same surname, followed by a complete first name beginning with the same letter as the initial. Again, "nothing before something."

Indexing Order

Name	*Unit 1*	*Unit 2*
Carson	Carson	
Carson Brothers	Carson	Brothers
J. Carson	Carson	J.
James Carson	Carson	James

Letters used as words. Consider any single letter as a word— not part of a cluster or part of an acronym.

Indexing Order

Name	Unit 1	Unit 2	Unit 3	Unit 4
NAPA Jobbers	N	A	P	A
NCR Accounting Company	N	C	R	Accounting
Pacific Car Company	Pacific	Car	Company	
R & B Auto Service	R	B	Auto	Service

Abbreviations. Abbreviations are indexed as if the words they represent are written out in full; hence, *Mme.* is indexed as *Madame.*

Indexing Order

Name	Unit 1	Unit 2	Unit 3
Mme. Sophie's Boutique	Madame	Sophie's	Boutique
Mr. Pete's Grocery	Mister	Pete's	Grocery
St. Alexis Hospital	Saint	Alexis	Hospital

Article *the*. When *the* is part of the name, it is disregarded in filing. If it is the initial word, it is placed at the end of the name in parentheses. If *the* occurs in the body of the name, it is placed in parentheses and disregarded.

Name	Indexing Order
The Cleveland Boat Company	Cleveland Boat Company (The)
Danny the Tailor	Danny (the) Tailor
Stanley of the Ritz	Stanley (of the) Ritz

Such words as *and, for, on, in, by,* and *of the* are disregarded in indexing and filing. However, they are placed in parentheses when writing names on folders and cards.

Hyphenated names. Hyphenated firm names are treated as separate names because they represent separate individuals. When listed among other proper names, the second name is regarded as a given name for alphabetizing purposes.

Name	Indexing Order
Branch-Merrill Company	Branch Merrill Company
Richard T. Branch	Branch, Richard T.

Winifred I. Wilson	Wilson, Winifred I.
Wilson-Wyman, Inc.	Wilson Wyman, Inc.

Hyphenated individual names are treated as one name because they represent one individual.

Name	**Indexing Order**
James A. Gladd-Monroe	GladdMonroe, James A.
Patricia Lloyd-Taylor	LloydTaylor, Patricia
Jane L. Marin-Jones	MarinJones, Jane L.

One- or two-word names. Names that may be spelled as one word or two words are usually considered to be one word.

	Indexing Order		
Name	*Unit 1*	*Unit 2*	*Unit 3*
Raybrook Cleaners	Raybrook	Cleaners	
Ray Brook Paint Company	RayBrook	Paint	Company
South East Electric Shop	SouthEast	Electric	Shop
Southeast Supply Company	Southeast	Supply	Company
Good Will Cleaners	GoodWill	Cleaners	
Goodwill Industries	Goodwill	Industries	

Individual surnames with prefixes. Prefixes such as *D', d', De, de, Del, Des, Di, Du, Fitz, l', La, Le, M', Mac, Mc, O', Van, Von,* and so on, are indexed as written and treated as one word.

	Indexing Order		
Name	*Unit 1*	*Unit 2*	*Unit 3*
D'Aoust, James	D'Aoust	James	
Darling, John E.	Darling	John	E.
De Lancett, Morris	De Lancett	Morris	
DeLancey, Lincoln	DeLancey	Lincoln	
MacDonald, George H.	MacDonald	George	H.
McCasland, Raymond A.	McCasland	Raymond	A.
Van Cour, Elsie A.	Van Cour	Elsie	A.
Von Ottenfeld, Oscar M.	Von Ottenfeld	Oscar	M.

Words ending in S. When a name ends in *s'* or *'s*, the *s* is considered part of the name.

Indexing Order

Name	Unit 1	Unit 2	Unit 3
Bob's Sport Shop	Bob's	Sport	Shop
Boy Scout Camp	Boy	Scout	Camp
Boys' Clothing Store	Boys'	Clothing	Store
Williams' Dry Cleaning	Williams'	Dry	Cleaning
William's Service Station	William's	Service	Station

Titles. A personal or professional title or degree is usually not considered in indexing and filing. When the name is written, the title is placed in parentheses at the end of the name.

Name	Indexed as
Dr. Richard P. Bellaire	Bellaire, Richard P. (Dr.)
Ms. Helen Hayles	Hayles, Helen (Ms.)
Grace M. Janson, D. D.	Janson, Grace M. (D. D.)

A religious or foreign title is considered as the first indexing unit when it is followed by a given name only.

Indexed and filed as

Brother Francis

Madame Eugenie

Prince Charles

Princess Anne

Sister Mary Megan

Married women's names. The name of a married woman is indexed according to the name by which she prefers to be known. Some women retain their maiden names after marriage, and this preference should be respected. A married name could be a woman's given first name, her maiden surname, and her husband's surname, or it could be her given first and middle names (or initial for the middle name) and her husband's surname. The title *Mrs.* is disregarded in filing, but it is placed in parentheses after the name. If signatures on correspondence from a married woman indicate that she prefers *Ms.*, then that is the title placed in parentheses after her name. The name of the husband may be given in parentheses below the woman's legal name.

Name	Indexing Order
Mrs. John F. Matson (Mary Nelson)	Matson, Mary Nelson (Mrs.) (Mrs. John F. Matson)
Mrs. Lucien (Louise S.) Platt	Platt, Louise S. (Mrs.) (Mrs. Lucien Platt)
Mrs. Robert (Mary Lee) Young	Young, Mary Lee (Mrs.) (Mrs. Robert Young)

Names with numbers. When a name contains a number, it is considered as if the number were written as a single unit and is spelled as it is pronounced.

	Indexing Order		
Name	*Unit 1*	*Unit 2*	*Unit 3*
A 1 Garage	A	One	Garage
The 400 Club	Fourhundred	Club (The)	
7th Ave. Building	Seventh	Avenue	Building

Geographic names. An easy rule to follow in arranging geographic names is to treat them as they are written. Each element in a compound name of a geographic location is indexed as a separate unit.

	Indexing Order			
Name	*Unit 1*	*Unit 2*	*Unit 3*	*Unit 4*
Mount Holly, New Jersey	Mount	Holly	New	Jersey
New Bedford, Massachusetts	New	Bedford	Massachusetts	
Newburgh, New York	Newburgh	New	York	

When the first element of a geographic name is not of English origin, that element is considered part of the first unit.

	Indexing Order	
Name	*Unit 1*	*Unit 2*
Des Moines, Iowa	DesMoines	Iowa
Las Vegas Hotel	LasVegas	Hotel
Los Angeles, California	LosAngeles	California
San Francisco, California	SanFrancisco	California

THE ASSOCIATION OF RECORDS MANAGERS AND ADMINISTRATORS INDEXING AND FILING RULES

ARMA, the Association of Records Managers and Administrators, Inc., in its book of indexing rules, *Rules for Alphabetical Filing*, has established three classifications for indexing: individual names, business establishment names, and government/political designations. ARMA recommends separating index units with the diagonal (/). ARMA rules are essentially the same as the ones listed previously, with the following differences:

1. The hyphenated company name is treated as one unit.

    Brown-Jacobs/Company/

2. Compound geographical names are treated as separate units.

    Las/Vegas/Construction/Company

    Del/Rio/Music/Store/

3. Company names that have compass points as part of the name are indexed as separate units.

Name	Indexing Order
North East Alignment	North/East/Alignment/
Southeastern Transfer	South/eastern/Transfer/

4. The *'s* is included as part of the indexing unit; that is, the apostrophe is disregarded.

Name	Indexing Order
Leon's Barbecue	Leon's/Barbecue/
Leons' Music Store	Leons'/Music/Store/

5. Company names that are numbers and written in figure form, such as 500 Club, are arranged in strict numeric sequence and are not spelled out. They are filed at the front of the entire alphabetic file.

Name	Indexing Order
1 Hour Cleaners	1/Hour/Cleaners/
7th Street Auto Shop	7(th)/Street/Shop/
8 Ball Eatery	8/Ball/Eatery/
400 Executive Clothiers	400/Executive/Clothiers/
500 Club	500/Club/

Government offices and departments. The name of a federal government office is indexed as follows:

1. *United States Government* (whether or not it is written as part of the name)

2. Principal word or words in the name of the department

3. Principal word or words in the name of the bureau

4. Principal word or words in the name of the division

Department of, Bureau of, and *Division of* are disregarded, but they are usually placed in parentheses.

Name	Indexing Order

Bureau of the Census
    U.S. Department of Commerce
	United States Government
	    Commerce (Department of)
	    Census (Bureau of the)

Office of Indian Affairs
    U.S. Department of the Interior
	United States Government
	    Interior (Department of)
	    Indian Affairs (Office of)

U.S. Postal Service
    Bureau of Accounts
    Division of Cost Ascertainment
	United States Government
	    Postal Service
	    Accounts (Bureau of)
	    Cost Ascertainment
	    (Division of)

Foreign government names. Names pertaining to foreign governments are indexed under names of countries and subdivided by title of the department; and then by bureau, division, commission, or board.

Name	Indexing Order

Republic of India
    Department of Energy
	India (Republic of)
	    Energy Department

Other political divisions. Names pertaining to other political divisions are indexed under the name of the political division and followed by its classification (such as state, county, or city); and then subdivided by the title of the department, bureau, division, commission, or board.

Name	Indexing Order

Bureau of Statistics
    State of Maine
	Maine, State (of)
	    Statistics (Bureau of)

Harris County
    Bureau of Personnel
	Harris, County (of)
	    Personnel (Bureau of)

Department of Safety
    City of Anaheim
	Anaheim, City (of)
	    Safety (Department of)

Banks. Banks are indexed under the names of the communities in which they are located, and then by bank name. The state is the last indexing unit.

Name	Indexing Order
First National Bank Cleveland, Ohio	Cleveland: First National Bank Ohio
Bank of New Jersey Newark	Newark: Bank of New Jersey New Jersey
Wells Savings Bank Wells, Maine	Wells Savings Bank Maine

If the name of the community is a part of the name of the bank, the name of the community is not repeated, but it is considered the first unit as it occurs.

Churches, schools, and other organizations. The names of churches, schools, and other organizations are indexed as follows. Cross-references may be used, when necessary, to file or find these names more efficiently.

Name	Indexing Order
American Legion	American Legion
University of California	California, University (of)
Lakewood Kiwanis Club	Kiwanis Club, Lakewood
First Lutheran Church	Lutheran Church, First
Martin Luther King High School	Martin Luther King High School
The Salvation Army	Salvation Army, The

Addresses. If two or more persons or firms have the same name but different addresses, alphabetize them according to city or town. If the persons or firms also have the same city or town name, then alphabetize according to the state name. If the persons or firms having the same name are in the same community but have different addresses, alphabetize these names according to the name of the street. If the same name has more than one address on the same street of that city or town, then index from the lowest to highest street number. 125 Main Street goes before 126 Main Street.

LONG-TERM FILE MAINTENANCE

When records become inactive in the office file, they should be transferred to storage files. Thus, the expensive filing equipment is used only for active material. The material that is removed from the active files and placed in the *inactive,* or *transfer,* files should be well arranged, so that no time is wasted in locating this material if it is needed. Many firms transfer the material in the files annually—the entire file drawer is transferred to the inactive file. The professional needs to make new guides and prepare new folders for the new files.

Records Management

Records management is the term for the systematic control of the maintenance, retention, protection, and preservation of records. Many business papers—from correspondence to reports and records—may not be needed in the future and can be destroyed to conserve file space. But other documents must be retained, sometimes indefinitely. Which documents to retain is determined by legal counsel or senior management. Duration may be a matter of federal or state statute, or it may be a management issue. For instance, a company will have to retain records of its incorporation indefinitely. Financial records must be retained not only for administrative purposes but also for government tax reports. Corporate historical documents are also frequently preserved by management, in case they want to catalog the growth of their organization. Historical records that identify the bases on which past decisions were made can also help with future decisions. Your responsibility is to know not only the length of time each document should be kept, but also the storage location of records that have been removed from file cabinets and relocated to a warehouse or other storage facility.

A time frame is usually set for purging file drawers or transferring files to a storage facility. You will also have a *retention schedule,* on which is listed instructions for how long each type of record should be kept. There will probably be instructions on the way specific documents should be treated—for instance, whether they should be transferred to an inactive file, destroyed, microfilmed, or scanned and put on CD for storage. The retention schedule is prepared by management in consultation with legal counsel. Although computer advancement enables the inexpensive storage of inactive files, government statutes still require original documents in many instances. The retention list will indicate those files that must be kept as hard copy.

If the guides and folders are going to be kept in the office, the transferred material should be labeled with the same captions as those in the active-file drawer.

If files are going to storage, they should be packed into file boxes and labeled to indicate their contents, dates, and so forth, so that they can easily be located when needed. It's also helpful to label boxes with a discard date.

Micrographics

Micrographics is the term used to designate reproduced information in miniature form on film. Storing information on microfilm has saved firms great amounts of money, space, and retrieval time. Records are photographed onto film in a microfilmer so that many small images in color or black and white

RECORDS RETENTION SCHEDULE

Here is an example of a retention schedule for various types of documents.

Classification	Document Type	Retention Time
Legal	Annual reports	Permanently
	Affadavits	10 years
	Contracts	5 years
	Copyrights	Permanently
	Correspondence	10 years
	Deeds, titles	Permanently
	Expired insurance policy	10 years
	Leases	6 years
	Licenses, federal, state, local	Permanently
	Maintenance and repair to facilities	10 years
	Mortgages	5 years
	Patents and trademarks	Permanently
	Research reports	20 years
	Speeches, publications	10 years
Personnel	Accident reports	8 years
	Attendance records	3 years
	Claims, workers' compensation	10 years
	Daily time reports	3 years
	Employee file (after separation)	5 years
	Medical folders	25 years
	Pension plan	Permanently
	Time cards	3 years
Manufacturing	Bills of materials	20 years
	Blueprints	30 years
	Correspondence	6 years
	Customer specifications	20 years
	Drafting records	8 years
	Inspection records	10 years

	Operating reports	10 years
	Production reports	5 years
	Quality control reports	5 years
	Test data	20 years
	Work orders	2 years
Accounting	Accounts payable ledger	6 years
	Accounts receivable ledger	25 years
	Bank reconciliation	2 years
	Bonds	Permanently
	Budget worksheets	6 years
	Capital stock records	Permanently
	Cash disbursement ledgers	6 years
	Cash receipt registers	15 years
	Check register	6 years
	Checks, cancelled	6 years
	Contracts	Permanently
	Correspondence	6 years
	Cost accounting records	6 years
	Dividend register	Permanently
	Donations	10 years
	Expense reports	6 years
	External audit reports	Permanently
	Financial statements	Permanently
	General journal	10 years
	Internal audit reports	10 years
	Inventory records	Permanently
	Invoices	6 years
	Payroll register, year end	Permanently
	Payroll register, weekly/monthly	15 years
	Profit and loss statement	Permanently
	Stock certificates, cancelled	15 years
	Stock ledger, reports and records	Permanently
	Trial balance sheets	Permanently

will appear on a reel of 16-millimeter or 35-millimeter film. Records can be viewed in enlarged form on a reader.

Storage on film is less expensive than on microfiche, but film is not as easy to handle. Microfiche is easier to use and makes retrieval of documents simpler, and consequently is better to use when the information is frequently referred to. Increasingly, however, companies are storing files on computer disks. Data stored on CDs can be sorted and then resorted alphabetically, numerically, or in many other ways. They can be easily retrieved, and cost is decreasing, which makes CD storage a convenient alternative to microfilming.

MANAGING MONEY

An office professional may be required to handle financial transactions during the work day. The mail may contain checks that need to be forwarded to the appropriate department. There may be payroll records or other financial records that must be processed and kept up to date. In some offices, an office professional may be responsible for petty cash, or handing out cash for travel and other business expenses. Whatever the transactions, they will need to be recorded. Such information may be used in preparing income tax returns and/or determining the profitability of the firm's operations.

Depending on your responsibilities, you need either to develop your own system or to follow your organization's established system to ensure that you keep track of these transactions. There will probably be different processes for different situations. For instance, you may need to keep only an informal record of incoming checks before putting them into interdepartmental mail, whereas you may have to keep a more formal record of cash given out for travel and other business expenses.

MANAGING CASH TRANSACTIONS

In today's parlance, cash transactions refer to cash and checks, but for the office professional they also include credit cards. Cash will come into the company from various sources, including fees collected for services, and payment of bills or accounts. For the executive assistant, there will also be personal funds of the employer such as salaries, interests, dividends, rents, and so on. An office professional who opens the mail on a regular basis will become used to seeing payments and should know how to route checks and credit card numbers in a secure manner.

It is important that all received monies be processed and deposited into the appropriate bank account on the day they are received. This procedure is the best insurance against thefts, robberies, and fraud. Examine checks to determine whether they are properly made out. Pay attention to the date; postdated checks cannot be deposited or cashed before the date written on the check. Set aside checks that are made out incorrectly and discuss them with your employer. If your company accepts credit cards and you receive credit card payments, they need to be processed through the credit card company and need an authorization number before they can be submitted.

The person who processes payments should also be responsible for the record keeping (entries should be made in the proper records). Arrangements for night deposits should be made if funds cannot be deposited before the bank closes.

HANDLING THE BANK ACCOUNT

Banks offer different services to client firms. The office professional needs to be familiar with the inner workings of the bank that the company uses. Such knowledge will be helpful when handling any problems that arise, and will help optimize opportunities for the company.

Making Bank Deposits

When cash is to be deposited in a bank, make out a deposit slip, detailing the specific checks and amounts. The company bank-deposit slips are usually imprinted with the company name and the bank account number. If these are not available, then fill out this information on a blank slip. The account number is important because it is the number, rather than the name, that the bank uses for its records.

Count the currency, and enter the total on the slip. If there are large quantities of coins, roll them in wrappers provided by the bank. List separately each check included in the deposit. Occasionally, traveler's checks or money orders may be a part of the deposit. Enter these in the same manner as ordinary checks. After all checks have been listed, add the amounts of all items on the slip and enter the total in the space provided. Deposit slips can be handwritten as long as writing and numbers are neatly written. If handwriting is illegible or the form is incorrectly filled out, the bank can reject it.

The bank will give you a receipt for the deposit. Retain the receipt until the bank statement is received, and then use it to check the statement to ensure that all deposits have been properly recorded.

Endorsing Checks

Technically, checks are written orders by which the depositor, known as the *drawer,* directs the bank, referred to as the *drawee,* to pay money to the *payee* or to a third party designated by the payee. Checks are sometimes made payable to *bearer,* a practice generally frowned upon because they are negotiated by simple delivery and can be cashed by persons who wrongfully receive them. Checks need not be made payable to real persons. Business checks are

BASIC BOOKKEEPING TERMS

Accrual method—An accounting system in which the right to receive payments and the establishment of obligations are recorded as transactions take place, rather than when cash is received or paid. Because both receivables and payables are matters of value, this system gives management a truer picture of the net worth than the cash method does.

Assets—Anything owned that has cash or exchange value. Collectively, the assets of a person or business are the means that may be used to offset liabilities. In accounting, the assets are all of the entries on a balance sheet, showing the entire resources of a person or business, which, when compared with liabilities, become a disclosure of net worth.

Balance sheet—A financial statement itemizing the assets, liabilities, and capital accounts of a business; and giving its net worth on a given date, such as the end of a fiscal year. A balance sheet is so called because it shows that the sum of the assets equals the total of the liabilities plus the net worth.

Bookkeeping—The work of keeping a systematic record of business transactions.

Capital—In accounting, the excess of assets over liabilities; the net worth of a business.

Cash method—An accounting system in which the receipts and payments of a business are recorded when made rather than when the transactions take place.

Current asset—Any of the liquid assets of a business, including cash, securities, goods, and materials that are expected to be sold or consumed within the fiscal year, and accounts receivable.

Current liability—Any of the liabilities of a business that are payable and that must be satisfied within the fiscal year.

Double-entry bookkeeping—A bookkeeping system in which a transaction is recorded as both a credit and a debit, in conformity with the accounting principle that assets equal liabilities plus net worth.

Expense—A cost met in doing business.

General ledger—The principal book of accounts for a business, in which all money transactions are recorded, including subsidiary accounts that may be summarized.

Income statement—A statement that summarizes the various transactions of a business during a specified period, showing the net profit or loss.

Journal—In accounting, the book in which the first entry of a transaction is recorded: Journal entries are chronological and are later posted to a ledger, in which they are classified by account.

Ledger—In accounting, the book of final entry, in which debits, credits, and all money transactions are recorded.

Liability—In accounting, any of the debts of a business, such as accounts and notes payable, obligations incurred but not paid, and long-term debentures.

Revenue—The aggregate of income to a business, individual, or government.

Single-entry bookkeeping—A bookkeeping system, used principally in small businesses, in which a transaction is entered only once.

frequently made out to "Petty Cash" or to "Payroll." A check is made payable to Payroll, for example, when money is needed to make up pay envelopes.

If a check is made out to a definite payee, such as the company or a specific person, there must be a matching signature on the back of the check. This signature is known as an *endorsement.* Endorsements are placed on the back of the check on the left-hand side. The endorser should sign the name exactly as it is written on the face of the check. If the name is misspelled or differs in any manner from the way it appears on the bank records, the payee should sign twice, first as it is written on the face of the check and then correctly. Many companies use stamps, which qualify as endorsements. You can also include the account number. It is also recommended that you note "For Deposit Only" to prevent checks from being cashed illegally.

Forms of Endorsement

There are three principal forms of endorsement: blank, in full, and restrictive.

Blank endorsement. In a blank endorsement, the endorser's signature is simply written across the back of the check. The effect of a blank endorsement is to make the check payable to the bearer. If it is lost or stolen, it can be cashed by the holder without further endorsement. Although commonly used, blank endorsements are not recommended. They should be made only at the time a check is being cashed or deposited at the bank.

*Blank Endorsement: Payable to
Bearer Without Further
Endorsement*

*Blank Endorsement:
for Misspelled Name*

Endorsement in full. In an endorsement in full, the endorser transfers the check to a designated party by writing the words "Pay to the order of," followed by the name of the person to whom payment is to be made, and then signs the check. A check so endorsed can be cashed or negotiated only after the person named in the endorsement has signed it. It is not negotiable by another person.

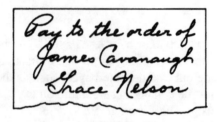

Endorsement in Full: Payable as James Cavanaugh Directs

Restrictive endorsement. In a restrictive endorsement, the endorser limits further negotiation of the check by writing definite instructions, above his or her signature, about what may be done with the check. Thus, a check might be made payable to one person only or it might be endorsed "For deposit only." Except when checks are being deposited in the bank, restrictive endorsements are almost never used. Business checks are usually endorsed for deposit with a rubber stamp; no written signature is needed.

```
FOR DEPOSIT ONLY IN
MECHANICS NATIONAL BANK
TO THE CREDIT OF
Grace Nelson
```

Restrictive Endorsement: Further Negotiation Prohibited

Dishonored Checks

A bank accepts checks for deposit subject to its final payment. If the drawer has directed the bank to refuse payment or if there are insufficient funds on deposit, the bank will return the check and charge it to the drawer's account. Such a check is known as a *dishonored check,* or an "NSF (nonsufficient funds) check." Informal arrangements for payment or redeposit of a dishonored check are usually made with the drawer. However, if the drawer is a stranger, it would be advisable for the holder of a dishonored check to take legal steps and file a formal notice of protest. In this way, the holder is assured of protecting full rights against the drawer. A fee is often also charged to the account holder for a refused check. This fee is usually charged back to the drawer in addition to the regular payment.

Dishonored checks that have been returned by the bank should be deducted from the bank balance on the depositor's cash records, and then be redeposited or filed for safekeeping until the drawer has made settlement. Any fees that may have been paid for the protest or collection can rightfully be collected from the drawer.

Bank Statements

At regular intervals (usually monthly, or sometimes upon request of the depositor), the bank renders a bank statement, showing what has taken place in the account since the last statement was prepared. It also shows the present balance, according to the bank's records. The statement shows the balance carried forward from the previous statement, all deposits and all charges made to the account during the period, and the balance on the date the statement was rendered. Sometimes sent along with the statements are canceled checks, credit memos, and debit memos. Otherwise, the bank keeps these documents on file for reference, for a period of time—usually five years.

Today, many financial institutions provide checkbooks that make self-carbon copies of checks written. These copies remain in the check register and are used to balance the account at the end of the statement period, just like the traditional canceled and returned checks.

Canceled checks are the depositor's checks that have been returned to the bank, charged against the account, and stamped "PAID." *Credit memos* are notices of amounts added to the account for such sums as interest allowed by the bank or proceeds of items left with the bank for collection—notes and bond coupons, for example. *Debit memos* are notices of deductions made from the account for service charges, interest on bank loans, and the like.

Bank Reconciliation

Seldom will the balance showing in the checkbook agree with the balance reported on the bank statement, even though no errors have been made in either place. Disagreement results from the following causes:

■ Deposits that were made near or after the date of the statement have not yet been posted on the bank records. They do, however, appear in the checkbook.

■ Credits that have been made to the account by the bank, as indicated on the credit memos, have not yet been entered in the checkbook.

■ Checks issued by the depositor and deducted in the checkbook are still outstanding; that is, they have not yet been presented to the bank for payment and therefore do not appear on the bank statement.

■ Charges that have been made against the account by the bank, as indicated on the debit memos, have not yet been entered in the checkbook.

■ Errors have been made in the checkbook, in the bank's records, or in both places.

As soon as possible after receiving a statement, the depositor should locate the reasons for differences between the bank statement and the checkbook, and find the correct balance in the account. This is done on a bank reconciliation statement, prepared by following these steps:

1. Compare deposits entered in the checkbook with those recorded on the bank statement. Check discrepancies against deposit slips to determine which record is correct. Make a note of deposits that do not appear on the bank statement and credits made by the bank that have not been added in the checkbook.

2. Take checks returned by the bank or self-carbon copies in the checkbook and arrange them in numerical order. Compare them with their stubs or other notations in the checkbook, taking careful notice to see whether the amounts agree. Make a note of differences. Place a check mark or other symbol on stubs of the checks that have been returned. Prepare a list of the outstanding checks, noting the check numbers, the dates, and the names of the payees. Do not include certified checks on this list because they have already been charged against the account. Make a note of any bank charges that have not been entered in the checkbook.

3. Arrange the information that has been assembled on a bank reconciliation statement. The form and the preparation of this statement are explained and illustrated in the following material.

If the checkbook and bank statement are both correct, the balances can be brought into agreement and the reconciliation is complete. If the accounts cannot be reconciled after adjustments have been made for omissions. there is probably an error in addition or subtraction in the checkbook. Check the check stubs, paying particular attention to the balances carried forward from one stub to another.

Bank Reconciliation Statements

Bank reconciliation statements are prepared in three ways:

1. Adjustments are made to the balance reported by the bank to bring it into agreement with the checkbook balance.

2. Adjustments are made in the checkbook balance to bring it into agreement with the balance shown in the bank statement.

3. Adjustments are made to both balances to get the correct balance.

Because neither of the first two methods provides the correct balance, the third method is the preferred procedure and is the one explained here. The sources of the data are the bank statement and the checkbook or a cash ledger account, if one was prepared.

Comparison of the deposits that were made during the month with those recorded on the bank statement reveals that the bank has not entered a deposit of $1,000 made on July 31; this amount is added to the balance reported by the bank. Comparison of the canceled checks returned by the bank with the checks drawn during the period shows that the following checks are still outstanding:

Check No.	Date	Payee	Amount
633	7/22	Bean & Co.	$2,180
634	7/28	Blue Cross	$50
			$2,230

The total of the outstanding checks is deducted from the balance reported on the bank statement. Adding the unrecorded deposits and deducting the outstanding checks takes care of all omissions on the bank statement. The correct bank balance is determined to be $6,098.

The bank statement shows a service charge of $2 that has not been entered in the cash records; this amount is deducted from the checkbook balance. Now, the corrected checkbook balance is also $6,098, and it has been proved that no errors have been made.

After the reconciliation has been completed, errors should be corrected and entries should be made in the depositor's cash records and checkbook for any omissions (such as the service charge discussed previously), so that the records will reflect the correct balance. Adjustments in the checkbook can be made on the stub for the last check drawn. It is not necessary to correct all preceding balances. Any bank errors uncovered in the reconciliation should be reported to the bank immediately.

The bank reconciliation statement should be filed for future reference. It will prove useful when the next reconciliation is made. The canceled checks are receipts for payments that have been made. They should be kept on file as long as proof of payment might be necessary.

Reconciliation Statement (July 31)

Balance on bank statement	$7,328
Deposits made after date of statement	1,000
Add	$8,328

Checks Outstanding

Check No.	Date	Payee	Amount
633	7/22	Bean & Co.	$2,180
634	7/28	Blue Cross	50
			$2,230

Deduct checks outstanding	2,230
Corrected bank balance	6,098
Balance according to checkbook	6,100
Service charge not recorded	2
Corrected checkbook balance	$6,098

Reconciliation Statement

Investigating Outstanding Checks

Ordinarily, checks should clear through the bank and be returned to the depositor within a few weeks after issue (this is not the case with self-carbon checks). Checks that have been outstanding for unreasonably long periods of time should be investigated. Outstanding checks not only are annoying when bank accounts are being reconciled, but also pose a question as to what may have happened to them. Perhaps the checks have been lost or mislaid by the payee. Communication with the payee is in order.

If the payee claims not to have received a check, a new one will have to be issued in its place. This should be done, however, only after a stop-payment notice has been filed on the old check. How to stop payment on a check is described later in this chapter.

HANDLING CASH PAYMENTS

Large organizations issue credit cards to their managers to use for business expenses. In smaller firms, a manager may use a personal card to handle some of his or her operating expenses. Just as the office professional checks outstanding bills for accuracy, the professional needs to review credit card bills and compare them to credit card receipts, to ensure the accuracy of the bills before preparing a check.

Compare the charges listed on the statement with the sales slips that are attached or other supporting evidence, and make sure that proper credits have been allowed for returns and payments that have been made on the account. The mathematical accuracy of all calculations on the statement should be verified.

Prompt payment of all bills is desirable; on some bills, payment on or before a given date is essential. Pay particular attention to insurance premiums because policies lapse if premiums are not paid before a certain date. Also pay attention to those bills that are subject to some form of additional charge if payment is not made within a stated period. Bills that allow for a cash discount if paid within a certain time should be earmarked for timely payment. For example, the expression "2/10: n/30" stands for a 2 percent discount if paid within ten days; if not taken, the total is due within thirty days. In terms of annual notes, this is the equivalent of almost a 35 percent interest charge if the discount is not taken. One method of ensuring payment at the right time is the use of a tickler file, in which bills are filed by the dates on which they should be paid.

Occasionally, payments must be made in a foreign currency. The easiest means of making remittances to foreign countries is a draft, payable in the funds of the country to which payment is to be sent. Drafts can be purchased at any bank. Personal checks can be used in some instances; however, this poses the problem of exchange rates and presents the possibility of over- or underpayment. The exchange rates fluctuate.

Writing Checks

Exercise care in writing checks. It is a good policy to fill in the check stub first; this prevents you from possibly drawing a check without recording it. On the stub, list the date, the check number, the name of the payee, and the reason for the payment. The reason for payment should contain enough information to permit later entry in the cash records. Fill in the check with the number (if not preprinted), the date, the name of payee, the amount in both figures and words, and the signature. Make sure the check is written legibly, and don't leave any blank spaces that might be used to alter the check. The amount in figures is placed close to the dollar sign, and the amount in words is started close to the left side. The amount in words should agree with the amount in figures. In case of disagreement, the bank may refuse to honor the check. If the check is

Example of a Filled-Out Check

honored, the amount written in words governs. If the amount of the check is less than one dollar, it is customary to cross out the word "Dollars" and write "Only . . . cents."

Information about the payee and amount of the check can be typed or handwritten, depending on managerial preference. Many organizations prefer typed checks, simply because some individuals' handwriting is indecipherable.

Titles such as "Dr." or "Rev." are not used; it is "Ben Kildare," not "Dr. Ben Kildare." "Mrs." is used only in connection with the husband's name; it is either "Mrs. Roy Roe" or "Ruth Roe." Checks issued to organizations should be made payable to the organization, not to some individual in the organization. Likewise, checks should be made payable to companies rather than to their agents. Checks for insurance premiums, for example, should be drawn in favor of the insurance company rather than the agent who handles the account.

It is not wise to sign blank checks. If this is necessary when the employer will be absent from the office, keep the checkbook in a place where it will be safe from theft. Checks, like money, are a medium of exchange and should be guarded as carefully as money.

Erasures and alterations should never be made on checks. Banks are reluctant to accept a check if there is any suspicion that it has been tampered with. If you make a mistake in preparing a check, write the word "VOID" across the face of the check and on its stub. If the checks are prenumbered, don't discard the spoiled check; keep it with the canceled checks so that there can be no question concerning the whereabouts of a missing check.

Certified Checks

Often, checks for large amounts drawn by a person whose financial status is unknown to the payee must be certified by the bank before they are issued. To secure certification, the depositor takes a completed check to the bank. After the cashier has ascertained that the account has sufficient funds to cover it, the cashier stamps the check "CERTIFIED" and signs it. Immediately upon certification, the amount of the check is charged against the depositor's account.

There can be no question concerning whether funds are available for payment when the check is presented. As far as the bank is concerned, it has already been paid. Thus, in a bank reconciliation, a certified check is never outstanding because it has been charged in advance.

Certified checks should never be destroyed. In the event that they are not sent to the payee, they should be redeposited in the bank.

Stopping Payment on a Check

The drawer of a check has the power to stop payment on it at any time prior to its presentation to the bank for payment. This is accomplished by filing a stop-payment notice at the bank on a form that the bank will provide. Oral notice is insufficient. So that the bank can identify the check when it is presented, it will ask for information such as the number of the check, its date, the name of the payee, and the amount. If a check is lost, file a stop-payment notice immediately.

As soon as the stop-payment notice is filed with the bank, mark the check stub "Payment stopped." The amount of the check should then be added to the current balance. This can be done on the check stub open at the time; it is not necessary to go back and correct all preceding balances.

Petty Cash Fund

It is good policy to make all payments by check because a check provides a written record of the transaction and serves as a receipt. But it is impractical to write checks for small amounts to cover items such as collect telegrams, postage due, carfare, supper money, and incidental purchases of office supplies. In some instances, too, cash is needed immediately. To meet these needs, it is customary to set up what is generally called a "petty cash fund." Operation of the petty cash fund is described in the following paragraphs.

Establishing the petty cash fund. First, decide how much cash should be placed in the fund. This is determined by the expenditures that are anticipated. The amount should not be too high, yet it should not be so low that too-frequent reimbursements are required. When the amount has been set, draw up a check, payable to Petty Cash. Cash the check and place the funds in a locked cash box or drawer, generally referred to as the petty cash drawer. One person should be responsible for the fund, and this person alone should have access to it.

Payments from the petty cash fund. All payments from the petty cash fund should be supported by documentary evidence in the form of a petty cash voucher, showing the date of payment, the name of the payee, the reason for payment, and the amount paid out. The petty cash voucher is initialed by the person making payment and signed by the person who has received the cash. Printed forms for this purpose can be purchased at any stationery store.

Petty Cash Voucher

Paid vouchers are placed in the petty cash drawer or in a special envelope kept for this purpose. In addition, some firms maintain a petty cash record. This is simply a form on which paid vouchers can be summarized. Columns are provided for the voucher number, date, name of payee, explanation of payment, and a summary of the expenditures made. Seldom is there a real need for such a record; the petty cash vouchers themselves usually provide an adequate record. However, in a company with a system of bookkeeping that accounts for every expenditure, regardless of how small, the inclusion of petty cash payments in the accounting books as part of the daily record may be the best procedure.

Replenishing the petty cash fund. Whenever the cash in the petty cash fund gets low, the fund is replenished. A check is written payable to Petty Cash for the amount that has been spent from the fund. The check is cashed, and the proceeds are placed in the petty cash drawer. After replenishment, the cash in the fund should amount to the fund originally established. If replenishment of the fund is taking place too often, consideration should be given to increasing the size of the fund.

BOOKKEEPING

There are two reasons for properly recording the income and expense transactions of any business operation. The first reason is to determine the profitability of the business. When a company is able to calculate the profit or loss of the operation, and then analyze in detail the individual items of income and expense, the company is in a position to make decisions with greater knowledge. The second reason is to gather the necessary information required by governmental tax agencies such as the Internal Revenue Service. These tax reports not only require a calculation of net income (income less total expense), but also require detailed substantiation of individual amounts.

The preparation of these financial statements is usually the responsibility of the accountant. Much of the initial work, however, may be done by the bookkeeper, and a professional may be called upon to handle these bookkeeping duties. The next section briefly describes these duties. It should be understood that some of these tasks can be handled with little or no experience, while others require complete training as an accountant.

Business Records

Careful records of all payments, expenses, and other transactions must be kept to determine the profits (or losses) of a business. Some of the tasks involved in keeping complete business records are:

- Recording business transactions originally in journals. Most companies use what is referred to as a *double-entry* system that has a debit and credit entry for each item.

- Posting the journal to the ledger. There will be a general ledger, and there may be subsidiary ledgers for specific accounts, such as accounts receivable and accounts payable.

- Calculating a trial balance of all accounts in the ledger to determine whether the accounts are in balance in terms of debits and credits.

- Adjusting journal entries to bring all accounts up-to-date. For example, any bills owed at the end of the year are recorded, even though they will not be paid until the next year.

- Preparing the financial statements, primarily the Balance Sheet and the Income Statement. This usually involves the use of a worksheet.

The first two items, and possibly the third, are considered to be work normally done by the bookkeeper. The last two items are more often the job of the accountant. How a professional fits into this process will depend upon the practice of the individual company.

Tax Records

Aside from the bookkeeping described previously, there is a need to keep adequate tax records. Every business must pay a tax on its profits. A corporation pays its own income tax; income from a partnership or an individually owned business is added to the personal tax return of the individual owner. In each case, there must be proof of the amounts recorded in the tax returns for income and expense. Save all receipts.

A sales invoice, a bill, a receipt for cash payment—all of these can be useful in providing the necessary documentation. A filing system that allows the accountant to find the necessary papers easily should be maintained.

A filing system can be set up on the basis of (1) date, with bills and invoices filed according to month; (2) type of expense—for example, office supplies or utilities; or (3) type of document—for example, invoice, cash receipt, or bill. Combinations of these systems are often used. The main point is that the system should be based on a common-sense approach that other people can follow. The professional is in a central position to see to it that the filing is correctly handled.

Travel and Entertainment Expenses

There are specific expense items for which the IRS requires a detailed record. An example of this type of expense and the additional recordkeeping involved is the travel and entertainment deduction (T & E). Adequate records include the following:

■ The amount of the expenditure

■ The dates of departure and return for each trip, and the number of days spent on business

■ The business purpose of the expenditure

■ The place of travel or entertainment

■ The nature of the business relationship of the person(s) being entertained to the taxpayer

Documentary evidence in the form of credit card stubs and receipts of paid bills is required for all expenditures for lodging while traveling away from

TRAVEL EXPENSE REPORT

Day	Date	Mil./Dr.	Location	Hotel	Meals	Ent'm't	Tel/Tel	Air	Gas/Oil	Other	Park/Tolls	Other	TOTALS
Sun.													
Mon.													
Tue.													
Wed.													
Thu.	8/12		Kansas City	28.50	21.75	45.00	2.30	82.73	10.30		50.00		240.58
Fri.	8/13		" "	--	19.80				10.50				30.30
Sat.													

Name: Harriet Blasko
Sales No.
Dept. No. 510-076
Date 8/16
Approvals *PBM*
Business Purpose: Annual Convention of Purchasing Agents
Debit Acct. Amt.
Credit Acct. Amt.

TOTALS 270.88

ITEMIZED ENTERTAINMENT RECORD

Date	Location	Business Purpose	Persons Ent'ed/Business Relationship	Amount
8/12	Jet Night Club	Inquiry on discounts for processing equipment	Elvin Hawes & Adele Vasquez, Acme Products	45.00

Miles @ 10¢

TOTAL	270.88
Less Airline Charges	82.73
Less Other Charges	
TOTAL	188.15
Cash Advance	
Due Me	188.15
Returned Herewith	

DETAIL OF OTHER EXPENDITURES

Date	Item	Total
8/12	cab; airport - hotel	10.30
8/13	" hotel - airport	10.50
8/12	Convention Registration fee	50.00

INSTRUCTIONS
1. Receipts for lodging, the customer copy of airline tickets, receipts for supplies and each item over $25 should be attached to the report.
2. Meal charges may be included in the report if the employee is away from home "overnight."
3. Include tips for meals and taxis in meal and transportation charges. Tipping for other services should be listed under "Other" expenses and itemized in the space provided.
4. Under "Other" expenditures include items such as luggage tips, supplies, postage, valet, and laundry.
5. Charges for transportation should be identified, such as bus, taxi, train, or rental car. Rental car receipts should be attached to the report.
6. If the space provided for entertainment is inadequate, use a separate memorandum for the overflow.
7. Expense reports are to be submitted weekly and should be sent to the office no later than the Friday following the week in which the expenditures occur.

Signed *Harriet B Blasko*
Send Check To: Harriet Blasko, Purchasing Dept.

Expense Report

home and for any expenditure over the amount specified by the Internal Revenue Service. It is good practice to record all expenditures in an account book or diary, and to attach receipts, paid bills, and other substantiating documents to the back of the page on which the expenditure is recorded. Employers will expect professionals to handle this type of detailed recordkeeping. Usually the employer will turn over the raw information to the professional and expect the professional to put it together in a formal record.

Automobile Expense Record

The taxpayer who uses a personal automobile in connection with business or employment is entitled to deduct automobile expenses (in total if the auto is used exclusively for business, or in part if it is used for both business and pleasure) on the income tax return. Expenses include not only all the operating costs, but also a reasonable allowance for depreciation. To ensure receiving full benefit from allowable deductions, the taxpayer should keep careful account of expenses and mileage on an automobile-expense record. An assistant can keep the record by using information supplied by the employer or, better yet, by making entries from bills that are routinely filed. The calculation for depreciation can best be made by the accountant responsible for preparing the tax return.

If records are not kept on automobile expenses, an optional tax-deduction method is allowed by the IRS. A standard mileage rate for business use each year, instead of a record of the actual operating and fixed expenses and a separate deduction for depreciation, may be used by an individual. Interest payments on loans, and state and local taxes (other than the gasoline tax) attributable to the business use of the car are deductible in addition to the standard mileage rate.

Always check current IRS booklets for detailed information and for rules on necessary record keeping.

RECORD OF AUTOMOBILE UPKEEP FOR THE   Month of *January* 1994

DATE	MILEAGE	GASOLINE No. Gals.	GASOLINE Amount		OIL AND GREASE		STORAGE and PARKING		AUTO REPAIRS		CLEANING AND WASHING		ACCESSORIES		MISCELLANEOUS	
1																
2	22,346	10	11	40												
3							2	00								
4											3	75				
5							2	75								
6					16	00			18	00					54	30
7		14	15	96												
29							3	15								
30		12	13	92												
31	24,180															
TOTAL	1,834				16	00	10	70	18	00	7	50			54	30

Automobile Expense Form

Employer's Personal Tax Records

A number of different nonbusiness expenses are deductible on the individual's personal income tax return. As with business expenses, it is important that there exist adequate evidence of the payment of these expenses.

The office professional may be called upon by the employer to keep an additional set of records for these personal expenses. The expense deductions include: contributions to charities, colleges, and so on; medical and dental expenses; interest on mortgages, loans, and so on; and taxes. The most important proof is the canceled check indicating payment. Although this is usually sufficient, more evidence is occasionally required. Thus, a file of the bills would be helpful in substantiating a tax deduction. The employer should turn over personal bank statements with the canceled checks, or at least the ones to be recorded, along with the bills received. The degree that the employer wants the professional involved in personal financial matters will obviously affect the amount of record keeping that will be necessary.

PAYROLL

The bookkeeper may be called in to handle the payroll of the company. This will involve calculating the net amount to be paid out, and keeping payroll records required for computing the various kinds of payroll taxes and for the government reports. The following section describes these procedures in some detail.

The federal government requires that the employer withhold from each employee's salary a sufficient amount that will add up to the amount of income tax due at year's end. The employee, when first hired, must fill out a form indicating the number of exemptions claimed. The number of exemptions is then used to calculate how much tax should be withheld for each salary level, according to IRS guidelines.

There also may be state and city income taxes that will require additional withholdings from the employee's payroll check. Although the general procedures are basically the same, it is important that the professional follow the specific requirements of each governmental agency.

Besides the various income taxes, the Federal Insurance Contributions Act (FICA) requires employees to pay a percentage of their salary as their contribution to the Social Security program. (There is a matching contribution that is paid by the employer.) The rate is fixed at a certain percentage of the annual salary, up to a given amount. After this figure is reached, no more FICA tax has to be paid. Each year FICA tables are prepared for the various salary levels.

The following example uses the figure 7.65% FICA tax to be withheld from the annual salary:

> Employee A, married with two children, may claim four exemptions. If A's weekly salary is $300, the payroll check is calculated as follows:

Gross Pay	$300.00
Less: Federal Income Tax Withheld	33.30
FICA Tax Withheld (7.65% × $300)	22.95
Total Withheld	− 56.25
Net Pay—Amount of Check	$243. 75

The illustration would have been more complex if state and city income taxes had been included. Besides the taxes that are withheld, the company sometimes withholds medical insurance, union dues, contributions to charity or retirement programs, and other agreed-upon items.

The monies withheld from the employee's paycheck have to be remitted periodically to the respective agencies. Thus, for example, the federal income tax withheld, plus the FICA tax withheld, and the employer's matching FICA tax contribution must be sent to the Internal Revenue Service (or a bank authorized to act as the depositor). How often this is to be done depends upon the dollar amount:

Dollar Amount	**Periodic Due Date**
Less than $500 a month	Every three months
More than $500, but less than $3,000 a month	Every month
More than $3,000 a month	Every two weeks

At the end of each three-month period, the IRS requires that a payroll tax return form be filed. Although this requirement normally is not the responsibility of the professional, keeping the detailed payroll records may be one of the duties. This will require a record of each pay period that shows the dates, hours, and earnings of each employee. Also required is a record of each employee's earnings that shows date of employment and discharge, Social Security number, rate or method of pay, and summary of wages and all deductions by quarter and calendar year.

There are additional reports required at the end of each year. These include the *Employer's Annual Federal Tax Return* (Form 940) and a *Wage and Tax Statement* (Form W-2) for each employee. On the state and local government level, quarterly and annual income and unemployment tax returns may be required, depending on state and local regulations.

> **TIP:** It is essential that any information you know about salaries be kept confidential. At many organizations, disclosure of this information to others can be grounds for dismissal. If office professionals deal with salary and tax records, they must be just that—professionals.

It is important to point out that the ability to manage all of these tax and payroll reports is normally *not* the responsibility of the professional. Usually, the company has an accountant who handles these items. However, the accountant may delegate much of the work to the bookkeeper or the professional, and act only as a supervisor. Therefore, it is helpful to be familiar with payroll procedures and tax reports, in case these areas become your responsibility.

When individuals think about office operations, they usually immediately think of record keeping. But record management isn't the only responsibility in office operations. As the role of office professionals grows, they

---

NECESSARY PAYROLL TAX FORMS

OOAN-7003   Employee Change of Name Form.

SS-4   For employers without an employer identification number.

SS-5   For employees without a Social Security number.

W-2   Employee's Wage and Tax Statements. The employer must provide these to the employee on or before January 31. Employers also send copies to the Social Security Administration and to state, city, and local tax agencies.

W-3   Transmittal of Income and Tax Statements. The employer sends this, along with every employee's W-2 forms, to the Social Security Administration. These statements are due on the last day of February. Because the W-3 form is scanned, entries must be typed in and no dollar signs may be used.

W-4   Employee's Withholding Allowance Certificate. Used to calculate federal and state income tax deductions. Employees are responsible for requesting any changes.

8109   Federal Tax Deposit Form. Employers must submit this form every time they deposit income tax and FICA deductions and contributions. The form must include the amount of tax deposited, the type of tax, and the tax period.

940   Employer's Annual Federal Unemployment Tax Return. The employer reports the amount already deposited during the year. This form is due on January 31 of the following year.

941   Employer's Quarterly Federal Tax Return. Employers report the amount of income taxes and FICA taxes deducted or contributed every three months. This form is due one month after the quarter ends.

will increasingly be involved in financial transactions, both incoming and outgoing. It's a very big responsibility. Aside from the monetary value, in this role you represent your company, and manage customers and vendors. It's imperative that you understand your responsibilities fully.

FOR MORE INFORMATION

If you can't find what you need from the phone numbers and Web sites listed in this chapter, you may need to expand your search.

- For more information on formal letters and their formats, consult "1001 Essential Letters," on the CD-ROM that accompanies this book. It has letter templates ready to load on your computer and use.

- For more information, check your local library or bookstore for the following books:

  - Association of Records Managers and Administrators. *Rules for Alphabetical Filing as Standardized by ARMA.*

  - Clements, Jonathan. *25 Myths You've Got to Avoid If You Want to Manage Your Money Right: The New Rules for Financial Success.* New York: Simon & Schuster.

  - Gallapher, Stephanie. *Money Secrets the Pros Don't Want You to Know: 365 Ways to Outsmart Your Banker, Broker, Insurance Agent, Car Dealer, Realtor, Travel Agent, Lawyer, Credit Agent.* New York: AMACOM.

  - General Services Administration. *A Guide to Record Retention Requirements.* Washington, DC: Government Printing Office.

  - Pool, John Charles, et al. *The ABCs of Personal Finance: An Essential Money Management Guide.* Shenandoah University Durell.

8

ORGANIZING PEOPLE AND TIME

◆

- **Organizing Meetings and Conferences**

  Planning

  Facilities

  Supplies

  Keeping a Budget

  Notification

  Teleconference and Video Conferences

  Minutes

- **Time Management**

  Basic Timesaving Strategies

  Manage the Executive Efficiently

- **For More Information**

A large part of the office professional's time and energy each day is taken up with managing multiple tasks effectively. This might range from structuring his or her own day and time to planning and managing others.

ORGANIZING MEETINGS AND CONFERENCES

Whenever people gather for a specific purpose—whether for weekly meetings or annual sales conferences—the event organizers must spend time and effort before, during, and after the activity to oversee both the event and its results. Even if the office professional does not attend the function as an active participant, he or she plays a crucial role behind the scenes. Even after the initial planning—and even when the office professional does not have to be onsite for the day or days of the meeting—he or she still must perform endless follow-up tasks. All arrangements should be checked and verified, if not by the office professional directly, then through someone else—and then the office professional should check with *that* person. Nothing can be left to chance. Nothing can be assumed to be okay.

In short, it takes enormous organizational skill to arrange a large-scale meeting or conference. Only those who have done it fully know the innumerable details involved. In fact, the task is so important and so time-consuming that many companies employ full-time meeting planners.

Because meeting planning accounts for only one part of an office professional's job, the skill may not always be fully acknowledged, even when the event is a success. But this is no place to cut corners and hope it won't be noticed. The meeting that ends in disaster makes both the organizer and his or her boss look bad and speaks poorly of the company.

PLANNING

In planning any meeting or conference, the most basic elements are the most important: Why is the event being called? Who are the people attending? How many people will be there? Where will they come from? How long will the meeting last? Obviously, a department-wide presentation of a new benefits package differs from a new-product presentation to overseas clients. A meeting to award salespeople differs from a meeting of the board of directors. Each event will have its own budget, atmosphere, setting, and so on—and each will treat the same element with a different procedure. For example, booking a professional speaker for a national conference is not the same as arranging for one of the company's retired sales stars to come back and give a motivational speech at an awards dinner. Similarly, the invitations sent to executives for an

COUNTDOWN FOR PLANNING MEETINGS AND CONFERENCES

This three-month countdown serves as a guideline for a mid-sized event. Because of their size, some functions might require a year or more of planning. Professional speakers also tend to book their engagements a year or two in advance. Adjust the early part of this schedule as needed.

Three Months Out

☐ Reserve the meeting location.

☐ Contact and draw up contracts with the conference center/hotel coordinator, the audiovisual coordinator, caterers, and others.

☐ Notify participants of dates and location.

☐ Make travel arrangements for participants.

☐ Contact the chamber of commerce, and select local events and entertainment venues for after-meeting sessions.

☐ Plan a program of structured group entertainment activities.

☐ Provide information on individual free-time entertainment possibilities.

☐ Plan agenda topics and book speakers.

☐ Send invitations to VIPs.

One Month Out

☐ Confirm menus, caterers, room arrangements, and business services and supplies with the conference center/hotel coordinator in writing.

☐ Confirm speakers and group entertainment events.

☐ Mail final agenda and information packets.

☐ Reconfirm RSVPs of participants.

One Week Out

☐ Ship materials to the conference center/hotel.

☐ Send a small backup supply of general office supplies, such as tape, shipping labels, paper clips, pens, pencils, note pads, badges, scissors, masking tape, magic markers, and so on.

continues

☐ Make arrangements with the conference center/hotel to collect, pack, and ship any unused materials back to your office.

48 Hours Prior to Departure

☐ Confirm arrival of conference materials.

☐ Reconfirm menus or catering arrangements.

Upon Departure

☐ Bring a master set of conference materials with you, just in case.

Upon Arrival

☐ Meet with the conference center/hotel coordinator and confirm all details.

☐ Meet with the audiovisual coordinator and confirm that required equipment is functional and in place.

☐ Walk through the meeting site.

☐ Introduce yourself to the bell captain and the maitre d' of the hotel(s).

☐ Confirm participants' room assignments with hotel registration.

☐ Confirm any special services to be rendered to participants, such as bed-time chocolates or complimentary breakfast.

☐ Confirm that the location of the meeting room(s) is clearly posted in the conference center/hotel lobby.

☐ Confirm that the speaker(s) have arrived, and introduce yourself.

☐ Review with the speaker(s) any audiovisual operating procedures that they might need to know.

Day(s) of the Meeting

☐ Do a final walkthrough of the meeting room(s) at least one hour prior to the beginning of the meeting each day.

☐ Confirm that all audiovisual equipment is functional and in place.

☐ Set up a command center so that you are instantly available during the meeting(s).

☐ Provide methods of contacting you in case of an emergency.

After the Meeting(s)

☐ Meet with the conference center/hotel coordinator to review billing.

☐ Confirm arrangements for the return of unused materials.

☐ Pay appropriate gratuities.

Back at the Office

☐ Distribute copies of the minutes to the appropriate individuals.

☐ Distribute, store, or destroy any unused materials, as appropriate.

☐ Review charges and receipts when they arrive.

☐ Write thank-you notes to speakers, VIPs, and conference center/ hotel staff.

in-house meeting will not be the printer-produced announcements and invitations sent about a meeting that attracts those from outside the organization.

Regardless of the size of the meeting, its purpose, or its location, the heart of its success always lies in the details.

The Offsite Large Meeting or Conference

The larger the meeting or conference, the more important it is to begin planning the physical setup first. For functions held in hotels or other outside facilities, preparations should begin at least a year ahead of time—longer, if possible. For the moment, agendas, invitations, and other details can wait. With the budget in mind, look for facilities that best match both the tone set by the participants and the space, location, and equipment needs of the meeting. Understand the terms used by hotels to describe set packages: What's the difference between a Full American, European, and Bermuda Plan? What about between a rack, flat, and run-of-the-house rate?

Take bids from several appropriate facilities. Each facility will want to know the date(s) of the meeting, the flexibility of the dates, the number of expected attendees, the type of meeting space desired, the need for overnight accommodations and for how many, and the number and type of meals prepared by the facility.

Although taking bids was once a time-consuming process consisting of multiple letters, faxes, and phone calls, online "request for proposals" systems now help search out those hotels worldwide that meet your criteria. After you select the venues you want to consider, the system sends a request for a bid. Make sure that submitted bids are completely itemized to ensure that all your points have been covered and to better compare results. Also make sure that each bid includes the facility's policy on gratuities and taxes (and the specific percentage for each), deposits, cancellations, no-shows, and other relevant points.

The In-house Meeting or Conference

Far fewer details require planning in this case, but reserving space still rates as one of the first things to do in planning an in-house meeting. Check with office management to see whether the desired room is available and to reserve both the space and any company audiovisual equipment required. If outside partici-

---

BOOKING SPEAKERS

No matter where the meeting is held, another element that requires advance planning is the booking of a speaker. For instance, your conference might include an industry professional who will present an informational program to all attendees at a general session or a motivational speaker who will address the closing banquet. Better-known or celebrity speakers book their schedules one and two years in advance. They sometimes work through a manager or agent, and charge a substantial fee. Don't plan on having a specific person attend (or mention it in early agendas) until you have a written contract. Until then, also investigate alternates because speakers' schedules—and your budget for them—can be subject to change.

When you confirm any speakers, make sure to finalize every term with them or their agents, including fees (if applicable), who will cover travel and hotel expenses, and any other special details, such as literature they might want to distribute or books to be sold.

Even non-professional speakers require advance notice. For example, if you work for an association or society, its annual conference might include a keynote speaker and several guest speakers—one or more of whom might be well-known. But the rest of the conference might consist of workshops given by the society's own members. These presentations will be generated by a call for papers about the conference theme, which is sent to the society's members six or nine months before the meeting date. The extra months are needed to gather and approve responses, and then to advertise the workshop topics when the conference notice is sent to the membership at large.

pants will be attending—whether from other divisions or other companies—see whether these people require hotel accommodations.

If the in-house meeting is large or lengthy enough, you also should make arrangements for meals and refreshments. These refreshments could be provided by the company's cafeteria (which is often serviced by an outside firm), by a caterer, or even by the hotel where guests are staying. If dealing with the hotel, find out whether delivery is included or if you must pick up the food. Because of the setup and clean-up involved, be sure to reserve a separate room for conference meals.

FACILITIES

Although meetings must be held *someplace,* they need not be limited to an official meeting room. Besides traditional places such as a company conference room, a hotel, or a meeting center, don't overlook an airport's business suite, the private dining room of a restaurant, or even a college auditorium or lecture hall during semester or summer break. The smaller the meeting, the more alternatives will be available. Just be sure that the venue can accommodate any special needs (such as audiovisual equipment or meals), that the place is easy to find, and that it's near sources of major transportation if out-of-towners are attending.

The Offsite Large Meeting or Conference

When your request for a bid has narrowed your search to a few choices, it's time to begin asking specific questions.

- How old is the facility? When was the last time substantial renovations were done?

- Where is the place located in terms of the airport or train station?

- What's the size of the available meeting room(s)?

- What are its furnishings?

- What audiovisual equipment is available? Is it available on your specific date?

- What are the overnight accommodations?

- What hotel amenities will be available to your group (restaurant, pool, steam room, golf course)? Are extra charges involved?

- What entertainment or extracurricular activities are available for attendees of multiday conferences? What can the facility arrange?

- What other conferences or events are being scheduled at the same or overlapping times as yours? Check not only those being held at the facility itself, but also those in the same town or city.

The best way to make a final decision on a facility is to personally inspect the site, preferably as a surprise visit so that you see the facility as the average guest would. Check the general layout of the facility: its security measures and its loading docks and freight elevators (if equipment or elaborate exhibits will be shipped there). Go to its meeting rooms and check their acoustics, sound systems, temperature and lighting controls, ventilation, and other relevant features. Eat in the restaurant to check its quality and service.

Although this in-person inspection offers a good opportunity to see what details might be negotiable (cost or service breaks, for example), prices written in ink aren't written in stone until the contract is signed. So gather up your advantages and see what better deal the hotel or conference center can offer. You eventually will want to meet the conference coordinator because this person will be handling the actual planning and setup. But now you want someone who has the authority to negotiate and to provide you with extras: That's the sales manager—or, even better, the director of sales.

Why would a hotel or conference center be willing to negotiate the price it just stated? Here are some reasons:

- Your company will be renting a proportionately large amount of its space.

- You're holding a multiday conference.

- Many overnight accommodations are needed.

- The hotel or center is providing meals.

- It's the hotel's off-season.

- You know from prior company events at this hotel or center that the just-quoted price is high.

- This is a first-time visit to the site with a chance of repeat businessl.

- Your company has used this same site every year.

- Your company's repeated use proves a history of very few no-shows, or heavy food and beverage consumption.

All these things provide you with negotiating leverage. Obviously, the hotel won't cut its rate in half—nor should you expect it to, in all fairness—but it might make concessions. For example, if a large number of guests are staying for one or more nights, the hotel might include the daytime meeting rooms at no charge. Or it may include one free room for every X number reserved. Or it may give you the room reserved for the hospitality suite at no charge, provided that you use the hotel's food and liquor. If the hotel has its own audiovisual equipment, it might let you use the equipment at no charge. If VIPs are expected, the hotel might include pickup from and return to the airport, free newspapers, and/or complimentary fruit and cheese baskets. Depending on what else is scheduled at the time, the hotel might even include a complimentary suite—the perfect place for the company CEO if attending.

> **TIP:** Don't be intimidated by the word *negotiation*. It doesn't mean playing hardball or being nasty. In fact, you want to avoid pressure and bad feelings because you'll be working with these same people on an almost daily basis for a very long time—you want the relationship to remain cordial. If the sales manager doesn't automatically bring up the topic of "Here's what I can do for you," say something like, "Last year's site provided complimentary airport limousine service for our chairman. Is anything like that possible?"

Not every hotel will give you everything, and what one can or will give won't be the same as another. For example, a non-union hotel might include meeting room setup at no charge, which often means the conference coordinator personally sets up the room. In a union hotel, everything from unloading meeting equipment off the truck to plugging in a projector must be done by union personnel and thus comes at a price tag with little or no margin for negotiation. Substantial breaks on meals and liquor generally are not offered because they represent a high percentage of the hotel's profit. One exception for food could be if another large group will be attending at the same time as yours and already has planned its menu: If your group accepts the same menu, you might be able to get a break because the kitchen has to prepare only one type of meal rather than two. However, equipment, rooms, and services provided by staff are more likely to be negotiated because the hotel has them on hand anyway.

Whatever is negotiated as extra should be put into writing in the contract with the regular charges so that no misunderstandings occur later. This also protects you if there's a change of personnel before your event and you end up working with new people.

The In-house Meeting or Conference

The needs of both the large meeting or conference and the in-house meeting converge at the point of the actual room used for the presentation. Here are some questions to ask about the room.

- How large a group must it hold?

- What is the best seating arrangement: classroom style with all attendees at tables facing a podium, horseshoe style to encourage whole-group interaction, or roundtable style for small-group discussion?

WHO NEEDS A/V EQUIPMENT? WHO SUPPLIES IT?

For a room of even moderate size, a microphone is required for all speakers. Some speakers have distinct preferences: a cordless hand mike or a lapel mike. If the speaker has any sort of experience, he or she also will want other audiovisual equipment as a way to vary the presentation and engage the audience. Although this equipment might be as simple as a flip chart and markers, the question remains: Who provides it?

At least a month ahead of time, find out the speaker's needs and whether he or she will be bringing equipment. Does the speaker's LCD presentation require an LCD panel, projector, and screen; a projector and screen; or just a screen?

Then ask whether the hotel has this available or can arrange for it on that day. Many hotels and conference centers do not own their A/V equipment; they use an outside leasing firm, passing the cost along to you. Some have their own equipment and a staff trained to set it up.

Be specific in asking the speaker his or her needs, and be specific when conveying them to the hotel. The hotel can comply with your request only with a reasonable lead time.

■ What are the speakers' audiovisual requirements? Their needs could run from a flip chart and magic markers all the way to LCD or CRT projectors that show computerized graphics.

■ Is the existing sound system adequate? Will the speaker prefer a wireless lapel microphone to one attached to a stand? If the meeting is important, you might want to consider renting a sound system for the occasion.

■ How is the lighting and visibility? Will charts or slide screens be clearly seen? Do supporting columns block anyone's line of sight? For an in-house meeting, check the room ahead of time. That flickering fluorescent tube—annoying in itself—could be out by next week, and maintenance might not be able to respond as quickly as you need.

When you've finally decided upon a facility for the larger meeting or conference, get the name of the individual who will be directly planning your event. Titles may vary: convention service planner, conference manager, or conference coordinator. Try to meet in person and establish rapport as soon as possible. This is the individual you'll be calling more frequently as the months and weeks go by.

SUPPLIES

What sort of supplies or giveaways will attendees receive at the meeting? These will be determined not only by the size and importance of the event, but also by your budget.

On the one end, you might provide attendees only with a duplicate copy of the agenda at an in-house meeting; in this case, pads and pens are their own responsibility. At the other end, you might want to arrange for color-and-design coordinated materials at an outside conference that include agendas, maps, reports, name tags, handouts, certificates of attendance, certificates of achievement, pads, imprinted items such as pens or keychains, and imprinted folders or plastic bags to hold all the materials. Leave adequate time for getting bids and ordering these materials. New-product launches might be even more lavish, especially to get salespeople and buyers excited. For example, a bound first chapter of a book, sample sizes of consumables, or demo video game disks can be given away.

TIP: Don't forget your own emergency supply kit. Include all those little extras found to be useful over the years, such as extension cords, an assortment of batteries, and all-purpose duct tape. Among a dozen other uses, duct tape can fasten wires to the rug and quickly mend torn rugs—both reduce risks of tripping.

Beverages and light refreshments can prove to be an ongoing distraction if set up in the back of the meeting room; it's better to set them up in another room or the hallway outside and to make sure that lengthy presentations allow for a brief break.

Supplies for the speaker should include at the minimum a carafe of water and a glass. Tissues and hard candies for a dry throat also are helpful. Ask each speaker if there's anything else in particular he or she would appreciate having at the podium.

Shipping

Getting everything you need to the site—from printed agendas, supplies, and giveaways, to audiovisual equipment coming from your company—is another key last-minute detail, but don't wait until the last minute to plan it. The best method of transportation is one that gets the materials there quickly and safely—and that can be tracked at every point.

Even if you use overnight delivery, mail the supplies two or three days ahead of time. Delays can happen, and the hotel needs a day to sort through its daily mail and packages. Have each package clearly addressed to you if you're going to be onsite, or address it to the appropriate person from your company

PLANNING FOR GIVEAWAYS

Having even simple giveaway supplies such as pens or pads imprinted can take several weeks. The more elaborate the meeting giveaway, the more lead time is needed. Add in even more time if this is the first time you're using a particular item or particular company. Samples such as those mentioned previously won't be under your direct responsibility the way imprinted folders will because they are likely to come from other departments. You'll need extra time to coordinate efforts.

Also leave enough time to check the finished item personally before sending it to the conference. Even if you're running late and you've seen proofs or mocked-up items, don't have the finished batch sent directly to the meeting location. Proofs are not an infallible indicator of the finished product. If you worked for FAST—Frank's American Steak Temptations—you wouldn't want to find out the morning of the conference that you have 200 canvas bags imprinted FATS.

who is coordinating the event at that end. After this name, put the word "guest" to make it absolutely clear to the hotel: "To Jackie Sinisi, Guest/Hotel Hanover."

If you must use overnight shipping the day before the event, try air freight or counter-to-counter service. Find out which service or airline is being used; get phone numbers, tracking numbers, and delivery locations; and then get all this information to the person on the other end.

No matter what type of service you use or what lead time you have, ask the conference coordinator to notify you when the shipment has arrived.

KEEPING A BUDGET

Except for the in-house event, which typically involves very few expenses, few steps in meeting planning can be taken without having a budget. In the early stages of planning, this may be as exact as a precise dollar limit or as open as a comment from the boss such as, "Everyone complained about the food last year. Let's see about upgrading all the menus." Without at least a rough budget, the office professional doesn't know whether to take bids from economy sites or luxury sites, whether attendees or the company will be responsible for meals and/or lodgings, whether refreshments will be catered, or whether the office professional will be making a fast trip to the local bakery that morning.

First-time planners should look up files of past events. These will provide a general idea of what events cost, as well as provide a breakdown of dozens of easily overlooked items that must be included and itemized. Draw up some rough figures based on estimates: These can be adjusted later as you get actual costs and head counts.

Budget for 4-Day Annual National Sales Convention

Airfare	Est $ pp × Est #	Estimated Cost	Actual Cost
Coach	$500pp × 139	$69,500	$74,128
First class	$1,200pp × 8	$9,600	$9,003
Total	$79,100	$83,131	

Hotel Rooms	Est $ pp × Est # × 3 Nights	Estimated Cost	Actual Cost
Block	$150 × 160 × 3	$72,000	$69,723
Suite	$425 × 2 × 3	$2,550	0
Meeting	$375 × 4 × 3	4,500	$4,230
Hospitality	$525 × 1 × 3	$1,575	0
Total		$80,625	$73,953

Other expenses to be itemized include:

Food and beverages: Total number of breakfasts, coffee breaks, lunches, and dinners over the four days and three nights—multiplied by the number of people

Audiovisual expenses: Production of presentations, professional graphics designer (if desired), and equipment rental (if needed)

Promotional materials: Design, printing, and mailing of invitations and replies; imprinted pens, pads, and cups; and folders, bags, and name tags

And so on. Although airfare, space rental, and food and beverages constitute the greater share of almost every budget, these other items add up and can completely throw off a budget if forgotten or underestimated.

NOTIFICATION

During this preparation phase, when should the office professional notify the meeting's attendees? The larger the function, the more notice is preferred—as much as several months—because the event might involve considerable travel and a stay of one or more nights. This requires arrangements and schedule-shuffling on the part of each attendee. Smaller, in-house meetings need less advance notice, of course, but take into consideration the staff, directors, and other persons who do not reside close to the branch site where the meeting will be held.

For the simple in-house meeting, a phone call or brief memo serves as the usual form of notification. A conference is better announced through a written invitation, which also can give further particulars about the meeting location, hotel accommodations, and so on. A single list of those to be notified makes it handy to track when notification is actually sent and what the response is. Prepare your final list of attendees from this list.

Unless the list of invitees is too long (for example, an association membership generated from computer files), make sure that every name is spelled correctly and that the person's business title is up-to-date.

For all large meetings and for smaller in-house meetings where attendance is optional, request a reply. The written invitation should include a reply card and self-addressed envelope. All notifications should include the name of a contact person and a phone number and/or e-mail address.

Press Releases

For conferences and meetings that cover significant items, you might want to seek press coverage for the event. In calculating when to send press releases, allow for individual deadlines: Monthly trade magazines may require as much as three months' lead time, while daily newspapers and local news shows can provide overnight coverage if the topic is deemed important enough.

The Agenda

At some point after notification and before the meeting date, all attendees should receive a copy of the agenda, even though they also might receive a duplicate at the door at larger meetings. A meeting without an agenda is a meeting without a purpose. Even though at its simplest an agenda is just a list of topics to be covered, it helps prepare the participants to focus on key issues. It also alerts them to the time limits: Conclusions should be reached before a certain hour to allow for the next item. More detailed agendas might include copies of supporting documentation if attendees are expected to make decisions on the issues at the meeting.

> **TIP:** A helpful tip for preparing agendas—particularly more detailed ones—is to look at previous copies, which will help you decide on the appropriate style and format. The descriptions of the separate items and the supplementary documentation often originate in separate departments and require some coordination in pulling together the information. Estimate the time you'll need for preparation so that the agenda can be printed and distributed before the meeting. As you plan more meetings, keep detailed files so that you have documentation to which you can return. Templates also can be helpful for frequently held meetings.

Here are two examples of a simple agenda.

Agenda for Monthly Staff Meeting
January 15, 200_

SCHEDULE	EVENT	PLACE
9:30 a.m.	Call to Order	Suite 1215
	Old Business	
	Read Minutes of Last Meeting	
	Committee Reports	
10:00 a.m.	New Business	Suite 1221
	1. Peter Spinella— Demonstration of New Computer System for Accounting	
	2. Ravi Dalal— Overlooked Markets	
Noon	President's Report	Suite 1221
1:00-2:00 p.m.	Lunch	Suite 1232

Daily Agenda for a Conference
Monday, February 15, 200_

SCHEDULE	EVENT	PLACE
9:00 a.m.-Noon	Letitia Johnson, Philip Boyle	Harrison Rm
	Our New Line of Software	
Noon-1:00 p.m.	Informal Discussion	Harrison Rm
1:00-2:30 p.m.	Lunch	Sky Terrace
	Dorotea Chavez	
	Dealing with Executive Stress: New Techniques	

Tuesday, February 16, 200_

SCHEDULE	EVENT	PLACE
9:00-11:00 a.m.	Ben Isaacs, Ginny Williams	Columbia Rm
	Hardware: Old and New	
11:35-1:00 p.m	Plenary	Wintergreen Rm
	George Takahashi and Martin Snow Management Systems for Small Companies	
1:15-2:30 p.m.	Lunch	Sky Rm
	Karen Trainer	
	Businesses Run by Women	

Typical Simple Agendas

TELECONFERENCE AND VIDEO CONFERENCES

With today's leaner budgets and widespread staff and customers, companies often choose teleconferences or videoconferences as alternates to face-to-face meetings. A teleconference is simply a multiway phone meeting. Local phone companies or voiceconferencing services can provide teleconferencing within minutes by patching a third party into a conversation. Private branch exchange

TIPS FOR MAKING THE MOST OF A MEETING

- Remember, the purpose of any meeting is to communicate.

- Determine whether a formal or an informal format would facilitate communication—a formal format ensures greater organization and closer attention, and an informal format ensures more opportunity for brainstorming and creativity.

- Include only those people who are directly affected by the information you have to communicate.

- Try to keep the number of people in attendance to fewer than ten whenever possible.

- Hold meetings that include everyone and that cover a large range of topics quarterly or on an as-needed basis.

- Discuss three topics at the most in a single meeting, if possible.

- Hold more shorter meetings that cover fewer topics.

- Prepare an agenda—even if the meeting is an informal one.

- Designate a chairperson to keep things on track—even if the meeting is an informal one. The person calling the meeting is usually regarded as the *de facto* chairperson.

- Open the meeting in a friendly, congenial manner.

- Make eye contact with the participants, especially if you're speaking.

- Pay attention to your body language.

- Maintain a professional tone of voice.

- Clearly state the topic or problem.

- Make any presentations succinctly and get directly to the point.

- Guest speakers should speak for a maximum of 20 minutes, unless the meeting is a seminar.

- Listen to all viewpoints carefully.

- Utilize a white board or flip chart to track the discussion visually.

- Ensure that all views are expressed.

- Utilize techniques of constructive criticism.

- Accept comments and criticism in a professional manner.

- Keep disagreements on a professional instead of personal level.

- Maintain control of your emotions.

- Be sure to clear up any misunderstandings as they occur. Remember, a meeting's true purpose is to communicate.

- Set a time limit for the meeting and stick to it.

- Select a time for a follow-up meeting or second session, if necessary, before dismissing everyone.

(PBX) systems also can merge several lines. Although some teleconferencing calls must be operator-assisted, technology provides for complete automation in many cases, with callers using a special toll-free number and a password. Meetings can be set up so that either all callers participate, or only a few do while many more listen in. Teleconferences also can be easily recorded for transcription for those unable to attend.

Teleconferencing is popular for many reasons beyond the obvious cost savings over travel. Telephones are easy and not intimidating to use, and conferences can be set up within minutes. On the other hand, if the equipment is older or if standard speakerphones are used, voices can echo or create feedback; it's also necessary that only one person speak at a time or the other conversation will be clipped. In addition, participants must deal with the artificiality of group conversations aimed at a single point, confusion about who is talking unless speakers identify themselves, and the lack of visual cues and body language. Frequent teleconferences and familiarity with the other parties help avoid some of this limitations, as does advanced teleconferencing technology, which accommodates a more normal back-and-forth flow of conversation, including overlapping voices. Headsets and handsets provide the participants with their own microphones so that a crowd need not cluster around one point. Customized conferencing phones with special microphones and speakers also are available.

Videoconferences combine the audio benefits of teleconferences with images of the participants, either in full motion or in freeze-frame. This currently involves special technology because of the need to match up the hardware and software compatibility of each participant. Rather than purchase the expensive and always-changing equipment, many companies rent time by the hour in videoconference centers. However, the technology already exists to change any PC equipped with a video camera into a videoconferencing unit, which allows for spontaneous meetings. One exciting possibility is the creation of virtual meetings, in which participants actually will perceive the other attendees as being in the same room as themselves.

Despite the advantages of being able to see the speaker, many people are camera-shy and are reluctant to have themselves filmed. As with teleconferencing, the method sometimes can feel forced, particularly if participants have never met. Watching a single talking head on a screen can be as removed and boring as watching a dull newscast.

Methods to increase the effectiveness of both teleconferences and video-conferences are similar to producing more effective face-to-face meetings. Having the participants meet beforehand at some point is very helpful. Handouts, slides, and other graphics for all ends increases involvement, as does carefully planned use of questions to participants, small group discussions, group problem solving, and other regular meeting strategies.

MINUTES

The request "Take the minutes" can cause even experienced office professionals to hesitate. In the old days, *minutes* meant shorthand and a word-for-word account of the entire meeting. Because shorthand is required less frequently today, office professionals wonder how they'll ever keep up when asked to take the minutes now. In addition, the formality of minutes with their suggestion of legal overtones still seems to demand absolute word-for-word accuracy.

Although meetings of any significance require minutes, all this really entails is a point-by-point record of what happened during the meeting. Accuracy and completeness are necessary because the minutes might later be used as evidence to settle legal or tax disputes, but these qualities are trademarks of top office professionals anyway.

The first step in taking the minutes is to look at those for previous meetings; the hard copies are usually kept loose in a ring binder to be bound into volumes later. Each book contains a copy of the corporation's charter and bylaws at the beginning, followed by the minutes. Study these minutes for tone and style, the type of matters that come up during meetings, and the format used by your company.

Follow the format for capitalization, indentation, use of captions, and line spacing. Generally, an inch-and-a-half margin on all sides of every page is used, with double-spaced text and triple-spacing between separate points. Materials that are read into the minutes, such as letters or documents, are single-spaced; resolutions are single-spaced and indented. Numbers, including sums of money, are written in words first, with the numbers following in parentheses.

Although the format itself is strict, there's nothing inherently legal in minutes, so formats do vary slightly from company to company. It's possible to suggest reducing double- and triple-spacing to single- and double-spacing to save paper, or to suggest other changes that seem economical and reasonable.

The contents of most minutes begin with the meeting's time and place, a statement that the meeting was properly called with advance notice given (get a copy of the notice given), and the names of the chairperson and secretary (as well as the attendees). Key people who did not attend—in a directors' meeting, for example—are noted; stockholders should be noted, whether present in person or by proxy. If attendees come late or leave early, mention the names and the point at which they came or left because their absences during certain discussions or votes might later become important. State whether the minutes of the last meeting were read and approved or corrected, or whether the reading was waived. For these initial points, the language from previous minutes usually can be copied with only the pertinent changes made.

After this standard opening, note each item on the agenda as it is addressed in the meeting, plus items not on the agenda that spontaneously come up. For the most part, this is not a word-for-word transcription of the meeting; it is a summary of the points made and by whom, as well as a neutral interpretation of the feelings expressed. So, although an attendee might bang a desk and yell, "You're crazy. This idea will never work," the minutes might read, "Committee head Robert Green strongly disagreed with the proposal." Decisions are set down as resolutions; resolutions and motions must be recorded word for word. If you don't hear something clearly, it's acceptable and even desirable for you to interrupt the proceedings and ask to have a statement repeated.

Even so, meetings in general often can have vague conclusions. If you're not quite sure what happened or what was decided upon after the meeting, talk to the chairperson to make sure that your record is accurate. In any case, try to type up the minutes as soon as possible, while your memory is freshest. Occasionally, minutes must be corrected when they're read at a subsequent meeting. This is not necessarily a reflection on your accuracy—people might remember events differently. Put a single red line through the incorrect statement so that it still can be read, and insert the new one between the lines (a reason for double-spacing if minutes tend to be frequently corrected). If a substantial part of the minutes must be corrected, cross out the original in red, keep the original page, and then include a separate new page with the corrected version.

After a meeting or conference, you might have to distribute copies of the minutes to the attendees on paper or via e-mail, depending on the company's practice.

TIME MANAGEMENT

When surveyed about workplace concerns, office professionals list the following: handling stress, reducing paperwork, keeping up with ever-changing software, improving human relations, reading faster, and comprehending better. However, almost without exception, the single topic that appears most often on their lists is *time management.*

Some office professionals can deal with a tremendous workload within the normal working day without appearing frazzled. They rarely need to stay late to catch up on correspondence, get out a critical mailing, meet a deadline, or develop a training plan. As the popular saying goes, it's not that they work harder—they work smarter.

The key to working smarter is time management. This is both a skill and a discipline, but it can be mastered and can yield many benefits. Effective control and use of time can restore confidence and job satisfaction—and ultimately even help the office professional advance his or her career.

Effective time management begins with a few basic strategies regarding habits and overall working patterns. Concrete tools, such as planners and calendars, also can help organize the day more efficiently.

BASIC TIMESAVING STRATEGIES

No one best way exists to save time. What's best is what actually works for you, your work habits, and your job. The following strategies, however, do seem to be successful with many different types of people and activities. See which of these you can adapt to your own situation.

Analyze the Way You Use Time Now

Before you can draw up meaningful rules for streamlining your performance and managing your time, you must diagnose the specific problems that plague you. In short, try to determine how your time is now being spent, and then decide whether it is being used to the best advantage in each instance. After this analysis, you'll be able to plan how to make better use of your time in the future.

Just as a research-oriented employer might bring in a time-study expert to watch employees in action, you must watch *yourself* in action. Keep a log of your daily expenditure of time. To do this, jot down your activities every half-hour for a period of two weeks. Then study the log and focus on recurring items that cause you to use time inefficiently. Are they repeated interruptions by staff members that you're training? Frequent visits from co-workers who want to socialize? Numerous periods of waiting for the busy executive to return to the office to answer your questions?

With the patterns apparent, you will find it easier to change habits, draw up a more effective schedule, and eliminate wasted time.

Ask: "Is This the Best Use of My Time *Right Now?*"

Besides writing down activities as they are performed, ask yourself at several points during each day, "Is this the best use of my time *right now*?" If you have to arrange a meeting, but you're politely smiling through a coworker's third folder of vacation photos, the question can bring you back into focus. Get into the habit of asking it of yourself frequently and then—if the answer is *no*—do what *is* the most profitable use of your time at the moment.

This same question can be applied to groups of activities when you're trying to prioritize: "*Which* is the best use of my time?" Another way to phrase it is: "If I had time to do only *one* of these things, which should it be?" Together, these questions repeatedly should lead you to the most important, most profitable activity.

Sometimes, however, when you ask yourself this question, you might be in the middle of a routine duty (such as filing or delivering mail). Although these tasks might not be the most profitable use of your time, you really cannot choose between writing up a procedures manual and filing: Both must be done. Accomplishing both in the most effective manner is another element of time management.

Learn How to Delegate

Few situations are more frustrating than an executive who refuses to delegate responsibility to an office professional who is eager, qualified, and competent. When this executive at last enrolls in a time-saving seminar, learning how to delegate is one of the first lessons he or she will learn.

Are you guilty of the same behavior, clinging to every chore as if each one were of equal importance? Is it really necessary for you to photocopy agendas, staple newsletters, or run envelopes through a postage meter? Are clerical assistants available for such tasks? Assuming that help is available, executive office professionals should learn how to delegate. Properly trained, most assistants will be able to take over routine duties, freeing you for those tasks that you and only you were hired to do. This also frees you to take on even greater responsibilities, which, hopefully, the executive will in turn have delegated to you.

> **TIP:** When delegating to assistants, do not give them only the worst and most boring of your tasks; assign jobs that make delegation worthwhile to *them*. After all, you hope for the same consideration from the executive.

Live with a Schedule

Another useful step in time-saving organization is a daily schedule.

Of course, individual assignments will make it necessary to vary routines, but a general schedule for each day can be helpful. Here's a sample schedule.

Within that schedule, variations always will come up. Vendors might not come every day, and meetings don't always end when lunchtime is supposed to begin. You'll face coffee breaks, emergencies, and days you're working through a cold. Nevertheless, those office professionals who are guided in general by a flexible schedule often find they have extra minutes each day to accomplish the tasks they need to complete.

```
9:00-9:30 a.m.      -Play back telephone messages; sort and deliver
                     mail; file
9:30-10:00 a.m.     -Transcribe executive's taped notes
10:00-10:30 a.m.    -Executive's correspondence
10:30-11:00 a.m.    -Personal correspondence, follow-up memos
11:00-12:00 p.m.    -Take meeting minutes; transcribe them
12:00-12:45 p.m.    -Lunch
12:45-1:30 p.m.     -Meet with vendors; review written bids
1:30-2:30 p.m.      -Make business calls; set up appointments;
                     respond to inquiries and complaints
2:30-3:30 p.m.      -Staff training
3:30-4:30 p.m.      -Make conference arrangements
4:30-5:00 p.m.      -Meet with executive to discuss tomorrow's work
                     and changes to schedule
```

Sample Schedule

Know the Times You Work Your Best

A schedule enables the office professional to take advantage of his or her natural rhythms and to find the time of day for his or her own peak performance. Work is done faster when done at peak performance. In the previous example, the office professional is obviously not a morning person. As much quiet work as possible has been scheduled for the morning, while people contact has been scheduled for the afternoon.

Work with a "To Do" List

Going hand-in-hand with a daily schedule is the "to do" list, a compilation of outstanding matters that require the office professional's attention. A typical "to do" list might include the following:

- Write to the new sales rep.

- Call the service company about the copy machine.

- Order office supplies.

- Write and place a help-wanted ad for a clerk-typist.

- Call DHL for pickup of the letter to the Bangkok office.

- Confirm Ms. Behrman's night flight to Atlanta with Delta Airlines.

- Research dining etiquette for Ms. Behrman's Thailand trip next month.

- Order business cards for Ms. Behrman and self.

- Follow up on memo to marketing.

- Draw up the guest list for the retirement party.

The "to do" list should be drawn up at the start of the week, should be reviewed daily, and should be updated as progress is made.

Some tasks on the list, such as a phone call, will take five minutes; some will be multistep challenges, such as reviewing the minutes of all unit meetings for the previous year and preparing an executive summary. In addition, some tasks require immediate attention; others are long-range in nature.

After drawing up the "to do" list, group the routine tasks that can be promptly accomplished in one column; group the more complex and time-consuming tasks in another column. The tasks in each column can be prioritized so that the more important ones and/or the ones to which the executive gives greater weight appear at the top. Also divide the larger tasks into smaller parts, and do one part at a time.

Don't put every single activity of the day onto your list, just for the sake of crossing them off. Include only the important items that *must* be done and the items you're likely to forget if they're not in writing. Some people advocate limiting such a list to no more than the three most important jobs of each day so that the list doesn't seem overwhelming. Do what works for you.

Learn to Say "No"

The office professional naturally wants to cooperate not only with the executive but also with coworkers. This cooperation sometimes can lead to problems if the office professional takes on others' responsibilities and becomes so overburdened that his or her own work suffers.

For example, suppose your coworker Jack surfs the Web all day. As a result, he doesn't have enough time to complete an important assignment, so he asks for your help. This is not the first time this has happened. Although fellow employees should pitch in and help each other, this has become a case of your good nature and willingness to work being taken advantage of. You might say (in your sincerest voice), "Jack, I'm sorry, but I'm too busy with my own assignments to help you out again. Should I talk to Ms. Behrman about how over-scheduled you are?" This tactfully lets you say no without lecturing Jack about his misuse of the Internet, thus keeping relations between you cordial. It also should prevent Jack from asking you again because he will not want you to go to bat for him to Ms. Behrman, who will probably then want to know why he can't get his work done on his own.

As another example, suppose Ms. Behrman asks you to shop for her daughter's birthday present, return a purchase for a credit, pick up theater tickets, and so on. She tells you to take a two-hour lunch, to leave the office an hour early, or to punch in an hour late tomorrow as compensation. If this will make you late on projects, you might say, "Ms. Behrman, I'm always happy to help you out. My one question is that you also wanted the sales figures from the fourth quarter by nine o'clock tomorrow. Should I postpone the figures until a later time?" Now the executive will either see where the better use of your time lies or extend your deadline.

Handle Paper Only Once

One of the most frustrating—and time-consuming—elements of paperwork is the number of times each piece of paper is picked up. You read a memo and don't quite know what to do with it, so you set it down to make a decision later. When later comes, you have to re-read the memo to refresh your memory. And this is just a simple example. Some documents are handled four, five, or six times before they leave your desk.

The best way to handle paper is to deal with it quickly and to deal with it only once. You have nothing to gain from reading every word of every document, or from reading mail or a memo and then putting off action until a later time only to have to re-read it to refresh your memory. Just determine the importance of the paper the first time you handle it, and then immediately do one of four things: Take action, pass it on, file it, or throw it out. Don't keep it on your desk, where it's subject to multiple handling.

Avoid Interruptions

Often, a steady swirl of people winds around the office professional's desk, which naturally leads to both needless questions and socializing. The placement of your office furniture can help reduce both. A person who can be seen from the hallway is often the one who is interrupted. Consider moving your desk, if your situation permits it, to prevent direct eye contact with passersby.

Another source of interruptions is people who repeatedly ask the same questions. It may be well worth the time to write up a simple set of directions for these people and have them photocopy it for their own reference.

Of course, for some people, it's their job to be interrupted—the receptionist, for example. In all fairness, these necessary interruptions should be taken into account when other duties are assigned. However, if no receptionist is present, the first person encountered on entering the office—no matter what his or her title is—will end up filling that role and will be forced to deal with visitors, salespeople, deliveries, and so on. This situation must be addressed. The "front desk" could be made a rotating position, an official receptionist could be hired, or the front door could be locked and visitors buzzed in only when they have an appointment and have been identified by an intercom.

Don't forget the times when you interrupt yourself by making or taking personal phone calls. Try to limit these to lunchtime. Besides being time-eaters, personal calls are much more obvious to others than the caller assumes and can be detrimental to career growth.

Keep Your Desk Neat and Clean

An office professional should have a clean and orderly desk for many reasons: It makes a good impression on visitors and staff. It reflects well on the executive. It also is much easier and less distracting to work on the task at hand than if a dozen other assignments are sitting on the desk at the same time.

Another important reason for neatness is the countless time spent each week looking for something that's lost on a cluttered desk. This lost time spent searching for misplaced notes, files, or messages can never be retrieved. Use temporary file folders for the materials you're currently working on until they are ready to be filed in the central system.

MANAGE THE EXECUTIVE EFFICIENTLY

Though it's not often thought of in these terms, the time-savvy office professional also must learn how to manage the executive. Too much time is lost when the executive and the office professional are not working in synchronization. You waste time pulling multiple files for a meeting that the executive rescheduled, you make multiple phone calls only to discover that the executive already has called personally, and so on.

First thing every morning (or last thing every night), sit down with the executive to discuss what needs to be done next, which changes have been made in appointments and schedules, and what your own priorities and deadlines for the upcoming day are. Your strategies for managing time and the executive's strategies for managing time must be a team effort for either of you to be successful.

Tools for Time Management

Many products on the market today can help office professionals and executives manage their time more effectively. Some of these products are varieties of calendars, and some are types of worksheets for individual projects. Together with multicolored pens and markers, these tools can be very useful for gaining better control of time. They gather key information—from frequently called phone numbers, to a list of who's doing what on a project—into one place that can be grasped with just a single glance. Planners also can be used to track the amount of time spent on each project, which is invaluable for pricing what a project really costs and deciding whether it's worth doing again in the same way.

Software finally has helped resolve the issue of keeping two separate calendars (one for the office professional and one for the executive), with each inevitably having different appointments and tasks. Networked scheduling systems enable both the office professional and the executive to work from the same calendar so that each can see what the other has added or changed.

Wall and Day Planners

Day planners are the basic calendar tool: You write assignments inside a portable daily calendar. These planners might have a page for each day or, if not many notes are needed, a week to each double-page spread. Most people often write down only the due date of an upcoming job. But this is a bad way to jog

CALENDAR TIME

The early Roman calendar was based on the lunar month of 29½ days, and it had 354 days. But the solar year (the time it takes the Earth to circle the sun) is about 365½ days. The Romans added an extra month from time to time to bring the calendar into agreement with the seasons.

A more consistent calendar was instituted by Julius Caesar in 46 B.C. Its year had 365 days, with an extra day added in February every fourth year (leap year). The Julian calendar set the length of a month at 30 or 31 days, except for February.

By 1582, the calendar again was out of sync with the seasons. In October of that year, Pope Gregory XIII dropped ten days from the calendar to correct the error that had accumulated. To keep the error from recurring, the Gregorian calendar includes a leap year every fourth year, except in those centesimal years that can be divided by 400. Many countries adopted the new calendar at once, but Great Britain and its American colonies waited until 1752. Sometimes, two dates are specified for an early event: "Old Style" means the Julian calendar and "New Style" means the Gregorian calendar.

A year is divided into 12 months, 52 weeks, or 365 days (except in a leap year, which has 366 days):

Months with 31 Days		*Months with 30 Days (or Less!)*	
January	31 days	February	28 days
March	31 days	April	30 days
May	31 days	June	30 days
July	31 days	September	30 days
August	31 days	November	30 days
October	31 days		
December	31 days		

one's memory: When the day is actually here, it's too late to be reminded that the work is due. A more effective use of day planners is to break large jobs into smaller parts, to give yourself due dates for each, and to write them down. Write reminders of the coming due dates several days ahead of time so you'll know how you're progressing. And don't forget a starting date: Make an appointment for when you actually will begin a specific task.

If you're not quite sure how a job will be broken down, first brainstorm on a piece of scratch paper, and then copy the results to the planner. This minimizes cross-outs and squeezed-in notes. Even so, on a project you might want to use a pencil because Step A and Step B invariably become Step A1, Step A2, Step A3, and then finally Step B.

Also use planners to schedule an appointment with yourself. These extra hours of free time sprinkled throughout the week provide opportunities to catch up on unfinished business, do specific jobs, or just catch your breath. Don't simply promise yourself you will leave Friday morning from ten to eleven free; write down the appointment, or the time will disappear.

Just as you might add birthdays and anniversaries to a personal calendar, add to your planner any significant recurring business events. You might have never missed handing in the updated quarterly budget report—yet. It takes just minutes to add this routine to the calendar, and it can save you work and embarrassment later.

Keep your "to do" list in the day planner as well. At the end of each day, look at the planner, note the tasks you finished, and mark them off. Seeing each crossed-off item gives you concrete proof of how much you actually achieved that day. Then plan for the next day, making whatever notes and changes are needed. A simple way to prioritize the next day's list is to ask, "What would happen if I don't do *this*?" Prioritize according to consequences.

Use the executive's day planner to track travel and entertainment expenses; some planners come with handy pockets to hold the receipts. The executive need only turn the whole thing over to you at the end of a trip.

Because of its portability, a day planner is an excellent place for you to write down personal goals. The act of writing something down automatically gives the thing more importance in the mind; no longer just a wish, it has its own life and constitutes its own reality. Write down goals frequently until you achieve them.

Wall planners are ideal for larger projects that have interim deadlines (whether assigned or imposed by you) or that are multifaceted in other ways. Wall planners are also useful when whole jobs or pieces of jobs have been delegated to different individuals. Each person's separate progress can be noted on the planner; use a different color pen for each person for easy tracking.

Appointment Calendars

Perhaps the most important thing for the office professional to keep in mind regarding appointment calendars is that your calendar and the executive's always should agree. Changes in the one must be marked on the other as soon as possible. Not having identical appointment calendars is a frequent complaint of office professionals, one that must be addressed to the executive in straightforward terms. Because it is almost always the executive who has gone ahead and made changes without saying anything, it's usually the office professional's time that is lost. This can become a serious problem—one that not only wastes time unnecessarily, but also that can threaten the sense of teamwork that the executive and office professional need.

As mentioned before, software calendars that can be accessed by both the office professional and the executive can offer a solution to this problem.

Project Planners and Flowcharts

Rather than being keyed into the yearly calendar, project planners focus on a specific piece of work. They track a project from the initial planning stages until its very end, breaking down the elements as work progresses. Use color coding for each person involved in a project; you also might find it useful to break down the type of work by color as well.

Flowcharts can be an enormous timesaver, even though they function differently from calendar-type tools. A flowchart is a schematic tracking of a process. The simplest example is a family tree, which is a schematic tracking of a family name over time. A flowchart tracks a particular job or project. Where does the task originate? Where does it end? What are the many steps along the way? Each time a job changes hands, it should be noted on the flowchart.

The timesaving benefit of making a flow chart is that when you see how a piece of work is actually routed, patterns become more obvious. It's easier to see which steps take the longest or create a bottleneck, which steps duplicate each other, or which steps can be eliminated. A flowchart also presents a broad picture of how the separate elements of a group relate to each other.

Software programs are available for ready-to-use flow charts or to help in designing your own.

FOR MORE INFORMATION

If you can't find what you need from the phone numbers and Web sites listed in this chapter, you may need to expand your search.

- For more information on meeting planning, check your local library or bookstore for books. Meeting planning titles will most likely be found in the business/management section. Or search www.amazon.com with the keywords "meeting planning."

- For more information on time management, check your local library or bookstore in the self-help section.

- For more information on conference supplies and corporate give away items, check the Yellow Pages under "promotions". Marketing or promotional companies will be able to help you get these.

- For more information on shipping materials, see chapter 4.

9

HUMAN RESOURCES

◆

- **Organizational Structures and Charts**
- **Hiring a New Employee**

Deciding on the New Job	Handling Resumes and References
Finding Job Candidates	Interviewing
Advertising the Position	Preparing for a New Employee

- **Training and Supervising Employees**

Performance Reviews	Firing
Discipline	Severance
Scheduling	Unemployment

- **Employee Rights and Responsibilities**

Sexual Harassment	The Americans with Disabilities Act
Workplace Violence	The Family and Medical Leave Act
Diversity	

- **Benefits**

Health Benefits	Pay for Time Not Worked
Insurance	Employee Services
Retirement Plans	

- **Etiquette**

Dealing with Office Politics	Gift Giving
Dress	Dating
Invitations	Congratulations and Condolences
Parties and Social Functions	

- **For More Information**

Effective *human resources,* also known as personnel management, is the basis for a happy office and successful employees. Without employees, companies simply don't exist. Although the current strides in technology have greatly changed the way we do business and have reduced the time required for many tasks, no amount of technology will ever replace the presence and abilities of people in the office. Even as technology makes our workday easier, however, it also presents new challenges and increases expectations in areas such as productivity, personal service, and quality. Coupled with more time constraints, the challenge to ensure that staff is qualified, content, and well-cared for has never been greater. To address this, the science of human resources is evolving to meet the changes in the American workplace. Innovations, tips, and standards for creating a productive workplace continue to be created and revised, and many of these are discussed in detail here.

ORGANIZATIONAL STRUCTURES AND CHARTS

You can get a better perspective of your own company's human resources if you look at its organizational chart. Within companies, organizational charts serve as an invaluable tool to help understand reporting relationships, manage workflow effectively, and maintain good communications. During reorganizations, they enable the planners to better understand the way the organization currently operates and the impact that changes may have on current communications or workflow. Companies are structured to maximize productivity and performance, and organizational charts, correctly done, can provide both new employees and existing ones with clear direction about whom to consult on a specific matter and how to get information or assistance with a problem or project.

Office professionals may not plan the original organizational charts, but they often are asked to update them and/or oversee review and approval of the final charts prior to their distribution—which is also a charge they frequently are given.

If you are asked to do one of these tasks, know that you can get help from one of a number of software programs. The most popular is actually PowerPoint, which contains standard templates you can use. To do the work, you need to know the following:

■ The source of information. Whether it is a new chart or revisions to an old one, you need to have one resource to whom you can go, should questions arise about the accuracy of the chart. This person should also review the final draft prior to its distribution to the remainder of the organization.

- The number of levels within your organization that will be depicted on the chart. Some charts include all job titles and levels; others go only to the first supervisory level.

- Whether the chart will reflect both formal and informal (dotted line) relationships.

> **TIP:** When putting on paper the organization of your company, it's important to realize that the chart depicts the formal structure of your company, not necessarily the interactions that occur daily in your organization as work is accomplished.

HIRING A NEW EMPLOYEE

One human resources responsibility is hiring new employees. Most people think of hiring only as the interview, but there is more to it than that. Rather, recruitment begins when you determine the need for someone—whether a replacement upon loss of a staff member or addition of a new position. The process doesn't end until someone has been chosen to fill the position. Some human resource authorities would say that recruitment isn't completed until a new hire has been oriented to the employer.

As you can see, hiring isn't a single step but rather a process, and office professionals will often be involved in it. They will be the individuals who process much of the paperwork associated with recruitment. As their responsibilities grow, they increasingly are also finding themselves developing the paperwork, conducting the interviews, and making the final selection of a candidate.

DECIDING ON THE NEW JOB

When you begin the hiring process, it's unwise to work with past documentation without giving careful consideration to your current needs. The earlier description may no longer reflect the work as done by the former job holder, or it may be time to rethink how the work should be done and the qualifications of the person you need to do the tasks.

Staff Requirements

Are staff positions required to effectively and efficiently handle the workload? Would alternatives such as overtime, temporary staff, or outsourcing be a more cost-effective solution? Often, when workloads increase, the situation can be addressed with more temporary solutions or a redistribution of duties among existing employees.

Job Descriptions

Job descriptions should include specific functions, required duties, and the tools needed to fulfill the expectations of the position. The job description should also include a measurable method of evaluating the success of the employee. The job description should clearly define what each job contributes to the organization as a whole and should be reevaluated and updated, with the employee's input, at least once a year.

Look at the past job description. If one does not exist, sit down and develop one, identifying not only the responsibilities the job will entail but also the qualifications for the position and the measures by which the job holder will be evaluated.

Consider the reporting structure. How does the position relate and contribute to other jobs within the firm? What level of supervision will the position require? It is important to take into account the workload requirements of each position before assigning direct reports, because time spent on the functions of the position may preclude an employee from being able to effectively manage other employees.

FINDING JOB CANDIDATES

Finding and hiring new employees tops the list of unpleasant, difficult, and time-consuming tasks for most offices. The time and effort involved in screening and interviewing candidates can be disruptive in the office, and, if you're having trouble finding the right person, it can be just plain frustrating. The more critical it is to find and hire someone, the more pressure is felt—particularly if, in this interim period, the existing staff has to assume the work in addition to their regular tasks. The time involved and amount of personal interaction is distasteful for both the potential employer and the employee. It's no wonder, then, that services such as personnel or recruiting firms (headhunters) and temporary services continue to grow at bounding rates. Rather than conduct your own screening, you may want to hire an outside firm to do your initial screening. Until you find someone, you may want to bring on board a temporary worker contracted from a temporary agency.

An interviewer may have to go through hundreds of resumes—in print and online—to identify ten to fifteen likely prospects for a job. Phone calls have to be made to interesting candidates to set up interviews; the telephone tag that often ensues can make even this phase time-consuming. Some interesting candidates may turn out to want higher salaries than you are able to pay or may lack critical qualifications and thus have to be eliminated. Good interviews take an hour or more for each candidate, and they are often conducted at lunch or after work to accommodate candidates who can come for an interview only

AGENCIES CAN LEND ASSISTANCE

Sometimes you will be working solely with your own human resources department to find a person to fill a vacancy; other times, you and your company will also have the aid of a recruitment agency. It will undertake the initial screening process, including advertising for the position for you. For a fee upon your selection of several possible candidates from those the agency has found, the agency will identify one or two candidates for you to meet. Thus, you save the time you might have had to spend in reviewing resumes or interviewing lots of candidates to identify the one or two likely ones.

Depending on the nature of the position you are trying to fill, you may want to give an agency exclusivity in finding someone for the position. If you have had good experiences with an agency, you may want to allow it exclusivity for two weeks or so. If it's not successful, then you may want to alert other agencies to help you in your search. That firm that identifies the candidate you hire gets its fee. Often the fee is calculated on the basis of the annual salary of the position to be filled.

Besides recruitment or placement agencies, there are also temporary agencies that will identify for you individuals for short-term assignments. This is a good option when your company has a short-term assignment, lasting a few days or a few months, but for economic or organizational reasons doesn't want to commit to a full-time staff member. The temporary agency should provide you with someone who meets your job needs in the same way that a placement firm would identify candidates for a full-time position. Some temporary agencies are willing to contract to provide temporary help that can become full-time if circumstances change or if you are extremely impressed with the individual's abilities and want to hire that person.

at these times because they already have a job. One of the most depressing aspects of interviewing is that you may finally identify a wonderful candidate and call to tell the person the good news, only to learn that the individual has taken a job elsewhere.

ADVERTISING THE POSITION

Because of their ability to reach a large number of potential applicants at a relatively low cost, newspaper ads remain one of the most common methods of external recruiting. Newspaper ads are also very versatile and can be used to recruit for all types of positions from unskilled to top managerial. Running your ad in the Sunday edition will generate the greatest response; avoid holiday weekends, however, since many people leave town and may miss your ad.

If cost is an issue, consider running the ad on a weekday and running a smaller, more concise ad. While a larger ad may seem to be more effective because it catches the applicant's eye, people do not respond on the basis of an ad's size. Also consider placing your ad in a trade journal to reach a more specific group of applicants. Be aware, however, that longer lead times are usually required and the ad can become dated.

The placement of the ad will be influenced by the nature of the position you are attempting to fill. If it's a technical position and there is a technical organization with a "positions available" column in its membership newsletter or journal, you may want to advertise there even if it will lengthen the time needed to fill the position. As you move up to senior management positions, you may want to supplement the ad in the employment section of your newspaper with an ad in the business section of the same newspaper. For some critical positions, if you are willing to pay relocation fees, you may want to advertise outside your geographical area. The more difficult the position you have to fill, the wider your search should be and the more money you may have to spend in advertising for suitable candidates.

TIP: If you are located in a suburban locale, you may want to advertise not only in your own local newspaper but in newspapers from nearby metropolitan areas. You may find someone who is more willing to commute for your job.

You can choose from two types of ads:

- *Open ads.* In an open ad, the company name and address are included, as well as a contact person and a telephone or fax number, so that a direct response may be made. This type of ad will generate the greatest response and is particularly useful if your company has a recognizable name and a good reputation. You should, however, be prepared for a significant number of responses from unqualified applicants as well.

- *Blind ads.* In a blind ad, the company name is not listed, and responses to the ad are directed to a post office box or a box provided by the newspaper. This type of ad makes the responses much more manageable; however, it also decreases the number of responses. In addition, some qualified candidates may not respond to an unknown company.

JOBS ON THE INTERNET

Increasingly, companies are using the Internet to advertise job openings. Many ads provide an e-mail address for replies. Usually these are blind ads; the firms create a special e-mail address just for responses rather than give their identity. They may also set up a separate phone line or voice mail box to receive responses without identifying themselves. They may also take advantage of the many, many job boards that are growing on the web. For certain positions—like computer-related jobs—these postings make much more sense than an advertisement in a newspaper.

How Much Does It Cost?

Advertising in a newspaper isn't cheap. Rates are based on publication circulation; the larger a newspaper is, the higher the price you will have to pay. Of course, too, the wider the newspaper's distribution, the more likely it is that you will get many individuals from which to make your final selection. Most newspapers charge by the space—whether classified or display ads—rather than by the word. If you choose to identify your firm, you will have to provide your firm's logo. For a simple classified ad, you need only provide the copy for the ad. If you choose to pay the much higher price of a display ad in the business section of a newspaper, and you have a certain graphical idea in mind, you may want to provide artwork.

Whatever the medium or type of ad, use care when deciding what information you will include. At the minimum, the ad should state the type of position, required qualifications, method of response (phone, fax, P.O. box), and any information that should be forwarded, such as resume, salary history, and references. In addition, you may want to consider including in the ad a salary range, job location, identifying codes (if advertising for more than one position), and any other information you believe relevant to the position.

HANDLING RESUMES AND REFERENCES

Because the writer of a resume wants to gain your attention, he or she may exaggerate, omit negative information, and sometimes lie about his or her credentials. References are infrequently sent, but if you do receive any, you can expect that they will give a glowing report of the candidate's personality, work ethic, and qualifications. However, you shouldn't assume that the references are necessarily untrue. Just as you would investigate the facts in a resume during an interview with its writer, you will want to verify the facts in a reference.

This kind of investigation is unnecessary with every candidate, only those final candidates from whom you are making your final choice. Then it is imperative that you check resumes and references with an eye for implied and less-obvious indicators of the applicant's past.

During your search, you will receive resumes for several days, even weeks, after placing an advertisement. Give respondents about a week; then read those you have received and select five to ten candidates to screen either in person or via phone. Often a phone call will be sufficient to determine whether you want to see the candidate. If you have a human resources department, this initial screening can be handled by it.

You may want to label the resumes "A" (really interesting, most likely), "B" (maybe but some concerns), "C" (intriguing for some reason but unlikely to be worthy of consideration). Begin with the "As," then "Bs." If you find yourself at the "Cs," you may want to look at those resumes that have trickled in since you last screened the original stack, or you may want to extend your search, maybe even consider placing another advertisement. While reviewing resumes or references, you should pay particular attention to some of the following details:

- *Extended time between jobs.* This in itself is not necessarily indicative of a problem; however, it is important for an applicant to explain the gap, and you should, if possible, check the truthfulness of the explanation. Difficulty in finding a new position, being laid off, and taking time to return to school or care for a family member with an extended illness are all plausible explanations and should not deter an employer from considering a candidate for a position.

- *Glowing or excessively qualified reports.* It could be that you have uncovered the world's only perfect employee. However, if the employee's past history is excessively positive or fits the job qualifications perfectly, it's more likely that the candidate is selectively presenting one-sided information. When speaking about references, ask them for other contacts who may be able to provide further information.

- *Frequent job changes.* This may indicate a problem with the employee's work habits or ability to adjust within the work environment. It is important to request employer contacts and compare their stories with each other as well as with the applicant's version of why he or she left each position.

- *Vague, missing, or incorrect information.* It is not uncommon for applicants to be unable to provide some information; companies do close, people change jobs, and time may change some specifics without the applicant being aware. Some information, however, such as length of employment, salary, positions, and duties should be relatively stable. Depending on the disparity of the discrepancy, you may want to allow the applicant the option of providing corrected information before discounting him or her as a candidate. If further information is provided, it should always be checked.

INTERVIEWING

The process of interviewing has two sides. Even as the prospective employer should obtain as much information as possible regarding the applicant's ability to do the job and fit into the workplace, so too should the prospective employee use this opportunity to determine particulars of the job, such as the work level, hours, company personality, and his or her appropriateness for the position. There will be other issues, too, that prospective candidates

REFERENCES TODAY

Because of today's litigious environment, many firms discourage managers from giving references when they are asked for feedback on a former employee. The managers are told to refer the inquirer to human resources, where he or she may get only confirmation that the person did, indeed, work for the firm as indicated and may be told the circumstances under which the person left.

If you do get the chance to talk to a former supervisor, have a list of prepared questions that call for more than "yes" or "no" answers. For instance, you can ask the manager to describe the climate or culture of the company and ask how it was evident that the candidate fit within that climate. Then compare the climate described by the former supervisor to your current climate. If the job you have to fill demands someone who can juggle multiple assignments and work in a pressure-cooker environment, ask for examples of how the employee worked under pressure. Don't ask, "Can he work under pressure?" or, "Did she ever have any problems doing more than one task at one time?"

If a manager or another person has provided a written reference, you may want to call and ask for specifics about the glowing assessment. A personal reference is very different from a professional one, and is irrelevant unless it addresses some aspect of the job you are attempting to fill and there is no professional reference. If you can't check with a former employer, then you may want to talk to someone's professor or minister or rabbi about the candidate's trustworthiness and honesty if the person will be handling money or making decisions that could be self-serving.

BASIC INTERVIEW QUESTIONS

As the job of office professionals changes, they find themselves responsible for interviewing and making decisions about prospective hires. Here are some questions to consider:

Why do you wish to leave your current position?

What do you like most/least about your current position?

Which accomplishments are your greatest source of pride?

What is your educational/professional background?

Why does this position appeal to you?

Why are you the best candidate for this position?

What are your professional strengths/weaknesses?

What are your career goals?

What questions do you have for me?

may be looking at—some that we tend to ignore once we have worked at an organization over time, but that can influence a candidate's decision about working for you.

First impressions count. And not just from your perspective. Job candidates will be looking at your work space to decide if they want to work in your company. Ask yourself if you would work at your firm if you knew nothing about it except what you see; then look around you. Would a visitor to your office be turned off because it looked messy? You expect your candidates to come dressed professionally. What impression would you give, in turn, if you showed up in jeans, even if it was a dress-down day? What if you wanted a candidate to meet with others in your organization, but you asked the person to hang around for 15 minutes to a half hour to see someone because you hadn't prepared for this situation? It's these little details that can influence a prospective candidate's impression.

Other factors can help candidates have a successful interview experience with your company. If they are expected to meet with several people, help set up a schedule for them. Determine who will be responsible for getting them from appointment to appointment and try not to leave them alone for too long. The office professional can provide a very pivotal role in the interview process, whether sending a quick e-mail to remind everyone that a candidate will be in or screening initial interviews for an executive.

Think of the candidates you will be interviewing as visitors, and prepare for their visit. This includes deciding in advance how you will conduct the

---

QUESTIONS TO AVOID

Usually, when a candidate arrives in the office for an interview, they will need to fill out a standard employment form. Make sure your form clearly states that questions or discussion on the following topics are strictly prohibited by antidiscrimination laws.

- Age
- Race
- Sex
- National origin
- Religion
- Credit record
- Marital status
- Parental status
- Sexual orientation
- Disabilities

---

interview. The three most common types of interviews are unstructured, structured, and panel.

Unstructured. In an unstructured interview, the interviewer has only a general idea of which topics to cover. Unstructured interviews enable both parties to focus on the areas that are specific to the individual being interviewed as well as allow them to interact on a more personal level. This type of interview is most appropriate when the personality of the interviewee is of paramount importance. For example, employees, such as receptionists, who will need to deal with the public on a constant basis, fall into this category. This type of interview, however, also provides the greatest opportunity to be swayed by the presentation of information, personal tastes and prejudices, and the interviewing skill of both parties.

For the most part, you will want to avoid unstructured interviews. Although they can give you insights into the character and personality of the candidate, they often give little information about previous job history or qualifications for the position you are attempting to fill.

Keep in mind that unless you are constantly alert in an unstructured interview, an articulate candidate can move the interview in directions that will show them only in a good light.

Structured. A structured interview resembles an oral questionnaire as the interviewer has a prepared list of questions he or she asks each interviewee.

This interview type, by its prepared nature, ensures consistency and minimizes personal interjection. Validation studies have shown that the patterned interview consistently predicts job success and is applicable for almost any position. You need to be a little flexible if you use this style, however. You should be willing to allow a candidate to lead the discussion for brief periods, and you should be willing to return to a comment by the candidate to get more insights.

Panel. Panel interviews require the participation of several individuals to interview the candidate at the same time. The panel members then discuss their impressions and reach a consensus regarding each interviewee. Panel interviews harvest the greatest amount of information on each candidate and allow for the least amount of personal influence. Panel interviews are, however, costly and time-consuming, and can make interviewees highly uncomfortable.

Note that as organizations move toward self-directed teams with responsibility for hiring new members, team-conducted interviews are occurring.

A version of a panel interview is one in which a candidate is interviewed separately by several members of the organization, rather than just the individual to whom the candidate would be reporting. Such an interview allows the company to get more than one person's perspective of the candidate. Usually the other individuals who participate would be peers of the new employee. Sometimes the person to whom the individual would report may ask his or her superior to meet with the final candidates in order to get a second view of them.

Which type of interview is preferable? There are benefits to be had in all three. You may want to choose the best from each. You might want to have a prepared list of questions that are critical to making a good hiring decision. On the other hand, you want to be flexible. If the candidate says something that interests you, you may want to pursue the issue unless you feel that the person is trying to distract you from another issue that would put him or her in a poor light. If so, after you have pursued the candidate's track, return to the original question that prompted the side trip.

If you aren't sure which of two candidates to choose or if you still have some doubts about an applicant, you may want to get a second opinion, either from a colleague or your own manager. Ask the candidate(s) back for a second interview with this other person.

In some cases, you will want others in your company to give their view of a candidate. If you want to conduct a panel interview, you may want to e-mail all likely participants to set up a schedule for a joint interview or a series of single interviews with your final applicant(s). The most important thing is to be sure that those with whom you want the applicant(s) to meet have sufficient advance notice.

PROS AND CONS OF TEMPORARY SERVICES

There are many benefits of temporary workers. Companies don't have to deal with the time, energy, and expense of hiring new employees, and some hard-to-find skills are more readily accessible through temporary agencies. Organizations often need extra help only for a limited time. Finally, in many instances, the hourly rate paid to temporary workers is less than what a full-time employee would have to be paid. For these reasons, over 3,000 agencies currently provide temporary employment for over 2.5 million people, representing a $3 billion industry. And that figure is growing.

Before hiring temps, however, your company should consider the dangers and drawbacks. Because they are placed and screened by their agencies, little, if any, information is provided regarding their skills and employment history. Often the temp who is sent may simply be the most available, not the most qualified. And because temps are employees of their respective agencies, a significant amount of control over their work habits is lost. Finally, as the name implies, temps have little or no reason to remain at an assignment when faced with a better employment prospect, and a significant amount of turnover is to be expected.

Here are a few considerations to keep in mind both when you call the agency and when the temp has arrived at your office:

- Tell the agency how long the position is needed. Do you need a data entry person for a week or an executive assistant for six months?

- Tell the agency whether it is a temp-to-perm situation. Some temp agencies get a commission if the person is hired and thus will send you a person looking for a permanent job. Other temps don't want permanent positions. Giving the agency this information in advance will prevent you from getting a person who doesn't want to stay.

- Make sure you gauge the amount of in-house training that the temp will need to the job length and the difficulty level. For example, you don't want to spend a lot of time training a temp if the job lasts only a week, or if the agency sends a different person every week. Let the agency know there is training involved.

- Make sure you monitor the performance of a temp. Remember, if the person isn't working out, you can call the agency and request another person. Of course, it's a two-way street and if the temp isn't happy, he or she can request reassignment also.

PREPARING FOR A NEW EMPLOYEE

Introducing a new employee immediately is imperative to making him or her feel comfortable and welcome in strange new surroundings. While generally it is the responsibility of the new employee's boss to make the introductions, when this is not possible, someone else, especially a co-worker, should take the responsibility. On the new employee's first day, wait until he or she is situated at his or her desk or office, then introduce yourself with a handshake, a smile, and a sincere "Welcome." It is also a good idea to tell the new employee where you sit and what your function is. Offer to take the employee around the office with a simple comment such as "Come on, I'll show you around."

Combine your introductions with a tour of the areas of the office with which the employee will come in frequent contact during the workday, including the kitchen area, restrooms, mailroom, and other facilities. Introduce the employee to his or her co-workers first, support staff second, and, if possible, executives last. When introducing the employee, include the function of both parties. For example, "John, I'd like for you to meet Bob Smith, our new director of marketing. Bob, this is John Anderson, our public relations manager." Avoid mentioning the person whom the new employee is replacing, since this can lead to embarrassment on the part of the new employee, as well as hostility or sadness from co-workers, depending on the circumstances surrounding the replacement.

After the tour, take the employee back to his or her work area. Take your leave with an offer of future assistance. For example, "I'm right over here. If you need anything, please don't hesitate to let me know." Remember that he or she will probably not be able to remember everyone's name or location at the office, so checking back periodically is a good idea. Above all, ensure that the employee feels comfortable and welcome.

You should prepare for the new employee before he or she arrives. Take a look at his or her workstation. Does the individual have all the supplies he or she will need the first week on the job? Has systems been notified that the person should be on the network? Has the switchboard been informed so that calls can be forwarded? Even more basic, if the job is new, does the desk have a phone and a computer and all other equipment the individual will need to get to work?

This kind of thinking is as applicable to the arrival of a temp as it is to a new hire. Most importantly, you want to set aside time in the morning to spend with the individual to review the job description and tasks and give him or her the first assignment. And you should be available for a few minutes at the end of the day to see how the individual has done.

If there are individuals you wish the new employee to know, you should schedule meetings prior to his or her arrival. Taking your new hire to lunch is another way to say, "Welcome aboard."

TRAINING AND SUPERVISING EMPLOYEES

Increasingly office professionals have to train coworkers as well as temps and interns. They may also have their own employees, such as assistants and temps, to supervise. These responsibilities are relatively new to many office professionals but are becoming more common, and all office professionals should be prepared to take them on.

It is the supervisor's responsibility to ensure that the employee grows professionally. Training and supervision are tools that can aid in this effort. The employee's supervisor should assign the training and determine the appropriate level of supervision.

The functions of training and supervision are both critical to the well-being of employees and employers. Unfortunately, these duties are too often pushed aside in the attempt to keep up with increasing workloads and a diminishing workforce. The ramifications of poorly trained and supervised employees are severe enough to endanger the future of the organization. It is imperative, therefore, to ensure that sufficient time, expertise, and importance be devoted to these areas.

PERFORMANCE REVIEWS

As you assume supervisory duties, one such duty will be providing feedback to those who report to you—even conducting performance reviews.

Performance reviews are an essential tool in determining how well an employee is doing his or her job. They provide the employee with valuable feedback about the areas in which he or she is excelling and also the areas that may need improvement. For the supervisor, this same information can be used to determine in which areas, if any, further training or closer supervision may be required. Performance reviews may also provide information on which an employer can determine promotions, raises, or bonuses as well as required corrective action and terminations.

For many office professionals, this responsibility represents a new and uncomfortable role—making judgments about others' work. Thus, it is important to keep in mind the positive goal of this task: providing feedback that the individual can use to perform his or her job better.

There are several different types of performance reviews; however, most require an accurate reflection of the job components and the criteria used for appraisal. The two most common are the subjective and the objective review.

- *Subjective reviews.* Subjective reviews evaluate the employee on personal attributes such as leadership, ability to work with others, and flexibility. These personal attributes are also referred to as *performance factors*. Subjective reviews are popular because their general nature allows companies to use the same form across all areas. They require little training to be effectively completed and give a clear picture of the employee's work habits. By their subjective nature, however, it is difficult to uniformly apply the same criteria to each employee, and personal feelings may distort the evaluation.

■ *Objective reviews.* Objective reviews evaluate specifically defined behaviors and quantifiable outcomes such as level of output, measurable tasks, and attendance. These reviews are often composed from employee feedback, and include objectives culled from the employee's job description. These reviews are popular because of their effectiveness in evaluating actual job performance. However, the time and the effort involved in creating and applying them are substantial, and as a result, they are often incorrectly applied, or avoided altogether.

DISCIPLINE

Disciplining employees is never a pleasant task. Through effective supervision and open communication, most problems can be resolved before they ever reach the stage of punitive action. Situations do arise, however, that require direct address, even in the best-run organizations. This process is known as the *corrective action process* and involves four steps.

1. Oral warning

2. First written warning

3. Final written warning

4. Termination

When addressing these situations, it is important to remember several things:

■ Always explain the disciplinary action in private so that you do not embarrass the employee.

■ Focus on the problem or behavior rather than the employee or the employee's personality.

■ Keep an open mind and listen carefully to the employee's comments and explanations.

■ Sincerely offer your support and help to rectify the problem.

If you are relatively new at applying discipline, it is best to go by corporate rules. Talk to your own supervisor to ensure that you are clear about corporate policy in issuing discipline; then follow that policy closely. Here are some general guidelines.

When administering an oral warning, explain the situation and its ramifications as they affect the company's well-being. Ask for the employee's input, and attempt to discover any underlying problems or situations you may not be aware of that may be contributing to the situation. Ensure that the employee is clear on all points, and seek his or her commitment to correct the problem.

If, after a reasonable amount of time, no improvement is visible, the first written warning is in order. The first written warning is the first official documentation of a problem, and can be used by both parties in later disputes or legal action. Take care, therefore, to fully document all aspects of the problem and the ramifications. Also document the fact that an oral warning has already been provided. Detail the expected improvement of the situation, the benchmarks that will determine the improvement, and the time frame in which this improvement is expected. Provide a space for the employee to sign acknowledging receipt of the warning as well as a space for his or her comments or rebuttal. Provide a copy for the employee and one for his or her personnel file.

If the problem persists, the final written warning is in order. The final written warning should contain the same information as the first written warning, but with the additional information that the employee has received a first written warning and that failure to rectify the situation will result in termination.

SCHEDULING

While most scheduling is a direct result of the requirements of the office, some flexibility in scheduling should exist. Creative and alternative scheduling can be implemented to accommodate the special needs of employees. By doing this, an employer can reduce lateness and absenteeism as well as boost the morale of employees. Three of the most popular approaches to alternative scheduling—flextime, the compressed workweek, and time-sharing—are discussed next.

Flextime

Of the three types of alternative scheduling, flextime is the most common approach. An employee works a required number of hours during an established time period and then has the flexibility to make up the remaining hours at his or her discretion. For example, the employee must be at the office between the hours of 11:00 A.M. and 3:00 P.M.; however, the balance of the eight-hour workday can be covered either before 11:00 A.M. or after 3:00 P.M.

Compressed Workweek

The compressed workweek is gaining in popularity and involves determining the required number of hours that must be worked per week and then compressing these hours into a set number of days (usually four). For example, a forty-hour workweek compressed into four days would require the employee to work ten hours per day for four days, rather than the standard eight-hour day over a five-day period. Other variations involve a two-week cycle of nine-hour days followed by a three-day weekend.

Time-sharing

Some office professionals share either their jobs or their offices, or both, with a second person. Individuals may come to the same workstation on alternate days, working at home in between. Neither one has to work in the office every day, and each can work at home effectively given new office technology.

FIRING

One of the most distasteful jobs you may have to perform is to fire someone. In cases involving ongoing problems, termination is unfortunately the only option available after disciplinary and other supervisory options have been exhausted.

Employees can be fired for any number of reasons. As a general rule, however, most terminations can be grouped into one of two categories:

1. Ongoing problems that have been brought to the employee's attention a number of times without satisfactory improvement or change. Terminating an employee in this case is the final step in what is known as the *corrective action process.*

2. Immediate termination for gross misconduct. Actions that would prompt this type of firing include being physical violent; being under the influence of, or buying or selling, drugs or alcohol while at work; falsifying credentials or company documents; and stealing company property. This process is known as *termination for cause.*

For legal recourse, any employee who is fired should receive an official letter on company letterhead that specifies the reasons for termination, the effective date, and any prior corrective action.

As a supervisor, you may find yourself having to make a termination decision about an employee after counseling shows no improvement. If you work for a manager who has terminated a staff member, you may find yourself typing the termination documents or otherwise having access to the records. From a professional standpoint, these documents are confidential. Their contents should be kept secret; you should not talk to anyone about them.

SEVERANCE

Depending on the circumstances of the termination, an employer may decide to offer the terminated employee *severance pay.* Severance pay is a voluntary allowance based on a preset formula, generally the length of time an individual has been employed. Recent trends have broadened to include other severance benefits such as use of company equipment (fax, computers, etc.) to assist in looking for another job, the right to apply for other jobs within the company, and the continuation of such benefits as health insurance. The benefits are referred to as a *severance package*.

When companies downsize or reorganize and have to let staff go, they frequently provide severance packages to those terminated. Some companies that are downsizing will offer generous packages to those who volunteer to be let go or who choose to take early retirement.

UNEMPLOYMENT

Employees who are terminated are generally eligible for *unemployment compensation benefits*. The purpose of unemployment compensation benefits is to provide income to a person seeking a job. Unemployment benefits are administered jointly by federal and state agencies, so eligibility requirements, compensation levels, and length of coverage vary. Terminated employees file a claim at the state unemployment office. The unemployment office mails the terminating company a questionnaire requesting such information as salary, length of employment, and details regarding the termination. This information, together with the employee's input, is used to determine the employee's eligibility for benefits.

Benefits are paid by the *Unemployment Compensation Fund*. This fund is supported solely through mandatory employer contributions, except in Alabama, Alaska, and New Jersey where employees also contribute. Employer contributions are determined by the number of unemployed people receiving benefits, so it is in an employer's best interest to keep firings to a minimum.

EMPLOYEE RIGHTS AND RESPONSIBILITIES

A variety of legal issues affect the office professional these days. Both state and federal government continue to pass and reform legislation. At the same time, rulings in the court system have a direct effect on policy and enforcement. While the aim of this increasing legislation is generally to protect and aid both employers and employees, compliance has become a nightmare. A variety of information regarding legal issues in the workplace is available directly from the government and, where appropriate, contact information has been provided in the following sections. This information is presented for informative purposes only; for any situation with legal or potentially legal ramifications, consult an attorney directly.

SEXUAL HARASSMENT

Sexual harassment is *"uninvited and unwelcome verbal or physical contact directed at an employee because of his or her sex."* Because sexual harassment is so subjective, however, it is often difficult to define which behaviors are unwanted. Overt action, such as groping, is clear and unambiguous, but more subtle actions such as sexually explicit jokes, gestures, or even pet names could be considered unwanted by someone—even if the same behavior would be acceptable to someone else.

Employees of either sex can be harassed by members of either sex. A principle of sexual harassment is that the person being harassed will be vulnerable if he or she objects to the harasser's behavior. While it's currently correct that sexual harassment doesn't legally go up the corporate ladder, the way the courts are handling the hostile workplace issue, the definition may soon change to find sexual harassment going up and down the corporate ladder. As sexual harassment is still largely determined by the relationship of the people involved, the first and most important step to stopping offensive behavior is to tell the person to stop.

It is the responsibility of employers to educate employees about their firm's policy. This issue should be treated with a high degree of seriousness, with a very carefully worded policy that tells employees these things are not permitted in the workplace. The policy should be disseminated, communicated, and accessible. In addition, it is important that the policy be enforced and be nonthreatening so that employees don't fear repercussions if they speak up. One bit of advice, if you think yourself a victim of harassment, immediately bring the matter to the attention of two parties, one male and one female.

WORKPLACE VIOLENCE

Physical violence or the threat of physical violence is not acceptable in any form in the workplace. Physical violence or the threat of physical violence from an employee is grounds for immediate termination or *termination for cause*. This area is not confined to employees, however; previous cases have included clients, suppliers, delivery personnel, and others with whom an employee comes in contact within a normal workday.

Courts have ruled that employers have a responsibility to provide a safe workplace for their employees and have ruled against employers in situations where an employee has suffered injury, been attacked, or been threatened while at work. In any situation where an employee is harmed or threatened, he or she should immediately inform management and, if the situation warrants, the appropriate legal authorities.

So far we have been talking about physical violence, but there is also emotional trauma, which can stem from verbal abuse. Sometimes the abuser is a colleague, sometimes a supervisor, a client, or a vendor or one of his or her representatives. While such abuse doesn't leave physical scars, it does impact self-esteem and performance. If you feel that you are being verbally abused—harangued or taunted by another—report such conduct to human resources or to your manager if he or she isn't the abuser. If your own supervisor is guilty of this, then go over his or her head. Often the intervention of a third party will put an end to such behavior.

Unfortunately, the Occupational Safety and Health Act does not cover verbal abuse, although it does cover situations that could lead to physical violence. When the problem lies with your manager and it continues, sometimes your only solution is to seek a transfer to another part of the company.

DIVERSITY

Workforce diversity is a growing reality. In 1987, 48 percent of the population entering the American workforce consisted of American-born white males; in the year 2000, this figure is projected to be a mere 15 percent. People of various ages, races, genders, physical abilities, sexual orientations, religions, socioeconomic classes, education, and national origins will continue to enter the American workforce in growing numbers. Even as this diversity creates challenges, it also provides for substantial benefits and opportunities. While misunderstandings in the office are bound to arise as a result of differences in behaviors, beliefs, and communication styles, the key to understanding people is learning to respect their differences. Hatred, prejudice, racism, sexism, ageism, and homophobia cannot be tolerated in the workplace in any form. The disruptive nature of such attitudes only hinders employees from achieving their full potential.

Even as more legislation is enacted, and courts rule to protect employees, it is heartening to observe the astonishing number of companies that have embraced diversity with such steps as broader recruitment, diversity training, and the establishment of inclusive policies and procedures. These steps pay off as study after study proves that companies who value a diverse workforce have saved million of dollars, lowered employee turnover, and improved their methods and products. There is a wealth of resources available, including training programs, videos, books, and consulting firms to address any aspect of diversity. Diversity in the workplace will continue to grow, directly mirroring the increasing diversity in the world in which we live.

THE AMERICANS WITH DISABILITIES ACT

Over 40 million Americans are disabled in some capacity. Recent studies have shown that over two-thirds of these people are unemployed, and over 80 percent of those unemployed would like to be employed. In response, the

Americans with Disabilities Act (ADA) was passed in 1990 to provide any disabled person with, among other things, equal access to employment.

ADA covers anyone who has a physical or mental impairment that limits one or more major life activity. Examples include blindness, deafness, or mental retardation; incapacitation in such areas as standing, walking, or speaking; and life-threatening illnesses such as cancer, epilepsy, or AIDS. Individuals who have a record of being substantially limited in any of these areas are also covered. For example, an individual who had cancer but has since recovered may qualify even though no visible impairment may remain. Finally, the act also applies to anyone who is regarded as being substantially limited. "Regarded," however, is subjective, and new interpretations are constantly being raised through ongoing discrimination lawsuits, further adding to the confusion.

The ADA is a complicated act divided into titles dealing with areas as broad as access to public transportation and services. Title I, *Fair Employment for People with Disabilities,* is specifically directed to employment issues. It prohibits discrimination in such areas as hiring, benefits, and medical examinations by any business that has fifteen or more employees. Title III, *Reasonable Accommodation,* requires employers to address qualified employees' physical and mental limitations. Accommodations include wheelchair ramps, Braille signage, or modified work schedules. Accommodations that would place an undue hardship on a business financially or logistically, or would otherwise have a negative impact on other employees, are exempt. Be aware, however, that this is extremely subjective and defined on a case-by-case basis. For specifics, clarification, or questions, contact the Office of the ADA or the Equal Employment Commission.

Office of the ADA
U.S. Department of Justice
P.O. Box 66738
Washington, DC 20035
800-669-4000

U.S. Equal Employment Opportunity Commission
1801 L Street NW
Washington, DC 20507
800-663-4900

THE FAMILY AND MEDICAL LEAVE ACT

To allow family members the opportunity to help each other without jeopardizing their work situation, as well as allow employees to take leaves of absence for personal illness without loss of employment, Congress passed the Family and Medical Leave Act (FMLA) in 1993.

The FMLA applies to any employee who must care for a child recently born, adopted, or placed in the employee's care through a foster agency, or who must care for a child, spouse, or parent with a serious health condition or illness requiring continuing treatment. Employees with a health condition that directly affects their own professional performance are also eligible. Employees must have worked for the company at least twelve months and worked at least 1,250 hours during that time. Employers with fewer than fifty employees and any branch office with fewer than fifty employees within a 75-mile radius are exempt. Employers may also exempt the 10 percent highest-paid employees if their absence would cause "substantial and grievous injury" to the company.

The Act grants eligible employees twelve weeks of leave per year to address these issues, with the guarantee that, on return, the worker will be returned to his or her formal position or its equivalent in pay benefits and working conditions. Payment during this leave is at the discretion of the employer, and employees are not eligible for unemployment benefits. Employees may also be required to exhaust their accumulated vacation, personal, and sick time first. Leave may be taken intermittently or all at once, again at the discretion of the employer. Employers must continue to pay any health-insurance premiums; however, if the employee paid any part of the premium, he or she is still responsible for it during the leave. The Act is enforced by the U.S. Labor Department, which can be contacted for further information at:

The U.S. Department of Labor
200 Constitution Avenue NW
Washington, DC 20210
800-366-0547

BENEFITS

Benefits, also known as *indirect compensation,* fall into three major categories: protection programs, pay for time not worked, and employee services. *Protection programs* ensure that employees and their dependents are cared for in the event the employee is incapacitated. These programs include pension, unemployment, disability, and medical benefits. *Pay for time not worked* covers vacation, personal days, and holidays as well as time during the day such as rest periods or lunch breaks. *Employee services* consist of "perks," which vary enormously, and may include such standard benefits as employee counseling, assistance programs, scholarship or tuition assistance, day care for children, food services, use of company vehicles, and expense accounts.

Benefits also fall into one of two different types. *Mandated benefits* are required by law, and their guidelines are determined by legislation and government entities. Examples of mandated benefits include Social Security, workers' compensation, and unemployment insurance. *Voluntary benefits* are not required by law, and the decision to provide them, as well as their terms and conditions, is largely left to the employer. Examples of voluntary benefits include medical and dental plans; life, health, and disability insurance; and savings, stock, or retirement programs.

Through indirect compensation, employers hope to attract and retain employees, increase morale and job satisfaction, and enhance their own image. Accomplishing all this while remaining cost-effective is, however, tricky because benefits packages usually average around a third of payroll costs. Several of the more standard benefits are discussed next.

HEALTH BENEFITS

Health benefits are an excellent form of protection for employees and their families. They can include health and dental plans and insurance, vision care, and even discount memberships to gyms and health clubs. Coverage may be *basic,* covering only one aspect of an employee's health needs, or *comprehensive,* covering several or all medical requirements. Employees may be responsible for a percentage of the cost of these benefits, the percentage being determined by the employer.

An employee can get coverage for his or her own medical expenses and those of dependents, such as children or a spouse, and, in some organizations, for a "domestic partner."

The three most common types of coverage are health maintenance organizations, known as HMOs; indemnity and reimbursement plans; and preferred provider organizations, known as PPOs. Each is discussed next.

Health Maintenance Organizations (HMOs)

In *health maintenance organizations,* or HMOs, a predetermined network of hospitals and doctors provides medical services to employees and their dependents for a monthly fee. HMOs have become increasingly popular through their attention to preventive care and their ability to offer one-stop shopping for most or all health care needs. Patients are assigned a primary care physician, usually a general practitioner or internist, who refers patients to specialists within the network, as needed. Patients who receive medical care outside of the network are not covered and are responsible for all charges incurred. HMO patients usually pay a small fee, called a *copayment,* each time they see their medical practitioner. The copayment is for services rendered within the network and for medication.

Indemnity and Reimbursement Plans

Indemnity and reimbursement plans are also referred to as traditional health insurance. Patients are free to select health care from any physician or hospital and are responsible for a percentage of the cost up to a predetermined limit. In an indemnity plan, physicians and hospitals bill the insurance provider directly for services rendered, with the patient paying the balance at the time of service. In a reimbursement plan, as the name implies, the patient is responsible for all charges incurred at the time of service and later files a claim with the insurance provider for reimbursement.

Preferred Provider Organizations (PPOs)

Preferred provider organizations, or PPOs, are a fusion of HMOs and traditional indemnity and reimbursement plans. PPOs are similar to HMOs in that a predetermined network of hospitals and doctors agrees to provide medical services to employees and their dependents for a set fee. PPOs allow patients to see physicians outside of the network, however, and still cover a percentage of the costs. This coverage is referred to as *point of service* (POS). Copayments for services within the network are substantially lower than those outside of the network in order to encourage patients to seek care within the network.

INSURANCE

A variety of insurance is almost always available to employees, particularly since it is one of the least expensive benefits an employer can provide. Insurance is popular with employees, as well, and the cost to employees for premiums is usually nominal. The importance of insurance should not be underestimated. Disability insurance, for example, provides income for employees or their dependents in the event that the employee is incapacitated. Other types of insurance provide income for retirement or payment in case of accidental loss of life or the loss of a sense or limb. Several popular forms of insurance are discussed next.

Life Insurance

There are various types of life insurance, including *whole life,* in which a policy, once fully paid, pays survivors whenever the employee dies; and *group term,* in which an employee must die during the policy term in order for payment to occur. Employers are free to decide which types, if any, they will offer. Most employers will pay the premiums for a set amount of coverage and allow their employees to purchase additional coverage as needed. Premiums are tax-deductible for both employer and employees, further enhancing life insurance's accessibility and popularity. Life insurance for employees with families is of major importance to ensure that survivors of the deceased have the necessary funds for burial costs and also as a means of replacing, at least partially, the income of the deceased.

Accidental Death and Dismemberment Insurance (AD&D)

Similar to life insurance, *AD&D insurance* provides a lump sum payment to the survivors of a deceased employee. As the name implies, however, the condition of death must generally be accidental and unforeseen as opposed to extended illness, for example. AD&D will also provide payment to the employee in the event of the loss of a sense or limb. These payments are generally less, although specifics vary from provider to plan.

Disability Insurance

Disability insurance provides income to an employee who suffers a debilitating injury or illness. There are two types of disability insurance: *short-term* and *long-term;* and both are designed to supplement state and federal disability programs. Corporate programs vary, but most employers pay the entire premium for short-term disability insurance since the premiums are small and tax-deductible; some companies self-insure their employees directly. Long-term disability insurance is usually part of a group policy in which the premium payments are split between the employee and employer. Because of these costs, short-term disability insurance is more common, being offered by 80 percent of employers as opposed to 70 percent for long-term.

RETIREMENT PLANS

Retirement plans have evolved to reflect the changes in the American workforce and to reflect recent legislation such as the Employee Retirement Income Security Act (ERISA). About 85 percent of all office workers are covered by their employer's pension programs, as opposed to 50-percent coverage in the general population. A recent trend is to offer retirement to younger employees. This enables employers to promote new employees more quickly, lower costs, and provide for better morale within the workforce. Retirement plans, once offered, must be available uniformly to all employees at least 21 years of age who have worked 1,000 hours or more within the past twelve months. Retirement plans fall into two categories: defined benefit and defined contribution.

Defined Benefit

Defined benefit plans are rapidly disappearing, reflecting the changes in the American workforce. Under a *defined benefit plan,* employers invest enough to pay a guaranteed, predetermined amount, usually a percentage of the employee's salary, upon the employee's retirement. This type of plan requires no contribution from the employee, involves enormous financial commitment from the company, and requires adherence to heavy administration and government regulations. Originally designed to encourage employees to stay with a company for life, defined benefit plans remain the domain of large corporations because of their expense. As the American workforce continues to move toward self-employment, contractual employment, and small business, defined benefit plans will continue to diminish.

Defined Contribution

Defined contribution plans continue to proliferate, replacing defined benefit plans. Employees in *defined contribution plans* have the opportunity to invest in their retirement themselves, up to a given percentage of their annual income. This money, along with a set portion from their employer, goes into a savings and investment program.

The most popular defined contribution plan today is the *401(k) plan* in which employees invest regularly on a pretax basis. Most employers make matching contributions, which are vested to the employee after a set amount of time. While still regulated by the government, 401(k) contributions and investment earnings are tax-free, allowing accelerated growth of employees' retirement accounts and further adding to the popularity of the 401(k) plan. Heavy tax penalties exist to discourage early withdrawal, although many plans do make provisions for employees to borrow from their accounts.

Investors suggest that you should be investing as much as 10 percent of your pretax income, or $3,000 per year if you are earning $30,000 annually, in a 401(k) to ensure sufficient retirement funds.

PAY FOR TIME NOT WORKED

Paid time off, such as holidays and sick days, is so commonplace in the office environment that employees are often under the impression that it is a mandated right. Make no mistake, offering pay for time not worked under any condition is completely determined by employers. It is also one of the most expensive benefits offered, accounting for about 10 percent of the average company's payroll costs. Still, paid time off continues to grow. For example, the average number of paid holidays per year in 1955 was six compared to today's twelve. Employers have long since recognized the effect of these benefits on employee morale and the need for time-off benefits as employees juggle the demands of their personal and professional life. Payment for time not worked falls into two categories: on the job and off the job.

On the Job

In the past, office workers were officially given a 15-minute coffee break about midmorning and a second formal coffee break between noon and the end of the day. During these time periods, everyone took time off. At the end of that time, everyone was expected to get back to work. Lunch, too, was structured, with 30 minutes being the norm rather than the 60- and 90-minute lunch times common today.

Generally, today's offices aren't so regimented. Most managers understand that their employees need some time to rest and socialize, and will say little about breaks or lunch times. On the other hand, abuse of the privilege can incur criticism from a supervisor. Excessive abuse by the staff as a whole can generate a very restrictive approach, with managers prowling the workplace to see if some worker has a newspaper out or is staring into space.

If you need a break, it is better to take a walk outside the building. Since confusion about a lunch break can arise if you eat at your desk, you may want to take your lunch breaks in the office cafeteria or nearby coffee shop.

Off the Job

Paid time off when you are off the job includes paid vacation, personal and sick days, and holidays. It also include less orthodox time off, such as floating holidays, bereavement days, and accommodations for jury duty. These benefits may be offered on an accumulated basis, may have eligibility requirements, or may be carried over from year to year. Since these benefits are strictly voluntary, conditions and specifics are as different as the employers who offer them. Most employers apply their policies uniformly, however, and have written policies available for new employees or employees who request them.

EMPLOYEE SERVICES

Employee services have changed considerably as companies have discovered the positive impact such services can have on productivity. Given the time constraints that we live under, these services can be of real value. For example, some companies contract to provide their employees with concierge services that range from picking up cleaning to picking up tickets for a children's outing.

During summer months, many companies offer a number of half days on Fridays. During the winters, in the two-week period between Christmas and New Year's, some offices close; others implement dress-down days. Many companies in summer allow dress-down everyday; the rest of the year, they allow dress-down every Friday. Some firms have a tradition of summer picnics or other social events for the company as a whole.

Other special benefits for employees can include company-paid snacks or dinners for those who work late in the evening, even limousine service home; child care; tuition reimbursement; and, increasingly, health club memberships or, at least, a portion of the membership fee. Employees at a certain level within their organization may get special perks, from extra vacation time to a company car.

For employees with personal problems, companies offer employee assistance programs (EAPs) that provide personal counseling and help with everything from drug or alcohol addiction to delinquency in a child to eldercare.

ETIQUETTE

The daily news is full of reports about huge, faceless entities that are merging with other companies, implementing new technology, or addressing stock fluctuations. When business is conducted on such a mega scale, we can easily forget that it is people who conduct business, not faceless entities. It is important, therefore, that we learn to treat each other with respect and consideration in the workplace. Office etiquette provides common-sense guidelines on how to do this in the easiest manner. Office etiquette increases the quality of life in the workplace, contributes to employee morale, and embellishes the company image—all with a minimum of effort. Having a knowledge of office etiquette is a quality that can separate an assistant from an office professional and can draw attention to his or her promotability.

General guidelines on some of the most common office situations follow. Two excellent and comprehensive sources of more detailed information are *Amy Vanderbilt's Complete Book of Etiquette* and *Letitia Baldrige's Complete Guide to Executive Manners.*

- When greeting a visitor to the office in your supervisor's absence, introduce yourself by name, then title, and ask, "May I help you?"

- When you answer the phone, don't just identify your company; identify yourself, as well. Say, "This is (your name)."

- Always introduce a younger person or junior person to an older or more senior person. An exception is that staff people should be introduced to clients or customers.

- Exchange business cards at the start of a meeting. Offer your card by saying, "May I give you my card?" if the other person doesn't offer his or hers. If you are given a card by another, offer yours in turn. Take the card and keep it before you if seated. Treat the card with the same respect as you do the person who is there with you. You can put the card in your Rolodex after the individual has left.

- If you are attending a large group meeting, the chair will likely ask each member to introduce himself or herself, going around the room. When you introduce yourself, give both your name and job title. If you don't know many people, take the opportunity before the meeting to introduce yourself to as many people as you can.

- Greet visitors and offer to take their coats. If they must wait for your manager, lead them to a chair and tell them you will return for them shortly. If the wait is longer than you thought, revisit to assure them that you haven't forgotten them.

- If you have been asked to help with a visitor—for instance, to take him or her on a tour of the office—introduce yourself to the visitor. If you must absent yourself from the visitor for a period of time, be sure to leave him or her in a colleague's care. Introduce the visitor to your colleague and tell the visitor when you will be back. When the visit is over, escort the guest to the office door and thank him or her for coming.

DEALING WITH OFFICE POLITICS

When people interact with each other on a daily basis, politics are bound to arise. It is important to keep office politics to a minimum by treating everyone fairly and refraining from participation in politics; this includes gossiping with or about co-workers. When conversation becomes uncomfortable, try to direct the conversation to a more neutral topic, or simply excuse yourself and leave. Gossip will almost always make its way back to the original person and lead to hostility, discomfort, and an unhappy work environment.

Avoiding gossip in today's offices is hard. But, if you want to be seen as a professional, it's imperative that you neither repeat gossip nor begin it yourself. If a co-worker wants to share some gossip with you, and you don't want to offend the person, you can use the excuse that you are too busy to hear.

THE ASSISTANT/BOSS PARTNERSHIP

In today's organizations, you and your boss are a team. Thus, it's imperative that you help your teammate look good. This means that you have to make that little extra effort to see that your boss is on time for meetings and that his or her letters do not have typographical errors. You also should ensure that your boss completes work on schedule by alerting him or her to due dates and assisting whenever you can. Never put your boss in a position to be surprised by a mistake. Let him or her know if there is a problem so that, together, you can resolve the problem.

The more you can make your boss look good, the better you will look. Many office professionals have built reputations based on their support of their boss. The demonstration of their professionalism ultimately resulted in obtaining their own managerial position. Being a partner with your boss may be the best career move you can make.

DRESS

Even though many offices have relaxed their dress standards, allowing employees to dress casually, it is critical that your clothing and grooming still portray a professional image. The most important aspect of dressing well for the office is appropriateness. What is acceptable in one office may not be appropriate in another. Banking and law, for example, still command a much more formal appearance than more creative industries such as journalism. Your position within the office should also be reflected in the way you dress. CEOs, for example, are expected to dress formally at all times, regardless of the policy for the office at large. Finally, employees who have direct contact with clients or others outside of the company should adopt a more conservative dress to portray a favorable and professional image.

If you are unsure whether your clothing is appropriate, a good model to follow is the dress of co-workers you respect. Other sources of information include consultants and salespeople in clothing stores, fashion magazines, books and other media, and friends or family with a good sense of style. When determining what is appropriate, consider your coloring and body type. Avoid trendy fashions and fads because they quickly go out of style. Invest in the best fabric and workmanship you can afford. It pays off in the long run because good-quality clothing wears better, never goes out of style, and looks better on you.

For men, a well-fitting suit is almost always appropriate dress in an office environment, and men should invest in a minimum of three good-quality suits. Styles and types vary and project different images, and should be carefully chosen to reflect the image of the individual and the profession. A double-breasted suit, for example, is considered more formal than a three-button suit, which is currently considered very stylish. A navy blue blazer should also be a staple in an office professional's closet. This garment is incredibly versatile and can be worn in place of a suit in the office as well as worn in more casual environments. Long-sleeved shirts project a better image than short-sleeved and are more appropriate for the office. If a man does wear a short-sleeved shirt, however, he should remember not to remove his jacket while in view of the public. Ties should subtly complement the colors, textures, and patterns of both the suit and the shirt, and should never be loud or distracting. Lace-up, dress shoes are most appropriate for the office, although tasseled loafers are also considered acceptable. Shoes should be clean, well-polished, and in good condition.

Women have much more versatility in what is acceptable dress in the office. With that versatility, however, comes more decisions. A professional woman's closet should contain a minimum of three business suits. Business pants suits are completely appropriate; however, a skirt suit is still considered more formal and professional. Daytime dresses are also a staple of office wear and should be chosen with care to project a good image. Women should also invest in good-quality blazers that can be coupled with skirts or pants. Blouses are the easiest garment to replace as fashion changes, so they can be stylish and project a more personal image. Blouses for the office should, however, remain somewhat conservative and subtle. Women should always wear stockings in the office. Hose with patterns, pictures, or runs is not appropriate and should be replaced. Shoes should be flat or medium-heeled, cleaned daily, and in good condition.

Always in Style by Doris Pooser is an excellent resource to help create your own personal style.

INVITATIONS

Invitations to office parties and socials should directly reflect the formality of the function. If the office is gathering after work to celebrate a co-worker's birthday, for example, it is fine to invite people verbally. A formal dinner or holiday party, however, requires a printed invitation that contains the time, date, location, dress, and type of function. In either case, it is a good idea to have a prepared list of invitees to ensure that no one is accidentally overlooked and omitted. For formal functions, the list also serves as a check-off of who has responded to an RSVP. On printed invitations, hand-write on the envelope the name of the recipient and also the address if the invitation will be mailed. Distribute printed invitations at least four weeks in advance; for verbal invitations or informal get-togethers, a week or two is sufficient.

Your responsibilities to your manager may include screening invitations to events and responding for him or her. You may want to discuss this issue with your boss to be sure that a key business opportunity isn't inadvertently declined. Until you are certain, it is better to take the information if the invitation is via phone. If he or she receives a printed invitation, make sure that your boss knows about it and has told you whether to accept. If your boss chooses to accept, note it on his or her calendar and also on yours when you make the acceptance..

If your boss decides not to attend, you still need to call. That's what *RSVP* means—*Respondez s'il vous plait* (Reply, if you please—in French). If your boss wants to take a guest, ask about this when you call. If there is a question of dress, you can use this occasion to ask about that, too.

If your boss will need the invitation to enter the gathering, you may want to keep it in your own work files and give him or her the invitation on the day of the event.

PARTIES AND SOCIAL FUNCTIONS

Office parties and social functions boost morale, encourage people to celebrate, and promote interaction on a personal level. They also vary greatly, depending on the event, the size of the company, and available resources.

When planning a party, take into consideration the size, cost, objective, theme, and image you wish to project. Preparing for a large function can quickly become overwhelming; the menu, guest list, location, decorations, and entertainment must all be decided on. In these situations, hotel and restaurant facility managers, caterers, and professional party consultants are an excellent source of information and ideas.

When attending an office party, use the opportunity to mingle and meet and talk with co-workers you don't know well or with whom you have little contact at the office. Keep conversation light and avoid office politics as a topic. Above all, maintain a professional image. While the purpose of the party is for employees to enjoy themselves, remember that anything said or done will be remembered the next day at the office. When alcohol is served, drinking in moderation is of paramount importance.

Here are some questions to ask yourself as you plan the party:

- Given the purpose of the occasion, where is the best location for it?

- Is this party solely for staff members, or should clients or customers be invited?

- Will guests bring family members—not just a spouse but children? If so, how should I adapt the menu?

- Should there be background music? If so, live or recorded?

- Should I arrange for transportation home if the event lasts late into the night?

GIFT GIVING

Corporate gift giving in the United States is a $2 billion industry. This is not surprising; giving gifts has long been an ingrained part of American culture. Gifts to clients and employees promote goodwill and loyalty, and let people know they are appreciated. Whenever possible, it is important to carefully select gifts that are individualized and will be personally appreciated rather than mass distributing identical items. In larger companies, budget guidelines can be set for representatives of individual departments, and gift purchasing can be on a smaller and more personal level. Even gifts to thousands of employees or clients can be creatively done so as to impress the recipient with your thoughtfulness. Tickets to sporting or cultural events; parties or receptions for employees, clients, and their guests; and gift certificates for products or services are good examples of gifts designed to make the individual feel singled out and appreciated.

In addition to a company's budgetary constraints, there are other reasons to keep the cost of corporate gifts in perspective. While there is no limit on what can be spent, excessively expensive gifts may make the recipient feel uncomfortable, may be construed as bribery, or may violate gift recipient rules of other companies. In addition, the IRS limits the tax-deductible amount for business gifts to $25. Twelve of the most popular gift items, which are not excessively expensive, are:

- Gift subscriptions
- Pen and pencil sets
- Clocks
- Coffee mugs
- Hats
- Food baskets

- Desk folios and folders
- Calendars
- Calculators
- Golf items
- Liquor
- Desk sets

Most of these gifts can also be imprinted with your company's logo. However, to avoid having your gift construed as cheap or an attempt at free advertising, you may want to consider imprinting the logo in an inconspicuous place or perhaps printing it only on the wrapping paper—or leaving it off altogether. Finally, a handwritten note or card should accompany every gift.

Personal gifts

A gift marks a special relationship with a person and should never be given by rote or obligation. Employees who give their coworkers gifts are under no obligation to give something to everyone; however, it is best to be as inconspicuous as possible to avoid hurt feelings. It is generally accepted that gift giving goes down the corporate ladder, so consideration should be given to staff and employees to show appreciation for their support. Employees are free to give their bosses a small token of their esteem, but the expense should be kept to a minimum and excessively personal gifts, which could be misconstrued, should be avoided.

DATING

In a perfect world, interoffice romance would not occur at all. The opportunity for hazardous situations is just too great. The reality, however, is that we spend most of our waking hours in the office, and attraction doesn't always conform to what is in our best interests. Because romance on the job will affect how an employee is perceived by his or her coworkers, care should be taken to keep the repercussions to a minimum. A few tips follow.

1. Be wary of a romance with someone from the same department. Even in the best of circumstances, you will both be under intense scrutiny, and your romance is going to be a topic of conversation in the office. In the event that the romance does not work out, you will be left in the

uncomfortable situation of having to face and work with the other person on a daily basis.

2. Under no circumstances engage in a romance with your boss or an employee who reports to you. The possible repercussions are severe enough to endanger your job. Should you find yourself involved in a mutual attraction, seriously consider transferring to a different department or finding a new job.

3. Keep your personal life private. Even though gossip and rumors may eventually circulate through the office regarding your romance, avoid providing verbal and behavioral confirmation as well as making references to your personal life.

4. In every area of the company, refrain from public displays of affection, pet names, arguments or disagreements, and plans for personal time. This includes cafeterias, break areas, and parking lots. Also avoid being together alone in isolated areas or behind closed doors.

5. Show no favoritism, and set priorities as always.

CONGRATULATIONS AND CONDOLENCES

Letters and cards of congratulations and condolences are in excellent taste. It is always appropriate and uplifting to let someone know how highly he or she is regarded both in celebration and in times of mourning. Such a gesture also demonstrates your thoughtfulness. Even though the two circumstances are opposites, several rules apply to both situations.

Don't let the opportunity pass you by. Write your note as soon as you hear the news. Delays imply that the news isn't as important to you as to the recipient. If you have learned of the event after the fact, address the situation with a simple phrase such as "I've only just recently returned from vacation and heard the great/terrible news." Available time should not constrain your response. If your time is limited, a two- or three-sentence note or a signed card is all that is required.

The same advice applies to your boss's response. Often, your boss will get so involved in office details that he or she will forget to ask you to send his or her requests/congratulations. Knowing your boss, you need to judge whether you should purchase a card for his or her signature and brief message.

Address the situation directly, and keep your response sincere and concise. Use a straightforward phrase such as "I was very happy to learn of your recent promotion" or "I was saddened to learn of the death of your mother." While writing congratulations, avoid gushing or using insincere flattery. When writing condolences, be as concise as possible to avoid making the recipient feel worse in an already difficult time.

Don't refer to other business or news or ask for favors. This is not an opportunity to "sneak one in." There will be time later to address circumstances that may arise due to the situation. Congratulations should never refer to how you can benefit from the situation. When writing condolences, it is appropriate, however, to let the recipient know you are available for anything he or she may need with a simple phrase such as "Please don't hesitate to let me know if there is anything I can do to help."

FOR MORE INFORMATION

If you can't find what you need from the phone numbers and Web sites listed in this chapter, you may need to expand your search.

- For more information on placing an ad for a job, call your local newspaper. Their classified advertising department will be able to assist you.

- For more information on temporary employment agencies, look in your Yellow Pages under "employment agencies."

- For more information on human resources, organizational management or employee management, check the business section of your local library or bookstore.

- For more information on your state's labor laws, including compliance requirements for ADA and other legislation, check your government listings for Labor Relations.

- For more information on your company's exposure to lawsuits regarding sexual harassment and other workplace issues, check with you attorney or local labor relations board. Seminars and on-site training courses are often available.

- For more information on business etiquette, check your local bookstore for the business category and business life subcategory.

10

TRAVEL PLANNING

◆

- **Business Travel Today**
- **The Itinerary**

    Compiling the Details
    Making Reservations
    Internet Travel Services

- **International Travel**

    International Airline Travel
    Passport, Visa, Immunizations, and Customs
    Getting Extra Business Help While Away
    Money: Yours and Theirs
    Legal Help Abroad
    Medical Help Abroad
    Renting and Driving Cars in Other Countries
    Business Etiquette Abroad
    Post-Travel Tasks

- **For More Information**

As advanced communications turn the world into a global village, businesses increasingly consider the entire country their market—and are rapidly expanding their interests into international areas as well. That means travel is the norm these days, no longer the exception. Sales people roam further and further to meet new clients, executives scour new locations for sources of cheaper manufacturing, and technical staffs shuttle between remote offices. Even the office professional, who years ago rarely left the office, now might accompany the boss to give a sales presentation, go on-site to arrange a conference, or fly cross-country to staff a trade show. All employees, including office professionals, are more likely today to go anywhere to make and maintain contacts, attend meetings and conventions, present lectures, and just relax.

Making travel arrangements for the entire staff often is a key part of the office professional's job. To ensure a smooth, enjoyable, and profitable trip, the office professional must be familiar with everything from the best means of transportation to the culture and politics of the intended location. And that's in addition to overseeing the innumerable details of collecting all the supplies and documents needed to make the trip a success.

BUSINESS TRAVEL TODAY

Once considered a perk, business travel is now more often seen as a chore, a disadvantage that sometimes prompts people to change or refuse jobs. After all, travel is time-consuming to prepare for and to do, employees often lose productive work time enroute, and travel isolates employees not only from their families, but from the critical events of everyday company life.

Good office professionals can do a lot to solve these problems. They track the traveler's mileage to upgrade flights for more comfort. They make seamless arrangements that don't force the traveler into either sprinting to connections or killing hours during changeovers. They route travel on airlines with up-to-date business lounges. They discover—and avoid—the worst travel times at individual airports. They facilitate communications between the traveler and the office, both en route to and at his or her destination. They make sure that the traveler has the necessary files and documents for business purposes. And, depending on their work, office professionals may be handling these same details for half a dozen different people traveling to half a dozen different destinations.

Large organizations sometimes have in-house travel services that handle all the pertinent arrangements. If the company has such a department, the office professional submits the details (such as arrival and departure dates, hotel requirements, and so on), and then helps coordinate the information with the traveler. The in-house travel service works out the itinerary with the traveler's approval, makes reservations for transportation and accommodations,

FINDING A GOOD TRAVEL AGENCY

The choice of a travel agency is crucial, not only to the success of any specific trip but also to the company's overall success as well. If the executive is late for a meeting because he or she missed a connecting flight that was too closely timed, if the hotel that was a "good deal" is actually so shabby that it gives a poor impression, or if the executive ends up overseas three days too early in one place and two days too late in another because of jumbled last-minute changes to the itinerary—these problems can result in a loss of clients and a drastic drop in profits.

Although many large companies put out bids or surveys before choosing an agency (and repeat this process at intervals), most companies want an agency they can use all the time. Today's business demands instant responses. If the company's manufacturing plant in Thailand is facing a crisis, the office assistant can't spend two weeks polling agencies about their practices. A reliable agency delivers every time, taking care of the major details of travel and transportation and also providing extra services for its clients. Therefore, the office professional will want to choose an agency that will do the following:

- Prepare a tentative itinerary, which the executive can approve or change.

- Handle all the arrangements for travel and transportation, for hotel reservations, and perhaps for sightseeing and other extracurricular activities.

- Arrange to have a rental car waiting for the executive at the destination point, if desired; explain relevant driving concerns; and arrange for necessary documents in a foreign country.

- Handle both personal and baggage insurance, if desired.

- Provide information about exactly which documents will be needed for foreign travel (such as passports, visas, and health and police certificates) and how to obtain them.

- Obtain as many of these documents as possible (certain documents must be obtained by the traveler personally).

- List the vaccinations required by each country to be visited.

continues

- Supply the name of a desirable hotel in the country of destination, and provide a letter of introduction to the hotel manager if the executive's accommodations are not finalized ahead of time.

- Inform the traveler of the country's culture, politics, and customs that might affect his or her business dealings.

- Alert the traveler to state department travel advisories regarding the political climate in areas to be visited.

Because an agency's true capability to handle these items will not be discovered until its services actually have been engaged, what should the office professional look for in selecting a travel agency?

Begin with recommendations from other departments and divisions, from fellow office professionals, and from the company's clients and vendors. Whether you have recommendations or must make cold calls from the telephone book, ask each agency the following questions:

- *What is the agency's professional affiliation?* Membership in professional travel societies usually indicates at least a minimum level of competence because certain qualifications must be met before the agency is awarded membership. The most important of these is the American Society of Travel Agents (ASTA). Other key organizations are Airline Reporting Corporation (ARC), International Air Transport Association (IATA), Meeting Planners International (PI), and Cruise Line Industry Association (CLIA).

- *Are one or more of its agents certified?* To become a certified travel counselor or certified travel consultant (CTC), an agent must log hours of study of a set curriculum. Certification is a good indication of the personnel's professionalism.

- *Can the agency write its own tickets?* Although many agencies today write e-tickets, written tickets are still very common. (An e-ticket is an electronic version of your ticket filed with the airline. To travel on an e-ticket, the traveler only needs a confirmation number and identification.) Having the capability to issue an airline ticket on the spot shows that the agency has experience and financial strength.

- *Does the agency specialize in corporate travel?* Package tours require very different planning from the more difficult individualized itineraries of business executives. Look for an agency that is familiar with the needs of business travelers.

■ *Is its technology up-to-date?* A fully computerized office can find you the best travel schedules and rates instantly and can make adjustments for changes on either end.

■ *Does it have a 24-hour toll-free phone number?* It's important that the agency can be reached after hours and on weekends through a toll-free phone number. This helps the traveler whose flight arrangements have been fouled up or whose sudden change in plans require new departure times.

■ *Is the agency multilingual?* An agent's capability to communicate in the language of the destination country can help prevent problems.

■ *Does it supply recordkeeping?* If the agency can supply a fully itemized bill matched to the itinerary afterward, a large part of the recordkeeping duties are done. This itemization can satisfy requirements for both company reimbursements and tax purposes.

■ *Will the agency provide recommendations from other business travelers?* The agency's willingness to do so often says as much as any customer's individual comments about it.

If this search does not yield a satisfactory agency, contact the American Society of Travel Agents (www.astanet.com/) for members closest to you. This organization can be reached at 1101 King Street, Alexandria, VA 22314; 703-739-2782.

When it comes to the particulars of the executive's trip, the agency relies largely on the information that comes from the office assistant. He or she should provide the agency with the executive's name, business and home telephone numbers, credit card number (if necessary), detailed information on dates and times of desired arrival and departure for each city to be visited, and the type of transportation preferred. Although the agent will report periodically on the progress made, it is the office professional's responsibility to keep in touch with the agent to see that tickets and reservations arrive at the office in plenty of time to check the dates, times, destinations, and so forth before they are turned over to the traveler.

If the office professional makes the arrangements without the use of an agency, he or she must see to all the details personally. All these details will be brought together in the itinerary.

and obtains confirmations. The details then are sent to the executive's office well before the departure date.

If a company does not have its own in-house travel department, it is often wise to use an outside agency. The services generally are free (except for rail travel), are backed by more specific experience and contacts than office professionals have in this area, can usually obtain better and faster service than an individual, and can save untold hours of time and effort.

However, even if help is available through an in-house agency or an outside firm, the office professional still plays a major role in travel planning. Not only does the office professional have the responsibility of providing the agencies with all the information regarding destinations, arrivals, departures, and accommodations, but he or she is also responsible for following up. If the department or agency makes the wrong arrangements or overlooks a detail, it's up to the office professional to catch the mistake and correct it.

The office professional also might be responsible for making sure that details of travel plans comply with the company's travel policies. This goes far beyond obtaining the proper signatures to authorize a trip beforehand, and collecting and filing receipts afterward. It involves planning both travel and accommodations within a limited budget—and sometimes within strict procedures. For example, some companies designate a travel level for each employee, which could mean that only CEOs fly first-class and only top executives fly business class. Middle managers, sales people, and other staff might be limited to coach, even if they've accumulated enough frequent-flyer miles to upgrade their own ticket. Accommodations are similarly graded. Policies might also require the filing of a travel profile, a document on file with the travel planner including preferred seating, meals, cars, and so on. Travel policies also might include handling appropriate accommodations, filing travel profiles, tracking personal days, or submitting an executive's frequent-flyer miles to an airline.

THE ITINERARY

For the most part, business travel has come to mean air travel. This means that the office assistant's travel-planning duties will largely involve booking flights and perhaps arranging for a rental car at each destination. But what sounds simple in theory becomes complicated in practice.

For example, let's say that an executive must fly from San Francisco to Washington, DC, and asks the office professional to book a nonstop flight from California's Oakland Airport to Washington's Ronald Reagan Airport. A simple request, right? Then the assistant discovers (or already knows from experience) that neither Oakland nor Ronald Reagan handles nonstop, coast-to-coast flights. Before coming up with alternatives, the assistant needs to know which is most important to the executive: leaving from Oakland, taking a nonstop flight, or arriving directly at Ronald Reagan. Knowing the traveler's priority determines whether the alternative is a flight from Oakland to Chicago with a brief layover, and then a flight from Chicago into DC; or whether it's a nonstop flight from San Francisco into Washington Dulles Airport with a limo, bus, or rental car ride into DC.

This is just the smallest example of the kind of creative thinking that an assistant must use when making travel plans. And given how ordinary business travel has become for just about every industry, the assistant must be ready to come up with creative solutions on any given day.

COMPILING THE DETAILS

An itinerary is a travel schedule, a chronological listing of each place to be visited, the separate appointments at each location, and the method of transportation between each point. To begin compiling an itinerary, ask the traveler his or her destination, the dates of the trip, the preferred time and method of travel, hotel accommodations, the daily appointments (if known), the preferred airports, and whether any options are possible. Write these facts up as a tentative itinerary, or enter them in a file.

Keep in mind the company's travel policy when drawing up even the initial itinerary, and include flights that fit the fare requirements. Some companies require only that flights be booked the standard 14 or 21 days in advance. Others require that the cheapest flight must be booked, no matter what. In addition, some policies might not allow the traveler to choose the method of transportation.

OBTAINING REFUNDS FOR UNUSED TICKETS

With today's hectic schedules that are always subject to change, travelers might need to change travel plans en route. In such a case, the traveler is entitled to a refund on the unused portion of the ticket. The airline should be informed immediately when the need for cancellation becomes apparent.

If the ticket was handwritten and not an e-ticket, the ticket must be physically returned to the travel agency or airline before the traveler can be issued a refund or credit, depending on the company's policy. If the unused ticket is mailed, include a cover letter mentioning the date of the flight, departure city, destination, ticket number, flight number, credit card number, and cost. Keep the letter in a follow-up folder to make sure that the company credit card is actually credited with the refund or to track credits to be applied to the next trip.

Charles Murray

Itinerary February 19, 200_

Tuesday, February 19 (New York to Raleigh)

10:00 a.m.	Leave West Side Airline Terminal, New York, by limousine or van for Newark airport.
11:10 a.m.	Leave Newark airport on Eastern Airlines Flight #275 (lunch). (Ticket attached)
1:19 p.m.	Arrive Raleigh. Van to Hotel Hilton. (Reservation attached)
2:00 p.m.	Yvonne Lee, Office Manager at Raleigh branch, will pick you up at the Hilton. Conference scheduled at branch office. (File #1 in briefcase)

Wednesday, February 20 (Raleigh)

9:00 a.m.	Yvonne Lee will pick you up at the hotel for inspection of Raleigh plant. (File #2 in briefcase contains facts and statistics on plant operation)
1:00 p.m.	Lunch with Yvonne Lee and Neil Jordan, Raleigh Plant Manager.
3:00 p.m.	Conference with plant shift managers.
8:00 p.m.	Company dinner at Hotel Hilton. (Speech in File #3 in briefcase)

Thursday, February 21 (Raleigh to Winston-Sale, via Greensboro)

9:30 a.m.	Yvonne Lee will pick you up at the hotel and drive you to the airport.
9:56 a.m.	Leave Raleigh on Delta Airlines Flight #101. (Ticket attached)
10:18 a.m.	Arrive Greensboro airport. Limousine or van to Winston-Salem Hotel in Winston-Salem. (Reservation attached) Lunch at hotel.
3:00 p.m.	Appointment with John Spaaks, Office Manager at Winston-Salem branch, and Teresa Kopecky, Sales Director. Hotel Winston-Salem, Green Room. (File #4 in briefcase)
7:00 p.m.	Dinner at Bill Lawson's home. (Telephone 722-1234)

Sample Itinerary (page 1 of 2)

If no limitations exist concerning the travel method, obtain complete information on all airlines and railroads serving the city of destination, including arrival and departure times and the costs of each. Also include information about car rental agencies at the various destinations. List all the choices available, and let the executive decide which to use.

As further pieces of information about the trip are gathered, the assistant can fill in the details of the itinerary. These details might include departure

---

Friday, February 22 (Winston-Salem)

9:00 a.m.　　Golf with Bill Lawson.

1:00 p.m.　　Conference with staff at Winston-Salem offices. (File #5 in briefcase)

8:00 p.m.　　Company dinner at Winston-Salem Hotel. (Speech in File #6 in briefcase)

Saturday, February 23 (Winston-Salem to Greenville via Asheville)

9:02 a.m.　　Leave Winston-Salem on Southern Airlines Flight #501. (Ticket attached)

10:10 a.m.　　Arrive Asheville. Limousine or van to Greenville Hotel in Greenville. (Reservation attached) Lunch at hotel.

2:00 p.m.　　Conference with Greenville branch office manager Nasim Borzorg at Greenville Hotel, Mezzanine Lounge. (File #7 in briefcase)

7:00 p.m.　　Company dinner at hotel. (Speech in File #8 in briefcase)

Sunday, February 24 (Greenville to Columbia)

3:00 p.m.　　Leave Greenville/Spartanburg airport on Southern Airlines commuter flight #38. (Ticket attached)

4:00 p.m.　　Arrive Columbia. George Lewis, Office Manager, will meet you at the airport. Magnolia Hotel. (Reservation attached)

Monday, February 25 (Columbia)

9:00 a.m.　　Conference at Columbia offices. George Lewis will pick you up at the hotel. (File #9 in briefcase contains statistics and progress reports from this branch)

7:00 p.m.　　Dinner meeting of Columbia staff at Magnolia Hotel. (Speech in File #10 in briefcase)

Tuesday, February 26 (Columbia to New York)

10:00 a.m.　　George Lewis will pick you up to take you to the airport.

11:07 a.m.　　Leave Columbia on Eastern Airlines Flight #666 (lunch). (Ticket attached)

2:33 p.m.　　Arrive Newark airport. Limousine to New York offices.

Sample Itinerary (page 2 of 2)

times, optional flight times, layovers, connections, arrival times, ground transportation, times and locations of appointments, people attending appointments, reference material needed for each, special meals, scheduled events, and so on.

In planning an itinerary, bear in mind that while en route to each destination, the traveler must have the time and a place to eat regularly, to rest, to travel from a terminal to the place of an appointment, and so forth. Therefore, the following information should be included in the schedule:

- Eating locations (plane, train, hotel, restaurant).

- Sufficient time to travel from the place of arrival to the appointment.

- Event times, listed in both the time zone of the destination and the time zone of the home office.

- Two copies of the final itinerary, meeting files, confirmation documents, and any other relevant travel information—one for the traveler and one for the office professional. Keep yours handy, in case the traveler calls while on the road with a problem. Additional copies of the schedule alone may be given to supervisors, family members, and others in the organization who might need to contact the traveler.

MAKING RESERVATIONS

For both domestic and international travel, the phone proves handy for finding information and making reservations quickly. The major airlines all have toll-free numbers listed in the Yellow Pages of the phone book (see the following section for numbers and Web site addresses). Most major hotel chains and car-rental agencies also maintain international branches, so arrangements for both can be made easily from the office. The Yellow Pages have toll-free numbers for these, too.

To make a plane reservation, call the reservation desk of the airline and give your boss's name, the name and address of the firm, the credit card number, the desired flight number, the city of departure and city of destination, and the time the flight is scheduled to leave. If the flight is already filled, or if a considerable change in departure time has occurred, ask for alternatives. If none of the suggestions is acceptable, ask to be put on standby, and then try to make reservations on another airline. As soon as a reservation is available and confirmed, immediately cancel the other arrangements, including the standby reservation.

When a reservation has been confirmed, ask for the confirmation in writing, and get the confirmation number over the phone. All future conversations and transactions will refer to that number—keep it safe and make sure that the traveler has a copy. Reservations for hotel rooms and rental cars also will give you a confirmation number.

When renting a car, be persistent in asking for the lowest rate possible. Check for promotional offers that may be lower than the corporate rate. Also know the travel itinerary before making the reservation; a difference in a few dozen driving miles per day can result in a lower-priced category. Before the reservation is finalized, check such details as late charges, city and state sales taxes, fuel charges, drop-off charges, insurance extras, backup cars in case of breakdown, emergency services, and so on.

If the executive travels frequently, the office professional may want to add the following resources to the office reference library:

TRAIN TRAVEL

Trains are of decreasing importance as a travel method in the United States: Disappearing railroad connections to desired cities reflect this. A rail trip takes longer than air travel and can be more expensive. However, some executives may not be able to fly (for health reasons, for example). For specific details about available rail destinations, call Amtrak at 800-872-7245.

Once overseas, however, trains still provide a viable form of transportation. Your travel agent will be able to supply you with information about the condition of the railroads in any particular country.

- *The Official Airlines Guide.* This guide provides information on airlines that service each city in the United States, its possessions, and Canada. It also includes information on car rental and taxi service in each city. The book is available by writing to *The Official Airlines Guide,* 2000 Clearwater Drive, Oak Brook, IL 60521; or by calling 800-323-3537.

- *Hotel and Motel Red Book.* This guide lists hotels and motels by city and state; indicates the number of rooms, rates, and plans (e.g., American, with meals; European, without meals); lists recreational facilities; gives toll-free telephone numbers for each; and indicates whether the hotel or motel is part of a chain. A special section lists the number and types of meeting rooms of various seating capacities, along with their audiovisual capabilities. Published annually, the *Hotel and Motel Red Book* is available from the American Hotel and Motel Association Directory Corporation, 1201 New York Avenue NW, Washington, DC 20036.

- *AAA Tour Books.* These guidebooks from the American Automobile Association describe one or more states per volume and list motels, hotels, inns, restaurants, and recreational spots for automobile travelers. Books for every state are available from local AAA offices and are free to members.

INTERNET TRAVEL SERVICES

More travel information is now available on the Web, and with encryption techniques improving, more actual transactions are being conducted. Travel is no exception to this; it's an industry that has embraced the Web enthusiastically from the beginning. Not only is it possible to research, book, and pay for an entire trip online, but Web sites also enable you to indicate seating preferences and meal selection, discover the length of travel time, find out about fare restrictions, hunt for fare discounts, and more.

An especially valuable feature of online travel services is the capability to compare up-to-the-minute flight prices and times. A few of these services are PC Travel (located at pctravel.net), easySabre (at easysabre.com) and the Official Airline Guide Electronic Travel Services (go to the home page at www.oag.com).

For comprehensive services that provide one-stop shopping for air travel, hotel reservations, and car rental, check expedia.com, previewtravel.com, travel.com, and airtravel.net.

Sites that specialize in booking air travel and providing discounted tickets are airline-fares.com, 4airlines.com, air-fare.com, and bestfares.com. For hotel and motel information and reservations, check travelWeb.com and hotelamerica.com.

Airlines, hotels, or car rental agencies also can be reached at their individual home sites. Here are several, with their Web addresses and toll-free numbers.

Travel Services: Web Sites and 800 Numbers

Company	Web Address	800 Number
Airlines		
Airline Aer Lingus	aerlingus.ie	800-474-7424
AeroMexico	aeromexico.com	800-237-6639
Air Canada	aircanada.com	800-776-3000
American Airlines	aa.com	800-433-7300
British Airways	britishairways.com	800-247-9297
China Air	china-air.com	800-227-5118
Continental	flycontinental.com	800-523-3273
Delta	delta-air.com	800-221-1212 (Dom) 800-241-4141 (Int'l)
El Al	elal.com	800-223-6700
Finnair	finnair.com	800-950-5000
Iberia	iberia.com	800-772-4642
Japan Airlines	japanair.com	800-525-3663
Korean Air	koreanair.com	800-438-5000
Lan-Chile Airlines	lanchile.com	800-488-0070
Lufthansa	lufthansa.com	800-645-3880
Northwest Airlines	nwa.com	800-225-2525 (Dom) 800-447-4747 (Int'l)
Qantas	qantas.com	800-227-4500

Swissair	swissair.com	800-221-4750
TWA	twa.com	800-221-2000
United Airlines	ual.com	800-241-6522
US Airways	usair.com	800-428-4322

Hotels and Motels

Best Western	bestwestern.com	800-780-7234
Embassy Suites	embassysuites.com	800-362-2779
Hilton	hilton.com	800-445-8667
Holiday Inn	holidayinn.com	800-465-4329
Howard Johnson	hojo.com	800-446-4656
Hyatt	hyatt.com	800-233-1234
Marriott	marriott.com	800-228-9290
Radisson	radisson.com	800-333-3333
Sheraton	sheraton.com	800-325-3535

Car-Rental Agencies

Alamo	goalamo.com	800-327-9633
Avis	avis.com	800-831-2847
Budget	budgetrentacar.com	800-527-0700
Enterprise	enterprise.com	800-327-8007
Hertz	hertz.com	800-654-3131
National	national.com	800-227-7368
Thrifty	thrifty.com	800-367-2277

INTERNATIONAL TRAVEL

The world is now a global village, meaning that today's traveler is as likely to be flying to Riyadh as to Richmond. But although the frequency of flying overseas has increased to the point of everyday business, international travel still requires extra preparations to smooth the trip and extra care to smooth the face-to-face encounter.

To begin planning, you'll need a bit more basic information. In addition to the list of countries to be visited and the trip dates, you'll need to find out the following:

- *Any requirements that the United States has for travelers.* Most of these requirements include customs for travelers re-entering the country and limits and/or fees based on the nature and amount of items being brought back. Business samples could be exempt from these limits or fees;

however, the business traveler must fill out specific exemption forms. Likewise, no more than $10,000 may be brought into or taken out of the country without filing a report.

■ *Any requirements that the destination country has for travelers.* These requirements vary from place to place and can include a visa for entry, a return ticket, sufficient funds for the stay, vaccinations, health insurance, and, in some cases, a test for Human Immunodeficiency Virus (HIV/AIDS). Some countries also limit the amount of currency that can be brought into or taken out of its borders.

■ *Any conditions imposed on business travelers that are not imposed on tourists.* For example, business travelers cannot use a tourist visa; they must obtain a business visa. Next, assemble a list of the names, nationalities, and citizenship of all employees who will be traveling; the countries to which they will travel; and the length of the trips. You'll need this basic information as you determine who needs visas, entry permits, and other official documents.

> **TIP:** Once again, assembling a detailed travel folder for each traveler is important. For foreign travel, it is useful to provide each traveler with a small ticket case (easily obtainable from travel agencies or office supply stores) for all transport tickets, official travel documents, and a passport. Travelers should be advised to keep this ticket case with them at all times.

In making foreign transportation arrangements, the agency or in-house travel service should be competent and experienced not only in international travel, but in corporate travel as well. Arranging a package tour to Italy, where a group of tourists could then be handed off to a sightseeing bus, differs significantly from arranging the detailed itinerary of a jewelry executive who will meet with a dozen new and prospective sources of Italian silver chains. If the agency is not fully experienced, make sure that you find a service that specializes or has some skill in international corporate travel. It's also invaluable that the agency have a toll-free number to call anytime for problems. This number can be helpful for the traveler on the road who might have lost a ticket, missed a connection, or changed his or her schedule.

> **TIP:** Although travel agencies often provide basic information about foreign countries, it's helpful for the visitor who is new to a particular place to have a guidebook, which the office assistant can pick up at most bookstores. A good guidebook can brief travelers on the country's customs and local sites and provide information on hotels and restaurants as well.

Travel is sometimes a bit different in foreign countries. In Europe, for example, it's common (and not that expensive) to hire a car and driver for the few days an executive might be in town. It's also more common to take the bus. Taxis are ubiquitous, but as in the United States, check first to make sure that they'll be available on both ends before committing your traveler to taxis between meetings. Train travel is much more common; between London and Paris it now replaces a short shuttle flight or a bumpy channel ferry. See what works best for your travelers and their schedules. In some foreign countries, guides are required (or at least recommended). Often, foreign business contacts can help arrange local transportation, a translator, or a guide, if necessary.

TIP: When scheduling a trip, bear in mind that many countries celebrate holidays and holy days that differ from those in the United States. Make sure that you check a calendar for the country of travel. This will prevent the executive from scheduling a business lunch in Saudi Arabia during Ramadan, when business clients are likely to be fasting till sundown; or from counting on bank services in Sri Lanka on May 22, National Heroes Day, which is also a bank holiday.

Make sure that you keep track of time differences as well. Make a note on the itinerary so that travelers know when they can call the office—and so the office knows when to call them. Nothing is as annoying for travelers as spending a late night out at a long business dinner, only to be rung up by the office shortly after going to bed.

INTERNATIONAL AIRLINE TRAVEL

For domestic flights, travelers have the option of first-class, business class, or economy (coach). The main differences arise in the size and comfort of the seats, the types of meals, and the amount of leg space. First-class travelers enjoy wider seats and more leg room. They are served restaurant-like meals and complimentary alcoholic beverages. Business-class passengers sit in slightly smaller seats, have no middle seats in the rows, and eat meals similar to those in first-class. The coach section of the plane accommodates many more passengers; thus, there's decreased leg room and the seats are set much more closely together. Meals are less elaborate, and alcoholic beverages are purchased separately.

On international flights, travel classes offer a much larger range of service. First-class often offers seats that recline for sleeping, elaborate multicourse meals, and fine wines and liquors. International business class is similar to domestic first class and is quite comfortable for business travelers. International coach or economy service is similar to coach service in the United States. Keep in mind that services will also vary depending on the airline, the region, and the length of the flight. Short flights won't provide the services that long flights do.

If you are booking travelers on international first- or business class, make sure you clarify with the ticket agent the services actually being offered, and weigh these against the traveler's needs. For example, in most cases the executive can fly business class (instead of first-class) and arrive just as comfortably for considerably less cost. On the other hand, if no business class is provided and the executive is expected to arrive in Europe rested for a morning meeting, it may be worth the additional cost to fly first-class. Always confirm your company's travel policy before upgrading.

Business- and first-class passengers are usually granted use of special terminal lounges. In larger international airports such as Tokyo, London, or Paris, these lounges include such services as meals, showers, and valet service.

PASSPORT, VISA, IMMUNIZATIONS, AND CUSTOMS

Every country has some requirements for visitors, although these vary widely from place to place. For a country-by-country listing, visit the State Department's Web site at http://travel.state.gov. Although the list is updated once a year, political events can rapidly change both the climate of a country and its travel status. For up-to-date changes, check the same Web site for the State Department's list of travel warnings and consular information sheets. The consular information sheets list the location of the U.S. embassy or consulate, health conditions, minor political disturbances, facts about currency, and entry penalties for each country.

Passport

All U.S. citizens traveling abroad should carry a passport at all times. This is strongly recommended, even in countries such as Mexico and Canada, where one is not required. These countries require proof of U.S. citizenship anyway, which the passport proves. In all cases, emergency itinerary changes, accidents, and sudden medical or legal problems may be handled more smoothly if a passport can be shown.

Before departure, two photocopies of the passport's identification page should be made to help facilitate replacement if the passport is lost or stolen. One copy should be kept with the traveler, and one should be kept at the office.

Anyone requiring a passport can apply for one at a passport agent's office; through a clerk of a Federal court, state court, or court of record; through a judge or clerk of a probate court; or through a designated postal clerk. Passport agencies are located in Boston, Chicago, Honolulu, Houston, Los Angeles, Miami, New Orleans, New York, Philadelphia, Portsmouth (New Hampshire), San Francisco, Seattle, Stanford (Connecticut), and Washington, DC. For passport information, contact Passport Services, Bureau of Consular Affairs,

1425 K Street NW, Washington, DC 20524; or call 202-647-0518. Forms are available from your local post office. Downloadable, printable passport applications are also available from the following Web site: www.travel.state.gov/passport_services.html.

The traveler should allow several weeks for a passport because processing normally takes 25 days. An expedited passport can be arranged in about three working days, but this requires an additional fee, as well as proof (such as plane tickets) that the applicant is leaving the country in less than two weeks (or in less than three weeks if a visa is also required). Expedited passports can be applied for in person at one of the passport agencies, but note that lines tend to be longest during the first half of the year, from January to July. These passports also may be applied for by mail, but payment for overnight return delivery must be included.

For all passports, the applicant is required to show proof of citizenship (birth certificate with embossed seal, certificate of naturalization, baptismal certificate, or voter registration certificate). Two full-face, front-view passport photos also must be presented. Many photo shops offer this service and develop the picture while the traveler waits. After a passport is issued, it is valid for 10 years.

A passport may be renewed by mail by submitting the previous passport if it has been less than 12 years since originally issued. In addition, the traveler's name on the original passport must be the same. If the name has been changed by marriage or a court order, the passport still can be renewed by mail if proper documentation of the name change is provided.

Visas

In addition to a passport, some countries require visitors to obtain permission to enter that country through a document called an entry permit or a visa. Call the consulates or embassies of the countries to be visited for their current requirements. (A travel agent or library should be able to provide the address and telephone number.) Also check the visa requirements posted on the State Department's Web site (http://travel.state.gov). If a visa or entry permit is necessary, the traveler must present a passport at the consulate and fill out a form. Some countries do not charge for their visas; others base the fee on the length of the visit. Be sure that you know the dates involved when applying. Because the length of time necessary to process a visa varies by country, this must be done well in advance of the set departure date.

Immunizations

The country's consulate determines which immunizations are needed, if any. A Certificate of Vaccination, as well as the shots themselves, can be obtained at a local board of health. The traveler also should be sure that personal immunizations are up-to-date, including those for measles, mumps, rubella, polio, diphtheria, tetanus, and pertussis. An increasing number of countries now require foreigners to be tested for Human Immunodeficiency Virus (HIV) prior to entry, especially for long-term visits.

Customs

To help the traveler avoid difficulties when entering the country of destination and returning to this country, the office professional should obtain information about customs regulations. The details can be found in pamphlets issued by the U.S. Treasury Department, located at the Bureau of Commerce in Washington, D.C. Further information can be obtained from the travel agent arranging the trip, from the individual consulates, and from the Department of Customs Web site at www.customs.ustreas.gov/.

Customs requirements vary depending on the individual country. Mexico, for example, limits the value of goods brought into the country to $300; Israel requires that all equipment (including laptops, cameras, and video cameras) be registered.

GETTING EXTRA BUSINESS HELP WHILE AWAY

Often travelers will find that they need office or secretarial services to help them conduct their business while away. It's very common, especially in Europe, for the hotel itself to have an extensive business center. This will accommodate business people in the hotel for just a day or two, as well as business people there for longer stays. Services can include faxing to and from the travelers' office at odd times; printing, copying or typing files; and arranging for private conference rooms or for a temporary assistant or secretary. If the company has several people in the hotel at once who need space for meetings or formal entertaining, it might be worthwhile to book a suite. Private rooms that accommodate several people often can be added on to the suite. Dining rooms or common rooms can be used for small meetings, lunches, dinners, or receptions.

If the hotel does not offer these services, or if the executive expects frequent or long-term office requirements, it is possible to rent furnished offices and office services in almost any country on a daily, weekly, monthly, or annual basis. The hotel concierge can be a great help in referring foreign business travelers to the appropriate place. The in-house hotel business center also can make recommendations if their own facilities do not suffice.

Services to expect from such companies include the following:

- Private office space/conference rooms/showrooms
- Business mailing address
- Mail-collecting and forwarding service
- 24-hour telephone answering service

- Multilingual office-assistant services

- Communication services, including photocopying, dictation, fax, telex, modem

- Internet, teleconferencing, videoconferencing

- Document safekeeping

In addition, these companies might provide assistance in making business contacts in the country in which the executive rents space or services, or in obtaining legal and financial advice. Costs, of course, vary depending on the space or services required.

MONEY: YOURS AND THEIRS

Don't wait too long before purchasing funds for the traveler's trip. Between the time a trip is first booked and the actual departure, the exchange rate can vary widely. Follow the rate in the financial pages of the newspaper, and buy when the dollar is strong. Because the rate changes daily, do not buy funds with a check or a credit card. By the time the check is actually cashed or the credit-card order actually processed, the rate can be much lower. Electronic transfer is best.

Traveler's checks are probably the safest and most convenient form in which to carry money while traveling abroad. They can be cashed easily in most cities, and in case of loss or theft, they can be replaced when a report is filed with the bank or agency from which they were purchased. For this purpose, the traveler should keep a copy of the checks' serial numbers in a place other than a wallet; a copy of the serial numbers also should be kept at the home office. Travelers' checks are usually available in the currency of the country to be visited and can be bought in the United States when the exchange rate is optimal. Also keep in mind that the exchange rate, as well as the service charge, can vary from bank to bank.

The office professional should obtain for the traveler a small amount of cash in the local currency to pay for taxis and porters on arrival. Banks may be closed at the destination, or the tired traveler simply might wish to leave the airport quickly without battling the crowds to cash a check. U.S. banks with an international department or currency exchange branches usually can provide a limited amount of funds in the desired currencies. Currency dealers, hotels, and most international airports are other sources, but a bank offers the best rate of exchange. Although the exchange rate on the "black market" may be tempting, it's inadvisable, foolish, and possibly even dangerous to use it.

When large amounts of cash will be needed in a foreign country, it is best to arrange for a line of credit with a U.S. bank before leaving. This line of credit then can be used to obtain funds from associated banks en route.

Some countries have currency restrictions that limit the amount of local currency that may be brought into or taken out of its borders. Check with the appropriate consulate or embassy for the latest information.

LEGAL HELP ABROAD

Legal difficulties abroad can be as complicated as legal difficulties at home, particularly in suits involving drug trafficking, personal injury, divorce, child custody, nationality, paternity, wills and estates, immigration violations, customs violations, drunk driving, and so on. Because of the complicated and varied legal systems in many other parts of the world, it is advisable to consult a law firm with experience in these matters. One such firm is the International Legal Defense Counsel, which is staffed by experienced American attorneys and has been providing this type of assistance for many years. The address is 111 South 15th Street, 24th Floor, Philadelphia, PA 19102; 215-977-9982.

The U.S. citizen must remember that he or she is subject to the laws and regulations of the country being visited. These laws sometimes differ significantly from those in the United States and might not provide the civil liberties taken for granted in this country. Laws also differ significantly from country to country and sometimes involve unexpected criminal penalties. For example, a traffic accident in Japan automatically becomes a criminal offense if an injury is involved. In case of arrest, the traveler should immediately contact the U.S. consul, whose range of services includes providing a list of local attorneys, providing information about the country's legal procedures, relaying information and requests to family and friends, and more. However, the services themselves are limited to the country's laws: A consul cannot get the traveler released on the simple basis of being an American citizen.

MEDICAL HELP ABROAD

A few simple first-aid items carried in a personal emergency kit can help cure uncomplicated illnesses and make life much more comfortable. Such items include aspirin (or an aspirin substitute), bandages, an antiseptic cream, a thermometer, sunscreen, antihistamines, nasal decongestants, antidiarrheal medication, and sunglasses. An extra pair of prescription glasses—or at least a written copy of the prescription (available from the traveler's optometrist)—should be included in case glasses are broken or contact lenses are lost.

If the traveler takes medication, it should be carried in its original container with the prescription attached; this will lessen problems with customs or during security checks in the foreign country. The name of the medication, along with the doctor's name and telephone number, should be carried separately in case the medication is lost. A letter from the doctor is also useful. Even with the written prescription and letter, however, certain medications that are legal in the United States might be considered illegal narcotics in the country to be visited. For example, Japan prohibits inhalers and allergy and sinus medication. Check the particular country's consul beforehand. If the medication is necessary, it may be possible for the consul to recommend a native doctor who can prescribe a similar (though not illegal) drug as a replacement for the duration of the trip.

Before traveling overseas, it is advisable to contact a travelers' clinic in the major city nearest the company. These clinics offer counseling on travel health, especially in countries in which water or disease problems exist. The clinics receive continual updates from the Centers for Disease Control in Atlanta and the World Health Organization to provide this information to their clients. One such clinic is the International Travel Clinic, 601 North Caroline Street, Baltimore, MD 21287; (410) 955-8931. As an alternative, the traveler can consult his or her private physician.

Another suggestion is to join the International Association for Medical Assistance to Travelers (IAMAT), a nonprofit, donation-supported foundation. Its home page is www.sentex.net/~iamat/; the address is 417 Center Street, Lewiston, NY 14092; 716-754-4883. No membership fee is required, although donations are accepted. Upon joining, the member will be sent a directory of doctors serving in 125 countries and territories worldwide. The physicians have been educated in international medical practices, with skills meeting Western standards. All speak English and are available to members 24 hours a day. A fixed fee is charged for office visits and house or hotel calls, as well as for holiday and Sunday visits. The traveler also will receive a Travelers Clinical Record (to be completed by a family doctor and carried with the traveler) in addition to world immunization and malaria risk charts.

Another organization that provides personal and medical service for international travelers is International SOS Assistance, Inc., 8 Neshaminy Interplex, Suite 207, Trevose, PA 19053; 215-244-1500. If the local medical center is inadequate, International SOS Assistance arranges for the patient to be evacuated to the nearest medical facility for treatment of the illness or injury. After stabilization, the patient is returned to facilities near home. More details are available by contacting the organization directly.

Most major hotels around the world also have a doctor on call and can make arrangements with the nearest clinic or hospital to treat guests who become ill.

In case of serious illness, the U.S. consul can help in finding appropriate medical services and medical evacuation.

Medical Insurance

Before departure, the traveler should determine what, if anything, his or her existing health insurance covers. Some policies provide coverage outside the United States, while others do not. Very few pay for medical evacuation back to this country, which may cost as much as $10,000. Check with either the

COMPILING A TRAVEL FILE

Each copy of the complete file (the traveler's and the office professional's) should contain the following, whether as documents or spreadsheets, copies of e-mail, or scanned-in forms:

- An appointment calendar listing the days, dates, and times of each meeting
- The name and address of each company to be visited
- A list of the individuals to see and their positions in the company
- A list of the officers and executives of the organization
- A list of the individuals with whom the executive has had contact in the past (other than those with whom appointments are scheduled), and the circumstances of these contacts
- Telephone numbers of the company and individuals to be seen
- Past correspondence with the firm or individual
- Letters or memos concerning the problem to be discussed
- All confirmations for hotel accommodations
- All confirmations for transportation, airline tickets, and other relevant materials
- Directions from hotels to meetings
- Miscellaneous items, such as notes for speeches and descriptions of customs for foreign countries

Except for necessary hard-copy documents (such as hotel confirmations, contracts, and so on), much of the previous information might be stored on disk for the traveler's laptop. Be sure that the battery is fully charged before the executive leaves—security checkpoints will ask that the laptop be taken out of its case and turned on. Also check to see what electrical adapters, if any, are needed for power sources in the places to be visited.

An excellent way to arrange all this travel material is with an accordion folder with section dividers. Mark the tabs with headings such as "Flights," "Hotel," "Car rental," "Jackson meeting," "Lundquist contract," and so on. In each section, put all the information pertinent to that subject; for example, a Meeting section would contain copies of correspondence about the meeting's subject, relevant files and documents, directions to the meeting location, method of transportation, names and phone numbers of people to be seen, and so on. Keeping all the information at an executive's fingertips simplifies the many problems of traveling. Then when the executive first arrives and the hotel says, "We have no record of your reservation," he or she can immediately turn to the Hotel section and pull out a copy of the confirmation letter without having to rummage.

employer or the insurance agent to get all the details of coverage, including exceptions, deductibles, maximum limits, and procedures to follow in case of need.

If the traveler is not covered by an existing policy, contact International Health Service, Georgetown University Medical Center, 3800 Reservoir Road, NW, Washington, DC 20007; 202-687-1872 for information.

RENTING AND DRIVING CARS IN OTHER COUNTRIES

If a traveler intends to drive overseas, the office professional should check with the embassy or consulate of each country for its requirements for a driver's license, road permits, and automobile insurance. If possible, also obtain road maps of the countries.

Although many countries do not recognize a U.S. driver's license, most will accept an international driving permit, which the traveler should obtain before departure. The State Department has authorized only two organizations to issue international driver permits: the American Automobile Association (AAA) and the American Automobile Touring Alliance. To obtain an international driving permit, the traveler must be at least 18 years of age and must present two passport-size photos and a valid U.S. driver's license.

Even with the international permit, however, it is wise to check with the consulate for requirements for drivers. Each country has its own age requirement for licenses, which may supersede the requirements for the international permit. In addition, many countries require a road permit, which is used in place of tolls on highways. The traveler could be fined if found driving without one. The consulate also can advise the traveler on road and parking signs, speed limits, insurance requirements, and other key information. Great Britain, for example, is not the only country whose drivers drive on the left side of the road.

Much of the procedure of renting a car overseas is similar to renting one at home. The traveler should read the rental agreement carefully to note significant differences, as well as to check for such details as late charges, city and state sales taxes, fuel charges, drop-off charges, back-up cars in case of breakdown, emergency service, and so on. Car-rental agencies usually provide automobile insurance, but it is often minimal. The traveler should purchase the equivalent of what he or she uses at home.

The traveler should be especially aware of the country's borders when driving a rental car. Cars rented in certain countries are not allowed in others. For example, a rental car from Austria is not allowed into Greece, luxury rentals are not allowed into Italy, and rental cars in Morocco must stay completely within its borders. Again, the office professional should check with the individual embassy beforehand.

BUSINESS ETIQUETTE ABROAD

Although people are more alike than different, they can easily take offense when their differences are ignored or unintentionally insulted. To be effective, the international business executive must make an effort to have a passing knowledge of the cultures and customs of the countries to be visited— especially their etiquette rules.

The following practices may vary greatly from culture to culture: religious customs, dietary laws, table manners, humor, style of dress, gift-giving practices, privacy issues, degrees of formality in person and in writing, tipping, local superstitions, and more. International etiquette involves many elements, each of which differ among countries. The next sections describe just a few that affect business travelers.

Timeliness

Although punctuality is a valued courtesy for Americans, it is a critical element of etiquette for the Germans, Romanians, and Japanese. On the other hand, clients in the Middle East, the Caribbean, and many Latin countries have a much more relaxed notion of time. Because being a half-hour late for an appointment is not necessarily an offense, the traveler should not necessarily read a hidden meaning into it if he or she is made to wait in these countries.

Gifts

At some point during the trip, the traveler is likely to be a dinner guest either at a restaurant or in the home of a business client. Although it is almost universally accepted for a guest to bring a gift (except in China, where gift-giving is discouraged), what makes it suitable varies from place to place. For example, the common gift of wine in the United States would offend a client in an Islamic country. Candy, pastries, or fruit make a safe choice for most countries, and small age-appropriate gifts for the host's children are encouraged. Souvenirs from the United States, such as landmark-site gift-shop items or foods such as maple syrup or macadamia nuts, are both intriguing and inoffensive.

Flowers are usually welcome, but be careful not to offend within that broad category. In some countries (Belgium, Italy, Luxembourg, and Spain), chrysanthemums suggest funerals; in Japan, chrysanthemums are acceptable as long as they are not the ones reserved for the imperial family. Roses suggest a lover's intimacy in Germany, Switzerland, and Poland and therefore are unsuitable for a business contact. The number and color of flowers in the arrangement is also important and varies from country to country.

Imprinted Items

No matter how expensive the gift and how subtle the imprint, items with the traveler's company logo should not be considered when the traveler is a guest. Some countries such as Japan consider imprinted items to be in poor taste in all situations.

Gift-wrapping

In Germany and Japan, the wrapping is as important as the gift inside. In Japan, several hundred ways to wrap gifts exist, each one having a different meaning. No matter which country, what looks like bright paper and festive ribbons may seem gauche to the recipient. Consult a local gift shop for help.

Body Language

A quick and firm handshake appropriate in the United States becomes much softer in France, is repeatedly frequently throughout a conversation in Latin and Middle-Eastern countries, and is seldom used at all in the East. Eye contact in France is maintained much longer than is the custom in the United States. Hispanic, southern European, and Middle-Eastern people also maintain a long and steady eye contact, while people in Asian countries are more likely to avoid direct eye contact altogether.

Common gestures in the United States may have unsuspected meanings in other countries, so the traveler should be conscious of hand and foot movements. Pointing with one's finger is rude in Asian countries, for example, as is crossing the legs. Middle-Eastern countries also dislike crossing the legs. Shorthand expressions also carry a risk of offending one's contacts: In many areas of the world, the "V-for-Victory" sign of two extended fingers is a vulgarity.

Formality

The American business traveler who is accustomed to using first names and knowing a great deal of personal information about clients should be prepared for a higher degree of formality in other countries. The safest course is to address all people by their surnames (Mr. Dudley, Señora Ramirez, Monsieur Guignard), unless specifically invited to do otherwise. Information about the other person's family could be sparse, and relationships may take longer to develop.

HANDLING BUSINESS WHILE THE BOSS IS AWAY

One of the ways the office professional is most useful to the traveling executive is by handling matters smoothly and capably while he or she is away. Following are a few basic steps:

- *Set a chain of authority.* Prior to departure, the office professional should work out with the executive which matters should be forwarded at once to his or her attention, which should be forwarded to other executives, and which should be handled personally. If some of these matters fall beyond the office professional's usual area of responsibilities, the executive should send a memo to everyone involved, granting the assistant authority to act in his or her absence.

- *Adjust the calendar.* While the executive is still in the office, cancel or reschedule appointments that fall during the business trip. Also make sure that the executive signs any documents or forms that will be needed in the office during this period.

- *Know how to make contact.* Even if the executive does not wish material to be forwarded, the office professional might need to contact the traveler about an urgent item. The executive's itinerary should be handy and up-to-date with any changes, and the assistant should know at all times how and when (depending on the time change) to make contact—whether through e-mail, fax, phone, telegram, or cablegram. If the traveler is calling in on a regular basis, keep a list of issues that need to be resolved, and address them all at once.

- *Know what to tell callers.* The executive may not wish people outside the company to know that he or she is away from the office, where he or she is, or for how long the trip will last. Before departure, establish what should be said and if there are any exceptions.

- *Keep a record.* The office professional should keep a log of each day's events, which can be used to provide a brief recap when the executive returns. Some travelers might even want the log forwarded to them regularly through fax or e-mail, especially if the trip is lengthy.

- *Divide incoming work.* Though the traveler is away, his or her work continues to pile up. So that the executive is not overwhelmed upon return, it is helpful for the office professional to prioritize the material. This can be done simply though the use of separate manila folders. Urgent items that must be handled at once by the executive can be placed in one folder, copies of work forwarded to other executives can go into another folder, and copies of what the assistant handled personally can go into still another folder. Additional folders can be made for less-critical items such as magazines and newsletters, advertising, and so on.

■ *Provide a transition period.* When the traveler returns, he or she might need a period of adjustment to cope with jet lag, the sometimes considerable difference in climate and environment, and the piles of materials labeled Urgent. The office professional should try to keep visitors, appointments, and phone calls to a minimum for a day or two to allow for a smoother transition.

The style of correspondence used in these countries reflects this formality. The flowery introductions and closings now considered to be old-fashioned in the United States are considered a point of etiquette elsewhere. The traveler should take his or her cue from the host. The office professional also should take cues from correspondence arriving from abroad and should imitate its style when preparing responses.

In addition, formal customs might mark business occasions, such as ordering champagne in Germany to signify the closing of a deal. It would be rude to refuse, so the traveler should at all times be prepared to follow the lead of his or her host.

This brief overview indicates how varied and complicated international business etiquette can be. The office professional can be of enormous help here by compiling pertinent information for the traveler about the country to be visited. Just one of the sources that can be tapped is *Letitia Baldrige's New Complete Guide to Executive Manners,* published by Macmillan, which is available from both amazon.com and barnesandnoble.com. In addition, information is available from the Industry and Trade Division of the Department of Commerce in Washington, D.C. The State Department also publishes *Background Notes,* pamphlets on 170 countries that provide brief factual information on culture, history, geography, economy, government, and current political situation. To purchase copies, contact the Superintendent of Documents, U.S. Government Printing Office, Washington, DC 20402; 202-512-1800. Select issues are also available on the State Department's home page at www.state.gov or by fax-on-demand by calling 202-736-7720. The country's own consulate is an ideal source of information, as is the travel agency handling the executive's trip.

POST-TRAVEL TASKS

Upon the traveler's return, the office professional might have to deal with urgent items: contracts, rush orders, special requests by clients, and so on. When the immediate tasks have been handled, the assistant should sort through the materials brought back by the executive and either file them or pass them on for the appropriate action. Thank-you notes to clients for their hospitality should be written for his or her signature. These notes should always be handwritten by the executive personally, but often the assistant can provide a few helpful phrases to get the process started.

Unused currency and traveler's checks in the foreign denomination may be kept if the country is a frequent destination. They can be converted to dollars if trips are infrequent or if the exchange rate is favorable.

The travel agency should already have been notified that all bills not already charged to a credit card must be sent to the attention of either the executive or the assistant. As bills and credit-card statements come in, the office professional should check them carefully before forwarding them to the accounting department or preparing an expense report. This includes can-celed checks and credit-card statements, which should be kept for proof of expenses paid.

Expense Reports

Many of the expenses incurred by the traveler abroad are reimbursable. They also might be tax-deductible (either personally or by the company), which requires detailed and accurate recordkeeping. The office professional often coordinates and maintains these records. But can encourage the executive to keep good recordkeeping habits, which will simplify these task reporting tasks.

Some travelers compile their own expense reports. Not only do they total up how much is owed them in each category (or by day), but they also usually attach receipts for documentation of all expenses. When the traveler prepares his or her own expense report, the office professional should look it over to make sure that it conforms to protocol before passing it along for sig-nature. Other travelers—usually executives with their own assistants—will turn expense reports over to their assistants. The assistant then compiles the report, based on the form provided, and assembles the appropriate receipts. Daily records should be annotated as fully as possible: A credit-card slip for a restaurant meal should note who was present and what business was discussed.

Records and receipts should be turned over to the office professional as soon after the trip as possible so that questions can be addressed while the trip is still fresh in mind. If the executive travels frequently, a routine biweekly or monthly timetable might be more convenient for handling records.

If the executive has combined business and pleasure on a trip (for exam-ple, has brought his or her family along or extended the length of stay for sightseeing), make sure that the records clearly show which expenses are purely personal.

In case records are lost or stolen, check the company policy for how to handle reimbursements and tax deductions.

Travel-planning duties are an increasingly important part of any office assistant's job, but, fortunately, resources for travel planning are also increasing. For further information on international travel, check the library, bookstores, Web sites, travel agencies, government agencies, and foreign consulates.

FOR MORE INFORMATION

If you can't find what you need from the phone numbers and Web sites listed in this chapter, you may need to expand your search.

- For more information on locating travel agencies, try your local Yellow Pages under travel.

- For more information on travel agency associations and obtaining ratings for agencies, try a Web search for the organization you want, or call information for 800 numbers.

- For more information on e-tickets and if they are the right solution for your travel needs, call any airline directly or check on the Web site.

- For more information on State Department travel advisories, immunization advisories or other international travel requirements, check the State Department Web site (http://travel.state.gov) or call your nearest U.S. consulate.

- For more information on obtaining a passport including requirements and time limits, call the passport agency in your city or your local post office.

- For more information on business customs, holidays, and etiquette for foreign travel, check your local bookstore or library in the business section. You can also check the travel section for any guidebooks or phrase books you might need.

GRAMMAR AND PUNCTUATION GUIDE

◆

- **Introduction**
- **Grammar**
- **Punctuation**
- **Capitalization**
- **Numbers**
- **Compound Words**
- **Usage**
- **Abbreviations**
- **Forms of Address**

INTRODUCTION

This reference contains a complete and concise review of English grammar as well as the basic rules of punctuation and capitalization. It also contains guidelines for the proper treatment of compound words including many commonly used business and technical terms. The section on numbers outlines the proper way to include numbers in both formal and informal writing. The usage section clarifies the appropriate use of words and expressions that are often confused or misused. The rules and guidelines in all sections are clearly illustrated with hundreds of examples. Also included are handy alphabetical lists of standard abbreviations, abbreviations of units of measure, and Latin abbreviations with definitions for each entry. Finally, for letter writing, useful tables indicate the correct forms of address for government and religious officials. With this reference in hand, you will never again be puzzled by such questions as the following:

- Does *XYZ Corporation* need a singular or plural verb?
- Is it *differ from* or *differ with* in this sentence?
- Does this sentence need a comma or a semicolon?
- Should the word *English* in English literature be capitalized?
- Should *1984* be spelled out at the beginning of a sentence?
- Which compound words need a hyphen and which do not?
- What is the difference between *abbreviate* and *abridge*? *allege* and *claim*? *farther* and *further*?
- Are abbreviations acceptable in a letter or report?
- How do you address a letter to a member of Congress?

GRAMMAR

This section provides a brief review of English grammar, concentrating on common errors.

PARTS OF SPEECH

Noun

A noun is a word used to name a person, place, idea, thing, or quality.

Shakespeare, Paris, desk, truth

Pronoun

A pronoun is a word used in place of a noun.

I, we, who, these, each, himself

Verb

A verb is a word or group of words that denotes action, occurrence, or state of being. The verb, together with any words that complete or modify its meaning, forms the predicate of the sentence.

am, has washed, ran, will be seen

Adjective

An adjective is a word that describes or limits (modifies) the meaning of a noun or pronoun.

higher morale, *net* income, *rolling* stone

Adverb

An adverb is a word that modifies a verb, an adjective, or another adverb. It answers the questions where, how or how much, or when.

write *legibly,* long *enough,* *very* high production, do it *soon,* go *there*

Preposition

A preposition is a word used to relate a noun or pronoun to some other word in the sentence.

at, in, by, from, toward

Conjunction

A conjunction is a word used to join words, phrases, or clauses.

and, but, nor, since, although, when

Interjection

An interjection is an exclamation that expresses strong feeling.

Ah! Nonsense! Shh! Bravo!

Note that the part of speech (grammatical function) represented by a given word is determined by its use in a sentence. For instance, *but* may be an adverb, a preposition, or a conjunction, depending on how it is used.

PHRASES AND CLAUSES

Phrases and clauses are groups of grammatically related words that function as a single part of speech (*noun, adjective,* or *adverb*) or as a sentence.

Phrase

A phrase is a group of grammatically related words *without a subject, a predicate, or both.* A phrase is used as a *noun, adjective,* or *adverb.* Phrases are classified as:

Prepositional:	Put the finished letter *in the mail.* (also adverbial phrase)
	The man *in the red swimsuit* is looking for attention. (also adjective phrase)
Participial:	The woman *giving the talk* speaks with conviction. (also adjective phrase)
Gerund:	*Skiing deep powder* is both exciting and challenging. (also noun phrase)
Infinitive:	Our purpose is *to eat as inexpensively as we can.* (also noun phrase)
	The teacher assigned work *to be done quickly.* (also adjective phrase)
	She ran *to catch the horse.* (also adverbial phrase)

Clause

A clause is a group of grammatically related words containing both a subject and a predicate.

Independent (or main) clauses make a complete statement and are not introduced by any subordinating word. When it stands alone, it is a simple sentence.

We will return the favor.

Dependent (or subordinate) clauses cannot stand alone as simple sentences, usually because they are introduced by a subordinating word. Dependent clauses are classified as:

Adjective:	This is the man *who wrote to us for information.*
	I have the video *he is looking for.* ("that" understood)
Adverb:	*As soon as you have finished icing the cake,* bring it to the table.

Noun:	*Whoever conducts the meeting* will be able to answer your questions.

Can you tell me *what my charges will total?*

TYPES OF SENTENCES

Simple Sentence

A simple sentence contains only one independent clause. This does not mean, however, that it must be short. It may include many phrases, a compound subject or predicate, and/or a number of modifiers.

The prisoner escaped.

You should run to the store next door and buy as many tortillas as you can.

Compound Sentence

A compound sentence contains two or more independent clauses, each of which could be written as a simple sentence.

You may want to vacation in the Bahamas, or you may prefer Acapulco instead.

Complex Sentence

A complex sentence contains one independent clause and one or more dependent clauses.

Since the freeway was jammed, we looked for an alternate route.

Compound-Complex Sentence

A compound-complex sentence contains two or more independent clauses and one or more dependent clauses.

Since they moved to town, the river flooded three times, and the stores all shut down.

PARTS OF A SENTENCE

The basic parts of a sentence are the *subject, verb,* and *complement. Modifiers* and *connectives* support this basic sentence structure—modifiers by making the meaning more exact and connectives by showing the relationship between parts.

Subject

The subject of a sentence is the word or group of words that names the thing, person, place, or idea about which a sentence makes a statement. These words or groups of words can include *nouns; pronouns; gerunds; infinitives; demonstrative, interrogative,* and *indefinite pronouns; phrases;* and *clauses.*

Nouns and **pronouns** are the single words most often used as subjects.

> The *director* called the meeting for 3 o'clock. (noun)

> *He* wants everybody to attend. (personal pronoun)

Gerunds and, less often, **infinitives,** are two verbals that may also be the subject of a sentence.

> *Walking* is good exercise. (gerund)

> *To run* is more tiring than to walk. (infinitive)

Demonstrative, interrogative, and **indefinite pronouns** are among the other parts of speech used as subjects.

> *That* is going to be a difficult task. (demonstrative)

> *What* are your plans for doing it? (interrogative)

> *Everyone* is eager to have you succeed. (indefinite)

Phrases serving as a noun may be the subject of a sentence.

> *Adopting that kitten* was the smartest thing he did.

> *To learn as many languages as possible* is his objective.

Clauses in their entirety may be used as the subject.

> *Whoever answers the telephone* will get a chance to win the prize.

> *Whether the wild burro has been released or not* will determine our action.

Verb

The verb tells what the subject itself does, what something else does to the subject, or what the subject is. Verbals, although they come from verbs, cannot serve as verbs in the predicate of a sentence. (For more on verbs and verbals, see the comprehensive section that follows.)

There are three types of verbs: *transitive verbs; intransitive verbs;* and *copulative* or *linking verbs.*

Transitive verbs take a direct object.

He *hit* the ball.

Intransitive verbs take no direct object.

She *fell* down.

Copulative or **linking verbs** take a predicate noun or predicate adjective.

Jim *is* captain.

Jim *seems* strong.

The properties of a verb are *number, person, tense, mood,* and *voice.* To indicate these properties we either change the form of the verb itself or add other verb forms called *auxiliary verbs—be, have, can, may, might, shall, will, should, would, could, must, do.*

Number tells whether the verb is singular or plural.

Person tells whether the first person (*I*), second person (*you*), or third person (*he, it, she*) is performing the action. A verb and its subject must agree in number and person. (This problem of agreement—so essential to the writing of clear sentences—is discussed in the section on Agreement and Reference.)

Tense is the means by which we show the time of an action—whether it happened in the past, is happening in the present, or will happen in the future.

Mood (indicative, imperative, subjunctive) indicates the manner of assertion—statement, command, wish, or condition.

Voice is the property of a verb that indicates whether the subject is performing or receiving the action of the verb. A verb in the *active voice* tells what the subject is doing; a verb in the *passive voice* tells what is being done to the subject.

The *athlete completed* his training on time. (The verb *completed,* in the active voice, tells what the subject, *athlete,* did.)

The *cereal was dropped* on the floor. (The verb *was dropped,* in the passive voice, tells what was done to the subject, *cereal.*)

Complement

The complement is the word or group of words that follows the verb and completes its meaning. A complement may be a *direct object,* an *indirect object,* a *predicate nominative,* or a *predicate adjective.*

Direct objects are nouns or other parts of speech functioning as nouns that receive the action of the verb.

He gave the *map* to the tourist. (*Map* is the direct object of the verb.)

We are trying *to launch a probe to Jupiter.* (The infinitive phrase is the direct object of the verb.)

Give me *whatever information you have.* (The noun clause is the direct object of the verb.)

Indirect objects are nouns or other parts of speech functioning as nouns that indicate to whom (what) or for whom (what) the action of the verb is done.

He gave [to] *her* the tickets. (*Her* is the indirect object of the verb; *tickets* is the direct object.)

Give [to] *whoever answers the door* the bouquet of flowers. (The noun clause is the indirect object of the verb.)

David did [for] *Jerry* a big favor. (*Jerry* is the indirect object; *favor* is the direct object.)

Predicate nominatives are also called predicate nouns, predicate complements, or subjective complements. The predicate nominative follows copulative, or linking, verbs and renames the subject. It can be a noun, a pronoun, a verbal, a phrase, or a clause.

Noun:	He is *chairman* of the committee.
Pronoun:	They thought the author was *she.*
Gerund:	My favorite exercise is *swimming.*
Infinitive phrase:	The purpose of this experiment is *to test the new engine.*
Noun clause:	The next president should be *whoever is best qualified.*

Predicate adjectives are adjectives (or adjective phrases) appearing in the predicate that modify the subject. A predicate adjective occurs only after copulative, or linking, verbs.

The flower smells *sweet.*

The meeting we are planning for Tuesday will be *on that subject.*

This material is *over my head.*

He appears *enthusiastic* about learning to dance.

Modifiers

Modifiers are single words, phrases, or clauses used to limit, describe, or define some element of the sentence. These are classed as either *adjectives* or *adverbs*. A modifier is said to "dangle" when it cannot attach both logically and grammatically to a specific element in the sentence. (For more on modifiers and modification, see the comprehensive section that follows.)

Adjectives describe or limit the meaning of nouns or pronouns.

> The *wily* raccoon was caught in the *baited* trap and transported to an *animal* shelter for *medical* tests.

> The statistics *on juvenile crime* are alarming. (prepositional phrase used as an adjective)

> The report *submitted by the audit committee* is being studied. (participial phrase used as an adjective)

Adverbs modify verbs, verbals, adjectives, or other adverbs. They answer the questions where, how or how much, when, and why?

> We will hold the meeting *here.* (Where?)

> The car accelerated *rapidly.* (How?)

> Spending *excessively,* he ran out of funds. (How much?)

> Let's eat the lasagna *as soon as it is finished cooking.* (When?)

> Pete went downtown *to buy a tie.* (Why?)

Connectives

Connectives join one part of a sentence with another and show the relationship between the parts they connect. Connectives joining elements of equal rank include: *coordinate conjunctions, correlative conjunctions,* and *conjunctive adverbs.* Connectives joining elements of unequal rank include: *subordinate conjunctions, relative pronouns,* and *relative adverbs. Prepositions* are also some of the most important connectives. (For more on the usage of these and other connectives, see the Connectives section.)

Coordinate conjunctions are perhaps the most frequently used connectives. They join sentence elements of equal grammatical importance—words with words, phrases with phrases, independent clauses with independent clauses. The commonly used coordinate conjunctions are:

> *and, but, or, nor, for, yet*

Correlative conjunctions work in pairs to connect sentence elements of equal rank. Each member of a pair of correlative conjunctions must be followed by the same part of speech. Examples of these conjunctions are:

> *either . . . or, neither . . . nor, not only . . . but also, both . . . and*

Conjunctive adverbs connect independent clauses and show a relation of equal rank between them. Although the clause introduced by the conjunctive adverb is *grammatically* independent, it is *logically* dependent upon the preceding clause for its complete meaning. These are some conjunctive adverbs:

> *therefore, however, consequently, accordingly, furthermore, moreover, nevertheless*

Subordinate conjunctions introduce dependent adverb clauses and join them to independent clauses. Some of these conjunctions are:

> *before, since, after, as, because, if, unless, until, although*

> **NOTE:** The subordinate conjunction *that* introduces a noun clause:
>
> When he calls, tell him that *I had to leave for a meeting.*

Relative pronouns not only introduce noun and adjective clauses but also act as pronouns within their own clauses. These pronouns include:

> *that, which, who, whom, whatever, whichever, whoever*

> The salesperson *who called for an appointment* has just arrived. (adjective clause)

> Tell me the news *that you just heard.* (noun clause)

Relative adverbs introduce subordinate clauses. The most common of these connectives are:

> *how, where, when, while*

Prepositions show the relationship between a word that follows them, called the object, and a word before them to which they relate. Some prepositions are:

> *to, of, by, from, between, in, over, under, for*

Verbals

Verbals are nonfinite verbs used as a noun, an adjective, or an adverb. A nonfinite verb can never stand as the only verb in a sentence. There are three verbal forms: *infinitives, participles, gerunds.* (For more on verbs and verbals, see the Verbs and Verbals section that follows.)

Infinitives (to go, to run, to see, etc.) may act as a noun *or* an adjective *or* an adverb.

>I like *to swim.* (noun)

>A book *to read* is what she wants. (adjective)

>He went *to play* golf. (adverb)

Participles may be either a present participle (going, seeing, feeling, etc.) or a past participle (having gone, having seen, having felt, etc.). A participle acts *only* as an adjective.

>*Going* to the store, Jamal slipped. (adjective)

>*Having seen* the entire movie, Judy left the theater. (adjective)

Gerunds (knowing, running, hearing, etc.) act *only* as nouns.

>Charlie enjoys *running.* (noun)

>*Dancing* is a good way to enjoy music. (noun)

NOUNS AND PRONOUNS

A noun names a person, thing, idea, place, or quality. There are five classes of nouns: *proper, common, collective, concrete,* and *abstract.*

Pronouns stand in place of nouns. The six classes of pronouns are: *personal, relative, interrogative, indefinite, demonstrative,* and *reflexive.*

Proper Nouns

A proper noun names a particular place, person, or thing. The writer's chief problem with proper nouns is recognizing them in order to capitalize them.

>Atlanta, Mr. Jones, the Commissioner of Education, Form 1040

Common Nouns

A common noun names a member of a class or group of persons, places, or things.

>hope, banana, education, form

Collective Nouns

A collective noun, singular in form, names a group or collection of individuals. The chief problem with collective nouns is determining the form of the verb to use with the collective noun. For this reason, it is discussed at length in the section on agreement and reference.

> committee, jury, council, task force

Concrete Nouns

A concrete noun names a particular or specific member of a class or group.

> apple, *not* fruit; chair, *not* furniture

Abstract Nouns

An abstract noun names a quality, state, or idea.

> beauty, truth, objectivity

> Notice that common nouns can be concrete or abstract.

Personal Pronouns

The personal pronoun shows which person (first, second, or third) is the subject. Personal pronouns are troublesome because of their many forms; they change form to indicate number, person, and case.

The personal pronouns are:

> I, my, mine, me, you, your, yours, he, his, him, she, her, hers, it, and its, *and their plurals*—we, you, they, it, our, ours, your, yours, their, theirs, us, and them

Relative Pronouns

The relative pronoun serves two purposes: (1) it takes the place of a noun in the clause it introduces, and (2) like a conjunction, it connects its clause with the rest of the sentence.

The relative pronouns are:

> who, whom, which, that, what, whoever, whomever, whichever, whatever

> The relative pronoun has the same number, person, and case as its antecedent.

Interrogative Pronouns

The interrogative pronoun is the same in form as the relative pronoun, but different in function. The interrogative pronoun asks a question.

who ⟶ refer to persons
whom

what   refers to things

which   refers to person or things

As an adjective, *which* and *what* may be used.

. . . which book? . . . what time?

Indefinite Pronouns

The indefinite pronouns listed here are singular, as are most indefinites:

another, anyone, each, either, everyone, no one, nothing . . .

Demonstrative Pronouns

The demonstrative pronouns (*this, that, these, those*) point out or refer to a substantive (usually a noun) which has been clearly expressed or just as clearly implied. They may be used as pronouns

These are the letters he wants.

or as adjectives

Bring me *those* letters.

Reflexive Pronouns

The reflexive pronouns are compound personal pronouns:

myself, yourself, yourselves, himself, themselves, ourselves, herself, itself

A reflexive pronoun emphasizes or intensifies a meaning. It is not set off by commas.

I *myself* will see that it is done.

The director *himself* gave the order.

You will take it to her *yourself.*

A reflexive pronoun often appears as the direct object of a verb; its antecedent, as the subject of the verb.

I taught *myself* how to type.

He hurt *himself* when he fell.

It can, however, be the object of a preposition,

He finished the job by *himself.*

He was beside *himself* with joy.

the indirect object of a verb,

I bought *myself* a new suit yesterday.

They gave *themselves* a pat on the back.

or a predicate nominative.

I am just not *myself* today.

They just were not *themselves* at the party.

In formal usage, the reflexive pronoun is not used where the shorter personal pronoun can be substituted for it with no change in meaning.

Not: Both the director and *myself* endorse the policy.

But: Both the director and *I* endorse the policy.

Avoid the following pronoun errors:

The use of *hisself* for *himself.*

The use of *theirselves* for *themselves.*

The use of *myself* or *yourself* instead of the personal pronoun *me, I,* or *you* in such constructions as "The secretary and *myself* opened the mail. It's ideal for a professional person such as *yourself.*"

CASE

Case is the property of a noun or pronoun which shows, either by inflection (change in form) or by position, the relation of the word to other parts of the sentence.

English has three cases: *nominative, objective,* and *possessive.*

All nouns and a few pronouns keep the same form in the nominative and in the objective cases. Consequently, we must depend on the position of these words in the sentence to indicate their function. Since nouns don't change form to indicate nominative and objective case, our only real difficulty with them comes in the formation and use of the possessive case.

On the other hand, some pronouns are inflected (change form) in the nominative and objective cases, as well as in the possessive. Because of this, the case of pronouns causes us more trouble than does the case of nouns.

Nominative Case

The nominative (or subjective) case is used primarily to name the subject of a verb or the predicate complement after a copulative, or linking, verb (such as *seem, appear,* or any form of *be*).

Not: Either *she* or *me* will be responsible.

But: Either *she* or *I* will be responsible. (Either *she* will be . . . or *I* will be . . .)

NOTE: An appositive, which is a word or group of words standing next to another word and denoting the same person or thing, is always in the same case as its antecedent (the word to which it stands in apposition). Therefore, if the antecedent is in the nominative case, the appositive must also be in the nominative case. If the antecedent is in the objective case, the appositive is also in the objective case.

Not: The representatives, *John and me,* are to meet on Friday.

But: The representatives, *John and I,* are to meet on Friday. (*John and I* are to meet. . . .)

Subject of a Verb in a Main Clause

A noun or pronoun serving as the subject of a verb (except the subject of an infinitive) is in the nominative case.

I was late for work this morning.

He is planning to finish his pancakes this morning.

Neither *she* nor *I* had heard of this before.

The culprits, *she and I,* were reprimanded.

Subject of a Relative Clause

A relative pronoun (*who, whoever, which, whichever*) used as the subject of a clause is in the nominative case.

Give the letter to *whoever* answers the door.

You'll want to decide *whichever* is best.

The clause itself may be a subject or an object; however, the case of the relative pronoun depends upon its use *within the clause.*

Whoever is selected must board the plane immediately.

The pronoun *who* used as the subject of a verb is not affected by a parenthetical expression such as *I think, he believes, they say* intervening between the subject and the verb.

She is the person *who* I think is best qualified. (*Who* is the subject of the clause.)

We asked Susan, *who* we knew *had always been* a climber of mountains. (*Who* is the subject of the clause.)

Ms. Mann is the attorney *who* we suppose *will prepare* the brief. (*Who* is the subject of the clause.)

Subject of a Clause Introduced by *than* or *as*

If the word following *than* or *as* introduces a clause, even if part of the clause is understood, that word must be in the nominative case. But if the word following *than* or *as* does not introduce a clause, it must be in the objective case. To test whether the word should be in the nominative or objective case, complete the clause.

He has been here longer than *she.* (than *she has*)

Mary is a better mathematician than *I.* (than *I am*)

They were as late as *we* in filing our tax returns. (as *we were*)

We were seated as promptly as *they.* (as *they were*)

In the following examples, the word following *than* or *as* may be in either the nominative or the objective case, depending on the intended meaning. If there is any chance your meaning might be misunderstood, complete the clause.

She likes this work better than *I.* (than *I like it*)

She likes this work better than *me.* (than *she likes me*)

I have known John as long as *she.* (as *she has*)

I have known John as long as *her.* (as *I have known her*)

Words Following Forms of *be* (Predicate Nominative)

A noun or pronoun following a form of the verb *be* (except for the infinitive if it has its own subject) must be in the nominative case. (This word is called the *predicate nominative*—or, if a noun, the *predicate noun.*) The general rule applying to this construction is that the word following the verb *be* must be in the same case as the word before the verb. Imagine that the verb *be* has the same meaning as the equals sign (=) in mathematics.

> Not: They thought I was *him.*

> But: They thought I was *he.* (*I = he*)

A noun or pronoun following the infinitive *to be* is in the nominative case if the infinitive has no subject.

> He was thought to be *I.*

> My brother was taken to be *I.*

NOTE: You may have trouble when one or both of the members of the compound subject or predicate nominative are pronouns. Try this simple test: Decide which case would be appropriate if *one* pronoun were the simple subject or predicate nominative, and then use the same case for both.

> Example: The new chairmen are *he* and *I.*

> Reverse positions: *He* and *I* are the new chairmen.

> Example: If any one of the free agents is chosen, *it* should be *he.*

> Reverse positions: If any one of the free agents is chosen, *he* should be *it.*

> Example: The *author* was thought to be *I.*

> Reverse positions: *I* was thought to be the *author.*

These examples show the proper forms for formal use. In informal English, the objective case forms are often encountered.

Direct Address

Direct address is a construction used parenthetically to direct spoken language to some particular person. Nouns or pronouns in direct address are in the nominative case and are set off by commas. This construction will cause little trouble, since proper names, which are the main examples of direct address, do not change form to indicate case.

Jim, come here for a minute.

It is true, *sir,* that I made that remark.

Tell me, *doctor,* is he showing much improvement?

Objective Case

The objective (or accusative) case is used chiefly to name the receiver or object of the action of a verb, or to name the object of a preposition.

When one part of a compound expression (joined by a coordinate conjunction) is in the objective case, all other parts of the same expression must also be in the objective case.

When you reach the station call either *him* or *me.*

The work was given to *you* and *me.*

When the antecedent of an appositive is in the objective case because it is serving a function that requires that case, the appositive must also be in the objective case.

The teacher has appointed *us, you and me,* to the group.

He gave *us passengers* a copy of the schedule.

The principle is basic to *us Americans.*

Direct Object of a Verb or Verbal

A noun or pronoun serving as the direct object of a verb or verbal is in the objective case.

The driver returned *him* to his home.

My father called *him* and *me* to come back inside.

They will invite *us fans* to the football game.

Whomever you called on Monday night is certainly upset.

BUT

Call *whoever* is responsible before the alarm sounds.

I enjoyed meeting *him.*

I didn't intend to ask *them* again.

Having called *him* and told *him* of our plan, we left for the evening.

We have a letter from her cousin thanking *us* for our courtesy.

Indirect Object of a Verb or Verbal
A word used as the indirect object of a verb or verbal is in the objective case.

The ballplayer gave *me* his autograph.

The supervisor assigned *him* and *me* the task of cleaning up the boardroom.

The inspector showed *us employees* the operation of the meat grinder.

A letter giving *him* authority to represent his mother is being prepared.

Object of a Preposition
A noun or pronoun serving as the object of a preposition is in the objective case.

From *whom* did you receive the letter? (*Whom* is the object of the preposition *from*.)

> **NOTE:** *But* is a preposition when *except* may be substituted for it with no change in meaning.
>
> Everyone is going but *me*.

A special troublemaker is the compound object *you and me* after the preposition *between*. Do not say *between you and I;* say *between you and me*.

Subject of an Infinitive
A noun or pronoun used as the subject of an infinitive is in the objective case.

I want *him* to have this car.

We expect *him* to finish that job.

They invited *her and me* to attend the reception.

Whom will he cast to play the lead character?

Words Following Infinitive *to be*
The verb *to be* takes the same case after it as before it. Since the subject of an infinitive is in the objective case, a word following the infinitive is also in the objective case.

They thought him to be *me*. (Reverse, to test choice of case: They thought *me* to be *him*.)

We assumed the author of the letter to be *him.* (Reverse: We assumed *him* to be the *author . . . .*)

They did not expect the representatives to be *him and me.* (Reverse: They did not expect *him and me* to be the *representatives.*)

Subject of a Participle and of a Gerund

The subject of a participle is in the objective case. The problem comes in determining whether a verbal is a participle or a gerund. Both may have the same form (the *-ing* form of the verb), but only the subject of the *participle* is in the objective case. The subject of the *gerund* is in the possessive case.

Imagine *him flying* an airplane. (The verbal *flying* is a participle modifying *him,* and the pronoun *him* is in the objective case.)

Imagine *his flying* to Paris. (The verbal *flying* is a gerund, and the pronoun *his* is in the possessive case.)

His rushing to catch the plane was in vain. (*Rushing* is a gerund, and its subject must be in the possessive case.)

We watched *him rushing* to catch the plane. (The verbal, *rushing,* is a participle modifying *him;* therefore, the subject, *him,* is in the objective case.)

NOTE: In the gerund expression *its being,* the subject that follows must be in the objective case.

In our search for the thief, we never thought of its being *him* (not *he*).

Possessive Case (and Its Proper Punctuation)

The possessive (or genitive) case is used to indicate possession.

Possessive of Singular Words

To form the possessive of singular words not ending in *s* (including the indefinite pronouns), add the apostrophe and *s.*

the *student's* report; the *neighbor's* car; the *widow's* cat; *anyone's* guess; *somebody's* coat

NOTE: When *else* is used with an indefinite pronoun, form the possessive by adding the apostrophe and *s* to *else,* rather than to the indefinite pronoun.

somebody's coat	But: *somebody else's* coat
anyone's idea	But: *anyone else's* idea

To form the possessive of singular words ending in *s,* add the apostrophe and *s* or simply the apostrophe alone.

Singular form	Possessive form
boss	boss's or boss'
hostess	hostess's or hostess'

NOTE: The possessive of some proper names ending in *s,* however, is traditionally formed by adding only the apostrophe:

Jesus' disciples	Moses' staff

Some names of more than one syllable ending in *s,* as well as some ancient Greek names, also form the possessive in this way:

John Quincy Adams' presidency

Epimenides' paradox

The apostrophe is omitted in some organizational or geographical names that contain a possessive thought. Follow the form used by the organization itself.

Harpers Ferry	Pikes Peak
Governors Island	Citizens National Bank

Do not use the apostrophe in forming the possessive of the personal and relative pronouns. The possessive forms of these pronouns are:

Relative: whose

Personal: her, hers (*not* her's) his, their, theirs, our, ours, my, mine, your, yours, its

NOTE: *Its* is the possessive form of the personal pronoun *it*; *it's* is a contraction of *it is*. Similarly, *whose* is the possessive form of the relative pronoun *who*, and *who's* is a contraction of *who is* or *who has*. The examples below illustrate the correct use of these words.

Its operation is simple.
It's (*it is*) simple to operate.

Don't drive that car; *its* tires need changing.
Don't drive that car; *it's* in need of new tires.

Whose mailbox is that?
Who's (*who is*) going with me?

Theirs is in the closet.
There's very little time left.

Possessive of Plural Words

To form the possessive of a plural word not ending in *s*, add the apostrophe and *s*.

men's, children's, women's, people's

To form the possessive of a plural word ending in *s*, add the apostrophe only.

All of the *mechanics'* tools were lost.

NOTE: Avoid placing the apostrophe before the final *s* of a word if the *s* is actually a part of the singular or plural form. To test, first form the plural; then add the correct possessive sign.

Not: ladie's

But: ladies'

(*Ladies* is the plural form; since the word ends in *s*, add the apostrophe alone to form the possessive, *ladies'*.)

Use of the *of* Phrase to Form Possessive

Use the *of* phrase in forming the possessive to avoid the "piling up" of possessives.

Not: The *taxpayer's wife's income* must be reported.

But: The *income of the taxpayer's wife* must be reported.

Not: Her *brother's friend's bicycle* was red.

But: The *bicycle of her brother's friend* was red.

In order to avoid an awkward construction, use the *of* phrase to form the possessive of names consisting of several words.

Not: The local chapter of the National Association of Radio and Television Broadcasters' first meeting was held Thursday.

But: The first meeting of the local chapter of the National Association of Radio and Television Broadcasters was held Thursday.

Not: The Director of the Alcohol and Tobacco Tax Division's report . . .

But: The report of the Director of the Alcohol and Tobacco Tax Division . . .

Use the *of* phrase to avoid adding a possessive to a pronoun that is already possessive.

Not: We are going to a *friend of mine's* house.

But: We are going to the *house of a friend of mine.*

Possessive of Compound Words

Form the possessive on the last word of a compound word, whether or not the compound is hyphenated. A point to remember is that even though the plural of a compound word is formed by adding *s* to the principal noun in the compound, the possessive is always formed by adding the sign of the possessive to the last word in the compound.

Singular	Singular Possessive
notary public	notary public's
comptroller general	comptroller general's
supervisor in charge	supervisor in charge's

Plural	Plural Possessive
notaries public	notaries public's
comptrollers general	comptrollers general's
supervisors in charge	supervisors in charge's

If a possessive is followed by an appositive or an explanatory phrase, form the possessive on the explanatory word.

That was *Mr. Smith the auditor's* idea.

I was acting on my *friend John's* advice.

Have you read the *senator from Arizona's* speech?

If the appositive or explanatory words are set off by commas, the possessive may be found on both the main word and the explanatory word.

Either: This is *Mary, my assistant's,* day off.

Or: This is *Mary's, my assistant's,* day off.

Either: I sent it to *Mr. Smith, the collector's,* office.

Or: I sent it to *Mr. Smith's, the collector's,* office.

NOTE: The methods just illustrated are grammatically correct ways to show possession; they do, however, sound awkward. To be more effective (and just as correct), try using an *of* phrase to form the possessive of compound words.

Not: This is the supervisor in charge's office.

But: This is the office of the supervisor in charge.

Not: I was acting on my friend John's advice.

But: I was acting on the advice of my friend, John.

Not: I sent it to Mr. Smith's, the collector's, office.

But: I sent it to the office of Mr. Smith, the collector.

Joint, Separate, and Alternative Possession

When two or more people possess the same thing jointly, form the possessive on the last word only.

She is *Mr. Smith and Ms. Henry's* cousin. (She is cousin to both people.)

These pictures are from *John and Mary's* vacation trip.

I bought my coat at *Woodward and Lothrop's.* (*store* understood)

> **NOTE:** When one of the words involved in the joint possession is a pronoun, each word must be in the possessive.
>
> This is *John's, Bob's,* and *my* neighborhood.
>
> Have you seen *Mary's* and *his* new home?

When it is intended that each of the words in a series possess something individually, form the possessive on each word.

Barbara's and *Mary's* singing are certainly different.

The *drivers'* and the *owners'* associations are meeting here this week.

When alternative possession is intended, each word must be in the possessive.

I wouldn't want either *John's* or *Harry's* job.

Is that the *author's* or the *editor's* opinion?

Possessive of Abbreviations

Possessives of abbreviations are formed in the same way as are other possessives. Ordinarily the possessive sign is placed after the final period of the abbreviation where one is present.

Singular Possessive	Plural	Plural Possessive
MD's	MDs	MDs'
Dr.'s	Drs.	Drs.'

John Blank, *Jr.'s* account has been closed. (Note that there is no comma after *Jr.* when the possessive is used.)

Parallel Possessives

Be sure that a word standing parallel with a possessive is itself possessive in form.

Not: *His* work, like an *accountant,* is exacting.

But: *His* work, like an *accountant's,* is exacting.

Not: The *agent's* job differs from the *auditor.*

But: The *agent's* job differs from the *auditor's.*

Not: *His* task is no more difficult than his *neighbor.*

But: *His* task is no more difficult than his *neighbor's.*

Possessive with a Gerund

A noun or pronoun immediately preceding a gerund is in the possessive case. A gerund is a verbal noun naming an action. A participle, which may have the same form as a gerund, functions as an adjective; its subject is in the objective case.

Our being late delayed the meeting.

Mr. Jones's being late delayed the meeting.

You can always depend on *his* being a good friend.

Jim's singing the anthem made all the difference.

Washington's being the capital makes it different from other cities.

NOTE: There are two exceptions to this general rule:

Do not use the possessive case for the subject of a gerund unless the subject immediately precedes the gerund. If the subject and gerund are separated by other words, the subject must be in the objective case.

Not: I can see no reason for a *man's* with his background *failing* to pass the test.

But: I can see no reason for a *man* with his background *failing* to pass the test. (Without intervening words: I can see no reason for a *man failing* to pass the test.)

There are no possessive forms for the demonstrative pronouns *that, this, these,* and *those.* Therefore, when these words are used as subjects of a gerund they do not change form.

Not: We cannot be sure of *that's* being true.

But: We cannot be sure of *that* being true.

Not: What are the chances of *this'* being sold?

But: What are the chances of *this* being sold?

He/She

Traditionally, the personal pronoun *he* has been used in English when the gender of its antecedent is unknown.

Each child (boy or girl) develops at *his* own pace.

This usage is still widely accepted, but it is changing. If you prefer a more neutral form (he/she, for example), or if you think your reader may be offended, use instead a form of *he or she.*

Each child develops at *his or her* own pace.

Since the *he or she* form is somewhat clumsy, a frequent repetition of it may make your writing awkward. Avoid the problem by rewording.

All children develop at *their* own pace.

Take care to make pronouns and antecedents consistent within a passage.

AGREEMENT AND REFERENCE

Many grammatical errors result from failing to make different parts of a sentence agree in number, person, or gender.

The verb must agree with the subject in number and in person. If the subject is singular, the verb form must also be singular; if the subject is in the third person—*she, it, he*—the verb must be in the third person. The chief problem is identifying the true subject of the sentence and determining whether it is singular or plural.

The pronoun must agree with its antecedent (the word to which it refers—sometimes called its *referent*) in number, in person, and in gender. Of the three, gender causes the writer the least difficulty. The chief problem is identifying the antecedent and determining its number, person, and gender.

Often the subject of the verb is also the antecedent of the pronoun. You might think that this would greatly simplify things, and to some extent it does, for once you have determined that the subject-antecedent is singular, you know where you stand—both verb and pronoun must likewise be singular. A word of caution: be consistent. Don't shift from a singular verb (which properly agrees with its singular subject) to a plural pronoun later in the sentence.

Subject Problems

The first step in making the parts of a sentence agree is to identify the subject. In this section, therefore, we will discuss only those subjects that may present special problems.

Collective Words

A collective is a single word that names a group of people or things. Although usually singular in form, a collective is treated as either singular or plural according to the sense of the sentence.

A collective is treated as singular when members of the group act, or are considered, as a *unit*.

The survey committee *is visiting* the district this week.

The national office evaluation team *has* five trips scheduled for this quarter.

A collective is treated as plural when the members act, or are considered, *individually*.

The jury *are* unable to agree on a verdict.

The national office evaluation team *pool* the data *they* gather and *prepare their* report.

Common collectives include:

assembly, association, audience, board, cabinet, class, commission, company, corporation, council, counsel, couple, crowd, department, family, firm, group, jury, majority, minority, number, pair, press, public, staff, United States

Company names also qualify as collectives and may be either singular or plural. Usually those ending with a plural signifier such as *s* are plural.

Flowers, Inc., *mails its* advertisements in envelopes with floral decorations.

Jones Brothers *have sent their* representative to the conference.

Short collectives include the following short words. Though seldom listed as collectives, these words are governed by the rule for collectives. They are singular or plural according to the intended meaning of the sentence.

all, any, more, most, none, some, who, which

When a prepositional phrase follows the short collective, the number of the noun in the phrase controls the number of the verb. When no such phrase follows, the writer signals the intended meaning by the choice of the singular or the plural verb.

Some of the *work has been done.*
Some of the *returns have been filed.*

Most of the *correspondence is* routine.
Most of the *letters are* acceptable.

Is there *any* left? (any portion—any money, any ink)
Are there *any* left? (any individual items—any forms, any copies)

Which is to be posted? (which one?)
Which are to be posted? (which ones?)

Either: None of the items *is* deductible.
Or: None of the items *are* deductible.

> **NOTE:** Many writers treat *none* as singular in every instance, since it is a compound of *no one*. This usage is correct. It is equally correct, however, to treat *none* as plural (meaning *not any*) when it is followed by a prepositional phrase that has a plural object. Those who want to emphasize the singular meaning often substitute *not one* for *none*:
>
> *Not one* of the birds *is* building a nest.

Special collectives include certain words called *abstract collectives* by some grammarians. These words are also treated as collectives, even though they do not name a group of persons or things. Their singular form is used when they refer to qualities, emotions, or feelings common to a group of persons or things; or to actions common to such a group. Their plural form is used when this common or general idea is not present.

Use the singular under such circumstances as these:

attention	We called their *attention* to the plan's advantages. (not *attentions*)
consent	Several gave their *consent* to the guru.
failure	The dogs' *failure* to heed commands delayed their finding new homes.
interest	Their *interest* was in winning at all costs.
sense	Our interpretation is based on the *sense* of the amendment.
work	Rain will not interfere with their *work*.

Use either the singular or the plural with:

opinion	The students and their teacher expressed their *opinion* (or *opinions*) on the matter.
time	The only *time* these restrictions are in order is when the airlines . . . *OR* The only *times* these restrictions are in order are when the airlines . . .
use	What *use* (or *uses*) can be made of the timber?

Units of Measure

When a number is used with a plural noun to indicate a unit of measurement (money, time, fractions, portions, distance, weight, quantity, etc.), a singular verb is used. When the term is thought of as individual parts, a plural verb is used.

> *Ten years seems* like a long time.

> *Ten years have gone* by since I last saw him.

> *Twenty-one pages is* our homework for each day.

> *Twenty-one pages are* needed to finish the job.

When fractions and expressions such as *the rest of, the remainder of, a part of, percent of,* etc., are followed by a prepositional phrase, the noun or pronoun in that phrase governs the number of the verb.

> *Four-fifths* of the job *was* finished on time.

> *Four-fifths* of the students *were* finished on time.

> The *rest* (or *remainder*) of the work *is* due Friday.

> The *rest* (or *remainder*) of the cards *were* mailed today.

> What *percentage* of the information *is* available?

> What *percentage* of the items *were* lost?

Confusing Singular and Plural Forms

It is sometimes hard to tell by its form whether a word is singular or plural. Some words that end in *-s* may be singular, and some seemingly singular words may be plural.

These words are singular, though they may seem plural in form:

> apparatus, news, summons, whereabouts

> The *news* is disturbing.

These words are plural, though they are singular (or collective) in meaning:

> assets, earnings, means (*income*), odds, premises, proceeds, quarters, savings, wages, winnings

> His *assets are* listed on the attached statement.

> *Earnings are* up this quarter.

> The *odds are* against our getting home on time.

> The *proceeds are* earmarked for the most needy.

These words may be either singular or plural, depending on their meaning, even though they may seem plural in form:

ethics, goods, gross, headquarters, mechanics, politics, series, species, statistics, tactics

Ethics is a subject on which he is well qualified to speak.

His business *ethics are* above question.

Statistics is the only course I failed in school.

The *statistics prove* that I am right.

A *gross* of pencils *is* not enough.

A *gross* of pencils *are* being sent.

These nouns are plural, though they may appear to be singular because they have foreign or unusual plural forms.

The *analyses* have been completed. (*Analyses* is the plural of *analysis.*)

What *are* your *bases* for these conclusions? (*Bases* is the plural of *basis.*)

Some interesting *phenomena are* disclosed in this report. (*Phenomena* is the plural of *phenomenon.*)

His conclusion seems sound, but his *criteria are* not valid. (*Criteria* is the plural of *criterion.*)

Hyphenated compound nouns usually take their pluralization on the important part.

editors-in-chief, daughters-in-law

Solid compound nouns always take their pluralization at the end of the word.

stepdaughters, spoonfuls, bookshelves

Indefinite Pronouns

These indefinite pronouns are singular. When they are used as subjects, they require singular verbs; when used as antecedents, they require singular pronouns.

anybody, anyone, any one (any one of a group), anything, each, either, every, everybody, everyone, every one (every one of a group), everything, neither, nobody, no one, nothing, one, somebody, someone, some one (some one of a group), something

Anyone is welcome, as long as *he or she* (not *they*) behaves appropriately.

Any one of the men *is* capable of doing it. (written as two words when followed by a phrase)

Each of us *is* obliged to sign *his or her* own name.

Either of the alternatives *is* suitable.

Everyone must buy *his or her* book for the course.

Every one of the relatives *wishes* to sign the card. (written as two words when followed by a phrase)

Everything seems to be going smoothly now.

Neither of the plans *is* workable.

No one believes that our plan will work.

Someone has to finish this dessert.

Even when two indefinite pronouns are joined by *and,* they remain singular in meaning.

Anyone and everyone is invited.

Nothing and *no one escapes* her attention.

When *each* or *every* is used to modify a compound subject (subjects joined by *and*), the subject is considered singular.

Every ticket holder and *fan has sent* in a request.

When *each* is inserted (as a parenthetic or explanatory element) between a plural or a compound subject and its plural verb, neither the plural form of the verb nor the plural form of the pronoun is affected.

Region A, region B, and region C *each expect* to increase *their* investments.

They *each want* the same thing.

The customers *each have requested* permission to change *their* method of payment.

Many a (unlike *many*) is singular in meaning and takes a singular verb and pronoun.

Many a new leaf falls prey to insects during its first few weeks.

But: *Many new leaves* fall prey to insects during *their* first few weeks.

More than one, though its meaning is plural, is used in the singular.

More than one vacation plan *was* changed last night.

More than one detail *is* often overlooked.

These words are plural:

both, few, many, several, others

Both of us *have received* new assignments.

Few will be able to finish *their* work on time.

Many plan to leave in the morning.

Several writers *have submitted their* stories.

Others have not yet *finished theirs.*

Relative Pronouns

The verb in a relative clause must agree in number and in person with the relative pronoun (*who, which, that, what*) serving as the subject of the clause. The relative pronoun, in turn, must agree with its antecedent. Therefore, before we can make the verb agree with the relative pronoun, we must find the antecedent and determine its person and number.

Have you talked with the man *who was* waiting to see you? (*Man* is the antecedent of the relative pronoun *who,* and the verb *was* must agree with this antecedent in person and number.)

Where are the books *that were* left on the table? (The verb in the relative clause—*were*—must agree with the relative pronoun—*that*—which must agree with its antecedent—*books.*)

We *who have* met him do not doubt his ability. (The relative pronoun is *who;* the verb in the relative clause is *have;* the antecedent of the relative pronoun is *we.*)

In sentences that contain the phrases *one of the* or *one of those,* the antecedent of the relative pronoun is not *one,* but the plural words that follow.

One of the tools *that were* on my table has disappeared.

Here is one of the men *who are* moving the piano.

One of the women *who are* attending the conference is wanted on the telephone.

Who, that, or *which* may be used to refer to a collective noun. When the members of the group act, or are considered, as a unit, either *that* or *which* should be used—*that* is usually preferred if the group comprises persons rather than things. *Who* is used when the persons comprising a group act, or are considered, individually.

The editorial suggests that there *is* a *group* of citizens *that* is unhappy with progress.

We have heard from an *association* of homeowners *who feel* strongly opposed to cutting down trees.

Subjects Joined by *and*

When two or more subjects are joined by *and,* whether the subjects are singular or plural, they form a compound subject, which is considered plural.

The *date and the time* of the party *have* not been decided.

The *host and his guests are* giving their toasts.

The *coins, pencils, and other papers are* on the table where you left *them.*

He and I will deliver *our* newspapers in the morning.

Phrases or clauses serving as subjects follow the same rule. When two or more phrases or clauses serving as the subject of a sentence are joined by *and,* the resulting compound subject is considered plural.

Rising early in the morning and taking a walk before breakfast make a person feel invigorated all day.

That your work is usually done properly and *that you are usually prompt are* the factors I considered.

Exception: When the subjects joined by *and* refer to the same person or object or represent a single idea, the whole subject is considered singular.

Ham and eggs is a traditional American breakfast.

The *growth and development* of our country *is* described in this book.

The article or personal pronoun used before each member of the compound subject indicates whether we see the subject as a single idea or as different ideas.

My teacher and friend helps me with my problems. (one person)

My teacher and *my friend help* me with my problems. (two people)

The lead actress and star of the film *has* arrived.

The lead actress and *the star* of the film *have* arrived.

Subjects Joined by *or* or *nor*

When singular subjects are joined by *or* or *nor,* the subject is considered singular.

> Neither the *cat nor* the *mouse knows* that *he* is being watched.

> *One or* the *other* of us *has* to go.

> Neither *love nor money is* sufficient in such situations.

> Neither *heat nor cold nor sun nor wind affects* this material.

When one singular and one plural subject are joined by *or* or *nor,* the subject closer to the verb determines the number of the verb.

> I believe that *she or* her *sisters have* the keys to the car.

> I believe that her *sisters* or *she has* the keys to the car.

When one antecedent is singular and the other antecedent is plural, the pronoun agrees with the closer antecedent.

> Is it the general or the rebels who *merit* praise?

> Is it the rebels or the general who *merits* praise?

NOTE: Because your reader may be distracted by your use of a singular verb with a subject containing a plural element, place the plural element nearer the verb whenever possible.

> *Ask* him whether the *card or* the *letters have* been signed.

> Neither the *equipment nor* the *drivers are* capable of maintaining that pace.

When the subjects joined by *or* or *nor* are of different persons, the subject nearer the verb determines its person.

> I was told that *she or you were* to be responsible.

> I was told that *you or she was* to be responsible.

Shifts in Number or Person

Once you establish a word as either singular or plural, keep it the same throughout the sentence. Be sure that all verbs and all pronouns referring to that word agree with it in number.

Not: Because this *country* bases *its* economy on voluntary compliance with *its* tax laws, we must all pay our share if *they are* to carry out the necessary functions of government.

But: Because this *country* bases *its* economy on voluntary compliance with *its* tax laws, we must all pay our share if *it is* to carry out the necessary function of government.

Not: A *person needs* someone to turn to when *they are* in trouble.

But: A *person needs* someone to turn to when *he or she* is in trouble.

Not: When *one* has had a difficult day, it is important that *they* be able to relax in the evening.

But: When *one* has had a difficult day, it is important that *one* (or *he or she*) be able to relax in the evening.

Be consistent. If you decide that a collective is singular, keep it singular throughout the sentence—use a singular verb to agree with it and a singular pronoun to refer to it. If you establish the collective as plural, see that both the verb and the pronoun are plural.

The committee *has* announced *its* decision.

The committee *have* adjourned and gone to *their* homes.

Our staff *is* always glad to offer *its* advice and assistance.

Most indefinite pronouns are singular and require singular verbs and pronouns.

Not: *Has anyone* turned in *their* report?

But: *Has anyone* turned in *his or her* report?

(The indefinite pronoun *anyone* takes both a singular verb and a singular pronoun.)

Do not apply a verb form from one part of the sentence to another (elliptically) unless the same form is grammatically correct in both parts.

Not: The *numbers were* checked and the total verified.

But: The *numbers were* checked and the *total was* verified.

Avoid shifting the person of pronouns referring to the same antecedent.

Not: When *one* is happy, it often seems as if everyone around *you* is happy, too.

But: When *one* is happy, it often seems as if everyone around *one* (or *him or her*) is happy, too.

Not: *As the ship* entered *her* berth, *its* huge gray shadow seemed to swallow us.

But: As the *ship* entered *its* berth, *its* huge gray shadow seemed to swallow us.

or: As the *ship* entered *her* berth, *her* huge gray shadow seemed to swallow us.

Structure Problems

Usually it is easy for us to identify the subject or antecedent and determine its number and person. But occasionally a puzzling sentence comes along. The subject is there, as clear as can be, but something in the structure of the sentence tries to make us believe that another word is the subject.

Verb Precedes Subject

When the verb precedes the subject in the sentence (either in a question or in a declarative sentence), locate the true subject and make the verb agree with it.

Are the *lamp* and the *bookcase* in this room?

Walking down the hall *are* the *men* we were waiting for.

Clearly visible in the sky *were* the *kites* he had previously admired.

From these books *come some* of our best *ideas.*

To us *falls* the *task* of repairing the environment.

Among those attending *were* two former *teachers.*

Where, here, and *there* do not influence the number or person of the verb when introducing a sentence. In such sentences, find the real subject and make the verb agree with it.

Where *are* the individual *sessions* to be held?

Where *is* the *case* filed?

Here *are* the *songs* for which we were waiting.

Here *is* the *song* for which we were waiting.

There *are* two *books* on the table.

There *is* a *book* on the table.

What, who, which, the interrogative pronouns, do not affect the number of the verb. Again, find the subject of the sentence and make the verb agree with it.

What *is* the *point* of your argument?

What *are* your *recommendations* on this problem?

Who *is* going to accompany you to the dentist?

Who, in this group, *are* members of your family?

Which *is* the *light* that he means?

Which *are* the *standards* that we are to apply?

The expletives *it* or *there* may introduce the verb and stand for the subject, which comes later in the clause. *It* requires a singular verb, even when the real subject is plural. Following *there,* the verb is singular or plural according to the subject which follows it.

It *is* solutions we are looking for, not problems.

It *is* doubtful that he will start today.

There *are* enclosed five copies of the pamphlet you requested.

There *is* attached a letter from your mom.

NOTE: Avoid confusing your reader by using the expletive *it* and the personal pronoun *it* in the same sentence.

Not: I haven't read the book yet; *it* has been hard for me to find time for *it.*

But: I haven't read the *book* yet; I haven't been able to find time for *it.*

Words Intervening Between Subject and Verb

The presence of explanatory or parenthetical phrases, or other modifiers, between the subject and verb does not change the number or person of the subject. Locate the real subject of the sentence and make the verb agree with it.

His sworn *statement,* together with statements from other witnesses, *was* heard in court.

The *amount* shown, plus interest, *is* due within 30 days.

The *letter* with its several attachments *was* received this morning.

Our *manners,* like our speech, *are* indicators of character.

The *policeman,* instead of the agents who had been assigned the case, *is* scheduled to visit our neighbor.

His *appraisal,* including extensive notes on the furnishings of the office, *was* well received.

That *fact,* in addition to our already large file on the case, *means* our assumptions were correct.

No one but those present *knows* of this bargain.

Subject and Predicate Differ in Number

After forms of the verb *to be* we often find a construction (called the *predicate nominative*) which means the same thing as the subject. When the predicate nominative differs in number from the subject, the verb must agree with the element that precedes it (the subject).

Our main *problem is* writing complete stories and keeping them short enough for fast reading.

Writing complete stories and keeping them short enough for fast reading are our main problem.

As always, the *question was* sufficient funds.

As always, *sufficient funds were* the question.

The electrician said that a dangerous *problem is* the old lines.

The electrician said that the *old lines are* a dangerous problem.

Construction Shift and Parallelism

Use the same grammatical construction for each of the words or ideas in a sentence if these words or ideas require balance, according to the meaning that the sentence is conveying.

Not: *Singing* and *to dance* are not permitted here.

But: *Singing* and *dancing* (or *To sing* and *to dance*) are not permitted here.

Not: The children are learning the value of *courtesy* and *being kind.*

But: The children are learning the value of *courtesy* and *kindness.*

Special Problems of Pronoun Reference

Pronouns should follow as closely and as logically as possible the antecedent (subject) to which they refer.

Ambiguous Antecedents

Do not use forms of the same pronoun to refer to different antecedents.

Not: The letter is on the conference table *that* we received yesterday.

But: The *letter that* we received yesterday is on the conference table.

Indefinite Antecedents

Be sure that the reference to an antecedent is quite specific.

Not: The copies of these letters were not initialed by the writers, so we are sending *them* back. (What are we sending back? The copies, the letters, or the writers?)

But: We are sending back the copies of the letters because *they* were not initialed by the writers.

Not: When you have finished the book and written your summary, please return *it* to the library. (What is going to be returned, the book or the summary?)

But: When you have finished the book and written your summary, please return the book to the library.

Implied Antecedents

As a general rule, the antecedent of a pronoun must appear in the sentence—not merely be implied. And the antecedent should be a specific word, not an idea expressed in a phrase or clause. *It, which, this,* and *that* are the pronouns that most often lead meaning astray. Any of these pronouns may refer to an idea expressed in a preceding passage if the idea and the reference are *unmistakably* clear. But too often the idea that is unmistakably clear to the speaker or writer is nowhere to be found when the listener or reader looks for it.

Not: Although the doctor operated at once, *it* was not a success and the patient died.

But: Although the doctor performed the *operation* at once, *it* was not a success and the patient died.

or: Although the doctor operated at once, the *operation* was not a success and the patient died.

Vague Reference

The usage illustrated below—the impersonal use of *it, they,* and *you*—is correct, but may produce vague, wordy sentences.

Not: In the instructions *it* says to make three copies.

But: The instructions say to make three copies.

Not: In the letter *it* says he will be here on Thursday.

But: The letter says he will be here on Thursday.

or: He says, in his letter, that he will be here on Thursday.

Not: *They* say in the almanac that we are in for a cold, wet winter.

But: The almanac predicts a cold, wet winter.

Not: From this report *you* can easily recognize the cause of the accident.

But: From this report *one* can easily recognize the cause of the accident. (The first example is correct if the writer is addressing his remarks to a specific person.)

or: The cause of the accident can be easily recognized from this report.

VERBS AND VERBALS

We know that, as their main function, verbs describe an action or a state of being on the part of the subject. But verbs also tell *when* the action took place or *when* the state existed. This property of verbs is called **tense.**

Tense

English has six tenses: three simple tenses (**present, past,** and **future**) in which an action may be considered as simply occurring; and three compound—called **perfect**—tenses in which an action may be considered as completed. (To be *perfected* means to be *completed.*)

Present Tense:	I walk, he walks
Present Perfect Tense:	I have walked, he has walked
Past Tense:	I walked, he walked
Past Perfect Tense:	I had walked, he had walked
Future Tense:	I shall walk, he will walk
Future Perfect Tense:	I shall have walked, he will have walked

Each of the six tenses has a companion form—the **progressive** form. As its name indicates, the progressive says that the action named by the verb is a continued or progressive action. The progressive consists of the present participle (the *-ing* form of the verb—that is, *walking*) plus the proper form of the verb *to be.* The progressive forms of the verb *to walk* are:

| Present Tense: | I am walking, he is walking |
| Present Perfect Tense: | I have been walking, he has been walking |

| Past Tense: | I was walking, he was walking |
| Past Perfect Tense: | I had been walking, he had been walking |

| Future Tense: | I shall be walking, he will be walking |
| Future Perfect Tense: | I shall have been walking, he will have been walking |

The present tense and the past tense also have an **emphatic** form, which uses *do, does, did* as auxiliaries:

| Present Tense: | I do understand, she does understand |

| Past Tense: | You did understand, they did understand |

We indicate tense by changing the verb itself or by combining certain forms of the verb with auxiliary verbs. The verb tenses from which we derive every form of a verb are called **principal parts.** The principal parts of a verb are:

The Present Tense:	talk, write
The Past Tense:	talked, wrote
The Present Perfect:	have talked, has written

Verbs are classified as **regular** (or *weak*) and **irregular** (or *strong*), according to the way in which their principal parts are formed. Regular verbs form their past tense and present perfect tense by the addition of *-ed* to the infinitive:

Present Tense	Past Tense	Present Perfect Tense
talk	talked	has (have) talked
help	helped	has (have) helped
walk	walked	has (have) walked

The principal parts of irregular verbs are formed by changes in the verb itself:

Present Tense	Past Tense	Present Perfect Tense
see	saw	has (have) seen
say	said	has (have) said
go	went	has (have) gone

Principal Parts of Troublesome Verbs

Some irregular verbs are particularly troublesome. The following list shows how the principal parts of these irregular verbs change to reflect the tense.

Present Tense	Past Tense	Present Perfect Tense
abide	abode, abided	has abode
arise	arose	has arisen
bear (carry)	bore	has borne
bear (bring forth)	bore	has borne
bid	bade, bid	has bid, bidden
bide	bode, bided	has bode, bided
bleed	bled	has bled
broadcast	broadcast, broadcasted	has broadcast(ed)
burst	burst	has burst
chide	chid, chidded	has chid, chidded, chidden
choose	chose	has chosen
cleave (adhere)	cleaved	has cleaved
cleave (split)	cleft, cleaved	has cleft, cleaved, cloven
cling	clung	has clung
drink	drank	has drunk
drown	drowned	has drowned
flee	fled	has fled
fling	flung	has flung
flow	flowed	has flowed
fly	flew or flied	has flown
forsake	forsook	has forsaken
freeze	froze	has frozen
grind	ground	has ground
hang (a picture)	hung	has hung
hang (a person)	hanged	has hanged
lay (place)	laid	has laid
lead	led	has led
lend	lent	has lent
lie (rest)	lay	has lain
light	lit, lighted	has lit, lighted
raise	raised	has raised

continues

PRINCIPAL PARTS OF TROUBLESOME VERBS *continued*

Present Tense	Past Tense	Present Perfect Tense
rid	rid, ridded	has rid, ridded
ring	rang	has rung
set	set	has set
sew	sewed	has sewed, sewn
shrink	shrank, shrunk	has shrunk, shrunken
sink	sank, sunk	has sunk
sit	sat	has sat
ski	skied (rhymes with *seed*)	has skied
slay	slew, slayed	has slain
slide	slid	has slid, slidden
sling	slung	has slung
slink	slunk	has slunk
smite	smote	has smitten
spring	sprang, sprung	has sprung
steal	stole	has stolen
sting	stung	has stung
stink	stank, stunk	has stunk
stride	strode	has stridden
strive	strove, strived	has striven
swim	swam	has swum
swing	swung	has swung
thrust	thrust	has thrust
weave	wove, weaved	has woven
wring	wrung	has wrung

NOTE: When two forms are given, one or the other may be restricted to a particular sense of the verb. Consult a dictionary to establish if this is so.

He wove fine cloth.

She weaved in and out of traffic.

Past Tense vs. Past Perfect Tense

The past perfect indicates that the action or condition described was completed (perfected) earlier than some other action that also occurred in the past. Distinguish carefully between this tense and the simple past tense.

> When I *came* back from lunch, she *finished* the letter. (Both verbs are in the past tense; therefore, both actions happened at approximately the same time in the past.)

> When I *came* back from lunch, she *had finished* the letter. (Again, both actions occurred in the past, but the use of the past perfect *had finished* tells us that this action was completed before the other action.)

> We *discovered* that a detective *was following* us. (Both actions happened at the same time in the past.)

> We *discovered* that a detective *had been following* us. (He had been following us some time before we discovered it.)

Mood

The mood of a verb tells what kind of utterance is being made. An English verb may be **indicative, imperative,** or **subjunctive** in mood.

Indicative Mood

The indicative mood—used to make a statement or ask a question—is used in almost all our writing and speaking.

> The planting *was scheduled* for May 15.

> What *is* the correct form to be used?

> It *seems* likely to rain.

Imperative Mood

The imperative mood expresses a command, a request, or a suggestion. The subject of an imperative sentence is ordinarily the pronoun *you* (not expressed, simply understood.)

> *Lock* the safe before you leave the office.

> *Let* me give you directions to the interstate.

> Please *sign* the receipt before returning it to us. (Note that the word *please* may be inserted with no effect on the use of the imperative, but often with a desirable effect on the listener or reader.)

Probably the greatest mistake we make in using the imperative mood is in *not using it enough.* An order or a request stated in the imperative is usually not only more emphatic but much more quickly and easily understood.

Indicative: It would be appreciated if you would open the envelope promptly.

Imperative: Please open them envelope promptly.

Subjunctive Mood

The subjunctive expresses a hypothetical or conditional situation, or an indirect command. It is going out of use in English, but the subjunctive can still be seen in the following forms:

The third person singular present (which in the indicative has an -*s* and in the subjunctive has none):

Indicative: The plane usually *arrives* on schedule.

Subjunctive: Should the plane *arrive* on schedule, we will be able to make our connection.

Indicative: The detective *prepares* his reports as soon as he completes a case.

Subjunctive: We suggested that the detective *prepare* his reports immediately.

The forms of the verb *be:*

He requested that we *be* there.

If I *were* rich, I would buy a house.

Present: If he *were* able to do it, I am sure he would.

Past: If he *had been* able to do it, I am sure he would have.

Uses of the subjunctive include the following:

1. To express a wish not likely to be fulfilled or impossible to be realized:

   I wish it *were* possible for us to approve the loan. (It is *not* possible.)

   I wish she *were* here to hear your praise of her work. (She is *not* here.)

   Would that I *were* able to take this trip in your place. (I am *not* able to go.)

   I wish I *were* able to help you.

2. To express a parliamentary motion:

   I move that the meeting *be* adjourned.

   Resolved, that a committee *be* appointed to study this matter.

3. In a subordinate clause after a verb that expresses a command, a request, or a suggestion:

He asked *that* the flowers *be* watered in his absence.

It is recommended *that* this office *be* responsible for preparing the statements.

We suggest *that* he *be* aware of the situation.

We ask *that* he *consider* the possibility of a reversal.

It is highly desirable *that* they *be* given the keys to the apartment.

4. To express a condition known or supposed to be contrary to fact:

If this *were* up to me, we wouldn't be going.

If I *were* you, I wouldn't wait in the car.

5. After *as if* or *as though*. In formal writing and speech, *as if* and *as though* are followed by the subjunctive, since they introduce as supposition something not factual. In informal writing and speaking, the indicative is sometimes used:

He talked *as if* he *were* an expert on karate. (He's not.)

This drawing looks *as though* it *were* the work of a master.

Shifts in Mood

Be consistent in your point of view. Once you have decided on the mood that properly expresses your message, use that mood throughout the sentence or the paragraph. A shift in mood is confusing to the listener or reader; it indicates that the speaker or writer himself has changed his way of looking at the conditions.

Not: The hospital suggests that newborns *be* fed by their mothers and *should be* changed by their fathers. (*Be* is subjunctive; *should be*, indicative.)

But: The hospital suggests that newborns *be* fed by their mothers and *be* changed by their fathers.

Voice

Voice indicates whether the subject of the verb is performing or receiving the action described by the verb. There are two voices: **active** and **passive.**

If the subject is performing the action, the verb is in the active voice.

The *mechanic fixed* our car.

The *article summarizes* the problem.

The *hostess asked* that everyone be seated.

If the subject is being acted upon, the verb is in the passive voice. (The passive form always consists of some form of *be* plus the past participle.)

Our *car was fixed* by the mechanic.

The *problem is summarized* in this article.

Everyone was asked by the hostess to be seated.

Active and Passive Voice

In general, the active voice is preferable to the passive: it is simpler and more direct. If, however, you wish to emphasize the action itself or the object of the action and not the agent, use the passive.

Smoking is prohibited. (emphasizing the object, smoking)

Lori is employed by the college. (emphasizing Lori)

Shifts in Voice

Shifts in voice—often accompanied by shifts in subject—usually occur in compound or complex sentences. Although it is not essential that all clauses in a sentence be the same in structure, any unnecessary shifts may result in a disorganized sentence. Therefore, unless you have a good reason for changing, use the same subject and voice in the second clause that you used in the first.

Not: As *I searched* through my dresser drawers, the missing sock *was found.* (The first subject is *I*—its verb is active; the second subject is *sock*—its verb is passive.)

But: As *I searched* through my dresser drawers, *I found* the missing sock. (Subject is *I* in both clauses; both verbs are active.)

MODIFIERS

Modifiers are words or groups of words that describe, qualify, or limit another word or group of words.

Classification of Modifiers

Modifiers fall generally into two categories: **adjectives** (and phrases or clauses used as adjectives) and **adverbs** (and phrases or clauses used as adverbs). Sometimes the form of the modifier clearly shows whether it is an adjective or an adverb; sometimes the form is the same for both.

Adjectives describe, limit, or make more exact the meaning of a noun or pronoun (any substantive).

> He liked the *red* car.

> The dresser *that is made of oak* is my favorite.

Adverbs describe, limit, or make more exact the meaning of a verb, an adjective, or another adverb.

> He liked the *enchantingly* beautiful actress.

> Run around the track *as quickly as you can.*

Articles

Articles are a type of adjective. The indefinite articles are *a* and *an,* and the definite article is *the.* Use *a* before words beginning with a consonant sound, *an* before those beginning with a vowel sound.

> *a* desk, *a* book

> *an* agent, *an* error, *an* unusual occurrence, *an* honor (the *h* is not pronounced)

The article used before each of two connected nouns or adjectives signals that the words refer to different people or things.

> We elected *a* secretary and *a* treasurer. (two persons)

> He uses *a* tan and green typewriter. (one machine, two colors)

Do not use *a* or *an* after *sort of, kind of, manner of, style of,* or *type of.*

> Not: What *kind of a* book do you want?

> But: What *kind of* book do you want?

Do not use *the* before *both.*

> Not: We'll buy *the both* of them.

> But: We'll buy *both* of them.

The following words may be either adjectives or adverbs depending on their use:

> above, bad, better, cheap, close, deep, early, fast, first, hard, late, long, much, only, quick, slow, very, well

Adverbs with Two Forms

Some adverbs have two forms—one ending in *-ly,* the other not. The longer form is nearly always correct and is preferable in formal writing. The short form is properly used in brief, forceful sentences (in commands, such as the road sign "Drive Slow") and may be used informally. The *-ly* form should, however, always be used to modify an adjective.

Following are examples of adverbs having two forms:

cheap, cheaply	direct, directly	sharp, sharply
clear, clearly	loud, loudly	slow, slowly
deep, deeply	quick, quickly	soft, softly

Sometimes the meaning desired will determine which form should be used. Notice that either *direct* or *directly* may be used when the meaning is "in a straight line," but *directly* is the only choice when *soon* is meant.

NOTE: In informal speech, we sometimes drop the *-ly* ending from some often-used adverbs. This practice is not appropriate in formal writing.

Correct usage:

> I am *really* glad you could come. (Not *real* glad)

Adjectives and Adverbs (Degrees of Comparison)

Adjectives and adverbs change form to show a greater or lesser degree of the characteristic named by the simple word. There are three degrees of comparison.

Positive Degree

The positive degree names the *quality* expressed by the adjective or adverb. It does not imply a comparison with, or a relation to, a similar quality in any other thing.

> *high* morale, a *dependable* worker, work *fast,* prepared *carefully*

Comparative Degree

The comparative degree indicates that the quality described by the modifier exists to a greater or lesser degree in one thing than in another. It is formed by adding *-er* to the positive degree or by inserting *more* or *less* before the positive form.

> Our club has *higher* morale now than ever before.

> Jan is a *more dependable* worker than Tim.

> She can work *faster* than I.

> This meal was prepared *more carefully* than the one we had last night.

Superlative Degree

The superlative degree denotes the greatest or least amount of the quality named. It is formed by adding *-est* to the positive degree of the adjective or adverb or by inserting *most* or *least* before the positive form.

> That club has the *highest* morale of any club.

> Jan is the *most dependable* worker in the office.

> This is the *most carefully* prepared meal I have ever eaten.

The comparative degree is used to refer to only two things, the superlative to more than two.

> This boat is the *longer* of the two.

> This boat is the *longest* of the three.

Using *-er* and *-est* vs. *more* and *most*

There is no difference in meaning between *-er* and *more* or between *-est* and *most*. Either method may be used with some modifiers. However, most adjectives of three syllables or more and almost all adverbs are compared by the use of *more* and *most* (or *less* and *least*) rather than by the endings *-er* and *-est*. In choosing which method should be used with the modifiers that may take either method, you may base your choice on emphasis. By adding *-er* and *-est* to the root word you emphasize the *quality,* while by using *more* or *most* you stress the *degree* of comparison.

> Should I have been *kinder* or *harsher* in handling that call?

> That boat is the *longest* of the three.

> Should I have been *more firm* or *less firm* in handling that caller?

> Of all the forms, this one is the *most simple* and that one is the *least simple* to fill out.

Irregular Comparisons

Some modifiers are compared by changes in the words themselves. A few of these irregular comparisons are given below; consult your dictionary whenever you are in doubt about the comparison of any adjective or adverb.

Positive	Comparative	Superlative
good	better	best
well	better	best
bad (evil, ill)	worse	worst
badly (ill)	worse	worst
far	farther,	farthest, further, furthest
late	later, latter	latest, last
little	less, lesser	least
many, much	more	most

Problems with Comparison (Adjectives and Adverbs)

Some adjectives and adverbs express qualities that do not admit freely of comparison. They represent the highest degree of a quality and, as a result, cannot be improved. Some of these words are listed below.

complete	infinitely	square
correct	perfect	squarely
dead	perfectly	supreme
deadly	perpendicularly	totally
exact	preferable	unique
horizontally	round	uniquely
immortally	secondly	universally

However, there may be times when the comparison of these words is justified. If we use these modifiers in a relative or approximate sense, they may be compared. But proceed with care. It is usually better, for example, to say *more nearly round* or *more nearly perfect* than *rounder* or *more perfect*.

Comparison with *other* and *else*

When we use the comparative in such an expression as *this thing is better than any other,* we imply that *this thing* is separate from the group or class to which it is being compared. In these expressions we must use a word such as *other* or *else* to separate the thing being compared from the rest of the group of which it is a part.

Not: Our house is cooler than any house on the block. (The mistake here is not separating the item being compared—*house*—from the group to which it is being compared.)

But: Our house is cooler than any *other* house on the block. (Our house is one of the houses on the block.)

Not: He has a better record than any coach in our conference.

But: He has a better record than any *other* coach in our conference. (He himself is one of the coaches in the conference.)

Incomplete Comparison—Improper Ellipsis

When you make a comparison between two items, be sure that both terms of the comparison are named. Violation of this rule places the burden on the listener or reader, who may or may not clearly understand which of two items you are comparing. Be sure the listener or reader knows exactly what you mean when you say:

There have been more successful ad campaigns in our district this year. (Do you mean *more than in any other district?* or *more than in any previous year?*)

Whenever a comparison is not completed, the meaning of the sentence is obscured.

Incomplete comparison with possessive:

Obscure: Joe's letter states the problem better than John. (We cannot tell whether it is *John* or *John's letter* that is stating the problem.)

Improved: Joe's letter states the problem better than *John's*.

Ambiguous: John's proposed form is less complicated than management.

Improved: John's proposed form is less complicated than *management's*. (Or: than the one proposed by management.)

Incomplete comparison with conjunction:

Obscure: This text is as good, if not better than that one. (Because of the omission of the second *as* after *good,* this sentence reads " . . . as good *than.*")

Improved: This text is as good *as,* if not better than, that one.

or: This text is as good as that one, if not better.

Obscure: This book is shorter, but just as comprehensive as that one.

Improved:	This book is shorter *than,* but just as comprehensive as, that one.
or:	This book is shorter than that one, but just as comprehensive.

Incomplete comparison with verb:

Ambiguous:	I enjoy this kind of work more than John. (This could be interpreted as: I enjoy this kind of work more than I enjoy *John.*)
Improved:	I enjoy this kind of work more than John *does.*
Obscure:	I have known him longer than John.
Could mean:	I have known him longer than John *has.*
or:	I have known him longer than *I have known* John.

Split Infinitives

Inserting an adverb between *to* and the rest of an infinitive creates a split infinitive. In the past, writers have been told unequivocally to avoid this construction and to reposition the adverb or recast the entire sentence. Today, however, this rule has been relaxed to a great extent, even by careful writers. Still, avoiding the split infinitive can result in clearer, more graceful writing.

Not:	He wished to *completely* forget the matter.
But:	He wished to forget the matter *completely.*

Verbals and Verbal Phrases as Modifiers

Verbals are sometimes used as modifiers, either singly or in phrases.

To get the most out of the course, you must study regularly. (infinitive phrase modifying *you*)

Rising, the lion roared. (present participle modifying *lion*)

The card, *signed by all of us,* was mailed today. (past participles modifying *card*)

The letter, *having been corrected,* was dropped in the mailbox. (perfect participle modifying *letter*)

Dangling Verbal Phrases

A dangling phrase is one that cannot logically modify the noun or pronoun to which it refers. Corrective action may be taken in either of two ways: (1) by changing the subject of the main clause to one that the phrase can refer to, or (2) by changing the phrase itself into a dependent clause, so that it has a subject of its own.

Dangling: *To get the most out of this course,* careful *study* is necessary. (The phrase cannot logically modify *study;* it dangles.)

Corrected: *To get the most out of this course, you* must study it carefully.

or: If you are to get the most out of this course, you must study it carefully.

Dangling: *To apply for this job,* an *application* must be completed. (Dangles; an *application* can't apply.)

Corrected: *To apply for this job,* the *applicant* must complete an applicaton.

or: When the applicant applies for the job, an application must be completed.

Dangling: *By summarizing the information,* a clear *picture* of the situation was presented. (Dangles; a *picture* cannot perform the act of summarizing information.)

Corrected: *By summarizing the information, we* were able to present a clear picture of the situation.

or: After we had summarized the information, a clear picture of the situation was presented.

An infinitive or a participial phrase that modifies the whole sentence—designating general action rather than action by a specific agent—may be correctly used without relation to the subject of the main clause.

Generally speaking, these plants grow better in sunlight.

To summarize, Albuquerque has many spectacular sunsets.

Prepositional Phrases as Modifiers

The prepositional phrase can serve as an adjective or adverb.

The letter was addressed to the office *of the registrar.* (adjective modifying *office*)

They have gone *to the rally.* (adverb modifying *have gone*)

A prepositional phrase *dangles* when it does not, both logically and grammatically, refer to the subject of the main clause.

Dangling: *With much effort,* the *assignment* was completed on time.

Corrected: *With much effort, we* completed the assignment on time.

Dependent Clauses as Modifiers

Dependent clauses can serve as adjectives or adverbs. Parts of a dependent clause are sometimes omitted because the missing elements can be easily supplied. These incomplete clauses are known as **elliptical clauses.** An elliptical clause must be able to modify, both logically and grammatically, the subject of the main clause. If it does not, it dangles.

Dangling: *Unless compiled by early June,* we cannot include the figures in this year's crop report.

Corrected: *Unless compiled by early June,* the figures cannot be included in this year's crop report.

or: Unless *the figures are* compiled by early June, we cannot include them in this year's crop report.

Dangling: *While making his periodic tour of the state,* a few changes in the planned itinerary were necessary.

Corrected: *While making his periodic tour of the state,* he made a few changes in the planned itinerary.

or: While *he was* making his periodic tour of the state, a few changes in planned itinerary were made.

Relative Pronouns Introducing Clauses

Be careful to select the correct relative pronoun to introduce the adjective clause. *Who* refers to persons; *what, that,* and *which* refer to things; *that* usually refers to things, but is sometimes used to refer to persons.

The trainer *who tamed this lion* has had extensive experience.

The homework assignment, *which is due tomorrow,* will contain that information.

The time card *that you have been submitting weekly* will be required once a month from now on.

Placement of Modifiers

Modifiers should be placed as close as possible to the words they modify. This is true whether the modifier is a single word, a phrase, or a clause. In English, sometimes the only way the reader can tell which word is being modified is by the location of the modifier. It's often simply a matter of proximity.

Many ambiguous (and unintentionally humorous) sentences result from the misplacement of modifiers.

Modifier Between Subject and Verb

Wherever possible, avoid placing the modifier between subject and verb and between verb and object.

Not: The driver, *to save money on fuel,* switched to a smaller car.

But: *To save money on fuel,* the driver switched to a smaller car.

Single Adverbs

Some adverbs—*only, almost, nearly, also, quite, merely, actually*—are frequent troublemakers. Be sure they are placed as close as possible to the words they modify.

Example: The problem can *only* be defined by this committee.

Could mean: *Only* this committee can define the problem.

or: This committee can *only define* the problem, not solve it.

Do not use *hardly, only, scarcely, barely*—so-called subtractive adverbs—together with a negative construction. If you do, you will have a double negative.

Not: They *haven't only* a single blanket.

But: They *have only* a single blanket.

Not: He *hasn't scarcely* done anything worthwhile.

But: He *has scarcely* done anything worthwhile.

Phrases and Clauses

Phrases and clauses, like single-word modifiers, should be placed as close as possible to the words they modify; this way there will be no danger of their attaching themselves to the wrong sentence element.

Not: We need someone to design buildings *with architectural experience.*

But: We need someone *with architectural experience* to design buildings.

Not: Mr. Dough has resigned from Congress after having served four years *to the regret of all the members.*

But: *To the regret of all the members,* Mr. Dough has resigned from Congress after having served four years.

Relative Clauses

Relative clauses should also be placed immediately after the word they modify, since they attach themselves to the sentence element nearest them.

Not: The man has an appointment *who is waiting in my office.*

But: The man *who is waiting in my office* has an appointment.

Not: She mentioned the number of cases closed by agents in her group *which are over a year old.*

But: She mentioned the number of cases *over a year old* which have been closed by agents in her group.

Squinting Constructions

Avoid **squinting** constructions—that is, modifiers that are so placed that one cannot tell whether they are modifying the words immediately preceding them or those immediately following them.

Obscure: The city agreed *after the papers were signed* to allow the march.

Could mean: The city agreed to allow the march *after the papers were signed.*

or: *After the papers were signed,* the city agreed to allow the march.

Obscure: He agreed *that morning* to marry her.

Could mean: He agreed to marry her *that morning.*

or: *That morning,* he agreed to marry her.

CONNECTIVES

Four kinds of words can serve as connectives: **prepositions, conjunctions, relative pronouns,** and **relative adverbs.** Each not only connects two sentence elements but also shows the relationship between them.

Prepositions

A preposition *connects* the word, phrase, or clause that follows it (its object) with some other element in the sentence *and shows the relationship* between them. A preposition can be a single word (*to, with*) or a phrase (*according to, as well as, because of, contrary to*).

Prepositional Idioms

The use of many prepositions in English is purely idiomatic: there is no logical reason that one preposition is wrong and another correct in a given expression. There are no rules for choosing the correct preposition; the idioms must simply be memorized. Study the following list of some of the more common prepositional idioms.

accede **to**	We cannot *accede to* the request.
accessory **of**	He was an *accessory of* the criminal.
accessory **to**	He was an *accessory to* the act.
accommodate **to**	He finds it hard to *accommodate* himself *to* new situations. (changed conditions)
accommodate **with**	We *accommodated* her *with* a loan of five dollars.
accompany **by**	Sheba was *accompanied by* a friend. (a person)
accompany **with**	The flowers were *accompanied with* a note. (a thing)
accountable **for**	I am *accountable for* my actions.
accountable **to**	I am *accountable to* my parents.
accused **by**	He was *accused by* the customer of giving poor service.
accused **of**	Edwin was *accused of* eating the last cookie.
acquiesce **in**	The commissioner *acquiesced in* the decision.
acquit **of**	The group was *acquitted of* the crime.
acquit **with**	She *acquitted* herself *with* honor.
adapt **for**	The stairway was *adapted for* our use.
adapt **from**	The movie was *adapted from* the book.
adapt **to**	Evelyn finds it difficult to *adapt to* new procedures.
adequate **for**	His golf game was not *adequate for* the course.
adequate **to**	Her ability was *adequate to* the job.
averse **to**	Fernandez was not *averse to* hard work.

advise **of**	The skaters were *advised of* the new regulations.
affix **to**	A stamp was *affixed to* the container.
agree **on**	They cannot *agree on* the best course of action.
agree **to**	They state that they *agree to* the compromise.
agree **with**	The boys and their fathers *agree with* us.
amenable **to**	Francis was *amenable to* our suggestion.
analogous **to**	This situation is *analogous to* the one we faced last year.
annoy **by**	The librarian was *annoyed by* the frequent interruptions.
annoy **with**	I was *annoyed with* many of the suggestions.
apparent **in**	Marv's attitude is *apparent in* his actions.
apparent **to**	The trouble is *apparent to* everyone.
append **to**	A rider was *appended to* the bill.
appreciation **for**	The student had a deep *appreciation for* the arts.
appreciation **of**	He expressed *appreciation of* their hard work.
appreciative **of**	They are *appreciative of* Jim's efforts.
authority **in**	Dr. Rollin is an *authority in* the field of radiology.
authority **on**	Professor Haslem is an *authority on* Renaissance literature.
basis **for**	They had a sound *basis for* agreement.
basis **in**	Janet's argument has no *basis in* fact.
cater **to**	This magazine *caters to* coin collectors.
commensurate **with**	His salary was *commensurate with* his abilities.
comply **with**	We must *comply with* the request.
concur **in**	We *concur in* the decision of the survey committee.
concur **with**	One member did not *concur with* the others.
conform **to**	All campers must *conform to* the regulations.
consist **in**	Her chief value *consists in* her ability to work with others.
consist **of**	The handbook *consists of* mathematical formulas.

consistent **in**	Parents should be *consistent in* rearing their children.
correspond **to**	His description of the planet *corresponds to* the known facts.
correspond **with**	Lakeisha has been *corresponding with* her boyfriend.
demand **from**	What did Oscar *demand from* them in payment?
demand **of**	They had *demanded* an accounting *of* the company funds.
differ **from**	Trent's estimate of the amount due *differs from* Jarlyn's.
differ **in**	We *differ in* our political opinions.
differ **on**	They *differ on* the amount to be assessed.
differ **with**	I *differ with* him about the evaluation method to be used.
discrepancy **between**	There is a *discrepancy between* the two totals.
discrepancy **in**	There is a *discrepancy in* Felix's account.
displeased **at**	Jeff was *displeased at* the way the employee wasted time.
displeased **with**	Rolando was *displeased with* Michael's comments.
eligible **for**	He is *eligible for* the job.
equivalent **in**	His shirt and mine are *equivalent in* size.
equivalent **of**	This is the *equivalent of* a full payment.
equivalent **to**	Each payment is *equivalent to* a week's salary.
excepted **from**	He was *excepted from* further responsibility.
excluded **from**	This item may be *excluded from* the questionnaire.
exempt **from**	This type of income is *exempt from* tax.
expect **from**	What favor do you *expect from* your friend?
expect **of**	What does Bacon *expect of* his assistant?
familiar **to**	The name is *familiar to* me.
familiar **with**	I am quite *familiar with* motorcycles.
find **for**	The jury *found for* the defendant.

furnish **to**	Adequate supplies were *furnished to* them.
furnish **with**	Please *furnish* us *with* background information on this matter.
habit **of**	Carlos made a *habit of* checking his facts.
identical **with**	That case is *identical with* the one I am working on.
identify **by**	The girl was *identified by* the tattoo on her arm.
identify **with**	He was *identified with* the opposing members.
ignorant **of**	He was *ignorant of* his rights.
improvement **in**	The *improvement in* his singing was soon noted.
improvement **on**	His second pasta dish was an *improvement on* the first.
inconsistent **with**	Cruelty is *inconsistent with* civilized behavior.
infer **from**	We *infer from* Karen's statement that she plans to visit Paul.
influence **by**	The actors were all *influenced by* the director's exhortations.
influence **on (upon)**	The moon at perigee has a dramatic *influence on* (*upon*) the tides.
influence **over**	The minister had a strong *influence over* his congregation.
influence **with**	Mark referred frequently to his *influence with* those in authority.
inform **of**	Patients should keep their doctors *informed of* any changes in their health.
inherent **in**	A capacity for growth is *inherent in* all people.
insert **in**	This pin should be *inserted in* the slot.
intercede **for**	My best friend *interceded for* me.
intercede **with**	Doug *interceded with* the board in my behalf.
invest **in**	The police said he had *invested* the money *in* stocks.
invest **with**	She was *invested with* full power to act.
irrelevant **to**	This statement is *irrelevant to* the matter under discussion.

irrespective **of**	They decided to appoint him *irrespective of* the criticism that might result.
liable **for**	Trudi is *liable for* damages.
liable **to**	The employee is *liable to* his employer.
liberal **in**	He was very *liberal in* his views.
liberal **with**	My boss was *liberal with* her praise.
necessity **for**	There is no *necessity for* our launching the boat.
necessity **of**	We are faced with the *necessity of* reducing travel expenses.
oblivious **of (to)**	He was *oblivious of* (*to*) the effect that his remarks had on his friends.
precedent **for**	Is there a *precedent for* this action?
precedent **in**	His decision established a *precedent in* law.
recompense **for**	Miguel was fully *recompensed for* the time he spent on the job.
reconcile **to**	We have become *reconciled to* our fate.
reconcile **with**	Our views cannot be *reconciled with* his.
similarity **in**	I agree that there is much *similarity in* their appearance.
similarity **of**	The *similarity of* these odd vegetables caused a great deal of confusion.
similarity **to**	This camera shows a *similarity to* one I have.
talk **of**	The traveler *talked* long *of* his experiences.
talk **to**	The teacher *talked to* his class.
talk **with**	The lawyer *talked with* her client.
transfer **from**	He has been *transferred from* his former position.
transfer **to**	They *transferred* him *to* another department.
unequal **in**	The contestants were *unequal in* strength.
unequal **to**	She was *unequal to* the demands placed on her.
use **for**	He had no *use for* the extra table.
use **of**	She made good *use of* her opportunity.
wait **for**	Marci seemed to be *waiting for* someone.

Placement of Prepositions

It is now considered acceptable to end a sentence with a preposition.

What did you do that *for?*

We had too many ideas to talk *about.*

Superfluous Prepositions

In formal writing, avoid superfluous prepositions.

Not: He is standing near *to* the ledge.

But: He is standing near the ledge.

Not: When are you going to start *in* to write that letter?

But: When are you going to start to write that letter?

Faulty Omission of Prepositions

The preference in more formal writing is to repeat the preposition before the second of two connected elements.

He seemed interested *in* us and our problems.

He seemed interested *in* us and *in* our problems.

He was able to complete the renovation *by* planning carefully and working diligently.

He was able to complete the renovation *by* planning carefully and *by* working diligently.

In the so-called *split* (or *suspended*) construction, in which two words are completed by different prepositions, be especially careful to use both prepositions.

Not: He has an interest and an aptitude *for* his work.

But: He has an interest *in* and an aptitude *for* his work. (Commas may be used in this construction: He has an interest in, and an aptitude for, his work.)

Not: They were puzzled and concerned *about* her erratic behavior.

But: They were puzzled *by* and concerned *about* her erratic behavior.

Conjunctions and Parallelism

Sentence elements are said to be *coordinate* (or *parallel*) when they are of equal rank (of equal importance) both grammatically and logically.

Determining equal grammatical importance is relatively simple: words = words; phrases = phrases; subordinate clauses = subordinate clauses; principal clauses = principal clauses.

Elements not grammatically equal (not parallel) are shown in this example:

> His main virtues are *that he is sincere* and *his generosity.* (a clause linked to a word)

Improved:

> His main virtues are *that he is sincere* and *that he is generous.* (two noun clauses, now parallel; noun clause = noun clause)

> His main virtues are his *sincerity* and his *generosity.* (two words)

Coordinate Conjunctions Showing

The coordinate conjunctions, including *and, but, or, nor, for, yet, moreover,* are the connectives most frequently used to show that two ideas are equal (are parallel). Notice in the following illustrations that the two ideas connected are parallel.

> The *director and* the *assistant director* will attend the meeting. (connecting a word with a word)

> He is a man *of great capability but of little experience.* (connecting a phrase with a phrase)

> He said *that he had filed a claim for a refund but that he had not heard anything further from this store.* (connecting a subordinate clause with a subordinate clause)

> *I was eager to attend the seminar; moreover, I knew that the exchange of ideas would be helpful.* (connecting an independent clause with an independent clause)

Correlative Conjunctions Showing Coordination (Parallelism)

The correlative conjunctions—*either . . . or, neither . . . nor, not only . . . but also, both . . . and, if . . . then, since . . . therefore*—work in pairs to show that words and ideas are parallel (equal in importance).

> *Either* the *doctor or* the *lawyer* must attend. (connecting a word with a word)

> The report is designed *not only to present a list of the problems facing us but also to recommend possible solutions to these problems.* (connecting a phrase with a phrase)

The significant point in the use of pairs of correlatives is that each member of the pair must be followed by the same part of speech (same grammatical construction). That is, if *not only* is followed by a verb, then *but also* must be followed by a verb; if *either* is followed by a phrase, *or* must likewise be followed by a phrase.

Not: *Either* fish of this type are much fewer in number *or* are not easily caught. (*Either* is followed by a noun, *fish;* or is followed by a verb phrase.)

But: Fish of this type *either* are much fewer in number *or* are not easily caught.

Not: His reply *not only* was prompt *but also* complete.

But: His reply was *not only* prompt *but also* complete.

When this plan is not followed, the result is "faulty parallelism." To turn faulty parallelism into effective parallelism, sometimes we need add only a word or two.

Not: The picnic was a disappointment *not only* to me *but also* my boyfriend. (*Not only* is followed by the prepositional phrase *to me; but also* is followed by a noun.)

But: The picnic was a disappointment *not only* to me *but also* to my boyfriend. (Note that each of the correlative conjunctions is followed by a prepositional phrase.)

Not: His assignment was *both* to conduct the course *and* the evaluation of it.

But: His assignment was *both* to conduct the course *and* to evaluate it.

> **NOTE:** The correlative *as . . . as* is used both affirmatively and negatively; the correlative *so . . . as* is used only negatively.
>
> This melon is *as* sweet *as* that one.
>
> This melon is not *as* sweet *as* that one
>
> This melon is not *so* sweet *as* that one.

Troublesome Conjunctions

and vs. *also*

Also, a weak connective, should not be used in place of *and* in sentences such as:

He writes poems, stories, *and* (not *also*) art reviews.

and etc.

The abbreviation *etc.* stands for the Latin *et cetera,* meaning *and so forth.* Obviously, then, an additional *and* is not only unnecessary but incorrect.

Not: He used all our paper, pencils, pens, *and etc.*

But: He used all our paper, pencils, pens, *etc.*

and which, and who, but which

Avoid using *and which, and who, but which, but that,* etc., when there is no preceding *who, which,* or *that* in the sentence to complete the parallel construction.

Not: We are looking for a car more economical to operate *and which* will be easy to maintain.

But: We are looking for a car *which* will be more economical to operate *and which* will be easy to maintain.

too many *and's*

Avoid stringing together a group of sentence elements connected by *and's.*

Not: The evaluation of the training program was planned *and* conducted *and* reported to the appropriate officials.

But: The evaluation of the training program was planned and conducted; then it was reported to the appropriate officials.

and vs. *but*

Use *and* to show addition; use *but* to show contrast.

Not: The boy and his mother have been called to a short meeting, *and* the principal will be out of the office all afternoon.

But: The boy and his mother have been called to a short meeting, *but* the principal will be out of the office all afternoon.

and or *but* to begin a sentence

We may begin a sentence—or even a paragraph—with *and, but,* or any other coordinating conjunction. A coordinate conjunction or a conjunctive adverb at the beginning of a sentence is often a handy signpost for the reader, pointing out the direction this new sentence will carry him.

as, since, because

These conjunctions can be used interchangeably to introduce clauses of cause or reason.

Because the book was due at the library, I returned it.

Since the book was due at the library, I returned it.

As the book was due at the library, I returned it.

However, *since* and *as* have another function: *since* introduces clauses of sequence of time, and *as* introduces clauses of duration of time. Because of the double function of these two words, we must be careful to use them only in sentences in which they cannot be misunderstood.

Not: *Since* this study was conducted to analyze the effects of . . .
(Could mean: *Since the time that* the study was conducted . . .)

But: *Because* this study was conducted to analyze the effects of . . .

Not: *As* I was writing the lab report, he gave the correct answers to Beth. (Could mean: *During the time that* I was writing the lab report . . .)

But: *Because* I was writing the lab report . . .

NOTE: When an *as* or *since* clause comes last in the sentence, the meaning of the conjunction can be made clear by the punctuation of the clause. If *as* or *since* is used as a time indicator, the clause it introduces is not set off from the sentence. But if the conjunction introduces a clause of cause or reason, the clause is set off.

There have been several changes in policy *since* the committee released its findings. (No punctuation; *since* means *since the time that.*)

There have been several changes in policy, *since* the committee released its findings. (. . . *because* the committee released its findings)

---

as vs. *that* or *whether*
Avoid using *as* in place of *that* or *whether* to introduce clauses following such verbs as *say, think, know.*

Not: I don't know *as* I believe you.

But: I don't know *that* I believe you.

or: I don't know *whether* I believe you.

if vs. *whether*
If is used to introduce clauses of condition or supposition.

We will stay *if* the fish are biting.

If you cannot answer the phone immediately, please ask Erin to do it.

Whether introduces clauses indicating an alternative. The alternative may be expressed in the sentence or understood.

It will not make any difference *whether* John agrees or disagrees with the outcome of the polling.

Please let me know *whether* you received the check.

Today, many grammarians endorse the use of either *if* or *whether* in such constructions as:

Please let me know *if* (or *whether*) you received the check.

I wonder *if* (or *whether*) he is qualified for that position.

If there is any danger that the reader may fail to understand the meaning, use the preferred *whether*.

whether vs. *whether or not*

It is not essential that *or not* be used with *whether* to complete the alternative choice. These words may be added if they are needed for emphasis.

Either: Please let me know *whether or not* you received our letter.

Or: Please let me know *whether* you received our letter.

that introducing parallel clauses

When either *that* or *which* introduces one of a series of parallel clauses, the same conjunction must introduce the other clauses in the series. Do not shift conjunctions or omit the conjunction in later clauses.

Not: He said *that* he would call me before noon and his brother would meet me. (conjunction omitted)

But: He said *that* he would call me before noon and *that* his brother would meet me. (conjunction supplied)

Shift in conjunction:

Not: We painted the boat *that* we liked so much and *which* we bought.

But: We painted the boat *that* we liked so much and *that* we bought.

proper omission of *that*

That may be omitted in noun clauses (especially those following such verbs as *say, think, feel, believe, hope*) and in adjective clauses, if the meaning of the sentence is clear.

Noun clauses:

He said (*that*) he would call me before noon.

I hope (*that*) we can finish this painting today.

Adjective clauses:

The book (*that*) I asked for is out on loan.

The instructions (*that*) she gave were perfectly clear.

faulty repetition of *that*

Do not use *that* twice to introduce the same noun clause. This error most often occurs in a long sentence in which a long interrupting expression occurs between *that* and the rest of its clause.

Not: I am sure you can appreciate *that,* in order to serve as many guests as possible, *that* we must open the veranda.

But: I am sure you can appreciate *that,* in order to serve as many guests as possible, we must open the veranda.

when

Avoid using *when* to introduce a definition unless the definition pertains to time.

Not: Their first important step in the improvement of the conditions was *when* they thoroughly surveyed the situation. (The step was not "when.")

But: Their first important step in the improvement of the conditions was *the thorough survey* of the situation.

Correct usage: Three o'clock is *when* the meeting will be held.

where

Avoid using *where* to introduce a definition unless the definition pertains to place or location.

Not: A sentence is *where* you have a subject and a verb. (A sentence is not "where.")

But: A sentence is a group of words containing a subject and a verb.

Correct usage: The large conference room is *where* the meeting is being held.

Avoid substituting *where* for *that.*

Not: I saw in the bulletin *where* the new law has been put into effect.

But: I saw in the bulletin *that* the new law has been put into effect.

while **vs.** *when*

While indicates duration of time; *when* indicates a fixed or stated period of time.

> *When* I return to work, I will take you out to lunch. (at that fixed time)

> *While* I am shopping, I will look for that skirt. (During the time I am shopping . . .)

while **vs.** *though, although, and, but*

While pertains to time and should not be substituted loosely for *though, although, whereas, and,* or *but.*

Not: *While* I did not remember the woman's name, I thought I could recognize her face.

But: *Although* I did not remember the woman's name, I thought I could recognize her face.

Not: I assembled the material for the manual *while* he wrote the outline. (Could mean: *during the time that he . . .*)

But: I assembled the material for the manual, *but* he wrote the outline.

PUNCTUATION

The purpose of punctuation is to clarify the meaning of written language. In general, punctuation marks should prevent misreading by bringing out clearly the author's intended meaning.

APOSTROPHE

Do not space to set off an apostrophe.

1. In a contraction, insert an apostrophe in place of the omitted letter or letters.

> have + not = haven't

> we + are = we're

> let + us = let's

> class of 2001 = class of '01

2. When indicating possession, the apostrophe means *belonging to every-thing to the left of the apostrophe.*

> lady's = belonging to the lady
>
> ladies' = belonging to the ladies
>
> children's = belonging to the children

Observe the following forms:

> man's, men's
>
> hostess's, hostesses'
>
> prince's, princes'

In set phrases, nouns ending in *-s* or *-ce* and followed by a word begin-ning with an *s* may form the possessive by adding an apostrophe only, with no following *s*.

> for goodness' sake
>
> for old times' sake

In compound nouns, the *'s* is added to the element nearest the object possessed.

> comptroller general's office
>
> John White, Jr.'s account
>
> attorney at law's fee

Joint possession is indicated by placing an apostrophe on the last element of a series; individual or alternative possession requires the use of an apostrophe on each element in the series.

> soldiers and sailors' home
>
> Brown & Nelson's store
>
> men's, women's, or children's clothing
>
> editor's or proofreader's opinion

Possessive pronouns do not take an apostrophe.

> its (belongs to it)
>
> theirs

Do not confuse *its* with the contraction *it's* (it is).

3. Use an apostrophe to form the plural of numbers and letters, and words referred to as words.

49'ers	a's, 7's, ¶'s
YMCA's	three R's
2's, 3's,	*but* twos and threes

Observe the following forms:

ands, ifs, and buts

do's and don'ts

ins and outs

Years may be typed as follows:

1990's or 1990s, the '90s, *not* the '90's

BRACKETS

Do not space to set off brackets from the material they enclose.

1. Brackets are used to enclose interpolations that are not specifically a part of transcribed or quoted material. An interpolation in brackets is often a correction, an explanation, or a warning that the material quoted is in error.

"The bill had *not* been paid." [Emphasis added.]

"July 3 [sic] is a national holiday."

2. Brackets are used to enclose parenthetical material within a parenthesis.

(The result [see fig. 2] is most surprising.)

COLON

Check carefully the spacing for colons. See each example below.

1. Use a colon after the salutation in a business letter.

Dear Board Member:

2. Use a colon (or a slash) to separate the initials of the dictator from the initials of the typist. Do not space after the colon.

RLT:pop

3. Use a colon to separate hours from minutes. Do not space after the colon.

    The eclipse occurred at 10:36 A.M.

4. A colon may (but need not always) be used to introduce a list, a long quotation, and a question.

    My question is this: Are you willing to punch a time clock?

5. Use a colon before a final clause that extends or explains what is said in the preceding matter.

    Railroading is not a variety of outdoor sport: it is a service.

6. Use a colon to indicate proportion and a double colon to indicate ratio. Space before and after the colon.

    concrete mixed 5 : 3 : 1

    1 : 2 :: 4 : 12

COMMA

Leave one space after the comma.

1. The salutation of a personal letter is followed by a comma.

    Dear Mary,

2. The complimentary close of a letter is ordinarily followed by a comma, though this use is optional.

    Cordially yours,

3. An appositive must be set off by commas.

    Jim Rodgers, my next-door neighbor, is an excellent baby-sitter.

4. A noun of address is set apart by commas.

    When you finish your homework, Jeff, please take out the garbage.

5. Use commas to set off parenthetical words.

    I think, however, that move might not be wise at this time.

6. When two or more adjectives (called coordinate adjectives) all modify a noun equally, all but the last must be followed by commas. Test: if you can add the word *and* between the adjectives without changing the sense of the sentence, then use commas.

    The jolly, fat man stood at the top of the stairs.

7. An introductory phrase or clause of five or more words is usually followed by a comma.

   Because the prisoner had a history of attempted jailbreaks, he was put under heavy guard.

8. After a short introductory phrase, the comma is optional. The comma should be used where needed for clarity.

   As a child she was a tomboy. (comma unnecessary)

   To Dan, Phil was friend as well as brother. (comma clarifies)

   In 1978, 300 people lost their lives in one air disaster. (comma clarifies)

9. A comma is not generally used before a subordinate clause that ends a sentence, though in long, unwieldy sentences, use of such a comma is optional.

10. A comma precedes the coordinating conjunction unless the two clauses are very short.

    The boy wanted to borrow a book from the library, but the librarian would not allow him to take it until he had paid his fines.

    Roy washed the dishes and Helen dried them.

11. Words, phrases, or clauses in a series are separated by commas. The use of a comma before *and* is optional. If the series ends in *etc.,* use a comma before *etc.* Do not use a comma after *etc.* in a series, even if the sentence continues.

    Coats, umbrellas, and boots should be placed in the closet at the end of the hall.

    Pencils, scissors, paper clips, etc. belong in your top desk drawer.

12. A comma separates a short direct quotation from the speaker.

    She said, "I must leave work on time today."

    "Tomorrow I begin my new job," he told us.

13. Use a comma to indicate that you have omitted a word or words, such as *of* or *of the.*

    President, XYZ Corporation

14. Use a comma to separate a name from a title or personal-name suffix.

    Linda Feiner, Chairman

    Carl Andrew Pforzheimer, Jr.

15. Use a comma when first and last names are reversed.

    Bernbach, Melissa

16. Use a comma to separate parts of addresses.

> Please come to a party at "The Old Mill" on Drake Road, Cheswold, Delaware.

The use of a comma between the name of a city and a two-letter postal abbreviation of a state is optional. Do not use a comma between the postal abbreviation of a state and the ZIP code.

> Cleveland OH 44114

> Scarsdale, NY 10583

17. A comma may or may not be used to separate parts of a date. But note that in European and military style dates the comma is never used.

> We will be leaving for Paris on October 6, 1999.

> I think she will arrive on April 14 1998.

> He joined the navy 31 October 1956.

18. A comma ordinarily separates thousands, millions, billions, and trillions. There is no space before or after the comma.

> 75,281,646

19. A nonrestrictive adjective phrase or clause must be set off by commas. A nonrestrictive phrase or clause is one that can be omitted without changing the meaning of the sentence.

> Our new sailboat, which has bright orange sails, is very seaworthy.

A restrictive phrase or clause is vital to the meaning of a sentence and cannot be omitted. Do not set it off with commas.

> A sailboat without sails is useless.

20. A comma must be used if the sentence might be subject to different interpretation without it.

> He saw the woman who had rejected him, and blushed.

21. If a pause would make the sentence clearer and easier to read, insert a comma.

> Inside the people were dancing. (confusing)

> Inside, the people were dancing. (clearer)

> After all crime must be punished. (confusing)

> After all, crime must be punished. (clearer)

The pause rule is not infallible, but it is an acceptable resort when all other comma rules fail to suit the situation.

DASH

Leave no space on either side of a dash.

1. You may use a dash—or parentheses—for emphasis or to set off an explanatory group of words.

   The tools of his trade—probe, mirror, cotton swabs—were neatly arranged on the dentist's tray.

2. Dashes must be used in pairs unless the set-off expression ends a sentence or marks a sudden break in thought or speech that leaves a sentence unfinished.

   The elections will take place in November—if we remain at peace.

   "No! Don't open that—"

ELLIPSIS

An ellipsis is three spaced periods. If the material deleted includes a final period, type four spaced periods.

1. An ellipsis indicates that something has been left out of a quoted text.

   "The country is excited from one end to the other by a great question of principle. On that question the Government has taken one side."

   becomes

   "The country is excited . . . by a great question . . . . On that question the Government has taken one side."

2. Four spaced periods may be used to indicate that a sentence or more has been omitted. To indicate the omission of an entire paragraph or more, terminate the preceding paragraph with a period and ellipsis (four dots) and initiate the next paragraph with an ellipsis (three dots).

EXCLAMATION MARK

Leave two spaces after the exclamation mark.

1. An exclamation mark indicates strong feeling or emotion.

   Congratulations! You broke the record.

   Rush! Perishable contents.

   Don't touch that dial!

HYPHEN

There is no space on either side of a hyphen unless it is used at the end of the line.

1. Use a hyphen to divide a word at the end of a line.

2. Use a hyphen to connect the elements of some compounds. (See the section on Compound Words.)

3. Use a hyphen to separate the letters of a spelled word.

   In front of the children she asked me if I had brought the c-a-n-d-y.

PARENTHESES

Do not space to set off parentheses from the material they enclose.

1. Use parentheses to set off matter that is not intended to be part of the main statement or that is not a grammatical element of the sentence, yet important enough to be included.

   This case (124 US 329) is not relevant.

   The result (see fig. 2) is most surprising.

   The Galesburg (IL) Chamber of Commerce

   A reference in parentheses at the end of a sentence is placed before the period, unless it is a complete sentence in itself.

   The specimens show great variation. (See pl. 6.)

   The specimens show great variation (pl. 6).

2. Use parentheses to enclose a figure following a spelled-out number in a legal document.

   The tenant shall vacate within thirty (30) days.

3. Use parentheses to enclose numbers or letters designating items in a series.

   The order of delivery will be (a) food, (b) medicines, and (c) clothing.

PERIOD

Leave two spaces after the period at the end of a sentence.

1. Use a period at the end of a sentence that makes a statement, gives a command, or makes a polite request in the form of a question that does not require an answer.

   I am brushing up on my archery skills.

   Give generously of yourself.

   Please read that menu to me.

2. Use a period after some abbreviations, including the initials of a personal name. (See the comprehensive section in this volume on abbreviations.)

   Gen. Robert E. Lee led the Confederate forces.

3. Use a period as a decimal point in numbers. Do not leave a space before or after the period.

   A sales tax of 5.5 percent amounts to $7.47 on a $135.80 purchase.

QUESTION MARK

Leave two spaces after the question mark.

1. Use a question mark at the end of a direct and genuine question.

   Why do you wish to return to Peru?

2. Do not use a question mark after an indirect question; use a period.

   He asked if they wanted to accompany him.

   I wonder where the fire is.

3. A direct question must end with a question mark even if the question does not encompass the entire sentence.

   "Daddy, are we there yet?" the child asked.

   The man cried "Who would do such a thing?" when he saw his vandalized car.

4. Use a question mark (within parentheses) to indicate uncertainty as to the correctness of a fact.

   John Carver, first governor of Plymouth colony, was born in 1575 (?) and died in 1621.

QUOTATION MARKS

Do not space to set off quotation marks from the material they enclose.

1. All directly quoted material must be enclosed by quotation marks. Words not quoted must remain outside the quotation marks.

   "If it is hot on Sunday," she said, "we will go to the beach."

2. An indirect quote must not be enclosed by quotation marks.

   She said that we might go to the beach on Sunday.

3. When a multiple-paragraph passage is quoted, each paragraph of the quotation must begin with quotation marks, but ending quotation marks are used only at the end of the last quoted paragraph.

4. A period always goes inside the quotation marks, whether the quotation marks are used to denote quoted material, to set off titles—such as chapters in a book or titles of short stories—or to isolate words used in a special sense.

   Jane explained, "The house is just around the corner."

   The first chapter of *The Andromeda Strain* is entitled "The Country of Lost Borders."

   Pornography is sold under the euphemism "adult books."

5. A comma always goes inside the quotation marks.

   "I really must go home," said the dinner guest.

   If your skills have become "rusty," you must study before you apply for the job.

   Three stories in Kurt Vonnegut's *Welcome to the Monkey House* are "Harrison Bergeron," "Next Door," and "Epicae."

6. A question mark goes inside the quotation marks if it is part of the quotation. If the whole sentence containing the quotation is a question, the question mark goes outside the quotation marks.

   He asked, "Was the airplane on time?"

   What did you really mean when you said, "I do"?

7. An exclamation mark goes inside the quotation marks if the quoted words are an exclamation, outside if the entire sentence including the quotation is an exclamation.

   The sentry shouted, "Drop your gun!"

   Save us from our "friends"!

8. A colon and a semicolon always go outside the quotation marks.

   He said, "War is destructive"; she added, "peace is constructive."

9. Words used in an unusual way may be placed inside quotation marks.

   A surfer who "hangs ten" is performing a tricky maneuver on a surfboard.

10. A quotation within a quotation may be set apart by single quotes (apostrophes).

    George said, "The philosophy 'I think, therefore I am' may be attributed to Descartes."

SEMICOLON

Always single-space after a semicolon.

1. A semicolon may be used to join two short, related independent clauses.

   Anne is working at the front desk on Monday; Pedro will take over on Tuesday.

   Two independent clauses must be joined by a conjunction (and comma) or by a semicolon (or colon) or must be written as two sentences. A semicolon never precedes a coordinating conjunction. The same two clauses may be written:

   Autumn had come to our mountain home, and the trees were almost bare. (Use a comma when conjoining longer independent clauses.)

   Autumn had come to our mountain home; the trees were almost bare. (Use a semicolon when conjoining two independent clauses.)

   Autumn had come to our mountain home. The trees were almost bare.

2. A semicolon may be used to join two independent clauses which are connected by an adverb such as *however, therefore, otherwise,* or *nevertheless.* The adverb must be followed by a comma.

   We went to the track; however, the race was rained out.

   You may use a semicolon to join one clause with the next; however, you will not be incorrect if you choose to write two separate sentences.

   We went to the track. However, the race was rained out.

   If you are uncertain how to use the semicolon to connect independent clauses, write two sentences instead.

3. A semicolon should be used to separate a series of phrases or clauses, especially when those phrases and clauses contain commas.

> The old gentleman's heirs were Margaret Whitlock, his half-sister; James Bagley, the butler; William Frame, companion to his late cousin, Robert Bone; and his favorite charity, the Salvation Army.

CAPITALIZATION

1. Capitalize the first word of a complete sentence.

> Your favorite television program is on now.

2. Capitalize the first word of a quoted sentence.

> The bookkeeper said, "Please identify your personal long-distance phone calls."

Do *not* capitalize the first word within quotation marks if it does not begin a complete sentence.

> "I tore my stocking," she told us, "because the drawer was left open."

3. Capitalize the letter *I* when it stands alone.

4. Capitalize the first letter of the first, last, and each important word in the title of a book, play, article, etc.

> "The Mystery of the Green Ghost"
>
> A Night at the Opera

5. Capitalize a title when it is used with the name of a person, group, or document.

> Senator Jane Doe is a leading figure in the Republican Party.

Do *not* capitalize the same type of title when it does not make a specific reference.

> The congressman is a liberal; his opponent is a conservative.
>
> It would be useful for our club to write a constitution.

6. Capitalize days of the week, months of the year, and holidays, but do *not* capitalize the seasons.

> Labor Day, the last holiday of the summer, falls on the first Monday in September.

7. Capitalize the points of the compass only when referring to a specific place or region.

> Many retired persons spend the winter in the South.

Do not capitalize the points of the compass when they refer to a direction.

> The birds were flying south.

8. The only school subjects that are regularly capitalized are languages and specific place names used as modifiers.

> Next year we will offer French, English literature, biology, mathematics, European history, and ancient philosophy.

9. A noun not regularly capitalized should be capitalized when it is used as part of a proper name.

> Yesterday I visited Uncle Fester, my favorite uncle.

10. In a letter, capitalize all titles in the address and closing.

> Mr. John Jones, President

> Mary Smith, Chairman of the Board

Capitalize the first and last words, titles, and proper names in the salutation.

> Dear Dr. Williams,

> My dear Sir:

Capitalize only the first word in a complimentary closing.

> Very truly yours,

11. Capitalize all proper names—including, but not limited to, the names of people (*John F. Smith*); buildings (*World Trade Center*); events (*Veterans Day*); places (*Panama*) and words formed using those places (*Panamanian*); organizations (*The United Fund*); and words referring to a sole God (*Allah*).

Some words derived from proper names have lost their proper-name meaning and have acquired an independent meaning in a different context. Many of these words are no longer capitalized. Below is a list of some lowercased derivatives of proper names. Consult a dictionary if in doubt.

angstrom unit	artesian well	bourbon whisky
apache (Paris)	astrakhan fabric	bowie knife
argyle wool	bologna sausage	britannia metal

burley tobacco	herculean task	neon light
cashmere shawl	holland cloth	newton
chesterfield coat	italic type	oriental rug
china clay	japan varnish	osnaburg cloth
chinook salmon	jersey fabric	oxford cloth
coulumb	joule	parkerhouse roll
curie	klieg light	pasteurized milk
degaussing apparatus	knickerbocker	petri dish
delftware	kraft paper	philistinism
diesel engine	lambert	pitman arm
dotted swiss	lynch law	pitot-static tube
fedora hat	lyonnaise potatoes	portland cement
frankfurter	macadamized road	quisling
frankfurt sausage	madras cloth	quixotic idea
fuller's earth	maraschino cherry	roentgen
gargantuan	maxwell	surah silk
gauss	mercerized fabric	timothy grass
georgette crepe	merino sheep	utopianism
gilbert	morocco leather	venturi tube
graham bread	navy blue	zeppelin

NUMBERS

SPELLED OUT

1. Two general rules apply to expressing numbers. One or the other should be followed consistently within a piece of writing.

   a. Spell out numbers through nine; use figures from 10 on.

   two people

   three times as large

   14 recommendations

    b. Spell out numbers through ninety-nine; use figures from 100 on.

        eighty-six apples

        forty people

        163 pages

2. Any number that begins a sentence:

    Nineteen eighty-three was the company's best year.

    Two hundred forty workers were hired.

3. Centuries, round numbers, and indefinite expressions:

    hundreds of men

    the early seventies, *but* the 1890s, mid-1964

    the nineteenth century

4. Large numbers in very formal writing such as legal work. Use the following forms as models:

    sixteen hundred and twenty

    exactly four thousand

    fifty-two thousand one hundred and ninety-five

    nineteen hundred and eighty-four

5. Fractions standing alone or followed by *of a* or *of an:*

    one-half inch

    three-fourths of a pie

    one-third of an acre

6. Ordinal numbers less than one hundred:

    twentieth century

    eighty-second congress

    Fifth Fleet

    Twelfth Avenue

EXPRESSED IN FIGURES

1. Numbers over one hundred within ordinary text:

   Enrollment reached 16,847.

   952 ballots

   101 districts

2. All numbers in tabular material.

3. Measurements of physical properties in scientific or technical writing, and any number used with a symbol or abbreviated unit of measurement:

20/20 vision	43 mm
6 pounds	13 lb. 2 oz.
32° F	1 yd.
17½"	8:30 A.M.

4. Serial numbers, including numbers designating the pages and other parts of a book:

   Bulletin 756

   pages 322–345

   diagram 4

5. Years:

53 B.C.	in A.D. 7
1925	1255 B.C.E.

6. Fractions that would be awkward if spelled out:

   8½-by-11-inch bond

7. Decimal fractions and percentages:

   10.5 percent return

   $83.95

   a grade point average of 3.42

8. All numbers referring to the same category in a single passage if the largest is over one hundred:

   Of the 137 delegates at the twelve o'clock meeting, only 9 opposed the plan.

LARGE NUMBERS

Large numbers are usually expressed in figures; however, numbers from a million up which end in four or more zeros may be expressed in text by combining figures and words. In the examples that follow, preference is based on the ease with which the number can be grasped in reading.

Figures:	299,789,655
Preferred:	299,789,655
Figures:	$12,000,000
Preferred:	$12 million
Acceptable:	12 million dollars
Figures:	3,250,000
Preferred:	3.25 million
Acceptable:	3¼ million
or:	three and one-fourth million
or:	three and one-quarter million
Figures:	9,000,000 to 1,000,000,000
Preferred:	9 million to 1 billion
Acceptable:	nine million to one billion

ROMAN NUMERALS

It is generally preferable to use Arabic numbers, as they are more easily understood than Roman numerals.

A repeated letter repeats its value; a letter placed after one of greater value adds to it; a letter placed before one of greater value subtracts from it; a dashline over a letter denotes multiplied by 1,000.

I	1	X	10	XL	40
II	2	XV	15	XLV	45
III	3	XIX	19	XLIX	49
IV	4	XX	20	L	50
V	5	XXV	25	LV	55
VI	6	XXIX	29	LIX	59
VII	7	XXX	30	LX	60
VIII	8	XXXV	35	LXV	65
IX	9	XXXIX	39	LXIX	69

LXX	70	C	100	CM	900
LXXV	75	CL	150	M	1,000
LXXIX	79	CC	200	MD	1,500
LXXX	80	CCC	300	MM	2,000
LXXXV	85	CD	400	MMM	3,000
LXXXIX	89	D	500	MMMM or MV	4,000
XC	90	DC	600		
XCV	95	DCC	700	V	5,000
XCIX	99	DCCC	800	M	1,000,000

Dates

MDC	1600	MCMLXX	1970
MDCC	1700	MCMLXXX	1980
MDCCC	1800	MCMXC	1990
MCM or MDCCCC	1900	MM	2000
MCMX	1910	MMX	2010
MCMXX	1920	MMXX	2020
MCMXXX	1930	MMXXX	2030
MCMXL	1940	MMXL	2040
MCML	1950	MML	2050
MCMLX	1960	MMLX	2060

COMPOUND WORDS

A compound is a union of two or more words; it conveys a unit idea that is not as clearly or quickly conveyed by the component words in unconnected succession. Compounds may be spelled open (with a space), solid (with no space), or with a hyphen.

Since ours is a fluid, changing language, the rules that follow can only provide guidelines to common practice. Word forms constantly undergo modification. Two-word forms often acquire the hyphen first and are later printed solid. Sometimes the transition is from open to solid, bypassing the hyphenated form. The trend recently has been toward solid spellings; for instance, the once-common spellings *life style* and *life-style* have now generally given way to *lifestyle*. Check a current, reliable dictionary for guidance.

GENERAL RULES

1. In general, omit the hyphen when words appear in regular order and the omission causes no ambiguity in sense or sound.

banking hours	fellow citizen	real estate
blood pressure	living costs	rock candy
book value	palm oil	training ship
census taker	patent right	violin teacher

2. Words are usually combined to express a literal or nonliteral (figurative) unit idea that would not be as clearly expressed in unconnected succession.

afterglow	eye-opener	newsprint
bookkeeping	forget-me-not	right-handed
cupboard	gentleman	whitewash

3. Unless otherwise indicated, a derivative of a compound, that is, a compound which is derived from another compound, retains the solid or hyphenated form of the original compound.

coldbloodedness	outlawry	X-rayer
footnoting	praiseworthiness	Y-shaped
ill-advisable	railroader	

4. Except after the short prefixes *co, de, pre, pro,* and *re,* which are generally typed solid, a hyphen is used to avoid doubling the same vowel or tripling the same consonant.

Solid	**Hypenated**
antiaircraft	semi-independent
cooperation	thimble-eye
preexisting	ultra-atomic
semiannual	shell-like

SOLID COMPOUNDS

1. Consider solid (as one word) two nouns that form a third when the compound has only one primary accent, especially when the prefixed noun consists of only one syllable or when one of the elements loses its original accent.

airship	cupboard	footnote
bathroom	dressmaker	locksmith
bookseller	fishmonger	workman

2. Consider solid a noun consisting of a short verb and a terminal adverb, except when the use of the solid form would interfere with comprehension.

blowout	pickup	*BUT* cut-in
flareback	runoff	run-in
giveaway	setup	tie-in
hangover	throwaway	
makeready		

3. Compounds beginning with the following nouns are usually considered solid.

book(end)	mill(work)	snow(fall)
eye	play	way
horse	school	wood
house	shop	work

4. Compounds ending in the following are usually considered solid, especially when the prefixed word consists of one syllable.

(blue)berry	(devil)fish	(lime)light
blossom	flower	like
boat	grower	wise
book	hearted	woman
borne	holder	maker
bound	house	making
brained	keeper	man
bush	keeping	master

mate	stone	woman
mill	store	wood
mistress	tail	work
monger	tight	worker
owner	time (*not* clock)	working
piece	ward	worm
power	way	wort
proof	weed	writer
room	wide	writing
shop	wise	yard
smith		

5. Consider solid *any, every, no,* and *some* when combined with *body, thing,* and *where*. When *one* is the second element, print as two words if meaning a single or particular person or thing. To avoid mispronunciation, print *no one* as two words at all times.

anybody	everywhere	somebody
anything	everyone	something
anywhere	nobody	somewhere
anyone	nothing	someone
everybody	nowhere	
everything	no one	

BUT Any one of us may stay.

Every one of the pilots is responsible.

6. Consider solid compound personal pronouns.

herself	oneself	thyself
himself	ourselves	yourself
itself	themselves	yourselves
myself		

7. Consider solid compass directions consisting of two points, but use a hyphen after the first point when three points are combined.

northeast	north-northwest
southwest	south-southeast

UNIT MODIFIERS

1. Except as indicated in the other rules in this chapter, type a hyphen between words, or abbreviations and words, combined to form a unit modifier immediately preceding the word modified. This applies particularly to combinations in which the second element is a present or past participle.

Baltimore-Washington road	long-term loan
collective-bargaining talks	long-term-payment loan
contested-election case	lump-sum payment
contract-bar rule	most-favored-nation clause
drought-stricken area	multiple-purpose uses
English-speaking nation	no-par-value stock
fire-tested material	part-time personnel
Federal-State-local cooperation	rust-resistant covering
German-English descent	service-connected disability
guided-missile program	tool-and-die maker
hard-of-hearing class	two-inch-diameter pipe
high-speed line	ten-word telegram
large-scale project	a 4-percent increase, the 10-percent rise
law-abiding citizen	U.S.-owned property

2. Where meaning is clear and readability is not aided, it is not necessary to use a hyphen to form a temporary (or made) compound. Restraint should be exercised in forming unnecessary combinations of words used in normal sequence.

atomic energy power	high school student; elementary school grade
bituminous coal industry	income tax form
child welfare plan	land bank loan
civil rights case	land use program
civil service examination	life insurance company
durable goods industry	mutual security funds
flood control study	national defense appropriation
free enterprise system	

natural gas company

parcel post delivery

per capita expenditure

portland cement plant

production credit loan

public utility plant

real estate tax

small businessman

Social Security pension

soil conservation measures

special delivery mail

speech correction class

BUT no-growth policy (readability aided); *NOT* no growth policy

3. When the second element is a present or past participle and the unit modifier does not immediately precede the thing modified, omit the hyphen.

The effects were far reaching.

The shale was oil bearing.

The area is drought stricken.

The reporters are best informed.

These cars are higher priced.

4. Use without a hyphen a two-word modifier when the first element is a comparative or superlative.

better drained soil

best liked books

higher level decision

highest priced apartment

larger sized dress

better paying job

lower income group

BUT lowercase, uppercase type (printing)

upperclassman

bestseller (noun)

lighter-than-air craft

higher-than-market price

5. Do not use a hyphen in a two-word unit modifier when the first element is an adverb ending in -ly. Do not use hyphens in a three-word unit modifier the first two elements of which are adverbs.

eagerly awaited moment

wholly owned subsidiary

unusually well preserved specimen

very well defined usage

longer than usual lunch period

very well worth reading

not too distant future

often heard phrase

> *BUT* still-new car, because still is an adverb and new is an adjective
>
> ever-rising flood

> still-lingering doubt
>
> well-known lawyer
>
> well-kept farm

6. Proper nouns used as unit modifiers—either in their basic or derived form—retain their original form, but the hyphen is used after combining forms of proper nouns.

Latin American countries	*BUT* Winston-Salem festival
North Carolina roads	Washington–Wilkes-Barre route
a Mexican American	African-American program
South American trade	Anglo-Saxon period

7. Do not confuse a modifier with the word it modifies.

American flagship	light blue hat
American-flag ship	old-clothes man
average taxpayer	prudent stockholder
canning factory	service men and women
competent shoemaker	stockownership
elderly clothesman	tomato-canning factory
elementary school teacher	well-trained schoolteacher
gallant serviceman	wooden-shoe maker
income-tax payer	

8. Where two or more hyphenated compounds have a common basic element and this element is omitted in all but the last term, the hyphens are retained.

two- to three-ton trucks

8-, 10-, and 16-foot boards

moss- and ivy-covered walls, *NOT* moss and ivy-covered walls

long- and short-term money rates, *NOT* long and short-term money rates

BUT twofold or threefold, *NOT* two or threefold

goat, sheep, and calf skins, *NOT* goat, sheep, and calfskins

American owned and managed companies

preoperative and postoperative examination

9. Omit the hyphen in a unit modifier containing a letter or numeral as its second element.

abstract B pages	grade A milk
article 3 provisions	class II railroad

PREFIXES, SUFFIXES, AND COMBINING FORMS

1. Compounds formed with prefixes and suffixes are typed solid, except as indicated elsewhere.

*after*birth	*in*bound	oper*ate*
*Anglo*mania	*infra*red	*out*back
*ante*date	inner*most*	out*let*
*anti*slavery	*inter*view	*over*act
*bi*weekly	*intra*specific	*pan*cosmic
*by*law	*intro*vert	*para*centric
*circum*navigation	*iso*metric	partner*ship*
*cis*alpine	kilo*gram*	*peri*patetic
clock*wise*	lone*some*	*plano*graphy
*co*operate	man*hood*	plebis*cite*
*contra*position	*macro*biotics	*poly*morph
*counter*charge	meat*less*	port*able*
cover*age*	*meso*thorax	*post*script
*de*cry	*meta*genesis	*pre*exist
*demi*tasse	*micro*phone	*pro*consul
*ex*communicate	*mis*state	procure*ment*
*extra*curricular	*mono*gram	*pseudo*science
*fore*tell	*multi*color	pump*kin*
geo*graphy*	*neo*phyte	*re*enact
home*stead*	*non*neutral	*retro*spect
*hyper*sensitive	north*ward*	self*ish*
*hypo*center	*off*set	*semi*official

spoon*ful*	*thermo*couple	twenty*fold*
*step*father	*trans*onic	*ultra*violet
*sub*group	*trans*ship	*under*coat
*super*market	*tri*color	*un*necessary

2. Consider solid words ending in *like,* but use a hyphen to avoid tripling a consonant or when the first element is a proper name.

lifelike	*BUT* bell-like
lilylike	Florida-like
girllike	Truman-like

3. Use a hyphen or hyphens to prevent mispronunciation, to insure a definite accent on each element of the compound, or to avoid ambiguity.

anti-hog-cholera	re-cover (cover serum again)
co-op	re-sort (sort again)
mid-ice	re-treat (treat again)
non-civil-service	un-ionized position
non-tumor-bearing tissue	

4. Use with a hyphen the prefixes *ex, self,* and *quasi.*

ex-governor	quasi-academic	self-control
ex-serviceman	quasi-argument	self-educated
ex-trader	quasi-corporate	*BUT* selfhood
ex-vice-president	quasi-young	selfsame

5. Unless usage demands otherwise, use a hyphen to join a prefix or combining form to a capitalized word. (The hyphen is retained in words of this class set in caps.)

anti-Arab	post–World War II	*BUT* nongovernmental
un-American	post–Second World War	overanglicize
non-Government	pro-British	*OR* transatlantic

6. The adjectives *elect* and *designate,* as the last element of a title, require a hyphen.

president-elect	ambassador-designate
mayor-elect	minister-designate

NUMERICAL, SCIENTIFIC, AND TECHNICAL COMPOUNDS

1. Do not type a hyphen in scientific terms (names of chemicals, diseases, animals, insects, plants) used as unit modifiers if no hyphen appears in their original form.

carbon monoxide poisoning	*BUT* screw-worm raising
guinea pig raising	Russian-olive plantings
methyl bromide solution	white-pine weevil

2. Chemical elements used in combination with figures use a hyphen, except with superior figures.

polonium-210

uranium-235; *BUT* U^{225}; Sr^{90}; 92^{U234}

Freon-12

3. Use a hyphen between the elements of technical compound units of measurement.

candle-hour	light-year
horsepower-hour	passenger-mile
kilowatt-hour	

IMPROVISED COMPOUNDS

1. Use with a hyphen the elements of an improvised compound.

blue-pencil (v.)	one-man-one-vote principle
18-year-old (n.)	stick-in-the-mud (n.)
first-come-first-served basis	let-George-do-it attitude
know-it-all (n.)	how-to-be-beautiful course
know-how (n.)	hard-and-fast rule
make-believe (n.)	penny-wise and pound-foolish policy

BUT a basis of first come, first served; easy come, easy go

2. Use a hyphen to join a single capital letter to a noun or participle.

H-bomb	X-raying
I-beam	T-shaped
V-necked	U-boat

USAGE

This section is a guide to the correct use of words and phrases that are frequently misused.

abbreviate—means *to shorten by omitting.*
abridge—means *to shorten by condensing.*
   New York is *abbreviated* to NY, Tennessee to TN.
   In order to save time in the reading, the report was *abridged.*

ability—means a *developed, actual* power.
capacity—means an *undeveloped, potential* power.
   He now has fair writing *ability,* but additional courses in college will
      develop his *capacity* beyond the average level.

above—Avoid *above* except in business forms where it may be used in refer-
   ence to a preceding part of the text.
   In normal writing use *foregoing* or *preceding,* instead of *above.*
   Unacceptable: The *above* books are available in the library.
   Acceptable: The *above* prices are subject to change without notice.

accede—means *to agree with.*
concede—means *to yield,* but not necessarily in agreement.
exceed—means *to be more than.*
   We *accede* to your request for more evidence.
   The candidate *conceded* the victory to his opponent.
   My expenses often *exceed* my income.

accept—means *to take when offered.*
except—means *excluding.* (preposition)
except—means *to leave out.* (verb)
   I *accept* the proposition that all men are created equal.
   All eighteen-year-olds *except* seniors will be called.
   The final report will *except* all data that doesn't conform to standards.

access—means *availability.*
excess—means *too much.*
> The lawyer was given *access* to the grand jury records.
> Their expenditures this month are far in *excess* of their income.

in accord with—means in agreement with *a person.*
> I am *in accord with* you about this.
in accordance with—means in agreement with a *thing.*
> The police officer acted *in accordance with* the law.

acoustics—when used as a singular noun means the *science* of sound.
> *Acoustics* is a subdivision of physics.

acoustics—when used as a plural noun denotes the *qualities* of sound.
> The *acoustics* of Carnegie Hall are incomparable.

acquiesce in—means *to accept,* with or without objection.
> Although there is some doubt about your plan, I *acquiesce in* its adoption.

ad—is a colloquial, clipped form for *advertisement;* it is not to be used in formal writing. Other colloquial words of this type are *exam* (*examination*), *auto* (*automobile*), *lab* (*laboratory*), *demo* (*demonstration*), and *dorm* (*dormitory*).

adapt—means *to adjust* or *change.*
adopt—means to *take as one's own.*
adept—means *skillful.*
> Children can *adapt* to changing conditions very easily.
> The war orphan was *adopted* by the general and his wife.
> Proper instruction makes children *adept* in various games.

addicted to—means *accustomed to by strong habit.*
subject to—means *exposed to* or *liable to.*
> People *addicted to* drugs or alcohol need constant medical care.
> The coast of Wales is *subject to* extremely heavy fogs.

addition—means *the act or process of adding.*
edition—means *a printing of a publication.*
> In *addition* to a dictionary, she always used a thesaurus.
> The first *edition* of Shakespeare's plays appeared in 1623.

advantage—means *a superior position.*
benefit—means *a favor conferred or earned* (as a profit).
> He had an *advantage* in experience over his opponent.
> The rules were changed for her *benefit.*
> NOTE: To *take* advantage *of,* to *have* an advantage *over.*

adverse—means *unfavorable*.
averse—means *disliking* or *reluctant*.
He took the *adverse* decision in poor spirit.
Many students are *averse* to criticism by their classmates.

affect—means *to influence* or *to pretend*. (a verb)
effect—means *an influence* or *result*. (a noun)
effect—means *to bring about*. (a verb)
Your education must *affect* your future.
He *affected* a great love for opera, though in fact it bored him.
The *effect* of the last war is still being felt.
A diploma *effected* a tremendous change in his attitude.

affection—means *feeling*.
affectation—means *pose* or *artificial behavior*.
Alumni often develop a strong *affection* for their former schools.
The *affectation* of a Harvard accent is no guarantee of success.

affinity—means an *attraction to a person or thing*.
infinity—means an *unlimited time, space, or quantity*.
She has an *affinity* for men with beards.
It is impossible to visualize an *infinity* of anything.

after—is unnecessary with the past participle.
Not: *After having checked* the timetable, she left.
But: *Having checked* the timetable, she left.

aggravate—means *to make worse*.
exasperate—means *to irritate* or *annoy*.
Her cold was *aggravated* by faulty medication.
His inability to make a quick recovery *exasperated* him exceedingly.

ain't—is an unacceptable contraction for *am not, are not,* or *is not*.

aisle—is *a passageway* between seats.
isle—is *a small island*.

alibi—is an explanation on *the basis of being in another place*.
excuse—is an explanation on *any basis*.
The *alibi* offered at the trial was that he was twenty miles away from the
   scene of the crime.
His *excuse* for failing on the test was that he was sick.

alimentary—refers to *the process of nutrition.*
elementary—means *primary.*
    The *alimentary* canal includes the stomach and the intestines.
    Elementary education is the foundation of all human development.

all ready—means *everybody or everything ready.*
already—means *previously.*
    They were *all ready* to write when the teacher arrived.
    They had *already* begun writing when the teacher arrived.

all-round—means *versatile* or *general.*
all around—means *all over a given area.*
    Rafer Johnson, decathlon champion, is an *all-round* athlete.
    The police were scouring for evidence for miles *all around.*

all together—means *everybody or everything together.*
altogether—means *completely.*
    The boys and girls sang *all together.*
    This was *altogether* strange for a person of her age.

all ways—means *in every possible way.*
always—means *at all times.*
    She was in *all ways* acceptable to the voters.
    Their reputation had *always* been spotless.

allow—means *to give permission.*
    Acceptable: The teacher *allows* adequate time for study in class.
    Unacceptable: I *allow* I haven't ever seen anything like this.

allude—means *to make an indirect reference to.*
elude—means *to escape from.*
    Only incidentally does Coleridge *allude* to Shakespeare's puns.
    It is almost impossible for one to *elude* tax collectors.

allusion—means *an indirect reference.*
illusion—means *a deception of the eye or mind.*
    The student made *allusions* to his teacher's habits.
    Illusions of the mind, unlike those of the eye, cannot be corrected with
        glasses.

alongside of—means *side by side with.*
alongside—means *parallel to the side.*
    Bill stood *alongside of* Henry.
    Park the car *alongside* the curb.

allot—means *apportion.*
alot—is an unacceptable spelling for *a lot. A lot,* meaning *very much,* should
be avoided in formal writing.
They *allotted* the prize money equally among the winners.
Not: We like the proposal *a lot.*
But: We like the proposal *very much.*

alumnus—means *a male graduate.*
alumna—means *a female graduate.*
With the granting of the diploma, he became an *alumnus* of the school.
She is an *alumna* of Hunter College.
NOTE: The masculine plural form of *alumnus* is *alumni* (*-ni* rhymes with
hi). The feminine plural form is *alumnae* (*-ae* rhymes with *key*). Use
alumni when referring to both men and women.

amend—means *to correct.*
emend—means *to correct a literary work; to edit.*
Our Constitution, as *amended* by the Bill of Rights, was finally ratified.
Before publication, several chapters of the book had to be *emended.*

among—is used with *more than two persons or things.*
NOTE: *Amongst* should be avoided.
between—is used with *two persons or things.*
The inheritance was equally divided *among* the four children.
The business, however, was divided *between* the oldest and the youngest
one.

amount—applies to quantities *that cannot be counted one by one.*
number—applies to quantities *that can be counted one by one.*
A large *amount* of grain was delivered to the store.
A large *number* of bags were delivered.

and etc.—is unacceptable for *etc.,* a Latin abbreviation meaning *and other
things.* It is best to use *etc.* only when you are sure your reader will understand what other items or kinds of items you are referring to—for instance,
when referring to a list of things already mentioned in full. Beware of *etc.*
as a cover for vague or sloppy thinking.

annual—means *yearly.*
biannual and **semiannual**—mean *twice a year.*
biennial—means *once in two years, every two years.*
The Saint Patrick's Day parade is an *annual* event in New York City.
Some schools have *biannual* promotion, in January and June.
The *biennial* election of congressmen is held in the even numbered years.

another such—is *acceptable.*
such another—is *unacceptable.*
  Another such error may lead to legal prosecution.
  After his illness, he seemed *quite another* (**not** *such another*) person from
    what he had been.

ante—is a prefix meaning *before.*
anti—is a prefix meaning *against.*
  The *ante*chamber is the room just before the main room.
  An *anti*fascist is one who is opposed to fascists.

anxious—means *worried.*
eager—means *keenly desirous.*
  We were *anxious* about our first airplane flight.
  We are *eager* to fly again.

Any other—indicates a comparison. Do not use *any* by itself for a comparison.
  He likes France better than *any other* country.

anywheres—is *unacceptable.*
anywhere—is *acceptable.*
  We can't find it *anywhere.*
  Similarly, use *nowhere* (**not** *nowheres*) and *somewhere* (**not** *somewheres*).

appraise—means *to set a value.*
apprise—means *to inform.*
  The jeweler *appraised* the diamond at a very high value.
  We were *apprised* of their arrival by the honking of the car horn.

apprehend—means to *catch the meaning of something.*
comprehend—means *to understand a thing completely.*
  At first I didn't *apprehend* his true intent.
  It is often difficult to *comprehend* the Euclidean postulates.
  NOTE: Apprehend may also mean to take into custody.
  The sheriff succeeded in *apprehending* the rustler.

apt—suggests *habitual behavior.*
likely—suggests *probable behavior.*
liable—suggests an *exposure to something harmful.*
  Children are *apt* to be rather lazy in the morning.
  A cat, if annoyed, is *likely* to scratch.
  Cheating on a test may make one *liable* to expulsion from school.

argue—means *to prove something by logical methods.*
quarrel—means *to dispute without reason or logic.*
  The opposing lawyers *argued* before the judge.
  The lawyers became emotional and *quarreled.*

artisan—means *mechanic* or *craftsman.*
artist—means *one who practices the fine arts.*
  Many *artisans* participated in the building of the Sistine Chapel.
  The basic design, however, was prepared by the *artist* Michelangelo.

as—(used as a conjunction) is followed by a verb.
like—(used as a preposition) is not followed by a verb.
  Do *as* I do, not *as* I say.
  Try not to behave *like* a child.
  Unacceptable: He acts *like* I do.

as good as—should be used *for comparisons only.*
  This motel is *as good as* the next one.
  Do not use *as good as* to mean *practically.*
  Unacceptable: They *as good as* promised us a place in the hall.
  Acceptable: They *practically* promised us a place in the hall.

as if—is correctly used in the expression, "He talked *as if* his jaw hurt him."
  Unacceptable: "He talked *like* his jaw hurt him."

as per—is poor usage for *according to* or *in accordance with.*
  He assembled the bicycle *in accordance with* (**not** *as per*) the directions.

as to whether—is *unacceptable. Whether* includes the unnecessary words *as to.*
  I don't know *whether* it is going to rain.

ascent—is *the act of rising.*
assent—means *approval.*
  The *ascent* to the top of the mountain was perilous.
  Congress gave its *assent* to the President's emergency directive.

assay—means *to try* or *experiment.*
essay—means *to make an intellectual effort.*
  We shall *assay* the ascent of the mountain tomorrow.
  Why not *essay* a description of the mountain in composition?

astonish—means *to strike with sudden wonder.*
surprise—means *to catch unaware.*
 The extreme violence of the hurricane *astonished* everybody.
 A heat wave in January would *surprise* us.

at—should be avoided where it does not contribute to the meaning.
 Acceptable: Where shall I meet you?
 Unacceptable: Where shall we meet *at*?
at about—should not be used for *about.*
 The group will arrive *about* noon.

attend to—means *to take care of.*
tend to—means *to be inclined to.*
 One of the clerks will *attend to* my mail in my absence.
 Lazy people *tend to* lack ambition.

audience—means *a group of listeners.*
spectators—refers to *a group of watchers.*
 Leonard Bernstein conducted a concert for the school *audience.*
 The slow baseball game bored the *spectators.*
 NOTE: A group that both watches and listens is called an *audience.*

average—means *conforming to norms or standards.*
ordinary—means *usual, customary,* or *without distinction.*
 A book of about 300 pages is of *average* length.
 The contents of the book were rather *ordinary.*

back—should **not** be used with such words as *refer* and *return* since the
 prefix *re-* means *back.*
 Refer to the text if you have difficulty recalling the facts.

balance—meaning *remainder,* is *acceptable* only in commercial usage. Use
 remainder or *rest* otherwise.
 Even after the withdrawal, his bank *balance* was considerable.
 Three of the students voted for John; the *rest* voted for Jim.

bazaar—is a *marketplace* or a *fair.*
bizarre—means *odd* or *strange.*
 We are going to the *bazaar* to buy things.
 He dresses in a *bizarre* manner.

being that—is *unacceptable* for *since* or *because.*
 Acceptable: Since you have come a long way, why not remain here for the
 night.

berth—is a *resting place.*
birth—means *the beginning of life.*
The new liner was given a wide *berth* in the harbor.
She was a fortunate woman from *birth.*

beside—means *close to.*
besides—means *in addition.*
He lived *beside* the stream.
He found wildflowers and weeds *besides.*

better—means *recovering.*
well—means *completely recovered.*
Ivan is *better* now than he was a week ago.
In a few more weeks, he will be *well.*

both—means *two considered together.*
each—means *one of two or more.*
Both of the applicants qualified for the position.
Each applicant was given a generous reference.

bouillon—is a *soup.*
bullion—means *gold* or *silver* in the form of bars.
This restaurant serves tasty *bouillon.*
A mint makes coins out of *bullion.*

breath—means an *intake of air.*
breathe—means *to draw air in and give it out.*
breadth—means *width.*
Before you dive in, take a very deep *breath.*
It is impossible *to breathe* under water.
In a square, the *breadth* is equal to the length.

bridal—means *of a wedding.*
bridle—means to *hold back.*
The *bridal* party was late to the church.
You must learn to *bridle* your temper.

bring—means *to carry toward the person who is speaking.*
take—means *to carry away from the speaker.*
Bring the books here.
Take your raincoat with you when you go out.

broach—means *to mention for the first time.*
brooch—means an *ornament* for clothing.
At the meeting, one of the speakers *broached* the question of salary increases.
The model was wearing an expensive *brooch.*

bunch—refers to *things.*
group—refers to *persons* or *things.*
This looks like a delicious *bunch* of bananas.
What a well-behaved *group* of children!
NOTE: The colloquial use of *bunch* applied to *persons* should be avoided.

burst—is acceptable for broke.
bust—is unacceptable for broke (or broken).
Acceptable: The balloon burst.
Unacceptable: My pen is busted.

business—is sometimes incorrectly used for *work.*
Unacceptable: I went to *business* very late today.
Acceptable: He owns a thriving *business.*

but—should **not** be used after the expression *cannot help.*
Acceptable: One cannot help noticing the errors.
Unacceptable: One cannot help but notice . . .

byword—is *a pet expression.*
password—is *a secret word uttered to gain passage.*
In ancient Greece, truth and beauty were *bywords.*
The sentry asked the scout for the *password.*

calculate—means *to determine mathematically.* It does **not** mean *to think.*
Some students still know how to *calculate* on an abacus.
Unacceptable: I *calculate* it's going to rain.

calendar—is *a system of time.*
calender—is *a smoothing and glazing machine.*
colander—is *a kind of sieve.*
In this part of the world, most people prefer the twelve-month *calendar.*
In ceramic work, the potting wheel and the *calender* are indispensable.
Vegetables should be washed in a *colander* before cooking.

Calvary—is *the name of the place of the Crucifixion.*
cavalry—is *a military unit on horseback.*
Calvary and Gethsemane are place-names in the Bible.
Most of our modern *cavalry* is now motorized.

can—means *physically able.*
may—implies *permission.*
    I *can* lift this chair over my head.
    You *may* leave after you finish your work.

cannon—is a *gun* for heavy firing.
canon—is a *rule* or *law,* usually of a church.
    Don't remain near the *cannon* when it is being fired.
    Churchgoers are expected to observe the *canons.*

cannot help—must be followed by an *-ing* form.
    We cannot help *feeling* (**not** *feel*) distressed about this.
    NOTE: *cannot help but* is unacceptable.

can't hardly—is a double negative. It is *unacceptable.*
    The child *can hardly* walk in those shoes.

capital—is *the city* or *money.*
capitol—is *the building.*
    Paris is the *capital* of France.
    The *Capitol* in Washington is occupied by the Congress. (The Washington
        Capitol is capitalized.)
    NOTE: *capital* also means wealth.

catalog—is a *systematic list.* (also **catalogue**)
category—is a *class* of things.
    The item is precisely described in the sales *catalog.*
    A trowel is included in the *category* of farm tools.

cease—means *to end.*
seize—means *to take hold of.*
    Will you please *cease* making those sounds?
    Seize the cat as it rounds the corner.

censer—is *a container which holds burning incense.*
censor—means *to examine for the purpose of judging moral aspects.*
censure—means *to find fault with.*
    One often finds a *censer* in church.
    The government *censors* films in some countries.
    She *censured* her husband for coming home late.

center around—is *unacceptable.* Use *center in* or *center on.*
    The maximum power was *centered in* the nuclear reactor.
    All attention was *centered on* the launching pad.

certainly—is an *adverb*.
sure—is an *adjective*.
> He was *certainly* learning fast.
> *Colloquial:* He *sure* was learning fast.

cession—means *a yielding*.
session—means *a meeting*.
> The *cession* of a piece of territory could have avoided the war.
> The legislative *session* lasted three months.

childish—means *silly, immature*.
childlike—means *innocent, unspoiled*.
> Pouting appears *childish* in an adult.
> His *childlike* appreciation of art gave him great pleasure.

choice—means *a selection*.
choose—means *to select*.
chose—means *selected*.
> My *choice* for a career is teaching.
> We may *choose* our own leader.
> I finally *chose* teaching for a career.

cite—means *to quote*.
sight—means *seeing*.
site—means *a place for a building*.
> He was fond of *citing* from the Scriptures.
> The *sight* of the wreck was appalling.
> The Board of Education is seeking a *site* for the new school.

climate—is the average weather *over a period of many years*.
weather—is the *hour by hour* or *day by day* condition of the atmosphere.
> He likes the *climate* of California better than that of New York.
> The *weather* is sometimes hard to predict.

coarse—means *vulgar* or *harsh*.
course—means a *path* or a *subject of study*.
> He was shunned because of his *coarse* behavior.
> The ship took its usual *course*.
> Which *course* in English are you taking?

comic—means *intentionally funny*.
comical—means *unintentionally funny*.
> A clown is a *comic* figure.
> The peculiar hat she wore gave her a *comical* appearance.

comma—is *a mark of punctuation.*
coma—(rhymes with *aroma*) means *a period of prolonged unconsciousness.*
    A *comma* should never separate two complete sentences.
    The accident put him into a *coma* lasting three days.

common—means *shared equally* by two or more.
mutual—means *interchanged.*
    The town hall is the *common* pride of every citizen.
    We can do business to our *mutual* profit and satisfaction.

compare to—means to liken to something *which has a different form.*
compare with—means to compare persons or things with each other *when they are of the same kind.*
contrast with—means to show the *difference between two things.*
    A minister is sometimes *compared to* a shepherd.
    Shakespeare's plays are often *compared with* those of Marlowe.
    The writer *contrasted* the sensitivity of the dancer *with* the grossness of the
        pugilist.

complement—means *a completing part.*
compliment—is *an expression of admiration.*
    His wit was a *complement* to her beauty.
    He received many *compliments* on his valedictory speech.

comprehensible—means *understandable.*
comprehensive—means *including a great deal.*
    Under the circumstances, your doubts were *comprehensible.*
    Toynbee's *comprehensive* study of history covers many centuries.

comprise—means *to include.*
compose—means *to form the substance of.*
    Toynbee's study of history *comprises* seven volumes.
    Some modern novels are *composed* of as little as three chapters.

concur in—must be followed by *an action.*
concur with—must be followed by *a person.*
    I shall *concur in* the decision reached by the majority.
    I cannot *concur with* the chairman, however much I respect his opinion.

conducive to—means *leading to.*
conducive for—is *unacceptable.*
    Your proposals for compromise are *conducive to* a settlement of our
        disagreement.

conform to—means *to adapt oneself to.*
conform with—means *to be in harmony with.*
    Youngsters are inclined to *conform to* a group pattern.
    They feel it is dangerous not to *conform with* the rules of the group.

conscience—means *sense of right.*
conscientious—means *faithful.*
conscious—means *aware.*
    Man's *conscience* prevents him from becoming completely selfish.
    We value her because she is *conscientious.*
    The injured man was completely *conscious.*

considerable—is properly used *only as an adjective,* **not** as a noun.
    Acceptable: The fraternal organization invested a *considerable* amount in
        government bonds.
    Unacceptable: He lost *considerable* in the stock market.

consistently—means *in harmony.*
constantly—means *regularly, steadily.*
    If you choose to give advice, act *consistently* with that advice.
    Doctors *constantly* warn against overexertion.

consul—means *a government representative.*
council—means *an assembly which meets for deliberation.*
counsel—means *advice.*
    Americans abroad should keep in touch with their *consuls.*
    The City *Council* enacts local laws and regulations.
    The defendant heeded the *counsel* of his friends.

contemptible—means *worthy of contempt.*
contemptuous—means *feeling contempt.*
    His spying activities were *contemptible.*
    It was plain to all that he was *contemptuous* of his co-workers.

continual—means happening *again and again at short intervals.*
continuous—means *without interruption.*
    The teacher gave the class *continual* warnings.
    Noah experienced *continuous* rain for forty days.

convenient to—should be followed by a *person.*
convenient for—should be followed by a *purpose.*
    Will these plans be *convenient to* you?
    You must agree that they are *convenient for* the occasion.

copy—is *an imitation of an original work.* (not necessarily an exact imitation)
facsimile—is *an exact imitation of an original work.*
The counterfeiters made a crude *copy* of the hundred-dollar bill.
The official government engraver, however, prepared a *facsimile* of the bill.

core—means the *heart of something.*
corps—(pronounced like *core*) means *an organized military body.*
corpse—means *a dead body.*
The *core* of the apple was rotten.
The *corps* consisted of three full-sized armies.
The *corpse* was quietly slipped overboard after a brief service.

corespondent—is *a joint defendant in a divorce case.*
correspondent—is *one who communicates.*
The *corespondent* declared that he loved the other man's wife.
Max Frankel is a special *correspondent* for the *New York Times.*

corporeal—means *bodily as opposed to spiritual.*
corporal—means *bodily as it pertains to a person.*
Many believe that our *corporeal* existence changes to a spiritual one after
death.
Corporal punishment is not recommended in modern schools.

could of—is unacceptable for *could have.* Similarly, avoid *should of, must of,*
and *would of.*
Not: I *could of* won.
But: I *could have* won.

credible—means *believable.*
creditable—means *worthy of receiving praise.*
credulous—means *believing too easily.*
The pupil gave a *credible* explanation for his lateness.
Considering all the handicaps, he gave a *creditable* performance.
Politicians might prefer to address *credulous* people.

decease—means *death.*
disease—means *illness.*
His friend is *deceased.*
Leukemia is a deadly *disease.*

decent—means *suitable*.
descent—means *going down*.
dissent—means *disagreement*.
    The *decent* thing to do is to admit your fault.
    The *descent* into the cave was treacherous.
    Two of the nine justices filed a *dissenting* opinion.

deduction—means *reasoning from the general* (laws or principles) *to the particular* (facts).
induction—means *reasoning from the particular* (facts) *to the general* (laws or principles).
    All men are mortal. Since John is a man, he is mortal. (*deduction*)
    There are 1,000 oranges in this truckload. I have examined 100 from various parts of the load and find them all of the same quality. I therefore conclude that the 1,000 oranges are of this quality. (*induction*)

deference—means *respect*.
difference—means *unlikeness*.
    In *deference* to his memory, we did not play yesterday.
    The *difference* between the two boys is unmistakable.

definite—means *clear, with set limits*.
definitive—means *final, decisive*.
    We would prefer a *definite* answer to our *definite* question.
    The dictionary is the *definitive* authority for word meanings.

deprecate—means *to disapprove*.
depreciate—means *to lower the value*.
    His classmates *deprecated* his discourtesy.
    The service station *depreciated* the value of our house.

desirable—means *that which is desired*.
desirous—means *desiring* or *wanting*.
    It was a most *desirable* position.
    She was *desirous* of obtaining it.

despise—means *to look down upon*.
detest—means *to hate*.
    Some wealthy persons *despise* the poor.
    I *detest* cold weather.

desert—(pronounced DEZ-ert) means *an arid area.*
desert—(pronounced di-ZERT) means *to abandon;* it is also *a reward or punishment.*
dessert—(pronounced di-ZERT) means *the final course of a meal.*
  The Sahara is the world's most famous *desert.*
  A husband must not *desert* his wife.
  Execution was a just *desert* for his crime.
  We had plum pudding for *dessert.*

device—means *a way to do something.* (a noun)
devise—means *to find the way.* (a verb)
  A hook is a good fishing *device.*
  Some fishermen prefer to *devise* other ways for catching fish.

differ from—is used when there is a difference *between things.*
differ with—is used when there is a difference *in opinion.*
  A coat *differs from* a cape.
  You have the right to *differ with* me on public affairs.

different from—is *acceptable.*
different than—is *unacceptable.*
  Acceptable: Jack is different from his brother.
  Unacceptable: Florida's climate is *different than* New York's climate.

discover—means *to find something already in existence.*
invent—means *to create something that never existed before.*
  Pasteur *discovered* germs.
  Whitney *invented* the cotton gin.

discreet—means *cautious.*
discrete—means *separate.*
  The employee was *discreet* in her comments about her employer.
  Since these two questions are *discrete,* you must provide two separate
    answers.

disinterested—means *impartial.*
uninterested—means *not interested.*
  The judge must always be a *disinterested* party in a trial.
  As an *uninterested* observer, he was inclined to yawn at times.

divers—(pronounced DI-vurz) means *several.*
diverse—(pronounced di-VERS) means *different.*
  The store had *divers* foodstuffs for sale.
  Many of the items were completely *diverse* from staple foods.

doubt that—is *acceptable.*
doubt whether—is *unacceptable.*
   Acceptable: I *doubt that* you will pass this term.
   Unacceptable: I *doubt whether* you will succeed.

doubtless—is *acceptable.*
doubtlessly—is *unacceptable.*
   Acceptable: You *doubtless* know your work; why, then, don't you pass?
   Unacceptable: He *doubtlessly* thinks that you can do the job well.

dual—means *relating to two.*
duel—means *a contest between two persons.*
   Dr. Jekyl had a *dual* personality.
   Alexander Hamilton was fatally injured in a *duel* with Aaron Burr.

each other—refers to *two persons.*
one another—may also refer to *more than two persons.*
   The two girls have known *each other* for many years.
   Several of the girls have known *one another* for many years.

economic—refers to the *subject of economics.*
economical—means *thrifty.*
   An *economic* discussion was held at the United Nations.
   A smart shopper is usually *economical.*

either . . . or—is used when referring to choices.
neither . . . nor—is the *negative* form.
   Either you *or* I will win the election.
   Neither Bill *nor* Ellen is expected to have a chance.

elegy—is a *mournful or melancholy poem.*
eulogy—is a *speech in praise of a deceased person.*
   Gray's "*Elegy* Written in a Country Churchyard" is a melancholy poem.
   The minister delivered the *eulogy.*

eligible—means *fit to be chosen.*
illegible—means *impossible to read* or *hard to read.*
   Not all persons are *eligible* to be president.
   His childish handwriting was *illegible.*

eliminate—means *to get rid of.*
illuminate—means *to supply with light.*
   Let us try to *eliminate* the unnecessary steps.
   Several lamps were needed to *illuminate* the corridor.

else—is superfluous in such expressions as the following:
   Unacceptable: We want *no one else* but you.
   Acceptable: We want *no one* but you.

emigrate—means *to leave one's country for another.*
immigrate—means *to enter another country.*
   The Norwegians *emigrated* to America in mid-1860.
   Many of the Norwegian *immigrants* settled in the Midwest.

enclosed herewith—is *redundant.*
enclosed—is *acceptable.*
   You will find *enclosed* one copy of our brochure.

endorse—means to write on the back of.
   Acceptable: He endorsed the check.
   Unacceptable: He endorsed the check on the back.

enormity—means *viciousness or great wickedness.*
enormousness—means *vastness.*
   The *enormity* of his crime was appalling.
   The *enormousness* of the Sahara exceeds that of any other desert.

enthused—should be avoided.
enthusiastic—is preferred.
   Acceptable: We were *enthusiastic* over the performance.
   Unacceptable: I am truly *enthused* about coming.

equally as good—is *unacceptable.*
just as good—is *acceptable.*
   Acceptable: This book is *just as good* as that.
   Unacceptable: Your marks are *equally as good* as mine.

everyone—is written as one word when it is a *pronoun.*
every one—(two words) is used when *each individual* is stressed.
   Everyone present voted for the proposal.
   Every one of the voters accepted the proposal.
   NOTE: *Everybody* is written as one word.

every bit—is used colloquially for *just as.*
   Acceptable: You are *just as* clever as she is.
   Colloquial: He is *every bit* as lazy as his father.

everywheres—is *unacceptable.*
everywhere—is *acceptable.*
   We searched *everywhere* for the missing book.

every which way—meaning *in all directions* is colloquial.
every way—is *acceptable.*
He tried to solve the problem *every way* he could.

exceed—means *going beyond the limit.*
excel—refers to *superior quality.*
You have *exceeded* the time allotted to you.
All-round athletes are expected to *excel* in many sports.

except—is *acceptable.*
excepting—is *unacceptable.*
Acceptable: All *except* Joe are going.
Unacceptable: All cities, *excepting* Washington, are in a state.
NOTE: Don't use *except* for *unless.*
He won't consent *unless* you give him the money.

exceptional—means *extraordinary.*
exceptionable—means *objectionable.*
Exceptional children learn to read before the age of five.
The behavior of exceptional children is sometimes *exceptionable.*

excessively—means *beyond acceptable limits.*
exceedingly—means *to a very great degree.*
In view of our recent feud, he was *excessively* friendly.
The weather in July was *exceedingly* hot.

expand—means *to spread out.*
expend—means *to use up.*
As the staff increases, we shall have to *expand* our office space.
Don't *expend* all your energy on one project.

factitious—means *unnatural* or *artificial.*
fictitious—means *imaginary.*
His *factitious* enthusiasm did not deceive us.
Jim Hawkins is a *fictitious* character.

faint—means *to lose consciousness.*
feint—means *to make a pretended attack.*
The lack of fresh air caused her to *faint.*
First he *feinted* to the left; then he lobbed the ball over the net.

farther—is used to describe *concrete distance.*
further—is used to describe *an extension of time or degree.*
Chicago is *farther* from New York than is Cincinnati.
I'll explain *further* my point of view.

feel bad—means to feel ill or sorry.
feel badly—is *unacceptable.*
   Acceptable: I *feel bad* about the accident I saw.
   Unacceptable: I *felt badly* when I saw her fall.

fever—refers to an *undue rise of temperature.*
temperature—refers to the *degree of heat* which may be normal.
   We had better call the doctor—he has a *fever.*
   The *temperature* is 80 degrees.

fewer—refers to *persons or things that can be counted.*
less—refers to *something considered as a mass.*
   We have *fewer* customers this week than last week.
   I have *less* money in my pocket than you have.
   But idiom: One *less* thing to worry about.

financial—refers to money matters in a *general sense.*
fiscal—refers to the *public treasury.*
   Scholars are usually not *financial* successes.
   The government's *fiscal year* begins July 1 and ends June 30.

flout—means *to show contempt for.*
flaunt—means *to make a display of.*
   He *flouted* the authority of the principal.
   She *flaunted* her wealth.

flowed—is the past participle of *flow.*
flown—is the past participle of *fly.*
   The flood waters had *flowed* over the levee before nightfall.
   He had *flown* for 500 hours before he crashed.

forbear—means *to refrain from doing something.*
forebear—means *ancestor.*
   Forbear seeking vengeance.
   Most of the family's *forebears* came from Ghana.

formally—means *in a formal way.*
formerly—means *at an earlier time.*
   The letter of reference was *formally* written.
   He was *formerly* a delegate to the convention.

former—means *the first of two.*
latter—means *the second of two.*
   The *former* half of the book was prose.
   The *latter* half of the book was poetry.

fort—means *a fortified place.*
forte—means *a strong point.*
   A small garrison was able to hold the *fort.*
   Conducting Wagner's music was Toscanini's *forte.*

forth—means *forward.*
fourth—*comes after third.*
   They went *forth* like warriors of old.
   The *Fourth* of July is our Independence Day.

freeze—means *to turn to ice.*
frieze—is *a decorated band in or on a building.*
   As the temperature dropped, the water began to *freeze.*
   The *friezes* on the Parthenon are wonders of art.

funny—means *humorous* or *laughable.*
   That clown is truly *funny.*
   Funny meaning *odd* or *strange* is a colloquial use.

genial—means *cheerful.*
congenial—means *agreeing in spirit.*
   Genial landlords are rare today.
   A successful party depends on *congenial* guests.

genius—means *extraordinary natural ability, or one so gifted.*
genus—means *class* or *kind.*
   Mozart showed his *genius* for music at a very early age.
   That flower probably does not belong to the *genus* of roses.

gibe / jibe—(pronounced alike)—both mean *to scoff.*
   We are inclined to *gibe* at awkward speakers.
jibe also means *to agree.*
   The two stories are now beginning to *jibe.*

got—means *obtained.* Colloquially, *got* conveys a sense of *obligation* or *possession.*
   He *got* the tickets yesterday.
   Not: We *have got* no sympathy for them.
   But: We *have* no sympathy for them.
   Colloquial: You've *got* to do it.
   I've *got* two cats.

gourmand—is *one who eats large quantities of food.*

gourmet—(rhymes with poor-MAY) is *one who eats fastidiously; a connoisseur.*

His uncontrollable appetite soon turned him into a *gourmand.*

The *gourmet* chooses the right wine for each course.

graduated—is followed by *from.*

He *graduated* (or *was graduated*) *from* high school in 1997.

Unacceptable: He *graduated* college.

NOTE: A *graduated* test tube is one that has markings on it to indicate volume or capacity.

guess—is *colloquial* for *think* or *suppose.* I *think* I'll go downtown.

habit—means an *individual* tendency to repeat a thing.

custom—means *group habit.*

He had a *habit* of breaking his glasses before each ball game.

The *custom* of the country was to eat fish raw.

had ought—is *unacceptable.*

You *ought* not to eat fish if you are allergic to it.

hanged—is used in reference to a *person.*

hung—is used in reference to a *thing.*

The prisoner was *hanged* at dawn.

The picture was *hung* above the fireplace.

healthy—means *having health.*

healthful—means *giving health.*

The man is *healthy.*

Fruit is *healthful.*

heap—means a *pile.*

heaps—is *slang* in the sense of *very much.*

Slang: Thanks *heaps* for the gift.

Lots is also *slang* for very much.

holy—means *sacred.*

holey—means *with holes.*

wholly—means *completely* or *altogether.*

Easter Week is a *holy* time in many lands.

Old socks tend to become *holey* after a while.

We are *wholly* in agreement with your decision.

hypercritical—refers to a person *who finds fault easily.*
hypocritical—refers to a person *who pretends.*
Don't be *hypercritical* about meals at low prices.
It is better to be sincere than to be *hypocritical.*

idle—means *unemployed or unoccupied.*
idol—means *image* or *object of worship.*
Idle men, like *idle* machines, are inclined to lose their sharpness.
Some dictators prefer to be looked upon as *idols* by the masses.

immunity—implies *resistance to a disease.*
impunity—means *freedom from punishment.*
The Salk vaccine helps develop an *immunity* to poliomyelitis.
Because he was an only child, he frequently misbehaved with *impunity.*

imply—means *to suggest* or *hint at.* (The speaker *implies.*)
infer—means *to deduce* or *conclude.* (The listener *infers.*)
Are you *implying* that I have disobeyed orders?
From your carefree attitude, what else are we to *infer?*

inclement—(pronounced in-CLEM-ent) refers to *severe weather,* such as a
heavy rainfall or storm. It does **not** mean threatening.
Because of the *inclement* weather, we were soaked to the skin.

indict—(pronounced in-DITE) means *to charge with a crime.*
indite—means *to write.*
The Grand Jury *indicted* him for embezzlement.
Modern authors prefer the expression *to write,* rather than *indite;* the latter
is now a stuffy sort of expression.

ingenious—means *skillful, imaginative.*
ingenuous—means *naive, frank,* or *candid.*
The *ingenious* boy created his own rocket.
One must be *ingenuous* to accept the Communist definition of freedom.

inside / inside of—When referring to time, use *within.*
She is arriving *within* two hours.

irregardless—is *unacceptable.*
regardless—is *acceptable.*
Not: *Irregardless* of the weather, I am going to the game.
But: *Regardless* of his ability, he is not likely to win.

irresponsible—means *having no sense of responsibility.*
not responsible for—means *not accountable for something.*
    Irresponsible people are frequently late for appointments.
    Since you came late, we are *not responsible for* your having missed the
       first act.

its—means *belonging to it.*
it's—means *it is.*
    The house lost *its* roof.
    It's an exposed house, now.

join together—means to *unite* or *connect.* Omit the redundant *together.*
    Acceptable: I want to *join* these pieces of wood.
    Unacceptable: All of us should *join together* to fight intolerance.

judicial—means *pertaining to courts or to the law.*
judicious—means *wise.*
    The problem required the *judicial* consideration of an expert.
    We were certainly in no position to make a *judicious* decision.

kind of / sort of—are *colloquial* for *rather.*
    What *kind of* car do you prefer?
    We are *rather* disappointed in you.

last—refers to *the final member in a series.*
latest—refers to *the most recent in time.*
latter—refers to *the second of two.*
    This is the *last* bulletin. (There won't be any other bulletins.)
    This is the *latest* bulletin. (There will be other bulletins.)
    Of the two most recent bulletins, the *latter* is more encouraging.

later on—is *unacceptable* for *later.*
    Later, we shall give your request fuller attention.

least—means *the smallest.*
less—means *the smaller of two.*
    This was the *least* desirable of all the locations we have seen.
    We may finally have to accept the *less* desirable of the two locations we
       last saw.

leave—means *to go away from.*
let—means *to permit.*
    Leave this house at once.
    Let me remain in peace in my own house.

legible—means *able to be read.*
readable—means *able to be read with pleasure.*
Your reports have become increasingly *legible.*
In fact, I now find most of them extremely *readable.*

lengthened—means *made longer.*
lengthy—means *annoyingly long.*
The essay, now *lengthened,* is more readable.
However, try to avoid writing *lengthy* explanations of obvious facts.

levy—means *to impose a tax.*
levee—means *an embankment.*
It is the duty of Congress to *levy* taxes.
The Mississippi River is contained by massive *levees.*

libel—is *a written and published statement injurious to a person's character.*
slander—is *a spoken statement of the same sort.*
The unfavorable references to me in your book are *libel.*
When you say these vicious things about me, you are committing *slander.*

lightening—is the present participle of *to lighten.*
lightning—means *the flashes of light accompanied by thunder.*
Lightening the pack made it easier to carry.
Summer thunderstorms produce startling *lightning* bolts.

line—meaning *occupation* is *unacceptable.*
Acceptable: He is in the engineering *profession.*
Unacceptable: What *line* are you in?

lineament—means *outline* or *contour.*
liniment—is *a medicated liquid.*
His face had the *lineaments* of a Greek Adonis.
After the football games, we all applied *liniment* to our legs.

loan—is a *noun.*
lend—is a *verb.*
The bank was willing to grant him a *loan* of $500.
The bank was willing to *lend* him $500.

lonely—means *longing for companionship.*
solitary—means *isolated.*
Some people are forced to live *lonely* lives.
Sometimes *solitary* surroundings are conducive to deep thought.

luxuriant—means *abundant growth.*
luxurious—implies *wealth.*
>One expects to see *luxuriant* plants in the tropics.
>The *luxurious* surroundings indicated both wealth and good taste.

majority—means *more than half of the total number.*
plurality—means *an excess of votes received by the leading candidate over those received by the next candidate.*
>*Example:*   A received 251 votes.
>   B received 127 votes.
>   C received 123 votes.
>A received a *majority,* or one vote more than half of the total.
>A received a *plurality* of 124 votes over B.

many—refers to *a number.*
much—refers to *a quantity in bulk.*
>How *many* inches of rain fell last night?
>I don't know, but I would say *much* rain fell last night.

material—means *of or pertaining to matter.*
materiel—(accent the last syllable) is French, and means *material equipment,* the opposite of *personnel (manpower).*
>His *material* assets included an automobile and two suits of clothing.
>The small army was rich in *materiel,* poor in personnel.

may—is used in the *present tense.*
might—is used in the *past tense.*
>We are hoping that he *may* come today.
>He *might* have done it if you had encouraged him.

it's I—is always *acceptable.*
it's me—is *acceptable* in informal speech or writing.

It's he / This is she / It was they—are always *acceptable.*
It's him / This is her / It was them—are informal.

measles—is plural in form, singular in meaning.
>*Measles* is now a minor childhood disease.
>NOTE: *Mumps* and *shingles* are also singular in meaning.

medieval—means of or pertaining to *the Middle Ages.*
middle-aged—refers to persons *in the middle period of life.*
>Serfs and feudal baronies were part of *medieval* times.
>According to the Bible, the *middle-aged* man has thirty-five more years of life to look forward to.

Messrs.—(rhymes with *guessers*) is the plural of *Mr.*
Misters is *unacceptable.*
The meeting was attended by *Messrs.* Smith, Jones, Brown, and Swift.

metal—is a type of *substance.*
mettle—means *spirit.*
Lead is one of the more familiar *metals.*
One had to admire his *mettle* in the face of a crisis.

minutiae—(pronounced min-EW-she-ee) is the plural of *minutia,* and means *minor details.*
A meticulous person spends much time on *minutiae.*

Mmes.—(pronounced me-DAM) is the abbreviation for *Mesdames,* the plural of *Madam.* It introduces a series of names of married women.
The party was attended by the *Mmes.* Jones, Smith, and Wilson.
The plural of *Miss* is *Misses.*

moneys—is *the plural of money.* (also monies)
We shall vote on the disposition of the various *moneys* in the treasury.

moral—means *good or ethical;* also, an *ethical lesson to be drawn.*
morale—(pronounced more-AL) means *spirit.*
The *moral* of the story is that it pays to be honest.
The *morale* of the troops rose after the general's inspiring speech.

most—is an adverb in the *superlative degree.*
almost—is an adverb meaning *nearly.*
He is the *most* courteous boy in the class.
It's *almost* time to go to school.

nauseous—means *causing sickness.*
nauseated—means *being sick.*
The odor is *nauseous.*
I feel *nauseated.*

naval—refers to *ships.*
nautical—refers to *navigation and seamen.*
John Paul Jones was a famous *naval* commander.
A *nautical* mile is a little longer than a land mile.

neither—means *not either of two,* and should **not** be used for *none* or *not one.*
Neither of his two books was very popular.
Of the many plays he has written, *not one* (or *none*) was good.

noplace—is *unacceptable* for *no place* or *nowhere*.
You now have *nowhere* to go.

nohow—is *unacceptable for regardless.*
Unacceptable: I can't do this nohow.

notable—means *remarkable.*
notorious—means *of bad reputation.*
December 7, 1941, was a *notable* day.
At that time, the *notorious* Tojo commanded the Japanese forces.

nothing more or less—is *unacceptable* for *nothing more nor less.*
Using correct English is *nothing more nor less* than a matter of careful
practice.

nowhere near—is *unacceptable* for *not nearly.*
The work was *not nearly* finished by nightfall.

nowheres—is *unacceptable.*
nowhere—is *acceptable.*
The child was *nowhere* to be found.

number—is singular *when the total is intended.*
number—is plural when the individual units are referred to.
The *number* of pages in the book is 500.
A *number* of pages were printed in italic type.

obligate—implies a *moral or legal responsibility.*
oblige—means *to do as a favor* or *to accommodate.*
The principal felt *obligated* to disqualify himself in the dispute between the
pupils.
Please *oblige* me by refraining from discussing this matter with anyone
else.

observance—means the *act of complying.*
observation—means the *act of noting.*
In *observance* of the new regulation, we shall omit further tests.
His scientific *observations* became the basis for a new rocket theory.

occupancy—refers to *the mere act of occupying,* usually legally.
occupation—means *the forceful act of occupying.*
According to the lease, the tenant still had *occupancy* of the apartment for
another month.
The *occupation* of the town by troops worried the townspeople.

oculist or ophthalmologist—is an MD who *treats diseases of the eye.*
optometrist—is a person who *measures the eye* to prescribe glasses.
optician—is a person who *makes the glasses.*
    An *oculist* is also called an *ophthalmologist.*
    An *optometrist* may also be an *optician.*

of any—(and *of anyone*) is *unacceptable* for *of all.*
    His was the highest mark *of all.*

off of—is *unacceptable.* Omit *of.*
    He took the book *off* the table.

OK—(or *okay*) is used for *acceptable* or *approved* in informal business and informal social usage. Avoid the use of OK in formal situations.

on account of—is *unacceptable* for *because.*
    We could not meet you *because* we did not receive your message in time.

oral—means *spoken.*
verbal—means *expressed in words,* either spoken or written.
    In international intrigue, *oral* messages are less risky than written ones.
    Shorthand must usually be transcribed into *verbal* form.

ordinance—means *regulation.*
ordnance—refers to *guns, cannon, and the like.*
    The local *ordinance* restricted driving speeds to 35 miles an hour.
    Some rockets and guided missiles are now included in military *ordnance.*

ostensible—means *shown* (usually for the purpose of deceiving others).
ostentatious—means *showy.*
    Although he was known to be ambitious, his *ostensible* motive was civic
        pride.
    His *ostentatious* efforts in behalf of civic improvement impressed no one.

other . . . than—is acceptable.
other . . . but—is unacceptable.
other . . . except—is unacceptable.
    Acceptable: We have no *other* motive *than* friendship.

other—is an adjective and means *different.*
otherwise—is an adverb and means *in a different way.*
    What you did was *other* than what you had promised.
    I cannot look *otherwise* than with delight at the improvement in your work.

out loud—is *colloquial* for *aloud*.
He read *aloud* to his family every evening.

outdoor—is an adjective.
outdoors—is an adverb.
We spent most of the summer at an *outdoor* music camp.
Most of the time we played string quartets *outdoors*.
Out-of-doors is *acceptable* in either case.

part from—*a person*.
part with—*a thing*.
It was difficult for her to *part from* her classmates.
It will be difficult for him to *part with* his car.

party—refers to a *group*, **not** an *individual*.
person—refers to an *individual*.
A *party* of men went on a scouting mission.
Who is the *person* you came with?
NOTE: *Party* may be used for the word *person* in a legal document.

pedal—means *a lever operated by foot*. (avoid foot pedal)
peddle—means *to sell from door to door.*
It is impossible to ride a bicycle without moving the *pedals*.
The traveling salesman *peddling* brushes is a thing of the past.

percent—(also **per cent**) expresses *rate of interest*.
percentage—means *a part or proportion of the whole*.
The interest rate of some banks is 4 *percent*.
The census showed the *percentage* of unmarried people to have increased.

persecute—means *to make life miserable for someone*.
prosecute—means *to conduct a criminal investigation*.
Some racial groups insist upon *persecuting* other groups.
The District Attorney is *prosecuting* the racketeers.

personal—refers to *a person*.
personnel—means *an organized body of individuals*.
The general took a *personal* interest in every one of his men.
He believed that this was necessary in order to maintain the morale of the
personnel in his division.

physic—means *a drug.*
physics—is *a branch of science.*
physique—means *body structure.*
>   A doctor should determine the safe dose of a *physic.*
>   Nuclear *physics* is one of the most challenging of the sciences.
>   Athletes must take care of their *physiques.*

plenty—is a noun; it means *abundance.*
>   America is a land of *plenty.*
>   There is *plenty of* (**not** *plenty*) room in the compact car for me.
>   *Plenty* as an adverb is *colloquial.*
>   The compact car is *quite* large enough for me.

pole—means a long stick.
poll—means *vote.*
>   We bought a new *pole* for the flag.
>   The seniors took a *poll* to determine the graduate most likely to succeed.

poorly—meaning *in poor health* is *unacceptable in formal usage.*
>   Grandfather was feeling *in poor health* all last winter.

pour—is *to send flowing with direction and control.*
spill—is *to send flowing accidentally.*
>   Please *pour* some cream into my cup of coffee.
>   Careless people *spill* things.

practicable—means *usable* or *workable* and is applied only to objects.
practical—means *realistic, having to do with action.* It applies to persons and
>   things.
>   There is as yet no *practicable* method for resisting atomic bomb attacks.
>   *Practical* technicians, nevertheless, are attempting to translate the theories
>   of the atomic scientists into some form of defense.

precede—means *to come before.*
proceed—means *to go ahead.* (*procedure* is the noun)
supersede—means *to replace.*
>   What are the circumstances that *preceded* the attack?
>   We can then *proceed* with our plan for resisting a second attack.
>   It is then possible that Plan B will *supersede* Plan A.

prescribe—means *to lay down a course of action.*
proscribe—means *to outlaw* or *forbid.*
>   The doctor *prescribed* plenty of rest and good food for the man.
>   Some towns may *proscribe* various forms of expression.

principal—means *chief* or *main* (as an adjective); *a leader* (as a noun).
principle—means *a fundamental truth* or *belief.*
His *principal* supporters came from among the peasants.
The *principal* of the school asked for cooperation from the staff.
Humility was the guiding *principle* of Buddha's life.
NOTE: *principal* may also mean a sum placed at interest.
Part of his monthly payment was applied as interest on the *principal.*

prodigy—means a *person endowed with extraordinary gifts or powers.*
protégé—means *someone under the protection of another.*
Mozart was a musical *prodigy* at the age of three.
For a time, Schumann was the *protégé* of Johannes Brahms.

prophecy—(rhymes with *sea*) is the noun meaning *prediction.*
prophesy—(rhymes with *sigh*) is a verb meaning *to predict.*
The *prophecy* of the three witches eventually misled Macbeth.
The witches had *prophesied* that Macbeth would become king.

put in—meaning *to spend, make,* or *devote* is *colloquial.*
Every good student should *spend* (or *put in*) at least four hours a day
  studying.
Be sure to *make* (or *put in*) an appearance at the council meeting.

rain—means *water from the clouds.*
reign—means *rule.*
rein—means *a strap for guiding a horse.*
The *rain* in Spain falls mainly on the plain.
A queen now *reigns* over England.
When the *reins* were pulled too tightly, the horse reared.

real—meaning *very* or *extremely* is *colloquial.*
He is a *very* handsome young man.
He is *really* handsome.

reason is because—is *unacceptable* for *reason is that.*
The *reason* young people do not read Trollope today *is that* his sentences
  are too involved.
Avoid *due to* after *reason is.*
The *reason* he refused *was that* he was proud (**not** *due to* his pride).

rebellion—means *open, armed, or organized resistance to authority.*

revolt—means *similar resistance on a smaller scale.*

revolution—means *the overthrowing of one government and the setting up of another.*

Bootlegging has sometimes been referred to as a *rebellion* against high whiskey taxes.

An increase in the grain tax caused a peasants' *revolt* against the landowners.

Unpopular regimes are often overthrown in violent *revolutions.*

reckon—meaning *suppose* or *think* is *unacceptable.*

I *think* it may rain this afternoon.

recollect—means *to bring back to memory.*

remember—means *to keep in memory.*

Now I can *recollect* your returning the money to me.

I *remember* the occasion well.

reconcile to—means *resign to* or *adjust to.*

reconcile with—means *to become friendly again with someone;* also, *to bring one set of facts into harmony with another one.*

I am now *reconciled to* this chronic ache in my back.

George was *reconciled with* his parents after many years.

How does one *reconcile* the politician's shabby accomplishments *with* the same politician's noble promises?

regular—meaning *real* or *true* is *colloquial.*

Colloquial: He was a *regular* tyrant.

Preferred: He was a *true* tyrant.

respectably—means *in a manner deserving respect.*

respectfully—means *with respect and decency.*

respectively—means *as relating to each, in the order given.*

Young people should conduct themselves *respectably* in school as well as in church.

The students listened *respectfully* to the principal.

John and Bill are the sons *respectively* of Mr. Smith and Mr. Brown.

reverend—means *worthy of reverence or respect.*

reverent—means *feeling or showing respect.*

Shakespeare, the *reverend* master of the drama, still inspires most readers.

Sometimes a too *reverent* attitude toward Shakespeare causes the reader to miss much of the fun in his plays.

rob—One *robs a person or institution.*
steal—One *steals* a *thing.*
They *robbed* the man of his money.
He *stole* my wallet.

rout—(rhymes with *stout*) means *a defeat.*
route—(rhymes with either *boot* or *stout*) means *a way of travel.*
The *rout* of the army was near.
The salesman has a steady *route.*

same as—is *colloquial* for *in the same way as* and *just as.*
The owner's son was treated *in the same way as* any other worker.
Avoid *same* as a pronoun, except in *legal* usage.
If the books are available, please send *them* (**not** *same*) by parcel post.

self-confessed—is *redundant* for *confessed.* Omit *self.*
He was a *confessed* lover of chocolate.

sensible of—means *aware of.*
sensitive to—means *affected by.*
I am very *sensible of* my shortcomings.
He is *sensitive to* criticism.

shape—meaning *condition* is *colloquial.*
The refugees were in a serious *condition* (or *shape*) when they arrived here.

show up—meaning *to expose* is *unacceptable.*
It is my firm intention to *expose* (**not** *show up*) your hypocrisy.

simple reason—is *unacceptable* for *reason.* Omit the word *simple* in similar
expressions: *simple truth, simple purpose,* etc.
Unacceptable: I refuse to do it for the *simple reason* that I don't like your
attitude.
Acceptable: The *truth* is that I feel tired.

simply—meaning *absolutely* or *extremely* is often redundant.
Not: The performance was *simply* thrilling.
But: The performance was thrilling.

size up—meaning *to estimate* is *colloquial.*
The detectives were able *to estimate* (or *size up*) the fugitive's remaining
ammunition supply.

sociable—means *friendly.*
social—means *relating to people in general.*
   Sociable individuals prefer to have plenty of people around them.
   The President's *social* program was just another waste.

sole—means *all alone.*
soul—means *human spirit.*
   He was the *sole* owner of the business.
   Man's *soul* is unconquerable.

some time—means *a portion of time.*
sometime—means *at an indefinite time in the future.*
sometimes—means *occasionally.*
   I'll need *some time* to make a decision.
   Let us meet *sometime* after noon.
   Sometimes it is better to hesitate before signing a contract.

somewheres—is *unacceptable.*
somewhere—is *acceptable.*

specie—means *money as coins.* (*Specie* is singular only.)
species—means *a member of a group of related things.* (*Species* is singular and plural.)
   He preferred to be paid in *specie,* rather than in bank notes.
   The human *species* is relatively young. (singular)
   Many animal *species* existed before man. (plural)

stand—meaning *to tolerate* is *colloquial.*
   I refuse *to tolerate* (or *to stand for*) crime.

state—means *to declare formally.*
say—means *to speak.*
   Our ambassador *stated* the terms for a ceasefire.
   We *said* that we would not attend the meeting.

stationary—means *standing still.*
stationery—means *writing materials.*
   In ancient times people thought the earth was *stationary.*
   We bought writing paper at the *stationery* store.

statue—means *a piece of sculpture.*
statute—is *a law.*
   The *Statue* of Liberty stands in New York Harbor.
   Compulsory education was established by *statute.*

summons—is singular; *summonses* is the plural.
We received a *summons* to appear in court.
This was the first of three *summonses* we were to receive that week.

surround—means *to enclose on all sides*. Do **not** add *on all sides* to it.
The camp was *surrounded* by heavy woods.

take in—is *colloquial* in the sense of *deceive* or *attend*.
We were *deceived* (or *taken in*) by her charming manner.
We should like to *attend* (or *take in*) a few plays during our vacation.

tasteful—means *having good taste.*
tasty—means *pleasing to the taste.*
The home of our host was decorated in a *tasteful* manner.
Our host also served us very *tasty* meals.

tenants—are *occupants.*
tenets—are *principles.*
Several *tenants* occupied that apartment during the first month.
His religious *tenets* led him to perform many good deeds.

tender—means *to offer officially or formally.*
give—means *to donate* or *surrender something willingly.*
The discredited official decided to *tender* his resignation.
He *gave* testimony readily before the grand jury.

testimony—means *information given orally only.*
evidence—means *information given orally or in writing.*
He gave *testimony* to the grand jury.
The defendant presented written *evidence* to prove he was not at the scene
of the crime.

that there / this here—are *unacceptable*. Omit *there, here.*
That person is taller than *this* one.

their—means *belonging to them.*
there—means *in that place.*
they're—means *they are.*
We took *their* books home with us.
You will find your books over *there* on the desk.
They're not as young as we expected them to be.

theirselves—is *unacceptable* for *themselves.*
Most children of school age are able to care for *themselves* in many ways.

therefor—means *for that.*
therefore—means *because of that.*
>One day's detention is the punishment *therefor.*
>You will, *therefore,* have to remain in school after dismissal time.

these kind—is *unacceptable.*
this kind—is *acceptable.*
>I am fond of *this kind* of apples.
>(*These kinds* would also be *acceptable.*)

tortuous—means *twisting.*
torturing—means *causing pain.*
>The wagon train followed a *tortuous* trail through the mountains.
>The *torturing* memory of his defeat kept him awake all night.

track—means *a path* or *road.*
tract—means *a brief but serious piece of writing* or *a piece of land.*
>The horses raced around the *track.*
>John Locke wrote a famous *tract* on education.
>The heavily wooded *tract* was sold to a lumber company.

ulterior—means *lying beyond or hidden underneath.*
underlying—means *fundamental.*
>His noble words were contradicted by his *ulterior* motives.
>Shakespeare's *underlying* motive in *Hamlet* was to criticize the moral climate of his own times.

unique—means *the only one of its kind,* and therefore does not take *very, most,* or *extremely* before it.
>The First Folio edition of Shakespeare's works is *unique* (**not** *very unique*).
>NOTE: The same rule applies to *perfect.*

upwards of—is *colloquial* for *more than.*
>There are *more than* (or *upwards of*) one million people living in Idaho today.

valuable—means *of great worth.*
valued—means *held in high regard.*
invaluable—means *priceless.*
>This is a *valuable* manuscript.
>The expert gave him highly *valued* advice.
>A good name is an *invaluable* possession.

venal—means *corrupted.*
>The *venal* councilwoman accepted the bribe.

veracity—means *truthfulness.*
truth—is *a true statement, a fact.*
> Because he had a reputation for *veracity,* we could not doubt his story.
> We would have questioned the *truth* of his story otherwise.

via—means *by way of* and should be used in connection with travel or motion only.
> We shipped the merchandise *via* motor express.
> I received the information *through* (**not** *via*) his letter.

virtue—means *goodness.*
virtuosity—means *technical skill.*
> We should expect a considerable degree of *virtue* in our public officials.
> The young pianist played with amazing *virtuosity* at his debut.

virtually—means *in effect.*
actually—means *in fact.*
> A tie in the final game was *virtually* a defeat for us.
> We had *actually* won more games than they.

waive—means *to give up.*
wave—means *a swell* or *roll of water.*
> As a citizen, I refuse to *waive* my right of free speech.
> The *waves* reached the top deck of the ship.

whereabouts—is *colloquial* for *where* but only as a noun meaning *location.*
> Not: *Whereabouts* do you live?
> But: Do you know his *whereabouts?*

whose—means *of whom.*
who's—means *who is.*
> *Whose* is this notebook?
> *Who's* in the next office?

would have—is *unacceptable* for *had.*
> I wish you *had* (**not** *would have*) called earlier.

ABBREVIATIONS

Established abbreviations are acceptable in all but the most formal writing. For reading ease, use only well-known abbreviations. If it is desirable to use an abbreviation that may not be familiar to the reader, spell out the word or phrase in parentheses after the abbreviation the first time you use it. After this first definition, the abbreviation may be used without further explanation. Abbreviations should be consistent throughout a text.

PUNCTUATION

1. In general, an abbreviation follows the capitalization and hyphenation of the original word or phrase. Each element may or may not be followed by a period. The current trend is to omit the periods where they used to be required. Note, however, that abbreviations of courtesy titles, initials, addresses, business names, calendar dates, and Latin terms generally retain their periods.

AFL-CIO	NATO	SW (in an address following a street name)
KGB	NT (New Testament)	USMC

2. Periods are omitted from abbreviations of units of measure in scientific or technical writing:

cm^3	FM	g
dB	ft-lb	km

In non-technical writing, abbreviated units of English measure may be typed with or without periods. Use a period if leaving it out would create confusion.

3. Abbreviations with periods should be typed without spaces, except for initials in personal names:

A.D.	R. S. Baker, MD
etc.	T. S. Eliot

The initials of American presidents, however, are typed without spaces or periods:

JFK	RMN	WJC

GEOGRAPHIC TERMS

1. You may abbreviate *United States* when preceding *Government* or the name of a Government organization, except in formal writing. Spell out *United States* when it is used as a noun or when it is used as an adjective in association with names of other countries.

US Government

US Congress

US Department of Agriculture

US monitor *Nantucket*

USS *Brooklyn* (note abbreviation for ship)

BUT The position taken by the United States, British, and French governments.

2. With the exceptions just noted, the abbreviation US is used in the adjective position, but is spelled out when used as a noun.

US foreign policy	*BUT* foreign policy of the United States
US economy	the economy of the United States
US attorney	United States Code (official title)
US troops	United States Steel Corp. (legal title)

3. Words in an address are usually spelled out. Where brevity is required, the following abbreviations may be used. Note that compass directions do not use periods.

Ave.—Avenue	Pl.—Place	NE—Northeast
Bldg.—Building	Sq.—Square	NW—Northwest
Blvd.—Boulevard	St.—Street	SE—Southeast
Ct.—Court	Terr.—Terrace	SW—Southwest
Dr.—Drive		

4. Spell out the names of the US states and territories when they are used alone or follow another name (such as that of a city) in ordinary text. If space is limited, as in tabular work, use the abbreviations given on the left. Use the official two-letter postal abbreviations with ZIP code for anything being mailed. The names of countries are usually not abbreviated.

Ala.	AL	Fla.	FL
Alaska	AK	Ga.	GA
Ariz.	AZ	Guam	GU
Ark.	AR	Hawaii	HI
Calif.	CA	Idaho	ID
Colo.	CO	Ill.	IL
Conn.	CT	Ind.	IN
Del.	DE	Iowa	IA
DC	DC	Kans.	KS

Ky.	KY	Okla.	OK
La.	LA	Ore.	OR
Maine	ME	Pa.	PA
Md.	MD	PR	PR (Puerto Rico)
Mass.	MA		
Mich.	MI	RI	RI
Minn.	MN	Amer. Samoa	AS
Miss.	MS	SC	SC
Mo.	MO	S. Dak.	SD
Mont.	MT	Tenn.	TN
Nebr.	NE	Tex.	TX
Nev.	NV	Utah	UT
NH	NH	Vt.	VT
NJ	NJ	Va.	VA
N. Mex.	NM	VI	VI (Virgin Islands)
NY	NY		
NC	NC	Wash.	WA
N. Dak.	ND	W. Va.	WV
Ohio	OH	Wis.	WI (or Wisc.)
		Wyo.	WY

NAMES AND TITLES

1. Use abbreviations in company names as they are shown on the company's letterhead.

    J. Dillard & Sons, Inc.

2. Where brevity in company names is required, the following abbreviations may be used:

Bros.—Brothers	Inc.—Incorporated
Co.—Company	Ltd.—Limited
Corp.—Corporation	&—and

Do not abbreviate *Company* and *Corporation* in names of Federal Government units.

Metals Reserve Company

Commodity Credit Corporation

3. In other than formal usage, you may abbreviate a civil or a military title preceding a name if followed by the person's given name or initial as well as the surname.

Adj.—Adjutant	LTJG—Lieutenant, junior grade)
Adm. (or ADM)—Admiral	
Asst. Surg.—Assistant Surgeon	Maj.—Major
	Maj. Gen.—Major General
Brig. Gen.—Brigadier General	M. Sgt.—Master Sergeant
	Pfc. (or PFC)—Private, first class
Capt.—Captain	PO—Petty Officer
Col.—Colonel	Prof.—Professor
Comdr.—Commander	Pvt.—Private
Cpl.—Corporal	Rear Adm.—Rear Admiral
CWO—Chief Warrant Officer	2d Lt.—Second Lieutenant
1st Lt.—First Lieutenant	Sfc.—Sergeant, first class
1st Sgt.—First Sergeant	Sgt.—Sergeant
Gen.—General	SGM (or Sgt. Maj)—Sergeant Major
Gov.—Governor	
Lt. (or Lieut.)—Lieutenant	S. Sgt.—Staff Sergeant
Lt. Comdr.—Lieutenant Commander	Supt.—Superintendent
	Surg.—Surgeon
LTC (or Lt. Col.)—Lieutenant Colonel	TSgt.—Technical Sergeant
LTG (or Lt. Gen.)—Lieutenant General	Vice Adm.—Vice Admiral
	WO—Warrant Officer

4. Use the following abbreviations after a name:

Jr., Sr.

2d, 3d, II, III (not preceded by a comma)

5. Fellowships, orders, etc.:

   BPOE (Benevolent and Protective Order of Elks),

   KCB (Knight Commander of the Order of Bath)

6. *Sr.* and *Jr.* should be used with the full given name and initials, and in combination with any title.

   Anthony Baxter Jones, Jr.; *or* A. B. Jones, Sr.

7. Do not use titles such as *Mr., Mrs., Ms., Dr.,* or *Esq.* in combination with another title or with abbreviations indicating academic degrees.

   John Jones, MA, PhD; *not* Mr. John Jones, MA, PhD

   David Roe, MD; *not* Dr. David Roe, MD, *nor* Mr. David Roe, MD

   Gerald West, Esq. *not* Mr. Gerald West, Esq., *nor* Gerald West, Esq., PhD

8. Although academic degrees are abbreviations of Latin terms, the punctuation and, in some cases, the spacing are often omitted.

   MA, PhD, LLD

9. When a name is followed by abbreviations designating religious and fraternal orders and academic and honorary degrees, arrange the abbreviations in this sequence: Orders, religious first; theological degrees; academic degrees earned in course; and honorary degrees in order of bestowal.

   John J. Jones, DD, MA, DLit

   Richard R. Row, CSC, PhD, LLD

PARTS OF PUBLICATIONS

Abbreviations may be used to designate parts of publications mentioned in parentheses, brackets, footnotes, lists of references, and tables, and followed by figures, letters, or Roman numerals. Note that these abbreviations retain their periods.

App., apps.,—appendix, appendixes

art., arts.—article, articles

bull., bulls.—bulletin, bulletins

cl., cls.—clause, clauses

chap., chaps.—chapter, chapters

col., cols.—column, columns

fig., figs.—figure, figures

no., nos.—number, numbers

p., pp.—page, pages

par., pars.—paragraph, paragraphs

pl., pls.—plate, plates

pt., pts.—part, parts

sec., secs.—section, sections

subchap., subchaps.—subchapter, subchapters

subpar., subpars.—subparagraph, sub-paragraphs

subsec., subsecs.—subsection, subsections

supp., supps.—supplement, supplements

vol., vols.—volume, volumes

CALENDAR DIVISIONS

When brevity is required, you may abbreviate the names of months—except May, June, and July—when used with day, or year, or both.

Jan. Feb. Mar. Apr. Aug. Sept. (or Sep.) Oct. Nov. Dec.

Similarly the names of days of the week may be abbreviated.

Sun. Mon. Tues. Wed. Thurs. Fri. Sat.

STANDARD WORD ABBREVIATIONS

AA or **A.A.,** Alcoholics Annonymous, antiaircraft, Associate in Arts, Administration on Aging

AAA, American Automobile Association, antiaircraft artillery

AB or **A.B.** or **BA** or **B.A.,** bachelor of arts

abbr. or **abbrev.,** abbreviated or abbreviation

ABC, American Bowling Congress; American Broadcasting Company; atomic, biological, and chemical

abs., absolute, abstract

AC or **A.C.,** alternating current, Athletic Club

A/C, air conditioning

acct., account, accountant
ACDA, Arms Control and Disarmament Agency
ACTH, adrenocorticotropic hormone
ACTION, not an acronym, but an independent Federal agency
AD or **A.D.,** active duty; Anno Domini, in the year of our Lord
ADP, automatic data processing
AEC, Atomic Energy Commission
AEF, American Expeditionary Force (or Forces)
AFB, Air Force Base
AFL-CIO, American Federation of Labor and Congress of Industrial Organizations
AID, Agency for International Development
aka, also known as
ALR, American Law Reports
AM or **A.M.,** *ante meridiem,* before noon; master of arts (see also **MA** or **M.A.**)
AMC, American Maritime Cases
Am Dec, American Decisions
AMG, Allied Military Government
Am Repts, American Reports
AMVETS, American Veterans of World War II, Amvet(s) (individual)
antilog, antilogarithm
API, American Petroleum Institute
APO, Army and Air Force Post Office (overseas)
App DC, District of Columbia Appeal Cases
App Div, Appellate Division
APPR, Army Package Power Reactor
approx., approximate, approximately
ARC, American Red Cross, AIDS-related complex
ARPA, Advanced Research Projects Agency
ARS, Agricultural Research Service
ASCS, Agricultural Stabilization and Conservation Service
ASME, American Society of Mechanical Engineers
ASN, Army Service Number
Asst. Surg., assistant surgeon
AST, Atlantic Standard Time
ASTM, American Society for Testing and Materials
AT, Atlantic Time
Atl, Atlantic; Atlantic Reporter; **A.(2d),** Atlantic Reporter, second series
AUS, Austria, Army of the United States
AWL, Absent With Leave
AWOL, Absent Without Official Leave
BAE, Bureau of Agricultural Economics
BCG, (bacillus Calmette-Guerin), anti-tuberculosis vaccine
BDSA, Business and Defense Services Administration

Bé, Baumé
BEC, Bureau of Employees' Compensation
bf, boldface
BIA, Bureau of Indian Affairs
BIS, Bank for International Settlements
Blatch Pr Cas, Blatchford's Prize Cases
bldg., building
BLit(t) or **B.Lit(t)** or **Lit(t)B** or **Lit(t).B.,** Bachelor of Letters (or Literature)
BLM, Bureau of Land Management
BLS, Bachelor of Library Science, Bureau of Labor Statistics
BNDD, Bureau of Narcotics and Dangerous Drugs
bo, back order, bad order, buyer's option
BS or **B.S.,** Bachelor of Science
CAB, Civil Aeronautics Board
CACM, Central American Common Market
c. and sc., caps and small caps
CAP, Civil Air Patrol
CARE, Cooperative for American Relief Everywhere, Inc.
cbd, cash before delivery
CCA, Circuit Court of Appeals
CCC, Civilian Conservation Corps, Commodity Credit Corporation
CCls, Court of Claims
CClsR, Court of Claims Reports
CCPA, Court of Customs and Patent Appeals
CCR, Commission on Civil Rights
CE, Christian (or Common) Era
CEA, Council of Economic Advisers, Commodity Exchange Authority
CEC, Commodity Exchange Commission
Cento., Central Treaty Organization
CFR, Code of Federal Regulations
CFR Suppl., Code of Federal Regulations Supplement
CIA, Central Intelligence Agency
CIC, Counterintelligence Corps
CJ, *corpus juris,* body of law; Chief Justice
CMS, Consumer Marketing Service
CO, Commanding Officer
COD or **cod,** cash (or collect) on delivery
col., collateral, collected, collector, college, colony, color, column
COL, cost of living
Comp. Dec., Comptroller's Decisions (Treasury)
Comp. Gen. Dec., Comptroller General Decisions
con., consolidated, consul, continued
CONELRAD, control of electromagnetic radiation (civil defense)
cos, cash on shipment, companies, cosine, counties
cosh, hyperbolic cosine

cot, cotangent
coth, hyperbolic cotangent
cp, candlepower, chemically pure, compare
CPA, Certified Public Accountant
CPI, Consumer Price Index
CPR, cardiopulmonary resuscitation
cr, credit, creditor
CRP, C-reactive protein
CSC, Civil Service Commission
csc, cosecant
csch, hyperbolic cosecant
CSS, Commodity Stabilization Service
CST, Central Standard Time
ct or **ct.,** cent, county, court
CT, Central Time
CWO, cash with order (cwo), Chief Warrant Officer
Dall, Dallas (U.S. Supreme Court Reports)
DAR, Daughters of the American Revolution
DATA, Defense Air Transportation Administration
dba, doing business as
dbh, diameter at breast height
DC, direct current, District of Columbia
DD or **D.D.,** Doctor of Divinity
DDS or **D.D.S.,** Doctor of Dental Surgery
DDT, dichlorodiphenyltrichloroethane
DEW, distant early warning (DEW line)
Dist. Ct., District Court
DLF, Development Loan Fund
Dlit(t) or **D.Lit(t)** or **Lit(t)D** or **Lit(t).D.,** Doctor of Literature
DMB, Defense Mobilization Board
DOD, Department of Defense
DOT, Department of Transportation
DP, dew point, displaced person, double play
DPH, Doctor of Public Health
DPHy, Doctor of Public Hygiene
dr, debit, debtor, drachma, dram
DSA, Defense Supply Agency
DV, distinguished visitor (Air Force) (see also **VIP**)
DVM, Doctor of Veterinary Medicine
Ecosoc, Economic and Social Council
EDT, Eastern Daylight Time
EEC, European Economic Community
EEE, Eastern Equine Encephalitis
EFTA, European Free Trade Association
EHS, Environmental Health Services

8°, octavo
emcee, master of ceremony
eom, end of month
EOP, Executive Office of the President
EPA, Environmental Protection Agency
ERP, European Recovery Program
ESSA, Environmental Science Services Administration
EST, Eastern Standard Time
ET, Eastern Time
Euratom, European Atomic Energy Community
Euromarket, European Common Market (European Economic Community)
Euromart, see Euromarket
Ex. Doc., executive document
FAA, Federal Aviation Administration
FAO, Food and Agriculture Organization
fas, free alongside ship
FAS, Foreign Agricultural Service
FBI, Federal Bureau of Investigation
FCA, Farm Credit Administration
FCC, Federal Communications Commission
FCIC, Federal Crop Insurance Corporation
FCSC, Foreign Claims Settlement Commission
FDA, Food and Drug Administration
FDIC, Federal Deposit Insurance Corporation
FDL, fast deployment logistic (ship)
Fed, Federal, Federation
FHA, Federal Housing Administration, Farmers Home Administration
FHLBB, Federal Home Loan Bank Board
FICA, Federal Insurance Contributions Act
FLSA, Fair Labor Standards Act
FM, frequency modulation
FMC, Federal Maritime Commission
FMCS, Federal Mediation and Conciliation Service
FNMA, Federal National Mortgage Association (Fannie May)
FNS, Food and Nutrition Service
FOB or **fob,** free on board
FPC, Federal Power Commission
FPIS, forward propagation ionospheric scatter
FPO, Fleet Post Office
FPV, free piston vessel
FR, Federal Register (publication)
FRS, Fellow of the Royal Society, Federal Reserve System
FS, Forest Service
FSA, Federal Security Agency
FSS, Federal Supply Service

Fsuppl., Federal Supplement
FTC, Federal Trade Commission
FWS, Fish and Wildlife Service
GAO, General Accounting Office
GAR, Grand Army of the Republic
GARIOA, Government and Relief in Occupied Areas
GATT, General Agreement on Tariffs and Trade
GAW, guaranteed annual wage
GCA, ground-control approach
GCD or **gcd,** greatest common divisor
GCI, ground control intercept
GCT, Greenwich Civil Time
GI, gastrointestinal, general issue, Government issue
GMAT, Greenwich Mean Astronomical Time
GM & S, general, medical, and surgical
GMT, Greenwich Mean Time
GNMA, Government National Mortgage Association (Ginnie Mae)
GNP, gross national product
GPO, Government Printing Office
gr. Wt., gross weight
GS, Geological Survey
GSA, General Services Administration
GTS, gas turbine ship
HC, House of Commons
hcf, highest common factor
H Con. Res. (with number), House concurrent resolution
H Doc. (with number), House document
HE, high explosive
HHFA, Housing and Home Finance Agency
HHS, or **DHHS,** Department of Health and Human Services
HJ Res (with number), House joint resolution
HL, House of Lords
Hosp. Steward, hospital steward
How., Howard (U.S. Supreme Court Reports)
HR or **H.R.** (with numbers), House bill
H Rept. (with number), House report
H Res. (with number), House resolution
HUD, Department of Housing and Urban Development
IADB, Inter-American Defense Board
IAEA, International Atomic Energy Agency
ICBM, intercontinental ballistic missile
ICC, Interstate Commerce Commission, Indian Claims Commission
id, inside diameter
IDA, International Development Association
IF, infield, intermediate frequency

IFC, International Finance Corporation
IFF, Identification, Friend or Foe
ILO, International Labor Organization
IMCO, Intergovernmental Maritime Consultative Organization
IMF, International Monetary Fund
INS, Immigration and Naturalization Service
Insp. Gen., Inspector General
Interpol, International Criminal Police Organization
IOU, I owe you
IQ, intelligence quotient
IRAC, Interdepartment Radio Advisory Committee
IRBM, intermediate range ballistic missile
IRE, Institute of Radio Engineers
IRO, International Refugee Organization
IRS, International Revenue Service
ITO, International Trade Organization
ITU, International Telecommunication Union, International Typographical Union
JAG, Judge Advocate General
jato or **JATO,** jet-assisted takeoff
JD., *jurum doctor,* doctor of laws
JOBS, Job Opportunities in the Business Sector
Judge Adv. Gen., Judge Advocate General
KCB, Knight Commander of the Bath
LAFTA, Latin American Free Trade Association
lat. or **lat,** latitude
LC, Library of Congress
lc, lowercase
lcl, less-than-carload lot
lcm, least common multiple
L Ed., Lawyer's edition (U.S. Supreme Court Reports)
LitD or **Lit.D,** Doctor of Literature
LLB or **LL.B.,** Bachelor of Laws
LLD or **LL.D.,** Doctor of Laws
log, logarithm
long or **long.,** longitude
loran, long-range navigation
lox or **LOX,** liquid oxygen
LPG, liquefied petroleum gas
LST, Local Standard Time
LT, Local Time
LTL, less than truckload
lwl, load waterline
lwm, low watermark

MA or **M.A.,** Master of Arts, Maritime Administration, Manpower Administration

MAC, Military Airlift Command (formerly MATS)

maf, moisture and ash free (coal)

MAG, Military Advisory Group

MB, Manitoba, megabyte

MC or **M.C.,** Member of Congress, emcee (master of ceremonies)

MCA, Model Cities Administration

MD or **M.D.,** Doctor of Medicine, Medical Department

MDAP, Mutual Defense Assistance Program

mf, machine finish, medium frequency

Misc. Doc. (with number), miscellaneous document

mmf, magnetomotive force

mol wt, molecular weight

MOS, military occupational specialty

MP or **M.P.,** Member of Parliament, Military Police, Mounted Police

mp, melting point

MS, or **M.S.,** or **MSc,** or **M.Sc.,** Master of Science

MSC, Military Sealift Command

msl, mean sea level

MST, Mountain Standard Time

MT, Mountain Time

N, normal

NA, not available

NAC, national agency check

NAS, National Academy of Science

NASA, National Aeronautics and Space Administration

NATO, North Atlantic Treaty Organization

NB, New Brunswick

NBS, National Bureau of Standards

NCUA, National Credit Union Administration

nec, not elsewhere classified

nes, not elsewhere specified

net wt., net weight

NF, Newfoundland, National Formulary

NFAH, National Foundation on the Arts and the Humanities

n-fe, nitrogen-free extract

NFSN, French-Speaking Nations of NATO

NIH, National Institutes of Health

nl, natural log or logarithm

NLRB, National Labor Relations Board

NOAA, National Oceanic and Atmospheric Administration

noibn, not otherwise indexed by name

nop, not otherwise provided (for)

nos, not otherwise specified

NOS, National Ocean Survey (formerly Coast and Geodetic Survey)
NOVS, National Office of Vital Statistic
NPS, National Park Service
NS, naval station, new series, New Style, Nova Scotia, nuclear ship
NSA, National Shipping Authority
NSC, National Security Council
NSF, National Science Foundation
nsk, not specified by kind
nspf, not specifically provided for
NT or **N.T.,** New Testament, Northern Territory, Northwest Territories
OASDHI, Old-Age, Survivors, Disability, and Health Insurance Program
OASI, Old-Age and Survivors Insurance
OCD, Office of Civil Defense
OD or **O.D.,** Doctor Optometry, Officer of the Day
od, olive drab, outside diameter
OE, Office of Education
OEO, Office of Economic Opportunity
OEP, Office of Emergency Preparedness, Office of Emergency Planning
OIT, Office of International Trade
OK, OK'd, OK'ing, OK's
OMB, Office of Management and Budget (formerly **BOB,** Bureau of the Budget)
ON, Old Norse, Ontario
OSD, Office of the Secretary of Defense
OTC, Organization for Trade Cooperation
PA, physician assistant, Post Adjutant, power of attorney, public-address system
Passed Asst. Surg., Passed Assistant Surgeon
PBS, Public Broadcasting Service
PE, physical education, Prince Edward Island
Pet, Peters (US Supreme Court Reports)
Ph, phenyl
ph, phase
PHA, Public Housing Administration
Phar D, Doctor of Pharmacy
PhB or **BPh,** Bachelor of Philosophy
PhD or **Ph.D.,** Doctor of Philosophy
PhG, Graduate in Pharmacy
PHS, Public Health Service
pl or **pl.,** plate, plural
PO Box (with number), *but* post office box (in general sense)
pod, pay on delivery
por, pay on return
POW, prisoner of war
PP, parcel post, postpaid, prepaid

PPI, plan position indicator
ppi, policy proof of interest
pq, previous question
PQ, Province of Quebec
Private Res. (with number), private resolution
PST, Pacific Standard Time
PT, Pacific Time
PTA, Parent-Teacher Association
pto, please turn over
Public Res. (with number), public resolution
PX, Post Exchange
QT, on the quiet
racon, radar beacon
radar, radio detection and ranging
R & D, research and development
rato, rocket-assisted takeoff
RB, Renegotiation Board
RDB, Research and Development Board
REA, Rural Electrification Administration
Rev., Revelation, Reverend
Rev. Stat., Revised Statutes
rf, radio frequency
RFD or **R.F.D.,** Rural Free Delivery
Rh, Rhesus (blood factor)
RN or **R.N.,** Registered Nurse, Royal Navy
ROP, run of paper
ROTC, Reserve Officer's Training Corps
RR or **R.R.,** railroad, Right Reverend, Rural Route
RRB, Railroad Retirement Board
Rwy or **Rwy.,** Railway
SAC, Strategic Air Command
SACEUR, Supreme Allied Commander Europe
SAE, Society of Automotive Engineers
SAGE, semiautomatic ground environment
s and sc, sized and supercalendered
SAR, Sons of the American Revolution
SBA, Small Business Administration
SCAP, Supreme Commander of the Allied Powers (Japan)
S Con. Res. (with number), Senate Concurrent Resolution
S Doc. (with number), Senate document
SEATO, Southeast Asia Treaty Organization
SEC, Securities and Exchange Commission
sec or **sec.,** secant, seconds, secondary, secretary, section
sech, hyperbolic secant
2d, 3d, second, third

ser., series, sermon
Sf, Svedberg floatation
SHAPE, Supreme Headquarters Allied Powers (Europe)
SHF, superhigh frequency
shoran, short range (radio)
SI, Systeme International d' Unites
sin, sine
sinh, hyperbolic sine
SJ Res (with number), Senate Joint Resolution
SK, Saskatchewan
so, seller's option
sofar, sound fixing and ranging
sonar, sound, navigation, and ranging
SOP or **S.O.P.,** standard operating procedure
SOS, wireless distress signal
SP, Shore Patrol, Submarine Patrol
SPAR, Coast Guard Women's Reserve (*Semper Paratus—Always Ready*)
sp gr or **sp. gr.,** specific gravity
S Rept. (with number), Senate Report
S Res. (with number), Senate Resolution
SRS, Social and Rehabilitation Service
SS or **S.S.,** Social Security, steamship
SSA, Social Security Administration
SSS, Selective Service System
St., Saint, Strait, Street
Ste., SS., Sainte, Saints
Stat., Statutes at Large
STP, standard temperature and pressure
SUNFED, Special United Nations Fund for Economic Development
Sup. Ct., Supreme Court Reporter
Supp. Rev. Stat., Supplement to the Revised Statutes
Surg. Gen., Surgeon General
tan, tangent
tanh, hyperbolic tangent
TB, tuberculosis
TD, touchdown, Treasury Department, Treasury Decisions
TDN, total digestible nutrients
ter., terrace, territory
tlo, total loss only
tm, true mean
TNT, trinitrotoluene
TOFC, trailer-on-flatcar
Tp., township
TV, television
TVA, Tennessee Valley Authority

2,4-D, insecticide
uc., uppercase
UHF or **uhf,** ultrahigh frequency
UMTS, Universal Military Training Service (or System)
UN, United Nations
UNESCO, United Nations Educational, Scientific, and Cultural Organization
UNICEF, United Nations Children's Fund
URA, Urban Renewal Administration
USA or **U.S.A.,** United States of America, US Army
USAF, US Air Force
USAREUR, US Army, Europe
USC, United States Code
USCA, United States Code Annotated
USC Suppl, United States Code Supplement
USCG, US Coast Guard
USDA, United States Department of Agriculture
USES, US Employment Service
USIA, US Information Agency
USMC, US Marine Corps
USN, US Navy
USNR, US Naval Reserve
USP or **U.S.P.,** United States Pharmacopoeia
USS, US Senate, US ship
USSR or **U.S.S.R.,** Union of Soviet Socialist Republics
ut, universal time
VA, Veterans' Administration
VAR, visual-aural range
VCR, video cassette recorder
VHF, very high frequency
VIP, very important person (see also **DV**)
VLF or **vlf,** very low frequency
WAC, Women's Army Corps
wae, when actually employed
WAF, Women in the Air Force
Wall, Wallace (US Supreme Court Reports)
WAVES, Women Accepted for Volunteer Emergency Service
wf, wrong font
Wheat., Wheaton (US Supreme Court Reports)
WHO, World Health Organization
wi, when issued
WMAL, WRC, etc., radio stations
woc, without compensation
YT, Yukon Territory
ZIP Code, zone improvement plan code (Postal Service)

METRIC ABBREVIATIONS

Metric abbreviations are typed in lowercase, the same form being used for both singular and plural. The preferred abbreviation for *cubic centimeter* is cm^3, rather than *cc*.

Prefixes for Multiples and Submultiples			
T	tera (10^{12})	c	centi (10^{-2})
G	giga (10^{9})	m	milli (10^{-3})
M	mega (10^{6})	μ	micro (10^{-6})
k	kilo (10^{3})	n	nano (10^{-9})
h	hecto (10^{2})	p	pico (10^{-12})
da	deka (10)	f	femto (10^{-15})
d	deci (10^{-1})	a	atto (10^{-18})

Length		*Area*	
m	meter	m^2	square meter
mym	myriameter	mya	myriare
km	kilometer	km^2	square kilometer
hm	hectometer	hm^2	square hectometer
dam	dekameter	dam^2	square dekameter
dm	decimeter	dm^2	square decimeter
cm	centimeter	cm^2	square centimeter
mm	millimeter	mm^2	square millimeter

Volume		*Weight*	
m^3	cubic meter	g	gram
km^3	cubic kilometer	myg	myriagram
hm^3	cubic hectometer	kg	kilogram
dam^3	cubic dekameter	hg	hectogram
dm^3	cubic decimeter	dag	dekagram
cm^3	cubic centimeter	dg	decigram
mm^3	cubic millimeter	cg	centigram
		mg	milligram
		μg	microgram

Land Area		Capacity of Containers	
a	are	l	liter
ha	hectare	myl	myrialiter
ca	centiare	kl	kiloliter
		hl	hectoliter
		dal	dekaliter
		dl	deciliter
		cl	centiliter
		ml	milliliter

A similar plan of abbreviation applies to any unit based on the metric system:

Units Based on the Metric System			
A	ampere	V	volt
Å	angstrom	W	Watt
c	cycle (radio)	kc	kilocycle
dyn	dyne	kV	kilovolt
erg	erg	kVA	kilovolt-ampere
F	farad	kW	kilowatt
H	henry	mF	millifarad
J	joule	mH	millihenry
mho	(not abbreviated)	mF	microfarad (one millionth of a farad)
ohm	(not abbreviated)		

STANDARD ABBREVIATIONS FOR OTHER UNITS OF MEASURE

a, are (unit of area), atto (prefix, one-quintillionth)
aA, attoampere
abs, absolute (temperature and gravity)
AF or **af,** audio-frequency
AM, amplitude modulation
asb, apostilb
at, atmosphere, technical
atm, atmosphere (infrequently, A_s)
at wt, atomic weight
avdp., avoirdupois

b, barn, bit
B, bel
bbl, barrel
bbl/d, barrel per day
Bd, baud
bd ft, board foot
Bhn, Brinell hardness number
bhp, brake horsepower
bm, board measure
bp, boiling point
Btu's or **BTU'S,** British thermal units
bu, bushel
C, coulomb, Celsius (preferred), also Centigrade
C or **C.** or **c** or **¢** or **ct,** cent
°C, degree Celsius
cal, calorie
cal., caliber
cd, candela
cd-ft, cord-foot
cd/in^2, candela per square inch
cd/m^2, candela per square meter
cfm, cubic feet per minute
cfs, cubic feet per second
c-h, candle-hour
Ci, curie
cp, candle power
cP, centipoise
cSt, centistokes
cu ft (obsolete), see **ft^3**
cu in (obsolete), see **in^3**
cu yd (obsolete), see **yd^3**
cwt, hundredweight
D, darcy
d, day, degree, diameter, penny, pence, deci (prefix, one-tenth)
db or **dB,** decibel
dbu, decibel unit
dol, dollar
doz or **doz.,** dozen(s)
dr, dram
dwt, deadweight tons
EHF or **ehf,** extremely high frequency
EMF or **emf,** electromotive force
esu, electrostatic unit
°F, degree Fahrenheit
F, Fahrenheit; femi

fbm, feet board measure
fc, foot-candle
fL, footlambert
FM, frequency modulation
ft or **ft.,** foot, feet
ft^2, square foot
ft^3, cubic foot
ftH$_2$0, conventional foot of water
ft-lb, foot-pound
ft-lbf, foot pound-force
ft/min, foot per minute
ft^2/min, square foot per minute
ft^3/min, cubic foot per minute
ft-pdl, foot poundal
ft/s, foot per second
ft^2/s, square foot per second
ft^3/s, cubic foot per second
ft/s^2, foot per second squared
ft/s^3, foot per second cubed
G, gauss, giga (prefix, 1 billion), gravity
Gal, gal (acceleration)
gal or **gal.,** gallon
gal/min, gallons per minute
gal/s, gallons per second
Gb, gilbert
g/cm^3, gram per cubic centimeter
GeV, giga-electron-volt
GHz, gigahertz, gigacycle per second
gr, grain, gram, gross
h, hour, hecto (prefix, 100)
ha, hectare
hf, half, high frequency
HP or **hp,** horsepower
hph, horsepowerhour
Hz, hertz (cycles per second)
ihp, indicated horsepower
in, inch
in^2, square inch
in^3, cubic inch
in/h, inch per hour
inH$_2$O, conventional inch of water
inHg, conventional inch of mercury
in-lb, inch-pound
in/s, inch per second
K, karat, kayser, kilobyte, Kelvin (no degree symbol °)

k, karat, kilo (prefix, 1,000)
kHz or **khz,** kilohertz (kilocycles per second)
klbf, kilopound-force
kt, karat, kiloton, knot
L, lambert
lb or **lb.,** pound(s)
lb ap, apothecary, pound
lb, avdp, avoirdupois, pound
lbf, pound-force
lbf/ft, pound-force foot
lbf/ft^2, pound-force per square foot
lfg/ft^3, pound-force per cubic foot
lbf/in^2, pound-force per square inch
lb/ft, pound per foot
lb/ft^2, pound per square foot
lb/ft^3, pound per cubic foot
lb/in^{2}a, pounds per square inch absolute
lb/in^{2}g, pounds per square inch gage
lct, long calcined ton
ldt, long dry ton
LF or **lf,** low frequency
lin ft, linear foot
l/m, lines per minute
lm, lumen
lm/ft^2, lumen per square foot
lm/m^2, lumen per square meter
lm-s, lumen second
lm/W, lumen per watt
l/s, lines per second
l/s, liter per second
lx, lux
M, Roman numeral for 1,000
M#bm, thousand (feet) board measure
mD, millidarcy
meq, milliequivalent
M#ft^3, thousand cubic feet
Mgal/d, million gallons per day
MHz or **Mhz,** megahertz
mHz, millihertz
mi or **mi.,** mile
mi^2, square mile
mi/h, mile per hour
min., minute (time)
mol, mole (unit of substance)
ms, millisecond

MT, megaton
Mx, maxwell
N, newton
N•m, newton meter
N/m^2, newton per square meter
nmi, nautical mile
Np, neper
ns, nanosecond
N•s/m^2, newton second per square meter
nt, nit
Oe, oersted (use of **A/m,** amperes permeter, preferred)
oz or **oz.,** ounce(s)
P, poise
Pa, pascal
pct, percent
pdl, poundal
pF, water-holding energy
pH, hydrogen-ion concentration
ph, phot
pk, peck
p/m, parts per million
ps, picosecond
pt or **pt.,** pint(s)
pwt, pennyweight
ql, quintal
qt or **qt.,** quart(s)
R, rankine; roentgen
°R, degree rankine; degree reaumur
rad, radian
rd, rad
rem, rem
rms, root mean square
rpm, revolutions per minute
rps, revolutions per second
s or **s.,** second(s) (time)
S, siemens
sb, stilb
scp, spherical candlepower
s-ft, second-foot
shp, shaft horsepower
slug, slug
sr, steradian
sSf, standard saybolt fural
sSu, standard saybolt universal
stdft^3, standard cubic foot (feet)

Sus, saybolt universal second
t or **t.,** ton
tbs or **tbs.** or **tbsp** or **tbsp.,** tablespoon
thm, therm
Twad, twaddell
u (unified), atomic mass unit
var, var
VHF or **vhf,** very high frequency
Wb, weber
W/sr, watt per steradian
W/(sr•m^2), watt per steradian square meter
yd or **yd.,** yard(s)
yd^2, square yard
yd^3, cubic yard
yr or **yr.,** year(s)

LATIN ABBREVIATIONS

a., *annus,* year; *ante,* before
A.A.C., *anno ante Christum,* in the year before Christ
A.A.S., *Academiae Americanae Socius,* Fellow of the American Academy [Academy of Arts and Sciences]
AB or **A.B.,** *artium baccalaureus,* bachelor of arts
ab init., *ab initio,* from the beginning
abs. re., *absente reo,* the defendant being absent
AC or **A.C.,** *ante Christum,* before Christ
AD or **A.D.,** *anno Domini,* in the year of our Lord
a.d., *ante diem,* before the day
ad fin., *ad finem,* at the end, to one end
ad h.l., *ad hunc locum,* to this place, on this passage
ad inf., *ad infinitum,* to infinity
ad init., *ad initium,* at the beginning
ad int., *ad interim,* in the meantime
ad lib., *ad libitum,* at pleasure
ad loc., *ad locum,* at the place
ad val., *ad valorem,* according to value
A.I., *anno inventionis,* in the year of the discovery
al., *alia, alii,* other things, other persons
AM or **A.M.,** *anno mundi,* in the year of the world; *Annus mirabilis,* the wonderful year [1666]; a.m., *ante meridiem,* before noon
an., *anno,* in the year; *ante,* before
ann., *annales,* annals; *anni,* years
A.R.S.S., *Antiquariorum Regiae Societatis Socius,* Fellow of the Royal Society of Antiquaries

A.U.C., *anno urbis conditae, ab urbe condita,* in [the year from] the building of the City [Rome], 753 B.C.

BA or **B.A.,** *baccalaureus artium,* bachelor of arts

BS or **B. Sc.,** *baccalaureus scientiae,* bachelor of science

C., *centum,* a hundred; *condemno,* I condemn, find guilty

c., *circa,* about

cent., *centum,* a hundred

cf., *confer,* compare

CM or **C.M.,** *chirurgiae magister,* master of surgery

coch., *cochlear,* a spoon, spoonful

coch. amp., *cochlear amplum,* a tablespoonful

coch. mag., *cochlear magnum,* a large spoonful

coch. med., *cochlear medium,* a dessert spoonful

coch. parv., *cochlear parvum,* a teaspoonful

con., *contra,* against; *conjunx,* wife

C.P.S., *custos privati sigilli,* keeper of the privy seal

C.S., *custos sigilli,* keeper of the seal

D., *Deus,* God; *Dominus,* Lord; d., *decretum,* a decree; *denarius,* a penny; *da,* give

DD or **D.D.,** *divinitatis doctor,* doctor of divinity

D.G., *Dei gratia,* by the grace of God; *Deo gratias,* thanks to God

D.N., *Dominus noster,* our Lord

DSc or **D.Sc.,** *doctor scientiae,* doctor of science

d.s.p., *decessit sine prole,* died without issue

D.V., *Deo volente,* God willing

e.g., *exempli gratia,* for example

et al., *et alibi,* and elsewhere; *et alii,* or *aliae,* and others

etc., *et cetera,* and others, and so forth

et seq., *et sequentes,* and those that follow

et ux., *et uxor,* and wife

F., *filius,* son

f., *fiat,* let it be made; *forte,* strong

fac., *factum similis,* facsimile, an exact copy

fasc., *fasciculus,* a bundle

fl., *flores,* flowers; *floruit,* flourished; *fluidus,* fluid

f.r., *folio recto,* right-hand page

F.R.S., *Franternitatis Regiae Socius,* Fellow of the Royal Society

f.v., *folio verso,* on the back of the leaf

guttat., *guttatim,* by drops

H., *hora,* hour

h.a., *hoc anno,* in this year; *hujus anni,* this year's

hab. corp., *habeas corpus,* have the body—a writ

h.e., *hic est,* this is; *hoc est,* that is

h.m., *hoc mense,* in the month; *huius mensis,* this month's

h.q., *hoc quaere,* look for this

H.R.I.P., *hic requiescat in pace,* here rests in peace

H.S., *hic sepultus,* here is buried; *hic situs,* here lies; h.s., *hoc sensu,* in this sense

H.S.S., *Historiae Societatis Socius,* Fellow of the Historical Society

h.t., *hoc tempore,* at this time; *hoc titulo,* in or under this title

I., *Idus,* the Ides; i., *id,* that; *immortalis,* immortal

ib. or **ibid.,** *ibidem,* in the same place

id., *idem,* the same

i.e., *id est,* that is

imp., *imprimatur, sanction,* let it be printed

I.N.D., *in nomine Dei,* in the name of God

in f., *in fine,* at the end

inf., *infra,* below

init., *initio,* in the beginning

in lim., *in limine,* on the threshold, at the outset

in loc., *in loco,* in its place

in loc. cit., *in loco citato,* in the place cited

in pr., *in principio,* in the beginning

in trans., *in transitu,* on the way

i.q., *idem quod,* the same as

i.q.e.d., *id quod erat demonstrandum,* what was to be proved

J., *judex,* judge

JCD or **J.C.D.,** *juris civilis doctor,* doctor of civil law

JD or **J.D.,** *jurum doctor,* doctor of laws

JUD or **J.U.D.,** *juris utriusque doctor,* doctor of both civil and canon law

L., *liber,* a book; *locus,* a place

L, *libra,* pound; placed before figures, thus L10; if l., to be placed after, as 40l.

LAM or **L.A.M.,** *liberalium artium magister,* master of the liberal arts

LB or **L.B.,** *baccalaureus literarum,* bachelor of letters

lb., *libra,* pound (singular and plural)

LHD or **L.H.D.,** *literarum humaniorum doctor,* doctor of the more humane letters

LittD or **Litt. D.** or **Dlit(t),** *literarum doctor,* doctor of letters

LLB or **LL.B.,** *legum baccalaureus,* bachelor of laws

LLD or **LL.D.,** *legum doctor,* doctor of laws

LLM or **LL.M.,** *legum magister,* master of laws

loc. cit., *loco citato,* in the place cited

loq., *loquitur,* he, or she, speaks

L.S., *locus sigilli,* the place of the seal

l.s.c., *loco supra citato,* in the place above cited

L s.d., *librae, solidi, denarii,* pounds, shillings, pence

M., *magister,* master; *manipulus,* handful; *medicinae,* of medicine

m., *meridies,* noon

MA or **M.A.,** *magister artium,* master of arts

MB or **M.B.,** *medicinae baccalaureus,* bachelor of medicine

MCh or **M.Ch.,** *magister chirurgiae,* master of surgery

MD or **M.D.,** *medicinae doctor,* doctor of medicine

m.m., *mutatis mutandis,* with the necessary changes

m.n., *mutato nomine,* the name being changed

MS., *manuscriptum,* manuscript; MSS., *manuscripta,* manuscripts

MusB or **Mus. B.,** *musicae baccalaureus,* bachelor of music

MusD or **Mus. D.,** *musicae doctor,* doctor of music

MusM or **Mus. M.,** *musicae magister,* master of music

N., *Nepos,* grandson; *nomen,* name; *nomina,* names; *noster,* our; n., *natus,* born; *nocte,* at night

N.B., *nota bene,* mark well

ni. pri., *nisi prius,* unless before

nob., *nobis,* for (or on) our part

nol. pros., *nolle prosequi,* will not prosecute

non cul., *non culpabilis,* not guilty

n.l., *non licet,* it is not permitted; *non liquet,* it is not clear; *non longe,* not far

non obs., *non obstante,* notwithstanding

non pros., *non prosequitur,* he does not prosecute

non seq., *non sequitur,* it does not follow logically

O., *octarius,* a pint

ob., *obiit,* he, or she, died; *obiter,* incidentally

ob. s.p., *obiit sine prole,* died without issue

o.c., *opere citato,* in the work cited

op., *opus,* work; *opera,* works

op. cit., *opere citato,* in the work cited

P., *papa,* pope; *pater,* father; *pontifex,* bishop; *populus,* people; p., *partim,* in part; *per,* by, for; *pius,* holy; *pondere,* by weight; *post,* after; *primus,* first; *pro,* for

p.a. or **per ann.,** *per annum,* yearly; *pro anno,* for the year

p. ae., *partes aequales,* equal parts

pass., *passim,* everywhere

percent., *per centum,* by the hundred

pil., *pilula,* pill

PhB or **Ph.B.,** *philosophiae baccalaureus,* bachelor of philosophy

pm or **p.m.,** *post mortem,* after death

PM or **P.M.,** *post meridem,* afternoon

pro tem., *pro tempore,* for the time being

prox., *proximo,* in or of the next [month]

P.S., *postscriptum,* postscript; P.SS., *post scripta,* postscripts

q.d., *quasi dicat,* as if one should say; *quais dictum,* as if said; *quasi dixisset,* as if he had said

q.e., *quod est,* which is

Q.E.D., *quod erat demonstrandum,* which was to be demonstrated

Q.E.F., *quod erat faciendum,* which was to be done

Q.E.I., *quod erat inveniendum,* which was to be found out

q.l., *quantum libet,* as much as you please

q. pl., *quantum placet,* as much as seems good

q.s., *quantum sufficit,* sufficient quantity

q.v., *quantum vis,* as much as you will; *quem, quam, quod vide,* which see; qq. v., *quos, quas,* or *quae vide,* which see (plural)

R., *regina,* queen; *recto,* right-hand page; *respublica,* commonwealth

R, *recipe,* take

R.I.P., *requiescat,* or *requiescant,* in pace, may he, she, or they, rest in peace

R.P.D., *rerum politicarum doctor,* doctor of political science

t. or **temp.,** *tempore,* in the time of

tal. qual., *talis qualis,* just as they come, average quality

R.S.S., *Ragiae Societatis Sodalis,* Fellow of the Royal Society

S., *sepultus,* buried; *situs,* lies; *societas,* society; *socius* or *sodalis,* fellow; s., *semi,* half; *solidus,* shilling

s.a., *sine anno,* without date; *secundum artem,* according to art

S.A.S., *Societatis Antiquariorum Socius,* Fellow of the Society of Antiquaries

sc., *scilicet,* namely; *sculpsit,* he, or she, carved or engraved it

ScB or **Sc.B.,** *scientiae baccalaureus,* bachelor of science

ScD or **Sc.D.,** *scientiae doctor,* doctor of science

S.D., *salutem dicit,* sends greetings

s.d., *sine die,* indefinitely

sec., *secundum,* according to

sec. leg., *secundum legem,* according to law

sec. nat., *secundum naturam,* according to nature, or naturally

sec. reg., *secundum regulam,* according to rule

seq., *sequens, sequentes, sequentia,* the following

S.H.S., *Societatis Historiae Socius,* Fellow of the Historical Society

s.h.v., *sub hac voce* or *sub hoc verbo,* under this word

s.l.a.n., *sine loco, anno, vel nomine,* without place, date or name

s.l.p., *sine legitima prole,* without lawful issue

s.m.p., *sine mascula prole,* without male issue

s.n., *sine nomine,* without name

s.p., *sine prole,* without issue

S.P.A.S., *Societatis Philosophiae Americanae Socius,* Fellow of the American Philosophical Society

s.p.s., *sine prole superstite,* without surviving issue

S.R.S., *Societatis Regiae Socius or Sodalis,* Fellow of the Royal Society

ss., *scilicet,* namely (in law)

S.S.C., *Societas Sanctae Crucis,* Society of the Holy Cross

stat., *statim,* immediately

STB or **S.T.B.,** *sacrae theologiae baccalaureus,* bachelor of sacred theology

STD or **S.T.D.,** *sacrae theologiae doctor,* doctor of sacred theology

STP or **S.T.P.**, *sacrae theologiae professor,* professor of sacred theology
sub., *subaudi,* understand, supply
sup., *supra,* above
ult., *ultimo,* last month (may be abbreviated in writing but should be spelled out in printing)
ung., *unguentum,* ointment
u.s., *ubi supra,* in the place above mentioned
ut dict., *ut dictum,* as directed
ut sup., *ut supra,* as above
ux., *uxor,* wife
v. or **vs.,** *versus,* against; *vide,* see; *voce,* voice, word
v.—a., *vixit—annos,* lived [so many] years
verb. sap., *verbum [satis] sapienti,* a word to the wise suffices
v.g., *verbi gratia,* for example
viz., *videlicet,* namely
v.s., *vide supra,* see above

FORMS OF ADDRESS

The following are conventional forms of address in general use. They may be varied where appropriate. Use them as guides for other addresses.

All presidential and federal and state elective officials are addressed as *Honorable.* A person once entitled to *Governor, Judge, General, Honorable,* or a similar distinctive title may retain the title for his or her lifetime.

When a woman occupies the position, substitute *Ms.* for *Mr.* However, before such formal titles as *President, Vice President, Chairman, Secretary, Ambassador,* or *Minister,* use *Madam* or *Mme.* If in doubt err on the side of formality and use *Mme.* Use the title *Senator* for a female member of the Senate and *Ms.* for a female member of the House of Representatives, Senator-elect, or Representative-elect.

In most States, the lower branch of the legislature is the House of Representatives. In some States, such as California, New York, New Jersey, Nevada, and Wisconsin, the lower house is known as the Assembly. In others, such as Maryland, Virginia, and West Virginia, it is known as the House of Delegates. Nebraska has a one-house legislature. Its members are classed as Senators.

Academic or professional titles replace *Mr.* or *Ms.* Don't use two titles with the same meaning with one name: write *Dr. Paula White* or *Paula White, MD,* not *Dr. Paula White, MD* or *Ms. Paula White, MD.* Spell out all titles in an address except *Dr., Mr., Mrs.,* and *Ms.* Use *Ms.* for women generally, unless the woman addressed has expressed a preference for *Miss* or *Mrs.*

The term *pastor* applies to a minister who leads a congregation. It is appropriately used in conversation or direct address, but not in formal, written address.

Forms of Address

Addressee	Address on Letter and Envelope	Salutation	Complimentary Close
The President	The President The White House Washington, DC 20500	Dear Mr./Mme. President:	Respectfully,
Spouse of the President	Mr./Mrs. [full name] The White House Washington, DC 20500	Dear Mr./Mrs. [surname]:	Sincerely,
Assistant to the President	Honorable [full name] Assistant to the President The White House Washington, DC 20500	Dear Mr./Ms. [surname]:	Sincerely,
The Vice-President	The Vice-President United States Senate Washington, DC 20510	Dear Mr./Mme. Vice-President	Sincerely,
The Chief Justice	The Chief Justice of the United States The Supreme Court of the United States Washington, DC 20543	Dear Mr./Mme. Chief Justice: *or* Dear Chief Justice [surname]:	Sincerely,
Associate Justice	Mr./Mme. Justice [surname] The Supreme Court of the United States Washington, DC 20543	Dear Mr./Mme. Justice *or* Dear Justice [surname]:	Sincerely,

Addressee	Address on Letter and Envelope	Salutation	Complimentary Close
United States Senator	Honorable *[full name]* United States Senate Washington, DC 20510 *or* Honorable *[full name]* United States Senator *[local address]* *[City], [State] [ZIP]*	Dear Senator *[surname]*:	Sincerely,
United States Representative	Honorable *[full name]* House of Representatives Washington, DC 20515 *or* Honorable *[full name]* Member, United States House of Representatives *[local address]* *[City], [State] [ZIP]*	Dear Mr./Ms. *[surname]*:	Sincerely,
Committee Chairman	Honorable *[full name]* Chairman, Committee on *[name]* United States Senate Washington, DC 20510 *or* Honorable *[full name]* Chairman, Committee on *[name]* House of Representatives Washington, DC 20515	Dear Mr./Mme. Chairman:	Sincerely,

continues

Forms of Address (Continued)

Addressee	Address on Letter and Envelope	Salutation	Complimentary Close
Subcommittee Chairman	Honorable *[full name]* Chairman, Subcommittee on *[name]* *[name of parent Committee]* United States Senate Washington, DC 20510 *or* Honorable *[full name]* Chairman, Subcommittee on *[name]* House of Representatives Washington, DC 20515	Dear Senator *[surname]*: Dear Mr./Mme. *[surname]*:	Sincerely, Sincerely,
Speaker of the House of Representatives	Honorable *[full name]* Speaker of the House of Representatives Washington, DC 20515	Dear Mr./Ms. Speaker:	Sincerely,
Cabinet Members	Honorable *[full name]* Secretary of *[name of Department]* Washington, DC *[ZIP]* *or* Honorable *[full name]* Postmaster General Washington, DC 20260 *or* Honorable *[full name]* Attorney General Washington, DC 20530	Dear Mr./Mme. Secretary: Dear Mr./Ms. Postmaster General: Dear Mr./Ms. Attorney General:	Sincerely, Sincerely, Sincerely,

Addressee	Address on Letter and Envelope	Salutation	Complimentary Close
Deputy Secretaries, Assistants, or Under Secretaries	Honorable *[full name]* Deputy Secretary of *[name of Department]* Washington, DC *[ZIP]* *or* Honorable *[full name]* Assistant Secretary of *[name of Department]* Washington, DC *[ZIP]* *or* Honorable *[full name]* Under Secretary of *[name of Department]* Washington, DC *[ZIP]*	Dear Mr./Mme. *[surname]*:	Sincerely,
Head of Independent Offices and Agencies	Honorable *[full name]* Comptroller General of the United States General Accounting Office Washington, DC 20548 *or* Honorable *[full name]* Chairman, *[name of Commission]* Washington, DC *[ZIP]* *or* Honorable *[full name]* Director, Bureau of the Budget Washington, DC 20503	Dear Mr./Ms. *[surname]*: Dear Mr./Mme. Chairman: Dear Mr./Ms. *[surname]*:	Sincerely, Sincerely, Sincerely,

continues

Forms of Address (Continued)

Addressee	Address on Letter and Envelope	Salutation	Complimentary Close
Librarian of Congress	Honorable *[full name]* Librarian of Congress Library of Congress Washington, DC 20540	Dear Mr./Ms. *[surname]*:	Sincerely,
Public Printer	Honorable *[full name]* Public Printer US Government Printing Office Washington, DC 20401	Dear Mr./Ms. *[surname]*:	Sincerely,
American Ambassador	Honorable *[full name]* American Ambassador *[City]*, *[Country]*	Sir/Madam: (formal) Dear Mr./Mme. Ambassador: (informal)	Very truly yours, (formal) Sincerely, (informal)
American Consul General	*[full name]* or American Consul General (or American Consul) *[City]*, *[Country]*	Dear Mr./Ms. American Consul *[surname]*:	Sincerely,
Foreign Ambassador in the United States	His Excellency *[full name]* Ambassador of *[Country]* *[local address]* *[City]*, *[State]* *[ZIP]*	Excellency (formal) Dear Mr./Mme. Ambassador: (informal)	Very truly yours, (formal) Sincerely, (informal)

Addressee	Address on Letter and Envelope	Salutation	Complimentary Close
United States Representative to the United Nations or Organization of American States	Honorable *[full name]* United States Representative to the United Nations (or Organization of American States) Ambassador: *[local address]* *[City]*, *[State]* *[ZIP]*	Sir/Madame: (formal) Dear Mr./Mme. (informal)	Very truly yours, (formal) Sincerely, (informal)
Governor of State	Honorable *[full name]* Governor of *[name of State]* *[City]*, *[State]* *[ZIP]*	Dear Governor *[surname]*:	Sincerely,
Lieutenant Governor	Honorable *[full name]* Lieutenant Governor of *[name of State]* *[City]*, *[State]* *[ZIP]*	Dear Mr./Ms. *[surname]*:	Sincerely,
State Senator	Honorable *[full name]* *[name of State]* Senate *[City]*, *[State]* *[ZIP]*	Dear Mr./Ms. *[surname]*:	Sincerely,
State Representative, Assemblyman, or Delegate	Honorable *[full name]* *[name of State]* House of Representatives (or Assembly or House of Delegates) *[City]*, *[State]* *[ZIP]*	Dear Mr./Ms. *[surname]*:	Sincerely,

continues

Forms of Address *(Continued)*

Addressee	Address on Letter and Envelope	Salutation	Complimentary Close
Mayor	Honorable *[full name]* Mayor of *[name of City]* *[City]*, *[State]* *[ZIP]*	Dear Mayor *[surname]*:	Sincerely,
President of a Board of Commissioners	Honorable *[full name]* President, Board of Commissioners of *[name of City]* *[City]*, *[State]* *[ZIP]*	Dear Mr./Ms. *[surname]*:	Sincerely,
Protestant Clergy			
—Episcopalian	The Most Reverend Archbishop of (Canterbury or York) *[local address]* *[City]*, *[State]* *[ZIP]*	Most Reverend Sir *[full name]*: (formal) Dear Archbishop *[surname]*: (informal)	Sincerely, (formal) Sincerely, (informal)
	The Right Reverend Bishop of *[name of church]* *[local address]* *[City]*, *[State]* *[ZIP]*	Right Reverend Sir: *[full name]* (formal) Dear Bishop *[surname]*: (informal)	Sincerely, (formal) Sincerely, (informal)
—Lutheran	The Reverend *[full name]* Bishop of *[name]* *[local address]* *[City]*, *[State]* *[ZIP]*	Dear Bishop *[surname]*: (informal)	Sincerely, (informal)

Addressee	Address on Letter and Envelope	Salutation	Complimentary Close
—Methodist	The Reverend *[full name]* Bishop of *[name]* *[local address]* *[City], [State] [ZIP]*	Reverend Sir/Madam: (formal)	Sincerely, (formal)
—Baptist —Christian (church) —Episcopalian —Lutheran —Methodist —Presbyterian —Quaker	The Reverend *[full name]* *[Title], [name of church]* *[local address]* *[City], [State] [ZIP]*	Dear Mr./Ms. *[surname]*:	Sincerely,
Catholic Clergy			
—Roman	His Holiness The Pope Apostolic Palace 00210 Vatican City	Your Holiness:	Your obedient servant,
	His Eminence *[given name]* Cardinal *[surname]* Archbishop of *[Diocese]* *[local address]* *[City], [State] [ZIP]*	Your Eminence: (formal) Dear Cardinal *[surname]*: (informal)	Yours faithfully, (formal) Yours faithfully, (informal)

continues

Forms of Address (Continued)

Addressee	Address on Letter and Envelope	Salutation	Complimentary Close
	The Most Reverend *[full name]* Archbishop of *[Diocese]* *[local address]* *[City]*, *[State]* *[ZIP]*	Your Excellency: (formal) Dear Archbishop *[surname]*: (informal)	Yours faithfully, (formal) Yours faithfully, (informal)
	The Most Reverend *[full name]* Bishop of *[City]* *[local address]* *[City]*, *[State]* *[ZIP]*	Your Excellency: (formal) Dear Bishop *[surname]*: (informal)	Yours faithfully, (formal) Yours faithfully, (informal)
	The Reverend *[full name]* *[Title]*, *[name of church]* *[local address]* *[City]*, *[State]* *[ZIP]*	Dear Monsignor/Father *[surname]*:	Yours sincerely,
—Orthodox	His Holiness The Patriarch *[local address]* *[City]*, *[State]* *[ZIP]*.	Your Holiness:	Your obedient servant,
	The Most Reverend *[full name]* Metropolitan or Archbishop of *[Diocese]* *[local address]* *[City]*, *[State]* *[ZIP]*	Your Grace or Eminence: (formal) Dear Metropolitan or *[surname]*: Archbishop (informal)	Your obedient servant, (formal) Your obedient servant, (informal)
	The Right Reverend Bishop *[full name]* *[local address]* *[City]*, *[State]* *[ZIP]*	Right Reverend Bishop: (formal) Dear Bishop *[surname]*: (informal)	Yours faithfully, (formal) Yours faithfully, (informal)

Addressee	Address on Letter and Envelope	Salutation	Complimentary Close
—Roman and Orthodox	The Reverend [full name] [Title], [name of church] [local address] 00000	Dear Monsignor/Father [surname]:	Yours sincerely,
Jewish Clergy	Rabbi [full name] [Name of Congregation] [local address] 00000	Dear Rabbi [surname]:	Sincerely,
Islamic Clergy			
—Sunni	His Eminence [full name] The Grand Mufti of [area] [local address] 00000	Your Eminence:	Sincerely,
—Shiite	His Eminence [full name] The Ayatollah of [area] [local address] 00000	Your Eminence:	Sincerely,
—Sunni and Shiite	Imam [full name] [name of mosque] [local address] 00000	Imam [surname]:	Sincerely,

INDEX

G

Q

R

S

T

U

WEBSTER'S NEW WORLD™ 1001 ESSENTIAL LETTERS

When you don't have time to start from scratch, Webster's New World 1001 Essential Letters helps you get a head start on writing the perfect letter. From this extensive library of letters to fit every purpose, you can conduct a keyword search to find the right one. The CD's easy-to-use interface lets you customize letters in a flash.

System Requirements

- Windows® 3.1, 3.11 or Windows 95 or 98 operating system

- 486 SX 33 Mhz or faster processor

- 8 MB Minimum System Memory (RAM)

- 2 MB Hard Disk Space

- CD-ROM drive

- Compatible with Microsoft Word, WordPerfect, and MS Write word processing software.

Installation Instructions

Windows 95 and 98:

1. Insert Webster's New World™ 1001 Essential Letters disc into your CD-ROM drive.

2. From the Start Menu, select Run.

3. Type "d:\setup" (where "d" is the letter of your CD-ROM drive) and press Enter.

4. Follow the instructions that appear on the screen to complete the installation.

5. To start the program, click on the Start menu, roll your mouse over the 1001 Essential Letters Group, and choose the 1001 Essential Letters icon. You may also choose the Release Notes icon to learn more.

Windows 3.1 and 3.11:

1. Put the Webster's New World™ 1001 Essential Letters disc into your CD-ROM drive.

2. From the Program Manager, open the File Menu and then choose Run.

3. Type "d:\setup" (where "d" is the letter of your CD-ROM drive) and press Enter.

4. Follow the instructions that appear on your screen to complete the installation.

5. To start the program, double-click on the Program Group labeled 1001 Essential Letters from your Program Manager. Double-click on the 1001 Essential Letters icon to run the program, or choose the Release Notes to learn more.